THE LIFE AND TIMES OF RAÚL PREBISCH

The Life and Times of Raúl Prebisch 1901–1986

EDGAR J. DOSMAN

McGill-Queen's University Press
Montreal & Kingston • London • Ithaca

ISBN 978-0-7735-3412-4 (cloth)
ISBN 978-0-7735-3775-0 (paper)

Legal deposit fourth quarter 2008
Bibliothèque nationale du Québec

Printed in Canada on acid-free paper that is 100% ancient forest free (100% post-consumer recycled), processed chlorine free
First paperback edition 2010

This book was first published with the help of a grant from the Canadian Federation for the Humanities and Social Sciences, through the Aid to Scholarly Publications Programme, using funds provided by the Social Sciences and Humanities Research Council of Canada.

McGill-Queen's University Press acknowledges the support of the Canada Council for the Arts for our publishing program. We also acknowledge the financial support of the Government of Canada through the Book Publishing Industry Development Program (BPIDP) for our publishing activities.

Library and Archives Canada Cataloguing in Publication

Dosman, Edgar J.
The life and times of Raúl Prebisch, 1901-1986 / Edgar J. Dosman.

Includes bibliographical references and index.
ISBN 978-0-7735-3412-4 (bnd)
ISBN 978-0-7735-3775-0 (pbk)

1. Prebisch, Raúl. 2. Banco Central de la República Argentina – Biography. 3. United Nations. Economic Commission for Latin America – Biography. 4. United Nations Conference on Trade and Development. 5. Latin American Institute for Economic and Social Planning – Biography. 6. Latin America – Economic conditions – 20th century. 7. Latin America – Economic policy. 8. Economists – Argentina – Biography. 9. Executives – Argentina – Biography. I. Title.

HC172.5.P74D68 2008 338.092 C2008-903529-1

This book was typeset by Interscript in 10/13 Baskerville.

To the memory of David H. Pollock
Friend, Colleague, Pioneer

Contents

Acknowledgments ix

Illustrations xii

Introduction 3

1 Childhood: The Dreams of Tucumán 7

2 University in Buenos Aires 21

3 Apprenticeship 43

4 Taste of Power 62

5 Central Banker 89

6 Opening to Washington 117

7 The Pearl Harbor Squeeze 144

8 The Wilderness 168

9 Discovery of Latin America 188

10 Solitary Scholar 211

11 Triumph in Havana 231

12 Claiming ECLA 250

13 The Creation of Latin America 273

14 Paradise Lost 297

15 Return to Santiago 321

16 The Kennedy Offensive 350

17 Global Gamble 378

18 The Gospel of Don Raúl 410

19 Trials in Washington 442

20 Prophet 473

21 House of the Spirits 498

Acronyms 503

Notes 507

Bibliography 555

Index 583

Acknowledgments

If I can claim any success in achieving the goal of writing a comprehensive biography of Raúl Prebisch, it is largely thanks to the gracious collaboration of family, friends, and close associates of Prebisch, beginning with David H. Pollock, co-director of the project until taken by illness and death, and to whose memory this book is dedicated. He was everything a colleague can ever be, generous and wise, and a devoted friend of Prebisch's since 1951. I miss him dearly, and he is similarly mourned by scholars and practitioners in development. Along with David Pollock, the unstinting support and encouragement of Adelita Prebisch and Eliana Prebisch have been crucial in the research and drafting of the text and facilitating access to interviews with Prebisch family and others in Argentina, and I wish to underline my gratitude for their kindness and patience with my repeated requests for information and additional interviews. The Prebisch Papers in Santiago, collected and maintained by Adelita Prebisch, are an indispensable scholarly source; and the Prebisch Foundation, formed under the leadership of Eliana Prebisch in Buenos Aires, has published Prebisch's *Obras (Collected Works) 1919–1948*, making most of his writings available from this early period.

Since the United Nations inexplicably destroyed the entire registry files and archive of ECLA between its founding in 1948 through the Prebisch period to 1970, interviews were indispensable in assembling data and perspective, and the generous assistance of scholars, officials, and associates consistently demonstrated their commitment to Raúl Prebisch and his memory. A full list of interviews is provided in the bibliography, and I wish to thank every colleague who helped in this way.

Certain individuals deserve a special note of appreciation. Enrique Iglesias, with his unparalleled knowledge of both Dr Prebisch and inter-American relations, Rangaswami Krishnamurti, who also donated his personal papers to the project, and senior Argentine scholar José Nun offered consistent encouragement over the long years of preparation. Their vast experience and advice helped to bridge moments of uncertainty.

Among the others, Ernesto Malaccorto, Mario Bunge, and Julio Gonzalez del Solar were particularly invaluable sources on Prebisch's home and student years and the pre-1943 period in Argentina. For the ECLA and ILPES years Sir Hans Singer, Celso Furtado, Victor Urquidi, Enrique Iglesias, Alex Ganz, Alfonso Santa Cruz, Anibal Pinto, Adolfo Dorfman, Osvaldo Sunkel, Carlos Lleras Restrepo, Fernando Henrique Cardoso, Benjamin Hopenhayn, Oscar Bardeci, Ricardo Cibotti, Norberto Gonzalez, Robert Brown, Gert Rosenthal, William Lowenthal, José Nun, Sheila Pollock, Margery Fones, Lucy Jull, and Bodil Royem were extraordinarily helpful. Key Washington sources and officials from international financial institutions included Enrique Iglesias, William D. Rogers, Edward M. Bernstein, Jacques J. Polak, Lincoln Gordon, Sidney Weintraub, Viron P.Vaky, Nancy Birdsall, and Jerome Levinson. Key UN and UNCTAD advice was generously provided by Philippe de Seynes, R. Krishnamurti, Diego Cordovez, Yves Bertholet, Zamit Cutajar, and Jorge Viteri de la Huerta. Raúl Alfonsin, Bernardo Grinspun, Juan Sourrouille, Enrique Garcia Vasquez, Arturo O'Connell, Aldo Ferrer, and José Luis Machinea were particularly helpful on the subject of Prebisch's return to Argentina.

The Life and Times of Raúl Prebisch examines the interplay between the key themes of Prebisch's career – development ideas, institutions, the UN, Latin American integration, and international governance. For these contexts the book builds on rich existing literatures, particularly on Argentine history and Latin American political economy and multilateralism, and therefore owes a huge debt to Prebisch scholars in these fields. While the bibliography and notes reference these sources a number of Prebisch scholars were consulted individually in the course of the research. Without repeating earlier acknowledgements they include Joseph Love, Adolfo Guerrieri, Manuel Fernando Lopez, Carlos Mallorquín, Gregorio Weinberg, John Toye, Richard Toye, Ronald Sprout, and Eric Helleiner. I wish also to acknowledge the extensive correspondence with authors in Latin America, Europe, and North America during the project.

While acknowledging my personal responsibility for all errors or omissions, I wish to recognize the assistance of the archivists who facilitated access to Argentine, US, UN, and other regional and global sources, particularly Bárbara Duranti at the University Di Tella in Buenos Aires; José Besa Garcia and Carmen Vera Arndt in ECLAC, Santiago; Marilla B. Guptil, chief of processing at the UN in New York; Alison Hicks, IDB Felipe Herrera Library; Stella Villagran at the OAS; Charles Ziegler at the World

Bank; Katherine Nicastro and Sally M. Marks at the US State Department; Peter B. Field, US Department of Commerce; and David C. Mulford, Department of the Treasury. At York University, the library staff headed by Brent Roe, as well as CERLAC (Centre for Research on Latin America and the Caribbean) and CISS (Centre for International and Security Studies) actively supported the project, with special mention to Professors Louis Lefeber, David Dewitt, Aleks Nicolic, and Heather Chestnutt. Not least I wish to underline the financial support provided by the Canadian Social Science and Humanities Research Council.

I am particularly grateful to Robert Fothergill for editing the entire manuscript and to R. Krishnamurti, Manuel Uribe, Carlos Mallorquín, and Eric Helleiner for their detailed comments and suggestions as the text progressed. McGill-Queen's University Press, particularly Jonathan Crago, John Zucchi, Joan McGilvray, and Claude Lalumière, has been unfailingly attentive and supportive.

To life-partner Maureen Whitehead there is an extra appreciation – not just for tolerating so much time and resources diverted, or even the endless patience and encouragement to keep so complex a project alive – but for the quality of advice, research, and editing to make the *The Life and Times of Raúl Prebisch* a worthwhile biography. To Maureen and the whole family, an even greater thanks than last time around.

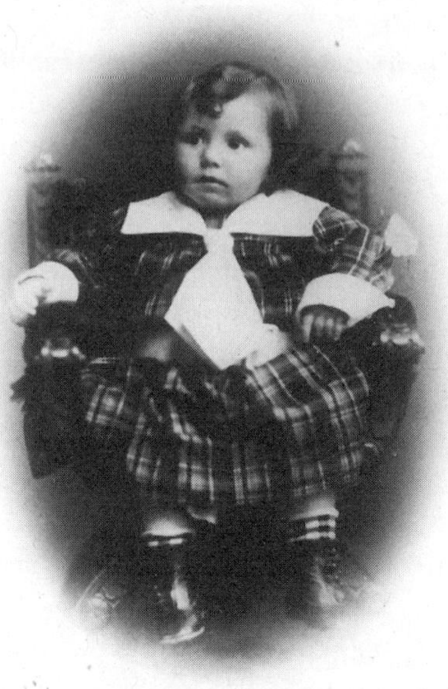

Raúl Prebisch at eighteen months.

The Prebisch family – Raúl on bicycle.

Raúl with Uncle Segundo Linares, Jujuy, 1911.

Military service, 1924–25.

Prebisch when he was undersecretary of finance, 1930.

Raúl and Adelita in Geneva, 1932.

Prebisch and the directorate of the Argentine Central Bank, 1935.

Raúl at the weekend house outside Buenos Aires.

Adelita at the weekend house outside Buenos Aires.

Prebisch meeting Chris Ravndal
(next to Prebisch) and the US delegation,
6 December 1941.

Prebisch in Havana, 1949.

From left, Gunnar Myrdal (ECE executive secretary), Raúl Prebisch, Dag Hammarskjöld, and P.S. Lokanathan (ECAFE executive secretary) in Bangkok, 1956.

Raúl and Adelita returning to Buenos Aires, October 1955.

John F. Kennedy launches the Alliance for Progress, 1961. Presbisch is third from the right.

David Pollock, Sidney Dell, and Raúl Prebisch: Forty Days around the World, 1963.

Prebisch launching UNCTAD, 1964.

Prebisch at UNCTAD headquarters in Geneva, 1965.

Prebisch at UNCTAD II, 1968 – the final appeal.

Raul Prebisch, Ambassador Amjad Ali (Pakistan), and chef de cabinet R. Krishnamurti.

Prebisch in New Delhi with Indira Gandhi, 1968.

Prebisch with Soviet Premier Alexei Kosygin, 1968.

Raúl's last team: the CEPAL Review, 1976.

Raúl Prebisch and Enrique Iglesias (centre) with ECLA executive secretaries, 1948–85 (from left, Carlos Quintana, Gustavo Martinez-Cabañas, Enrique Iglesias, Raúl Prebisch, and José Antonio Mayobre).

Prebisch and President Raúl Alfonsin, Buenos Aires, 1984.

Prebisch as prophet: Inaugural Conference, Centre for Research on Latin America and the Caribbean, York University, Toronto, 1978.

THE LIFE AND TIMES OF RAÚL PREBISCH

Introduction

I met Raúl Prebisch in 1978 and was determined to explore this most unusual figure among twentieth century personalities. His working life as economist spanned most of the twentieth century and the assessments of the man have tended to extremes: supporters have revered him and critics vilified him in equal measure. In part this book is a response to the strength of his personality; in part also to the challenges he faced in the political turmoil of his home country Argentina, Cold War Latin America, and North-South relations. *The Life and Times of Raúl Prebisch*, which traces Prebisch's development from childhood and student days through his work as an economist in Argentina, to his well-known regional leadership in the Economic Commission for Latin America (ECLA) and his international role as head of the United Nations Conference on Trade and Development (UNCTAD), attempts to present a balanced perspective on Prebisch's contribution to development economics and international institutions.

The main challenge, it became clear, was Prebisch himself – or rather integrating the personal and professional dimensions of this complex man. Prebisch was reticent about discussing his personal life, and it had been largely overlooked in the large but specialized literature on specific issues such as international trade or his UN career. Curiously, large segments of his life, such as the World War II period or the transition years between Argentina and the UN (1943–49), had not yet been systematically researched. Prebisch, in short, remained an enigma: only a biographical approach could capture the essential unity of his life and work.

The task, however, proved enormous, beginning with the sheer scope of the project. Prebisch began his studies in Buenos Aires in 1918 during the final phase of the First World War and when Argentina was in the First World; his thinking and writing mirror the entire course of Latin American economic thought in the twentieth century. Entering the United Nations in 1949 he was one of its leading figures for twenty-five years, and he remained intellectually active until his death in 1986. The many interrelated facets and personal challenges of this remarkable life had somehow to be uncovered and explained while avoiding a mini-history of the times in which he lived. The breadth and scope of my research allowed me to penetrate Prebisch's thoughts and feelings without sacrificing scholarly accuracy. In the end his life and work came together; and if the search for the essential Raúl Prebisch was more complex and much longer than anticipated, it was rewarded by a deeper personal understanding of a leader of rare accomplishment and enduring legacy.

Raúl Prebisch's funeral on 20 April 1986 was a busy affair in Santiago, Chile. There were the crowds, tributes, and dedications befitting an economist whose ideas had changed the twentieth century. A cardinal of the Church presided in Santiago's cathedral; presidents and dignitaries mourned with his family. Speaker after speaker intoned his enduring legacy as Latin America's Keynes, as the "father of development" whose charisma, warmth, and generosity changed the lives of those who knew him, as one of the few Latin Americans whose energy and leadership had made him a global personality.

But most of the mourners were middle-aged or older, colleagues who had known him in his prime, people retired from the United Nations who remembered Prebisch's heroic stature as a man of power and the embattled champion of economic justice and of the spread of material and social progress to all of humankind.

Where were the young? For them Prebisch's views seemed hopelessly old-fashioned compared with the new economics, and better consigned to the historical dustbin. Indeed his ideas about development and so-called "North-South" relations were massively out of favour in Ronald Reagan's Washington and the West in general, including his own Latin America. The essence of Prebisch's message had been the danger to all countries of polarization between rich and poor, and therefore the need for both sides to cooperate in their mutual long-term interest. By 1986 the mainstream had moved on to Margaret Thatcher and the "Reagan Revolution," leaving Prebisch and his dwindling band of supporters and followers from the old days in its wake as they bade farewell to their hero in his beautiful cliffside garden overlooking the Maipo River against the snow-covered Andes.

So complete was his eclipse that Prebisch has been neglected by biographers, the only great economist of the twentieth century to endure this doubtful distinction. By the end of the century, however, after twenty years of being dismissed as *passé*, or even dangerously misguided, the originality of his call to "civilize globalization" was rediscovered; by this time he was long since dead. Fashions were now reversed; even the famous twins of liberal capitalism – the World Bank and IMF – paid Prebisch the compliment of recognizing his work.

The Prebisch legacy, however, was unusually opaque. To many observers he remained an enigma, a puzzling figure with a fractured identity. Born in 1901, his life had spanned nearly the entire twentieth century; when he died in 1986, the Cold War was drawing to a close. His life therefore reflected the development of modern Latin America, its successes and failures; few careers reflected the contradictions and turmoil of this brutal century with such intensity.

Raúl Prebisch was an outsider, born the son of a German immigrant father in the traditional Argentine interior, arriving in the capital in 1918 as the First World War entered its climactic last phase. Educated at the University of Buenos Aires, he rose rapidly to become the country's most powerful economic manager, but the corrupt political regime that he served was overthrown by a military coup in 1943, and he himself was dismissed shortly thereafter for his pro-Allied views and defense of the autonomy of the Central Bank. After six years of search and rejection Prebisch finally joined the UN system in 1949, beginning with the Economic Commission for Latin America (ECLA) and as founding secretary-general of the United Nations Conference on Trade and Development (UNCTAD), a leading advocate for North-South dialogue and a powerful moral and intellectual force for international justice. Thus, unlike most economic thinkers, he was much more than an academic. Rather he was a person of diverse talents who not only produced new theories but also created institutions to give them form, from which emerged new policies and practices. Throughout his life Prebisch was driven by a search for "historical moments" in which the timing of a new concept could transform an organization into a movement. Theory, machinery, and policy: this powerful trinity linking an idea to a historical mechanism comprised the core of the Prebisch vision. Although a Latin American culturally embedded in his region, Prebisch's message was universal.

Few historical figures have been as vilified and misunderstood – or as uncritically acclaimed. Observers and critics saw two different lives and personalities. The CIA kept him under surveillance during the 1950s as a dangerous radical, but he was always firmly anti-communist and had worked closely with the US Embassy and US Federal Reserve a decade earlier. In Argentina he was viewed overwhelmingly as a symbol of the old oligarchy, but he disparaged the military and was never accepted by the elite. He loved Buenos Aires above all cities in the world, and when he returned in 1983 after democracy was restored there were no monuments to one of its most famous citizens.

Prebisch, quite simply, was hard to place. Even in his last years he radiated energy and charisma; he was amusing, articulate, and charming. Conversations with him were like living history; he grew older, but he never seemed to age. But while easy to meet, he was difficult to know; below his evident public accessibility Prebisch guarded his persona with an impenetrable inner reserve. He delighted in ideas and career anecdotes; but he never discussed the turbulent and conflicted personal life that so intrigued friends and foes. The inner struggles that underlay his thought and work remained hidden by reticence and vulnerability.

It has therefore seemed valuable to understand the Raúl Prebisch of fact rather than fiction, and to weigh the competing claims of supporters and critics. What really was his legacy? When his life and work are integrated some of the mystery is dispelled: despite the apparent contradictions, Prebisch's long public career demonstrates a remarkable unity of purpose and approach and a surprising coherence in his approach to innovation. From the young administrator who served the Argentine state to the economist who challenged the international economic system, he projected an ethical imperative that demanded commitment and left no justification for inaction – beginning with himself. Moulded by family and upbringing and repelled by the injustices he witnessed, strong in passion as well as intellect, he was an idealist among cynics, and ultimately a lonely and misunderstood figure, preoccupied that his work had failed in a country of broken promises and a continent of lost dreams.

1 Childhood: The Dreams of Tucumán

Buenos Aires was "something fantastic," Raúl Prebisch marvelled after his first stroll through the capital.[1] He was seventeen and had lived a sheltered life in the distant interior of Argentina without a sip of wine or a cigarette or holidays on the Atlantic coast. The train pulled into the station at noon on his birthday, 17 April 1918, surely an auspicious beginning for his new life as a university student in the national capital. Having only imagined the great city from boyhood in the far-off Andean mountains, he hoped the reality would equal these dreams.

From the station Raúl marvelled at the sights of Buenos Aires, gawking at street-corners like the provincial he was, his boyhood expectations hugely exceeded.[2] He saw for the first time the Plaza de Mayo, the central focus of Buenos Aires since 1580, an oblong square anchored by the elegant Casa Rosada (Government House), which faced the National Congress at the end of the Avenida de Mayo, where it met the Boulevard 9 de Julio. This was the widest street in the world, bold and grand, but no more so than the overall architecture of a capital into which most of the national wealth of Argentina had poured since independence in 1816.

Buenos Aires was comparable only with New York in vitality and modernity in the New World, a thriving cosmopolitan centre unique in Latin America. Its population had grown from 663,854 in 1895 to more than two million by Raúl's arrival; a hundred ships were in the port each day, making it the busiest in the southern hemisphere. A new subway had just been completed to complement the exclusive pedestrian sectors for shopping and restaurants; urban services such as mail and telephones were reliable and efficient; the city parks were proud urban symbols, and the city's cultural life had blossomed with the building of theatres and palaces by French architects. The premiere of *Il Trovatore* with Enrico Caruso at the El Cine Teatro in 1872 had set off a competition for luxurious settings that culminated in the opening of the 3,500–seat Colon Opera House in 1908 with Verdi's *Aida.* Henceforth Buenos Aires was part of the Milan, London, and Berlin ballet and music tour during the summer months. The mansions built along Avenida Alvear celebrated the unprecedented new wealth in the country, and the Jockey Club in Buenos Aires surpassed the opulence of New York clubs for high society. Nightlife of all kinds thrived, and the tango swept the city across its districts, from gritty Mataderos (or "New Chicago," from the old slaughterhouses on which it was built) to old Palermo with its Plaza Italia and monument to Garibaldi. Anything and everything could be experienced in this incredible city, and for Raúl every building or street corner had a special quality or historical meaning.

Prebisch's passionate love affair with Buenos Aires began that autumn in 1918. It captured his ambitions; he was determined to succeed and shape the future of a New World capital that would be the leader of the South American continent. As a young man, Raúl Prebisch stood on the threshold of a new life, but the special features of his personality had been formed during his childhood and school years in the remote provincial capital of Tucumán in Argentina's northwest Andean region.

Raúl Federico Prebisch Linares was born on 17 April 1901 in Tucumán to Albin Prebisch and Rosa Linares Uriburu. Raúl's mother, Rosa, was a product of the old Spanish colonial order in aristocratic Salta in the Andean Northwest of Argentina. The Linares family line could be traced directly back to the conqueror Francisco Pizarro, and Rosa's forebears included senators, bishops, and generals. The Uriburus, a tough, ambitious Basque family, arrived later in the 1750s from Guernica in Spain. Her great-grandfather, Joseph de Uriburu, presided over the family during the wars of independence, and the Uriburu clan remained one of the most powerful families of the oligarchy in the new Republic of Argentina during the next century. Rosa's grandfather, Pedro, one of Joseph's nine children, had married Cayetana Arias Cornejo from another traditional family in Salta; no house was grander than their mansion in the centre of the city. Rosa's mother, Luisa, was the youngest of their nine children and grew up while Pedro was active in politics, eventually presiding over the National Senate in Buenos Aires in the early 1860s. Thereafter his economic fortunes changed for the worse, and he lost the famous "Uriburu House" to wealthier relatives with a sounder economic base.[3]

Luisa Uriburu appeared to have escaped financial turmoil by marrying Segundo Linares y Sansetena, a member of a notable family in Salta whose brother was the local bishop and whose uncle was rich enough to own a private railway car. Indeed his early career as a capable minister in the provincial government and then as Senator of the Republic gave every indication of continuing success. But after a promising start his fortunes crumbled. After falling out with the political elite in the 1870s, he retired to the neighbouring capital of Jujuy where he taught Latin at the local Colegio Nacional and supplemented his income by consulting on legal matters, a small practice with few clients since he was not a trained lawyer. The family was short of funds, but they lived in faded elegance: their house, with multiple courtyards and one of the best libraries in Salta and Jujuy, covered an entire city block; its elegant stained-glass windows overlooked the main square and framed the snow-capped Andes. But Segundo Linares's money was gone, and this lifestyle was impossible to maintain. Clearly outside the rich and powerful branches of the Uriburu family, he and his wife raised their children in genteel poverty in their beloved but crumbling colonial mansion with its leaking roofs and aggressive termites. Rosa was raised with aristocratic sensibility tempered with financial desperation. Her sister had married back into money in a union with Julio Cornejo, a Conservative Party deputy in the National Congress, but Rosa was out of school at sixteen and her prospects were decidedly uncertain when she met her future husband and Raúl's father, Albin Prebisch.

Prebisch was a first-generation German immigrant who had recently found his way to Argentina from a village near Dresden in Saxony, where his family had a prosperous farm. His motivation for leaving Germany was not so much financial as to escape from the tedium of farming and rural life. Restless, anxious to get out of Europe and see the world, he began his global wanderings in England, where he made ends meet by teaching German, and then took a ship to India. Unhappy in the noise and confusion there, he set out again, searching for a frontier country where he could begin a new life; when his voyage around the world landed him in Buenos Aires, Prebisch knew at once that he had found his new homeland. Here lay a country of the future, a million miles square – so huge that Germany would fit inside it many times, and so geographically diverse that it included the Andean region, the rainforests of the northern lowlands, and the endless grasslands of the central pampas extending all the way to Patagonia. Here at last he felt welcome. In this New World dream country, seven thousand miles distant from New York or the English Channel, he could build the life he pleased.

Plunging into his new world and picking up Spanish as he went, Albin drifted from job to job, beginning in Buenos Aires but moving out of the capital to survey prospects in the sheep-raising south before heading to Mendoza, the central wine-growing province against the Chilean border. The vineyards of Mendoza were as unappealing as the sheep pastures he had just left in the south; he had finished with farming when he left

Germany and needed something else to satisfy his yearning for adventure. Albin therefore left for the distant Andean provinces and found a job in Jujuy with Mensajerias, an overland transport company with mules and horses shipping mail and coach passengers between northern Argentina and Bolivia. It was hard work, setting out from the compact colonial capital though indigenous areas and isolated mountain passes that were the only route between the two countries.

Albin met Rosa Linares Uriburu in 1887, when she was sixteen and he twenty-six. Although they were an unlikely couple given their social backgrounds, acquaintance quickly developed into a serious courtship. Her family disapproved; Segundo Linares was worried that Prebisch lacked both family and a stable position, and he fretted over losing his young daughter to a complete stranger who was a lapsed Protestant into the bargain. But Rosa had fallen in love, and Albin pressed. If this insistent foreigner attracted her affection, she represented for him a coveted link with the romantic colonial Argentina of his imagination. Segundo's opposition gradually yielded to necessity; his own financial situation was sufficiently precarious to prevent a veto, and Albin finally overcame parental hostility to his marriage proposal by promising that he and Rosa would have their children baptized and raised as Catholics.

If Albin Prebisch thought that marriage into a famous family would yield financial prospects and social recognition he was to be seriously disappointed. At first the couple remained in Jujuy, but life was not easy – their family was enlarged with the birth of their first child, Amalia, and the stagnant economy made work hard to find. Finally one of Rosa's wealthy uncles in Buenos Aires, Francisco Uriburu, arranged a job for Albin as an accountant in the local branch of the Bank of London, and they left for the capital with two children (a second daughter, Maria Luisa, having recently expanded the household). In Buenos Aires the young couple were treated like second-class relatives. The Francisco Uriburus were scions of society, and their sumptuous mansion at Lavalle 371, one of the most extravagantly appointed in Buenos Aires, was a hub of high society; Albin and Rosa were not welcome. It was not that all immigrants were excluded from the Uriburu house and the oligarchy it represented; the Bunges, Tornquists, Shaws, and Bembergs were welcomed and were also guests at their family ranch north of Buenos Aires, "Villa Elisa," with its 5,000 hectares and house built with materials imported from Europe, to which the symphony orchestra from the capital was invited to perform on special occasions. What these accepted immigrant families had in common were fortunes; serious wealth from anywhere could enter the Argentine upper class. Albin was a mere clerk, and the Uriburus left no doubt that they saw him as not fit to cross their threshold in town or country. Unable to tolerate the snub but still unwilling to break free from the family mystique, he left the capital to work on Francisco Uriburu's vineyards at Caucete, in San Juan province, located to the north of Mendoza along the Chilean border. However he found supervising 350 abject peasants who toiled for an absentee landlord in Buenos Aires even more unattractive than clerking in a major bank. He had not come all the way from a farm outside Dresden for this.

Albin Prebisch realized that he would have to make his own way, and he and Rosa, with three children (after the birth of their first son, Ernesto) returned to settle permanently in San Miguel de Tucumán. The new location was a happy choice. Sensing an opportunity, Prebisch decided to go into business for himself rather than work for others. He used his meagre savings supplemented with borrowed money to buy a small and struggling printing shop, La Velocidad. To the surprise of his relatives, he revealed a flair for entrepreneurship and rapidly built it into one of the largest printing establishments in northwestern Argentina. Capitalizing on an expanding regional market, he then diversified his operations, setting up a commercial sawmill and founding a major bookstore in Tucumán. Within twenty years of his arrival in Argentina with empty pockets, he had emerged as a respected businessman in the city, with sufficient free time to teach English at the local Colegio Nacional, be a director of the Banco Comercial de Tucumán, and serve as the Dutch Honorary Consul for Northwestern Argentina.

Albin Prebisch had correctly anticipated Tucumán's economic potential at the turn of the century. Although it was the smallest province in Argentina, comprising only 0.8 percent of the national territory, it was an agricultural paradise; nationally it was known as the "Garden of the Republic" or more poetically "America's Eden." When the enterprising Jesuits arrived they discovered that sugar cane could be grown profitably in these soils and sheltered valleys and had created a major sugar industry by the time of their expulsion from Spanish America in 1767. Fifty years later, in 1821, another Catholic dignitary, Bishop José Eduardo Eusebio Colombres, restarted sugar cane production and turned it into the backbone of the local economy, but it took the arrival of the railway from Buenos Aires in 1876 to open the national market.[4] Sugar production exploded from 5,000 to 135,000 acres, and priests gave way to oligarchs. Tariffs kept out cheaper Cuban and Brazilian sugar, and the region experienced a boom that created fortunes for its sugar barons.

When Albin Prebisch entered business in 1893, the national economy was in deep recession following the financial collapse of 1890, and it was far from clear when, or whether, it would recover. But he was correct in predicting an early recovery, although no one could have anticipated the pace of that growth. After 1896 the Argentine economy took off, and by 1914 it had become the world's leading exporter of meat and grain. To anchor its export trade economy, the railway network expanded from 2,516 km in 1880 to 16,563 in 1890 and 33,510 in 1914. By 1914 Argentina had entered the group of ten top trading nations with a per capita income double that of Italy and a third more than France. Enriched by a flood of 3.3 million immigrants from Europe between 1857 and 1914, the country was bursting with entrepreneurship and energy. Over three-quarters of industrial and commercial establishments were owned by foreign-born citizens. The most advanced public school system in Latin America had produced a large middle class with expectations of social mobility, and by 1914 Argentina had become the second wealthiest country in the world after the United States.

Tucumán shared in the economic boom with its expanding sugar refining industry, and the city recast itself as the pearl of the north. A tramway, a telephone system, and streetlights were built, as well as a new provincial legislature, a new University and National Secondary School, the Odeon Theatre, and the Fine Arts Museum. Grand banks and government buildings competed for attention in a city evidently on the move, and the rebuilding of the Belgrano, San Martin, and Alberdi plazas and the completion of the stunning 9 de Julio Park by the French landscape architect Carlos Thay made Tucumán a symbol of optimism in the future of Argentina. By 1914 it had become a major centre servicing the entire Argentine Andean region, growing to 91,000 people by 1914, unlike its sister cities, Salta and Jujuy, which stagnated at twenty-eight thousand and eight thousand respectively, and were envious of Tucumán's growth and vitality. They were depressed towns looking to the past; not so Tucumán, where there were opportunities for the quick and willing.

While Albin and Rosa Prebisch were not wealthy, his income permitted a comfortable middle-class life for the family, with a large house in the centre of the city enclosing courtyards lush with jasmine and gardenia, sheltering flocks of tiny hummingbirds much loved by Rosa. The rest of the children were born and raised here. Three sons, Ernesto, Julio, and Alberto followed the first two daughters; Raúl was the fourth and last boy. Another two daughters completed their family. Later Julio Gonzalez del Solar, Rosa's orphaned nephew, was also welcomed into the household. It was an open and friendly home where hospitality was generous, but there were no luxuries and Albin and Rosa did not own their house. Rosa made clothes for the children on her sewing machine and only occasionally brought out the family Dresden china. In contrast, Albin was a careful dresser, demanding tailor-made suits and English cashmere sweaters. Rosa maintained close relations with her own family in Jujuy, but the Prebischs lived outside the upper-class Uriburu circle and the local society of Tucumán and Salta. As in Buenos Aires, they were not invited to the great houses. Nevertheless a middle-class income meant that domestic servants could be hired for manual work, along with a full-time nanny.

An underlying social ambiguity surrounded the Prebisch family in Tucumán, given its evidently upper-class heritage but also the immigrant origins on Albin's side. While having a foreign-born father would not have been exceptional in Buenos Aires, Rosa's decision to marry an immigrant and raise her children in Tucumán gave them an uncertain social status. Buenos Aires was multiethnic like New York, where half the population were first-generation immigrants, and where these immigrants controlled a good portion of the city's wealth and financial power. The provincial city of Tucumán was a very different case; society remained stratified and traditional, and less than 5 percent of its population were immigrants. Raúl's family could not be in the Argentine oligarchy because his mother had married a first-generation German immigrant, nor was his family even remotely connected to the sugar barons in Tucumán. Immigrants were visible in the professions and local business; in Tucumán people knew their place, and family mattered. Albin was aware of this and insisted that his children identify with their mother's deep roots in Argentine history rather than the German heritage from which he had broken. He always spoke in Spanish to his children and would not tolerate the use of German at home for fear it would undermine the children's patriotism. While they were expected to learn foreign languages, particularly English and French (given their commercial importance in Argentina), he discouraged German at school and none of his children ever spoke the language or interested themselves in German culture or history. Albin's inculcation of national values proved effective: despite his evidently central European surname it never occurred to Raúl that he was anything other than an unhyphenated Argentine, and he was always offended by innuendos that he was a "foreigner."

By the time of Raúl's birth, his father had distanced himself emotionally from the family. The moment Albin stepped out of the family home he changed personality, and the demanding, dutiful parent who insisted on discipline and education was transformed into someone unrecognizably different. First, there was the Albin of the Tucumán German Club. Here he would revert to German at the first opportunity, eventually becoming the club's president and even reviving contacts with his birthplace in Saxony. Here he would smoke and drink; no alcohol or tobacco was allowed at home to corrupt the children or dull their appetite for success. Neither Rosa nor the children ever entered this world, although at the club Albin displayed their superior school report cards with parental pride.

Beyond the German Club, Albin Prebisch created another, entirely covert reality, which reflected a bohemian streak, a wildness and abandon Rosa could neither understand nor satisfy. In fact, the outwardly upright patriarch kept another household, woman and children, hidden on the other side of Tucumán. It was as if Rosa and her eight children formed the official household, but the marriage was not a success, or it was not enough; he also needed a different woman outside of society and convention. Unable to contain this passion, but also torn by guilt, he managed to conceal this secret life from Rosa and the entire family for twenty years in a busy shuttle between the two households, which left him increasingly less available emotionally for either – certainly for Rosa and their children. To Raúl his father seemed distant and cold, but he craved his affection and admired his independence, trying to please him through academic excellence.

Rosa therefore became a prime influence over her flock of children, guarding their development and their faith. The household was devoutly Catholic, and Raúl, like his siblings, proceeded through the steps of Holy Communion to Confirmation. The Linares-Uriburu tradition of conservatism and formality was followed at home and the Prebisch children never used the familiar form of address with their parents. Raúl's dependence on his mother grew in the absence of his father's affection, and Rosa became the central influence in his childhood. He in turn was his mother's favourite among the children with his quick sense of humour and evident intelligence. Family photographs show him in repose at eighteen months on the abundant maternal lap, confronting the camera with the amused, slightly ironic aspect characteristic of Raúl the adult. Even physically Raúl seemed drawn entirely from his mother's side of the marriage; he shared her features and the erect aristocratic Uriburu bearing. She gave her son an oil painting of her grandfather, Pedro Uriburu, with its startling likeness in features, eyes, and bearing. Rosa would sew special clothes for him to wear on National Day; she was unconditionally loving and the wellspring of his intellectual self-confidence. Her humanism was the source of Raúl's lifelong generosity and sensitivity to the underdog and human suffering, and he reciprocated his mother's affection with an unqualified loyalty in a lifelong intimacy that extended to her death in 1943.

In the absence of paternal support, Raúl's grandfather, Segundo Linares, played a fatherly role, his importance magnified by the complete absence of in-laws or family connections of any kind with his German relatives. The old crumbling mansion in Jujuy became Raúl's favourite vacation destination, where his grandfather would entertain him with colourful stories of the colonial days, embellished with library readings and walks together in the mountains. Segundo recognized Raúl as a future leader and encouraged his interest in Argentine history as they walked hand in hand through the narrow streets, his long white beard blowing in the sharp Andean winds, and the young boy became obsessed with his country – invoking his "four centuries of Argentine blood" – and determined to shape its future.[5]

Segundo Linares was a great storyteller, and it was from him rather than from his parents that Raúl learned the compelling history of family, region, and country. From his earliest years his grandfather instructed Raúl in the drama of the colonial past and the greatness of Argentina. He wove stories of Pizarro and his band of Spanish invaders creating garrison towns like Jujuy to guard the hostile passes; how to the immediate north of Tucumán lay its sister province of Salta, shaped like a boomerang, enclosing the even more remote Jujuy tucked in the farthest corner of the country against the Andean Cordillera and the borders of Chile and Bolivia; and how Tucumán (officially "San Miguel de Tucumán y Nueva Tierra de Promisión") was founded on 31 May 1565 by Diego de Villarroel and his troop of Spanish soldiers to defend their transportation routes from the Diaguita Indians, only to be swept away by a flood and forced to higher ground at the foot of San Javier mountain. Segundo described how Tucumán, Salta, and Jujuy prospered after their founding in the 1560s, sharing in the wealth of empire because they occupied a strategic location in the Spanish empire. Madrid's core interest was extracting wealth from the mines of Potosí in Bolivia for its royal monopoly over gold and silver and maintaining Lima as its colonial capital and centre of operations; therefore, the role of these three provinces was to protect the long overland colonial route from Lima across the Andean Highlands and then southward into Argentina, where it branched west at Cordoba over the Andes to the port city of Santiago, Chile. Raúl's grandfather recounted how Spanish policy had deliberately isolated Buenos Aires from the interior for two centuries to maintain Spain's control of precious metals because it had lost control of the South Atlantic after its naval defeat by England in 1588; this had resulted in the stagnation of Buenos Aires (or the "Puerto de Nuestra Senora de Santa Maria de Buenos Aires") so that it could claim no more than ten thousand inhabitants in 1750, two centuries after being founded in 1536, and still exchanged animal hides as the local currency despite all the king's gold and silver from the Andean mines.

But, Segundo continued, as Spain grew weaker and the silver and gold mines failed, the pull of Buenos Aires and the Atlantic grew stronger and forced King Charles III of Spain to reorder his colonial holdings by creating a new viceroyship of the Plate River in 1776 with its capital in Buenos Aires, which also included Tucumán, Salta, and Jujuy as well as Paraguay and Uruguay. Segundo recounted tales from the wars of independence and the exploits of the Uriburus in those wars – how the creation of the new viceroyship of the River Plate was too late and became the final stage in the collapse of Spanish rule in the Americas as the US and French Revolutions shook the New World, before Napoleon conquered Spain and Portugal to end the authority of the Spanish crown and unleash independence movements from one end of Latin America to the other. He described how British forces attacked Buenos Aires twice during 1806–07, and how the patriots repelled them in hand-to-hand fighting; how the viceroyship of the Plate River ceased to exist on 25 May 1810, and the patriots sent troops to free the rest of the viceroyship (including Uruguay, Bolivia, and Paraguay) from Spain, but how after long and bloody wars (including with Brazil, which wanted to annex Uruguay) these territories became independent countries and were lost to Argentina. Raúl's grandfather lovingly recalled the formal declaration of independence by a congress of Argentine statesmen and generals on 9 July 1816, which made Tucumán the "cradle of the nation." Segundo pointed out to Raúl that Tucumán had raised more than its share of national leaders, boasting landmarks such as Independence House, with its bronze busts of national heroes, and Independence Plaza, lined with flowering orange trees.

Alas, national independence spelled decline for the historic Andean region: Buenos Aires now became the economic and political centre of the nation; the shift of population and resources to the capital accelerated a parallel isolation and decline of the interior. As Buenos Aires dominated Argentina's political life, the picturesque colonial capitals of Salta and Jujuy watched their glory and leadership fade. Segundo Linares loved the Andes, but his years in Buenos Aires were equally unforgettable, and he filled Raúl's head with the beauty of the capital, its gomero trees and flowering jacarandas forming a sheet of purple colour over the city, and its romantic streets – Alvear, for example, which he compared with the Faubourg St Honoré in Paris, or Ayacucho, with its wrought-iron street lamps over the crowded cafés and sidewalks.

Young Raúl dreamt Argentine history, with his grandfather's mysterious fall from power in the capital only heightening his fascination. It moulded his sense of purpose in life; his mother and her ancient family represented the glory of the past, but also the promise of the future that he had a responsibility to honour. He took his legacy seriously; service to his country was expected and considered a bond with the many generations in the New World since 1565. Raúl was therefore devastated by Segundo's death in 1910 and became even more emotionally dependent on his mother. The subsequent decay of the old mansion in Jujuy pained him as it tottered toward demolition and was finally pulled down, with the complete loss of his grandfather's library.

Raúl Prebisch thus grew up between the old and the new Argentina. His mother represented the old oligarchy with colonial roots while his father was entirely a self-made person who owed nothing to connections. Salta and Jujuy were declining; Tucumán was a dynamic and growing city on the rise. But the old oligarchy remained a formidable power in the new economy of Argentina, and the Uriburu clan that would have nothing to do with the lowly Albin Prebisch family counted heavily in the region and Buenos Aires. They seemed to be everywhere. José Evaristo Uriburu had been vice-president and president of the Republic in 1885–88; Francisco Uriburu was a central figure in the ruling circles of Buenos Aires, a senator, minister of finance in the Province of Buenos Aires, and a leading banker in the national capital; Luisa, the older sister of Rosa's mother, had married General Teodoro Garcia, who had fought with Roca in the desert and been rewarded with a mansion in Belgrano; General José Felix Uriburu had been director of the elite Superior War School since 1907 and was a powerful figure in the military establishment. The provincial governments of Tucumán, Salta, and Jujuy were still run by the traditional oligarchy, which included Uriburus at the top of the social and business hierarchy.

Like his father, Raúl grew up with a middle-class disdain for the Argentine oligarchy, loathing in particular the sugar barons in Tucumán, whose labour practices made it the most socially backward province of the country. The exploitation of the sugar cane workers hung over the city like the smell of molasses from the twenty-six sugar mills ringing the booming city, a visceral reminder that left Raúl with a permanent revulsion against such injustice toward the weak. Here, also, Tucumán was a bridge between the new and old Argentina. While most sugar holdings were small, a few magnates led by Robustiano Patron Costas, owner of the largest sugar conglomerate in Argentina, dominated the industry. Also connected by marriage to the Uriburus, Patron Costas symbolized for Raúl the failings of the Argentine oligarchy, as well as its power; to complement his wealth, Patron Costas was also governor of Salta, a stalwart of the most intransigent wing of the Conservative Party, and he maintained close links with the Argentine military. General José Felix Uriburu was his closest personal friend. Between mid-May and August each year, Patron Costas and the other big owners hired thousands of migrant workers – Bolivian Indians, mestizo and black labourers – who worked in conditions rivalling those of colonial times. Tucumán thus became a backwater of social exclusion and poverty, having the highest illiteracy and infant mortality rates in the country. The migrants' shacks and makeshift shantytowns encircled the city; Tucumán was too small to hide their misery and the discrimination they suffered. Social violence against Indians was still widespread and broadly condoned. In 1903, a police chief and fourteen soldiers north of Tucumán attacked and killed one hundred Indians in retaliation for the alleged rape of a white woman.[6] Men, women, and children were tied to horses in groups of ten and dragged by their feet into the river, where their heads were cut off. There were no arrests.

As a child, Raúl played with Indian children during the harvest season, when they filled the streets of Tucumán begging for food; he refused to run inside and was scolded for associating with them.[7] His boyhood experience, therefore, was broader than that of children from most middle-class families in Argentina, and it was formative in his ethical development, making him part of Argentina's "generation of 1910," committed to balancing Argentina's economic success with a just society. His dislike of the oligarchy and military were therefore not accidental or derived from theory, and his pursuit of land reform and a modern state were similarly grounded in his experience growing up in Tucumán. But Raúl also grew up knowing how close he was to the powerful, that they were blood relatives of his mother, and therefore his own family as well. Altogether, his mother's legacy instilled an intimation of destiny, a calling to serve his country, and a responsibility for its future greatness, but also a love/hate relationship with the oligarchy represented by his own family.

Education played a central role in the Prebisch household in Tucumán; it was the key to success, and both parents demanded the highest grades in school. In turn, they were blessed with unusually gifted children, and the commitment to learning went beyond the mechanical issue of grades. The house was full of books, well-thumbed by his older brothers or sisters before Raúl got to them, and Rosa read all her children to sleep. For primary education Raúl was sent to the College of the Sacred Heart, run by French Jesuits, who taught a strict classical curriculum, with tough exams and demanding homework, to a largely middle-class group of children; the oligarchy sent its sons and daughters to the Mitre, Roca, and Rivadavia private schools. Raúl was a brilliant and headstrong pupil across the subjects taught in school, with his grandfather's love of books and with an intellectual self-confidence that astonished his teachers. The Prebisch family became mildly famous for the scholarly ability of their many children, but Raúl was the brightest of them all and regularly earned top prizes for his grades. The new Colegio Nacional, which Raúl attended for secondary school, was also of high quality and scarcely less regimented. His years there, coinciding with the First World War, were marked by a growing anti-German sentiment in Tucumán, which may have added to his own anti-German bias. Certainly the French Jesuits at the College of the Sacred Heart were passionate French nationalists – which meant hostility toward Imperial Germany. In his penultimate year, and for reasons which remain unclear, Raúl participated in a student strike at the Colegio Nacional, and his parents lodged him with his grandmother in Jujuy to complete his final year there rather than in Tucumán. Whatever the cause of the strike, and Raúl's role, it left no mark.

Unlike his gregarious brothers, Raúl was not interested in team or contact sports. From the beginning he was quiet and studious – a loner who had acquaintances but few friends. Apart from his mother and Segundo, he was closest to his old nanny, Mercedes Frias, or "Mametela," who remained devoted to Raúl and corresponded with him into the 1930s.[8] He preferred spending time at home reading, or with his mother or oldest sister, whose weakness left her unable to complete school or leave home. His one physical pastime was hiking in the surrounding hills, where he would disappear for long solitary walks on weekends. Raúl obviously missed his father. He was a quiet boy rather than a rebel, and a teenager without disciplinary problems, self-possessed, and firm in his likes and dislikes.

As Raúl neared the completion of secondary school, the choice of university and career became increasingly pressing. There was no doubt that Rosa's boys would go on to post-secondary education, and she insisted that they study in the capital rather than in the new University in Tucumán or the old colonial academy in Cordoba. Since Buenos Aires dominated Argentine life, her children were going to attend the best academic institutions the country could offer. Raúl himself was ready to move on, but he was uncertain about a career. His three brothers had made their choices and left home: Alberto was already a student of architecture; Julio was in medical school; and Ernesto was about to graduate as an engineer. This coverage of the obvious professions seemed to leave law for Raúl, and it was the traditional path for upward mobility in Argentina. But Raúl was not interested. He had seen a newspaper article regarding the new Faculty of Economic Sciences at the University of Buenos Aires, incorporated on 1 March 1914, and sent off for a prospectus.[9] He knew little about the subject, but the materials he received from the faculty in Buenos Aires intrigued him. It advertised itself as the foremost school of economics in Latin America, the only economics program that had, so far, established itself as a discipline separate from law.

Economics was a relatively new discipline in Latin America and a course of study that offered few job prospects compared with law. Within the academy in Argentina it had not attained the prestige that it had in the US, Britain, or the continental universities, nor was it seen as a stepping-stone for success in either the public or private sectors. When asked later what had stimulated his interest in economics, Raúl could only recount several boyhood anecdotes – a storekeeper complaining to one of his brothers about running out of change for a cigarette purchase and blaming it on the "financial crisis" – what was this crisis, he had asked? He overheard conversations with general references to inflation and land speculation in Argentina. "Why can't they print more money?" he asked his sister Amelia.[10] In any case, as his seventeenth birthday approached, Raúl elected to be a nonconformist and entered the Faculty of Economic Sciences in the university. In the end, his choice of career reflected his commitment to addressing the social question he had experienced in Tucumán. Its goal, or what Prebisch understood to be the principal object of enquiry in economics, was understanding the condition of business and labour in Argentina to improve the overall public good.

Boarding the train for the trip to the capital, Raúl was seen off by his mother, his sisters, and his grandmother with farewell presents of sweets and cured meats from the North. The inevitable dread of leaving behind family and home was real enough as they disappeared in the distance and the train descended into the wide horizon of the pampas en route to Buenos Aires, but it had already dissipated long before the train approached the city of dreams and promise.

2 University in Buenos Aires

On his arrival in Buenos Aires Raúl moved in with his widowed Aunt Luisa Uriburu de Garcia, whose old mansion in Belgrano served as the gathering place for the Uriburu-Linares-Prebisch flock in the capital. Her husband, General Teodoro Garcia, had fought with Roca against the Araucanian Indians, and his looming memory in the enormous faux-Moorish house with its large and well-groomed private park set the conservative tone for the large household. Raúl's uncle, Dr Julio Cornejo, who was a member of the National Congress, also lived in the house and venerated the general's memory and values, which included a lively hatred of economists. "Why do you do this sort of thing?" he would badger Raúl at dinner, maintaining a tiresome lecture until the poor student fled from the table. Nevertheless his Aunt Luisa somewhat moderated the shock Raúl experienced at the contrast between the worlds of an adolescent's Tucumán and Buenos Aires.[1]

Raúl's older brothers Alberto and Julio also lived with their aunt. All three shared a room with Ernesto, who was about to graduate and return to Tucumán. Albin provided fifty pesos a month for the older boys, and forty for Raúl, but Alberto was always short of money and invariably borrowed from Raúl at the end of each month. His brothers ridiculed him for his continuing religious orthodoxy and regular church attendance – they were now proud urban atheists. Raúl, at age seventeen, was too sheltered to participate in their nightlife in La Boca, the port area across the downtown core from upper-class Palermo and chic Recoleta, a sliver of land facing the Atlantic on one side and the Riachuelo River on the other. This had become the most lively and picturesque quarter of greater Buenos Aires, where a community of Italians, Greeks, Arabs, and Jews lived in precariously built but brightly painted houses (standing on piles to allow for floods), and the centre of brothels and nightlife of all kinds – the only place in the capital where the tango was not prohibited. Instead Raúl was a model student during his first year at the Faculty of Economic Sciences. Studious and disciplined, he maintained a Prussian schedule of eight hours of study each day in classes or the library. After 9:00 PM he would put aside his economics texts and read Cervantes, Shakespeare, and Balzac; he would then carefully prepare his agenda and work plan for the next day and go to bed. On Sundays he broke his routine by attending mass in the morning, followed by a movie.

Such an evident disregard for café life in the capital yielded a reputation as a social recluse, but Raúl felt blessed in his choice of discipline. His arrival in Buenos Aires and entry into the Faculty of Economic Sciences coincided with the opening of the last German offensive in the First World War, and with its failure the end of the war was imminent. For an aspiring economist like Raúl the challenges faced by postwar Europe and Latin America were of consuming interest, and the very turbulence and richness of life in Buenos Aires provided intellectual discoveries from one day to the next.

The governing Radical Party (Radical Civic Union: UCR) under President Hipolito Yrigoyen, born of the 1890s' financial and political crisis, was hard-pressed at this point during the First World War. Yrigoyen had won the 1916 national elections by a margin of only one electoral vote over the PAN, the conservative National Autonomist Party, which had ruled since 1880, when Roca took power in the interests of the traditional oligarchy and its newer moneyed allies in Buenos Aires. The Radical Party appealed to a broader constituency, particularly the emerging middle class; Yrigoyen's long political struggle therefore centred on one critical reform – ending a restricted and often corrupt voting system based on property in favour of universal, compulsory, and secret male balloting (as in North America and Europe, women did not have the vote) in national elections. But the PAN had not gone easily: Luis Roque Saenz Peña, elected in 1910 under the old system, had sensed eventual defeat on this issue and pre-empted the Radical platform in 1912 by passing the so-called Saenz Peña Law. But having reformed the electoral system, he (as well as Roca) suddenly died two years later, leaving no strong Conservative presidential candidate for the 1916 elections; so Yrigoyen had won, however narrowly.[2]

The result was a new government taking power at the height of World War I, amidst great expectations from the country and Radical Party followers. Instead there was disappointment and letdown; patronage spiralled, spending doubled, and the public debt increased eight-fold in six years with little to show for it. Yrigoyen seemed exhausted by success; having fought courageously all his life for the single objective of democratic reform, he had few other ideas about domestic or foreign policy. As the First

World War intensified after 1916 and allied pressure built for Argentine entry into the war against Germany, Yrigoyen could neither make a decision on war policy (remaining neutral even when Brazil declared war in 1917), nor cope with Argentina's mounting social problems as the conflict destroyed prewar trade patterns and businesses. Urban unemployment had tripled from 6.7 percent to 19.4 percent between 1914 and 1917, and inflation cut the real wages of industrial workers by one-third.[3] The result was an upsurge in strikes and labour violence, which employers countered with private police and paramilitary groups such as the Argentine Patriotic League. The Russian Revolution in November 1917 further radicalized the working-class districts and terrified the propertied classes. Change, even revolution, was in the air. The war in Europe was closely followed by all groups within the country. The majority of Argentine immigrants were from Italy (55 percent) and Spain (26 percent), but there were also strong communities from Britain, Germany, Eastern Europe (where the Jewish Colonization Association founded in 1891 had selected Argentina as a settlement area), and other countries. In 1910 three out of four adults in Buenos Aires had been born in Europe, bringing with them new political ideas and movements from the continent, such as socialism and anarchism. Alicia Moreau founded the Socialist Women's Centre in 1914 to provide care for middle-class women in the capital, and her upper-class counterpart Victoria Ocampo led the women's suffrage movement.[4]

Discontent and tension in the capital were deepening as Raúl arrived in Buenos Aires, and six months later there was a pitched battle between packinghouse workers and police. By January 1919, a metalworks strike degenerated into a week of street fighting between anarchist gangs and Patriotic League thugs that left over a thousand dead. The so-called "Tragic Week" stunned the country. President Yrigoyen called in the army to restore order but otherwise provided no clear leadership or initiatives for dealing with the causes of this class warfare.[5]

The result was a heated public debate in Buenos Aires on the future of the country, both within and outside the Congress. Modelled on the US Constitution, the Argentine Congress had two houses, a Senate and Chamber of Deputies; since the Senate remained under Conservative control, it could block reform legislation introduced by the government. However, the Chamber of Deputies was rich in the quality of discourse, if not necessarily in effectiveness. Besides the Radicals and Conservatives, it included the Argentine Socialist Party, which had been founded in 1896 by neurosurgeon Dr Juan B. Justo, the translator of Marx's *Capital* and Argentina's most internationally recognized intellectual in European circles. He advocated land reform to break up the large estates, labour rights and unemployment insurance to protect industrial workers, a welfare state, rural electrification and cooperatives, and free trade to lower food costs for consumers and prevent handouts to the corporate sector. *La Vanguardia* became the official newspaper of the Argentine Socialist Party. The party's base was in Buenos Aires, and in March 1914 it had defeated its Conservative opposition in the city by a margin of two to one in the elections for the Chamber of Deputies. Besides Justo, the Socialist Deputies included some of the best minds in the country – men like Augusto Bunge, Federico Pinedo, Alfredo Palacios, Nicolas Repetto and Antonio de Tomaso, all of whom were militant defenders of free trade to protect consumers against special interests. To the left of the Socialist Party was its bitter enemy, the new Moscow-dominated Argentine Communist Party, created in 1921, when the international socialist movement split into supporters and opponents of the Russian Revolution.

The Progressive Democrats formed another small but influential party headed by Lisandro de la Torre, a powerful Senator and cattle-raiser from Santa Fe province north of Buenos Aires. Born in 1868 into an old and wealthy family in Rosario, he studied law and local government in Buenos Aires, was elected as national deputy for the Radical Party between 1890 and 1893, but broke with Yrigoyen over party strategy and fought a duel with him, which left them mortal enemies for life. He thereupon founded the Progressive Democratic Party as an alternative to the Radicals and served again as a national deputy from 1912 to 1916. Hoping to appeal to the Conservatives in the 1916 elections, he only managed to split the anti-Yrigoyen vote and thereby facilitated a Reform Party victory. Lisandro de la Torre was, however, the best orator in the country and remained a colourful and potent political personality.

A vigorous press in Buenos Aires followed the debates in Congress and engaged the public; the normally dry subjects of trade, money, and inflation were recognized as major issues, linked to the revival of Europe and the global economy, and discussed everywhere in the capital. Buenos Aires was an exciting crossroads of new ideas and people and the metropolis of Latin America's artistic and literary world. Close links with Italian, Spanish, and French intellectuals such as Vilfredo Pareto and José Ortega y Gasset maintained a steady flow of news regarding developments in Europe.

The looming power of the US was also a more salient theme than before 1914. American seizure of Cuba, Puerto Rico, and the Philippines during the Spanish-US war of 1898 had had the effect of kindling fears of Washington throughout Latin America; and the nationalist impulse and renewal of the Mexican Revolution echoed throughout South America as writers sought anti-imperialist options.[6] The fascination and concern over the North American colossus were hugely magnified by the near defeat of

Britain and France in the First World War and the potential of even greater disparity in US-Latin American relations. What was the destiny of Latin America? Young Argentines were exploring their own inheritance and wanting to escape from the stranglehold of foreign ideas.

In contrast, the Faculty of Economic Sciences Raúl encountered seemed stodgy, complacent, and boring. From his opening class his experience with courses and professors was disappointing. He had expected an engaged faculty; he had anticipated quality teaching, and the prospectus had promised the first economics class using mathematical modelling in all of Latin America.[7] Instead his professors seemed out of touch with the postwar world, old-fashioned in teaching methods, unable to link theory and practice, uninterested in the international scene, and in any case busy elsewhere in the city with full-time jobs and never available for students. In theory the faculty had a large staff; in practice they were rarely available for teaching. The curriculum was deficient in the essential tools for quality teaching and independent research: languages, training in methodology and applied research, statistics, and comparative work. It was all too much like high school in Tucumán. The professors seemed content to rely on foreign textbooks and teaching materials and lacked the skills or interest for research that would help clarify the existing situation faced by Argentina's policymakers. It was very frustrating. Argentina confronted major postwar dilemmas, but the faculty seemed mesmerized by Europe and North America and therefore were unable to examine critically the Argentine economy in the international system. In fact his own faculty still taught economics as if the school were located in London rather than in South America. This was the case before the First World War, and it remained so after 1918, as if the war had been an unfortunate aberration with no lasting impact.

The orthodoxy remained the classical political economy imported from England before 1914, particularly the theory of comparative advantage.[8] Developed by David Ricardo and elaborated by his successors John Stuart Mill and Alfred Marshall, among others, this theory supported Latin American specialization in raw materials (in agricultural products in Argentina's case) for export to industrial countries in exchange for importing manufactured goods. The doctrine of comparative advantage also reflected the elite structure of prewar Buenos Aires. At its pinnacle were the English, who owned and controlled the railroads and much of the meat trade. Overwhelmingly reliant on its one trading and financial partner, Argentina was virtually a "sixth Dominion" of the British Empire. It was the most classic staple producer in Latin America; no other Latin American country except Cuba was more dependent on a single foreign market. In short, not only the wealthy English, but also the members of the Argentine oligarchy whose wealth came from the export of staples (primarily beef) to Britain, endorsed classical economic theory since it fit so well with the policies and trade patterns that created and protected it. Consuming 94 percent of total global beef exports in 1913, and therefore controlling the market, Britain relied on Argentina for 64 percent of these products. In the more technology-intensive chilled (as opposed to frozen) beef trade, Argentina was much farther ahead of its main competitors in Britain (Australia, New Zealand, and Canada) with 99.4 percent market share.

The Faculty of Economic Sciences reflected this pro-British stance, beginning with Dean Eleodoro Lobos, who had been minister of finance and agriculture in the last Conservative Governments before the 1916 Radical victory. While the outbreak of war in 1914 had thrown Argentina into a deep recession as exports to Britain fell and consumer goods and capital markets dried up – in effect subjecting it to a forced isolation in the international economy – neither this experience nor Britain's evident weakening relative to the United States as a world economic power had undermined the faculty's single-minded Anglo-Saxon identification when Prebisch enrolled in 1918. The assumption was that the prewar world centred on London would revive after the end of hostilities and that Argentina's future in the international economy could be secured by trade in staple products such as grain, beef, minerals, and coffee.

Outside the faculty, it was different. The theory of comparative advantage and the benefits of free trade were vigorously challenged by Alejandro Bunge, a professor at the National University of La Plata (UNLP). Bunge advocated industrialization as a complement to agricultural specialization, taking a different lesson from the First World War experience than Raúl's professors. He argued that Argentina had in fact benefited during World War I, when it could not get industrial imports at any price, because this forced isolation had nurtured a process of industrialization that was already under way before 1914. Industries allied to the export sector (such as meat-packing) had emerged and already accounted for no less than 17 percent of gross domestic product. Labour in machine-shops alone had grown from 28,000 in 1895 to 78,800 in 1914. Women already comprised 14 percent of the labour force, and two waves of industrial strikes had swept Argentina before the war, feeding socialist and anarchist unions. On industry's side employers had created the UIA (Argentine Industrial Union) as early as 1887 to lobby the national government on behalf of its members.[9] In Bunge's view, however, the war provided an additional powerful stimulus for industrialization, increasing the number of new factories from 48,000 to 68,000 between 1913 and 1923, with industrial employment increasing by almost 200,000 for a total of 600,000. He argued that these gains should not be squandered – that this sector should now be protected and encouraged to expand; there was no need to label these new industries "artificial" and kill them off by resuming unrestricted free trade with the industrial countries. Instead Argentina should reduce its dependence on Britain and the US by building its own capital goods industry; for all its apparent wealth, the country still lacked an iron and steel industry and therefore was in the weak position of importing virtually all of its higher-technology industrial goods while paying for them in agricultural sales to Britain.[10]

Raúl had no access as yet to people like Bunge. Classroom attendance was mandatory during his first year, but the effort was irrelevant given the quality of teaching. Raúl became so enraged by Professor Luis Roque Gondra's mechanical repetition of statistics on the Roman Empire in his seminar on Economic History that he and a new friend, Enrique Siewers, staged a class boycott and were sent in to Dean Lobos to explain themselves. Lobos listened to their demand that teaching be improved in the faculty and then consulted with Gondra – who to their surprise agreed to change the structure of the class. After the incident Dean Lobos took a special interest in the young Prebisch from Tucumán, giving him private weekly sessions each Thursday at 12:00 in his downtown law office. It was Raúl's first positive brush with the powerful in Buenos Aires. But aside from Dr Lobos there were few professors to whom he could turn for direction. Mauricio Nierenstein, secretary-general of the university, was interested in economic thought and promoted the translation of works by international figures such as American Henry George into Spanish. Salvador Oria, a young professor of public finance in the faculty, also encouraged Prebisch, but Oria was closely linked to the Radical Party and busy campaigning for a senior government appointment.

Raúl was thus largely on his own; unable to find the professorial supervision or research materials he sought, he immersed himself in library work instead. By his second year a new university reform law had been passed by the Yrigoyen Government eliminating mandatory classes, and he rarely attended faculty courses thereafter. "I studied by myself because I did not find anybody to guide me," he later noted.[11] He was therefore essentially self-taught and always regretted that he was at a disadvantage relative to peers in US or European universities because of the lack of disciplined course work in a serious economics program. But while continuing work on the English economists from Ricardo to Marshall, he also encountered Continental and US economists, and his thinking broadened. Raúl had underestimated – and came to respect – Gondra, for example, who introduced him to Continental economists such as Maffeo Pantaleone and Hugo Broggi.[12]

Nierenstein invited Raúl to translate a book by the Italian economist Enrico Barone, a follower of Léon Walras and Pareto, and through Lobos he also translated John Williams's PhD thesis, *Argentine International Trade Under Inconvertible Paper Money, 1880–1900*, which questioned conventional trade theory. But he lamented the "mediocrity" and "deficiencies" of the faculty and missed the challenge of a disciplined program. "My great aspiration at that time was to go to Harvard," Prebisch recounted, to study with Frank W. Taussig and the recently hired Williams.[13] There were also gaps. Although his reading included Marx's *Capital*, as well as some works by Lenin and the European socialists who had broken with bolshevism, he did not have access to Marx's earlier, more humanistic, writings.

Prebisch found that the faculty journal would publish his work, and while this *Journal of Economic Sciences* was not a refereed journal and remained well below international quality, it was at least a reliable outlet for youthful first articles. His short piece "La cuestión social," written when he was only nineteen, dismissed the relevance of Soviet-style Marxism in the Argentine situation, but this was an assertion rather than a reasoned conclusion, typically Catholic and conservative, reflecting his upbringing and current surroundings in Belgrano, home of the Buenos Aires Polo Club, embassies, and palaces.[14] During his first two years he wrote numerous short articles for the faculty's *Journal of Economic Sciences* on a variety of topics ranging from postwar stabilization in Europe to monetary issues, and reviews of articles or books published abroad supplemented by short commentaries. These early research notes of 1918–19 revealed little more than the future promise of a young but exceptionally talented and traditional student who wrote with confidence and fluid style. Even the most ardent admirer of Prebisch could claim no more from these articles.[15]

In 1920 a personal crisis challenged Prebisch's conservatism and expanded his intellectual and political horizons during his remaining university years. The first shock was discovering his Aunt Luisa dead of heart failure. He had returned unexpectedly after lunch to find that she had not awakened from her regular siesta; he was the first on the scene and it was the first time he had experienced death first hand. Besides losing a close friend, Raúl found himself without a place to live. He moved to lodgings not far away in Belgrano, but this time he lived alone. His two brothers had left Buenos Aires, Julio for Tucumán and Alberto for Paris to study with Le Corbusier; Raúl was now alone for the first time.

Coincidentally, Raúl's faith evaporated. In the middle of Sunday mass shortly after his aunt's funeral he suddenly and without warning lost belief. "A veil fell over my eyes" he noted, "I had to leave church."[16] In fact the change was part of a broader awakening provoked by the exposure of his father's secret family.[17] In mid-1920 Rosa finally uncovered the humiliating truth, and the secret spread quickly to Ernesto, who told his brothers and sisters. Angry and insulted, Raúl now realized that he had never known his father at all; he had not suspected anything like this to explain Albin's long absences on "business," or his constant criticisms of his family, or his aloofness and lack of emotional support. The curious lack of money despite his business successes was now readily understandable. It was a blow to Raúl because he had sought so hard to win his father's acceptance, and he admired his father's achievements, dynamism, work habits, and entrepreneurial spirit. He called it "good German blood." If Raúl's national commitment, intellectual self-confidence, and personal warmth bore the stamp of his mother and her family, he was also his father's son in energy, determination to succeed, and relentless capacity for work.

Raúl never forgave Albin for betraying the family while self-righteously demanding discipline from Rosa and their children. It was one thing for Argentine men to keep a mistress, and the practice was widespread in the interior; but it was another for a German like his father. During the next decade he rarely visited Tucumán and communicated only intermittently by letter despite his father's repeated overtures for reconciliation and protestations of parental affection. Nor did he meet or try to establish contact with his half-brothers and sisters on the wrong side of Tucumán. Like a lingering shadow, the sense of rejection by his father continued to haunt Raúl. "I hope relations with my son will be better that mine were with father," he concluded.[18] Raúl may also have reacted so strongly because he sensed his father's bohemian streak in himself and feared so unwelcome an inheritance.

The family crisis made him even more determined to prove himself and instilled a fanatical desire for financial independence from Albin. The result was a burst of activity in which he became as obsessed with work as his father and continued a joyless student lifestyle despite the new freedom from religious inhibitions. He had arrived as a first year student from the provinces without independent means, knowing that his future depended entirely on talent and energy. He now began an almost frantic work schedule, beginning with his first job on 1 September 1920 as teaching assistant, second class, at a salary of one hundred pesos a month. Financially it was a major step forward in what he called "the emancipation from my father,"[19] but it was also a tough assignment since he was given responsibility for the faculty's Research Seminar even though he had neither formal training in social science research methods nor fieldwork experience apart from his own ad hoc research.[20] He worked hard to prepare for seminars, and his success earned him a rapid promotion in August 1921 to first class assistant with a pay raise to 150 pesos a month.

Raúl also enrolled in Alejandro Bunge's seminar at the National University of La Plata and worked briefly as his assistant, leading a research group that compared purchasing power in Argentina and postwar Europe, publishing its findings under the title of "Salary Adjustment and Cost of Living" in the November-December 1920 issue of the *Revista Económica Argentina.* Bunge had just founded this journal in 1918 and had also recently published a major work, *Argentine Trade 1901–17*, one of the few reliable sources of data in Raúl's major field of interest.[21] Bunge was one of the more interesting scholars he had met since leaving Tucumán – a homegrown economist, unorthodox and multifaceted. Born in 1880, he was an engineer, leader of the Catholic Workers Group (Circulos de Obreros Catolicos), and Director of Statistics in the National Department of Labour from 1913 to 1915, before becoming director of the National Statistical Office, 1915–20, and again 1923–25. His training as an engineer inclined him to scientific methods, and he insisted that his students undertake fieldwork to support their findings. He thought big, and Raúl liked him. There was more to him than his well-known challenge to the theory of comparative advantage and support for industrialization. Bunge was well connected internationally, multilingual, and well-read. He intrigued Raúl by advocating the economic integration of Argentina and the other Southern Cone countries, Chile, Bolivia, Paraguay, and Uruguay.

If Raúl respected Bunge's knowledge and statistical fluency, the professor appreciated the younger man's seriousness and commitment to empirical research. He invited him to use the National Statistical Office in his teaching and research and suggested that Raúl work with him when his secretary was absent. Bunge also helped Raúl secure a position in the Faculty of Social and Legal Sciences at UNLP to teach a research seminar at a rate of 250 pesos per month beginning 4 April 1921. This was a more visible appointment as a full course director rather than as a teaching assistant, and it was in a new university outside Buenos Aires, where he felt a greater freedom than in his own faculty. The new city of La Plata, south of the capital, was home to the powerful provincial government of Buenos Aires, built in defiance of federal authorities after Buenos Aires was taken from them and declared the federal capital in 1880. Planned on a grand scale like Washington, DC, it was laid out as a grid of streets numbered in the American style creating blocks five hundred metres square with an overlay of radials converging on the central square in front of the provincial Parliament. The optimism of the decade was reflected in ambitious public buildings and a speculative bubble that burst in 1890, but UNLP was nevertheless created in 1906 as Argentina's third university (after Cordoba and

Buenos Aires) and was known for its progressive ambience. In this more open environment, Raúl vented his frustration with his faculty's backward curriculum by preparing a course outline with a stinging attack on the quality of university training in economics in Argentina. He advocated sweeping changes and now could finally implement the teaching methods that he found conspicuously absent at the University of Buenos Aires (UBA). Students and faculty must redesign their professional responsibilities, he insisted; dogma delivered from on high by part-time professors had to give way to scientific methods; and serious students must accept economics as a vocation rather than a part-time diversion. With his UNLP niche, Prebisch became more assertive personally and intellectually within his own faculty. Taking advantage of the 1918 University Reform, which ended compulsory attendance and granted students the right of co-governance, Raúl demanded a reshaping of the *Journal of Economic Sciences* with a joint faculty-student editorial board – which of course included him.[22] He also vigorously promoted links to European universities such as the University of Paris to enrich the curriculum and welcomed the visit of public finance specialist Gaston Jeze from that university even though certain faculty professors felt personally slighted by the addition of a foreign expert in their areas of concentration.

Despite his respect for Alejandro Bunge, Raúl rejected his advocacy of industrialization rather than free trade. While he agreed with Bunge that the economy had grown during the 1914–18 war, Raúl could not be persuaded that Argentina should support "artificial industries," nor would he accept comparisons with countries such as the US and Germany, which had built large competitive enterprises behind tariff walls before 1914. Bunge then challenged Prebisch with the experience of Canada, where similarities with Argentina were obvious. Canada had not been content with free trade; instead the federal government had introduced a national policy of high protective tariffs in 1879 and already by 1901 had a domestic steel industry for building its great railway systems. Now it had an emerging heavy industrial sector and had become one of the leading farm equipment manufacturers in the world after 1918, while Argentina seemed content to remain the world's largest pasture serviced by British-owned and -operated railways. Should not Argentina follow Canada's example and discard the belief that free trade was an immutable principle never to be challenged? Prebisch rejected this entire argument, turning the doctrine of comparative advantage against Bunge: Canada had unlimited and accessible supplies of high quality iron ore – Argentina did not, and it was therefore cheaper to continue to import steel. He also noted that Dr Josiah Stamp of the Royal Statistical Society in London (1919) had placed Argentina somewhat ahead of Canada in per capita income in 1914, confirming that the staples model remained the most efficient for Argentina in terms of resource allocation.[23]

Prebisch would develop a stronger bond with Alejandro's elder brother, Augusto Bunge, who occupied an even more conspicuous niche in Buenos Aires. The founder of empirical sociology in Argentina, Augusto Bunge was born in 1877 and completed his medical training at the age of twenty-three, after which he devoted himself to the promotion of public health and politics in Argentina.[24] He had toured Europe in 1906 while heading the industrial health section of the National Department of Public Health, and his book, *Las Conquistas de la Higiene Social* (1911), which advocated a German social-insurance model, remained the authority in the field for a decade. The two brothers came from a large and famous family, grandsons of Karl August Bunge von Reinessend und von Renschenbusch, who had arrived in 1827 as consul-general for Prussia and had stayed and married into the aristocracy. With his brother Hugo, Karl August had founded a huge business and banking conglomerate and amassed a significant fortune.

Neither grandson had entered business, preferring careers in the professions instead, but their similarity in this broad aspect gave way to sharp differences in ideology and politics. Unlike Alejandro, Augusto Bunge was a socialist who taught at UBA and served as a national deputy for the Socialist Party for five consecutive terms between 1916 and 1936. Prominent in the Argentine Socialist Party hierarchy, he also edited a party journal, *La Hora*, as well as the influential Buenos Aires daily *Critica*, and was one of the most passionate critics of Yrigoyen's social and labour policies. Augusto's sprawling house in the district of Florida was built when the wealthy families of the capital had moved north from San Thelmo south of the Plaza de Mayo after the yellow fever epidemic of 1871. But unlike his wealthy relations, Augusto was uninterested in money: he gave half his salary to the Socialist Party, and lived in such spartan conditions that his house lacked running water and indoor toilet facilities. He was, in short, a committed intellectual and writer caught up in a ceaseless campaign to reform his country, now teaching and lecturing, now writing or active in the Congress, translating Goethe's *Faust* into Spanish on weekends, and late in the evening still supervising the morning edition of *Critica,* the first of three each day.

Prebisch had admired Bunge from a distance after attending one of his sociology seminars during his first year at the university, but his main purpose in meeting him was political: Raúl had decided to join the Socialist Party of Argentina. Before his personal trials of 1920 he had regarded religion and socialism as incompatible, automatically rejecting the latter as atheistic. In Tucumán there had been no political debate in the family home; his father shunned all party involvement and such references as there were identified Rosa's family with the Uriburu relatives from Salta, including his uncle Dr Julio Cornejo, who proudly represented the landed oligarchy in the Conservative Party. Raúl later recalled meeting a fellow student promoting "socialism," but he had rejected this as an attack on religion and the incident left no lasting impression.

Now he could enter the national debate on the social question in Argentina with a new freedom and come to terms with the sociopolitical and industrial crisis he had witnessed since 1918. The Argentine Socialist Party interested Raúl far more than the other alternatives. He categorically ruled out the Conservatives. The Radicals were almost equally unattractive, already devoid of ideas, and with a leadership almost as exclusive as that of their Conservative rivals. Lisandro de la Torre's Progressive Democrats were also no improvement. Indeed, the failure of de la Torre's attempt to unite the Radicals and Conservatives after he broke with Yrigoyen summed up eloquently, for Prebisch's generation, the bankruptcy of Argentina's political class. The Yrigoyen-Lisandro de la Torre duel (complete with seconds and ceremonial pistols in leather cases), left a hole in de la Torre's jaw that had to be disguised with a beard. And if Raúl dismissed the pathetic anachronism of duelling he also rejected out of hand the Leninism of the Argentine Communist Party.

This left the Socialist Party, and he found much in its platform to his liking, beginning with its position on land reform, because he also viewed the concentration of land in the hands of a small class of largely absentee landlords as Argentina's crucially negative inheritance from Spanish rule. Unlike the US, Canada, or Australia, where land colonization had proceeded through a homestead policy for European immigrants, the power of the landed elite in Argentina continually frustrated the emergence of an efficiently farmed and numerically large agrarian sector. Few immigrants worked on the land, and much of the enormous countryside was practically empty. But the political power of the oligarchy continued, and its pursuit of special privileges for big agriculture (the Tucumán sugar barons made their fortunes with duties that kept out cheaper Brazilian imports) made nonsense of the official policy of free trade. The sugar plantations in Tucumán remained a vivid memory, where the suffering of marginalized migrant workers was much worse than that of the urban proletariat in Buenos Aires, even if they were too cowed to rebel. Fundamental reform was essential to break this power and integrate the agrarian sector more rationally within the Argentine political economy, and the Socialist Party was the standard-bearer of change. Veteran Alfredo Palacios, elected in 1904 (although evicted by the party between 1912 and 1916 for duelling), was a political economist of continental rank and the first Socialist member of Congress in all Latin America; others such as the younger brilliant protegé of Justo, Antonio de Tomaso, were outspokenly opposed to increases in the military budget, and this also attracted Prebisch; the very fact that Antonio de Tomaso had become the prime target of verbal abuse from General José F. Uriburu increased his respect for the party.[25]

The Socialist Party deputies in Congress dominated the parliamentary debates on Argentina's postwar economic and political future. If rhetoric alone could win, the party would long since have controlled Argentina; Socialist deputies were intellectuals rather than workers or provincial politicians from the interior, such as Raúl's uncle Cornejo, and they were both hardworking and intelligent, demonstrating a nonsectarian pluralism and breadth of opinion unique in the Argentine political spectrum. Broadly speaking the party had three identifiable camps or tendencies, united only in their opposition to Soviet-style communism and their support of free trade. Party Chairman Juan B. Justo was the undisputed leader and commanded the middle ground with a reformism modelled on the Bernstein wing of the German Social Democratic Party; he was, in short, a Marxist revisionist promoting change and accommodation within a democratic political framework. He was venerated by acolytes such as Nicolas Repetto and Enrique Dickmann. To his right was the gifted maverick lawyer Federico Pinedo, only six years older than Prebisch, who had led the legislative campaign for the creation of the Faculty of Economic Sciences and who remained a member of its governing council. The position of Pinedo on free enterprise and trade was so orthodox as to call into question his long-term commitment to social change or even democracy. The left of the party, championed by Augusto Bunge and Alfredo Palacios, demanded social transformation and gender equity. While it was a fractious party loaded with disagreements, there seemed to be room for all.[26]

Prebisch's decision to join the Socialist Party was a symbolic break with Catholicism and a repudiation of the Uriburu Conservative inheritance, and he turned to the left of the party with Augusto Bunge as his first contact. An introduction was soon arranged by fellow student Luis de Francesco, who had worked as Bunge's secretary, and Raúl was immediately welcomed into one of the most diverse and interesting social circles in Buenos Aires. The Bunge house was a gathering place every Sunday for radicals, refugees from Europe and Latin America, and interesting people of all kinds from across the political spectrum. During his first visits Raúl was embarrassingly socially inept: when Augusto saw him adding sugar and water to a glass of good Mendoza red wine he discreetly took him aside for a good-humoured fatherly chat. These rougher edges soon disappeared;

Raúl became a regular visitor and a close personal friend whom Bunge asked to be godfather for his son Mario. Raúl brought along boxes of treats sent from Tucumán. He also brought along his friends from the university, who were accepted into the generous Bunge flock as readily as Raúl himself.[27]

The Sunday debates in the Bunge household were always memorable. Thinkers from all over Latin America and Europe gathered to discuss ideas, international developments, and new theories over wine, coffee, and a permanent haze of cigarette smoke. Every session was special in its unpredictability. The foremost political topic of the day was the Russian Revolution and its implications for the spread of socialism in Europe and Latin America. The rise of Mussolini was also closely followed, a sensitive issue among Italian veterans and their families in Argentina after the First World War. So was the US growth of power during World War I and the evident unleashing of its Napoleonic instinct in the Caribbean Basin.

Encouraged by his experience with Augusto Bunge, Prebisch picked up the application forms to join the Socialist Party; coincidentally Bunge asked him to write an article for the party newspaper *La Hora* on postwar monetary policy and cost-of-living increases after the World War. Raúl agreed. He was researching this subject for a faculty seminar and had a text nearly ready for publication. In fact the article was completed and published with the title "Wages or Gold" before Raúl had submitted his membership application to the Socialist Party office. The Socialist Party had taken a clear stand on postwar inflation, maintaining that the gold standard, which had been suspended on 2 August 1914, should be reintroduced and that workers should be paid in gold rather than currency to protect their purchasing power. But Prebisch disagreed, arguing that it was both impractical and misguided because gold had also depreciated; without being disrespectful to Justo, he argued that he had understated the impact of this structural factor. The proverbial tempest-in-a-teapot occurred: the great Dr Justo himself intervened, complaining to Bunge that Raúl's piece confused both party and public opinion by openly contradicting the party's platform (as well as the leader's own well-known views on the sanctity of the gold standard). Justo even took the issue to the party governing council, which formally criticized Bunge for inviting a non-militant (and a mere student at that) to write for *La Hora*. Prebisch tore up his membership application when he heard what had happened and never joined another political party for the rest of his life.[28] But he retained his personal links with Bunge and the Sunday gatherings and joined several of Bunge's working groups (on the Railway Workers' Pension Fund, for example), which offered serious learning experiences. But the Justo incident permanently soured Prebisch on party politics, even though he supported the candidacy of Justo for dean of the faculty.

Prebisch now became even more a person apart. He craved a more serious research experience. He had come to Buenos Aires to write and to join the great debates of the day as a participant with something to add, and the difficulty of locating reliable information about the Argentine economy drove him to find like-minded students who shared this frustration and desire to write and undertake research. Other gifted young Argentines had indeed entered the faculty with the same sense of public commitment, among them Ernesto Malaccorto, Max Alemann, Enrique Siewers, Julio Silva, and Julio Broide, and they formed the inner core of a closely knit circle of friends and supporters with whom Raúl formed lifelong friendships. They were united by the belief that Argentina had come out of the war greatly strengthened as an international player and could become an important power if it managed its affairs successfully. Recognizing Raúl's intellectual qualities and academic virtuosity, they formed ad hoc research groups under his direction to examine outstanding public policy questions and publish reports to stimulate debate in a modest effort to link policy with university research and promote fieldwork for students.[29]

The scholarly results were soon evident. Raúl's research matured, and the range of his interests and scholarly energy expanded after 1920 with serious writing based on broader and more serious reading and presented with greater authority as his self-education deepened. Raúl's interest lay in trade and monetary policy. His two 1921 articles on the Brussels Conference of September 1920, in which he encountered and read John M. Keynes's *Economic Consequences of the Peace*, took up the question of postwar monetary stability and its implications for Argentina.[30] Not having had the luxury of prior advanced training in economic theory, he read back into the theoretical and historical literature after selecting an issue for research. This method risked a helter-skelter approach to the classics and required discipline to be effective, but Prebisch's remarkable article, "Notes On Our Money Supply," published in five succeeding issues of the *Journal of Economic Sciences* in 1921–22, proved his scholarly potential – even if so humble an outlet for this work guaranteed invisibility within the discipline. This misfortune does not detract from its boldness and insights.[31]

The article was technically a review of *La Moneda, el Credito y los Bancos en la Argentina*, a book on the history of banking in Argentina recently published by Norberto Piñero, a private banker and briefly minister of finance in 1913, who also taught a course in the faculty and had written an earlier book on this subject in 1916, *La Moneda Argentina.* But Prebisch's interest had also grown after his translation into Spanish of (now) Harvard Professor John H. Williams's book, the most authoritative book available on the subject by a professional economist of rank. Prebisch used the opportunity to review the banking sector since independence in 1810, examining historical records and available secondary sources, as well as the theoretical literature from European and American economists relevant to this field.

Piñero had written a descriptive and largely anecdotal account of the national banking system in a light text building from Buenos Aires's humble beginnings in colonial times, when it was a small Atlantic port, isolated from the interior by Spain's policy of favouring Lima as the heart of its Andean empire, and only gradually developing into a powerful city after independence in the nineteenth century. Piñero maintained that the business cycle in Argentina essentially replicated the European experience, in which excessive credit during prosperous times eventually produced imbalance and crisis through excess consumption and a flood of imports, with a resulting trade imbalance and flight of gold. However, an automatic correction would inevitably follow as interest rates rose to stop the bleeding and lure short-term capital back into the market – indeed this was one of the sacred assumptions of liberal equilibrium theory taught in the faculty. Beginning with the first Argentine bank (Banco de Descuento) in 1822, Piñero argued, governments and business had sought to accommodate the ebb and flow of the international market with increasingly sophisticated banking instruments, and step by step they had succeeded in laying the foundation for the great trading nation that Argentina had become by 1914. He concluded that the government should expand the powers of the Exchange Office to build on its successes.

Prebisch and his team undertook a detailed historical analysis of the boom-and-bust cycle from independence in 1810 to the First World War, trying to identify recurring features in each crisis, which could either verify Piñero's conclusions or point to other explanations. The research results demonstrated that neither Piñero nor the few other Argentine economists who had written in this field had researched the subject in depth. A closer analysis of the specific dynamic of each cycle and the role and behaviour of Argentine banks and governments showed a much more complex picture. International and Argentine markets were linked, to be sure, but instead of merely imitating the European experience, the boom-and-bust cycle revealed an interaction of factors peculiar to Argentina and absent in the European business cycle.

The very vulnerability of Argentina in the international economy propelled its banks into a depressingly familiar pattern of errors. A narrow taxation base and the lack of domestic capital markets made it dependent on international borrowing. Argentina had already borrowed heavily from London in 1824, creating a financial system largely destroyed in the 1824–26 war with Brazil. But banking institutions remained fragile for political reasons; property taxes were too unpopular to impose effectively, leaving customs receipts responsible for funding 90 percent of federal income and thereby leading to a crisis whenever the British chose to blockade its ports. The analysis of banking and monetary policy before and after speculative bubbles or when harvests failed or prices dropped showed a pattern repeated with almost monotonous regularity in which an immature banking system invited disaster by excessive loans and sale of bonds in European markets, thus provoking a boom in what Prebisch called "non-essential" imports and a speculative frenzy. This ascending part of the cycle was followed by severe crises, as in 1873 or 1891, when money dried up, abruptly halting speculation and plunging the country into recession.

The discovery "projected a new perspective on our monetary problems," Raúl noted.[32] There were vital policy, political, and psychological differences at play in Argentina relative to England or Europe. Money fled the country for safe havens during the downward part of the cycle, but, unlike in Europe, high interest rates alone could not reverse the outflow by halting capital flight and attracting new investment to fuel an economic recovery. Although accurate for Europe, the theory did not fit the Argentine reality. He used the terminology of "centre" and "periphery" for the first time in this article, terms that he would make famous twenty-five years later in his structuralist critique of liberal orthodoxy, but in this context they reflected the ongoing debate in Argentina regarding the relationship of Buenos Aires with the dependent interior of the republic.[33] Instead of the more balanced urban/rural development characteristic of Canada or the United States, the Argentine capital had extracted wealth from the interior until it dominated the economic, political, and cultural life of the country.

No one, including Raúl himself, realized the significance of what he had produced or its potential theoretical implications for the study of international trade and monetary policy. Prebisch had entered into the study of the business cycle, a neglected area of enquiry, which for decades had been separated from that of general economic theory and which in any case had never been applied systematically to dependent agricultural economies or to the role of international money markets and balance of payments. Raúl had discovered that, while local monetary mistakes by Argentine banks and governments did not cause the periodic crises (the international business cycle inevitably clobbered Argentina as well the developed countries), the *course, severity,* and *dynamics* of each crisis were indeed the product of local circumstances. Argentine authorities were not merely victims but also actors, and their decisions could mitigate or aggravate the impact of international recessions.

Raúl's work opened a huge opportunity for future investigation, but there was no one in Buenos Aires to tell him what he had done, and there is no indication that the article was reviewed or even read by his professors. Prebisch had taken his historical analysis to 1914 and promised to cover the war years later. He also underlined his interest in studying the "relationships of the money markets, or in other words, the functioning of the international monetary system."[34] But while his 1921 paper had ignited a lifelong interest in this subject, he had struck a conceptual barrier that disempowered him – namely the assumption that Argentine governments could not influence or correct the business cycle.

So rather than following this line of research, he moved on instead to additional work on postwar stabilization plans. Like the earlier major work it centred on the review of an economist's book on the subject, in this case *Stabilizing the Dollar: A Plan to Stabilize the General Price Level without Fixing Individual Prices* (1920), by US economist Irving Fischer.[35] Written with more theoretical flair than *Notes on our Money Supply*, with references to the English classical economists including Stanley Jevons and F.W. Taussig, as well as F.A. Fetter and Edwin Kemmerer from the US, Prebisch's review explored the complexity (but eventual necessity) of reintroducing the gold standard in the context of the growing financial destabilization in Western Europe. In fact, the situation deteriorated further with the French occupation of the Ruhr Valley and a fantastic surge of inflation in Germany that destroyed the deutschmark. Prebisch did acquaint himself with the work of Kemmerer, who would become the foremost US economic advisor to Latin American governments in the interwar years, but he wanted to move on from this subject as well.

In fact Prebisch was looking beyond the university: given the quality of teaching and resources in his subject in Buenos Aires there was nothing more for him here – the scholars he respected most, such as the Bunges or Lobos, were engaged public figures who could never be full-time researchers. He would have to go outside the university to learn more about his country. There was, of course, the possibility of continuing his training abroad as a professional economist; his brother Alberto had managed to get a scholarship to study with Le Corbusier in Paris. But there was no similar possibility in economics and graduate work for him in Europe or North America was therefore impossible for financial reasons. Raúl knew that university teaching in Argentina was not viable financially as a full-time career, and he therefore decided to leave UBA with a diploma as chartered accountant.

But the compelling reason was not money. The chief interest of his undergraduate work was policy rather than economic theory, and his evident goal was to understand Argentina's position in the international economy in order to serve his country in a practical job. His vocation, his mission, lay outside the university, which could never offer enough to satisfy his deeper ambition of service to the Argentine state.

Imperceptibly, but with a certain logic, Prebisch's choice of career was narrowing to the Argentine public service, but he did not arrive at this position from his flirtation with the Socialist Party. While he accepted its platform calling for the return of the gold standard and free trade, he was difficult to pin down ideologically after he rejected membership when crossed by Justo, and he showed no interest in the Radicals, Conservatives, or any of the other smaller parties. Yet it is a weak passion that can be extinguished by one disappointing experience, and Raúl's quick withdrawal from political engagement offered an important early clue to his intellectual development. He showed little enthusiasm for socialist doctrine or class analysis; his earliest writings on trade and monetary issues were concerned instead with understanding policy, cast largely within a liberal trade and monetary perspective. Nor could he accept the notion that the state was a mere tool of the oligarchy without autonomy; his own sense of power to shape events ruled out such determinism. The truth was that though Raúl was committed to social justice from his childhood in Tucumán, particularly the advancement of labour and human rights in Argentina after the First World War, he did not see his role as a reformer within party politics. While the social question drew him to Augusto Bunge and the left of the Socialist Party, he was to a remarkable degree indifferent to political campaigns and meetings, or demonstrations of any kind.

Instead Raúl was drawn to the belief that a technocratic elite could lead a reform process, using the state as an instrument of change rather than a tool of class or special interests. The Argentine state was weak; it could not even impose taxation on the elite, and fiscal reform was a measure of capacity and institutional development. Canada had implemented an income tax in 1917; Australia had also reformed its tax system; but every time an Argentine government had attempted a reform package it had fallen before political resistance in favour of the easy way out – external borrowing. From 1888 to 1896, for example, Argentina's indebtedness per capita had tripled. The country, in short, needed an administrative elite to modernize the public sector. In this sense it was Pareto, rather than Marx, who proved the most important influence on Prebisch's choice of vocation. Raúl had encountered his work while translating Barone during the 1922 presidential election campaign, and its results confirmed his disillusionment with Argentina's electoral politics.[36] Notwithstanding six years of blatant UCR (Union Radical Civica or Radical Party) patronage and broken promises, and the onset of a serious postwar recession, the well-oiled political machine of the Radical Party delivered another huge victory, with 235 delegates compared with sixty Conservatives, ten for Lisandro de la Torre's Progressive Democrats, and only twenty-two Socialists. Marcelo T. Alvear replaced Yrigoyen as president, but he was as much part of the oligarchy as his boyhood friend, General José F. Uriburu. Argentina's political stagnation confirmed for Raúl Pareto's diagnosis of corrupt liberal states. In Argentina, as in Italy and France, a speculative elite incapable of reform was endangering the future of the country. Pareto's vision of an alternative – a technocratic modernizing elite guiding the state with rational policymaking above special interests – therefore engaged Raúl at a critical moment and clarified his future roles in Argentine public life.[37]

An engineer by profession, born in Paris in 1848 to an exiled Genoa Marquis, Pareto was a lifelong opponent of both Marxism and the decadent liberal regimes he observed in Italy and France. He viewed socialism as simply an attempt to replace one elite with another, where the party bureaucracy spoke in the name of the proletariat, but was no less concerned about power than the capitalist state it wanted to supplant. The triumph of Leninism in 1917 confirmed his cynicism that Marxists were hypocritical about democracy. But the ruling groups in Europe formed so speculative, effete, irresponsible, and short-sighted an elite that they also richly deserved to fall. Although Pareto diagnosed a much more complex power struggle in societies than Marx, in the end he recognized only two elites within any society locked in a constant struggle over the ages: first, the governing elite in power; and second, the non-governing challenger. History demonstrated a continual process of challenge and replacement of ruling elites as they grew out of touch and unleashed sufficient fury from below for their overthrow and replacement. Wise governments would eliminate abuses by timely reforms in order to adjust and survive; if they failed and became flabby and corrupt the non-governing group would eventually rebel and take power in their place. Successful countries therefore depended on good government, and this required rational technocrats recruited on the single criterion of merit, who worked for the public rather than special interests. Prebisch understood from Pareto that the leadership of any successful society in the twentieth century depended on creating and sustaining such a modernizing elite, and nurturing it represented the principal challenge facing all countries if progress and justice were to be maintained.

This was an analysis that conformed to Raúl's observation of the political challenge in Buenos Aires; while the mainstream political parties were corrupt and merely played at change, the long-term needs of the country were being frustrated. The failure in land and social reform revealed the same disastrous tendencies as in Italy or France before 1922, while the opposition was too divided and internally fractious to develop an alternative platform for common action against the regime. The missing link in Argentina was an anchor in the state – a strong, trained, rational, and disinterested public sector that could carry on the work of the nation above the noise and chaos of the endless political battles, which led nowhere. Its credibility would stem from its quality and honesty; its legitimacy would come from performing essential roles. Prebisch and his colleagues were the first generation in Argentina that had the skills and idealism to claim this role of a modernizing elite within the state. He knew the energy and capacity of Malaccorto and his other friends, who shared his own commitment to Argentina and its future; like him, they saw the state as an instrument of change. Raúl, in short, was committed to serving Argentine society through policy and public service rather than partisan politics.

Raúl's choice of vocation in the public sector also resolved the ambiguities stemming from his early years in Tucumán; by choosing to reform the Argentine state from within the public service, above class and party politics, Raúl found an outlet for his idealism compatible with his mixed heritage. By an accident of birth he was outside the social networks that automatically conferred power; Raúl and all the Prebisch children knew that they would have to be self-made – that while their maternal link with the Linares-Uriburu clans provided a possible calling card and a source of personal status and confidence, it was too diluted to ensure work or social advantages. Tucumán left no room for a political vocation; Prebisch could not compete with Robustiano Patron-Costas, nor did he seriously consider this option. He never wanted to be a politician or felt himself to be presidential material. At the same time his entire early life, from Segundo Linares's tales of colonial days to his own encounters with indigenous children in the fetid slums of Tucumán, pressed him to serve his country.

If Raúl had now made a firm decision about his future career, he had no idea how he would find the right path toward his eventual goal of being an influential insider. He was only twenty-one years old; he had learned a great deal since arriving in Buenos Aires, but he had no experience outside the university. In short, Prebisch needed work.

3 Apprenticeship

Prebisch turned to Dean Eleodoro Lobos for advice on job openings. A deep international recession following the unwise overproduction and inflation of the first postwar years gripped the Argentine economy just as President Yrigoyen's term ended. The mood of the country was grim, and employment prospects poor. Lobos, whose dual academic and public policy careers offered a model for Raúl and whetted his appetite, agreed to keep an eye open and recommend him for promising opportunities.

Raúl could not have found a more effective ally. Lobos was a key interlocutor with the Buenos Aires elite, a former editor of the powerful daily *La Prensa*, one of the foremost lawyers in Buenos Aires, and a former minister of finance and agriculture under Conservative Saenz Peña from 1910 to 1916 before his appointment as the second dean of the faculty. But he was also close to the present Radical Government because his brother-in-law, Rafael Herrera Vegas, was appointed by Alvear as the new minister of finance. It did not take long for Raúl, who was then leading his research seminar at La Plata University, to receive an offer of a one-year contract in finance as secretary to a special budgetary commission set up by the minister, with a monthly salary of four hundred pesos.

Before Raúl could respond to finance, another and much more interesting opportunity arose from an unexpected quarter when Lobos was asked by the Argentine Rural Society (SRA) to locate an economist to work in their head office in Buenos Aires. Founded in 1866, the SRA was the lobby for the largest cattle-raisers, with the most elite membership in the country. Often seen as synonymous with the Argentine oligarchy, the SRA crossed party lines to include Radical oligarchs such as Yrigoyen and the current President Marcelo T. Alvear, as well as familiar Conservative figures such as the Uriburus, but it also remained open to new members depending on wealth. The SRA's major event each year was the July Agricultural Fair in

Palermo, which could not be missed by high society, and at which the president of the republic would appear in a horse-drawn carriage with cavalry escort, to award the grand prize at the closing ceremonies. But its goal was more than social. The SRA also promoted the modernization of agriculture and its members formed so powerful a national organization that they also led the Argentine Industrial Union (UIA), industry's main association, from its founding in 1887 until the war in Europe in 1914. The entire private sector stood in awe of the agro-industrialists.[1]

Dean Lobos immediately recommended Prebisch, who was then interviewed by SRA President Ernesto Bosch and a director, Enrique Uriburu. It was a formidable team, with both men charter members of the Conservative oligarchy. Bosch had been close to every Conservative president since the 1880s either as private secretary or minister, serving as minister of foreign affairs in Saenz Peña's government before the 1916 Radical victory. Uriburu was Francisco's son and heir, having inherited the family mansion on Lavalle 371, and now married to the daughter of ex-President Quintana. Twenty years older than his second cousin Raúl, Enrique Uriburu was a dealmaker in Buenos Aires, a key social figure in the capital, a part-time professor in the UBA Law Faculty, and of course he also retained the family estates. It was Raúl's first meeting with Uriburu since arriving in Buenos Aires four years earlier – like his parents he lay outside this social circle.

The SRA job involved setting up a new research office to study the causes and implications of the post-World War decline in international beef prices. Prebisch would have to work alone, without an assistant for statistical work, on one of the most important and controversial economic issues of the day. At the end of the interview Bosch offered him the job despite his reputation for socialist leanings and support for agrarian reform. He then asked about salary expectations. On this tricky subject Raúl was hesitant. He thought of holding out for three hundred pesos per month but decided to wait for an offer since he had no previous experience with private-sector rates and had forgotten to ask Lobos's advice on this point.[2] Wisely he let Bosch do the talking and was dumbfounded to be offered eight hundred pesos a month. He accepted and work began on 5 June.

The SRA wanted to know, and if possible to prove, that Argentine cattle producers were being manipulated by the big British and US meat-packing firms that controlled the transport of meat products to foreign markets with their monopoly of refrigerator cargo vessels. Since Britain had stopped importing live animals in 1900 after an outbreak of hoof-and-mouth disease in Argentina, the beef trade depended on shipping either frozen or chilled products in refrigerator ships, and this change in shipping technology gave a handful of British and US multinational firms

(Swift, Wilson, Armour, Smithfield, and Vesty) control of the market. Only the Sansenina Frozen Meat Company remained Argentine-owned. The meat-packers were therefore highly visible and prone to criticism on nationalist grounds, a familiar object of hatred in Buenos Aires during recessions. The meat-packers for their part argued that the international shipping conference set up in April 1914 to regulate the beef trade prevented ruinous fluctuations in the market and that their pricing reflected supply and demand as registered in the London Smithfield market. As Prebisch began his research prices were falling sharply, reaching one-half their 1920 values by 1923, and the SRA demanded state intervention to protect a core national industry against a foreign-owned and controlled monopoly; like the sugar barons of Tucumán it was pro free trade in general but more than willing to wrap itself in the flag to protect the special interests of its members.[3]

Prebisch's research project became even more politically hot as the crisis deepened; the SRA left no doubt that he was a consultant and that his findings were meant to support its lobbying position. Fresh out of university, Prebisch had landed a well-paying job, but he could not have found a tougher assignment. While the same charges against the meat-packing industry were being heard in other meat-exporting countries, in the US and Australia parliamentary commissions were at work to distinguish myth from reality. In Buenos Aires a young economist in his first work experience was caught between two business groups and their political allies.

In practice the research drew Prebisch into the complex dynamics shaping Argentina's most important export trade with Great Britain. This market was in transition after the war, but the insecurity went deeper than the bungled return to markets after 1918, with an immediate postwar boom to satisfy pent-up demand leading to oversupply and recession by 1921.[4] As before the war, Britain was the main global importer of meat; in 1921 it comprised 94 percent of the entire international market, with 64 percent in beef products and with Argentina accounting for 64 percent of these imports. Argentina was gaining on its Australian and Canadian competitors because consumer tastes in England were changing toward chilled rather than frozen meat, and here Argentina had a comparative advantage. Between 1920 and 1921 British imports of chilled beef more than tripled from 510,000 to 1,883,000 tons (in effect recovering from the steep drop-off during the war), and 90.7 percent of this product was shipped from Argentina. In effect Britain was the global market regulator, while Argentina was overwhelmingly its single largest import source.[5]

Considering the significance of the beef trade for the entire Argentine economy, it might have been expected that researchers in Buenos Aires would have specialized in the dynamics of this sector, but Prebisch found the opposite. Systematic work had not been undertaken in Argentine universities, and national statistics on the prices paid to ranchers by the meat-packing firms had never been collected in Argentina; without them an accurate overview of the industry from the farm gate to the London market was simply not possible. In one of his earliest research notes for the faculty journal he had reviewed the post-1918 efforts in many countries to upgrade their statistical capabilities; he now understood their significance in a modern state. In practical terms Raúl faced the task of filling this gap if he hoped to understand all the elements in the sector: prices paid to local producers; the structure of the producing industry; fluctuations in the London Smithfield market; the impact of shipping technology; prices on the local Buenos Aires Liniers livestock exchange; and finally the policy options of the Argentine state toward the meat-packing sector. Laboriously he began to assemble these data in the meat sector, with the assistance of the meat-packers, and this patient statistical research eventually yielded the first integrated analysis of the industry produced so far in Argentina.

Six months after joining the SRA Prebisch had amassed a credible statistical base for the study and was able to present a first draft of his findings to the directors. Unfortunately it was not the tame and supportive document they had been expecting. Instead he had prepared a carefully documented and balanced report, describing a complex dynamic in the sector that ruled out simplistic solutions. Clearly, he argued, the meat-packers took high profits and used their technological advantage to operate as a trust.[6] Obviously prices on the local and London livestock markets were not determined by supply and demand alone; given their small number the firms could unofficially divide the market among them to improve their profit margins. But Prebisch could not conclude that the markups by the meat-packers were the determining factor explaining the postwar collapse in prices and the existing rural crisis in Argentina. The main problems hurting Argentine producers stemmed from the oversupply of chilled beef and the price sensitivity of this product. British demand for chilled beef had risen rapidly, and prices would also have risen if the supply had not increased proportionately even more. Postwar Argentine producers in the great hinterland of the vast pampas were flooding the market and driving down prices. Too many cattle were being raised for too few consumers. Beyond this key factor, market conditions in the industry as a whole were imperfect, with 80 percent of Argentina's ranchers having fewer than two hundred head of cattle, leaving a fragmented producers' group without the market power to confront the well-organized meat-packers whose profits reflected their monopoly position.[7]

As a result Prebisch did not recommend government control of the meat-packing sector despite his criticism of price-fixing in the industry. The SRA was not happy. Bosch and Uriburu were no longer on the board after elections had resulted in a more protectionist leadership that was highly critical of his study. Successfully exploiting nationalist sentiment against the foreign-owned meat-packers and refrigerator cargo fleets, the SRA was almost insurrectionist in its denunciation of the so-called "meat trust" and insisted on government action to take it over and break its control. It was naïve of Prebisch to think that the SRA would accept a nuanced report with balanced recommendations, when the goal was immediate action, and his findings were dismissed in a direct appeal to President Alvear. The government gave in to SRA demands by establishing a minimum price for cattle brought to market, but the meat-packers retaliated by closing the Buenos Aires stockyards, provoking a major economic crisis. Within days Alvear back down and revoked the minimum price. The new SRA leadership now turned on Prebisch, blaming him for undermining its political campaign, and attacking him as pro-British and anti-nationalist. Prebisch was sacked without notice and had no opportunity to respond or explain his report in detail. "*Los violentos,*" as Prebisch called them, had prevailed.[8]

Dejected, Raúl went home to his mother in Tucumán, where he licked his wounds and completed the final draft of "Notes Regarding the Beef Crisis," published in January 1923 in the faculty's *Journal of Economic Sciences,* in which he laconically gave his title as "Ex-Director of Statistics, Argentine Rural Society."[9] It was written in an acerbic style, which did not curry favour with the country's most powerful lobby; he even attacked the SRA for its short-sightedness and tightfistedness in refusing to support scholarly research in the faculty dealing with this important economic sector. But Prebisch overestimated his setback. Academically the publications that emerged from his SRA work were visible and well received. Moreover he had not cut his links with the SRA; both Bosch and Enrique Uriburu remained strong supporters, and these men had influence well beyond the ranks of the SRA. In addition, the political row with the meat-packers was forgotten because of an upturn in the British economy, and the recovery in chilled-beef prices for Argentine cattle-raisers masked the temporary defeat of the SRA.

Eleodoro Lobos remained a powerful patron watching Raúl's fortunes, keen to ensure that the political trap into which he had fallen in the SRA would not compromise his career. He himself, like many Conservatives, approved of Prebisch's well-known demands for land reform, understanding with the Socialists that something had to be done.[10] He therefore intervened personally with the minister of finance to hire Raúl as a consultant to visit Australia and New Zealand and compare their income-tax legislation and administration with those in Argentina. In particular the minister wanted advice on income-tax reform: like Argentina they were agricultural countries, he noted in a letter to Raúl, but while they apparently had effective income-tax systems, his own advisors claimed that they were unworkable.[11] Since Australia in particular had a similar staples-based economy where growth was related to the export boom of land-extensive economies, it seemed to offer an important comparison. Since landowners in Argentina were resisting increased taxes it was obviously important to see what was happening on the other side of the world, where the colonial inheritance was different.

On 24 October 1923, Prebisch sailed for Wellington, via New York. *La Razon,* the Buenos Aires daily associated with the governing Radical Party, criticized his appointment as "a paid holiday at government expense," but for Raúl it was an important opportunity to travel abroad.[12] Arriving in New Zealand on 13 December, he worked for eleven days with Malcolm Fraser, head of the Bureau of Census Statistics, before proceeding to Australia and celebrating Christmas at sea with New Year's Eve in Melbourne, his first holiday season away from home. Prebisch found much to learn in Australia and New Zealand – so similar in economic structure to Argentina, but so different in every other way. He was struck by their equitable social structures relative to Argentina: servants were rare, and manual work was routinely performed by middle-class property owners. Expectations were completely different. Prebisch's teachers in the faculty had full-time domestic staff to clean and maintain their houses and gardens, while Malcolm Fraser, who was internationally famous, lived in a modest bungalow. In Argentina he and his wife would have maintained a fleet of servants. Australian wheat production was only one-quarter that of Argentina, but the ratio of owners and tenants and income distribution bore no resemblance to the Argentine countryside. A place like Tucumán, with its poverty-stricken migrant labourers, was unknown here.

Prebisch's research visit helped him clarify his views on Argentina's location in the world. In many respects, and despite its location, its political culture was very different from neighbouring Brazil and Chile, more highly developed economically and more urbanized with a larger middle class. But Argentina still shared the Latin American curse: like its neighbours it had inherited from colonial days a powerful oligarchy that directed the state within a dependent agricultural export economy. Geopolitically it was the strongest power in South America, locked in a rivalry of long standing with Brazil, and to a lesser extent with much smaller Chile. Bolivia, Paraguay, and Uruguay formed buffer states between Argentina and Brazil. But, in its internal structure and global trade relations, Argentina was closer to the small grouping of white European-settled overseas cereal producers comprising Australia, New Zealand, and Canada. Australia and New Zealand offered a particularly useful comparative perspective since they were also distant from the core economies, unlike Canada. Like Argentina they had a high land-labour ratio, a population shortage, and mass immigration. How had they fared in relative terms? Economically, according to Prebisch, both Australia and New Zealand lagged behind Argentina, and none of their cities could even remotely compare with spectacular Buenos Aires. But although not as wealthy (the per capita income of Australia was estimated at $1,590 compared with Argentina's $1,700), these British dominions were developing on a sounder base, while Buenos Aires lumbered on, secure in its sense of superiority. Land reform offered a good example of form versus content. In Argentina entire libraries were filled with books and projects dedicated to land reform, including the most arcane details – but nothing ever happened. In contrast, Prebisch could not locate a single published work in Australia on land reform. Through the good fortune of a different colonial legacy it was able to implement an effective homestead policy because the land was not already controlled by a local oligarchy at the time of immigration. This vital difference – an outmoded class system and concentrated land ownership in which the Argentine oligarchy was allied with the state and could always block reform – was a structural flaw that compromised an otherwise brilliant future.

In a speech delivered in English to the Henry George Club in Melbourne shortly after his arrival in Australia – fortified, no doubt, by his recent experience with the Argentine Rural Society – he underlined the negative effects of a dominant land-holding oligarchy on the economic and political life of his country and the need for land reform. He explained to his audience the colonial and postcolonial dynamic that had resulted in an extreme concentration of land in few hands, and absentee landlords in many cases, and therefore the failure of Argentina to develop a homestead policy comparable to the US or the British dominions. Since political power followed economic organization, a rational land-reform policy had proven impossible. Instead of a thriving and populated countryside, the huge Argentine interior was depopulated; instead of the homesteaders who had created a rural massmarket in the British dominions or the US, Argentina imported migrant labourers by the tens of thousand each year for the harvest. The Argentine elite gave a bad example of luxury in the midst of rural and urban poverty. "The gay night life, the jewels of the women, the generous flow of champagne in night clubs, and the brilliance of our Buenos Aires' cosmopolitan ambience," Prebisch concluded in Melbourne, "provoke exclamations by foreigners that it is the Paris of South America. Little consolation for the working classes, who drag out their lives between sweatshop and hovel!"[13]

Raúl narrowed his research to the two themes of income-tax reform and national accounts, working in the Department of Taxation in Melbourne with Sir George Knibbs, the director of Statistics, who was also a well-known demographer. Raúl discovered that Argentina was twenty years behind Australia in the modernization of the state; its stronger civil society was reflected in a more developed state in which an efficient civil service and taxation system were taken for granted. Unlike Argentina it had modernized its statistical system after 1920 in line with Britain, the US, and Canada, and it had introduced effective income-tax legislation by using an averaging formula to counteract annual fluctuations in farm incomes. The system worked, he reported in an article published in the *Argentine Journal of Economics*; taxpayers were willing to pay and were fined if they did not. Altogether Argentine public administration seemed soft by comparison, lacking innovation and depriving the country of the necessary tools and infrastructure to move forward. As a case in point, Argentina's National Statistical Office required new standards and technological innovation (such as adopting the Hollerith system used in Australia, which had automated record-keeping using perforated cards) if it was to maintain international standards. It was as if Australia's enormous contribution to victory in the First World War had strengthened and disciplined the state and brought capabilities and expectations into balance; Argentina had escaped war but retained a flabby state.[14] The way to keep peace in Buenos Aires was to postpone taxation.

The consultancy was meant to run until mid-April, but in late March the newly appointed Undersecretary of Finance Salvador Oria cabled Prebisch to return home immediately: President Alvear had changed ministers, and his contract was cancelled. Prebisch had long considered Oria a friend and supporter, and indeed this young professor had helped him prepare his course outline for La Plata University. But Raúl (without realizing it) had angered him by supporting the visit of Gaston Jeze in 1923, whose mild criticism of the Argentine economy had been condemned in *La Razon*.[15] Raúl had publicly mocked the newspaper's provincialism, not realizing that Oria had also opposed Jeze's visit to the Southern Cone since he considered himself the national expert on taxation policy and felt that Argentina had nothing to learn from either Jeze or Australia. Newly appointed to his position, Oria decided to teach Prebisch a lesson, terminating the consultancy and leaving him stranded far from home. Raúl was forced to complete his research at his own expense.

Prebisch began his long sea voyage home on 17 April with stops in Perth in Western Australia and then Europe, where he travelled in France, Italy, and England, before continuing to Argentina. Like his father, he discovered the joy of travel, and would also have visited the US if funds had been available. Having written on postwar adjustment in Western Europe from the considerable distance of Buenos Aires, he now had an opportunity to see Paris, Rome, and London for himself, but he was also on vacation and he enjoyed visiting the historic capitals of the old continent, reviving his French and finding books unavailable in Buenos Aires. His brother Alberto was part of the large Argentine community in Paris, studying with Le Corbusier. The two young men roamed the streets together, noting the poverty of postwar Europe with crowds of damaged veterans even in a victorious country. For all its problems Argentina seemed so obviously successful by comparison. Not only was it richer by far than Europe, but it was also at peace and not victimized by rival nationalisms. Raúl also used the trip to deepen his reading of Pareto and was all the more convinced of Argentina's potential as a rising power in the New World.

By the time he embarked at Cherbourg for Buenos Aires in early July, Prebisch was anxious to get back home, and when he arrived at the port the new prosperity of Buenos Aires struck him like a gale. The labour wars and dislocation of the immediate postwar years were over and the prewar optimism had returned. Capital again flowed into the country with investments increasing from 524 million to 2.6 billion pesos; business expanded as in the golden years before 1914. Prebisch rejoiced at being home, even if the political pressure for change had also been dissipated by the return of prosperity.[16] In neighbouring Uruguay the government used the economic revival as an opportunity to introduce long-delayed reforms, and social policy dominated Chilean politics as well. But in Buenos Aires there were fewer successes. Augusto Bunge kept demanding action and remained busy organizing public campaigns for reform, and his Sunday gatherings, to which Raúl returned with pleasure, remained as lively as ever. But Alvear's Radical Government took advantage of the 1920s hiatus to postpone action again on the social question; the fierce debates in the Congress in the first years over trade and monetary policy lost their edge in a premature sense of self-satisfaction in Buenos Aires, as if prosperity had returned for good. Buenos Aires was too prosperous to consider the seriousness of its social and economic deficiencies in the fool's paradise of the 1920s, or to challenge the doctrines of free trade and comparative advantage, which dominated the academic and political life of the capital.

While in Paris Raúl had worried about finding work after being out of the country for eight months, but he managed to resolve this problem aboard ship, where he encountered Argentina's minister of agriculture, Tomas Le Breton, who was returning to Buenos Aires after a round of visits to European capitals. Another powerful member of the Argentine oligarchy, Le Breton was a former president of the Argentine Rural Society and a close friend of Bosch and Uriburu. He had heard of Prebisch's experiences with the SRA in 1923 and wanted to hear his side of the story, and he also wanted to discuss the results of Australia's agricultural colonization program in New South Wales.[17] After an initial coolness Le Breton developed a liking for the younger man, and they discovered a common pleasure in long after-dinner walks on deck. As Prebisch discussed his work in Australia and New Zealand, as well as his impressions of postwar Europe, he gained another powerful patron in the capital.

The day before their arrival in Buenos Aires, during the final stop in Montevideo, Le Breton surprised Raúl by asking him if he would work for him, inviting him to go to Canada as consul-general to study its grain marketing system. But Prebisch, who had now been fired twice, had learned a lesson. "No," he smiled, "I lack experience."[18] He explained that without a career appointment he would be defenceless should ministers change, and he could not afford to leave Buenos Aires before his career was launched. Le Breton understood but still wanted Raúl to work for him as a personal consultant. The day after his return on 24 July 1924, Le Breton installed Prebisch in his office as special assistant at 800 pesos a month with the official title of Technical Advisor to the Under Secretary. Raúl was able to complete two reports for Le Breton on rural taxation and land colonization that drew on his research in Australia, and he remained a close day-to-day advisor of the minister. Much of this latter work concerned the accumulated backlog of land grant certificates: thousands remained outstanding from many years back, and Raúl was given authority to interview applicants and recommend either rejection or approval. The work was personally challenging, dealing face-to-face with frustrated people in emotion-charged circumstances, but it was only a job. Prebisch needed a career, and his interest flagged.

He also faced compulsory military service, which he had so far successfully avoided by remaining a university student. But now he could postpone no longer. Le Breton therefore gave him a leave of absence from January to April 1925, and Raúl enlisted with No. 1 Infantry Regiment Patricios, located on the outskirts of the capital. Raúl would shudder at the memory.[19] However brief this interlude of military service, it was one of the most unpleasant experiences of his life. He hated the cursing and swaggering male camaraderie of the barracks and the violence of the training. His lack of coordination amused the much younger recruits while angering the NCOs. Marching was torture as his frequent faux pas singled him out for NCO derision and punishment, to which he could only respond with silent and ineffectual rage.

During his last weeks in the barracks the University of Buenos Aires offered him an appointment on 1 March 1925 as acting professor of Political Economy, despite his lack of a doctorate in Economics and without a formal competition for the position. His former professors, Mauricio Nierenstein and Luis Roque Gondra, had appealed to the faculty's Board of Governors on Prebisch's behalf, realizing that only once before in 1883 had any faculty in the University granted such an exception, and then in Medicine. Raúl had established himself in university circles as a confident teacher and had earned the support of colleagues and particularly Dean Lobos with his publications – thirty-seven articles that showed a capacity and range of interests badly needed in the faculty. He had written on monetary policy and postwar stabilization, and he was the accepted authority on the Argentine beef trade; his experience from Australia had appeared in articles on taxation policy and land reform. He spoke three languages and was au courant with the academic and business literature in Europe and the US. Such breath of knowledge was rare in the faculty. Prebisch never felt that his appointment in the faculty had the same weight as an appointment to the great US or European universities, and perhaps for that reason he was evasive about his lack of advanced academic credentials. It meant a great deal for him to be called "Dr Prebisch," and he went so far as to sign his articles as "graduate of the Faculty of Economic Sciences." This error of judgement underlined a continuing insecurity and courted embarrassment by enemies who could throw "Prebisch the public accountant" in his face as a constant reminder of his unnecessary claim to being "Dr Prebisch."

Prebisch had coveted a professorship in the faculty with the opportunity to design and lead a research seminar; it was an opportunity to continue his academic work in international trade and monetary policy, and it was an invaluable link with students and economists. But the chair (titled Economic Dynamics), which involved one research seminar per year, was not enough to meet his financial needs or his ambitions. He had returned to Argentina to be a national leader in the public service, and he had been with Le Breton long enough to realize that he had to move on to advance his career. Le Breton understood Prebisch's choice and, although he wanted him to remain, supported him in a nationwide competition for a permanent position as Deputy Director of the National Statistical Office. Raúl applied and was selected for the job.

The new appointment was not a success. He had applied because he had seen in Australia the necessity of national statistics, and he realized that even compared with Brazil and Chile, not to mention the developed counties, Argentina was seriously deficient. Moreover, he had remembered the office under the exceptional stewardship of a first-class mind such as Alejandro Bunge, who was also committed to reform. But after arriving in his new job Raúl understood the obstacles to change. Even Bunge had not been able to break the resistance of his superiors to new ideas or new data-processing technology: even when the US agreed to give three Hollerith machines at no cost, the government refused. Bunge had now retired to edit the *Journal of Argentine Economics*, and the new director, Alfredo Lucadamo, lacked the standing and energy to break an ingrained bureaucratic resistance to interdepartmental cooperation or to obtain the resources required for an adequate National Statistical Office.[20]

Innovation was annoyingly difficult; the office remained addicted to the old colonial system of dictating numbers to clerks working in longhand at their ledgers, and Prebisch's efforts to introduce Hollerith data-processing came to nothing, until he rented a model for a staff demonstration. Although the effectiveness of the National Statistical Office depended on interdepartmental coordination, agencies jealously guarded their data or refused altogether to set up statistical sections. Raúl was convinced that population statistics should be correlated with trade and other economic indicators; he not only failed to get authority from the Statistical Office to lead this task, he also failed to convince the Hygiene Directorate of the Department of Health to begin this work. He had better success in the banking sector, where deposit and loan data since 1910 were assembled for the first time with the cooperation of the private banks. He could also take some credit for setting up the first National Statistical Conference held in Cordoba. In August 1925, Prebisch published an article outlining the existing deficiencies as well as the vital importance to the country of national data series as reliable as those of its competitors, closing with a challenge for the Alvear Government to introduce the reforms outlined by the British Empire Statistical Conference held in London in 1920.[21] But by the end of the year he was bored and worried that he might be stuck in a middle-paying job (eight hundred pesos) with diminishing interest and potential.

Intellectually Prebisch used his time in the National Statistical Office to prepare a more reflective article, "Notes on Demography," published later in Bunge's journal, which allowed him to develop his thinking on a subject that had interested him since arriving in Buenos Aires in 1918 and that had been stimulated by his work with Malcolm Fraser in Australia.[22] It also reflected a natural preoccupation as an immigrant's son and his concern for land reform and rural development in general. Raúl decided to correlate the rise and fall of Argentine business cycles, using a historical approach going back to the first reliable statistics in the 1860s, with population trends. He found an almost perfect correlation between export fluctuations on the one hand and marriage licences, births, and migration in Buenos Aires on the other. The study of demography was in its infancy; Prebisch therefore pointed out the importance for Argentine scholars to start working in this field with scholars abroad, because globalization implied interdependence. Argentina's birth rate, for example, depended on prosperity in Britain, given its symbiotic connection via staples production. Any sharp recession in Britain meant a certain crisis for Argentine trade and, with it, a sharp reduction in marriages and migration. Other population trends in Europe and North America had implications for Argentina as well. In England the sharp population rise associated with the Industrial Revolution in the nineteenth century had changed course after 1875 with greater prosperity and urbanization; moreover only the lowest uneducated classes were still having large families. The same was occurring in Canada (Quebec excepted), New Zealand, and Australia, which Raúl described (with Argentina) as "countries of recent colonization." The Argentine data (given the poverty of its national statistical services only Buenos Aires could be researched) suggested the same tendency. As prosperity advanced, parents chose to have fewer children but raise them with higher expectations, and greater availability of reliable methods facilitated voluntary birth control. Meanwhile in Brazil, Asia, and other non-European geopolitical areas the population increase was still alarming, as claimed by neo-Malthusian writers such as Cambridge Professor Harold Wright. In a bestseller released in 1926, he demanded international action by the West to safeguard the race from the fast-breeding Asian hordes. Prebisch refused to be drawn into Wright's argument, although he noted that Keynes's otherwise unremarkable introduction to the book was an indication of the future importance of the subject. Argentina's population problem was the imbalance between Buenos Aires and an interior so empty that it could not sustain local services; the country was like a head with no body, and the problem would eventually have to be addressed by the national government.[93]

Raúl felt trapped in the National Statistical Office; he couldn't stand a boss, even a good one, and there was limited career scope, given the lack of staff and freedom. He wanted out, but the alternatives were not immediately apparent either inside or outside the government. In this situation the last option Raúl could possibly have imagined for his release was the SRA, which he assumed he had alienated for good after his 1923 report on the meat trade and subsequent dismissal. But the big lobby had again renewed its executive board and was now led by Luis Duhau, who was a friend of both Bosch and Uriburu. Duhau had decided to visit the US, and since he spoke no English he needed an assistant. Uriburu and Le Breton recommended Prebisch for the position, given the quality of his earlier work, despite its subsequent fate at the hands of the SRA executive board.[24] In other ways beyond languages Raúl was a logical candidate for a travel companion: he had worked with US sources and periodicals since his first year in university; he had studied international trade and monetary policy; he had been in Australia and New Zealand; and he had worked for Tomas Le Breton in the Ministry of Agriculture. Prebisch was also willing to travel again. Stuck in a dull job, the prospect of visiting Washington was a relief, and he correctly saw it as a rare opening to understand the new issue of Argentine-US trade relations and appreciate the enhanced US role in international affairs after 1918. Duhau requested that the National Statistical Office release Raúl on loan, and they were soon bound for North America.

The US was a foreign-policy puzzle for Argentina, which had remained firmly in the British zone before 1914 despite the growth of US influence in the rest of Latin America. Britain had even managed to retain its dominant role in Argentina after the First World War despite the heavy costs incurred, and unlike in Mexico or the Latin countries in the Caribbean Basin the US had not displaced Britain as its main trader during the 1920s. But US investment was increasing rapidly in Argentina; a major new office in Buenos Aires was among the twelve branches set up in Latin America by the First National City Bank of New York during the war.[25] More important, Argentina's dependence on the US in the 1920s for the import of machinery was growing, particularly the new agricultural equipment required to keep up with rapid technological changes in this sector. Since the outer limit of the land frontier had been reached in Argentina in 1910, and since prices for wheat had not recovered from the war, increased production with new technology was the only way to maintain farm incomes.[26] Imports from the US were therefore bound to increase in the future because the US rather than Britain produced the technology and capital goods it required. This situation created a serious long-term dilemma for Argentina, namely the emergence of a trade triangle in which increasing imports from the US created a trade deficit that could only be paid with the surplus gained in Argentine beef and agricultural trade with Britain. The US was a temperate country producing largely the same range of commodities as Argentina, and thus didn't require Argentine agricultural products. There were other trade problems: most important, Argentine meat products were prohibited because of intermittent outbreaks of hoof-and-mouth disease.

Most of their three months abroad were spent in Washington, where Duhau had discussions on limiting US restrictions on imports of meat, wool, linseed oil, and other products from Argentina with officials in the

Hoover Administration. Raúl's role during the trip was to prepare background documents and speeches for Duhau, set up meetings with officials in the State Department and the Department of Agriculture, as well as with congressional staffers and legislators, and to be on hand to translate and follow up with the media as necessary. The mission was a discovery for both men, and the experience went well beyond trade; their continuing surprises left Prebisch and Duhau permanently close friends. Thrust into the tough world of Washington politics they quickly appreciated the complexity of US decision-making and consensus-building with a protectionist US Congress. Despite the official rhetoric, it fell to Duhau to preach the gospel of free trade – with few expectations of success.

The reality of US power was also indelibly imprinted on Prebisch's mind from that visit, and therefore the need to understand Washington and its institutions. Given the prewar British and European connection, the US was relatively unknown in Argentine society, and US civilization was poorly taught in universities. This included the banking system. During the visit Raúl had an opportunity to acquaint himself with the US Federal Reserve System or the "Fed," set up in 1913, which divided the US into twelve districts each with its own Federal Reserve Board, and which performed the normal duties of a central bank. What impressed him was its Research Department, which maintained close links with US universities and had achieved a high level of acceptance and credibility in the financial and business communities.[27]

While in North America Prebisch and Duhau also visited Canada to examine the grain elevator system set up to protect Western grain growers; they travelled to the Winnipeg Grain Exchange and studied the operations of the Wheat Board in Regina, where the introduction of quota books in local elevators had eliminated the intermediary operators, who still controlled the grain trade in Argentina. Canada was similar to Australia in lacking a cosmopolitan capital like Buenos Aires. As in Australia, Raúl experienced a sense of kinship with a major staples producer far from Britain and dependent on agricultural markets; and as in that earlier visit he saw how a modern state was creating a more solid basis for long-term growth than Argentina. The challenge at home was to build on its achievements and strengths and catch up with the British dominions by remedying Argentina's deficiencies with timely reforms.[28]

Duhau was impressed with Prebisch's work during the trip to North America, and with the support of his directors, including Enrique Uriburu, he asked him to stay on as his advisor and leave the National Statistical Office with its secure tenure. Prebisch proposed a counter-offer: would the SRA agree to produce an annual Argentine statistical yearbook with special reference to agriculture, but comprising all sectors including foreign trade? Despite his bad memories of the SRA from 1923 he was interested in pursuing Duhau's offer, but he was not willing to accept general advisory work without prior agreement on concrete tasks. He also knew from his work in the National Statistical Office that the national government itself would not produce an annual statistical yearbook – the Department of Finance refused to approve the necessary resources. Duhau not only agreed to Raúl's proposal but also asked him to undertake another special report on the meat industry; the SRA had set up a special commission to investigate the meat-packing firms again, following another round of criticism of the foreign-dominated "meat trust."

With this offer Raúl resigned from the National Statistical Office and plunged into the preparation of the first *Statistical Yearbook* on foreign trade in Argentina's history – this time with sufficient resources to undertake an adequate national survey. Entitled the *Anuario de la Sociedad Rural: Estadisticas Economicas y Agrarias*, it was a massive and unique tome that filled an important gap as a research and policy tool.[29] Simultaneously Raúl began his second task of preparing the report on the meat-packing industry in Argentina with high expectations, not just in the study itself but also because he felt that the publication would ensure his definitive appointment to the faculty professorship in Political Economy. He need not have worried, however, because the sudden death of Professor Nierenstein opened a permanent position that Prebisch would retain until 1948. Raúl could now inform his father that he no longer needed additional money from the family. Albin congratulated him in an affectionate letter. "You are the youngest son," he said, "but the first to become financially self-sufficient." He hoped Raúl would continue to send him his reports and newspaper articles and worried that Raúl was working too hard; he should be careful with his health, Albin warned, and in his next letter he included some money for entertainment. Raúl was unmoved. He remained sufficiently in need of affirmation from his father to send copies of his academic and newspaper publications, and relations were correct; but he still refused forgiveness and reconciliation.[30]

Neither of Raúl's SRA projects during 1927 prospered; both the *Statistical Yearbook* and the meat-packing report were tarnished politically by their association with the SRA and ultimately failed. It was of course absurd that the SRA, rather than the National Statistical Office, should have produced such a document. The *Statistical Yearbook* was indeed a much-needed national resource, but in the end the SRA was the instrument of the landed elite rather than the Argentine state. Duhau had agreed to Prebisch's offer because he had the skills and contacts for the task, but the publication would not survive his tenure with the SRA. His successor was given another assignment, and the project collapsed when the National Statistical Office once again refused to take up the challenge; Prebisch's 1927 *Statistical Yearbook* remained the single issue on the SRA shelves.

His report on the beef sector was even less successful. Entitled *The Meat-Packing Pool – The Necessity for State Intervention*, it advocated state regulation of the big firms that controlled shipping in the beef trade, given the strategic role of the industry in the economy for both consumers and producers. Prebisch argued that the inherent tendency toward collusion in the domestic meat market justified state intervention, but he stopped short of recommending nationalization.[31]

From a research perspective Prebisch's report was not comparable in quality with his 1923 work on the beef trade, but it remained an interesting case study of state policy in imperfect markets. Even before it was published, however, the report was condemned as self-serving propaganda for the most powerful interest group in Argentina, and critics of the SRA in Congress such as Lisandro de la Torre wanted his blood.[32] As in 1923, therefore, Raúl's report was a political bombshell that again exploded in Argentine politics; not only was 1926 a year of low prices, but Yrigoyen announced that he would run again for the presidency in the 1928 elections, and politicians from all sides were positioning themselves behind nationalist symbols. Raúl denied the allegation of SRA influence in his findings, praising Duhau and Uriburu for their trust and objectivity, but in the uproar his findings could not be judged on their merits and it was evident that he would have to resign.

Raúl now confronted a dilemma. His second period of work for the SRA in 1927 was as brief as the first in 1923, and certainly no happier, but he wanted to avoid a second experience of retreating to Tucumán nursing humiliation and empty pockets. Once again his career had ended in a blind alley of controversy and rejection. Although he had been in and out of many interesting assignments and jobs since leaving university, and had benefited from lengthy research trips to the US, Canada, Australia, New Zealand, and Europe, he had no firm or attractive prospects on the horizon. Moreover, at twenty-six he was no longer the wunderkind he had been on leaving the university at the age of twenty-one. He had tried a public sector job and found the National Statistical Office a stultifying experience, more than he could bear. He remained committed to Pareto's vision and his own destiny within the Argentine state – he was as unwilling now as before to go to the private sector. Worst of all Raúl was not only developing a reputation for opportunistic job-hopping but he was also becoming identified with the Conservative oligarchy because of his personal links with highly visible SRA members such as Ernesto Bosch, Enrique Uriburu, and Luis Duhau. Raúl dismissed such attacks as absurd. Both his experiences with the SRA had been disastrous – he had been sacked both times. Friendship from such powerful individuals did not imply an obligation to serve the interests of the oligarchy, and all the jobs he had obtained with or without their support had been earned on a strict merit principle rather than patronage. Nor did he believe that belonging to the upper class necessarily disqualified individuals such as Bosch or Duhau from serving their country as sincerely or effectively as their detractors from more humble origins. Ernesto Malaccorto, Raúl's closest lifelong friend, regularly endured Raúl's diatribes against the Argentine oligarchy and its military allies, and he dismissed any argument that his own work with the SRA had been biased on class or political grounds. His disdain for the oligarchy went back to his earliest memories of the sugar barons in Tucumán; and he had never hidden his views of the land question, either while travelling in Australia or at home when he openly spent every Sunday with a leading Socialist like Bunge. If Prebisch had wanted personal wealth he would long since have been in one of Argentina's private sector conglomerates.

Raúl was therefore uncertain of the future in 1927, worried that options were closing. He lived frugally, still moving from one boarding house to another. Socially the Bunge house had become Raúl's oasis, his one secure link with the intellectual life of the capital other than the group of old friends from university days and colleagues in the faculty. His academic appointment did not allay a growing anxiety at being on the sidelines, and his own scholarly research and writing had stagnated since the early 1920s. The university seemed even less relevant during the prosperous 1920s, preaching the status quo and the gospel of free trade while critics outside the sheltered academy were forecasting the end of capitalism. Raúl ventured into this debate only once with a tough rebuttal of visiting Spanish Professor Luis Olariaga's criticism that Argentina's foreign trade performance since 1918 had lagged behind that of Canada, Australia, and the US. Olariaga's methodology was evidently inadequate, Prebisch noted, slanted to provide some basis for his argument that the Argentine economy was in "crisis." Any objective assessment of the data revealed instead that Argentina's performance was about the same as that of its competitors. Even 1926, which was a weak year, hardly constituted the "crisis" claimed by the professor, and given Argentina's success in attracting new investment in the chemical, cement, textile, and newsprint industries this catastrophism of the left seemed ludicrous. Argentina was hardly a failure despite its deficiencies: internationally experts such as Saavedra Lamas, a senior professor of Labour Law at La Plata University, were active on the global scene, with Lamas invited to preside over the 1928 meetings of the ILO (International Labour Organization) in Geneva. In a world where child labour and racial segregation survived in the US, the richest country of all, and where the turmoil in Europe was far from resolved, Argentina's record in the 1920s was hardly disastrous. Raúl worried that the work of Olariaga and others like him provided comfort for special interests seeking government intervention and protectionism.[33] Meanwhile he supported the return of the gold standard on 25 October 1927, following Britain's decision the year before, hoping that it would solidify the return to stability and growth after the First World War.[34]

The opening he needed, the break that decisively changed Raúl's career, came unexpectedly in late 1927, when Duhau moved up from the presidency of the SRA to become a director of the Banco de la Nacion Argentina. The BNA was at the centre of Argentina's economy, the financial institution closest to a central bank. It had been created in 1891 to stabilize the sector after a devastating banking crisis and runaway inflation. Duhau called Raúl immediately to let him know that he would propose a new Office of Economic Research within the Bank on the model of the US Federal Reserve and that he would also recommend his appointment as its first director. Duhau had a major office in mind and was serious about committing resources; he assured Prebisch that he would have complete freedom to design the new office, select his team, and publish its work in a new journal. For Raúl this was the opportunity he had long sought, the ideal position from which to influence public policy, combining applied research with a secure and prestigious institutional base. Moreover the new directorate conferred status within the state and brought him into the first division of Argentina's economic managers. Both financially and professionally, Raúl's apprenticeship was over.

4 Taste of Power

The Raúl Prebisch of 1928 contrasted visibly with the youth who had arrived in Buenos Aires a decade earlier not knowing how to drink red wine. His lifestyle had matured. In 1925, having changed address eighteen times since his Aunt Luisa's death in 1920, he had finally left boarding houses behind for an apartment. But as his financial prospects advanced so did his ambition to buy a house of his own, and this symbolic confirmation of personal independence became possible with his major promotion at the National Bank in 1927.

A year later he moved into an elegant house at 1340 Luis Maria Campos. A narrow but soaring four-storey structure in the style of Le Corbusier, it was designed by Alberto on his return from Paris, the first structure of its kind in Buenos Aires. Malaccorto and Max Alemann, who shared the house, had ensuite bedrooms on the third floor, while Raúl occupied the master bedroom and study at the top with a terrace overlooking the city. Raúl also had located a good tailor; a comfortable income had made him a selective dresser like his father, and he always arrived at the BNA in expensive and immaculate suits. To all appearances he was one of Buenos Aires's most eligible bachelors, with a senior position close to the centre of power, and with an assured future.

Yet Raúl's continuing unidimensional lifestyle worried friends like Augusto Bunge. His work habits had not changed with greater financial security; without a discernible social life Raúl's disciplined schedule centred on his work alone. He still insisted on formal Spanish even with Malaccorto and Alemann, who were his closest friends; he was distant and severe, took no part in their parties, and had a reputation as a forbidding workaholic with a sharp tongue and a quick temper. Otherwise he was quiet and studious, like a retired academic. Raúl would walk for hours along the riding paths of Palermo on weekends, but he played no organized sports and rarely left work before 9:00 in the evening. The rich cultural life of Buenos Aires did not interest him; Malaccorto and Alemann could only rarely draw him out, even to the Colon Theatre, where he was known to fall asleep during plays and concerts. All of Raúl's energies remained focused on his work in a single-minded will to succeed.

Only at the Bunge house on Sundays after his regular long walk in the country would he loosen up to show the different and more playful personality hiding under his well-pressed blue suits. Throughout the 1920s Prebisch invariably attended these gatherings when he was in the city on weekends. He retained his admiration for Bunge and took seriously his role of godfather to young Mario. During these Sunday gatherings little Mario seemed to melt Prebisch's formality; he played puppets and word games, regaling the boy with impersonations of the Argentine oligarchy, or buying him outlandishly expensive birthday presents that horrified his parents – such as a set of twenty popular novels by "Hugo Wast" (Gustavo Martinez Zuviria), considered sexually suggestive, ultramontane, politically reactionary, and anti-Semitic. Mario responded with almost filial devotion, calling him "the most cherished and admired friend of my childhood," with Raúl obviously playing the role of Segundo Linares during his own childhood in Jujuy many years before.[1] Augusto Bunge and his wife had just lost their only and much loved daughter, and her early death deepened their affection for Raúl, who became almost a younger brother to Augusto. They sensed that he was on the brink and needed a wife urgently to avoid permanent bachelorhood and isolation from normal society.

Prebisch's new position was qualitatively different from his previous jobs: no longer an employee, at twenty-seven years of age he was now a director – a boss, with an opportunity to test his leadership ability. The BNA – deliberately severe and imposing, occupying a full city block and located immediately to the right of Government House in the Plaza de Mayo – offered a privileged niche for his work. The BNA's mandate was simple: to maintain sound money. Immediately behind it stood the National Mortgage Bank, another financial anchor of the country and guarantor of savings. Bank President Tomas de Estrada gave Prebisch his full support in transforming the previous small Office of Economics, Development and Statistics into a new Office of Economic Research modelled on the US Federal Reserve Board and European counterparts. A working group under Raúl's direction prepared a plan of operations for the new office and the design of a new publication, titled simply the *Economic Journal (Revista Económica)*. The goal was to establish a research team comparable in quality to those of other countries, providing the same backup to the authorities responsible for monetary policy, and it was not surprising that he chose Ernesto

Malaccorto as well as trusted friends including Max Alemann, Edmundo G. Gagneux, Julio Broide, and statistician Abraham Gerest. Raúl used his perch in the BNA to link up with other old friends from university days in the public and private sectors, and to identify rising talent committed to reforming the Argentine state. The new group was not merely gifted, but also united by a group spirit and commitment to quality, loyalty, and purpose in Argentine public policy – the nucleus of a modernizing elite that Prebisch saw as essential for rational state policy.

Prebisch's research office in the BNA provided a new element in Argentina: a group of young economists with the necessary resources to prepare economic reports for the minister of finance on request but also to present well-researched and carefully presented articles on the economy in the *Economic Journal*. Planned as a monthly, it sought a wider audience beyond the BNA, offering a regular and readable analysis of Argentina's economic and international trade prospects rather than scholarly or theoretically oriented articles. All articles were published as team research and remained unsigned, but because editor Prebisch reviewed each issue and established the publication schedule they all bore his personal stamp.

The timing, however, was decidedly unpromising. The first issue of the *Economic Journal*, which appeared on 1 January 1928, coincided with the growing turbulence preceding the Great Depression. While Raúl now had the opportunity for systematic work on his core interests since university days – monetary and trade policy – he confronted the task of interpreting the gathering international crisis and recommending appropriate responses to protect Argentina's economy. Political warnings were also evident. Yrigoyen was certain to return to power in the national elections scheduled for March 1928; the old man was intent on a comeback and controlled the electoral machine of the Radical Party throughout the country. But while he was ensured victory, he was also so widely disliked within his own party that a split could be foreseen.

As elsewhere, Raúl and his team initially misinterpreted the warning signs preceding the Great Depression, which began to affect Argentina before the United States. Wheat prices peaked in May 1927 and the commodity markets turned downward in 1928, but the *Economic Journal* argued in January 1929 that there was no reason to panic. Argentina had returned to the gold standard a year earlier, a step Prebisch had long advocated, and despite the negative trade picture he took an overall benign view of the business cycle, hoping for the same rapid recovery as had occurred after the previous mild recession in 1926. Six months later the *Economic Journal* again reassured its readers that the worst was over, noting that firm action had restored complete confidence in the German currency, and that Argentina's trade balance remained favourable. This issue ended with a warning that a rise in US interest rates was sucking gold across the Atlantic from all sides and could threaten international stability, but it counselled caution and continuity to ride out this newest downturn in the business cycle.[2]

In the midst of this preoccupation about the international economy, Prebisch faced an internal challenge within the Bank. The 1928 elections had indeed returned the Radical Party with Hipolito Yrigoyen as the new president; outgoing President Marcelo T. Alvear moved out of his way to become Argentine ambassador in Paris. Rumours circulated that Yrigoyen would eliminate the new Office of Economic Research in the BNA because he disliked Duhau and the other Conservative friends of Alvear responsible for its creation, and in any case it was certain that Estrada would be replaced as Bank President by one of Yrigoyen's friends. However the first months of Yrigoyen's administration, after his inauguration on 12 October, passed without incident. Then Estrada was fired, with Dr Carlos Botto becoming the new Bank president; Raúl and Malaccorto were certain they would soon be out on the street. These fears in the Research Office deepened when Prebisch was summoned to Botto's office and instructed to prepare a report on the gold standard: should Argentina stick to its policy of peso/gold convertibility, or should it be the first major country in the world to close its Exchange Office to halt the flood of gold to the US? Prebisch and his team rushed out a recommendation against closing the Exchange Office, arguing that the fundamentals in Argentina were sound. Unlike in earlier financial crises Argentina was not experiencing a speculative boom or inflation, and the money supply was in check. The preferred policy, therefore, was for Argentina to ride out the international storm and position itself for taking full advantage of the upswing of the cycle.

Raúl sent the report to the president and was given an appointment; he prepared for the worst when he saw bank staff along the way ignore him as if they already knew the Research Office was consigned to history. Instead Botto congratulated him. "Excuse me for not yet having made the acquaintance of a young man of your quality," he said. "Your report is excellent, and I sent it to President Yrigoyen, who enjoyed it very much." Prebisch left in a rush, noticing that bank staff in the corridors now stood at attention as he passed, to tell Malaccorto the good news that their Office of Economic Research was safe for the time being.[3]

In fact, nothing could save the gold standard, and Raúl's advice was promptly overtaken by events. Argentina faced ruin as the run on the peso accelerated, and in December 1929 the Yrigoyen Government had no option but to salvage its remaining gold reserves by closing the Exchange

Office. Confounded so completely by reality, and swallowing his pride, Raúl now accepted that the international depression was different than the downswing of a normal classic business cycle, and the *Economic Journal* turned away from counselling long-term optimism to documenting the growing financial and economic recession in Argentina and the declining terms of trade facing it in the global economy. By June 1930, the *Economic Journal* was blunt and bleak; all of Argentina's inherited structural weaknesses and vulnerabilities, which had been concealed during the 1920s, were now exposed. The export prices for its agricultural products collapsed, with receipts falling from 211 to 84 million pounds sterling between 1928 and 1933, while the prices Argentina paid for its industrial imports from the United States and Britain fell less steeply – indeed this deterioration in terms of trade averaged 45 percent in this period; GDP fell 14 percent from 1929 to 1932. This unprecedented situation created increasing demands for assistance as businesses and farmers faced ruin.[4] In this worry and turmoil the *Economic Journal* became essential reading, situating the country within the international economy and providing a context for understanding what was happening in Latin America and to its key partners Britain and the United States. With each month Raúl became an ever more influential advisor to Botto and the minister of finance.

President Yrigoyen seemed incapable of managing the government or responding to the depression, and by mid-1930 rumours began to circulate of a military coup. Old and nearly senile, he gave the impression of being alarmed at his misfortune in governing during this sudden adversity while his predecessor Alvear had presided over the happy 1920s; he watched the approaching tide of depression with resignation. He would not risk state intervention – he had inherited orthodox economic policy, and orthodox he would remain. But unemployment and bankruptcies rose and labour strife increased sharply. An anti-Yrigoyen faction spread within the Radical Party and grew bolder in its opposition after the 2 March 1930 elections for Congress revealed massive discontent with the president.

General José Felix Uriburu, a second cousin of Raúl's mother, and a group of Army officers began to plot a coup under the slogan "the fatherland is in danger."[5] Born in 1864, he had moved to Buenos Aires at thirteen, growing up in a wealthy neighbourhood beside his boyhood friend Marcelo T. Alvear. Rising quickly in the military, he was in the first graduating class of the War Academy created in 1900 with instructors from the German Army, and he was selected as its director in 1909 after two tours in Germany, where he met Field Marshall von Hindenburg. Heavily influenced by the geopolitical preoccupations of German military thinking regarding the threat of a two-front war, Uriburu feared the growing power of

Brazil and Chile, which forced Argentina to divide its forces between north and west. Besides the failing economy and Yrigoyen's passive response, Uriburu was upset by the lack of funding for the Army; anti-militarists in the Radical and Socialist Parties continued to block military appropriations. Then there was the Communist threat. To Uriburu's horror, the first Latin American Conference of Communist Trade Unions was held in June 1929 in Buenos Aires, and the Independent Socialists controlled the Federal Capital.

By August preparations for the coup were advanced enough for Uriburu to offer Lisandro de la Torre the Ministry of the Interior after the fall of Yrigoyen. De la Torre declined but did not betray the plot. General Agustin P. Justo, who had been Alvear's minister of war in the 1922–28 government, was careful to offer no more than moral support to Uriburu, in effect distancing himself from Uriburu's clique, and other officers, including Justo's protegé, Captain Juan Domingo Perón, were also far from enthusiastic about the coup's chances of success.[6] Meanwhile the opposition to Yrigoyen gathered force in the Congress and the press, forming a rare alliance of disaffected Radicals, Independent Socialists, Conservatives, and various other factions. Both houses of Congress were paralysed.

The weekly sessions in Augusto Bunge's home became increasingly less social and more politically intense as the crisis deepened in mid-1930. Constitutional democracy in Argentina had long seemed secure; fears of a rupture pressed even unemployment into the background as anxiety about the political future of Argentina gripped the capital. Positions were being taken; individuals and political parties were being forced to choose. If Yrigoyen's own Radical Party was divided, the Socialist Party was in even deeper turmoil, with the Independent Socialist Party having split from the main group in May 1927, taking with it with some of its leading personalities, such as Federico Pinedo, Antonio de Tomaso, and Augusto Bunge. On 10 July, Pinedo had signed a manifesto published in *La Nacion* declaring that Yrigoyen himself had annulled the Constitution by virtue of gross incompetence – meaning that he would support a military coup. Pinedo was not representative of either half of the socialist movement; he was so far to the right that he condemned Saenz Peña for granting universal male suffrage in 1912 as a dangerous sop to the illiterate mob in the capital. But even Augusto Bunge now supported the overthrow of President Yrigoyen on grounds of terminal failure, and more than any other group in society he represented the hard core of Argentine democracy. The whole of Buenos Aires seemed obsessed. Prebisch disagreed with this pro-revolutionary groundswell, calling military intervention "most inopportune" as well as dangerous and shortsighted.[7] He argued that, while Yrigoyen was incompetent, his term was already nearly half over, and that a military coup would only deepen rather than resolve the political crisis. He refused to accept the argument that only the military could provide the discipline required to lead the country in a time of crisis and depression.

At 7:30 AM sharp on 6 September 1930, General Uriburu arrived at the National Military College in the Buenos Aires suburb of San Martin for a second try at a coup, after an earlier attempt set for 30 August had failed. The director of the college and his cadets hailed him as national liberator, but the officers refused to join him in a march on the Plaza de Mayo in the capital, and most other military units in the region were also loyal to the Constitution. Faced by failure, Uriburu had to make a choice between being shot in the barracks or in the Plaza de Mayo, and with the instinct of a Prussian-trained soldier he decided to risk everything by leading his small band of supporters toward the centre of Buenos Aires. What happened next impressed Colonel Juan Perón, a young and rapidly rising Army officer, as divine intervention: the streets filled with people from every age, gender, class, and party in the tens of thousands, welcoming the military coup in a spontaneous orgy of public acclaim in the streets of the capital. Flowers greeted the soldiers as they entered the Avenida de Mayo, and the overwhelming civilian support overcame the reluctance of the military units that had refused to join Uriburu at the outset. Perhaps most important of all, Dr Alejandro Shaw, the doyen of Argentine financiers, guaranteed a favourable loan of 1 million pesos, which would stabilize the bond markets on the Buenos Aires and New York stock exchanges. It was a virtually bloodless coup, with Yrigoyen detained and sent to the island prison of Martín García in the Plate River.

Augusto Bunge was among those in the streets cheering Uriburu's success on 6 September in overthrowing the Radical Party. "We'll give them three months," he shouted, predicting that Uriburu would fall under his own weight and create the preconditions for a Socialist victory.[8] *La Nacion* and *La Prensa*, the country's two most prestigious newspapers, also supported Uriburu, with the former calling the coup "a real civic apotheosis." The American ambassador, John Barret, agreed, noting that "Argentina faces an era of progress." Most enthusiastic of all was German President Field Marshall von Hindenburg, Uriburu's hero and the first person he telephoned after the fall of the Yrigoyen Government.[9]

Prebisch did not share in the public festivities that filled the streets of Buenos Aires with wildly celebrating mobs. Instead he remained in his office tidying up the week's work, arriving home late and dining alone. Malaccorto was reading in his room next morning (7 September) when the telephone rang for Raúl. Answering the call, he said that Raúl had already left for his customary long Saturday walk through the Palermo Woods. But it was the new minister of finance, Dr Enrique S. Perez, on the line, and he wanted to speak urgently with Prebisch. When Malaccorto repeated that he had no way to contact Raúl and that he would return in several hours, Perez simply mentioned that he would call later. Raúl had often been pestered by his roommates with the prediction that he was destined to become undersecretary of finance; when he returned from his walk and was told that Enrique Perez had telephoned he laughed it off as yet another Malaccorto joke. Not only had there been no public announcement of Uriburu's new Cabinet, but there were many claimants more senior than himself for the prize of undersecretary. Moreover Raúl had no experience in running a large department; his only serious public sector experience was the small BNA Research Office staffed with proven friends from earlier days.

Before he could change clothes, however, the doorbell rang to announce the minister himself on the doorstep requesting a meeting with Raúl. Coffee was hastily brought to the fourth-floor study. Raúl had never met Perez, a formidable man more than forty years Raúl's senior, an establishment figure who had served as the last Conservative minister of finance before the First World War in 1910–14, so lined and wrinkled he almost crackled when walking. With oligarchic authority Perez invited Prebisch to serve as his undersecretary in the Provisional Government. Taken unawares by the offer, Raúl blurted out that he was neither wealthy nor had he the backing of powerful industrial interests in Buenos Aires. Perez replied that the BNA had presented a list of candidates on which he was the first choice, but Raúl guessed that Luis Duhau and Enrique Uriburu, both close friends and fellow SRA associates of Perez, had pressed for his appointment. Raúl wasn't asked whether he accepted or not. Instead Perez said only, "We start tomorrow." Prebisch called it a moment of "great exhilaration."[10] The offer was irresistible, but he did call Augusto Bunge for his advice; Bunge told him to accept. Officially Raúl would retain his formal position at the BNA as director of Economic Research while on leave to the Ministry of Finance; Malaccorto would become acting director.

At the age of twenty-nine Raúl had captured a position at the epicentre of the Argentine state. He moved immediately from the BNA to his new office in finance – not far, since the joint finance-agriculture building occupied the same location to the immediate right of the Casa Rosada – meeting the new Cabinet, which included Ernesto Bosch as minister of foreign affairs. So meteoric a rise left him temporarily disoriented, but Perez left no doubt that Raúl had to either take this huge department in hand or face the wilderness. Overhauling finance meant clearing up an administrative mess in which deliberately confused lines of accountability had produced a chaos of special deals negotiated in the corridors with the office of the undersecretary. With the support of Malaccorto, Max Alemann, and Israel Gerest, he launched a modernization program in which the huge department was reined in and divided into two divisions, finance and administration, with Prebisch himself heading the former and Alemann as the new budget director. It was evident that he had an unusual talent for administration, a mind of his own, and the confidence to manage effectively at the highest government levels; after two weeks Dr Perez called Prebisch to his office to confirm his appointment.[11]

This abrupt rise to power, however, ended the luxury of academic-style, arms-length research in the BNA Office of Research, where Prebisch had had time to reflect on concepts such as deteriorating terms of trade. As undersecretary of finance he now had to shoulder responsibility for tackling the Argentine crisis. There was no time to think as it deepened by the month. As trade and tax receipts collapsed, a yawning budgetary deficit loomed. Adopting the familiar orthodox policies practiced in other Western capitals, Raúl attacked it in an adjustment package designed to attract new capital, stabilize the economy, and prepare for an upturn in international markets. Public sector salaries were cut by 10 percent, and general expenditures were slashed far harder.[12]

At first Prebisch really believed that recovery was "just around the corner." But orthodox measures failed to revive the economy. Real wages fell by 20 percent from 1929 to 1932, and unemployment was sufficiently dramatic to reduce strikes from 119 in 1929–30 to only seventy-four in 1931–32.[13] The crisis in the countryside was even more profound than in the cities as prices for meat and grains remained low and forced many farmers into bankruptcy. Internationally the full dimensions of the Great Depression were becoming more obvious. Production of steel in Britain had dropped from 9.6 million tons in 1929 to 5.2 in 1931, and the country despaired of recovery. Ramsay MacDonald's Labour Government was reeling. In Brazil Getulio D. Vargas had deposed the elected government on 25 October 1930, six weeks after the Uriburu coup. The US Congress passed the Smoot-Hawley tariff in 1930, closing its markets for foreign imports. Argentina's best – indeed only – export customer was Great Britain, but Canada, Australia, New Zealand, and South Africa were demanding special imperial trade preferences in agricultural products to its disadvantage.[14] Pressure grew for special measures in Argentina as well. The banking sector in Argentina was also near collapse, but the government from General Uriburu down was terrified of inflation. The imminent failure of the BNA, however, produced the even worse nightmare of bankruptcy. Using this threat, Prebisch overcame official resistance to reviving old dormant legislation that authorized the BNA Exchange Office to advance paper for commercial operations, and he placed Malaccorto in charge of a special commission to supervise these transactions. There was no theory here at all; the only policy was survival, using the single criterion of trying and following practical initiatives that showed results.

After months of frustration with the evident failure to halt the economic slide, Raúl faced the additional aggravation of political turbulence. General Uriburu was not the tame father figure the multitudes who had celebrated the military coup had expected. Only four days after seizing power, Uriburu announced that he had suspended the Constitution, dissolved the Congress, and declared a dictatorship. He also set up a special section within the federal police to deal with labour and leftist organizers and to beat up and torture opponents; he followed the Nazi storm trooper model in organizing the Argentine Civic Legion by merging extreme nationalist groups, fitting its members with brown-shirted uniforms, providing military training, and issuing them weapons and ammunition from the War Ministry. Uriburu had turned to the most paternalistic and corporatist sectors of the Argentine establishment. The result was the rapid growth of both domestic and international opposition. He was now branded in London and Washington as a pro-fascist dictator, while the mainstream press deserted him. Within the military itself it was evident that Agustin P. Justo was far from happy with the Uriburu regime.

Confronted by an opposition it had underestimated, Uriburu's Provisional Government agreed to permit free and fair elections in the province of Buenos Aires in April 1931 on the assumption that the Radical Party was discredited and that General Uriburu's prestige would be strengthened by a triumphant victory. In fact the Radicals won handily, and Uriburu responded by annulling the results. Finance Minister Perez, like many of his conservative colleagues, had viewed Uriburu as a transitional figure whose ultimate respect for electoral democracy was not in doubt, and he resigned when so clear an electoral victory was reversed. Prebisch had to choose between staying and leaving with his minister. Initially he decided to resign, but changed his mind when Enrique Uriburu, Perez's replacement, appealed to him to stay with the argument that the end of the regime was in sight anyway. Not only was Uriburu gravely ill, but both General Agustin P. Justo and Lisandro de la Torre had convinced him to restore constitutional rule with national elections set for 8 November. Raúl knew that the new minister supported him without qualification, and with this added political support he now had more leverage to deal with the depression.

Political instability in Britain strengthened Prebisch's argument for greater innovation in Buenos Aires. Ramsay MacDonald's Labour Government, elected in 1929, had been feared by the right, but had been too timid in practice by far, and was finally brought down on 31 August 1931 by the European financial crisis. The subsequent National Government formed with MacDonald as pro forma prime minister was in fact dominated by familiar Conservatives beginning with Neville Chamberlain as chancellor of the Exchequer. The results were immediate and contradictory. The Labour Party, although feared by the right, had stuck to old policies, while the National Government unhesitatingly adopted radical measures. Britain abandoned the gold standard and devalued its currency, with the pound losing 20 percent of its value overnight. In November Board of Trade President Walter Runciman introduced legislation to impose duties of up to 100 percent on imports deemed to be entering in "abnormal" quantities. Free trade was replaced by protectionism, a revolution by the very conservatives in London revered in Buenos Aires as the bastion of sound laissez-faire principles.[15]

With times so out of joint the pursuit of principle in Buenos Aires had to give way to the real-world search for pragmatic measures to limit the damage. Prebisch realized that the mindless repetition of phrases such as "the recovery is just around the corner" or "there is light at the end of the tunnel" were clichés and wishful thinking, and that the Argentine state must now pursue its own mix of policies according to the single criterion of results – it could not afford to sit on the sidelines hoping for better times. It was not so much a conscious break with orthodox approaches as a realization that the disorientation in Argentina after 1929 was too deep to permit recovery with conventional approaches.

In October 1931 Prebisch reacted to Britain's abandonment of the gold standard by convincing his government to introduce exchange controls to stem the outflow of gold and facilitate payment of Argentina's hard-currency debt. For this he assembled another group, the Exchange Control Commission, with three representatives from private banks, including René Berger, who had arrived in Buenos Aires three years earlier from France, to avoid further devaluation and review exchange rates and export applications on a daily basis. The exchange rate was pegged, and the distribution of foreign exchange was rationed, distinguishing between essential imports, remittances of public utility companies and immigrants, personal travel, and non-essential and commercial transactions. These measures allowed Argentina to respond on its own terms to the round of competitive devaluations underway in the global economy. Prebisch also proposed import duties, and he decided that Argentina should explore setting up a modern central bank to manage the economy. This idea had already been explored by his group in the BNA before 1930, and now he assembled a group of five experts drawn from finance and the BNA to begin work on this project, chaired by BNA financial specialist Alberto Hueyo. Malaccorto was sent to Chile to examine the operations of its Central Bank.[16]

Most important, Prebisch decided to launch an overhaul of taxation policy with a progressive income tax on the Australian model he had seen in 1924. Tax reform was difficult politically because it directly affected General Uriburu's immediate supporters, and neither Enrique Uriburu nor Duhau believed he would approve it. Indeed both refused to present the issue, leaving Raúl to argue the case alone with the president. He had been meeting Uriburu each day at the end of the afternoon and had developed a close relationship of trust on matters of economic policy. He now pleaded with him that increasing revenue was an essential part of any program to stimulate the economy and provide support for struggling firms. The general reluctantly agreed – not on grounds of equity, but rather economic emergency – and the law was published on 19 January 1932. Prebisch eased the public relations issue by calling it a "revenue" rather than "income" tax. It was a key victory. "Never again would I enjoy such direct access to power – such complete confidence of the Minister, and such direct access to the President of the Republic," Prebisch later explained.[17]

Prebisch was overworked and exhausted, completely without social life apart from the company of Malaccorto and Alemann in their home, and he had not taken a day of vacation for three years. Moreover his friendship with Augusto Bunge, his strongest personal bond and destination in Buenos Aires, was endangered by conflict over Raúl's continuing to work for the military government. Bunge acknowledged his own error in supporting the military coup and supported Raúl's decision to work for the Provisional Government, but he now saw the 1930 coup as a fundamental turning point in Argentine political history and claimed that Prebisch's work indirectly strengthened the dictatorship by giving it legitimacy. Bunge was being harassed by the police; he threatened to break his relationship with Raúl if he stayed in his position. But Raúl refused, defending his decision to work for General Uriburu. He prided himself and his team on their honesty and commitment in serving the Argentine state during a period of domestic and international turmoil. They had finally got the income tax for which the Socialist Party had fought for a generation. Prebisch also viewed Uriburu as a simple and well-intentioned man, easily duped and manipulated by clever intriguers who painted him unfairly as a dictator. At a personal level Raúl had grown fond of Uriburu. Raúl recounted that the general had made a point of seeing his mother when he visited Tucumán in early 1931, recalling the days when they had played together as children in Salta.[18]

This painful confrontation with Bunge was resolved on 21 March 1932, when Prebisch unexpectedly resigned. The 8 November elections had been won by General Augustin P. Justo, now the new President of the Republic. Justo and his running mate for vice-president, Julio A. Roca, had defeated Lisandro de la Torre and Nicolas Repetto, but the victory was tainted because the Radical Party's candidate, Marcelo T. Alvear, was not allowed to return to Argentina to stand for election. When he was locked out the Radical Party boycotted the election, but it was generally agreed that Alvear would have won over the Justo-Roca team in a fair contest.

For opponents the fraudulent election symbolized the "infamous decade" of the 1930s, the so-called Concordancia, or Conservative revival with the Argentine Army playing a central role in the background behind a pseudo-constitutional facade. From another perspective the Concordancia reflected the political entropy suffered by the major parties in Argentina, in which the political centre was collapsing. Not only had the Socialist Party split after the Russian Revolution in 1917, and then again in 1927, but Nicolas Repetto had actually stood for vice-president with Lisandro de la Torre in November 1931 in a new formation called the Democratic-Socialist Alliance. After the election Antonio de Tomasso joined Justo's Cabinet as minister of agriculture, the most important portfolio after foreign affairs and finance, thus becoming the first Socialist ever to hold office in Latin America.[19] The Radicals and Conservatives were also split.

Prebisch did not resign from finance on principle; he left because Justo chose Alberto Hueyo as his new minister of finance, and the two men differed sharply in both style and substance. Hueyo was a wealthy and independent Conservative, a determined anglophile who admired everything English from his Scottish nanny and waistcoats to his cavalry twills, pipes, and blazers – and even spoke Spanish with an English accent. More important the two differed over approaches to inflation, and the formal occasion for Raúl's resignation was their disagreement over Hueyo's insistence on terms for a "patriotic" bond offering, which Raúl rejected as inflationary; he also rejected the Central Bank project proposed by Prebisch. In any case Hueyo turned more to private sector bankers for advice than to his own undersecretary, and Raúl found this lack of confidence intolerable.[20] On 21 March 1932, he handed in his resignation, and Bunge was delighted that his friend had finally come to his political senses. *Critica* viciously attacked Prebisch and rejoiced at his departure, calling him "the sphinx," and "the financial face of the dictatorship," whose departure was a prerequisite to saving Argentina.

Raúl badly needed a change. He remained an employee of the BNA, but applied for (and was granted) a two-month leave of absence for an extended trip to Europe, with Paris as his first destination. He intended to rendezvous with ex-President Uriburu, who had embarked on 12 March for Berlin, where he was to undergo an operation in an Army hospital. His condition deteriorated rapidly and forced emergency treatment in Paris; the surgery failed and Uriburu died on 29 March 1932, while Raúl's ship was in the middle of the Atlantic Ocean. Among his old friends only Ernesto Bosch was able to bid him farewell on his deathbed; Bosch had resigned from the government when Uriburu had vetoed Alvear's return and had been appointed Argentina's ambassador to the Conference on Disarmament in Geneva, but he had remained loyal to the general as a friend and rushed to his side in Paris for his final hours.

This was a poor start to the trip. When Raúl arrived in Paris he read the news of Uriburu's state funeral in Buenos Aires at which his boyhood nemesis, Robustiano Patron Costas, had delivered the eulogy. Depression-ridden Paris seemed remote from his happy memories of 1924, when he and Alberto had roamed the Left Bank and drunk cheap red wine long into the night; it now was short of joy and energy, as well as prosperity, preoccupied by the imminent triumph of Nazism in Germany. Rome was triumphalist; Berlin was terrifying. So far from providing a break from routine, Europe was depressing. His vacation was also damaged by a wounding insult from Buenos Aires, which caught up to him in Italy shortly after leaving Paris, when he was informed that Hueyo had frozen his salary by special ministerial decree on suspicion of concealing or removing a Treasury certificate after being fired. Hueyo even refused to authorize Prebisch's accumulated holiday entitlement, leaving him stranded without cash and requiring him to take a loan to remain in Europe.

Cutting back his planned two-month holiday, Raúl landed at the port in Buenos Aires and headed straight for the Ministry of Finance to confront Hueyo, showing him where the Treasury document in question was filed and personally locating the allegedly concealed certificate. Only then, after this entirely unsatisfactory break, did Prebisch return to his house at 1340 Luis Maria Campos, where Malaccorto and Alemann surprised him with a welcome-home party, but he was grumpier than ever.

Prebisch was at loose ends, upset and preoccupied. Although he retained his job at the BNA as director of Economic Research, he had tasted power. He prepared his seminar at the faculty; he took up the reins of the *Economic Journal*; he even advised Finance Minister Hueyo, who had elaborately apologized for his gaffe. Raúl pondered his future and the lessons of his brief period in power. He experienced the outsider's dilemma, the legacy of his Tucumán inheritance. He now realized fully his vulnerability and dependence on powerful patrons – he was without consistent political support, an institutional base, or serious wealth of his own. How could he move beyond a subordinate advisory role in the Argentine state into a position impervious to the flow of ministers and political appointees? How could he construct a core institution within the Argentine system from which he could direct an autonomous technical elite capable of modernizing the economy at a time of national emergency and political decay? Just when the Ministry of Finance was reorganized and with a new team in charge, political change at the top had eliminated him from the scene.

On 15 August Raúl's dark reflections were interrupted by a telephone call from Adela Moll inviting him on a blind date – a performance of the Comédie Française at the Colon Theatre. She was a friend of Ernesto Malaccorto and particularly Max Alemann, whose family had been close to the Molls for many years. Eight years younger than Raúl, she was diminutive in size and thus was called "Adelita" by her friends. The daughter of a German-Argentine businessman, bankrupted during the Great Depression, who had departed for Germany a year earlier, she gave piano lessons, sold life insurance, worked as secretary to Frau Keller, the wife of the German ambassador, and arranged music for the Colon Theatre to make ends meet. Her only sister, Alicia, lived in Holland, and she had two brothers (also older), Carlos in Spain and Alfredo, a local businessman in Buenos Aires.

Adelita explained to Prebisch that a group of eight friends including his two flatmates had tickets – expensive tickets at 15 pesos each – but that her date, an Englishman, had been called out of town at the last minute. Malaccorto, she continued, had suggested that he might be free. Would he come? She didn't want the ticket to go to waste. Adelita thought it unlikely that he would agree, given his reputation as an irritable bachelor, but Malaccorto felt he had changed somewhat recently – he seemed "more civilized" since he got back from Europe. Raúl said he would be delighted to come, and the two met for the first time.

After the show Raúl invited the whole group of eight back to his house for coffee, and, before Adelita left, Raúl invited her for dinner on Sunday. "Would you like to buy some life insurance?" she smiled. "I prefer you," he replied.[21]

The Bunges reacted quickly to this promising development; they knew the Moll family in the Buenos Aires German community and approved. Adelita's father Carlos had followed a similar path to that of Albin Prebsich as global wanderer before settling down in the capital, marrying French immigrant Alicia Buffe, and he had prospered in the export-import boom preceding the First World War. He had even been elected president of the prestigious German Club before the depression. Severely affected by the 1914–18 war, he had rebuilt his company and took his entire family on a visit to Germany in 1926, only to lose everything again in 1930 and be forced at seventy-two to return for good to the home of his birth as empty-handed as the day of his departure over fifty years before.

Mrs Bunge flustered to promote the romance and insisted that Adelita also come to their next Sunday meetings. But her efforts were unnecessary; by the time of Adelita's first visit the romance was irrevocable. Soon the two were seen together everywhere in the capital and five weeks later, on 21 September, they were engaged. Raúl's mother disapproved of an alliance to a woman she had never met and from a family she didn't know. Her eldest son, Ernesto the engineer, was happily married and well on his way to becoming president of the University of Tucumán. Alberto had also married well, not only into Buenos Aires society but also to a woman who could control his spending. ("Alberto," Maria Mercedes Lerena would bellow, "back to your drafting table.") But her other son, Julio, had made a disastrous choice that was threatening a promising medical career with depression and substance abuse.

Raúl himself was unconcerned, and the couple did not visit Tucumán for a formal introduction to his parents before their wedding, although Adelita took the initiative and wrote to her future mother-in-law on 10 October reassuring her that "All I want is to be his loyal friend. I love him so much that I cannot tell you what this means to my life."[22] When asked by Malaccorto whether he knew that Adelita's brother Carlos Moll was a fugitive and a convicted swindler who had skipped jail in Buenos Aires following a notorious business fraud, crossed the Plate River (abandoning wife and children) in a motor launch, and then forged an "e" on "Moll" in his passport to get a visa to Spain, where he had for the moment dropped out of sight, Raúl replied simply, "I am marrying Adelita, not Carlos." Enrique Uriburu told Raúl that he was a fool to damage a brilliant career with a marriage outside society, and that he should send her back to Germany instead. To Adelita, Raúl confided, "If I can't have you I won't marry anyone."[23]

Events now accelerated their marriage. At the request of the BNA the Argentine Government nominated Raúl to work in Geneva with the League of Nations' Preparatory Commission for the forthcoming World Economic Conference to be held in London the following summer. As director of the BNA Research Office Prebisch was a logical nominee; moreover he could scarcely refuse this invitation. The long-delayed World Economic Conference followed two years of fruitless international attempts to deal effectively with the Great Depression, and it was recognized as the most important conference since 1919. If successful it offered a unique opportunity to restore stability and growth in the international economy. Raúl was keen to take up this job at the Preparatory Commission and help the League play a successful role in economic diplomacy in London, anxious to believe that it could oversee new rules for an effective international trade regime to reverse the vicious cycle of protectionism since 1929. Saavedra Lamas was a strong supporter of the League, and was determined that Argentina reclaim its membership after walking out in 1920, when its absurd demand for universal Council membership without vote or application was overwhelmingly defeated.[24]

Accepting the assignment meant leaving quickly for Geneva. He requested, and received, another leave-of-absence without pay from the National Bank; he also asked Adelita to marry before the departure date of 25 October – or, he warned, they would have to wait a year. In fact Raúl did not want to go to Geneva alone, and Adelita was similarly committed to being with him. It was agreed that the marriage would be Catholic in deference to Raúl's mother, and it was scheduled for 9:00 AM on 25 October at Santo Cristo Church, the last possible opportunity since their boat was in the harbour and sailing for Geneva that evening. But a final problem occurred when their priest discovered a liturgical error; the couple had forgotten to post the customary banns, or announcements of intent to marry, on the three preceding consecutive Sundays, and he balked at proceeding with the ceremony. Raúl insisted that the service be held anyway, and finally threatened to find a Protestant minister or rabbi if the priest maintained his intransigence. To their relief he relented, although in poor humour, with a brief ceremony sandwiched between masses in a side chapel of the church with Adelita and Raúl wearing working clothes rather than the usual gown and formal suit. There was no reception; instead, both left the service immediately to clear away loose ends before departure. Augusto Bunge was their witness and signed the marriage certificate; Raúl's parents did not come from Tucumán. But a large group of friends gave them a memorable combined wedding party and send-off on board the *SS Duilio* in Buenos Aires harbour, and their life together began with a private champagne toast as the ship slipped out to sea with fireworks lighting up the city skyline.

Snapshots from the long European honeymoon frame a radiant couple – against the smooth Atlantic, on the boulevards on Lake Geneva on bridges over the Seine, in Amsterdam and Piccadilly. Before returning to Argentina Raúl gave Adelita a gold locket engraved with Austen Chamberlain's tribute to his wife. "She has been privy to all my plans, she has never divulged one. She has rejoiced in my successes, she has encouraged me in my disappointments, she has guided me with her counsel, she has warned me off dangerous courses, and she has never allowed me to forget the humanity that underlies all politics."[25]

Housing in Geneva had been arranged by Enrique Siewers, Raúl's old friend from the faculty, who now worked with the ILO (International Labour Organization). He had rented a well-appointed apartment for them in the Place St Pierre, the home of a French baroness. The idyllic circumstance included the discovery of winter after the summer heat of Buenos Aires and the surprise of frozen milk bottles in the morning, but a more romantic entrance to Europe could hardly have been imagined. A maid arrived each morning to clean and polish; they ate one meal at home and dined out for the rest. While Raúl worked at the League, Adelita hiked around the lake and in the snow-clad mountains around Geneva. There was time to travel given the League's leisurely work schedule, and they visited Italy ("like vagabonds," Adelita wrote), going from one interesting town to the next in local trains until they reached Rome, and then Paris. From Paris they travelled north to spend Christmas at her sister's home in Holland, where they were reunited with her parents, who arrived from Germany to see them. "This is the best present Raúl could have given me," she said. They accepted Raúl like a son, and he reciprocated, discovering that the Moll family was titled, with its own coat-of-arms, and owned one of the most distinguished houses on the Baltic coast. When they were back in Geneva on 6 January, apologizing for not having written earlier, Adelita wrote to Raúl's mother. "I am so happy with Raúl that I don't know how the time flies by."[26] Later in January they were successful in locating and making contact with the Albin Prebisch family in Germany, but this trip was a failure. Here also Raúl discovered that the Prebisch name was more recognized in Saxony that he had supposed, extending to the "Prebisch Gate," a natural bridge formation across a canyon in the nearby Hartz Mountains. While Adelita's parents were solidly anti-Nazi and worried by the growing power of Hitler in Berlin, Raúl's relatives were Nazi supporters and had already completed their genealogical tables proving undiluted Aryan purity. The beautiful countryside of Saxony surrounding the Prebisch lands and the splendid city of Dresden contrasted with a pervasive and suffocating sense of foreboding. Adelita and Raúl left as quickly as they could decently extricate themselves from a long-delayed family reunion and were relieved to be back in Geneva.

Raúl's months in Geneva from December 1932 to April 1933 were a forced-draft education in the theory and reality of international trade. Globalization, or the cross-border flow of goods, services, and capital, had reached an advanced stage before the First World War, only to break down definitively with the onset of the Great Depression. The US had played the lead role in the postwar recovery of the 1920s, having replaced Britain as the chief international lender, but after the 1929 stock market crash Washington took a wrong turn by undermining global trade with the Smoot-Hawley Act of 1930, thereby leaving its debtor countries without the ability to service their US loans. Foreign gold reserves poured into the US from around the world, but trade collapsed in a downward spiral of protectionism and competitive devaluation, taking down the US economy as well. Prebisch had witnessed the results firsthand in Buenos Aires, adopting state intervention in 1931 as a defensive measure under Uriburu.

But it was quite different to view the Argentine experience from the centre of Europe, and particularly from the League of Nations, which remained a bastion of free-trade orthodoxy. The League's Economics Department comprised earnest blue suits such as Sweden's Charles Rist, who stood in awe of official thinking in the Bank of England and US Federal Reserve. Underneath this blandness, however, and indeed stimulated by some of the League's own commissioned studies, Raúl encountered a crossroads of ideas and debates on international trade and precisely the terms of trade issue he had raised in the *Economic Journal* after 1928. The Swedish economist Gustav Cassel had produced a commissioned paper for the League in 1927, in which he noted that a "very serious dislocation of relative prices has taken place in the exchange of goods between Europe and the colonial world."[27] The "price-scissors" problem he had identified of a widening gap between industrial and agricultural prices in the late 1920s, which worsened as the depression advanced, was global in scope. Agricultural and raw materials producers were the "chief sufferers" from the deteriorating terms of trade that stemmed, he contended, from the protectionism, monopolies, and labour and trade unions of the industrial West. Eastern Europe, led by Romania, had tried unsuccessfully to create an agrarian bloc after 1930, and Romanian economist Mihail Manoilescu advocated protective tariffs and industrialization in Eastern Europe as a defense against declining terms of trade in his *Theory of Protection and International Trade.* Labour productivity, he argued, was always superior in industry than in agriculture – a different position from Argentina's Alejandro Bunge, who saw industrialization and agriculture as complementary and mutually reinforcing. Although Manoilescu's book was available in English, Prebisch neither read it nor did he meet Manoilescu (who may have been in Geneva for part of this period).[28] However Raúl did meet conservative financial advisors to the League's Economic Committee such as Britain's Sir Frederick Leith-Ross, with whom he lunched at the Beau Rivage Hotel and who shared with Raúl his worries about the commitment of the major Western governments to the World Economic Conference. Leith-Ross maintained his belief in a natural division of labour between industrial and agricultural producers, but he complained that protectionist policies in the leading industrial states were ruining the prospects for the recovery of international trade. He heard the same message from Jean Monnet in Paris when he visited Luis Duhau, who was serving as Argentina's ambassador to France. Later it was revealed that Norman Montagu, governor of the Bank of England, had stated that "nothing" would come out of the Conference, but Raúl on his arrival in Geneva was not at first cynical or discouraged by its prospects.[29] On 11 December 1932, he presented a paper from his minister of agriculture entitled "Suggestions Regarding the International Wheat Problem," which proposed a voluntary reduction of acreage to reduce the huge wheat surplus, which had ballooned to 18,200,000 tons when world commodity trade collapsed after 1929. Argentina itself had an exportable surplus of 2,907,000 tons. The price per bushel had also plummeted to $0.59 in 1932, falling from $1.35 in 1928. The International Wheat Conference, led by the four major exporters (Argentina, Australia, Canada, and the US), had met in London in 1931 without success. Raúl's text of the Argentine proposal therefore recommended that voluntary crop reduction be placed on the agenda for the International Economic Conference. Although the concept had been raised in 1931 the scope of the Argentine proposal made it a first in international economic diplomacy.[30]

Prebisch quickly shed his optimism. He had arrived in Geneva eager to work, but he found that the League and smaller countries such as Argentina counted for little among the world powers. The currency of international trade was power, and the "market" concealed the power relationships that stratified the global system into a core of dominant subjects with a broad band of heterogeneous peripheral objects. There was indeed a single global trading order, but with a hierarchy divided into two distinct groupings. At the apex were the Western industrial countries already identified by their membership in the League's Permanent Council (including the US, even though it was not a member of the League). At the bottom were the agricultural and raw materials-producing countries. Within this category were the large and politically independent but non-industrialized countries: Argentina, Canada, Australia, Eastern European states such as Romania, which depended on the trade rules set by the industrial powers. For all the size and comparative splendour of Buenos Aires, Argentina was as politely ignored in Geneva as Canada and Australia. No one seemed to care much about these producers whatever their impressive territorial size or per capita wealth, and Prebisch felt that he had been invited to work in Geneva as a mere symbolic overture to placate these far-flung regions. Argentina's 11 December proposal on voluntary acreage reduction was ignored. Smaller countries than Argentina were even more marginal at the

Preparatory Commission; Prebisch himself had no recollection of even meeting other Latin Americans in Geneva, and prepared to return home earlier than expected.

Scheduled to embark for Buenos Aires on the *SS Giulio Cesare* on 31 January, Raúl instead received a cable from the Argentine Government with instructions to remain in Europe until August, to join a mission to Britain headed by Vice-President Julio A. Roca to negotiate outstanding debt and trade issues. His stay to Europe therefore expanded from a relatively brief and targeted mission to a significantly longer and more complex diplomatic experience dealing with the two priorities facing Argentina in the Great Depression. Arriving in London in February after meeting the Roca delegation in Paris and accompanying it to Britain, Prebisch assisted the vice-president in a successful round of debt negotiations. Argentina had arrived with a clear strategy aimed at reducing interest rates, achieving a twenty-year amortization schedule, and avoiding a risk premium. Praised in the Buenos Aires press, the outcome was better than Roca had expected and eased the immediate crisis somewhat.

But the difficult part – trade – lay ahead. The success of Argentina's trade mission to Britain was vital for preventing the loss of its most important beef market, and with it any possibility of economic recovery. Argentina had developed a triangular pattern of trade with Britain and the United States in which it accumulated a significant surplus in trade with Britain, its primary export market. Exports to the US were limited: the US raised its own cattle and in any case had higher sanitary standards that kept out Argentine beef. The US, however, was increasingly important for industrial imports, and the surplus from British trade balanced the endemic deficit with the US. The beef trade remained the lifeline of the Argentine economy, and there was simply no alternative market to Britain. In effect the Great Depression had hit Argentina from two directions. First, it encountered the "price-scissors" faced by all agricultural producers as the price of exports fell relative to their imports of industrial products from advanced countries; second, its exports to Britain were threatened after London introduced high protective tariffs in 1931 and signed the Ottawa Accords a year later giving preferences to its former colonies (and Argentina's principal competitors) Canada and Australia. The British Government was fully aware of its leverage over Buenos Aires and already in 1929 had threatened to cut Argentine exports unless it was offered trade and investment concessions. President Yrigoyen had accepted this bitter pill in the D'Abernon Treaty (named after the British chief negotiator Viscount D'Abernon), but the 6 September 1930 military coup intervened and prevented its ratification. Now the British again threatened to block Argentine beef imports; with trade accounting for a quarter of Argentina's gross domestic product, the future of the economy lay with Vice-President Julio Roca and his delegation in London.

The bilateral trade negotiations between Britain and Argentina got under way on 12 April. Prebisch first served as expert, and then de facto secretary of a strong delegation including the prominent lawyer Guillermo Leguizamon, Dr Carlos Brebbia, and Miguel Angel Carcano, two of Argentina's leading agricultural experts, and Manuel Malbran, who was Argentine ambassador in London. The outlook for Roca and his delegation was not good, however, and even the first meetings with their British counterparts in the Carlton Hotel were most unpromising. Walter Runciman, president of the British Board of Trade, headed the British negotiations, and he wanted to exploit his position of strength. An old Lloyd George Liberal turned protectionist, his dry manner and acid tongue left no doubt that Britain wanted greater concessions than those offered in the failed D'Abernon Treaty three years earlier. Britain's adverse trade balance with Argentina had more than doubled from 18,100,000 to 38,000,000 pounds between 1913 and 1932.

Runciman in fact was in a bloody mood after the fighting and snubbing he had absorbed in Ottawa during the Imperial Economic Conference from 21 July to 20 August 1932. While the Argentines viewed the resulting trade preferences for its Canadian and Australian competitors as a proverbial sword of Damocles, the British thought they had been skinned. Its large delegation, including journalists, had arrived from London with the expectation of a mutually happy bargain with the King's loyal subjects, in which they would grant preferences in exchange for concessions on their manufactured products.[31] But having assumed an easy ride and barely prepared for the conference, the British not only confronted tough and professional negotiators but also found themselves sharply attacked as heartless imperialists whose stupidity in World War I had cost Canada 66,655 dead and another quarter of a million wounded. Now the old crew was coming back to suck the blood of Canadian and Australian farmers and destroy their new factories set up after the war. The climax came with an all-night negotiating session on 19–20 August, which Neville Chamberlain left in disgust but which narrowly avoided complete breakdown with an agreement that nevertheless left London very displeased.

Facing Roca in London on 11 April 1933, Runciman was in no mood to tolerate another fracas with delegations of uppity colonials, or semi-colonials in the Argentine case. Meeting in London meant that he had the British media to soften up the Argentines with their howling protectionism, and unlike in Ottawa his delegation this time did its homework.

Armed with tariffs as a weapon, the glacial Runciman was negotiating seventeen bilateral agreements with smaller agricultural producers, including Argentina, and he presented Julio Roca an unyieldingly tough package of demands with the same arrogance he would display five years later in bludgeoning Czechoslovakia to accept Hitler's demands. Prebisch was least resigned to Argentina's impossible mission. At one point he replied sharply to Runciman, for which he was criticized by Leguizamon in his own delegation. Roca subsequently learned that Leguizamon had been retained by British railway interests in Argentina and removed him from the meetings. But Roca was trapped. Member of a charter family in the Republic, he had already served as national deputy, ambassador, and governor of Cordoba before his vice-presidency under Justo. His father had even embedded public duty in Julio A. Roca's own name – the "A" standing for *Argentino.* Now in London, in the negotiation that would identify him in history books, he was bound to fail. An insomniac, Roca would pace during the night, or work on his translation of Shelley's *Adonais.*

Runciman was inflexible, and there was little room for manoeuvre since Argentina had no alternative to the British market; the terms of the draft Roca-Runciman Treaty announced on 1 May should not have surprised anyone following international trade politics during the depression years. While Britain guaranteed a quota of meat imports equalling 1932 sales (except in unforeseen circumstances) and promised not to raise tariffs on its wheat, the Argentine Government agreed to numerous conditions: tariff reductions on British industrial goods; benevolent treatment of British investment and preference to British machinery and vehicles over all other competitors; payment of Argentine debts to British creditors in sterling earned from foreign sales; and an agreement to reserve 85 percent of the meat export trade to Britain for the British-owned meat-packers in Buenos Aires.[32] In effect, Roca could not prevent Britain tying the foreign exchange that Argentina earned from its British beef exports to bilateral trade and investment privileges that would force a reduction in US exports to the largest economy in South America. As with the other bilateral trade agreements negotiated by Britain (a better bilateral deal than Runciman's agreement with Denmark, for example), the British press blasted him for not squeezing harder. Faced by these British editorials – "The Worst Bargain of All," or simply "Sold" – *La Nacion* in Buenos Aires praised the agreement as the best possible in an imperfect world and gave considerable space to the role of Prebisch in the negotiations. But for Raúl it was a painful demonstration of Argentina's international weakness. Roca left for home immediately on 10 May, with the actual signing date of the Roca-Runciman Treaty set for 27 September in Buenos Aires.[33]

Argentina's attention now turned to the much-heralded World Economic Conference in London scheduled to open on 12 June. Prebisch was again requested by the government to be part of the delegation, again as secretary, and he therefore remained with Adelita for another two months in the British capital. Tomas A. Le Breton was named as its head, with the delegation also including Ambassador Malbran, Carlos Brebbia (who came up from the International Agricultural Institute in Rome), Ernesto Hueyo (brother of the new minister), and Anibal Fernandez from Buenos Aires. Argentina hoped that traditional trade patterns could be restored in a revived multilateral order, and, notwithstanding his doubts from the preparatory session in Geneva, Prebisch shared the same sense of expectation and anticipation as governments and media around the world.

Earlier that year Raúl had opened the *Times* of London on 16 March to discover the first of four articles titled "The Means to Prosperity" by John Maynard Keynes, offering a new approach for reviving the multilateral trading order.[34] Prebisch knew little about Keynes, apart from his *Economic Consequences of the Peace* written in 1919 and the less than memorable 1926 introduction to Wright's *Population*. He was therefore taken aback by the daring concept and magisterial prose in the *Times*, as Keynes proposed a new path to attack the causes of the Great Depression and thereby revive growth and international trade. In essence Keynes advised the great powers to agree on a series of initiatives at the World Economic Conference to stimulate demand, clean up overburdened financial markets, and thereby re-ignite growth and the exchange of goods. A new international authority should be created to provide central banks with up to $5 billion equivalent hard-currency credit to restore activity in heavily indebted countries. He included Argentina with the US, UK, Germany, France, Japan, and Spain in a group of seven senior economies to receive the maximum $450 million and act as motors to revive the world economy. This dramatic reintroduction to the work of Keynes made a lasting impression on Prebisch, who rushed to acquaint himself with his previous work as scholar, journalist, bureaucrat, and most recently as a member of the National Economic Council set up in 1930 to meet monthly under Prime Minister MacDonald's chairmanship. It was an enviable record and career. In his *Times* articles Keynes had challenged Britain to take the lead at the conference "with concrete measures," and Raúl made the mistake of thinking that Keynes represented the official thinking of the British Government prior to the World Economic Conference. No doubt also flattered by Keynes's inclusion of Argentina among the top seven countries in his proposed plan, he suffered a premature lifting of spirits. For most signs suggested impending failure. Adolf Hitler's election as German Chancellor on 30 January deepened the gloom in Western Europe; he had already announced a policy of economic autarchy, massive rearmament, and the penetration of Eastern Europe. Across the Atlantic, the election of President Franklin D. Roosevelt had revived hopes of US international leadership, but these had diminished after his devaluation of the dollar on 19 April. While international developments reinforced the sense of urgency in London for the success of the World Economic Conference in combating the Great Depression and thereby reducing international tensions, it was difficult to see which great power would take the lead in reviving multilateralism when they all were themselves struggling for survival in a confusion of contradictory policies.

King George formally opened the great assembly on 12 June, and Prime Minister MacDonald himself presided, a sign of British seriousness lending hope that the Conference objectives of reviving trade, raising commodity prices, and stabilizing exchange rates and currencies would be realized. For once the United States was a participant in a major League event, with Secretary of State Cordell Hull leading a large delegation. But Maxim Litvinov and Hjalmar Schacht also arrived from Moscow and Berlin respectively, carrying a powerful scent of nationalism and militarism.

It was left to Neville Chamberlain to set the tone and give form to the Conference; as British chancellor of the Exchequer and host of the Conference his leadership role was vital to craft a consensus on the key points also acceptable in Washington. Without a coordinated Anglo-American effort, the prospect of success was dim. Chamberlain's speech was delivered in a rasping voice that gave a Dickensian overlay to an otherwise clichéd, arrogant, and fatuous address. His undoubtedly principled civil-service mind failed to hide a scorn for the less fortunate; unable to seize the moment with great ideas he was left invoking the virtues of discipline. "Weaned on a pickle," a Labour MP noted.[35]

Roosevelt's message was conveyed by radio on 3 July and then presented to the Conference by Cordell Hull. Not only was it barren of practical measures, it also alarmed delegates by blaming the crisis on the machinations of international bankers, and then destroyed hopes for a successful conference by rejecting the concept of an international agreement to regulate currencies as an intolerable League intrusion into US domestic affairs. Washington would deal with the Great Depression in its own way and in its own good time. Maxim Litvinov and Hjalmar Schacht spoke vigorously for the Soviet Union and Germany, with both seconding Roosevelt's condemnation of international financiers but agreeing on little else. The Soviet Union trumpeted its first Five Year Plan; Germany arrogantly rejected cooperation in building a new multilateral order, with Schacht attracting considerable applause. Prebisch saw Keynes in the corridors, but they did not meet; it was apparent that his proposals had little support. The high point of the Conference was the Guildhall banquet on 26 June, with a table including Birch's Punch, Gonzalez Sherry, Liebfraumilch Hock (1921), two champagnes (Bollinger 1923 and Geo. Goulet 1921), Offley Port (1910), and a superb 1814 brandy with assorted liqueurs.

Roosevelt's speech in effect ended the World Economic Conference, terminating the prospects for an early end to difficult times with a multilateral solution to the Great Depression; the Western leaders had decided to continue their pattern of ad hoc defensive measures in their short-term interests – bottom-feeding, so to speak, at the expense of the vulnerable. It was the last great international conference of the interwar years, and its failure a foretaste of the doom that awaited Europe. The Argentines now knew it was "*sauve qui peut*," with every country for itself in an unpleasant world. They were on their own, and Buenos Aires had to be agile to survive. The Roca-Runciman Treaty had to be swallowed and signed; vain expectations of collective action had to be avoided in a single-minded national mobilization to survive. Opportunities had to be seized where possible: the Conference failure convinced Canada and Australia as well as Washington to join Argentina in convening the International Wheat Conference on 21 August, at which agreement was reached on a series of modest measures to protect both importing and exporting countries, but it was not clear how they could be enforced.

After his European tour Prebisch was no longer an innocent, with Keynes and the World Economic Conference in London underlining his gathering conviction from Geneva that the laissez-faire theory and practice of pre-1914 globalization was damaged beyond recovery. He had jettisoned his prior neoclassical economic theory, already frayed by his year and a half of experience in the Ministry of Finance, and entered a new and uncharted world in which the choice of policy options would be based on the single criterion of effectiveness. He recognized that all countries, particularly large but vulnerable traders such as Argentina, required a stable international trade regime, but multilateralism depended on the leadership of the core economies, and more particularly the US and Britain, who had demonstrated their lack of interest at the London conference. Buenos Aires could not survive in a world of dreams; bilateralism was in the ascendant, and the Roca-Runciman Treaty was a lesson to Argentina's policymakers not to be laggards in understanding and adapting to the realities of international trade. To surmount the Great Depression, Argentina needed an activist state without the hoary academic baggage of the 1920s.

The corollary of Prebisch's new intellectual toughness was his ambition to return to Buenos Aires to take up where he had left off in 1932 as undersecretary of finance. After ten months away he was both homesick and determined to introduce new ideas and policies to end the Great Depression. Meanwhile a major Cabinet shuffle was under way in Buenos Aires, with Finance Minister Hueyo announcing his resignation on 28 June, leaving Argentina rudderless at the worst period in the Great Depression for Argentina. The other key portfolio, agriculture, had also become vacant when Minister Antonio de Tomaso unexpectedly died. President Justo therefore had an opportunity to renew his Cabinet appointing maverick Federico Pinedo as his new minister of finance with Luis Duhau brought back from Paris as his counterpart in agriculture. Pinedo asked Raúl to be his undersecretary; though they had clashed often during the Uriburu period, Raúl's experiences in Europe along with his previous successful stint as undersecretary made him a logical choice. But Luis Duhau also asked Raúl to serve as undersecretary in his ministry, an offer nearly as tempting as finance given the international trade problems in meat and grains; after their many long years of friendship it was a difficult request to turn down.

Raúl disliked having to take sides. Unwilling to choose one or the other, but interested in both, Raúl negotiated an unusual position outside the line bureaucracy as senior advisor to both ministers while retaining his formal job title with the BNA. Technically, therefore, he would remain director of the Research Office in the National Bank; in practice he would be available to both ministers, working full-time in developing a plan for national economic recovery. He was bursting with energy and determined to succeed where Geneva and the World Economic Conference had failed; he would be no less daring in Buenos Aires than John Maynard Keynes had been in London.

5 Central Banker

The Prebischs returned from Europe in late August to the damp and cold of the declining winter season in Buenos Aires, but Raúl was aglow with optimism. He knew, finally, what he wanted – if not yet how to get it.

Between meetings in London, Prebisch had pondered his dilemma: how could a rational, hard-working bureaucratic elite lead the state? Technocrats like himself had neither wealth nor power – no roots, party, or support – compared with the politicians, who came and went, appointing and dismissing officials with no consideration for ability or the future of the country. They claimed the authority of the state but were in fact accountable to no one. These were the "violentos," but they had power. Raúl's experience after 1930 had reinforced his belief that Argentina needed a managerial elite, but until he understood the British system he remained uncertain how to build and protect it.

Prebisch had visited Britain only once before, and then briefly, in 1924. Now he had time on his hands to study Whitehall and the informal power structure of government in London. The hapless Ramsay MacDonald was prime minister in the National Government, but in fact he was a figurehead within a Cabinet of much tougher men. Looking deeper below the Cabinet, however, even the bulldog Chamberlain and bully Runciman were eclipsed by the hidden figure of Montagu Norman, governor of the Bank of England, with his caste of clever officials extending seamlessly into Treasury. Here was real power, above political parties, an anchor of untouchable stability capable of ensuring continuity in the state. Protected by convention rather than statute, his status made him politically untouchable, but his shadowy hand provided the essential touchstone of continuity, legitimacy, and influence. Argentina needed an analogous institution as a backbone in the state; currently there was no shield against corruption or the erratic political shifts so characteristic of Buenos Aires.

Prebisch had been convinced of the need for a central bank since 1931, but it now dawned on him how such an institution could be structured to achieve so central a policy role that it would answer Argentina's predicament. It was a discovery – he knew he had found a breakthrough concept that could be tailored to Argentina's special circumstances. But he didn't know yet how he could design and lead such an institution at his young age. At thirty-two years he lacked seniority, and there was still a great deal of opposition in the country to creating a central bank.

While waiting for the World Economic Conference and the outcome of the Roca-Runciman beef talks in London, he had met Sir Otto Niemeyer, the acknowledged expert on Latin America in the Bank of England, who had recently returned from Buenos Aires. After Prebisch's departure in 1932 Alberto Hueyo had invited him to study the Argentine situation and prepare recommendations for the creation of a central bank; when Niemeyer learned that it was Raúl who had initiated this during his period as undersecretary, he invited the young couple to his country house for a weekend visit of long walks and whiskey-sodas. The talks convinced Raúl all the more that, while Sir Otto did not understand Argentina, the general concept of a central bank was essential for its future. But Hueyo had resigned, and when Justo had replaced him with Federico Pinedo, the entire project was shelved in favour of developing a national recovery plan. The dream of a central bank receded before this immediate challenge, therefore, but Prebisch was going back to a splendid job for which he felt prepared and confident, and he could scarcely ask for more.

Raúl and Adelita were happy to be home at last; the visit to Europe had lasted nearly a year, and now they could finally reoccupy their house at 1340 Luis Maria Campos. Malaccorto and Alemann had both married and moved, leaving the newlyweds with the agreeable task of creating a home together. The year abroad, with its wealth of experiences and personal happiness, had also given Raúl a new serenity and perspective on his father; he had finally come to terms with his hostility toward Albin with a new understanding of the turmoil hidden in restless wanderers. Raúl had not seen his father for years, but he increasingly recognized in himself Albin's peculiar blend of strengths and weaknesses. Anxious now for reconciliation, he planned an early trip to Tucumán with Adelita to rebuild the family.

But the trip to see his father was delayed; there was simply no time as Prebisch was summoned immediately by Pinedo and Duhau, his new masters, and given the task of coordinating the work of finance and agriculture for a first draft of the Economic Recovery Plan to be ready by November. He therefore reoccupied his office in the BNA and got down to work in a pattern of daily meetings with Pinedo, Duhau, and Enrique Uriburu, now BNA president.

This left Adelita with the work of equipping and furnishing the house, and it also meant travelling alone to Tucumán for her long-delayed first meeting with Raúl's family. Although she worried about arriving cold and unknown, the visit was mutually agreeable and an obvious success. Rosa Linares saw in Adelita a person of shared values beginning with affection for her favourite son, a friend as well as daughter-in-law, and the two women became close and lasting companions. Albin proudly introduced her to the German Union, which Raúl himself had never entered, delighted in her fluent German, and pointed with proprietorship to the Dutch flag flying over their house.

Prebisch's work designing the Economic Recovery Plan in late 1933 was of such consuming interest that he barely noticed the passing of weeks and the approach of the Christmas season. His calendar had one deadline only. For the first time since the Great Depression in 1929, a combination of national and international factors opened an opportunity for policy innovation in Argentina paralleling that in Washington under Roosevelt. As in the US, an irresistible pressure was mounting for government leadership. Argentine industrialists were clamouring for help, and the UIA was now led by Luis Colombo, a self-made immigrant millionaire who knew how to mobilize private-sector support.[1] The homeless were everywhere looking for food, even at Raúl's own door at 1340 Luis Maria Campos. Both ministers and President Justo accepted the need for a radical new departure, and the failure of the World Economic Conference cleared away any lingering loyalty to 1920s orthodoxy.

The Economic Recovery Plan was written by Prebisch – 100 percent according to Malaccorto, but it was announced by Minister Pinedo on 28 November 1933 to a full Congress.[2] While building on the tentative small steps taken after 1929, this package of measures struck a new direction in Argentine economic history. The first step – a major government bond offering to restructure the public debt – actually preceded the 28 November announcement. Launched on 13 November, its success was a precondition for the Plan, and Prebisch and Pinedo were initially worried. Prebisch planted an anonymous article in *La Nacion* predicting success, and this media vote of confidence may have helped to ensure that the offering met its target. Next the peso was devalued, easing to 15 per pound sterling, which had the effect of supporting Argentine exports.[3] The rigid exchange control system introduced in 1931 was also changed to a "prior permit" or dual exchange-rate system, where importers had to apply for a permit to obtain exchange at the official rate – or turn to the "free market," which according to law had to be 10 percent above the official rate. This differential was increased to 20 percent in 1935. Setting official exchange rates below foreign market values and forcing importers to apply for licenses discouraged imports and promoted the creation of subsidiaries. Tariffs were also raised to promote import substitution. In overall trade terms the system gave Britain a 15–20 percent price edge over US exporters since access to the cheaper official exchange rate was conditional on the importance of Argentina's exports relative to import needs.[4]

Meanwhile the surplus created by the exchange margin was used to fund public works projects to get people off the streets and provide money to buy goods from the new industries. A vast highway-building program was launched, and a national merchant marine was established. Real government expenditures expanded 50 percent over 1929. No fewer than 30,000 kilometres of all-weather highways and improved roads were to be added to the pre-1930 total of only 2,100 kilometres. Another thrust of the Economic Recovery Plan became apparent on 20 November, when the government created a wheat board (Junta Reguladora de Granos) on the Canadian model, which Duhau and Prebisch had examined during their trip to North America in 1927. This was followed by the new National Meat Marketing Board set up on 26 December. The pace of change continued. A month later, on 29 January 1934, one of Prebisch's pet projects since his student days was finally realized with Minister Duhau's announcement of the Official Colonization Plan, whereby the bankrupt farms now owned by the National Mortgage Bank and the BNA would be resold to farmers in an orderly way to resettle the countryside.[5]

The Economic Recovery Plan was well received nationally. Luis Colombo applauded the support of a more activist state; the public works projects finally offered jobs to the unemployed. But the British reaction pleased Prebisch best of all. In a backhanded compliment, they correctly saw the Economic Recovery Plan as a riposte to the Roca-Runciman Treaty, which evened the bilateral score; the new tariff barriers and other direct and indirect measures had the effect of squeezing out British imports, while the new highway program undercut the monopoly of the British-owned and -operated railway system.

Selling the Plan was a delicate public relations exercise. Much of Prebisch's time was spent writing articles for *La Nacion*, which were published as interviews with "senior officials with whom we have been in regular contact."[6] He was that contact, and the apparent ambiguity of the Justo Government over industrialization reflected the prevailing state of public opinion. On the one hand it was clear that the Economic Recovery Plan strengthened local demand and promoted import-substitution industrialization (ISI) using import controls, variable exchange rates, and large public works programs in an expansionist approach similar to Keynes's work, which Prebisch had absorbed in London. Officially, however, the authors of the Economic Recovery Plan justified it as an emergency response to the

Great Depression rather than a program to replace imports with national production and thereby transform Argentina from a dependent agricultural producer to a less vulnerable industrial economy. It would have been impossible to gain acceptance for the Plan if the objective of industrialization had been explicit and communicated as such to the public. Unlike in the US the mainstream Argentine press, including the quality *La Nacion* and *La Prensa*, as well the political parties including the Socialists, remained free traders and opposed any measures that risked an inflationary cycle. The nightmare memories of hyper-inflation in 1891 still hovered over Argentina, severely curbing the appetite for reform initiatives, and the Socialist Party still supported free trade on ideological grounds. The government therefore appeared alternately enthusiastic and apologetic.[7] In December 1933 Luis Duhau, who had previously opposed state intervention, gave a major speech in the Congress heralding the end of free trade and called on Argentines to depend on their own resources. Yet he also supported a US initiative for tariff reductions that month at the Pan-American Conference of 1933 and signed a bilateral trade agreement with Belgium on 17 January 1934. The team that planned the Economic Recovery Plan was not radically protectionist like Manoilescu in Romania, and Prebisch certainly cared less about textbooks than evolving a new balance between industry and agriculture in the uncharted waters of the Great Depression.

Prebisch's immersion in the Economic Recovery Plan was interrupted by the death of his father on 3 February 1934. He had suffered a sudden and completely unexpected heart attack, which left Raúl devastated. Nothing had ever gone right in their relationship, and now even the last hope of reconciliation had been lost to his unwillingness to spare even one week for Tucumán after his return from London. This time it was totally his fault; he had allowed himself to become absorbed in the Economic Recovery Plan to the exclusion of everything else, including his family. Now this ambiguous relationship would remain forever unresolved, and his earlier anger was swept away by a wave of sadness for opportunities lost. The funeral was sparsely attended, and one could sense an undercurrent of embarrassment and anxiety, as if unwanted inlaws might show up at the ceremony. In fact none did; the other secret family remained hidden, to Rosa's relief. Only eight days earlier Albin had been elected chair of the local German Union, and its members had turned out in force to hear the German vice-consul contribute a humiliating eulogy along the same lines as the Nazi-leaning *Deutsche La Plata Zeitung*, which had described his father as a "tireless defender" of "our beloved Fatherland and new German Empire."[8] Raúl grieved that his father had not been given an appropriate farewell. But this chapter was now definitively closed.

Raúl and Adelita returned from Tucumán to another personal blow. Augusto Bunge had long threatened to break with Raúl if he continued his work for the Concordancia, but he now delivered an ultimatum. Prebisch had to make a choice: unless he resigned, Raúl would no longer be welcome at his home, and they could no longer pretend to be friends. Bunge admitted that Justo was not a dictator in the style of Uriburu, but he still maintained an authoritarian regime, keeping a narrow oligarchy in power. Genuine Congressional control over the executive did not exist, nor had Justo abolished the Special Section or the Argentine Civic Legion. The 1932 change in government was cosmetic, merely another chapter in the Conservative Restoration, and it was unacceptable for Prebisch to work for it. Bunge was particularly upset with Raúl for agreeing to work for Pinedo, a turncoat and archenemy suspected of illegal land speculation in Bariloche, apart from his reactionary views. The issue was one of principle: if Raúl did not leave the Concordancia, they would never speak again.

Prebisch came over to the house at once to talk things over with his closest friend and confidant apart from Adelita. The confrontation was all the more painful because of their mutual affection and the special place Raúl occupied in the family as godfather to Mario. The Bunge house was almost like home, and the Sunday gatherings there were events not to be missed – a diversion from a heavy workload and a place where new and interesting people could always be encountered. Augusto Bunge was also a magnificent human being. Uncompromisingly principled, Bunge had denounced Stalinism when he visited the Soviet Union in 1933, repudiating his earlier book, *The Red Continent*, which had given a glowing account of Soviet triumphs naively assumed from afar, and he was one of the most outspoken Argentine opponents of Nazi Germany after 1933. *Critica* published three daily editions in a tireless duel with the conservative press, and Bunge's opposition to the regime risked harassment from the Special Section, whose gangs would periodically break up his Sunday meetings, arresting and jailing both Augusto and his guests.[9]

But Prebisch also had made a clear choice. He and Bunge were on different paths, reflecting fundamentally opposed responses to the crisis of the 1930s. While he admired Bunge's courage and his intellectual honesty, Prebisch's position was just as firm. He agreed on the lack of genuine democracy in Argentina, but saw that the left was as intellectually barren of economic ideas as the mainstream parties, equally incapable of offering a credible alternative to the Concordancia. In an age of fundamental transition such as the 1930s all the inherited orthodoxies appeared outdated and inadequate and to limit oneself to the self-absorption of Socialist politics seemed both self-indulgent and disempowering. There was obviously no impending revolution. What Prebisch did know was that the modernization of the state was necessary for Argentina, regardless of who was in power. Here, as a public servant, he could make a major contribution to his country, and he would not stand aside now when he knew what to do to improve the economy for the masses. Prebisch did not see himself as a tool of the oligarchy or the SRA, but rather as a professional economist and nationalist who had chosen to participate rather than protest from the sidelines, a patriot who was leading a modernizing elite from an institution he had created as his answer to the political failings of the Concordancia.

The two men parted with mutual regret. Saddened by the loss, Raúl turned and left the Bunge house for good, embracing his godson Mario outside the front door in a final farewell. "I am not a politician, Marucho," Raúl said. "I am a technocrat and believe in technocracy, and technicians are politically neutral."[10] Henceforth when Augusto and Raúl happened to meet on the street they would stride by each other in wooden silence. With this the Argentine left turned its back on Prebisch, identifying him with the Conservative restoration; he never met again with other prominent Socialist leaders such as Alfredo and Alicia Palacios.

These setbacks were counterbalanced by an unexpected telephone call from Pinedo, who, in his usual dry tone, asked Prebisch to prepare legislation for a new central bank. Pinedo stated simply that he had changed his mind, that the current banking crisis had brought several private banks in the country close to bankruptcy, and that the BNA had insufficient powers to deal with the emergency. A central bank was therefore unavoidable if the Economic Recovery Plan were to succeed. Prebisch was to lead a working group to design the new institution and draft the required legislation; Duhau and the Cabinet were in favour, and President Justo also supported the initiative personally, but it was a politically delicate topic and Prebisch would have to guard a strict secrecy.

Prebisch knew immediately that his lifetime opportunity had arrived. It was as if the emotional ordeal in Tucumán and now with Augusto Bunge had been rewarded with a unique and spectacular career breakthrough. If he had his way, the central bank he had in mind would be the core institution for economic leadership heretofore lacking in Argentina; following a concept he had developed gradually since 1930, it would have a unique structure and role, and Prebisch hoped that authoring the legislation would also yield the prize of directing it. At age thirty-three he stood on the threshold of an unprecedented leadership role; all his previous work was coming together in a grand synthesis much more quickly than he had thought possible. He had proven his administrative competence in managing finance under Uriburu; in Europe he had experienced international power politics firsthand; and since his return he had been absorbed in the Economic Recovery Plan. Designing the new central bank, the capstone project of his career, would modernize the Argentine state and equip it for international success.

When Pinedo added the central bank project to Raúl's other responsibilities, Adelita became even more "the widow Prebisch." He had two lives during 1934. On the one hand he mobilized a small project team staff headed by Edmundo Gagneux and René Berger to develop the concept; in fact Pinedo gave him free rein to design the new central bank, and as winter and spring progressed, the proposed legislation for a comprehensive reform of the entire sector took shape. On the other hand, and in parallel to the central bank initiative, Raúl continued his work with Duhau and Pinedo on the Economic Recovery Plan until late 1934, when the Justo Government finally introduced the new legislation in the Congress, after which he would be poised to assume a leadership role in the new institution.

In this latter role as advisor to the two ministers during 1934, Prebisch was gratified by an upswing in the Argentine economy. The first air-conditioned skyscraper in Latin America, the thirty-two-storey Art Deco Kavanagh Building at 1065 Florida, across from the flowering jacarandas in the Plaza San Martin, began construction in 1934, and the dramatic arrival of the *Graf Zeppelin* from Germany on 30 June underlined the return of Buenos Aires to the first league of world capitals. The long-awaited economic recovery was finally under way. Industry grew, and as Luis Colombo became more expansive, the government became more confident in promoting industrialization. On 19 July 1934, in a speech to the UIA written by Prebisch for Luis Duhau, the minister noted that "We have opened one era and closed another," committing the government to the "healthy and orderly growth" of the industrial sector and stressing not only job creation but also the new energy and entrepreneurial spirit that was transforming national values in Argentina.[11] In fact the basis was laid for a jump in industrial employment and new factories after 1935, compared with zero growth in the US and Canada (as the harvest failed again in North America) and with a weaker expansion in Australia. The onset of drought in Canada and the United States eliminated the international wheat surplus, easing the downward price pressure on Argentine farmers to the point where the Justo Government abrogated the 1931 International Wheat Agreement on 14 July 1934, charging that its two North American competitors had violated their commitments.[12] But prosperity could not be restored as quickly to other agricultural sectors given the low prices for beef exports; as Prebisch wrote in an article published on 16 June, "when the countryside is suffering in Argentina, everyone suffers except bondholders," and he and

Duhau proposed a series of measures to ease the pressure.[13] A meat export promotion board was announced on 3 August 1934, to match the subsidies used by competitors to market their products below market rates, with Duhau claiming an immediate success in selling ten thousand tons of beef to Italy.[14] A wine marketing board was set up on 8 November to aid the ailing producers in Mendoza, with a similar board for milk producers, in a continuing overhaul of the rural economy that Raúl had directed since his return in 1933.[15] Meanwhile Raúl continued his steady stream of articles for *La Nacion,* always without a byline, explaining government policy in complex areas such as the new exchange control system, or foreign-trade problems in the wheat and meat sectors.

But his heart lay in his other task of designing the Central Bank. While his 1931 internal report offered the actual point of departure for this work, the 1933 Niemeyer proposal would have to be presented as its initial point of reference in order to gain the support of the Argentine Congress. Niemeyer had a godlike reputation in banking and political circles in Buenos Aires; along with Edwin W. Kemmerer from the US Federal Reserve Board, he was considered expert without peer in an informal Anglo-American division of labour in Latin America. Kemmerer gave advice to the Andean region; Sir Otto dealt with the Southern Cone. It was as if no Latin government could set up a central bank without the blessing of one or the other representative of the two major Western powers. Niemeyer in 1933 had cleared the way for the Central Bank by rejecting all other alternatives, including the BNA's last-ditch effort to expand its own mandate rather than create a new institution, but his recommendations were of the generic variety that external consultants applied generally to Latin countries, without regard to their special needs and differences. He seemed unaware, for example, of the precarious situation of the banking sector in Argentina. The Niemeyer Central Banks were independent of the political executive but with limited powers apart from money supply; their emphasis was on sound money, not banking or monetary policy, and certainly not rescuing an entire sector near bankruptcy. In fact the Latin American central banks built with the advice of both Niemeyer and Kemmerer during the 1920s had not functioned well during the Great Depression; every South American country except Argentina had either failed to meet its international debt or was hovering at the edge of default.

Raúl acknowledged his debt to the British master, but in fact fundamentally reshaped the Niemeyer vision in his own image. As introduced in Congress on 28 March 1935, the Central Bank legislation offered a new approach to accommodate Prebisch's vision of Argentina's special needs. Instead of a financial institution with limited authority and regulatory instruments, the new Argentine Central Bank that he proposed would be the core central agency in the country's banking and financial system. First, the banking legislation brought under one roof the various banking activities that had developed separately in an ad hoc fashion and now required integration: the Treasury, the Exchange Control Office, Conversion Fund (Caja de Conversion), and certain BNA functions were merged into a single institution with one thousand employees. The gold standard remained suspended, and the Bank was free to adjust exchange rates and administer the exchange control system. Second, the transitional Institute for the Liquidation of Bank Investments was created as a mechanism for sanitizing the bankrupt commercial private banks by taking over their frozen assets in exchange for cash or redeemable bonds.[16] Two major banks were totally bankrupt – El Banco El Hogar Argentino and El Banco Argentino Uruguayo. El Banco Espanol de Rio de la Plata had greater questionable loans than capital reserves; and the BNA had lost a good percentage of its capital resources. With the creation of the Institute for the Liquidation of Bank Investments, to restore confidence in the system, the National Mortgage Bank was authorized to grant loans to expedite the sale of properties that had been seized or acquired. Third, the powers of the new Central Bank bore little resemblance to Niemeyer's concept of a largely passive role; instead it was allowed open market operations designed to manage the fluctuations of the international business cycle by absorbing excess financial flows in the upswing of the cycle and releasing them later in the downturn. It also managed a new office, the Superintendent of Banks, which supervised the private banks. Given these diverse functions on the one hand, and its policy role regarding money supply, interest, exchange-rate policy, and the management of import controls on the other, the Central Bank envisaged by Prebisch would be the heart of the Argentine financial system. He had drafted and supervised the legislation to create a unique hybrid with far-reaching regulatory powers over monetary policy, fortified by open-market operations in bonds, certificates, and Treasury bills that could absorb liquid funds by redeeming the government's foreign debt. Its control over the credit policies and practices of the domestic and foreign banks and its strategic position over foreign exchange added further to its stature. In general, and reflecting the enormous role of the external sector in the Argentine economy, the new institution was equipped to manage the business cycle as well as to check inflation.[17]

Finally, the new Argentine Central Bank was both closer to the state but also more independent of the political executive than the Niemeyer concept. Prebisch sought to institutionalize the autonomy of the Bank of

England in Argentine circumstances, and this required a unique public/private-sector balance. The new Bank was therefore created as a mixed enterprise, protected in both direct and indirect ways from political interference but constituted very clearly as the financial agent of the government reporting through the minister of finance. But its structure provided a far-reaching autonomy from the presidency. Of its twelve Directors, only one would be named by the government, with the remaining chosen from a wide base: one each by the BNA and the Bank of the Province of Buenos Aires and the other share-holding provincial banks; three others would be selected by the Argentine commercial banks; and an additional two would be chosen by an assembly of the foreign banks in the country. Finally four directors were to represent the major economic sectors: an agriculturalist, a livestock producer, a manufacturer, and a merchant. The board's responsibilities were restricted to administrative oversight and general policy; the financial policy of the government and the inspector of banks were outside its purview, remaining strictly matters between the president of the Bank represented by his general manager and the minister of finance. The president and vice-president had to be Argentine citizens, were to serve for seven years, and were to be selected by the government from a list of candidates picked by the board of directors representing their manifold shareholders. The general manager would be chosen by the president of the Bank and approved by the directors; he would be the chief executive officer to serve at the president's discretion without a fixed term. The two foreign bank directors on the board added another source of domestic leverage and international legitimization in a period of rising nationalism. Prebisch had taken the best features of the US and UK banking systems but moulded a truly national and powerful instrument to steer the economy independent of day-to-day political events; he had sought – and found – an equilibrium between public accountability and operational autonomy, between state power and the private sector.

Pinedo proposed Prebisch as founding president of the Central Bank, but General Justo balked because he considered Raúl at thirty-four too young for such a senior position. Instead he reached into the old Conservative establishment and named Ernesto Bosch as president with José Evaristo Uriburu as vice-president to confer legitimacy on the new institution. Bosch had enormous prestige domestically within the Conservative Restoration, while Uriburu (son of ex-President J.E. Uriburu, 1895–96) had been ambassador in London, had read history at Cambridge (which had also awarded him an honorary doctorate), cherished his stamp collection (one of the most impressive in Argentina) and membership in the Royal Historical Society, and therefore represented a valued interlocutor with the British Embassy. Prebisch knew Ernesto Bosch, to whom he owed his first job, while the older man admired and trusted Raúl. The two were logical and enthusiastic partners, and Raúl readily stood aside in favour of Bosch. He also thought himself insufficiently recognized in Argentina for the top job, but the position of general manager also suited him better because it controlled policy and administration while the president's functions were front office and honorific.

On 9 May 1935 Prebisch was officially named general manager, with Dr Bosch and the first board of directors already in place and an official Central Bank start-up date of 31 May. Only one jarring note marred the appointment. One of the new board members was not happy when Dr Bosch nominated Raúl – none other than Salvador Oria from previous acquaintance, who now surfaced as director of the Banco Popular Nacional and one of the representatives of the national banks. Oria could not block the appointment but protested that Raúl's salary should be below those of CEOs from the private banks. Bosch squashed him. Otherwise the Buenos Aires press was positive on Prebisch's appointment. At the inaugural reception on 6 June, Pinedo turned to Prebisch and asked who was going to pay for the champagne; Raúl smiled "You, my Minister." Pinedo declined: "No Sir! This lunch is on you."[18] Thereupon President Justo gave the toast and committed his government to respect the autonomy of the new Central Bank.

The youngest Central Bank chief executive in Latin America, Prebisch firmly and unequivocally took charge and established his leadership, chairing a four-person commission to give form and direction to the new entity and working out of the old Exchange Control Office until permanent quarters for an institution of this size could be located. His objective was the completion of preparatory work for the new Institute for the Liquidation of Bank Investments by 1936, and in fact Raúl opened the Institute's operations on 30 December 1935, with the four bankrupt banks absorbed by a new company called the Banco Espanol del Rio de la Plata.[19] But already by mid-July 1935 the financial markets had seen enough to register their verdict on the new system: the orderly consolidation taking place under Central Bank leadership had restored tranquility and stability; with the creation of the Central Bank and the rescue of the banking system the worst of the Great Depression was over for Argentina.

Argentina had never before possessed a comparable public sector institution devoted entirely to excellence, where hiring was completely subordinated to merit rather than family, wealth, ethnicity, or connections. It was staffed by a self-conscious managerial elite that called itself the

Prebisch "brains trust." The new building selected by the government on 275 San Martín was the old Foreign Exchange Office, across from the Templo de la Merced; it was imposing but rundown, and Adelita and the new staff joined Raúl on weekends during the renovation. Its location and architecture expressed Prebisch's vision of the Central Bank in the national economy: although its facade was impressive, with a bronze clock and marble entry, its entrances and the gateway to the basement vault understated its size, which in fact covered most of the block up to its other entrance at 266 Reconquista. Inside it was luxuriously appointed, beginning with the Bank's mission attached in gold letters in the foyer: *The first and fundamental task of the Argentine Central Bank is to preserve the value of our money*. It exuded quiet power.

Here immigrants and economists from established families competed equally and were accepted without distinction or discrimination as long as they survived the annual formal evaluations demanded of all employees including the general manager. Raúl lived on his salary; he did not speculate and offered a model for his troops. Indeed he ran the new Bank along military lines, with uniforms for the non-professional staff and formal suits for the rest, and inspected offices daily for tidiness. More important, he provided intellectual and administrative leadership, building the most cohesive and effective cadre of administrators in Argentine history and commanding their respect and loyalty. Conscious of their steering role in the economy and proud of their elite status in the state, Raúl's team bonded all the more behind a leader who could write his own reports, including the final drafting of each *Annual Report*. These reports were analytically based and thoroughly researched, serious and well-written documents on Argentina's economic prospects. Although a team research effort, their preparation was directed by Prebisch himself, down to insisting on professional editing to ensure fluid prose.

Prebisch moved his core team from the BNA to the Central Bank and created an expanded Office of Economic Research with the best library and resource centre in the country to help guide Central Bank operations and prepare its *Annual Reports*. In general Raúl had the luxury of building his institution without obligations: he could draw on his proven "brains trust" and widen it with the best talent in Buenos Aires, while placing key individuals in complementary positions in the senior public service. His goal was to staff the Central Bank with a world-class modernizing elite with links into the senior ministries, self-consciously adopting the Bank of England model of directing monetary policy from behind the scene. Malaccorto became undersecretary of finance, for example, working with Edmundo Gagneux, Max Alemann, Israel Gerest, Walter Klein, Roberto

Verrier, A. Muschietti, and the others in the Central Bank. The Prebisch team occupied the strategic centre of national economic decision-making, united behind a coherent vision of national policy and public sector innovation, able to coordinate its policies with finance and other ministries to provide the public and private sectors with continuity in troubled times.

For Prebisch the creation of the Central Bank was a moment of enormous personal satisfaction. He had worked toward this goal all his life, and it embodied his commitment to Argentina and its future. It was a truly national institution, above factions, dedicated only to the public good. But instead of receiving recognition for his work as a national milestone to be celebrated (not to mention for the evident success of the Economic Recovery Plan) he was overwhelmed by a virulent political storm in Buenos Aires.

This vindictiveness toward Prebisch had been building since the 1933 Roca-Runciman Treaty. Even before its official signing in Buenos Aires on 27 September by British Ambassador Sir Henry Chilton and the Argentine Minister of Foreign Affairs Carlos Saavedra Lamas, it had become the most detested foreign agreement in the history of the country, greeted with incredulity by an aroused Congress and public. Prebisch's long absence in Europe during 1932–33 had isolated him from the political scene in Buenos Aires, and he was unprepared for the fury. All the members of the negotiating team, including Prebisch, were vilified in the media as lackeys of the oligarchy and betrayers of Argentina's national honour, cynical manipulators willing to convert the country into Britain's "Sixth Dominion" for money. Luis Colombo organized a public demonstration of seventy thousand workers against the Roca-Runciman Treaty. Prebisch simply had not anticipated his notoriety in Buenos Aires and the personal nature of these attacks – even Malaccorto called it "a betrayal of Argentina" – as if the Roca delegation had committed a crime.

The very violence of the attacks suggested a certain pathology. Who could possibly believe that negotiations with Runciman, one of the most unpleasant men in England, would convert anyone into an anglophile? Roca, Prebisch, and every other member of the Argentine delegation had experienced the most depressing time of their lives – they deserved the compassion rather than the anger of their fellow citizens. But instead of blaming the real culprits for an unequal trade pact – the Depression, Britain, and the realities of Argentina's vulnerability – the opposition in Buenos Aires attacked local, and therefore more easily identifiable scapegoats, such as Roca and Prebisch, who could not possibly have achieved a different outcome. Indeed, in Raúl's case, he had joined the delegation almost by accident because he was already in Europe. Formidable Senator Lisandro de la Torre was smarting from his unsuccessful challenge to

Justo and Roca in the 1932 elections in combination with Socialist Nicolás Repetto, and he led the charge in this heroic fallacy, detecting a conspiracy of the SRA and meat-packers allied with the Justo Government – as if the Roca mission could have manufactured an option other than the British market out of thin air. Duhau and the SRA fumed at de la Torre's charge, insisting that they were the historic opponents of the foreign-owned meat-packers. At the inauguration of the Agricultural Fair in 1934 Duhau was so angry that he could hardly speak. "Imagine," he thundered, "the big beef-producers ... the SRA ... no one has fought harder to control the meat-packers!"[20]

Prebisch never apologized for his role in negotiating the 1933 Roca-Runciman Treaty, defending it as a necessary, if unpleasant, defensive measure required to maintain markets and buy time for restoring prosperity and economic growth. He argued that Argentina's inherent strength, under sound economic management, would permit a rapid recovery if breathing space could be achieved through a bilateral agreement with Britain, and in this the treaty was eventually successful. Once Argentina had rebuilt its public finances it could manage its way out of the Roca-Runciman Treaty, ignoring it just like the British or Germans would in similar circumstances. The way to get back at Britain was not to scream, but rather to undermine its railway monopoly in Argentina by building a network of competing roads. Prebisch admitted that the phrase in the treaty granting "benevolent treatment" to British investors had been a public-relations disaster – the adjective "equitable" might not have been as explosive, but overall he saw it as a reflection of the global trading system, which was breaking down into bilateral regimes.[21] Argentina was the victim of a staples model anchored in Britain, which could only be changed gradually through deliberate state policy. Yet his opponents, self-styled Argentine nationalists who endlessly repeated Prebisch's sell-out to Britain, seemed incapable of understanding this elementary fact.

During 1934 Prebisch ignored the insults and concentrated on his work, assuming that the attacks would diminish as recovery took hold, but this relative calm was broken by Lisandro de la Torre, who now launched another round of the "Meat Debate," which also reopened the unhealed wounds of the Roca-Runciman agreement. As in previous times of low prices and trouble on the land, there was a ready audience, and political opposition to Agriculture Minister Luis Duhau and his advisor Prebisch mounted within and outside Congress just as the Central Bank legislation was being drafted. De la Torre charged that the beef trade was rigged in a conspiracy pitting the beef barons of the Argentine Rural Society and their US and British allies in the meat-packing plants, refrigerator-cargo vessels, and stockyards against Argentine interests including his own wing of the cattle industry (the breeders) and the public. The meat-packers were again singled out as the main culprits, and de la Torre demanded a Congressional investigation into their alleged monopoly of the beef industry.

Week after week Prebisch was identified as the backroom advisor behind Duhau and Pinedo, directing policy in the Concordancia. On 23 August 1934 the Buenos Aires humorist "Titiritero" anticipated the looming contest with a football metaphor, with team captain Lisandro de la Torre and his ragged mates of poor ranchers and enemies of the establishment glaring heroically at their opponents the rich ministers, officials, the men of the Roca-Runciman treaty, the directors of the SRA, representatives of the foreign-owned meat-packing firms, railway barons, and the landlords of Buenos Aires province. On 14 September 1934 the personal attacks on the agriculture minister had reached a point where Prebisch wrote the text of a formal response for Duhau, calling attention to de la Torre's record in abusing erstwhile friends from across the political spectrum and making it clear that the senator himself was far from being the victim he claimed to be.[22] This tactic backfired when Lisandro de la Torre correctly identified Prebisch as the author of Duhau's letter and ridiculed him all the more.

By late autumn the Lisandro de la Torre campaign against Duhau and Prebisch momentarily exhausted itself with a vote to set up a special Senate Commission to study the meat industry again and report in mid-1935, but the government was evidently rattled. The Cabinet activated the Joint Commision established with Britain to broaden the investigation and requested that Sir Otto Niemeyer chair it because of his credibility in Argentina. Niemeyer did not consider himself an expert in the meat trade and declined; the British proved slow in providing information on the meat-packers and shipping lines. Instead the National Meat Board began its own investigations of the refrigerator-cargo shipping firms and identified one of them, Anglo Shipping, as evasive and suspicious.[23]

De la Torre now shifted his attention to Pinedo, the budget, and the Central Bank, adopting a broad populist cloth. "There has not been a word of consideration for the anxious state of the Argentine economy, ruined by the loss of value of our products," he cried, complaining about Pinedo's callousness. "This is quite logical given his fiscal policy. Only the capitalist merits consideration – not the consumer, the producer, industrialist or merchant." But Pinedo was a tougher opponent than Duhau and stood his ground, congratulating Prebisch in the Senate as "the most careful, hard-working and serious of his public servants."[24] The budget was duly passed, but political opposition broadened when the Central Bank legislation was introduced. *La Prensa* opened its campaign on 14 January 1935, claiming it to be inflationary, sprung on the country without meaningful debate, and designed for the sole purpose of rescuing the corrupt BNA. It correctly saw that the Niemeyer model had been changed but failed to understand the thrust of the new legislation and forecast a repetition of the 1891 crash. For thirty-nine consecutive days it ran long editorials condemning the project, comparing it unfavourably with Canada as well as the Bank of England and the US Federal Reserve. By 20 February the attack had become so bitter and unbalanced that Pinedo made an official response to *La Prensa* in *La Fronde*, denouncing its journalism as excessive and irresponsible.[25] Lisandro de la Torre's attack was different. Like *La Prensa* he attacked the bill because the government would have more control than under the Niemeyer approach, but he also criticized the private sector influence on the Board, taking aim at Leo Welch of the National City Bank of New York and Leopold Lewin of German Transatlantic, claiming that the Central Bank would be manipulated by these US and German interests. In fact it is doubtful if de la Torre had even read the proposed banking legislation.

Under Pinedo's political leadership, however, the Central Bank was approved in March despite these criticisms. President Justo took the extraordinary step of inviting opposition Senators to private meetings with him in the *Casa Rosada*, including Socialists Alfredo Palacios and Nicolás Repetto, to explain the new banking legislation and respond to their concerns. *La Prensa's* violent attacks eventually bored the public by their excess; even *Critica* came out in support of the new Central Bank. Lisandro de la Torre undermined his credibility in these debates by gross errors of fact that Pinedo quickly turned to his advantage. Moreover the senator from Santa Fe, it was suspected, was himself sufficiently financially compromised in the troubled banking sector that he had no alternative but to support the creation of the Institute for the Liquidation of Bank Investments.[26] Since the institute was included within a unified legislative package and could not be extracted from the bill, he could not stop the momentum of the Central Bank initiative.

But de la Torre now took his revenge in a spectacular rekindling of the "Meat Debate," which captivated the media and overshadowed all other issues in national politics. The new stage of the crisis began in June 1935, just as Prebisch and his new team were moving into the new Central Bank building, when the Senate commission issued its report concluding that the Argentine beef-trading system was fundamentally sound, although in need of regulatory reforms, which it addressed with a set of recommendations. These findings did not satisfy Senator de la Torre, who issued a dissenting report denouncing the greedy triumvirate of beef barons, government, and foreign shipping and financial interests, and accusing

Pinedo and Duhau of personal corruption and complicity in swindling Argentine meat producers and the Argentine state. Duhau, he charged, manipulated markets for the sale of his own cattle, and Ministry of Finance officials inadequately supervised the foreign shipping interests and deliberately obstructed the work of the investigating committee. These charges were magnified by the discovery of falsified accounting books of the shipping firm Anglo, seized by police in the hold of the SS *Morning Star* about to set sail for London. Prebisch spoke with Leith Ross at the British Treasury to examine the shipping lines from London, their control of the market, and their exorbitant profit margins. While Leith Ross agreed to undertake an audit, the British Government had no interest in pursuing the matter, and de la Torre chose to blame Buenos Aires rather than London for the impasse. Everyone knew the problem, but short of refusing to ship its meat products, Argentina lacked bargaining power. Prebisch challenged de la Torre to propose a boycott, but the Senator demurred, knowing that producers in Canada and Australia would replace Argentine meat in Britain. Nationalization was simply no option.

De la Torre decided to place Prebisch at the centre of the scandal, vilifying him with a bitterness and personal edge that often exceeded his attacks on Duhau and Pinedo. Unlike his ministers, Prebisch had no weapons for a counterattack except coaching Pinedo and Duhau during the debates, and neither could match de la Torre. Pinedo was cerebral and spouted reams of figures to disprove the attacks, but he was so cold a fish personally that he was mocked publicly as a candidate for self-inflicted frostbite. Duhau was rambling and ineffectual. Defenseless, Prebisch had to absorb de la Torre's personal insults from the benches. "I don't call him (Prebisch) *public accountant* to diminish him, because I bear no ill-will toward him [laughter in the Senate], but rather given my habit of telling the truth," de la Torre scoffed. "Mr Prebisch knows more than many doctors, but I understand that he has a doctorate in nothing whatsoever [laughter in Senate], not even in Economic Sciences, which is a cheap doctorate [laughter in Senate]."[27] He labelled Prebisch the "Minister without Portfolio," or "the Little Minister," as the power behind the throne manipulating both Duhau and Pinedo, writing their speeches and their reports. *Caras y Carretas* published a cartoon depicting Raúl in pin-striped trousers guiding his two ministers forward between outstretched arms and holding a briefing document in front of them with the caption, "And tomorrow, whom do we applaud or whistle at?"[28]

Public attention grew with the mudslinging and melodrama escalating into sensationalism when de la Torre challenged Pinedo to a duel with pistols to settle issues of personal honour. Pinedo accepted the challenge, to grotesque media infatuation. But both shots went wide of their mark, and they resumed verbal conflict in the Congress. De la Torre's popularity surged while Pinedo, Duhau, and Prebisch defended their personal and professional conduct and dismissed his charges of corruption. The animosity finally came to a head when a Conservative Senator shot and killed Lisandro de la Torre's friend and party colleague Senator Enzo Bordabehere – whereupon de la Torre unilaterally terminated the debate in a flourish and retired as the obvious victor in the public-relations war. None of his allegations was ever substantiated, but the mythology of Lisandro de la Torre as the persecuted patron of the weak driven to his death (he committed suicide in 1939) by vested interests in the Concordancia became entrenched as national legend.

Pinedo and Duhau offered their resignations and left the Cabinet at the end of the year. Prebisch was not in danger of losing his new position, but the affair succeeded in wounding his public image and reputation and enraging Argentine nationalists of all stamps. He retained the confidence of Bosch and the Central Bank directors, as well as of President Justo, and his day-to-day work with his staff in building the bank was not impaired. But the personal toll of overwork in this atmosphere of hostility finally affected his health, and at the height of the controversy in 1935 he became so ill with shingles that he had to leave the capital for a month to recuperate.

On his return to Buenos Aires he found that the political campaign against him had subsided.[29] To his relief his name gradually left the headlines, and he and Adelita could recover among family and loyal friends, withdrawing from society and becoming almost invisible in Buenos Aires. Although his position in the Central Bank made Prebisch a powerful figure within the state, it did not yield social recognition by the oligarchy for which he worked. Only very occasionally would Raúl and Adelita be invited to the homes of Ernesto Bosch, Luis Duhau, or Finance Minister Santamarina. Enrique Uriburu never invited Adelita once, as if she came from an unacceptably low immigrant class. Alberto was the more newsworthy Prebisch by far. Already a leading architect in Buenos Aires, he had recently built the Rex Theatre to general acclaim. But he now proposed a 140–metre obelisk in the centre of Buenos Aires on the Avenida 16 Julio as part of a grand scheme to rebuild the central artery of the capital on its 400th anniversary into an Argentine Champs Élysées. This concept polarized the public and preoccupied the media almost as much as the Lisandro de la Torre affair, eventually succeeding despite the Great Depression, and the obelisk converted Alberto into a celebrity: he became a professor of Architecture at the National Academy of Fine Arts, gained a seat on the board of the Colon Theatre and eventually was propelled into the Mayoralty of Buenos

Aires. Raúl and Alberto lived in different worlds: Alberto was in the Argentine *Who's Who* and a prominent guest in the great homes of the capital; Raúl in contrast was never invited to join the Jockey Club.

Instead the Prebisch home was reserved for family. Adelita's mother ("La Flia") had come from Germany to live with them after the death of her husband, Carlos, on 7 December 1934, and Tucumán provided a steady stream of visiting relatives. Ernesto was now president of the University of Tucumán, providing the progressive leadership that was attracting faculty and students from all over the country, and Ernesto Sabato, his nephew, was emerging as a leading writer in the capital. Complementing family and established friends such as Malaccorto and Alemann were Raúl's newer acquaintances from the business and diplomatic sectors, including Carlos Brebbia, undersecretary in the Ministry of Agriculture and then roving Argentine ambassador in Europe, Chris Ravndal from the US Embassy after his arrival in Buenos Aires in 1937, and Leo Welch from the National City Bank. René Berger and Raúl amused themselves by importing French wines. An ironic and amusing veteran of the 1914–18 war whose experience in the trenches had soured him on marriage and children, Berger became inseparable from Konrad Dutenbach of the German Embassy after they discovered that both had fought on opposite sides at the Somme; Dutenbach was therefore added to the Prebisch household until 1938, when Berger was posted to France. Prebisch and Adelita spent occasional weekends outside the city in a simple two-room country cottage that they bought with Edmundo Gagneux, planting trees and mowing hay with a scythe.

Prebisch's professional life centred on perfecting the Central Bank and managing the national economy. This was more than enough challenge. He had sought and achieved the position and leadership role he desired, and for this he did not need political headlines – quite the reverse. Like Montagu Norman in the Bank of England, he preferred a low public profile in Buenos Aires, secure in the knowledge that the Argentine Central Bank was quickly becoming recognized as indispensable in the capital and one of the most innovative financial institutions in Latin America, if not the world. Albin would have been pleased to note Raúl's disciplined work habits: arrival at 8:00 AM for a work day that lasted until 7:00 PM, with a bag lunch in his office followed by a short siesta on a reclining chair before returning to his desk. His one regular weekly outing was to the Faculty of Economic Sciences, where he revived his course on the international business cycle in 1936, once the Central Bank was established. The seminar offered not only a respite from a demanding workload but also an opportunity to test new ideas for the *Annual Report* in an academic setting and to hunt for new talent for his bank.

As the national elections of 1938 approached, the Central Bank was fully established as the core of the Argentine financial system. Already in 1936 its open market powers were expanded with the right to negotiate Treasury bills up to 100 million pesos and, in the next year, gold and Foreign Exchange holding certificates. To confront the 1937 boom, therefore, Raúl could orchestrate an anti-cyclical policy that he might have dreamt about in 1921 but never dared to think possible until the creation of the Central Bank; he expanded the market for domestic public debt with the sale of bonds and refinanced the debt to lower the burden of payments to leave more funds for employment programs and public works – whereas in 1932 only 5 percent of state expenditures were directed to public works compared with 29 percent for the debt, in 1938 public works had risen to 20 percent with funds for the debt dropping to 20 percent.[30] Foreign investment, including flight capital from Europe, was moving to industrial production rather than commodities production. While overall annual GDP growth did not return to the 5 percent level of the 1920s, Argentina was clearly outperforming both the US and Canada in economic growth; in 1939 GDP was 17 percent above the 1929 level. Not only was Argentina the one Latin American country with moderately sophisticated financial markets, it alone matched petro-rich Venezuela in South America by servicing its national debt. Brazil and Chile defaulted, in contrast, and while servicing its debt cost Argentina in growth relative to its neighbours, its decision elevated its international standing. Refugee capital flowed to Argentina as Buenos Aires emerged as a stable international financial centre. It was an exhilarating personal triumph for Prebisch, given the backdrop of crisis that surrounded the international economy; while credit for these successes was by no means Raúl's alone, the Central Bank had become the directing force in Argentina's fiscal, monetary, industrial, and international trade policy that he had envisioned on its creation.

Internationally, Argentina had also become a major player with an active regional and international foreign policy. The aristocratic Foreign Minister Saavedra Lamas, who married a president's daughter and wore the highest collars in the capital, had broken with Uriburu's geopolitical hostility to Brazil and Chile and instead had drawn his neighbours (along with the US, Peru, and Uruguay) into a successful six-power effort to end the bloody Chaco War between Bolivia and Paraguay. In 1936 Saavedra Lamas was awarded the Nobel Peace Prize for mediating an end to this conflict, which had cost more than 100,000 lives since 1932. Argentina's regional leadership role was additionally confirmed when Brazilian President Getulio Vargas made a state visit to Argentina in 1935, and the two countries opened a new period of bilateral dialogue led by Colonel José Maria Sarobe, who was sent as Argentine military attaché to Rio. With the strongest and healthiest economy in Latin America, Saavedra Lamas also felt confident enough to rebuild relations with Washington and Europe. Just as Argentina became known as the one major Latin country that paid its debt, so also it was increasingly respected as a reliable multilateral actor in the Americas. At the global level, Saavadra Lamas was elected to chair the League of Nations Council in 1937 in recognition of his Nobel Peace Prize, and with neither the US nor Brazil in the League, Argentina became its principal interlocutor state in the New World.

The Nobel Committee's presentation speech on 10 December 1936 awarding its Peace Prize to Saavedra Lamas underlined Argentina's advantages over Europe during the 1930s – its peaceful environment and its enviable political stability and prosperity. But below this external glitter Argentina's internal problems were serious and worsening, even if they were hidden from afar. It was true that the large middle class in Buenos Aires prospered, that kiosks in the new subway system were loaded with good and affordable books, and that the Mendoza vineyards and the beef pastures of the pampas provided food in an abundance unknown in Europe, and equivalent (if not superior) to the US. The dance halls of Buenos Aires were jammed, and the tango swept the country. The Conservative oligarchy was corrupt but also educated; General Justo was not a Pinochet. A personable man and an avid reader, his vacation house in Mar del Plata was not guarded. If the 1930s were a *decada infama*, it was either a soft dictatorship – a *dictablanda* – or a false democracy – a *democradura*. But that was the problem – its structure was unsound because the political system harboured a fatal contradiction. At the top was a narrow oligarchy that could not broaden beyond the rich banking and industrial circles of Buenos Aires, while the Argentina below this narrow elite was changing and booming – a growing and broadening body escaping the control of its tiny head.

The social and political turbulence beneath the Concordancia was therefore gathering force year by year. Industrialization was creating not only a large labour force in Buenos Aires, but also a growing underclass of migrants to the capital after the Economic Recovery Plan took hold in 1934. These so-called *cabecitas negras* occupied the slums around the inner city and were courted by the yellow press, such as *El Pampero*. Industrialization had also created big industrial towns like Rosario, Cordoba, and Tucumán in the interior, which for the first time could challenge the capital's dominance for the location of new factories. This new economy, with new entrepreneurs and workers demanding support by the central government, was typical of the 1930s phase of industrialization: it was based on the use of labour rather than capital and advanced technology and took place in small-scale plants producing goods that replaced imports. In this sense Argentina was following a trend in South America – Chile, for example, had substituted 90 percent of its imports with national manufactures by the mid-1930s. Major international investment had simply dried up for temperate South America, and it responded with a higher level of industrial activity in the 1930s relative to pre-Depression days than other regions in the world economy.[31] But because Argentina was the most advanced economically of the Southern Cone countries, and the most urbanized, the new economy transformed the social structure more dramatically, with a looming confrontation between the ossified Concordancia and the boiling masses in Buenos Aires and the interior, who were not being brought within the divided and foundering mainstream political parties. No leader, and no party, seemed capable of channelling this growing political force on the streets, and even the interest groups seemed split, with the Union of Argentine Industrialists representing the big businesses of Buenos Aires but unable to incorporate the new and smaller labour-intensive industries in the provincial cities.

Instead of broadening to adapt to these social changes, the Concordancia was narrowing and failing. It was keeping afloat through bargaining and manipulation and the hovering threat of military intervention; the 1938 national elections confirmed this pattern. Roberto Ortiz of the Concordancia became the new president, but he could not have won without the help of a fraudulent electoral system. A Radical who had broken with Yrigoyen in 1930, Ortiz had a talent for political cooperation and retained a measure of respect even among the party loyalists he had abandoned, but the army and General Justo himself remained the dominant political actors in the country. The faultlines in Argentina's political edifice, apparent during the 1920s, when they had brought out crowds in support of the 6 September 1930 Revolution, widened into cracks after 1938. The new industrial masses were restless, and there was an upsurge of religious and ethnic intolerance; pressures for change were building, but the political system was blocked.

National frustration created an anomie that affected all social actors and gave a magnified intensity to the ideological debate after the rise of fascism in Italy and Germany. The outbreak of the Spanish Civil War in 1936 directly affected the second largest community in Argentina and further polarized the population. It seemed that the political stalemate at home was so profound that it released Argentines to fight over the future of Europe. On May Day, pro and anti Franco and Mussolini forces locked in ferocious combat. Argentine political life was a bizarre world of conflicting images and lack of dialogue, with the great European struggle a metaphor of Argentina's insoluble political paralysis. The Concordancia itself was split in its response to political developments in Europe. General Justo was strongly anti-fascist and a year earlier had supported the founding of the Committee for the Struggle Against Racism and Anti-Semitism, which included senior personalities from across the political spectrum, including Augusto Bunge, but the military was split as the Spanish Civil War forced a choosing of sides. The long-standing admiration for the German Army characterized by General José F. Uriburu remained a powerful tendency and fed on the string of Nazi successes after 1936 and Franco's intervention in Spain against the Republican forces. The widespread anti-British feeling throughout Argentina (and the Concordancia's association with Britain) also generated sympathy for Germany's desire to overturn the humiliation suffered after World War I.

Prebisch's horizon was narrower. His concern was banking and the economy, and by 1938 he was again seriously worried, despite the excellent results of 1937. Argentina's relative success in dealing with the Great Depression did not ease his growing apprehension about the future as Britain, France, and Germany strengthened their sterling, franc, and mark blocs, while the United States used its bilateral clout to ensure one-sided "reciprocity" agreements. All were using their bargaining strength to shield themselves from the Great Depression rather than expanding international trade. Prebisch saw this undermining of the global trading system as self-defeating and illogical, but he had no illusions about the cost to Argentina as a small and vulnerable player still dangerously dependent on exports to one market. As if to drive this lesson home again, the British announced a new meat import tax and used it to force additional concessions from Argentina when the Roca-Runciman Treaty was renewed. Prebisch ruefully remembered his 1927 defense of Argentina's trade policy based on the theory of comparative advantage; ten years later the Achilles' heel of trade in staples and dependence on Britain was maddeningly obvious. The US market also remained closed after fruitless bilateral trade negotiations. Argentina confronted a difficult period internationally on the downward slope of the business cycle. The 1937 boom had flooded luxury-conscious Buenos Aires with imports, overheating the economy, and the US economy fell once more into recession. The drought in Canada continued, but Argentina would again face tough competition when climatic balance was restored, and international prices were certain to fall in the event of a wheat glut. In the pattern established since his return from London in 1933, Raúl continued his educative work on banking policy through unsigned articles in *La Nacion*.[32]

The gathering political crisis in Europe made these concerns increasingly urgent, since the German threat in Europe aggravated tensions in the whole structure of international trade. Prebisch insisted that trade with Nazi Germany be limited to hard currency operations; he wanted to prevent Argentina from getting sucked into dependent barter trade where essential agricultural products would be swapped for military hardware or worthless marks, as had happened in Eastern Europe. Unlike Brazil or Mexico, therefore, Argentina's trade dependence on Germany fell sharply after 1933, to only 5 percent of total exports and imports by 1939. Because of his influential role in the Central Bank, the German Embassy courted Prebisch, extending him a decoration in November 1937 signed by Chancellor Adolf Hitler, which was promptly consigned to his personal memorabilia.

Building on his European contacts from the Geneva and London years, Prebisch had a network of friends and associates who provided detailed private accounts of the diplomatic crisis. Carlos Brebbia, Argentine ambassador-at-large after 1938, travelling around the continent from his base in the Netherlands, and René Berger, who was now employed at the Banque de l'Union Parisienne in Paris, were his most trusted advisors in Europe. Both confirmed the rapid dissipation of hopes for peace after Neville Chamberlain's dramatic visit in September to see Adolf Hitler and discuss Czechoslovakia; instead the Munich Agreement had merely opened Central Europe to German arms without a fight while failing to contain Hitler's ambitions. By autumn 1938 the prospect of war could no longer be ruled out. Writing to Prebisch from Paris on 23 September 1938, René Berger ridiculed Chamberlain's "grotesque voyage," calling it "immoral" and "treason *vis-à-vis* Czechoslovakia" and predicting that 1939 would be the year of "the big settling of accounts." In France, Prime Minister Edouard Daladier and his Foreign Minister Henri Bonnet were "*imbéciles et vendus*, two tired men without ideas or character"; of Neville Chamberlain and Walter Runciman, who had taken the lead in forcing Czechoslovakia to accept Germany's demands, the less said the better. The pogrom against German Jews soon after Munich, known as *Kristalnacht*, deepened Berger's worries as Western leadership continued to weaken. France seemed unable to pull itself together despite the Nazi threat and its humiliation after Hitler tore up the Munich Agreement; France had become subservient to a British government and business class that appeared equally defeatist. British bankers seemed willing to do anything to avoid armed conflict with Germany. Carlos Brebbia, who had observed the Munich crisis from Budapest, reported Germany's rapid penetration into Eastern Europe using bilateral trade deals with weaker partners in which Berlin provided armaments, surplus goods, or unconvertible marks in exchange for valuable raw materials. "The great game is now under way," Berger predicted. Nazi Germany had captured the momentum before a cowering Europe and an isolationist United States. "It is impossible to overestimate the importance of these events for Argentina and South America," Berger wrote, "The months and years ahead will be vital for their future."[33]

While Berger and Brebbia reported the approach of war in Europe, Prebisch introduced measures to mitigate its financial and economic fallout. On 7 November 1938, he recommended a decree that expanded the powers of the Central Bank even more, strengthening its system of import controls to include all commercial transactions in the free market as well. Since all purchases of foreign exchange had to be authorized by a prior permit, it allowed the government to direct trade along bilateral lines or even to embargo certain imports in order to bargain effectively with competitors to ensure an overall trade balance. The policy was borrowed from the SRA slogan of the 1920s, "to buy from those who buy from us"; while it simply responded to the prevailing bilateralism in the international system, the Great Powers strongly opposed it. Washington complained that the policy was biased in favour of Britain because of the Roca-Runciman Treaty.[34]

In effect the November decree recognized that the Argentine trade and economic situation was the most difficult since the 1931–32 period. The predicted wheat surplus materialized as Canada and the US, with bumper crops, saturated international markets. Argentina also faced a foreign exchange problem, already apparent in two mild currency devaluations in 1938, which raised sufficient concerns in New York about the stability of the peso that Prebisch delayed a bond issue planned for spring 1939. In effect Prebisch had developed a contingency plan should war break out in Europe, but the immediate threat of conflict ebbed somewhat in the months after the Munich Agreement. Prebisch's actions prompted worries of excessive state intervention. Berger warned him not to go too far. "Argentina remains a veritable oasis of economic liberalism," he wrote, hoping it would remain so.[35] He saw no future in Europe for himself and returned to Buenos Aires in mid-1939 to a senior position with the Banco Francia.

By summer 1939 Argentina's prospects had not improved, and the whole fragile interwar structure of international trade appeared to be breaking down. Increasingly trade reflected purely political criteria as the powers struggled for position. In 1939, to balance Germany's growing influence in Eastern Europe, Britain purchased 500,000 tons of wheat from Romania rather than Argentina; similarly a 625,000 ton purchase from the US, again in preference to Argentina, reflected a desperate prewar British diplomatic opening to Washington. The US for its part was aggressively bartering wheat and cotton for rubber and other strategic materials. Argentina faced diminishing markets and the threat of another currency devaluation with the consequent loss of international confidence in the peso. In a letter to Brebbia on 15 July 1939, Prebisch shared his fears for Argentina's delicate financial situation in the face of the unlikelihood of finding markets for her wheat, the potential problem of declining international confidence in the peso, and the urgent need on behalf of Minister of Finance Dr Pedro Groppo, a close friend of both, to explore the possibility of a loan with Dutch bankers.[36]

Brebbia's initial discussions with banking and government officials in Amsterdam were positive, particularly at Mendelssohn's, where Prebisch had personal contacts. Its managing director, Fritz Mannheimer, was confident that a major loan could be negotiated in the near future. In a conversation on 16 July 1939, he assured Brebbia that Argentina was a "favoured country, far from the battle zone, and with a good credit rating despite the short-term financial short-fall."[37] Mannheimer explained, however, that the Dutch banks were still digesting a major loan to France of 155 million Florins to consolidate its debt. This loan, primarily Dutch with the participation of Switzerland, was essentially political, to shore up France as it prepared for war. But it was a Dutch political priority, Mannheimer explained, and all the banks were following on national security grounds. He himself, a Jewish exile from Germany, was a strong supporter of the plan. The delay, however, was problematic; Prebisch was disappointed and pressed for action. But on 10 August Mannheimer unexpectedly died, and the Argentine loan proposal was shelved. With it went any hope of easing the short-term problem with a European loan. Therefore on 21 August, Prebisch again tightened import controls by introducing a system of special foreign exchange permits in another attempt to bring the trade account into balance and halt the drain on Argentina's gold and foreign exchange reserves accumulated at such cost during the Great Depression. An article in *La Nacion* explained the special circumstances requiring this policy of a strict matching of imports with payments, adding that "the country is far from adopting the dangerous doctrine of autarchy."[38]

Argentina's decision went unnoticed, however, as the deepening Polish crisis consumed the Great Powers. On 23 August the surprise agreement between Stalin and Hitler to share spheres of influence in Eastern Europe opened the way for Germany's invasion of Poland. As the Polish Army crumbled, Britain and France finally were forced to act, and their ultimatum to Adolf Hitler and subsequent joint declaration of war on 3 September confronted the world with the reality of a second European conflict in twenty-five years. The Great Game indeed had begun.

The German invasion of Poland totally transformed the European financial scene. The Germans' easy victory over the Polish Army was no great surprise after the Nazi-Soviet pact, and this left Hitler free to turn his Army to the Western Front. Now menaced directly, the Western European governments were consumed by mobilization for war. While the private banks of Holland assured the Argentine Legation that they were only too ready now to get their money out to safe havens such as Argentina by buying Treasury bills, the Dutch Government had categorically refused to permit its Central Bank to facilitate the export of capital. Holland was putting 2 million florins a day into defense; Britain was investing every pound available – 6 million pounds sterling daily. Any European bank that underwrote a loan to Argentina in these circumstances would be labelled a traitor in both official and public opinion. Gold was flowing in a river to the United States as Europe borrowed to the limit at any cost. Europe, in short, meant flight capital for the New World, but for the duration of the war at least it was closed as a source of lending. New York was now the only alternative, the financial centre of the world.

Brebbia wrote Prebisch recommending caution. The shock of the rapid Nazi victory over Poland and its partition as Soviet forces moved into the country from the east closed out the 1930s as definitively as 1914 had terminated the nineteenth century. The "German Problem" had not been solved by the First World War; it would now be settled at far greater cost to the peoples of Europe and the international system. From the periphery in Buenos Aires, so far away but so linked to Europe with personal ties, black flags greeted the return to war and the new decade.

6 Opening to Washington

So long feared and anticipated, the Polish crisis and actual outbreak of war in Europe were not as traumatic as expected for Argentina. Local interest in Buenos Aires remained focused on the "Match of the Nations" under way at the Teatro Politeama, the much-anticipated international chess final that had brought grandmasters from all over the world to South America, including the now-warring Europeans and the Soviet Union. Despite conflicting nationalisms and recall by governments, the match went ahead anyway, but by its end Polish grandmaster Mieczyslav Najdorf had already lost his country; he took up permanent residence in Argentina as Miguel.

The spectacular German advance into Poland created an immediate financial panic, however, with the beginnings of a serious run on the Buenos Aires stock market and Argentine bonds, but decisive Central Bank action succeeded in stabilizing markets with the announcement that it would purchase all bonds sold by nervous investors and peg the peso to the pound sterling. By the end of the month an absolute calm had returned to Argentina's financial markets and pressure on the peso disappeared as the end of the German-Polish war restored an uneasy diplomatic interlude in Europe.

Prebisch had gambled that national and international confidence in Argentina's economy would return quickly if the strong hand of the Central Bank were seen to be in charge, and the events of 1939 proved him right. Investors were attracted by Argentina's inherent long-term strengths as a stable and prosperous democracy far from Europe's destructive wars and with the required strong financial institutions to adjust to external shocks. European capital flooded to Argentina as a safe haven. Between 11 and 20 September the Central Bank monitored the inflow of capital and adjusted the exchange rate daily against the pound sterling to cushion the adjustment, setting it finally at seventeen pesos to a pound with a higher rate of fifteen pesos to a pound for certain import categories.

On 4 December Raúl felt confident enough to float a 150 million peso bond offering to finance a major public works program; it was immediately subscribed, another mark of confidence in the Argentine currency and recognition of Central Bank prestige in the international financial community. Critics, as well as friends, could only applaud Prebisch's handling of the September 1939 emergency.

The most immediate effect of the war was the curtailment of trade with Germany. Like Roosevelt in Washington, Argentina's President Roberto Ortiz announced a policy of neutrality in which commercial relations were retained; but in practice German efforts to protect its commercial shipping proved futile as its ships were quickly swept from the oceans by a far superior British navy. Indeed Buenos Aires was treated to a ringside demonstration of German weakness when the warship *Graf Spee* was cornered by the British in the Plate River and blown up by its crew in Montevideo harbour in December 1939. In any case the loss of trade with Germany was not a major problem because bilateral trade had declined by over 50 percent since 1933, when Adolf Hitler came to power, and by 1939 comprised only 5 percent of Argentine exports and imports. The German-Argentine Economic Agreement of 1934 permitted each country to buy as much from the other as it sold, but no more. This halted chilled beef exports to Germany, although in 1935 Berlin agreed to a token quota of 25,000 tons. The decline in Argentine exports to Germany was later offset by increased Argentine orders from Britain and Western Europe as allied forces assembled for war. In fact Argentina picked up an unexpected bonus from the outbreak of war in 1939: ninety thousand tons of German shipping stranded indefinitely in Argentine harbours were sold at fire-sale price to the new Argentine merchant marine.

Once Argentina had adjusted to the onset of war it had to face the more complex problems created by the conflict in Europe. It was not clear how long it would last, or whether a diplomatic opening could be achieved before it spread further. Argentina's distance from the European battlefields could not protect it from the economic impact of the war, and the main problem was Britain, still Argentina's dominant trade partner and source of investments – four times larger than the US. In October, Britain stunned the Argentine Government by announcing its inability to pay for its meat and grain imports in pounds sterling. This blocking of the bilateral sterling account was a far more serious problem for Argentina than the loss of German trade, because it froze Argentina's primary source of foreign exchange, leaving a sterling surplus piling up until the war was over, but meanwhile creating a mounting Argentine trade deficit with the United States. The result was a foreign-exchange dilemma for the Argentine Central

Bank. While the British were technically only postponing payments until the war was over and they could resume normal commercial transactions, Argentine producers could take little consolation in the accumulation of a huge – but inaccessible – account: they needed their money immediately to survive. Moreover the country had to somehow pay for its US imports in convertible currency. If before 1939 the deficit of Argentine-US trade had been balanced by a trade surplus with Britain, the blocking of the sterling account presented a fundamental imbalance that threatened Argentina's long-term stability. While Argentina needed US imports to maintain its economic growth, it no longer could afford them.

Prebisch led the Argentine team trying to find a solution to this problem. But in a replay of the Roca-Runciman negotiations the British held all the advantages and were, in addition, desperate themselves. The new agreement was unilaterally imposed and totally one-sided. For Prebisch this humiliating experience ended his patience for good and made him determined to seek an alternative to a dependence the British kept abusing. While the Roca-Runciman Treaty was scheduled to expire on 25 January 1940, it was obvious that London would – and could – demand its renewal. Meanwhile, like a good colony, Argentina was expected to continue all remittances on its outstanding debt in Britain, and the British Embassy in Buenos Aires rubbed it in by not hiding its intentions. "It is fully admitted that Great Britain is waving the meat club and using this threat to preserve its preferential status," the US Embassy in Berlin reported to Secretary of State Cordell Hull.[1] Its broader policy, of course, was to force Argentina into a position of having to borrow from the United States to compensate for the blocked sterling, in effect transferring these credits to Britain as a wartime bonus.

Washington therefore became the key to any solution. International borrowing could delay the crisis, but it could not resolve the structural problem created by the war. The immediate need, therefore, was to negotiate a new trade agreement, but the long-term question concerned the future of Britain as Argentina's economic anchor. While London guaranteed payment after the war, its freezing of payments signalled the decline of power. The old empire was under threat, no longer powerful enough to prepare for battle with Nazi Germany as well as to maintain its international commitments: Argentina's star was fixed to a great power in evident decline while the US was emerging as the new dominant world leader; and however much Buenos Aires might resent the Napoleonic pretensions of the Monroe Doctrine, it had to recognize the opening of a new international order and adjust to geopolitical realities. Argentina's traditional foreign-policy orientation had sought to maintain a triangular relationship with

Britain and the United States, keeping these opposing poles in balance to maintain its autonomy and interests in the South Atlantic. But the new developments in Europe terminated this concept: the US was destined to be the new global centre of finance, trade, and technology whether Latin America liked it or not, and the entire Atlantic, North and South, would henceforth be in the US orbit. Argentina's challenge was to enter it on favourable rather than dependent terms.

Washington proved as difficult to deal with as London. It was hard to decide which was worse: the unselfconscious superiority of the Americans or the condescending arrogance from London. After the British debacle, Prebisch was entrusted by the Ortiz Government with the task of negotiating a reciprocal trade agreement with the US to reduce trade barriers and expand bilateral trade, thereby compensating for the blocking of sterling. Argentina's current account imbalance with the US in 1939 was unsustainable at 130 million pesos. But Raúl failed as completely as with the British. By 8 January 1940, and to the delight of the German press, the talks broke off definitively. The US State Department's later account of the failure in the Prebisch negotiations speaks for itself, noting the Argentine "lack of understanding of American character and conditions, as illustrated by their apparent assumption that the American proposition represented an extreme bargaining position, that requests for haste were attempts at pressure, and that the value of the tariff concessions was greatly exaggerated; and genuine disappointment at the failure of United States to improve its offer, especially as to imposition of customs quotas on two important products."[2] In plain English, this meant a US ultimatum for Argentina, either to capitulate and accept its terms or to leave with nothing. Prebisch chose nothing. High Argentine expectations of an agreement produced a backlash when the negotiations failed, but there was not yet sufficient urgency in Washington to look beyond domestic politics. The Americans rejected in principle the concept of "buy as much as you can sell," but in addition the Roosevelt Administration faced a campaign for re-election in 1940 and was unwilling to alienate domestic agricultural interests clamouring for protection.[3]

Argentina's dilemma, therefore, remained unresolved as the war continued into winter. The situation in Europe remained unclear into 1940, and all countries, Argentina included, awaited the next step. Stalin's attack on Finland in November 1939 and the Soviet Union's subsequent expulsion from the League of Nations diverted attention from Germany; Eastern Europe stabilized after the fall of Poland and the Western Front remained calm. Prebisch streamlined import restrictions to cope with a growing foreign-exchange deficit, tightening controls over luxury goods while facilitating the approvals process for essential products in the Bank's Office of

Exchange Control. Nevertheless investor confidence in Argentina – both foreign and domestic – remained strong. In early May 1940, Prebisch launched another 150 million peso bond issue: it was oversubscribed the first day.

Tension mounted in April with Hitler's successful occupation of Norway and Denmark; German and Allied forces massed along the French border. On 10 May the German Army launched an all-out attack on France through Belgium, occupying Paris on 13 June and forcing the French Government to capitulate a week later. The European balance of power was now destroyed, with Britain itself in imminent danger of attack. Italy jumped into the war on Germany's side, leaving Britain and Canada alone against a triumphant Hitler controlling Western Europe, while the Nazi-Soviet pact gave him a tranquil Eastern Front. The Argentine public was incredulous that the armies of France and Britain could have disintegrated within six weeks and that the British Army had fled at Dunkirk, leaving all its arms and heavy equipment to the Germans. The collapse of Western Europe directly affected Raúl and Adelita's friends and family, particularly her sister, who was now under German occupation in Holland. Although René Berger had returned to South America in 1939, Raúl's other French friends were either trapped or in exile. Adelita's brother Carlos was safe in Switzerland, however, and Brebbia had also moved from Holland to Berne, where he continued to cover the European situation for the Ministry of Foreign Affairs.

For the first time the Nazi threat seemed close rather than a far-distant menace concerning only the Old World, and this was brought home by German foreign policy toward South America. Confident of further victories, and to the applause of his local supporters such as *El Pampero* and *El Cabildo*, Hitler promised to resume trade with Argentina by October, after subduing Britain, adding to another round of stock-market panic in Buenos Aires comparable to the one in September 1939. Once again, however, the same firm action of the Central Bank in offering to purchase all bonds offered for sale quickly re-established confidence and calmed the stock and currency markets. But the stakes in the war were now much higher for Argentina. The scale of German victory meant that the world had changed radically and permanently for Argentina and Latin America. What remained of the Allied forces were now dependent on the US for their survival, not to mention eventual victory.

Raúl agonized over what to do. His Jesuit education in Tucumán had made him a francophile; he had visited Washington, but Paris remained for him the centre of culture. By background and inclination Western Europe was more congenial to him than the self-absorbed and arrogant

US, where politicians could demand free trade for everyone else but their own interest groups and insist on international human rights despite the racial discrimination at home. But as a realist he was drawn to Washington after the Western Europe he knew had been destroyed. He loathed the racism of German fascism. The pro-Nazi press in Argentina noisily criticized the many Jewish economists whom he had hired in the Central Bank and voiced its suspicions that he was himself of dubious background. He feared the rise of pro-fascist groups in Argentina and their ability to latch on to the nationalist banner. During the 1930s he had remained an apolitical technocrat, dedicated to serving his country despite a corrupt state. But after the fall of Western Europe a choice had to be made; the US was the key to Allied victory and much superior to the alternative. And there was another factor that underlined the growing attractiveness of the US relative to a Britain in decline: if the manner in which London blocked sterling summed up "perfidious Albion" for Prebisch, Americans seemed more open to new ideas and approaches. He recalled meeting Professor John Williams in 1934 in Buenos Aires when he was on a US mission to examine price and exchange-rate controls in Argentina. What a pleasant experience that had been! Williams, unlike Niemeyer, could listen as well as talk and could understand the conditions that had led Argentina to adopt new policies after 1930.

Argentina's relations with Washington therefore had to be changed from adversary to privileged partner in the Americas, and President Ortiz understood this challenge perfectly well. But Ortiz was now so ill that his government was moribund. It was the worst possible moment for a crisis of succession in the capital, and Raúl did not think that Vice-President Ramon S. Castillo could sustain the loyalty of the coalition supporting President Ortiz. Four days after the fall of Paris, and faced by growing governmental paralysis, Prebisch took action by establishing a direct link with the US Embassy. On 17 June 1940, he met secretly with embassy officials in Buenos Aires to inform them of Argentina's precarious economic and financial situation and to suggest a new opening in Argentine-US relations. While Raúl did inform Pinedo and Minister of Finance Dr Groppo, he acknowledged to US officials that his visit was outside official Foreign Ministry channels or presidential authorization and that he would deny it if word was leaked. Indeed he scorned the reliability of Argentina's foreign-affairs officials, suggesting to US Ambassador Armour that he invite a US expert to visit Buenos Aires as soon as possible to assess the situation. He appealed for a new beginning in their relationship, noting that "the Argentine Government was now probably better disposed toward the US and saw more nearly eye-to-eye with the US with respect to the European situation than any other American republic."[4] Raúl argued that Argentina had only two alternatives after the fall of France: to restrict trade with Britain and the US and therefore undermine support for the Allies at a time when German victories had substantially improved its public credibility in Buenos Aires; or to sustain shipments of food supplies to Britain and imports from the US by borrowing from commercial banks until Argentina's credit was exhausted. Neither option was compatible with US and Western interests. The former would undermine Argentina's vital role in the British war effort, while the second opened the possibility of Germany "breaching the American front."[5]

Instead, Prebisch suggested a third option, which he felt would solve the dilemma: a national recovery plan that would simultaneously promote the creation of a strong industrial economy as well as a new opening to the US in trade and foreign policy. The result would be both an economic turning point and a new US-Argentine understanding to cement Western Hemisphere relations in face of the Nazi threat. Argentina, the strongest economy in South America, would become the key US partner in Latin America, maintaining pace with Canada and coming out of the war with the same network and advantages. Such a new departure would require a package of US support measures including an Export-Import Bank loan to finance the exports of US products; an additional loan to cover immediate shortages after the loss of European markets; and the opening of US markets not merely to Argentine agricultural exports but also to new products that would replace the European suppliers shut out by the war.

Prebisch's de facto leadership role continued after his discreet visit to the US Embassy as President Ortiz's health collapsed; he was no longer effective and his ministers prepared to resign with him as soon as he left the capital. On 28 June 1940 Prebisch wrote a long article in *La Nacion*, in which he outlined a new national policy to promote economic recovery and industrial development. Meanwhile, he continued his discussions with the US Embassy to bring Lee Pierson, president of the Export-Import Bank, to Buenos Aires for initial discussions with the Central Bank. His own staff began drafting another national recovery plan.[6]

The authority of the national government was finally restored on 4 July, when Ortiz retired to Mar del Plata and Vice-President Ramon S. Castillo was elevated to acting head of government to shape a new Cabinet. Ortiz had been pro-Allied to the point of withdrawing government support for the anti-democratic Civic Legion, and it was widely expected that Castillo in his choice of ministers would try to distance himself from his predecessor. Instead Castillo, coming from the mining province of Catamarca, was more open to industrial development than Ortiz, and the surprise appointment of

Federico Pinedo and Julio A. Roca as his ministers of finance and foreign affairs, respectively, gave a clear signal of continuity. Pinedo had come around to the need for a pro-US orientation, and Raúl had kept in touch with him since their work together in 1934–35. Roca could also be counted on to support the opening to Washington and Brazil. No two Cabinet appointments could have been as agreeable for Prebisch – bearing in mind the association of both ministers with the debilitating political debates of the 1930s – and Pinedo had the leadership skills to steer the National Recovery Plan through the Cabinet and Argentine Congress.

Although the National Recovery Plan concept preceded Pinedo and was drafted by Raúl's team, particularly himself, Malaccorto, and Guillermo Klein, it became known simply as the Pinedo Plan, in view of his ministerial role. But this was irrelevant to the key point that Pinedo fully endorsed its main thrust, particularly to break free from the Atlantic Triangle concept and recognize the reality of US power in the Western Hemisphere. The Pinedo Plan was both a bold program to promote Argentina's national industry and a long-term strategic plan to assert regional leadership in the Southern Cone.[7] On the domestic side the government proposed the creation of a new industrial credit bank to promote industrialization, fulfilling a long-established demand of Luis Colombo's UIA and recognizing that Argentina had to strengthen growth with new state/private-sector tools. Borrowing from the French slogan "If construction is healthy, the economy is healthy," the subtitle of the Pinedo Plan also endorsed a massive housing program for the poor and medium-income earners in the Republic to stimulate employment (210,000 jobs were to be created) and the local construction materials market. It also committed itself to support agriculture with a new state agency that would buy unsold agricultural products, sell them overseas, and use the resulting profits to purchase necessary industrial imports. The Central Bank would finance the scheme by expanding credit and issuing government bonds to the commercial banks at 2 percent above the going interest rate for savings accounts. Each of the main sectors – agrarian, industrial, and urban – got something positive in the Pinedo Plan: business praised its support for industrialization, the public endorsed job creation and housing, and economic nationalists saw in it a clever plan to leverage ownership of the British-owned railways using Argentina's blocked sterling account in London as a down payment, with the balance to be paid over a period of sixty years. Based on the expansion of local demand and control of incomes, Pinedo defended the plan as a social conservative by arguing that "A sound economy and social structure based on general welfare and justice is as important for defense as a well-equipped army."[8]

The international trade thrust of the Pinedo Plan was equally central and quite a new departure for Argentina. It was not just a plan to promote national industry at any price; instead it promoted a particular strategy of national development that aimed at export competitiveness in the US and regional Southern Cone markets to guard against "artificial" industries that would be swept away when the war ended. The argument stemmed from what the authors called the "three wheel" dilemma of Argentine trade policy, the three wheels representing the UK, the US, and neighbouring Latin American markets. The first wheel had broken with the war and the blocked sterling account; this meant that Argentina would have to reorient its economy to the US and Brazilian markets. To accomplish this on a permanent basis, however, Argentina would have to produce and export quality products beginning with non-traditional agricultural goods but also including value-added products that would permanently replace the former European suppliers shut out of the Americas by the war. The British, of course, were not happy with the weakening of its leverage in the region, with the Embassy blaming "irresponsible political forces" for the Pinedo Plan. Prebisch and Pinedo, so long condemned by the popular press in Buenos Aires as irredeemable anglophiles, were now recategorized by the British as "radicals."[9]

Since the success of the National Recovery Plan depended on building new relationships with the US and Brazil, Pinedo, Roca, and Prebisch worked together closely during the winter and spring to lay the necessary diplomatic groundwork for successful missions to both countries. Given geographic proximity all three would travel together to Rio, but on 24 September Pinedo named Prebisch as chief of delegation for the trip to Washington. It was already clear that the approach of US presidential elections meant the postponement of his mission until the re-election of Franklin Delano Roosevelt on 4 November 1940.

Their first visit, therefore, was to Brazil, Argentina's historic rival in South America. Brazilian Foreign Minister Osvaldo Aranha welcomed the suggestion for a bilateral meeting and President Getulio Vargas invited his Argentine counterparts to a major conference on 3–6 October in Rio de Janeiro. It was a propitious moment to break their long legacy of discord with a new era of cooperation. Bilateral relations had been strengthened after 1930 under Presidents Vargas and Justo, and General José M. Sarobe's tenure as Argentina's military attaché in Rio had removed some of the historic distrust between the two militaries. The Great Depression and the outbreak of war in 1939 gave an additional impulse for regional cooperation, since both Argentina and Brazil needed expanded markets. During the Depression both had erected tariff barriers against each other; now Europe was at war, and both were dependent on the US. It was time to explore a larger regional market to diversify that dependence. At an inter-American conference in Havana earlier in 1940 the Brazilian and Argentine delegations had agreed to discuss a new trade initiative in light of the wartime emergency. The Pinedo Plan therefore revived a long-standing dream of the formation of a common market in the River Plate Basin, anchored by Brazil and Argentina but including Uruguay, Paraguay, and if possible Chile, which would bury their rivalry and together create a South American bloc in the world economy.[10] Pinedo had long been in favour of integration, but Prebisch took the initiative in 1940, insisting that instead of Argentina and Brazil duplicating sectors for local markets the two countries should promote sectoral specialization for a regional market. Fundamentally, the Pinedo Plan sought to reactivate the local economy and to expand and divert trade to "no-dollar" zones like Southern America as well as to "sterling" and "transferable exchange" areas.

The Brazil-Argentine Economic Conference was opened by Aranha on 3 October and brought together the key political and economic leaders from both countries. Respective Chambers of Commerce also participated in the discussions, as did Brazil's leading economists Octavio Bulhões and Eugenio Gudin from the Ministry of Finance. In a private meeting with Prebisch, Roca and Pinedo, President Vargas underlined his support for building a large regional market. "In place of the so-called Monroe Doctrine," Brazilian Finance Minister Costa Souza noted, "we are proposing a new era for the new circumstances: continental cooperation at the economic level without prejudicing the right of any country of the Americas to manage their internal affairs according to their individual needs."[11]

The underlying concept was a free-trade agreement beginning with sectoral accords, starting with wheat and textiles and working forward toward an increasingly comprehensive agreement on a step-by-step basis as regional integration deepened. Given the early stage of industrialization in both countries it seemed the right moment to determine relative sectoral comparative advantages, achieve an agreement on priorities, and thus build competitive industries with economies of scale capable of producing for a combined regional market; the alternative was to view each economy as a watertight compartment protected by import-substitution strategies. Examples of the benefits of regional cooperation were readily identified. Brazil was growing wheat and mixing manioc with flour because of its persistent trade deficit with Argentina, yet Brazil was the more advanced of the two in certain textile products. Brazil therefore agreed to expand wheat imports from Argentina in return for Argentina's purchase of Brazilian textiles worth 30 million pesos. As a safeguard both parties agreed that reasonable overall trade parity would have to be maintained as the integration process deepened, but they endorsed the logic of regional sectoral specialization to build export-capable industries across the Argentine-Brazil divide.

The formation of an Argentine-Brazilian trade grouping implied a potential diplomatic revolution in South America. But if the Rio Conference signalled a historic departure, both sides understood the challenge facing them in actually achieving this dream. The Argentine-Brazil rapprochement since 1930 remained fragile, and since neither country had a steel or capital goods industry both looked to the US and UK as their primary trade partners for developing their economies. But Aranha and Roca set a bilateral goal of a free-trade treaty, open to the neighbouring countries and as a step toward a regional customs union. In a special paragraph the two countries also supported a spirit of pan-Americanism, agreeing that Uruguay and Paraguay should be included in a Southern Cone trade agreement and that the participation of Chile should also be explored. To allay suspicions of exclusion, Prebisch had already sent a team to Santiago headed by Central Bank official Alizon Garcia to brief officials there on the Rio Conference. In more specific terms the two large countries tried to calm the fears of the smaller neighbours. Julio Roca met with his Uruguayan counterpart, Foreign Minister Alberto Guani, on 14 December in the border town of Colonia to endorse regional free trade and establish a bilateral Joint Ministerial Economic Commission. All the governments agreed to participate in a Cuenca del Plata Conference to be held 27 January-6 February 1941, comprising the five River Plate countries – Uruguay, Paraguay, Bolivia, Argentina, and Brazil – to take the first steps toward regional integration and set up a secretariat for this purpose in Buenos Aires.

The Rio agreement cleared the way for the Prebisch mission to Washington. Although the US criticized the prospect of a free-trade agreement or customs union in South America as a potential violation of the most-favoured-nation principle, the protest was surprisingly muted. Prebisch and Aranha argued that improved bilateral trade cooperation strengthened all South American economies and should be supported in view of the Nazi threat, and a press release from Sumner Welles during the Rio Conference ended by promising that despite its reservations about regional free trade pacts the US might accept a Southern Cone Accord. "It is to be hoped," Pinedo responded, "that human understanding has not become altogether blind to the creation of new forms of living together."[12] On the eve of Prebisch's departure for Washington, therefore, Argentina had scored a major diplomatic success that strengthened his hand in the forthcoming talks with US officials.

Prebisch arrived in Washington on 8 November 1940. His was the first foreign delegation to meet President Roosevelt after his re-election earlier that week. Prebisch's program for the US trip had been developed in close cooperation with US Embassy officials in Buenos Aires, particularly Christian Ravndal, secretary of the embassy, who travelled with him to Washington. Prebisch had prepared a detailed background paper that would become known in Washington as the Prebisch Memorandum, setting out the Argentine predicament with the war in Europe, and the need for a bilateral agreement with the US comparable with its wartime accords with China or Britain. The objective was a "special relationship," a unique relationship between Washington and Argentina. While the official purpose of the Prebisch mission was to seek financing from the US Government and the Export-Import Bank to accommodate its difficult foreign-exchange crisis, the underlying goal was to achieve a long-range program of closer economic and political cooperation between the two countries. Following a decade of bitter fighting Argentina and the US both faced a watershed in their relations, where an alliance appeared possible. With Nazi Germany threatening Britain and Western Europe under Nazi control, the two countries had something in common and needed one another. If the US was the anchor of North America, Argentina was the strongest power in South America. They were obvious partners who paid their debts and deserved some recognition for this good behaviour. Pinedo was reported as asking, "Why does the United States not face facts and shift its policy to one that will give the Americas preference?"[13] The objective of the Prebisch mission, therefore, was to forge a long-range financial, economic, and trade program to decrease Argentina's dependence on Europe, including initial soundings regarding the establishment of a Western Hemisphere free-trade area and eventually of a customs union encompassing the Americas from Canada to Patagonia. During Raúl's visit to the US, President Ortiz added his personal support for Western Hemisphere solidarity, appealing on 20 November for a broad program of cooperation in the Americas "to establish their defense against foreign perils."[14]

Prebisch was accompanied by his foreign-exchange expert, Eduardo Grumbach, and Roberto Verrier, head of the Central Bank's Economic Research Department. Settling into the Willard Hotel, Raúl began discussions with US Treasury and State Department officials the next day, while Adelita visited the battlefield at Gettysburg. They met Secretary of State Cordell Hull and Assistant Secretary Sumner Welles, who had served as Secretary in the US Embassy in Buenos Aires and spoke Spanish, as well as Henry Morgenthau, Harry Dexter White, and Daniel W. Bell from the US Treasury, Congressional leaders, and Nelson Rockefeller, who had recently been appointed coordinator of Commercial and Cultural Relations. With the help of Chris Ravndal, Prebisch explained the National Recovery Plan that Pinedo would be presenting to Congress on 14 November. He clarified the proposed industrial development program to alleviate US fears of protectionism and underlined that improved US-Argentine commercial relations would allow the Central Bank to lift import restrictions. The Prebisch Memorandum served as rationale for the specific credit request of the Argentine Government.

A stronger Argentine economy would have the additional effect of aiding Britain in its war effort, and Prebisch also used this argument of food security for promoting a special US-Argentina economic relationship. But although British officials met with their US and Argentine counterparts to discuss future plans, it was evident that the British resented Prebisch's mission to Washington and the concept of a special hemispheric link. They knew that it would be at their expense; a special US loan and Export-Import Bank support to Argentina would not merely be "financially unorthodox," as they complained to London, but it also gave the US an advantage in the Southern Cone that Britain could not match.

The British connection proved to be the main theme in Prebisch's interview with President Roosevelt, which was arranged by Felipe Espil, Argentina's ambassador to the White House. A protocol visit of three minutes had been agreed to, but Roosevelt kept Prebisch for an hour (with Raúl periodically leaping from his seat on missed signals that his time was up), mightily impressing Raúl with his charisma, cordiality, and aristocratic bearing. But FDR really wanted to talk about the mutual US-Argentine interest in limiting British power in the Western Hemisphere. Just as Roosevelt had bought the last British bases from the Caribbean and Atlantic waters for fifty old destroyers several months earlier in a deal of questionable loyalty, so he also supported the Argentine threat of nationalization of the British railways as set out in the Pinedo Plan. "They have to agree to save their skins," he concluded, noting that British-owned railways in South America were badly run in any case. But he also warned Prebisch that railway investments were a losing proposition – his family knew this all too well.[15]

Prebisch informed the US that the Pinedo Plan also included the creation of a new trade export corporation, the CAPI (Argentine Export Promotion Corporation), which had been approved on 29 November but not signed or released pending discussions with the US.[16] The CAPI concept preceded the arrival of Pinedo as minister, and Prebisch had actually discussed it with the embassy two months earlier, but he now wanted to place this initiative on his Washington agenda. The concept had emerged after the Central Bank was criticized by importers for restricting import and export permits for US products. Raúl had explained that Argentina required essential goods first and foremost, but that if the US were to import

Argentine manufactured goods, the Central Bank would reconsider its policy in favour of a program that would link such exports with US imports.[17] Ravndal supported the plan to help solve Argentina's ballooning trade deficit and encouraged Cordell Hull to accept it as well. In his description, the new Export Promotion Corporation was aimed at "winning a place in the American market for articles new in Argentina's export trade, but old in world commerce" by replacing the French, Italian, Polish, and Czechoslovakian exporters excluded by the war in Europe. Such new product areas could include cheese, ham, wine, and leather goods, but other new and unanticipated export articles might also be developed through a new form of private/public-sector cooperation.[18] "Exporting is not a function of government," Prebisch argued, but he insisted that "government must concern itself with making conditions favourable for export trade." He didn't know if it would work, but there was "no justification in pointing to obstacles as an excuse for not attempting to acquire a part of the orders American importers formerly placed in Europe."[19] The central idea was to woo Argentine producers out of the domestic market alone by giving them title to the foreign exchange created by exports with the right to use it for importing goods otherwise subject to import duties. The Central Bank would manage it, and US business leaders such as Leo Welch were already discussing the mechanics of such an organization. Prebisch hoped to find new approaches in meetings with the private sector in Washington and New York, but above all he wanted to ensure that the US would not retaliate by imposing countervailing duties to offset the foreign-exchange rate differential in Argentina.

By 5 December Washington had agreed to a $50 million stabilization loan for Argentina, along the lines of a similar agreement with China a week before, confirming a special relationship with Buenos Aires as unique in the region. As such it carried a special political significance. In the specific wartime circumstances the US was prepared to alter its relationship with Argentina. Together with an Export-Import Bank credit of $60 million at 4 percent per annum, Prebisch could return with a total commitment of $110 million. In a last-minute flare-up Prebisch refused a US Treasury demand that Argentina guarantee its loan with gold, although it was standard US practice at the time, arguing that Argentina had not reneged on its debt payments during the Depression. Finally Sumner Welles intervened on Raúl's side. "You made monkeys out of them," Ravndal confided.[20]

The language of the Argentina-US Joint Statement on 20 December 1940 reflected a change in bilateral rhetoric from hostility to cooperation. "This is a cooperative arrangement between old and good friends," it began. "Monetary authorities of the two countries expect to hold discussions in the same friendly spirit during the coming year; and it is hoped that these conversations will enable both countries to reap the greatest possible benefit from the workings of the present agreement." Henry Morgenthau hailed the compact as "practical proof" that the good-neighbour policy is "a living force among American Republics."[21] Media reports in the US praised Argentina's "remarkable adaptation to the loss of European markets after the fall of France" and also supported the National Recovery Plan as a recipe for recovery.[22] But the Prebisch mission and the warm afterglow in Washington had changed the bilateral relationship in ways unanticipated before his departure. Politically, Washington and the US media noted the transformation of US-Argentine relations following their December 1940 agreement. Prebisch's mission to Washington had been successful in establishing a framework for reviving a very complicated and poorly managed relationship. On the Southern Cone free-trade front, the Roosevelt Administration promised not to object to free-trade agreements with neighbouring states.[23]

Prebisch remained in Washington until 21 December, when he and Adelita went to New York to spent the Christmas holidays with her brother Alfredo, who worked at the IG Farben Head Office in the US. They went skiing in Vermont – or at least Alfredo tried the slopes. Raúl refused. He was more interested in US universities and decided to contact John H. Williams at Harvard, whom he had met personally in Buenos Aires in 1934. Williams was receptive; they met in Boston and discussed the possibility of complementing the new bilateral opening with US-Argentine academic cooperation. Since Williams had close connections with the US Federal Reserve, the concept emerged of a trilateral training program in which two or three young Argentine economists in the Central Bank would be selected for graduate studies at Harvard and would combine this theoretical work with an internship at the Federal Reserve during summer vacations. They would then return to the Central Bank in Buenos Aires and be replaced by other colleagues in rotation. For Prebisch the proposed program solved two problems. First, the quality of training in economics at the Faculty of Economic Sciences at the University of Buenos Aires remained substandard. Apart from his own seminar, there was nothing that could be called graduate level work at all. Harvard would therefore expose his gifted young staff to a quality curriculum with a faculty list that included Schumpeter, Haberler, Williams, Hansen, Mason, Harris, and W. Leontieff. Second, the combination of Harvard and the Federal Reserve Board provided the best platform for understanding monetary policy in the approaching postwar era. The openness of the US Government and its depth of talent gave it a strength entirely lacking in Buenos Aires. Here links between the private sector and universities were taken for granted, and information was more readily shared and respected. Since Argentina would be increasingly affected by US policy, the Central Bank required a better knowledge of US institutions, practices, and personalities. What better way to do this than to have a strong personal link with the ranking academic and banking institutions in the US itself? Walter R. Gardner at the US Federal Reserve considered Prebisch to have created one of the best Central Banks in the world and agreed immediately to the trilateral program, with the first graduate students to arrive for the Harvard fall semester. But Prebisch also saw the Harvard/Federal Reserve connection as part of a larger effort to stimulate regular visits of US scholars and bankers to the Argentine Central Bank for joint research or study projects to maintain his Argentine Central Bank's stature in the increasingly interconnected global financial system. The first US official from the Federal Reserve of New York to visit the Central Bank was scheduled to arrive in Buenos Aires in January 1942.[24]

Prebisch returned to Washington in early January 1941 on Cordell Hull's invitation to stay in the US and help relaunch the ill-fated negotiations for a reciprocal trade agreement, which had failed the previous year and produced an undercurrent of mutual resentment. Pinedo and Roca agreed, on condition that the talks remain secret and that all remaining obstacles be cleared away to prevent another failure.[25] The same problem remained as a year earlier: while Argentine exports were now doing better in US markets, the US still provided 30 percent of Argentina's imports but took only 16 percent of its exports. When he met Secretary Morgenthau to begin talks he pointed out the section on trade in Adolph Berle's new book *New Directions in the New World.* Berle, who had just been appointed assistant secretary of state for Latin America, had written, "The captain of a Salem bark trading out of New England to Whampoa in China, or to Valparaiso in Chile, planned to buy as well as to sell ... the Agents for General Motors in Brazil who export to sell ought to be the buyers for Brazilian coffee ... In other words, we must think a little less about 'selling' and a little more about 'trading,' which is, in its essence, exchange."

Meanwhile political opposition to the Pinedo Plan had grown in Buenos Aires. While it was approved in the Senate with broad support and few modifications, Pinedo faced a Chamber of Deputies in which the Radicals had the majority, and he opened a dialogue with its leadership in the hope of an early agreement. Many Radicals opposed it because Pinedo had been a lawyer for the railways and he was assumed to have a private interest in the deal. Others criticized the "financial oligarchy" represented on the Central Bank's board of directors, resenting the Central Bank for its steady accumulation of powers – if adopted the National Recovery Plan would be managed by a three-person commission within the Bank, extending its already enormous influence in regulating the economy.[26] It was noted that Prebisch had dominated the Washington mission, acting virtually as a Cabinet minister, and that, while a foreigner like Leo Welch of the National City Bank sat on the Central Bank's board of directors, Argentine Cabinet members remained at arm's-length from the Bank. For some Radical Parliamentarians, therefore, the Pinedo Plan represented a last-ditch effort by the corrupt coalition behind the Concordancia to establish a new legitimacy. Another and more obvious reason for Radical opposition to the Pinedo Plan was its popularity; approval would go far toward consolidating the Conservative revival, while its defeat would revive the old anger against Roca for the Roca-Runciman agreement and Pinedo during the "Meat Debate."[27]

But the outcome was not predictable, since the Radical Party also comprised factions across the entire political spectrum, including supporters of industrialization and strong pro-Allied advocates. While the Pinedo Plan hung in the balance, and might well have been approved before the provincial elections in Santa Fe on 16 December, the assassination of Radical Party candidate Conrado Risso Patron sharply lowered the political barometer. Two weeks later, on 5 January 1941, electoral fraud in Mendoza claimed the life of another Radical, Ernesto Matons. After two overt cases of fraud the UCR boycotted the Congress, opposing any cooperation with the government on anything including endorsing the National Recovery Plan, unless President Castillo intervened in these two provinces to restore due process. Unlike Ortiz, Castillo was too brittle to build political bridges with the Radicals; in place of dealing with the Santa Fe and Mendoza scandals he went on holiday to Mar del Plata. As a final offering the Radicals insisted that President Ortiz return to the presidency to mediate the dispute, but his health was too fragile. The Pinedo Plan thereupon collapsed, and both Pinedo and Roca resigned in an undignified and final exit from public life.[28] Brazilian Foreign Minister Aranha was so taken aback by the fall of Roca so soon after their meeting in Rio that he refused to attend the Cuenca del Plata conference in Montevideo, which opened on 27 January 1941.

The departure of Pinedo and Roca meant that, in Washington, Prebisch was now alone in bringing the US-Argentine trade negotiations to a successful conclusion. By 6 February agreement had been achieved on the main points: US tariff concessions in exchange for non-discriminatory treatment and concessions on import restrictions. Washington also agreed to downplay its criticism of the Brazilian-Argentine agreement. It was a relief for both governments, and although it was only signed on 14 October 1941, given the political complexity of both capitals, it was ratified with only minor changes. Hull noted his satisfaction that a bilateral accord was finally in place. "As you know," he wrote to Roosevelt, "We have sought over a period of years to bring about improved relations with Argentina, a matter which is of course of fundamental importance at this time."[29] Prebisch also found US private-sector support for the proposed Export Development Corporation when he visited New York on 11 January, and he recommended the publication of the decree in Buenos Aires three days later, with a State Department agreement to begin detailed work on this topic.

Prebisch left Washington for Buenos Aires on 15 February in a warm bilateral afterglow. His many weeks in Washington and New York had offered an opportunity to meet regularly with reporters and sensitize the press to Argentina's needs and special circumstances. For decades the US press had been hostile toward Argentina, and Raúl set about to change this image. He dramatized the impact of Britain's decision to block the sterling account by describing the increase in bankruptcies and unemployment, with unsold grain lying in the fields, the unsustainability and unfairness of it all. The US public was intrigued to learn that to save foreign exchange Argentines had been reduced to distilling corncobs into alcohol for liquid fuel. By the time of Prebisch's departure a more balanced media coverage of US-Argentine relations had evolved as a necessary precondition for building a closer bilateral relationship.[30]

Raúl and Adelita were now impatient to get home; they had been away for a full three months, but there was no escaping the boredom of wartime travel in the Americas, with one uncomfortable and bumpy flight after the next and numerous stopovers – Miami, Mexico, Panama, Lima, Santiago, and finally Mendoza, where they boarded a train for the last leg to Buenos Aires. Back in his office in the Central Bank Raúl found the order and tranquility of a well-managed institution run in his absence by deputy Edmundo Gagneux. The same could not be said for the government in a capital even more paralyzed by inter-party warfare than before his departure. Now, however, Prebisch had lost his chief supporters within the Castillo Cabinet.

Prebisch nevertheless soldiered on in the spirit of the Pinedo Plan, confident that a pro-US alignment would eventually prevail in Argentina. Nazi fortunes had diminished sharply since the fall of France. Germany had lost the air war in the "Battle of Britain," ending the threat of a German cross-channel invasion, and US policy had shifted definitively to support for the Allied cause beginning with a first shipment of arms after Dunkirk and the subsequent adoption of a lend-lease policy in March 1941, which permitted full-scale re-equipment of British-Canadian forces. Defense cooperation in the Americas under US leadership was inexorably expanding, and

Germany's military fortunes were waning. Hitler had to swallow his commitment to open trade with Argentina in 1940, and apart from submarines the oceans were now definitively under Allied control. Moreover the German invasion of the Soviet Union on 22 June shifted Hitler's war effort to the Eastern Front, enlarged the Allied coalition, and further undermined the likelihood of an eventual German victory. In public opinion the combination of the Battle of Britain and Soviet entry into the war reversed an earlier tide of pro-German sentiment in Argentina after war had broken out in 1939.

Maintaining his connection with the US Embassy, Prebisch continued plans for the creation of the Argentine Trade Promotion Corporation (CAPI) to promote exports to the US, which he had discussed with US officials during his Washington trip, and on 9 May the CAPI gained President Castillo's formal approval, setting up its offices at 559 Bartolome Mitre in downtown Buenos Aires with Josiah B. Thomas (formerly head of the local US Chamber of Commerce) as the first manager. Leo Welch was chosen president of a ten-person board of directors comprising two Argentine and eight US citizens, and its network included most of the big companies in Buenos Aires. All dealings of the CAPI were to be controlled by the Central Bank, reporting of course to the minister of finance, but as anticipated it was self-financing rather than supported by tax dollars and therefore avoided the political criticism of a publicly funded support for the private sector. Instead the CAPI would retain 4 percent of the dollar exchange produced by exports for its operating budget with the rest going to the shareholders of the corporation when they were successful in the US export market; US business leaders from John D. Rockefeller to commercial bankers encouraged the State Department to support the initiative, and a New York office opened in July as part of a major diplomatic campaign in the US. "The CAPI is making every effort to assure the Argentine exporter that this is not a temporary organization and that the opportunity exists for finding permanent and lasting markets in the United States, markets that can be retained even after the war," one New York banker noted.[31]

Pinedo travelled to the US to speak on behalf of the new initiative, and the private sectors in both countries were supportive.[32] Leo Welch's letter to Sumner Welles on 31 July requesting his official support was strongly endorsed by senior US officials. The CAPI, Duggan noted in a covering memo, "seems to be an unusually promising effort to develop new Argentine exports to this country." Sumner Welles replied that "All of the officers in this Department who have had anything to do with inter-American relations are, I believe, fully conscious of the need for the development of new complementary exports from Argentina to the US." Rockefeller's Inter-American

Development Commission set up a special committee in August to help identify new Argentine exports for US markets, a display was set up at Macy's in New York, and the Armour Research Corporation was retained to examine and strengthen trade opportunities. Chris Ravndal had now been posted in Washington, and he promoted this promising file from State's Latin America Division, with Josiah Thomas thanking him for his "splendid cooperation" in setting up his new office in New York. In general, Ravndal stood guard, ready to pre-empt charges that the Argentine Export Promotion Corporation was unfair to US suppliers in providing unilateral benefits to Argentina instead of demanding reciprocal treatment. "It would be in order for the Secretary to send the Corporation a word of welcome at this time," he suggested to Hull, noting that it was a product of his reciprocal trade program.[33]

Despite the failure of the National Recovery Plan, therefore, Argentine-US relations were thriving in a special relationship centred on an export-led industrialization policy and underwritten by the major firms on both sides. Luis Colombo strongly supported this new drive; official Washington as well as the US business community and wartime organizations were also on board. In Buenos Aires the Central Bank was working closely with the American private banking and business sector with its own representative on the CAPI board of directors. This benign climate in US-Argentine relations had the additional benefit of supporting the Argentine-Brazil economic agreement and its vision of a Southern Cone trade grouping. On 23 May 1941 the embassy commented favourably that the two countries were committed to a program aimed at "a progressive implantation of free-trade and eventual customs union" and that an approach was being made to include Chile as well.[34]

The economic results for Argentina during 1941 were surprisingly favourable; growth resumed and unemployment fell. Industry and commerce expanded while bankruptcies were down by 27.3 percent. Major strides had been achieved by Argentine industry, which now accounted for more than wheat and cattle combined. The expansion of inter-American trade, particularly with the US and Brazil, more than offset the loss of markets in continental Europe. New trade agreements with the US and Canada, and the opening of the CAPI, underlined a historic trade reorientation toward the Americas. Exports to the US doubled from 264 million pesos in 1940 to 562 million pesos a year later, and Argentina had been able to arrange shipping for this increase despite acute Allied shortages. Prebisch's grim expectations after the German invasion of France were therefore premature; the economic outlook had improved to the point where a special parliamentary committee had been appointed to study the import permit system with a view to the gradual elimination of import controls by the Central Bank. Indeed, by autumn 1941, given the strength of the economy and the money flooding into Argentina, Prebisch was able to eliminate most import controls. Prebisch's concern had now shifted to the control of inflationary pressures. Overall, Argentina's economic situation among the major economies in the world was enviable.

Prebisch's dilemma in 1941 was the inevitable politicization of the Central Bank as its powers increased and it became more visible as a political player; his increasing activism did not go unnoticed, and opponents wondered if he was general manager of the Central Bank or trying to be foreign minister and president. By mid-1941, to dilute the Central Bank's influence, his critics were endorsing the creation of a national economic council reporting directly to the president. The Radical Party continued to condemn the "financial dictatorship," and the US Embassy captured the sense of frustration and unease in Buenos Aires as wartime demands increased the powers and visibility of the Central Bank. According to Ambassador Armour there was "a widespread feeling here that the group which controls the policies of the Central Bank as well as the Ministry of Finance, and which is sometimes referred to as the 'brains trust,' has more or less a monopoly on the furnishing of expert advice to the President on economic matters, industry and technical matters connected with international trade and finance; and that some of the paternalistic views held by this group together with their arbitrary methods which it often considers necessary to follow, are not consistent with the best interests of the country."[35]

The pro-US tilt in Argentine trade policy during 1941 was supported by the successful containment of Nazi influence during the middle of 1941 through the vigorous efforts of the Argentine Congress and civil society supporters and the intervention of the Central Bank. During 1939–40 Germany's successes had resulted in important connections with powerful Argentine elites and alarmist predictions of a pro-Nazi coup circulated in the media. Augusto Bunge and his *Critica* denounced the encounters of German Ambassador Eduard Freiherr von Thermann with the Argentine social elite in the Jockey Club. Pro-Allied forces mobilized. Deputies led by Damonte Taborda warned that the German Embassy was actively promoting anti-democratic forces, particularly funding the Nazi-inspired newspapers *El Cabildo* and *El Pampero*, and successfully demanded the creation of the Parliamentary Commission on Anti-Argentine Activities, chaired by Taborda to investigate illegal German activities. The Commission asked the Central Bank to investigate the possible existence of financial links between the pro-Nazi press, the German Embassy and the two German banks that occupied the same building in Buenos Aires. Prebisch sent two teams of inspectors that came up empty-handed, but the third was headed by Malaccorto, and he found incriminating cheques from the Banco Germanico. Without asking the minister of finance, Prebisch personally delivered the evidence to Taborda in the Congress, giving him the concrete evidence he needed for a credible assault on the German Embassy.[36] On 17 September 1941 the *Washington Post* carried an editorial titled "Pulling Together" in which it applauded the subsequent Chamber of Deputies' censure of the German Ambassador Freiherr von Thermann for "overstepping the functions of his office and abusing his diplomatic privileges."[37] There was only one dissenting vote, and Thermann's position in Buenos Aires was now hopeless. However, Prebisch was targeted even more by Nazi sympathizers after the incident. He was already the permanent enemy of *El Cabildo* and *El Pampero* for cutting off their paper supplies using the Central Bank's rationing powers; now he received a direct death threat in an anonymous letter denouncing the "betrayal of his father's German blood." But Nazi Germany's influence in Argentina plummeted after the von Thermann affair and never recovered. The *Washington Post* noted that "the development is a testimony to the manner in which all America is moving together in this greatest of world crises." The British Ambassador in Buenos Aires concurred, referring to the so-called Nazi menace in mid-1941 as "an embarrassment rather than a direct threat." The Atlantic was closed – Germany simply could not access Argentina by sea or air. As the historian of the period underlined, the Argentine people had contained the Nazi threat by themselves before the end of 1941.[38]

But for all this positive economic and anti-Nazi news in 1941, a deepening crisis of political direction in Buenos Aires threatened to upset the pro-Allied balance of forces in the country. Three foreign-policy tendencies were competing within Argentina, each with a different political and social base. Pro-fascist supporters within and outside the armed forces endorsed a policy of neutrality given Germany's distance from South America and the obvious fact of naval inferiority and lack of an air link – neutrality was the most that Hitler or Mussolini could expect from any Argentine government. A second camp endorsed President Ortiz' pro-Allied declaration in 1939 since Argentine food supplies were vital for British food security and neutrality allowed their shipment across the Atlantic without fear of German submarine attack. Ironically, therefore, both Britain and Germany supported the same objective of neutrality in Argentine war diplomacy, and both were suspicious of US intentions in the Southern Cone. Castillo was a committed neutralist. The third tendency, which Prebisch endorsed after observing the eclipse of Western Europe and which was reflected in the Pinedo Plan, substituted the traditional Atlantic triangle paradigm in Argentine foreign policy with a realignment toward the US and Southern Cone integration.

The confusion and uncertainty about war diplomacy remained unresolved. Justo's compromise between the Radicals and Conservatives had come unstuck with the departure of Ortiz, and Argentina teetered at the edge of political instability. In Foreign Affairs Dr E. Ruiz-Guiñazú, Roca's successor, was a committed neutralist with close ties to Franco's Spain. He suspected that Washington intended to replace British influence in the Southern Cone by clamping a military stranglehold of its own over the region on the excuse of countering the German threat; and the British lobby around Castillo promoted this latent distrust of the US to maintain Argentine neutrality during the war and to maintain a postwar position of leverage in South America. President Castillo seemed trapped by contradictory pressures so evenly balanced that they yielded stalemate. Nothing seemed consistent or predictable; although it had rejected the Pinedo Plan in January, the Radical Party supported the creation of the Industrial Credit Bank on 30 September 1941.[39]

Moreover, the military was restive. Colonel Juan Perón's career since the military coup of 1930 had involved assignments on the Bolivian frontier and as military attaché in Chile, but his promotions were earned as professor of Military History at the Superior War School. Between February 1939 and January 1941, when he returned to Buenos Aires, he was based in Italy studying warfare in Europe. These were the years of apparently invincible German and Italian advance. He praised Hitler's Germany as "an enormous machine that functions with marvelous precision … where nothing – not even a tiny screw – was missing" and said that "Italian fascism achieved effective participation for popular organizations in the nation's life: something which had always been denied to the people. Until Mussolini came to power the nation was on one side and the worker on the other." A fellow officer, Colonel Enrique V. Gonzalez, lived in Germany in the same period and visited him in Italy. Both were active in a secret Army lodge, the GOU (Group of United Officers). Like many other officers who played cards at the German Embassy in Buenos Aires, they were disenchanted with the evident political chaos of the Concordancia.

The unrest in the military was not confined to pro-fascist elements; there were legitimate national security fears that concerned many other officers and that helped to undermine civil-military relations in 1941. For example, the Argentine military was indignant over US plans for a major naval base across the River Plate in Uruguay at Punte del Este. Agreed to on 11 September, the base dominated approaches to Buenos Aires and could only be seen as a threat; nationalists also argued that provocative US military manoeuvres in the South Atlantic were aimed as much at Argentina as at Nazi Germany. The deeper issue concerned the regional balance of power. New armaments were required for modernizing Argentina's defenses, and these had to be imported. But, with the German market closed and Europe needing every weapon available, the US dominated this market as well. It was therefore not surprising that the Argentine military feared that the US would favour Brazil – and this fear became reality in April 1941, when the US Export-Import Bank provided $20 million in credits to build a major state-owned steel complex in Brazil, the National Steel Company (CSN) Companhia Siderúrigica Nacional. President Vargas convinced Washington that, if the Americans refused, the Germans would finance it instead, given their strong position in Brazilian trade with 19 percent and 25 percent of its exports and imports. Unlike Argentina, Brazil had therefore played the German card to its advantage, while the conscious curtailment of bilateral trade by the Argentine Government after Hitler took power in 1933 left it with little leverage in Washington. Previous efforts by Brazil to build a national steel industry with foreign capital had failed, leaving it with only one small producer, Belgo Mineira, which was unable to fabricate heavy weapons. In response to the creation of the CSN the Argentine military urged the government to match Brazil's emerging heavy-industry capability. The politicians agreed, including the pro-Allied Radical Party. On 23 April a five-year rearmament program, including the purchase of aircraft, was adopted by the Castillo Government. On 9 October it followed up by creating the long-desired Direccion General de Fabricaciones, a special secretariat controlled by the military to build an independent arms-producing sector by expanding industrialization.[40]

At the diplomatic level, however, the Argentine-Brazil rapprochement was maintained, and on 21 November Osvaldo Aranha visited Buenos Aires to sign a bilateral agreement that endorsed regional free trade. Beneath the tension created by the personal dislike between the two foreign ministers a subregional concept was forming with a set of regional commissions in which the five countries were beginning to coordinate policy on functional areas such as customs and transport, and a regional office for Information and Economic Research was being organized in Buenos Aires. The practical result was a lowering of Argentine-Brazil rivalry in the buffer states, particularly Paraguay and Bolivia.

The inconsistency of the US contributed to the political uncertainty in Argentina; it was sometimes unclear whether the US was trying to save the world or to buy it and take over the Western Hemisphere for itself. When

Prebisch was in Washington he promoted an Export-Import Bank loan to build an oil pipeline from Mendoza to the Atlantic; US oil interests lobbied successfully against the project. When the Central Bank cut newsprint shipments to *El Pampero* and *El Cabildo* the US Embassy again launched an official protest on behalf of their US paper suppliers. The rapaciousness of the US in cornering Latin American strategic resources also affected US-Argentine relations. Having manoeuvred Bolivia into signing away its tin reserves in a long-term contract to feed the US war machine, the US informed Argentina in May 1941 that it wanted a similar deal for three-quarters of Argentina's tungsten production. The request was accompanied by an implied threat linking Argentina's flexibility on this issue to getting key exports such as tin-plate from the US. Prebisch turned down the offer flat. In a note to Ambassador Armour, he indicated that Argentina was "anxious to cooperate" but insisted not merely on a "substantial improvement" over the Bolivian deal but also an agreement at a price "not far below that paid by Japan" for diverting tungsten to the US. "The necessity of securing certain essential materials from the US," was an absolute quid pro quo, as was "due regard for producers and their employees."[41] Even the mild-mannered Carlos Brebbia worried about a world dominated by an overpowerful Washington with Europe in eclipse. "What will the Americans do now that they have all the world's gold in their possession?" he mused in a letter from Berne to Prebisch. "I sometimes imagine it may be like a person who has collected all the telephones in the world and can no longer ring up anyone."[42] In the Southern Cone the USA's increasing pressure on Paraguay was resented in Buenos Aires as interference in its sphere of influence (a free-trade agreement had been in operation since 1916).

Overall, however, the US-Argentine relationship remained on track. There were powerful voices in Washington sensitive to Argentina's interests, reciprocated in Buenos Aires as bilateral trade grew. The progressive deterioration of security in the Pacific as Japan extended its zone of influence also underlined the mutual interest in stabilizing and strengthening their "special relationship." The result was a series of positive steps that together marked an important rapprochement. In July 1941 there was a major public display of solidarity between US and Argentine armed forces, complete with parades and a fleet of B-17 Flying Fortresses flying into Buenos Aires. On 14 October the Argentine-US bilateral trade agreement was finally signed, ending a decade of fruitless negotiations and heralding greater cooperation. Certain other contentious struggles ended in success; in the end Argentina fended off a Bolivian-style capitulation to US threats and got a satisfactory price for its tungsten. But other irritants remained in both the security and economic areas, and the Roosevelt Administration therefore decided to send Chris Ravndal to Buenos Aires with a group of US diplomats to try to resolve outstanding problems. The date for these talks was set for Monday, 8 December 1941.

As Prebisch awaited the arrival of Ravndal on 6 December to drive him from the airport to his hotel, he could review a successful year, achieved under difficult circumstances. The reputation of his Central Bank had been confirmed again, and the missions to Brazil and particularly the US had been successful. He had become a key player in Argentine wartime policy. Despite the failure of the Pinedo Plan, the economy was expanding. In overall foreign policy, neutrality balanced the conflicting demands of political groups at home by feeding Britain while containing Nazi political influence. Meanwhile the US opening was moving ahead, including his special project of sending young Central Bank economists for training at the Federal Reserve and Harvard. In late June, Julio Gonzalez del Solar, Prebisch's younger half-brother, and Francisco Coire had left Buenos Aires for New York, steaming up the Brazilian coast and through the hot Caribbean ports-of-call on the SS *Argentina*.

That fall Prebisch had the luxury of memorable personal indulgences – designing a full set of new peso bills and relocating to a new residence designed by his brother at 134 Rivera Indarte in San Isidro, a prosperous suburb twenty-one kilometres north of the downtown on the coast. Friends called it the "second Casa Rosada." It was an oasis reserved for close friends and relatives – he now ventured even less into the world of theatre or the broader social life of the capital – and his few free hours were dedicated to planning the new two-acre garden set among tall elms and flowering dogwoods. Raúl also boasted a big green Packard – a fond companion that he drove with great pleasure. He had also bought a family antique from the sale of the contents of Enrique Uriburu's mansion at Lavalle 371: a wall-length desk with inlaid drawers and panels of superb woods. Uriburu had died of a sudden stroke, and the bankruptcy of an estate that included his father's immense inheritance shocked Buenos Aires society as much as his premature death. Raúl was too busy to attend the sale and sent Pedro Orradre, his secretary, with instructions to buy the desk at any cost. Orradre eventually persevered against rivals with a successful bid of two thousand pesos, equivalent to one month of Raúl's Central Bank salary.

Raúl and Adelita eagerly awaited Ravndal's visit to Buenos Aires. They had last been together in Washington, and he was almost family. They planned a barbecue for Sunday, 7 December, in the garden of roses and flowering trees. But Japanese forces attacked Pearl Harbor that morning, and Ravndal was recalled to Washington without the opportunity to pass by the house and say farewell to Raúl and Adelita. The aborted mission was a signal that a whole new era was beginning in which Argentine-US relations were suddenly captive to a much bigger game. South America would now be a military rearguard rather than a partner for Washington, and the term "special relationship" would have a different meaning. It was now a full scale World War, and all of Prebisch's successes were at risk.

7 The Pearl Harbor Squeeze

Prebisch could not have been surprised with his first task on Monday morning, 8 December, the day after Pearl Harbor. Another run of panic selling on the financial markets had broken out and had to be managed in the pattern that had become almost routine after the two earlier panics in September 1939 and with the fall of France in June 1940. Business reaction on the Buenos Aires Stock Exchange was no different in 1941, with nervous investors selling 93 million pesos for the security of government bonds offered by the Central Bank. With the return of stability the Bank then disposed of these purchases through direct sales and on the Stock Exchange. The operation was again swift and successful. The short-term problems created by the USA's entry into the war were therefore quickly resolved, and even Argentina's loss of trade with Japan was manageable, since bilateral exports had shrivelled up anyway during the crisis months before Pearl Harbor. The domestic political impact was more complex, and on 16 December Acting President Ramon Castillo declared a state of siege that further underlined his political isolation.

Argentina's long-term international prospects were suddenly in question. Although far from Japan and Germany and insulated from physical attack, its 1940–41 breakthrough in bilateral relations with the US was threatened by this new stage of the war. The logic of Argentina's policy since 1940 and its opening to Washington had been a regional leadership role in South America, in cooperation with the US, within a neutral Western Hemisphere (Canada excepted since it had been fighting from the beginning). Its policy of neutrality vis-à-vis Germany protected its primary role of supplying Britain with bully beef for its troops while tolerating, but containing, Nazi influence in Argentina. Argentina had the best of both worlds: it maintained strong ties with both Britain and the US as its leading external economic partners, but it also expanded relations with South American partners, particularly Brazil, to enlarge the regional market.

But Pearl Harbor eliminated this policy framework, destroying the delicate international balance that gave Argentina room for manoeuvre among the powers from 1939 to 1941. Instead the Grand Alliance against Germany and Japan left Argentina out of step with both Washington and the rest of Latin America. Although the US had been content to remain out of the war for over two years after September 1939 in an enviable and profitable rearguard role, the Japanese attack unleashed a furious crusading instinct; the Roosevelt Administration now demanded immediate Argentine entry into the war on its side as a test of loyalty. The Conference of Inter-American Foreign Ministers was called for 15–28 January 1942 in Rio de Janeiro to mobilize the Americas for war, with Sumner Welles clearly stating Washington's goal: "to obtain a joint declaration of all the American Republics that they feel it necessary to sever all relations with the Axis powers."[1] Argentina's predicament was both simple and fundamental: while its policy of neutralism was certain to incur the wrath of Washington, its internal divisions and nationalist tradition prevented joining the Allied war coalition. It was marching to a different drummer, and the collision course between Washington and Buenos Aires became apparent in the weeks preceding the Rio Conference.

Prebisch, as general manager of the Central Bank, was included in Argentina's delegation to Rio led by Foreign Minister Ruiz-Guiñazú with his team of Foreign Ministry officials and naval and Army advisors. As the constantly widening war brought greater centralization of trade and exchange controls, the Central Bank's role in the economy deepened to become even more the core financial institution in the Argentine state. Full-scale US mobilization after 7 December implied fewer exports of capital and consumer goods available to Argentina at any price and therefore the need for the Central Bank to ration imports and plan their replacement by local production. A week after Pearl Harbor, Prebisch informed the US ambassador that he would be participating in the Conference and asked him for an advance summary of the US recommendations that Sumner Welles would be presenting to his Inter-American colleagues.[2] Armour was supportive because he knew that Prebisch was in favour of breaking relations with Germany and Japan.

Prebisch had made his choice in 1940. Both ethical and political considerations made him a firm Allied supporter, and he advocated joining the war effort as soon as possible after Pearl Harbor. Quite apart from the moral issue of helping to defeat Nazism, Argentina's national interests dictated becoming the privileged ally of Washington in South America. After his trip to Washington and New York he had no doubt that Germany and Japan would be defeated and that the US would completely dominate the war effort and postwar reconstruction. An immediate war alliance with the US would consolidate Argentina's position as the anchor of Allied forces in the South Atlantic, yield the same industrial benefits of war production gained by Canada since 1939, and integrate Argentina within the diplomatic coalition shaping the postwar era. Prebisch's pro-US tilt had already worried the British a year earlier over the Pinedo Plan, but the stakes grew for them also after Pearl Harbor in the knowledge that, while US entry into the war would ensure military victory against Germany, it would probably also end their sphere of influence in Argentina. Underneath their wartime collaboration, therefore, London and Washington were rivals in South America, with the British Embassy fighting hard to maintain its traditionally close links with the Concordancia.

But Prebisch did not control Argentine foreign policy, and the Argentine delegation to the Rio Conference sailed for Rio de Janeiro on 8 January aboard the SS *Uruguay* plagued by division and uncertainty. Still acting in an interim capacity (assuming office as president of the republic only in July 1942), Ramon Castillo's position was far from strong, with his declaration of a state of siege both reflecting and deepening the political paralysis in Buenos Aires. The Argentine military lay in the background, but one sector of the Army and most of the navy supported the Allied cause while other groups including the GOU (Group of United Officers) were neutralists, some with a pro-Axis perspective. The political scene was divided and complex.[3] Pro-British and nationalist factions supported the existing policy of neutrality, while the pro-Allied forces in Buenos Aires clamoured for war with Germany. Foreign Minister Enrique Ruiz-Guiñazú was not easy to place ideologically. His conservative Catholicism, inherited from his years as Argentine ambassador to the Vatican, and his close family ties with Franco's Spain (and a daughter engaged to an officer in the Italian army), suggested corporatist leanings. Politically he had publicly restated his commitment to a policy of strict neutrality as late as 24 November 1941 during Brazilian Foreign Minister Oscar Aranha's visit to Buenos Aires to sign their bilateral trade treaty. But no one in Buenos Aires or abroad knew precisely where he stood. He had variously condemned Nazi atrocities in Eastern Europe, objected to the Soviet Union forming part of the Western Alliance, and supported greater ABC (Argentina, Brazil, and Chile) cooperation in resisting US influence in the Southern Cone; but he also on occasion had endorsed the principle of inter-American solidarity and cooperation. A narrowly legalistic lawyer, he was described privately by *La Prensa* journalist Gainza Paz as an "inflated idiot."[4]

In short, the Concordancia was in complete disarray at the critical moment of the twentieth century when a new international system was taking shape. Argentina's domestic crisis and the broader international transition had separate roots but were to become linked after Pearl Harbor, with Argentina's choice of Great Power alignment at Rio certain to be a determining factor in the struggle for power in Buenos Aires as well as its future prosperity.

Diplomats from the US roamed the region before the Rio Conference to enlist the majority of Latin American states in an inter-American defense coalition and therefore isolate those governments that preferred a policy of neutrality. In practice the only two states likely to resist moving away from neutrality were Argentina and Chile. By the opening of the Conference nine Latin countries had already followed the US lead and declared war on Germany, while Brazil and most of the rest were clearly sympathetic to breaking diplomatic relations. Aranha recalled Brazilian-US cooperation as allies during the First World War (when Argentina had chosen to remain neutral), and he informed Washington that he had no intention of supporting any grand gesture by Ruiz-Guiñazú at Rio against US-Latin American solidarity.[5] Chile was being courted by Argentina, but its reluctance to break relations had more to do with its long undefended coastline and the German submarine threat than conviction; Washington had no doubt about Chile's eventual cooperation in support of the draft resolution it was preparing for the Rio Conference. This left Argentina as the main target of US war diplomacy at Rio. By 4 January Cordell Hull thought that Ruiz-Guiñazú might well come around to the US position. "The Argentine people in their vast majority seem to be strongly opposed to the hesitant course so far followed by their Government," he noted. "I am inclined to believe however that Argentina will not permit herself to be placed in a minority of one at the meeting, even on an issue of this fundamental importance."[6] He knew from Prebisch that the majority of the Argentine delegation wanted to sever relations with Nazi Germany.

The opening chords of the Rio Conference on 15 January quickly lost their harmony, however, when Ruiz-Guiñazú made it clear Argentina would not join the inter-American wartime symphony and rejected the US resolution calling for the severance of relations with the Axis powers. Negotiations bogged down in a tough standoff. Ruiz-Guiñazú maintained that his government faced such political disunity in Buenos Aires that no major foreign policy decision was possible before the upcoming March elections for the Argentine Congress in which the Concordancia feared defeat, particularly in Buenos Aires. Brazil, in contrast, welcomed the US resolution and played a cooperative role with Sumner Welles and his delegation. Aranha had been posted to Washington as ambassador and was close to the Americans, making no secret of his distaste for Ruiz-Guiñazú; the Brazilian Foreign Ministry was primed to repeat its World War I cooperation with the

US and was neither surprised nor displeased at the evident disarray in Buenos Aires. As for Chile, the untimely death of President Pedro Aguire Cerda on 25 November gave its delegation the advantage of a lingering universal sympathy. Argentina, therefore, was the conspicuous holdout among the ABC countries and the pariah at Rio from Washington's perspective. After days of argument Sumner Welles walked out, breaking off the talks, and transmitted a warning to the Argentine Government through Prebisch that "the economic and financial assistance which the United States can give the other American Republics will necessarily be given only to those nations which are wholeheartedly and effectively cooperating with us in the defense of the hemisphere."[7] This threat implied serious hardships for Argentina, with the unmistakable message that Brazil would be rewarded for good behaviour at Argentina's expense.

Three days later, after gruelling negotiations, Ruiz-Guiñazú reversed his earlier position and agreed on a text, brokered by Brazil, for severing relations with Berlin. The Chilean foreign minister also accepted the wording, and it seemed that the diplomatic impasse had been resolved in a common pan-American defense agreement.[8] But Acting President Castillo refused to approve the tentative agreement and the deal collapsed, leaving the Argentine delegation in a hopeless position. Ruiz-Guiñazú effectively withdrew, his credibility shattered, and Prebisch became the interlocutor with the US and Brazilian delegations in the search for a face-saving compromise. Raúl's mission to Washington the year before had built sufficient confidence for the two sides to begin again and they found an opening in the wording of President Castillo's communication to Rio: he had rejected breaking relations with the Axis powers, but had also promised that "the Government was disposed to take all necessary steps to join in hemispheric defense."[9] Such language left some room for US and Argentine officials to devise a diplomatic formula. Eventually, and with a strong push from Prebisch, Castillo and Hull agreed to a text that endorsed "the cutting off during the present continental emergency of all commercial and financial intercourse between the Western Hemisphere and the nations signatory to the Tripartite Pact and the territories dominated by them as well as suspending commercial and financial activities prejudicial to the welfare of the American Republics."[10] Sufficiently flexible of interpretation, it allowed the delegations to leave Rio with a rhetorically robust communiqué claiming yet another pan-American milestone.

The wording of this clause, adopted as Resolution V of the Rio Declaration, was indeed imprecise enough to permit both Argentina and the US to claim success, but in practice it poisoned wartime US-Argentine relations. If Argentina could retain its policy of neutrality, Washington gained a multilateral instrument to force compliance on Buenos Aires. The vagueness of Resolution V in defining "activities prejudicial to the welfare of the American Republics" guaranteed misunderstandings and accusations of bad faith, with the US certain to demand the curtailment of German activities in Argentina, both public and private, to a level equivalent with severing relations, and to have no hesitation in punishing Argentina for foot-dragging. Castillo for his part was bound to see US behaviour on Resolution V as extreme and interventionist, as nothing more that a convenient US club with which to beat Argentina.

The Roosevelt Administration and the US public reacted to the outcome of the Rio Conference by labelling Argentina as a traitor to the Allied cause and world peace. Enraged US officials turned their backs on Argentina in a highly personalized attack, beginning with Secretary Cordell Hull, whose anti-Argentine crusade after Rio surprised his own staff. "I can't say I admire [Hull's] policy toward Argentina," Merwin Bohan, who joined the embassy staff in early 1942 as counsellor for Economic Activities, explained. "It was a regular old Tennessee feud, and every time he could sneak around the tree and see an Argentine in the sights of his musket he'd let go at him. It really became a personal vendetta ... I really ... feel that Mr. Roosevelt more or less gave Argentina to Mr. Hull to play with, to keep him out of his hair."[11] The US media accused the Castillo Government of pro-Nazism and opened a press war against Argentina, reversing the growing harmony in Argentine-US relations that had developed during 1940–41. "You can imagine the effect that the position of our Government has produced in this country," Julio Gonzalez del Solar noted to Prebisch in a letter from Harvard University on 10 February.[12] If Julio Gonzalez had hoped that the US public would make a distinction between the government and the Argentine people, he was proven wrong. The US media campaign against Argentina as principal traitor of the Free World accelerated after the Rio Conference, deliberately nourished by the abundant wartime propaganda myths against Argentina fabricated by US and British intelligence, which were accepted and broadcast at face value.

Prebisch therefore had good reason to be troubled at Rio – a sudden and deep chill in US-Argentine relations had destroyed his 1940–41 opening to Washington. The bilateral trade treaty, so recently signed on 14 October and so much the result of his own work (Ambassador Armour had noted to Hull that it "was due in large measure to his cooperative work") was dead.[13] The CAPI could not grow and prosper in an atmosphere of US public hostility toward Argentina. The only intact remnant of his US tour was the Federal Reserve/Harvard/Central Bank training and exchange program, and that was also threatened.

President Vargas's announcement on 28 January that Brazil had broken relations with Nazi Germany and Japan also reversed the Brazil-Argentine partnership that had emerged during 1940–41, terminating this brief period of forward momentum toward a South America Common Market. Such a vision ended with the Rio Conference, and the renewal of bilateral rivalry in the context of open US support for Brazil implied the return to an Argentine-Brazilian arms race including a stepped-up struggle for influence in the buffer states of Paraguay, Bolivia, and Uruguay. Brazil's temptation to challenge Argentina for leadership in the South Atlantic was too strong to be resisted, particularly since Germany's defeat before Moscow in December and Japan's relatively insignificant capabilities implied an Allied victory. In August 1942, Brazil declared war and fought alongside the Allies with an infantry brigade in Italy, cementing a postwar Brazil-US military and economic alliance that would underwrite an era of unprecedented expansion. For its part the US would inherit Germany's prewar trade with Brazil, while Argentina lost out everywhere; Castillo and Ruiz-Guiñazú possessed neither the internal political coalition nor Brazil's long-term strategic vision to understand and adapt to the emerging international order. Brazil therefore became the key US partner in South America, leaving Argentina increasingly isolated. For Washington, Brazil's geographic extension toward Africa was of strategic importance for war operations in the Atlantic and North Africa theatre; in South America, Brazil provided a pro-Allied counterweight to Argentina. Ironically, Argentina got no credit for its cold shoulder to Nazi Germany and uninterrupted debt servicing during the 1930s, while Brazil got privileged treatment after Rio despite defaulting and maintaining close commercial relations with Germany right up to Pearl Harbor.

Prebisch's troubles, however, did not end here. Beside the broader prospect of diplomatic isolation lay a more immediate problem – the Central Bank as the battleground of Argentine-US relations. Resolution V of the Rio Declaration referred to the curtailment of "financial and commercial intercourse" with the Axis powers, and this meant that the Central Bank, which regulated the activities of these sectors, would become the focal point of US surveillance until such time as Argentina entered the war. This crossfire became evident even before Prebisch left Rio in a high-profile dispute over newsprint imports from the US. The evening before departure he received a telephone call from Edmundo Gagneux that President Castillo had ordered the Central Bank to restore the paper shipments for *El Cabildo* and *El Pampero,* which it had cut in 1941. The Bank had no option but to comply, whereupon the US Embassy demanded that Prebisch refuse Castillo's request on grounds of aiding enemy propaganda and thereby contravening Resolution V of the Rio Declaration. Raúl reminded Ambassador Armour that the US had earlier attacked the Central Bank when it ended paper imports for the pro-fascist newspapers, protesting officially against the barring of US products. President Castillo had now used this US *démarche* as a rationale for demanding that the Central Bank reverse its decision; Washington's inconsistency had played directly into Castillo's hands. "The newsprint problem was a very involved and difficult one," an embarrassed embassy official acknowledged.[14]

Embarrassment did not stop the US from demanding closer and closer scrutiny over Central Bank transactions as well as maintaining the privileged non-official relationship with Prebisch that had developed with his secret visit to the US Embassy on 17 June 1940 after the fall of Paris. But US intelligence never trusted Prebisch. The first US efforts at spying before Pearl Harbor were sufficiently amateur to be laughed off by the US Embassy in Buenos Aires as the excessive enthusiasm of FBI Director J. Edgar Hoover. (On 8 October 1941, for example, the US secretary of state quoted "a confidential source of unknown reliability" to the effect that Adelita Prebisch and Central Bank employee Francisco Coire had a contact within the German Embassy and were both security risks, although it was not clear whether Raúl Prebisch was part of this network or not.[15] Adelita had indeed worked for the wife of the German ambassador, but that was in 1932 before her marriage and the Nazi takeover, after which Herr Keller was dismissed. While Francisco Coire indeed worked for the Central Bank, he was busy studying public administration at the Littauer Centre at Harvard University.)

But Pearl Harbor and the militarization of Washington elevated the credibility of US intelligence whatever its accuracy, and this affected official perceptions of Prebisch. J. Edgar Hoover's letter of 22 January 1942 to Adolf Berle, copied to Naval Intelligence and the G-2 War Department, noted that Prebisch was "anti-democratic and reactionary" as well as "vain and ambitious" and "completely dominated by his Nazi relations who have convinced him that Argentina must treat with the United States as one 'world power' would treat with another."[16] Even Ambassador Armour wasn't completely convinced that Prebisch was what he seemed. "He gives the impression of talking frankly and sincerely, and he gives every evidence of being a good friend of the United States," the ambassador noted to Hull before the Rio Conference, and he continued that "Mrs. Prebisch, who is an unusually charming person, gives every appearance, like her husband, of being friendly toward the United States."[17] But he wondered if this was too good to be true and whether J. Edgar Hoover was right that Raúl and Adelita Prebisch were dissembling. "Dr Prebisch is probably extremely shrewd and there are those who say that if he is now really friendly toward the United States, it is because he considers that to be good policy. There are those who say that he is at heart pro-totalitarian, and that his wife and a brother of his wife, have pro-Nazi leanings, but how true these charges are is not known."[18] Adelita's brother Alfredo Moll was called pro-Nazi because he had worked in New York with I.G. Farben until the US-German declaration of war, and this was sufficient for Washington to add his name to the blacklist. Added to this, and repeated in Armour's list of Raúl's possible shortcomings, was the feeling that he retained a pro-British trade bias and was responsible for the decline of US exports to Argentina in the 1930s. By mid-1943 this US ambivalence toward him had led to wiretapping his Central Bank office.

Unfortunately for Prebisch the US focus of attention on the Central Bank created a corresponding suspicion in Argentine government and military circles that he was unpatriotic – or "anti-patria," as *El Pampero* and *El Cabildo* regularly referred to him. The image of the Central Bank as part of the "financial dictatorship," as a foreign-dominated institution grown too powerful and out of government control, was already widespread before 1941 and provided the raw material for a new groundswell of hostility for its alleged links with the US Embassy. Both Prebisch and President Dr Bosch were concerned by the degree of public alienation but could not agree on countermeasures. Bosch refused Prebisch's suggestion that they counterattack with articles in the mainstream press, either *La Prensa* or *La Nacion*, rebutting accusations against the Central Bank item by item; he would not accept what he felt would be the politicization of the Central Bank or the admission that *El Cabildo* or *El Pampero* should be given the dignity of a response.[19]

After Pearl Harbor, foreign exchange and import controls took on a new significance as the war changed production and consumed materials previously available to Argentina. The result was a further widening of Central Bank powers. On 15 June, a decree gave it new powers to control all operations, including the movement of funds, accounts, and bonds between Argentina and European countries, Japan, and China. It was therefore natural that the US would target it as its principal economic intelligence source in Buenos Aires. The Central Bank and the Argentine Government had introduced rigorous controls over German activities the year before. Prebisch had already rationed the German Embassy to an allowance of 200,000 pesos per month, which permitted only a skeletal operation. The Central Bank had already closed the dollar-currency market with the exception of sales up to $100 for travellers to the US, and it had provided the US Embassy its data on Axis investments. The latter figures showed virtually no German (about $9 million) investments, and Japanese holdings of less than $3,000, and there was hardly any trade because of the deliberate Argentine policy since 1933. Where was the enemy? This was frustrating for US intelligence, and the Americans suspected a hidden network of remittances by Axis-controlled firms and front organizations, including the suspiciously large flight capital to Argentina, which had increased from 13 million pesos in 1937 to 325 million in 1941. Since Argentina was both the largest economy in Latin America and the holdout at Rio, it became a special concern for the US Board of Economic Warfare seeking to snare all vaguely suspicious companies on the blacklist, called the Proclaimed List of Axis Companies.[20]

On 5 August 1942 US officials met Prebisch to demand that the Bank provide them with information on "foreign-funds control and related matters."[21] They had gone directly to private banks asking for information on their accounts with firms on the US Proclaimed List, or companies that were suspected to have an Axis link, but found them unwilling to comply. United States policy refused such firms access to US credit (such as from the Export-Import Bank), and the embassy needed Central Bank help in providing this information on its shareholding banks. Of course they also wanted detailed information on Argentine banks whether or not they were seeking US credits. The US Government considered access to "full details" as a right justified by the Rio Agreement, even though it saw no responsibility to share its evidence for putting firms in Argentina on the blacklist in the first place. Argentine banks viewed this US demand as both interference and access to market opportunities for US companies positioning for the postwar period. Prebisch said that the embassy was "creating an unfavourable impression." The US officials were offended and resolved to get much tougher with the Central Bank. Merwin Bohan, the new US counsellor for Economic Affairs in the embassy, gloated that Argentina was going to reap the bitter fruit of its own restrictive trade practices of the 1930s and be shut out of US export permits. "Somewhat ironically for a country that has long clung to the policy of 'buy from those that buy from us,'" he noted, "Argentina cannot obtain at any price many of the goods that it wishes to import from the United States and other countries."[22]

Prebisch's dilemma was, what to do? To a certain extent the US had a legitimate concern with security, which he shared – there were pro-Nazi groups in Argentina. The problem was the exuberant US exaggeration of the threat and their missionary fervour in getting their hands on German property in Latin America. In markets, investments, defense – in everything – Argentina needed the US more than ever, and the Central Bank had to keep an open line to the embassy. As a compromise the Central Bank agreed to provide banking information and to assign inspectors to monitor firms (like the two German banks) on the Proclaimed List to ensure that no funds were applied to Axis uses.[23] But US demands grew exponentially. In March 1942 Prebisch had already suggested a new procedure to reduce bilateral venom with a system called "Consignee Control," in which a joint Central Bank-US Embassy monitoring process would verify Argentina's compliance with Resolution V of the Rio Declaration. Specifically, the Central Bank would share information regarding all Argentine foreign remittances on a monthly basis with officials of the US Embassy and allow it to review the government-approved list of Certificates of Necessity for import licences before their recommendations were sent to the Board of Economic Warfare in Washington. The government delegated this task to the Central Bank, but critics howled that allowing the US a right of prior agreement on import licenses represented an intolerable intrusion into Argentina's internal affairs. Prebisch argued that the system kept the Central Bank's overall supervisory role intact, while offering a transparent mechanism to reduce tension and deflect further US demands. The brute fact was that Argentina needed US goods because there was no alternative source.

Consignee Control was a rational but dangerous response to managing Argentine-US economic relations. First, it needed priority attention from Washington with sufficient time and resources to work effectively, and although Prebisch's friends, such as Chris Ravndal, understood and supported the system, the war theatres in Europe and Asia were the top US priorities, and attention to Latin America slipped. Prebisch's concept required a larger staff at the US Embassy in Buenos Aires, and Washington stalled. Ravndal wrote to Raúl on 31 August 1942 after returning from Buenos Aires, where he had discussed the growing tension over export controls. "My dear Raúl," he wrote, "the plans we worked out with you with respect to decentralization of export control are maturing much more slowly than I had anticipated. There seems to be no question at all regarding the principles involved and I believe I may say that the basic idea has been accepted by the government."[24] He thought that the Consignee Control system would probably not be in effect before the end of the year, and in fact an agreement on procedures was only finalized with the Central Bank on 7 January 1943.

By then, however, Argentine-US relations had deteriorated seriously. Castillo was anti-communist, anti-American, and pro-British, seventy-one years old, and troubled by the results of the March 1942 elections, which challenged the Concordancia with a Radical/Socialist majority in the Chamber of Deputies and total defeat in Buenos Aires. The state of siege declared in December continued. In foreign policy he was not about to change Argentina's policy of neutrality.[25] Argentina's economic prospects had also dimmed; before Pearl Harbor Argentina's 1941 recovery had prompted favourable predictions for 1942, but in April the Central Bank warned of trouble ahead, and the US Embassy also reported impending difficulties. In September Washington approved a new "Economic Policy toward Argentina" that outlined an Allied strategy including Canada, Britain, Brazil, Uruguay, and Mexico, squeezing Argentina by denying it critical imports such as coal, petroleum equipment, and heavy weapons. The US meanwhile staged provocative naval manoeuvres in the Plate River in view of Buenos Aires to rub in its wartime isolation and to impress on Argentina's military the contrast with Brazil, which now enjoyed a privileged access to modern arms, courtesy of its Washington connection.

The arrogance of the US became insufferable. Its embassy swelled in size with wartime operatives. By early 1943 Bohan was proud of his eighty-two-person Economic Unit housed in the Boston Bank Building, with another eighteen in commercial intelligence. It was, as he put it, "a unified and smoothly functioning economic agency."[26] Hoover and the other US intelligence services were busy locating Nazi plots in Buenos Aires and rooting out German economic influence and investments in the Americas in a sweeping effort to eliminate German communities, as if ethnicity confirmed guilt and sanctioned blacklisting and expropriation. The British Embassy noted the "seemingly directionless dynamism of the swollen US diplomatic, quasi-diplomatic, intelligence and military establishment in Buenos Aires."[27] Each Argentine compliance with increasingly intrusive US requests would only result in new and more extreme demands, always presented unilaterally as if Washington knew best and had unfettered rights of interference throughout Latin America. US belligerence strengthened Castillo's resistance to what he felt was a two-faced US war effort and his determination to maintain an independent foreign policy against what he felt were Washington's hegemonic pretensions in the Americas; he criticized the unfairness of a US policy that could neither substantiate a German threat nor appreciate the value of Argentina's policy of neutrality in supporting the British war effort. The "Nazi Menace" in Argentina was hugely exaggerated: British Ambassador Sir David Kelly had already noted in 1941 that it was "an embarrassment rather than a threat"; a year later he reported that it was "not in the running" any longer as an economic, political, or cultural competitor.[28] Washington acted as if Argentina's only duty was to obey orders and not ask questions; Castillo and a powerful current in Buenos Aires reciprocated with a stubborn refusal to comply. The bilateral temperature rose accordingly.

Secretary of State Hull seemed to want revenge for imagined slights of the past, becoming so paranoically hostile that Ambassador Armour tried to reason with him against undermining Prebisch and the Central Bank as friends of the Allied cause. On 28 August 1942, Hull held Prebisch personally responsible for following orders from his own government and rejected his own embassy's advice that Washington should strengthen Prebisch's position and the Central Bank rather than undermine them. "You should inform Prebisch," Hull wrote, "that the known pressure exerted by the Foreign Office leaves the (US) Department with no alternative but to recognize that the Central Bank's controls of necessity have to be relaxed frequently irrespective of what the independent desires of the Central Bank may be." Hull continued, "The Department must reject the view of the Central Bank that the latter's approval of transactions which benefit the enemy insulates the commercial banks consummating those transactions against the application of United States controls."[29]

Prebisch gambled for time. The challenge was to keep the lid on US-Argentine relations until military realities changed perceptions on both sides and allowed the rebuilding of the amiable relationship that had blossomed in 1940–41. Once the war was over, he reckoned, bilateral relations would improve again and vindicate the Central Bank's thankless task of administering the Consignee Control system. As the fortunes of war definitively turned in 1942–43 it appeared for a while that an end to the post-Pearl Harbor nightmare in US-Argentine relations was in sight. In November 1942, Ambassador Armour reported a significant improvement; while the Argentine Government strongly rejected a speech by Sumner Welles on 8 October alleging that Argentina was allowing its soil to be used by Nazi agents, it nevertheless arrested twenty senior Germans. The Nazi military defeats in North Africa and Italy and above all at Stalingrad in February 1943, as well as the earlier crushing Japanese naval defeat at Guadalcanal in 1942, threw Axis forces on the defensive and opened the final phase of the war. There was no longer any conceivable military threat to the Americas, nor anything – economically, politically, or arms shipments – that Germany could offer to its remaining supporters in Argentina or the Americas. Nazi influence in Argentina would now atrophy, Prebisch reckoned, and US pressure on Argentina would begin to relax.

But he was wrong: US-Argentine relations deteriorated in 1943, and the Central Bank was caught in a situation made more difficult with each passing month after Consignee Control became fully operational on 7 January 1943. Meanwhile US relations with Brazil deepened with President Roosevelt's first presidential visit; he met with President Vargas on board a US destroyer on 28 January after the Allies' Casablanca meeting, while US demands on

Argentina sharply intensified in an inverse relationship with the actual German security threat to the Western Hemisphere. On 4 March, the US State Department approved a policy memorandum that opened a new campaign of "economic warfare" (as Bohan called it) determined to cut the last ties between Nazi Germany and Argentina.[30] Officially communicated to Prebisch and the Argentine foreign minister on 27 March by both the US and UK ambassadors, the "new" approach simply built on the Consignee Control policy already in place, but behind a strategy of punitive sanctions for any Argentine deviations from the Rio Declaration. Bohan told Prebisch that absolutely no US export permit to Argentina would be allowed without a certificate of necessity approved by the Board of Economic Warfare (BEW). Such approvals would only be allocated to the degree that the US Embassy and the BEW considered Argentina a reliable partner.

The US, using the Central Bank as its instrument, tightened the noose, "which should, within a period of months," Bohan argued on 26 April 1943, "begin to close industries and cause unemployment."[31] As the policy matured, by May 50 percent to 60 percent of the Central Bank's applications for import licences were being rejected, including those for essential materials such as replacement parts for the oil and transportation sectors. Bohan crowed that "ruthlessness is as much a part of economic warfare as it is of physical warfare, and if we are going to clean up the situation through Consignee Control, bomb splinters will occasionally injure the innocent in spite of every effort we may make to be fair to every Tom, Dick and Harry claiming to be an importer." He vowed "to barricade the last remaining highway between the Axis and the Western Hemisphere ... Let Argentina read itself out of the community of Western nations."[32] In a childish display of pique Cordell Hull cut Prebisch out of the international preparations for the International Monetary Fund and the World Bank, even refusing him a visa for attending the 1943 United Nations International Monetary and Food Conference in Washington. Bohan reported that Prebisch was very upset but remarked that "a bit of egoistic deflation will do no harm."[33]

Prebisch challenged Bohan and the US Embassy to provide evidence for their charges against individuals and firms under surveillance by the army of US and British agents living it up in Buenos Aires. Where was the Nazi threat? Who were the "confidential sources" making allegations? Malaccorto was blunt in his reports on German-owned firms that were legally registered and were doing nothing illegal: "the Argentine Government is not convinced that the operations of the totalitarian firms are, in fact, inimical to the security of the Western Hemisphere."[34] The Central Bank similarly rejected the US decision to treat Winterhilfe (donations and small family remittances to needy relatives in Germany) as evidence of Nazi penetration of Argentina and a pan-American security threat. Prebisch wondered if Bohan expected the Argentine Central Bank to become simply another US instrument in its campaign to supplant British (and German) interests. He warned Bohan that US demands were becoming unreasonable and endangered the credibility of the Central Bank as the financial agent of the Argentine Government. Was the US fighting Nazi Germany or Argentina? Pressure by the US on the Central Bank had already turned to demands for petroleum concessions as a condition for import permits. Bohan thought it only fair that Argentina should open the sector to Standard Oil companies as compensation for US wartime sacrifices in defense of the free world.

Prebisch meanwhile bent farther and farther to satisfy US demands. Bohan insisted that he provide the US Embassy with monthly statements of Argentine remittances abroad. He agreed. Bohan demanded that the Central Bank block a payment of 15.5 million pesos to the Siemens Group for local construction projects, for no other reason than that Siemens was a German-controlled company on the US blacklist. Prebisch again agreed, reluctantly, since Argentine neutrality gave him no legal basis for doing this. Bohan pressed on: the Central Bank should also block future remittances to the Dresdener Bank. Raúl saw no legal basis for such action, but said he would ask Pinedo's advice. On Pinedo's urging, he again agreed. With each concession to ward off US retaliation this dangerously intimate relationship with the embassy undermined the Central Bank's official channels with the government. A habit of "non-protocol" contacts, or confidential communications not sanctioned by or communicated to the Argentine Government, had developed between Prebisch and the US Embassy since 1940, strengthened by Raúl's personal ties with Chris Ravndal and US bankers closely linked with the Central Bank and the embassy. In August 1942, for example, Ravndal requested from Washington that his letter to Raúl should be delivered "at the discretion of the Embassy" – that is, without routing it through foreign affairs in the normal diplomatic practice – and the letter asked for sensitive data that only the Central Bank possessed. "If you could give us a better idea as to Argentina's flag shipping you will have at your disposal, it would be a great help," Ravndal noted.[35] Prebisch was being drafted into the role of agent to the US Embassy. By mid-1943 Bohan and US Embassy officials took for granted this direct access to Prebisch as a channel for obtaining or giving confidential information they wanted to conceal from the Foreign Ministry or the presidency. The ill-fated Consignee Control system deepened the expectations of this special relationship, and the line between compliance with Resolution V of the Rio Declaration and providing intelligence for the US Board of Economic Warfare became blurred. By 1943 the US Embassy was demanding confidential copies of ship manifests from all Argentine ports; the Cabinet or Foreign Minister Ruiz-Guiñazú would never have authorized their disclosure to the Americans.

Relations with the US Embassy took another nosedive in 1943 when Bohan's Consignee Control system broke down in the corridors of wartime Washington. Lobbyists were active with Congress and officials, and the quickest way to get action from the Board of Economic Warfare was to cut a special deal. While Bohan and Prebisch prepared their lists in Buenos Aires and sent them to Washington, Board officials disregarded them and approved export licences for Argentina on the lobbying of firms with sufficient political influence to bypass the Consignee Control system altogether. The notions of overall war requirements and consistent policy simply had no effect. In practice this could mean that Argentine businesses would get additional US imports – but not necessarily the scarce goods required to fill the shortages threatening its wartime economy. The essential goods priorities set by the Central Bank had to be respected if national production was to be maintained; for example, it was only the Herculean efforts by the engineers of the state oil company Yacimientos Petroliferos Fiscales that kept the company operating at all, but its equipment shortages were becoming dramatic and would soon affect output if not met. Prebisch was irritated. He called Bohan on 24 May to tell him that he felt used. The Central Bank, he said, "cannot allow its prestige to be undermined by American inefficiency."[36] Bohan agreed that both of them had been disregarded in Washington but claimed he was helpless against the Washington lobbyists. He complained to the State Department that the result in Buenos Aires "was a complete loss of prestige – both for the Bank and the Embassy, and for that matter for the entire export control system."

Ironically, and despite the US policy of economic warfare, Bohan's predictions of hunger and mass unemployment in the streets of Buenos Aires failed to materialize. Instead the Argentine economy expanded during 1943. It turned out that Argentina retained significant international leverage despite US hostility; its beef production was necessary for the Allied war effort, and Cordell Hull had to ensure continued Argentine beef exports for Britain. The US private sector's interest in Argentina similarly continued, and the Export Promotion Corporation set up at 9 Rockefeller Square in New York survived and indeed planned branch offices in Chicago, San Francisco, and New Orleans. Moreover, Britain and the US also maintained their disagreement over wartime policy toward Argentina, with London strongly favouring continuing neutrality to protect beef shipments from German submarine attacks while the US pressed Buenos Aires to enter the Grand Alliance. Resenting Washington's aggressive intervention in Argentina, Britain undercut the US policy of economic warfare by brokering an Allied contract for the entire Argentine meat surplus until 30 September 1944. "It is now difficult for opponents to argue that the regime is isolated," Bohan lamented.[37] Indeed Argentina remained a haven for so much European capital fleeing the war that Prebisch's problem in the Central Bank was controlling inflation. Industrial growth was stimulated by the arrival of European entrepreneurs who were impressed by Argentina's inherent strengths, spurring industrial investments such as the steel factory of Santa Rosa, opened in 1943 by a French industrialist who had moved permanently to the New World. Key Argentine industrialists like di Tella, with factories throughout the Southern Cone, were living examples of successful European immigrant entrepreneurship beyond the reach of Washington.

From inside the Central Bank Prebisch advocated postwar planning; governments in the industrial countries were already hard at work, and the Central Bank's 1943 *Annual Report* repeated the urgency of beginning a serious national debate on what it termed "inward-directed growth," or "*hacia adentro*."[38] Support for industrialization was growing rapidly. The Argentine military demanded more direct state support for the arms industry. Luis Colombo and the UIA pleaded for an Industrial Credit Fund or Bank to do for industry what the BNA had done for the ranchers and farmers. Advised by Alejandro Bunge, Colombo feared a government retreat after the war from its current level of support for industry, and he created a centre in mid-1942 to drum up support for industrialization. This new Institute for Research and Industrial Conferences invited Carlos Saavedra Lamas, now rector of the University of Buenos Aires, to be its president, and he lost no time in recommending that a new national commission on social and economic reconstruction meet in August 1943 to begin work on postwar planning.[39] Most of Argentina's industries built since 1930 to replace imports were vulnerable; industry had expanded by 22 percent during the war and now accounted for 50 percent of overall national production, transforming the traditional agricultural base and soaking up labour. Industrial growth had also made the country less Buenos Aires-centred, with plants also spread around the towns and provinces of the interior.[40] Labour had not only grown but also made up some lost ground between 1940 and 1943, and these numbers alone suggested that Argentina was destined to become Latin America's leading industrial nation, even poised to take its place as a fully developed industrial power after the Second World War. But there were also serious weaknesses in Argentine industrialization, inadequacies that had to be corrected if this promising seedling were not to wilt and die. Most of the new war industries were low in productivity because they were sheltered in a domestic market cut off from the outside world by the war. There were exceptions, and Argentine exports had grown with Brazil (and other Latin neighbours) despite the de facto termination of the 14 November 1941 bilateral trade treaty after the two countries parted ways following the Rio Conference. Typically the new plants were small and labour-intensive, serving local markets rather than competing abroad; Argentina did not yet possess significant heavy industrial sectors. Once the war ended they risked being swept away by North American competition. Prebisch felt that Argentina faced this threat with better tools than after the First World War, given its much improved financial and credit situation. The postwar reality would pose a major threat to the new industrial base, and success required the right balance of state support for the private sector, but Raúl expressed optimism that a solid base had been constructed. His thinking on this problem was further reflected in a new decree on 20 April 1943 designed to channel the floating capital seeking a safe haven in Argentina into productive investment. The article he wrote for *La Nacion* explaining the new regulations related it to the work of Keynes in trying to restore a stable international credit and payments system to expand trade and open markets for Argentine products.[41]

Instead the immediate threat facing Argentina came from domestic political tensions that were sharpening in late 1942 as the end of the Castillo period loomed. Elections were set for September 1943, but there was no obvious successor to shore up the Concordancia. Increasingly leading personalities realized that Argentina had to prepare for the postwar era, but the government was paralysed. A political vacuum had emerged in the capital just when Argentina most needed top-level leadership to deal with its diplomatic isolation and postwar reconstruction. The Radical Party could still marshal Marcelo T. Alvear, even if he was old and exhausted. There seemed to be no young blood in the Concordancia as a credible presidential successor to Castillo who could lead its party, the Partido Democrata Nacional, to victory. Finally General Agustin P. Justo decided to make a political comeback in a last-ditch effort to head a coalition with broad public support and experience. Justo remained the most powerful figure in the Concordancia, and he had always rejected Castillo's policy of neutrality. After Pearl Harbor he had advocated breaking relations with Germany and, when Castillo took the other path, volunteered to serve in the Brazilian Army. From his earlier pro-British days he had shifted to a US orientation, and by late 1942 was clearly concerned to reduce tension with Washington and restore a working relationship between their respective governments and militaries.[42] Justo could count on the support of Saavedra Lamas, Pinedo, and Julio A. Roca, and he retained a wide appeal in both Socialist and Radical circles as well. In December 1942, for example, Pinedo paid special homage to President Roosevelt and the need for Argentina to support US leadership in the war effort.[43] Prebisch supported Justo's candidacy because the general was committed to restoring a consistent foreign policy to Argentina after the waffling of Castillo, and he had sufficient prestige to ensure a strong relationship with both the US and Britain. Raúl believed that no other person on the political spectrum was more likely to succeed in leading Argentina in the postwar period, given his record in adjusting to the Great Depression.

Prebisch had never campaigned actively before, but he could not hold back when the country was in such danger, and he therefore made contact with the ex-president and offered his services as informal advisor. He helped prepare Justo's important address to the British Chamber of Commerce on 22 November, which supported the victory of the Allies and explained his views about creating a just and equitable international order. The speech stressed the need for close cooperation between the US and the UK in creating a stable trade and financial system, and, in a comment aimed to clarify his views on the national economy, Justo underlined the need for "a firm and sustained industrial development with the most open support of the state so long as it is not 'artificial' or anti-economic."[44]

This attempt of the Concordancia to put together a credible post-Castillo leadership failed when General Justo died in January 1943. He was irreplaceable; there was no comparable candidate on the political horizon, and within months the options facing Argentina changed even more decisively when other key figures passed away. Roberto Ortiz and Marcelo T. Alvear both died, leaving the Radicals in disarray, while Julio A. Roca's sudden death at home in the family townhouse at 579 San Martin removed another credible senior figure who had been active since the Revolution of 6 September 1930. Nevertheless national elections were set for September 1943, and the Concordancia had to come up with a new leader. After difficult negotiations the final result was a bleak compromise among the factions, Robustiano Patron Costas – the same Patron Costas whom Prebisch had detested from his youth in Tucumán. President of the Senate and now acting vice-president, he still retained his vast sugar estates, whose migrant workers still lived in conditions that earned him the national nickname of "Indian Slave Driver." His elevation to presidential candidate completed the political polarization of Argentina. It was a bitter outcome for Raúl, trapped into working with an impossible choice. In April he attended an agonizing lunch with Patron Costas, the British financier Evelyn Baring, and several Argentine counterparts, in which they assessed his views on war diplomacy and the economy: Patron-Costas was hopeless. The outgoing Castillo had made many political enemies with his mistakes, but the new leader of the Concordancia was disliked by all the Great Powers, including the US, Britain, and Germany, as well as by virtually all Argentines from the unhappy working classes clamouring for attention to the increasingly restive military.[45]

Alejandro Bunge's death on 24 May further complicated the future of the shaken Concordancia because he had become a critical interlocutor between the government and the business community. For the Central Bank Bunge had offered a direct contact with the UIA business lobby, providing a welcome voice of moderation and common sense at a time of growing political turbulence. At a personal level Prebisch sensed that a whole generation was leaving the scene before his eyes. Bunge had been a mentor and a scholar ahead of his time in promoting industrialization and regional integration, and in his last book, published in 1940 with the title *A New Argentina*, he had paid Raúl the compliment of endorsing the concept of a technocratic elite to lead national development.[46] Raúl thought of his father's funeral in Tucumán and all that had happened since. Not many of the people he had worked for were around any more, Augusto Bunge wouldn't speak to him, and now he faced a certain confrontation with Patron Costas.

Ten days later, on 4 June 1943, a military coup toppled Castillo and sent him into exile, terminating the Concordancia and abruptly changing the terms of debate over Argentina's future. Led by General Arturo Rawson, the coup was launched to pre-empt the election of Robustiano Patron Costas, but it altered the political landscape of Argentina as decisively as its Uriburu-led predecessor had done on 6 September 1930. The coup was well planned, and it proceeded efficiently and without significant opposition after troops occupied the Presidential Palace. But no sooner was President Castillo deposed than the military leadership fell out among themselves over the succession, and for two days it was not at all clear who would emerge as president. The confusion was enormous, with the government of the republic virtually in limbo as Rawson tried to establish control. Debate mounted on appointments for the chief portfolios, particularly finance and foreign affairs; at one point Malaccorto found himself in de facto control of the entire ministry. Finally General Pedro Pablo Ramirez replaced Rawson and established authority with an announcement of senior appointments that calmed the capital. The Central Bank was left undisturbed, and this decision calmed the markets. Jorge Santamarina was appointed minister of finance on 7 June, the only civilian minister in the

Cabinet, and Malaccorto remained his deputy and chair of the Permanent Inter-Ministerial Committee on Economic Policy. Santamarina was a former BNA president and a charter member of the oligarchy; his continued presence was reassuring to the elite, but he was insecure in his tenure and worried about his isolation in the military government.

Foreign reaction was favourable. The appointment of pro-Allied Admiral Segundo V. Storni as minister of foreign affairs was well received domestically as well as in Washington and London. The US Embassy had been unenthusiastic about the prospect of dealing with Patron Costas and reported that the 4 June coup favoured US interests because Ramirez would prove to be more pro-Allied than President Castillo. Argentine quotations rose in London, as did the Stock Exchange in Buenos Aires. Both the Brazilian and US press showered praise,[47] with the *New York Times* volunteering that Rawson and Ramirez inspired "respect and confidence."[48] The mainline Buenos Aires newspapers also applauded the military coup and the final end of the power struggle evident since the illness and withdrawal of President Ortiz in 1940.

Few tears were shed initially in Buenos Aires for the fall of the Concordancia; it had collapsed from within with only a final push from the barracks, and there was little surprise that Patron Costas had been denied power. But the competition among military leaders puzzled observers as they tried to interpret the implications of the coup for domestic and foreign policy. Initially they thought General Ramirez might contain the more extreme nationalist and pro-Axis agitation in Argentina, and at first he appeared to court the US colony in Buenos Aires with the same affection as Castillo had shown to the British. Admiral Storni, the new foreign minister, was pro-US and determined to reverse the poor bilateral relationship; he attended the 4 July reception at the US Embassy, and it was rumoured that the Cabinet had hovered four times on the brink of breaking relations with Nazi Germany. In regional relations Storni revived integration efforts stalled since Pearl Harbor; Argentina and Chile agreed in principle to establish a customs union, and the formation of a joint commission was to be celebrated with a bilateral ceremony in Buenos Aires on 24 August.

Other signs pointed the other way and suggested that the impact of the 4 June Revolution would be more radical than it first appeared. The military coalition that overthrew Castillo had a hard core; behind Rawson and Ramirez lay a more focused and coherent group led by Colonel Juan Domingo Perón, leader (or at least co-leader) of the GOU, with a corporatist ideology and an affinity for the fascist experiments in Italy, Germany, and Spain. Ramirez named him undersecretary of war after the coup and therefore placed him in a position to consolidate a power base. Perón had the will to power and a vision of Argentina's future, which made him a formidable opponent, but he remained in the background after 4 June and was not well known as yet outside military circles. The clearest signal that the 4 June Revolution was a break with the past came with the appointment of Colonel Elbio Anaya as minister of education. As a junior officer in the early 1920s, Anaya had suppressed the peasant uprisings in Patagonia with exceptional brutality, and he had approved a pedagogy "which has its roots in the depths of national tradition and the sentiments of the Argentine nation which has provided above and beyond all else a *falange* of proud citizens, men of property, God-fearing and lovers of the fatherland." A new crackdown on civil society now followed, which far exceeded the periodic crackdowns and inefficient censorship of the defunct Concordancia. Augusto Bunge, now president of the Democratic Commission for Aid to Countries Fighting Nazi Racism, was arrested along with a thousand others, and his library was burnt by a gang from the Civic Legion. The military government also appointed so-called *interventors* to take over the universities in Argentina, thereby silencing opposition from this quarter. Grants of citizenship were also suspended for the duration of the war. The official rationale for this repression was that the pro-democratic groups provided a cover for communist activities. Nobel Prize winner Saavedra Lamas resigned in protest, but the loss of the most internationally respected person in the country seemed not to worry Ramirez and his colleagues.

In the midst of this political change sweeping Buenos Aires Raúl's mother died in Tucumán on 23 June, and, although it was not unexpected, the death of the old matriarch deeply affected him. Adelita, who had been adopted by Rosa Linares as a daughter, spent the last weeks at her side as a growing circle of children, relatives, and friends gathered in Tucumán. But the political crisis had kept Raúl in the capital, and she was gone before he could bid a suitable farewell in person. The immense funeral in Tucumán added to a depressing year already full of worries. For despite the first reassuring reaction of the military government toward the Central Bank, the revolution left it more exposed and vulnerable. A decree permitting it to issue bond certificates to the public as well as to the banks had completed its central agency architecture within the state, allowing it the freedom it needed to balance fluctuations in the economy, but such measures fuelled attacks on its vast powers as a corporate-dominated state within a state. For the Radical Party and the left the Central Bank embodied the "financial oligarchy" running the country. Prebisch was criticized for his close relations with the US Embassy, and the Nazi-influenced press never forgave him for his part in the expulsion of German Ambassador Von Thermann. But there was also a groundswell of opposition from unusual quarters, such as the virulent crusade against the Central Bank in the slums of Buenos Aires led by a Catholic priest named Father Mendivel.[49] He had brought together all the charges against Prebisch and his "Brains Trust" (tool of the oligarchy; puppet of the US Federal Reserve; sycophant of Harvard University) under the war cry of "*anti-patria*" in a powerful public mobilization of working-class deprivation and democratic failure. Shortly before the June coup Raúl invited Father Mendivel to the Central Bank to see for himself that nothing sinister was going on and explained the Central Bank's national role and structure and the procedures that guaranteed accountability. Mendivel seemed perplexed and left stammering; Prebisch also visited his parish to answer questions. But the campaign against the Central Bank continued, and Prebisch could only assume that it was being encouraged by factions within the 4 June revolution itself.

Then on 1 August Augusto Bunge died. It seemed impossible that the grim succession of deaths in 1943 could continue, and this one was even more painful because the two friends had been stubborn enough not to speak since their break in 1934. Both had assumed a long life in which the other would eventually yield, but in this bitter year Augusto had followed his brother to a premature death at age sixty-six, and the estranged friends could never make up for this time lost. Yet for all these years, and despite their rupture, Bunge had left his will deposited with Raúl as a mark of the special affection and trust he continued to hold for him. For Raúl, Augusto Bunge represented a civility and quality of culture and citizenship without parallel in Buenos Aires; he had taken Raúl in when he was fresh from the provinces and encouraged him at every stage of his rise to influence. At the funeral Raúl gave the will to his godson Mario with a tenderness befitting their joint memory of so great a man as his father.

As he bade farewell he told Mario – and only he would know – that he was leaving that evening for Washington. The purpose of this trip remains mysterious. He did not inform Adelita of the visit, and the US documents referring to his conversations are among the hundreds of pages blacked out by zealous US archivists guarding the intelligence records of the war years.[50] Raúl never spoke about this trip, and only these US memoranda could have revealed whom he met and what they discussed. Since there was no international conference to attend it can be assumed that he went for private consultations with US officials. No copies of these conversations remain, and US intelligence reports from Buenos Aires on 23 June, 23 July, and 2 August, which probably dealt with this visit, were also destroyed by US censors. He probably argued the need for a new and less interventionist US policy in Argentina, which would strengthen domestic support for pro-Allied forces like the Central Bank, rather than undermining them by provoking resentment. He almost certainly told the Americans that the Consignee Control system had to be scrapped.

Prebisch knew that his trip to Washington was risky, but his conviction that the West must defeat Hitler as soon as possible was reinforced by family developments. Adelita's sister lived in Holland, and they knew from her the realities of the Nazi occupation. In addition, Raúl had heard a first-hand account of the Nazi death camps in mid-1942 when Adelita's brother Carlos crossed the Atlantic from Europe to Buenos Aires to visit his estranged wife and their two daughters, whom he had not seen for a decade. Carlos knew what was going on in Europe because he had joined the German underground movement and was ferrying Jews and other endangered people across the border into Switzerland. He had completed an ethical metamorphosis: the fugitive who had excaped prison in Buenos Aires and fled to Spain under an assumed name had become a humanitarian anti-Nazi who risked his life if caught by the Gestapo. When Carlos returned to Europe to continue the good fight, Raúl realized that he himself had no moral alternative to promoting a pro-Allied policy during the war, and all the evidence suggests that this motivation underlay his decision to go to Washington. Prebisch undoubtedly took the same laborious route to Washington as in 1940, boarding a train to Mendoza and then taking the uncomfortable DC-3 to Santiago, Lima, Panama, Mexico City, and Miami; by mid-August the same itinerary had brought him back in Buenos Aires, where he resumed his leadership of the Central Bank.

But the political pressures were growing. In his commitment to his country and the Allied cause, Prebisch found himself squeezed ever tighter between Washington and the Argentine military government.

8 The Wilderness

Adelita opened the morning edition of *La Nacion* on 19 October 1943 to a headline announcing the resignation of Raúl Prebisch as general manager of the Central Bank. Breakfast was not yet ready and Raúl was shaving. She ran upstairs immediately. "You didn't tell me that you had resigned."[1] Prebisch rarely discussed his work at home, but this was a bit much. Unfortunately it was news to him as well; the new government had fired him without warning. After eight years of power at the centre of the Argentine state, Prebisch faced a sudden and unexpected assault on the institution that he had created and that dominated his life and work.

Prebisch forgot breakfast and drove immediately to the Central Bank, where his confused and worried staff waited. Colonel Enrique Gonzalez from the president's Office was already in his office and handed him an envelope containing his letter of dismissal. He didn't agree personally, Gonzalez told Raúl, but these were his orders, and he departed immediately without further comment, leaving Raúl in disbelief. By law the Central Bank general manager was accountable to the Bank president, in this case Dr Bosch; it was illegal for the political executive to fire him. Prebisch hoped that the press had merely leaked a rumour, a not abnormal feature of the poisonous political life of the nation's capital, but after Gonzalez' visit he knew there was no way to avoid a crisis that could destroy both him and his life's work – the Central Bank itself. Additional news arrived confirming the sacking of other senior members of the Prebisch team – including Malaccorto in finance – in a sweeping move that removed several ministers, deputy ministers, deputies, financial experts, and university professors. By this time Alfredo Moll, now living in Buenos Aires after returning from New York, had heard the news on the radio and rushed to see Adelita at 134 Rivera Indarte, since he feared that Raúl would also be arrested by the police.

Prebisch should have anticipated his dismissal. He had felt a severe political chill on his return from Washington in mid-June, and attacks on the "dictator" Prebisch and his "brains trust" had gathered strength in the government-sanctioned press. Argentine-US relations were again in decline as the US Embassy finally decided that the Ramirez Government was even more intractable and dictatorial than its predecessor. Cordell Hull decided to escalate US pressure after Mussolini was overthrown and arrested in July 1943, in the belief that tougher action would strengthen the pro-Allied opposition. Hull therefore rejected Foreign Minister (Admiral) Storni's request for US weapons on the grounds that Argentina had failed to live up to the Rio Declaration. The strategy was misguided; not only was Argentine society too controlled by the military to allow mass demonstration, but the hardening of US policy only achieved the early departure of pro-Allied Storni from the Cabinet. These developments removed all bilateral ambiguity, and Washington now changed its policy from Consignee Control to putting intense pressure on Argentina to break relations with Germany and Japan.

Because the new US policy focused on Ramirez and the military rather than the Central Bank, the Bank had seemed to gain elbow room, so to speak, after Prebisch's return from the US. The end of the Consignee Control system eased its isolation and allowed it to concentrate on running the economy and preparing for the postwar period. Prebisch's relationship with Minister of Finance Santamarina remained correct if not personally close; they met each morning, and Raúl was entrusted with writing the minister's speeches related to banking and international finance. A new bond offering on 23 August yielded over 400 million pesos, the most successful in Argentine history.[8]

The Ramirez Government supported industrialization more openly than Castillo. In August it opened a direct line to the private sector by creating a special commission including Luis Colombo representing the beef industrialists of the UIA and José Maria Bustillo, president of the Sociedad Rural, to advise the minister of finance, signalling stronger government-business collaboration in future. Moreover the arms industry now became an even higher national priority. The military arms corporation FM (Fabricaciónes Militares) had been created on 9 October 1941, before Pearl Harbor and the subsequent US cut-off of arms to Argentina after the Rio Conference; with the advent of the military government, existing enterprises were consolidated and brought under the leadership of General Mario A. Savio, who was a first-class organizer and military entrepreneur, determined to modernize Argentina's weaponry and defense to compete with Brazil and Chile. The FM was campaigning for a modern steel sector as well as investments in other heavy industries such as chemicals, vehicle production, optical equipment, and machine tools and therefore added another strong voice for industrialization.

Ramirez also approved the creation of the Industrial Credit Fund, to be administered by the Central Bank. Raúl had unsuccessfully promoted this concept in the 1940 Pinedo Plan, but it took the military government to see its merits and actually take this important decision. Santamarina's announcement of the new policy to the UIA on 1 September was so drowned by applause that he could barely complete his speech.[3] The text of Santamarina's address, written by Prebisch, struck a new note of optimism regarding the prospect of Argentine exports. The new Industrial Credit Fund finally gave Argentine companies access to a type of credit that its foreign rivals had long enjoyed; there was now every prospect of their success in international trade. The speech called for the "systematic application of a coherent industrial development policy," which required both industrialization and an international trade policy. "This country also needs a vigorous foreign trade," he noted, "and as active as possible. This goal does not contradict a vigorous industrial development policy ... It is evidently in our interest that our exports grow as rapidly as possible in order to maintain importing as many essential goods as we can."[4] However the military government also insisted that 60 percent of the Industrial Credit Fund be reserved for the FM, which embodied a state-led investment strategy with national security rather than commercial criteria. But the fact that the Ramirez Government agreed to place responsibility for the Fund in the Central Bank was another signal of confidence, and Prebisch could not be more open in his advocacy of Argentine industrialization. He had also been able to liquidate two-thirds of Argentina's external debt with Britain, buying it at favourable interest rates and harnessing the inflow of wartime capital, thereby removing a long-term financial burden on the national economy and allowing the government to plan for the future with greater confidence.[5]

Prebisch was confident that the Central Bank could ride out the storm of wartime politics and that Argentina would come into the postwar era with the advantage of a healthy and growing industrial economy. During the Concordancia period he'd had friends and allies in government who were able to support the Central Bank politically. However, after the death of Justo, Prebisch had no links with the military establishment, and after 4 June this problem became acute. When it became clear that Perón was the key player behind the 4 June revolution, Raúl asked Finance Minster Santamarina to arrange a closed meeting with him, hoping that a frank exchange on the national economy and banking policy would dispel the many negative rumours about the Central Bank. Prebisch knew little about Perón, except that he was a leader in the GOU and close to Ramirez. In fact the two men had certain things in common. They were close in age – Perón was six years older – and both were protegés of General Agustín Justo, supported industrialization through import-substitution, and endorsed the creation of a regional market comprising the ABC countries and the three smaller countries of Uruguay, Paraguay, and Bolivia. Perón's specific ideas and policies regarding industrialization were not clear in early 1943, and Raúl at this point did not predict an irreconcilable divergence on this question – indeed there were better-known military protagonists of a national armaments industry such as General Savio of Fabricaciónes Militares. Prebisch believed that if he and Perón could meet and talk privately he would be able to explain convincingly the role of the Central Bank in the national economy and its special importance in preparing for the postwar period.[6] But the encounter with Perón did not materialize, even though Santamarina did arrange a private meeting between Perón and himself. The minister failed to invite Raúl because he wanted to monopolize this contact with a rising personality in the country.

As late as mid-October, during a major political shake-up in the capital, Prebisch remained convinced that both he and the Central Bank were safe. Even when Santamarina had been replaced by military loyalist Cesar Ameghino, he insisted in a conversation with US officials on 15 October that he had no intention of leaving the Central Bank at a time when it needed "calm and serenity."[7] Like many others in the capital, he was taken aback by these appointments of the military government. Colonel Anaya had been replaced in the Ministry of Education by Gustavo Martinez Zuveria, the pulp novelist ("Hugo Wast") who was a throwback to the Inquisition, a Catholic fundamentalist who believed that the military as an institution brought the discipline and order required to complement the introduction of compulsory Catholic instruction in all Argentine universities. This appointment in particular had Buenos Aires shaking its collective head; at least Anaya had been a soldier from the ranks, but why had Ramirez placed "Hugo Wast" in the Cabinet of Argentina? Raúl recalled Augusto Bunge's horror when he had bought Mario his novels; it was incredible to think that this man now had power.

Prebisch did not realize that this Cabinet shift would also sweep him off the political stage. On 15 October, shortly after Raúl's conversation with embassy officials, *La Nacion* and *La Prensa* defied the government by publishing an open letter signed by 150 leading academics and personalities, including Bernardo Houssay, Argentina's first Nobel Prize winner for Science, calling for the restoration of democracy and pan-Americanism.

Supported by Interior Minister General Luis Perlinger, Gustavo Martinez fired many of them on 17 October; Houssay was never reinstated. The attack on universities prompted the resignation of Alfredo Palacios, now the president of UNLP; like the loss of Saavedra Lamas some months earlier, it was a blow to the international reputation of Argentina's system of higher education. The regime's campaign to eliminate potential opposition was only beginning, and Prebisch had no suspicion that he himself was on the list until Adelita read about his "resignation" in the first edition of *La Nacion* on 19 October.

When Colonel Gonzalez left his office, Prebisch ordered his staff back to their regular assignments until Bank President Bosch and his directors were informed and could meet to discuss the crisis. Bosch was furious with the government when Raúl called him with the news, and he refused to accept his "resignation," demanding instead an immediate interview with the president of the republic to denounce his illegal intervention in the internal affairs of the Bank. But times had changed; when the call was not returned it was evident that Bosch had little influence within the new regime. With this Prebisch decided to submit his own letter of resignation on 19 October. For the next twenty-four hours President Ramirez ignored Bosch, who finally was told that if he wanted to question the decision he should see Gonzalez. But when Bosch repeated his demand that the order to fire Prebisch be rescinded (and that in any case the matter only concerned his board of directors), he was acidly instructed to submit a letter to the new minister of finance outlining his concerns. This was not promising, nor did he receive a response to his letter. Swallowing his pride, on 21 October Bosch then met the minister of finance, who informed him that nothing could be done – although like Gonzalez he regretted the loss of so valuable a public servant as Raúl Prebisch. The decision to fire him had been made at the presidential level and was final.

But the Central Bank Directors refused to accept Prebisch's resignation by a margin of eleven to one. Meeting the next day in an emergency session, only Cosme Massini Escurra of the BNA voted against him; even Emelio F. Cardenas, President Ramirez' personal representative on the board, abstained, noting that he agreed personally with the majority and would not join Massini Escurra against Raúl. Thus fortified in their resolve, Bosch and the board of directors were determined to confront the military government on its flagrant disregard for the law in Prebisch's dismissal. Prebisch was gratified by the support of his board and knew that he enjoyed the unconditional loyalty of his Bank staff, but he realized things were different in the capital. The legacy of the Uriburu connection, the Roca-Runciman pact, and the famous "meat debate" had come to fruition.

He could read the nation's newspapers: the nationalist press widely supported the government's dismissal of him and the others, exulting in the fall of the so-called "*anti-patria*."[8] The *anti-patria* were disloyal traitors to their own country, friends of the US Embassy, British plutocrats, bankers, and Jews. The inclusion among them of so many professionals with foreign sounding names – starting with Raúl himself, and including Max Alemann, Malaccorto, and Jacobo Weiner – was hardly coincidental. The suggestion was clear that this was a group influenced by Jews, and that by decapitating its leaders the 4 June revolution had liberated Argentina from a conspiracy operating within the state. That this nonsense should appear in the nationalist press, particularly *El Cabildo* and *El Pampero*, did not surprise Prebisch. It was of much more concern that the mainstream press such as *La Nacion* and *La Prensa* failed to come to his defense. The silence of *La Nacion* was a particularly severe blow, since he had worked so closely with its editorial staff during the last decade. In fact the newspaper had supported the 1943 military coup for bringing down the Concordancia and defended it for months before publishing its open letter on 15 October.

After the Central Bank Directorate refused to accept his resignation, Prebisch spent two days in individual interviews with leaders in the business and banking community. By 22 October, after having thoroughly assessed his options, he had made his decision. He wrote again to Bosch insisting that, for the sake of the Bank, the board accept his resignation. Three days later, at a second extraordinary meeting, the board saw no option and Prebisch's departure was confirmed. Prebisch could have encouraged the directors of the Central Bank in their refusal to accept his dismissal. Flattering as their support was, however, he would require more broad-based backing if he was going to fight the government for his job. And he didn't have it. The Argentine public associated Prebisch with the discredited Concordancia; the nationalist press called him the "dictator." His consultations with representatives of the big national conglomerates including the Shaw, Tornquist, and DeBary empires and forty other leading businessmen and bankers had shown him that he had no significant support in the domestic private sector. He realized that the military government had successfully co-opted the leadership of the UIA and other business groups with its strong commitment to industrialization. Not a single Argentine firm offered him a job – the word was out to blackball him; only the foreign banks and the US Embassy supported him, but in the political climate of the day this support was counter-productive, to say the least.

Prebisch was caught unawares. He had come to believe that the he and his "brains trust" had become indispensable and that no rational government, military or civilian, corrupt or honest, would destroy such an asset or even allow it to be weakened. He had been lulled into a false sense of security, thinking that the Central Bank had sufficient international linkages and domestic support to remain immune from Argentina's political epidemics. In the end, Pareto's model of a "modernizing elite" had exploded in his face. Politics mattered; democracy and the rule of law mattered. Prebisch had sought to isolate the Central Bank from politics in Argentina, leaving the political fray and the Jockey Club to his social betters, but it hadn't worked in the end.

There was now the future to consider. A forced resignation was painful, but Prebisch thought it would be a pause rather than a permanent termination. He still had the overwhelming support of the Central Bank's board of directors. Bosch was eighty years old, and Prebisch was the obvious successor, and he also retained strong support within state agencies and the Ministry of Finance. In short his early reinstatement was quite possible once the government came to its senses or political circumstances changed. Prebisch also reasoned that the orientation of the Central Bank, not to mention the great bulk of his staff, would more likely survive should he resign now without forcing a major confrontation with the military government; if his personal unpopularity had become a liability to the Bank, his removal would make it less subject to political interference and criticism.

Rather than immediate policy differences, the issue behind his dismissal from the Bank was Prebisch himself and the institutional power he represented. With the collapse of political parties during the Concordancia the military and the Central Bank formed the two institutional anchors of the state: the military dominated the political scene, and the Central Bank regulated the economy. A logical and inevitable collision was building; Prebisch, in the view of the military, had become too powerful and independent, and too close to the US Embassy. Since 1942 he had increasingly exposed himself politically with his pro-Allied stance, including his link with the US Embassy outside of official channels and his overt political support for Justo; his August trip to Washington was the final evidence that he had become too powerful to be tolerated. If the US Embassy was wiretapping the Central Bank it was unlikely that the military remained uninterested in Prebisch's contacts with the Americans. As the Central Bank accumulated international influence through its networks and emerged as a major power centre not directly controlled by the state, the military government decided to remove a powerful opponent and strike a blow at the independence of the Bank itself.

The US Embassy closely watched these events unfold, correctly seeing that a fundamental divide over the future of Argentina had opened with the forced departure of Prebisch from the Central Bank. Ambassador

Armour and Bohan held an immediate four-hour emergency session at the embassy with Leo Welch and Lansing Silcox from the First National Bank of Boston, and the group recommended a new era of uncompromising toughness, escalating pressure, and a general freezing out of Argentina. "No one doubts that the Government is aiming to obtain control of the Central Bank," Armour explained to Cordell Hull, "and the general feeling is that it is only a question of time until this objective is achieved."[9] Prebisch's departure from the Bank ended the embassy's direct access to a key power centre in the state, which could not easily be replaced. "We are fully cognizant of the responsibility we assume in recommending a vigorous course of action." Bohan noted, and accentuated his overt hostility to the regime with an awkward misquotation of the familiar aphorism attributed to US Judge Hartz: "We assure you that we are not guided by Judge Bean's philosophy of giving the culprit a fair trial and then hanging him, but rather by the unknown jurist who observed that 'we may be in error but we are no longer in doubt.'"[10] Argentine-US relationships now deteriorated definitively; by January *Time* had categorized Argentina as "fascist" and an "enemy."[11] Full-scale US sanctions to undermine its economy were being applied. Bohan's work was now finished, and he left Buenos Aires for Washington.

And what of Prebisch? Washington sensed its responsibility in his downfall, with Assistant Secretary Adolph Berle recognizing his "sterling cooperation with the cause of the US and UN [the Allies]."[12] He suggested that Prebisch be invited to the US. "It occurs to me that it might be well to make some arrangement for Mr Prebisch to visit the US under Government auspices or those of some organization such as the American Bankers' Association." That was it – a visit as recompense for good deeds; history had moved on, and Prebisch was now in the superfluous rearguard of the Allied cause.

The moment he lost the protection of the Central Bank, Raúl faced personal danger in Buenos Aires. His house was under police surveillance; Pinedo had already been arrested. With Alfredo Moll's assistance he left that evening for refuge with friends from the German community, Oswaldo Altgelt and his wife, who lived at an isolated location five kilometres from Mar del Plata. In fact agents from Military Intelligence confronted Adelita the next morning and entered the house at 134 Rivera Indarte looking for Raúl; they toured the house and left when Adelita refused to speak with them. Only his *chef de cabinet*, M.A. Martinez (who continued to address him as "*gerente*" – "boss"), knew his whereabouts and arranged for the delivery of letters and personal articles to Mar del Plata, but on 2 November Raúl telephoned Adelita to tell of her of his safe arrival.

At first he was too restless for anything except pacing in the garden, and for two weeks he still hoped that his absence was temporary and that he would soon be reinstalled. On 2 November Adelita sent a message with reports of a campaign within the Bank for his reinstatement and of rumours of an impending reversal of government policy. Julio Gonzalez del Solar would be coming to the house that evening to report on the situation. But hope faded during the next week and nothing came of these efforts. By 14 November Adelita wrote again acknowledging the failure. They now faced difficult times. It was easier for her, she noted, because she and her family had already lost everything in the Great Depression. "What I want most of all," she wrote, "is to be your true friend, and to be helpful in these difficult days of your life. Don't worry about me. Everything will work out."

The sudden termination of his salary shook Prebisch from the lethargy of depression. Decisions had to be taken. Since the government stopped his salary precisely on 22 October, providing no separation pay, compensation, or benefits, and since no other public service options were available, Raúl and Adelita had to sell their car, with the proceeds from the Packard paying off the last instalment of their mortgage. This left them with no debts, but without income they could not afford to remain in their house and would have to rent it immediately. Marcelo, the son of Dean Eleodoro Lobos, who had befriended Raúl on his arrival in Buenos Aires, offered Adelita and her mother temporary quarters in their small garden house nestled among the hills and lemon groves 8 km from San Isidro. Adelita accepted the offer and was left alone to find tenants and prepare 134 Rivera Indarte for lease while making the garden house with three small rooms and tiny kitchen habitable. She also sold their half-share of the vacation property to Gagneux and used this for furniture for the new quarters. Friends pitched in, helping to make curtains and fix the kitchen and bathroom. On 8 November Adelita gave a dinner party – a farewell to the beautiful house in which they had lived for less than three years, and which she hoped to reoccupy soon, and a celebration of the wedding anniversary of Julio and June Gonzalez del Solar. By the end of the month, when the new tenants arrived, the Lobos garden house had been converted into a cozy little home for Adelita and her mother, with a few inconveniences – groceries, for example, were 8 km away and Adelita had to get them on a bicycle.

Raúl still lived with the Altgelts in Mar del Plata, but fear of the police had dissipated. For the regime Raúl Prebisch was only a threat as head of a powerful state agency; he was not a challenge to them once removed from public office, particularly if he remained far from the capital. This new security eased life at Mar del Plata, where family guests began to visit again, his address and telephone number were freely circulated, and he became a more visible resident in the community. But the prettiness and isolation of Mar del Plata, with its long walks along the sea, only underlined for Raúl the pain of his sudden rupture from power and the accompanying sense of loss in his life. His first month away from the Central Bank, with its deluge of letters of support, appreciation, outrage, and condolence from the great banking houses around the world, as well as from his former employees, underscored his isolation from the worlds he knew and loved. Now he had nothing. Julio Silva, who worked in the Bank and came from a wealthy family, pleaded with Raúl and Adelita to live free in one of their houses for as long as they wished, and to accept this offer "from the heart, not as an obligation to repay, but rather as my debt of gratitude for your gift of confidence in allowing me to work at your side for seven years."[13] But he refused charity. He similarly refused offers from foreign banks encouraging him to join the private sector abroad; the national banks continued to shun him.

The change was too abrupt. Raúl had always lived for his work, and his life had contracted overnight from one of the busiest and most interesting in the capital to the nothingness of forced retirement. Before 19 October his decisions shaped the economy and made daily news; now he was a disgraced observer on the sidelines. From the beauty and gardens of 134 Rivera Indarte he had landed in cramped quarters with leaf mould and couch grass. A terrible driver, Prebisch nevertheless coveted luxury cars; now even his Packard was also gone. His position in the Economics Faculty was also in doubt. He did not know if he would be acceptable to the regime as a professor at the university; he could only guess whether his dismissal from the Central Bank had made him persona non grata for other public positions in the capital. The people he most admired, such as Palacios and Saavedra Lamas, had resigned in protest against the military government; by crawling back in disgrace he would be giving a message of weakness. In any case there would be no teaching until the spring semester, and the faculty was an intellectual backwater compared with the Central Bank. He could not get up enough energy to contact the faculty.

What was he to do in the wilderness – cultivate his garden? Prebisch loved gardens and their design but his idea of gardening did not extend to weeding raised beds or planting begonias. He designed; Adelita worked. Raúl had inherited a distaste for manual labour and was not inclined to sports apart from walking. Adelita was more resourceful, a stronger and more serene person than Raúl; she simply accepted setbacks and got things done, manual or not. Coming from a genuinely titled family in Germany she was immune to snobbery.[14] In contrast Raúl was sensitive and easily wounded; he would turn repeatedly to Adelita, beginning with this first major crisis in 1943, to help him through tough times. He needed her unfailing common sense and good humour to stop his raging and regretting and get back to work. By the last week of November he had accepted the new reality and the need to begin a new life.

Prebisch decided to use his retreat to the country to write a book on his experiences as Central Bank general manager; if he was no longer welcome inside the government and no one would offer him a job, he could at least present his views to the public in a book. For fifteen years, since his entry into the BNA and then in the Ministry of Finance and Central Bank, he had been an insider in the economic management of the world's leading emerging economy; however small a consolation, his forced resignation certainly gave him the luxury of spare time for writing. Since the outbreak of war in 1939 his schedule had been so overwhelmingly hectic that he could barely direct seminars in the faculty. He had directed official publications such as the Central Bank *Annual Reports* and had ghostwritten *La Nacion* articles where he was identified as "a senior government official," but he had been a practitioner rather than a scholar – a technocrat in the governing establishment. Now Prebisch finally had the time to think through the lessons of his experience since 1928 and also to write freely since he no longer had a stake in the current military regime. Of course his motivation was practical as well as financial. A book would keep him in the Buenos Aires loop and prepare for his return to public life once Ramirez and the generals were themselves history; it never occurred to Prebisch that he might never regain a position of influence in his country.

Prebisch's original idea was to write a largely descriptive personal memoir to document and reflect on the lessons of the Central Bank years while they were still fresh in his memory. No detailed publication existed on the origins and working of the Argentine Central Bank; Raúl knew this story from the inside and better than anyone else. Financial and monetary policy were of fundamental importance to Argentina; the Central Bank had been created because the alternatives had failed, and the role it had played since 1935 represented an important chapter in Argentine history. Essentially it meant integrating his personal experiences between 1928 and 1943 with his writings and lecture material in the faculty. He had kept no journal, but Adelita had preserved what she could over the years. Most of his team remained in the Bank to assist with information. Prebisch knew he could offer an unmatched assessment of Argentina's response to the Great Depression during the 1930s, and it was best to write the story at once while his memory was fresh.

But he soon decided on a much more ambitious book. To be credible in a period of unparalleled international and national turbulence, it should deal not only with the past; it would also have to look to the future. The challenges that faced Argentina in the Great Depression and the war would be followed by new and different problems after the peace; and solutions would prove just as difficult to achieve. What lessons for future policy could and should be extracted from the Central Bank experience? What monetary policy should Argentina adopt after the war? More generally, how could past experience best serve a successful Argentine transition to peace? Prebisch therefore prepared a three-part book proposal: the first section would deal with his theoretical approach; the middle part would cover monetary and banking policy in the 1930s; and a final part would assess Argentine prospects and policy options after the Second World War. The rather dry and technical title, "Money and the Rhythm of Economic Activity" ("La moneda y el ritmo de la actividad economica"), was deceptive.[15] Instead of a narrow academic project with a conventional focus and structure, Prebisch set out a bold framework that went far beyond monetary policy. Just as his decision to document his Central Bank experiences had led him to look at future policy options, so the study of Argentina's prospects also forced him to interpret Argentina's place in the international economic system. The original project had therefore expanded into an undertaking that required him to clarify his own thinking on fundamental principles. Writing with the confidence of a senior manager, he left no doubt where Prebisch the economist stood on his theoretical assumptions in 1943 – he offered a unique and prophetic blend of theoretical radicalism and Keynesian state activism, with a banker's concern for sound money and the private sector. He challenged conventional Western liberal economists by reversing the assumptions of equilibrium and comparative advantage in the international economy, and he proposed developing a theoretical approach more in line with intuition, observation, and his own experience. In effect, *Money* incorporated a set of five interrelated propositions regarding markets and the state.

Prebisch began with the fundamental question: what were the national purposes of financial and monetary policy in Argentina? He was unequivocal that the proper functioning of the economy required an activist state to achieve three basic public policy goals: avoiding a boom-and-bust cycle by controlling the violent ups and downs in agricultural prices and other foreign trade impacts on the economy; strengthening development and maintaining full employment; and stimulating the fastest possible rate of economic growth. Only these goals would enable Argentina to fulfill its "enormous potential," and only an activist state building on the type of calculated interventions devised by the Central Bank could shield Argentina from its permanent vulnerability relative to the industrial countries. Just as

Argentina had been forced to abandon free trade and evolve tools like the Central Bank during the Great Depression, it would also have to manage its way through postwar challenges or face marginalization. National development after the war would not happen automatically; only an activist state could ensure that Argentina remained a full partner – rather than a dependency – in the emerging global economy.

Prebisch's second proposition concerned his concept of "inward development" (*desarrollo hacia adentro*). Industrialization had come to play a central role in Argentina's economic development and import substitution and other state policies were required to maintain its momentum. He asked: why must Argentina pursue industrialization? Because it faced unequal relationships with its industrial trading partners; neither the doctrine of comparative advantage nor the workings of the business cycle automatically benefited it. Prebisch maintained that the terms of trade for agricultural commodity producers like Argentina were in historical decline and that a "persistent fall in the international prices for exports" could be expected in the future. His position on declining terms of trade came from his experience since 1930 in different government positions and insights gained in Geneva; if economists in developed countries still clung to the doctrine of comparative advantage in international trade, Prebisch had learned differently. He had watched Argentine farmers selling grain against rising costs long enough to convince him of this reality.

But Prebisch also located a deeper structural imbalance than declining terms of trade in the international system – the functioning of the business cycle. According to liberal Western economists the market mechanism benefited all countries – the large industrialized or small agricultural economies alike – and the business cycle regulated the periodic ebbs and flows in the international economy. Prebisch disagreed. He had already concluded in his 1921 *Notes* that the business cycle in Argentina created an atypical boom-and-bust phenomenon because it lacked the self-correcting mechanisms characteristic of industrial economies. Since then he had lived through the post-1918 crash, the boom of the 1920s, the Great Depression, the post-1934 recovery, and finally the Second World War. He now concluded that the international economic system functioned with a permanent disequilibrium because the business cycle operated differently for industrial countries like Britain and agricultural countries like Argentina. Without vigorous intervention to control cyclical fluctuations and to strengthen purchasing power and employment through industrialization, Argentina would remain extremely vulnerable to external shocks. "To resist subordination of the national economy to foreign movements and contingencies," he wrote, "we must strengthen out internal structure and achieve an autonomous functioning of our economy." Argentina could not develop an autonomous economy while remaining primarily a producer of commodities.

Prebisch's third proposition, however, set limits on the role of the state in promoting industrialization. He demanded "an intelligent regime" (or "smart state," in later economic parlance), which implied the "judicious management" of state powers without stifling productive forces. Excessive state intervention would be as damaging as a naive acceptance of the doctrine of comparative advantage. While the state must support industrialization, he argued, the economy as a whole must remain led by the private sector. Don't stifle the private sector, Prebisch warned. "Monetary policy serves little or no use if it suffocates private initiative and the spirit of enterprise which absolutely requires the profit motive to promote an overall climate of confidence." Argentina therefore required a private/public-sector partnership to succeed.

Prebisch's fourth proposition addressed the role of trade in development. At the international level he underlined the need to restore an open trading system. He had witnessed the breakdown of global trade into blocs (Prebisch referred to them as "watertight compartments") during the Great Depression and had lived with the damage it had created. Restoring globalization after the war, therefore, with a soundly based multilateral trade and credit system, was a precondition for Argentina and all other countries – and few shared Argentina's high stakes. "It is essential to avoid what happened after the First World War," Raúl noted. "Inward development" strategy did not imply withdrawal from the international economy or hostility to industrial powers. "The participation of our country in the international economy has to be as intensive as possible," he stressed. "To the measure that imports grow, particularly essential materials and durable and capital goods, they will permit exports and permanent foreign investment ... this country must export and therefore has to import." Export promotion was essential and excessive protectionism had to be avoided. Prebisch looked forward to a postwar period when policies such as "buy from those who buy from us" could be laid to rest and when import controls could be simplified. Harry Dexter White and John M. Keynes were preparing a conference for July 1944 to devise a postwar plan to revive trade and stabilize the international economy, and he hoped for US leadership in ensuring their success.

In Prebisch's view the imperative of postwar trade and industrialization policy required a judicious combination of import substitution and export promotion rather than blanket protectionism. "A policy of autarchy is as absurd as free trade," Prebisch concluded, "with 'noxious' consequences ...

This possibility of increasing imports under an intelligent regime, and a policy of prudent monetary stimulation where indispensable, will favour an intensive industrial development with the natural effect of attracting immigration to other economic sectors as in earlier days of economic and demographic growth." Argentina's challenge was to develop a trade policy that reflected its own needs.

Fifth, a competitive private sector after the war implied building on the viable industrial sectors created during the war while eliminating the inefficient and uncompetitive industries that had emerged during the enforced protectionism of World War II. Prebisch's same caution applied to state expenditures that must remain prudent and non-inflationary: "There must be a reasonable equilibrium between the role of the state and the play of individual interests in economic life." He warned against the politics of extremes. A balance had to be ensured between productivity and social policy to maintain growth rather than excessive public expenditure. Prebisch was obsessed over inflation – he was clearly worried about the military government overspending on payouts and armaments. The Argentine economy was already at full employment and in danger of overheating, and the government should therefore resist political pressures for inflationary expenditures. Although Argentina had to improve conditions among the poor, Prebisch appealed for a social policy coordinated with national economic productivity to prevent deficits and inflation. "One must bear in mind that the common denominator of social policy is the increase in production. Without this a stable increase in the level of income for the masses cannot be sustained." Argentina could only maintain its high ranking if the government adopted the correct policy mix; domestic policy had to encourage sustained growth because Argentina depended as much on the state as on international trade to shape the conditions for prosperity.

Despite the many uncertainties, Prebisch forecast a positive future for Argentina. Obviously its prosperity was not automatically guaranteed by the relative success during the last decade. But as a senior manager he felt that it had all the policy tools it needed to achieve stability and growth. Argentina's success in managing the Great Depression and the war experience had given it new confidence and international ranking; it had made great strides since 1930 and could look forward to the postwar era with confidence rather than fear as a powerful young actor on the international scene.

Prebisch's *Money* raised many theoretical questions. His views on the historical decline in global terms of trade, his hypothesis of structural disequilibrium in the international economic system, his call for industrialization, and his concepts of "inward development" and "smart state" were of extraordinary scholarly interest.[16] His approach could be called "civilizing globalization"; he saw no other choice for Argentina but to embrace globalization, strengthen trade links with its neighbors; recognize the decline of Britain, and accept that US leadership was inevitable in the emerging international system. He saw many problems ahead, but he insisted that Argentina itself, beginning with the state, could not avoid responsibility for policy choices. While he believed in the inequality of the existing international system for commodity producers, Prebisch was not a revolutionary critic of Western capitalism. He expressed no anger or bitterness; instead he was confident that Argentina could develop the tools it needed to meet the postwar uncertainties.

Nevertheless, when taken together, Prebisch's propositions in 1943 presented a major theoretical challenge to traditional liberal orthodoxy. For him, the latter doctrine had too many gaps; it simply couldn't explain Argentina's predicament. "My long involvement with the practice of monetary policy over the last fifteen years has constantly persuaded me of the need to return to the theoretical foundations of the system to improve our understanding and management of concrete problems," he wrote. The operation of the international economy presents "such distinct characteristics in our economic life that their explanation requires an alternative theoretical explanation than that appropriate for industrial countries." This "alternative explanation" claimed an embedded disequilibrium between industrial and agricultural countries within a unified global system. There was no automatic harmony in the international economic system, and no "magic of the marketplace"; instead there was an unequal power relationship that could only be remedied by deliberate state action. Prebisch's posing of this *structural critique* of liberal theory opened a new perspective in the study of international economics with serious consequences for development policy.

Prebisch completed his book proposal on 13 December, but Argentine publishers showed no interest. No one recognized its scholarly importance and innovation. There was nothing of comparable interest in the economics literature, and, apart from its theoretical novelty, the book would have provided a valuable study of an emerging economy from an insider's perspective. Perhaps its title concealed the full range of his enquiry; its proposed three-part structure – theory, Central Bank experience, and policy implications – may have seemed too dry. Perhaps the book's attractiveness would have been increased by a Latin American, rather than Argentine, focus. Perhaps Prebisch erred in presenting it without evocative imagery – like "core" and "periphery" – which he had used in 1921. Most probably the proposal was simply too far ahead of its time and was lost in the political turmoil of Buenos Aires during the Second World War. One can only speculate on the impact of this book had it been written and published in 1944, but in the end all that remained was the proposal itself, an essential benchmark of his thinking at the immediate close of his Central Bank career.

The debacle of the book project plunged Raúl into depression. Oscar Altgelt, an avid flyer who owned a small Cessna, tried unsuccessfully to divert Raúl with plane rides around the countryside and up and down the coastline. Raúl was determined to revive his theoretical work as soon as possible, but without the Central Bank he was alone and without resources – he no longer had a research team, access to the Central Bank library, or a vehicle for publishing his work. Prebisch knew that his background and career were atypical and dutifully acknowledged the limitations of his training compared with full-time professional economists in North American or European universities. But he felt he was on the right path because the policy tools he developed in the Central Bank had been effective in the real world; he spoke of the Argentine "reality" because he lived it; he criticized existing theory because he had wrestled with money and international finance since the Great Depression; and he understood intuitively that the Argentine case was simply different from that of the US or the UK.

So strong was his need for an institutional base to regain his creative self that he decided to swallow his pride and revive negotiations with the Faculty of Economic Sciences, presently in a state of chaos as the military government reorganized the university administration and the students and faculty remained out on strike. But backwater or not, the faculty was better than the boredom and futility of Mar del Plata or the garden house in San Isidro. Julio Gonzalez del Solar did the advance work in a first meeting with the Faculty of Economic Sciences on 27 December, carrying a letter from Raúl requesting his full-time reinstatement. The new dean was confident – even excited – by the prospect of Prebisch's return, recognizing him as a major addition to the faculty complement. Moreover, official hostility toward Prebisch had waned during the months since his dismissal. He was flattered, for example, that Ministry of Finance officials were contacting members of his old Central Bank team to find unobtrusive ways of seeking his advice. He thereupon agreed to direct two seminars each year at the faculty beginning in April 1946, but he turned down all administrative assignments to concentrate on research and teaching.[17]

Although his isolation was ending and he yearned to return as soon as possible to Buenos Aires, Raúl and Adelita became increasingly short of cash. Their savings were running out and the failure of the book proposal meant the end of any dreams of an advance. His university position in Argentina was largely honorific, and the rent from 134 Rivera Indarte barely covered essentials. Neither he nor Adelita had private incomes, and she was as unlikely as Raúl to be employed in Buenos Aires. He badly needed a job.

On 22 December an unexpected letter arrived from the Mexican Embassy that transformed his professional and financial prospects.[18] A month earlier the Bank of Mexico had sent an exploratory note to Prebisch in Mar del Plata via the Mexican Embassy in Buenos Aires, sounding him out regarding a possible visit. With nothing else on the horizon he had immediately accepted the invitation in principle, indicating that he would be prepared to consider a formal invitation. But nothing happened, and he stoically assumed that the issue had been dropped or that the Ramirez Government had vetoed it with a note of protest. He had received a similar invitation from Uruguay shortly after his dismissal, and that too had not materialized.[19] In any case he needed a job rather than a diversion. On 19 December, however, Prebisch reminded the Mexican Ambassador, in a note delivered by Alfredo Moll, that he had not received a reply to his earlier letter. To his surprise, the Embassy delivered a formal invitation from the Bank's Deputy Director-General Rodrigo Gomez, proposing a three-month visit, with extensive trips throughout Mexico to acquaint him with the country, but centred on a series of seminars dealing with Prebisch's experiences as general manager of the Argentine Central Bank. The Bank of Mexico offered to cover all his expenses and asked him to fix a date and suggest an honorarium. Clearly moved by this astonishing break in his fortunes, he replied on Christmas Day that he would accept whatever they offered; as for a date he suggested 5 January to allow his return in early April to prepare his faculty seminar.[20] When the Mexicans offered an incredible US$5,000, Prebisch's short-term financial crisis was over. He could now think of returning to the capital, living again with his family in normal circumstances, and even buying a small car. Adelita immediately began a search for larger and more accessible quarters than the Lobos garden house in San Isidro, eventually finding a modest house in Buenos Aires that would be available on Raúl's return from Mexico City.

The Mexican invitation restored Prebisch's confidence. As much as he needed the money, he needed to get back into circulation. His greatest pain after being dismissed from the Bank was isolation; the Bank of Mexico was fully in the network with Allied governments in reshaping international monetary policy, and he now had a means of access to a world denied him in Argentina. Not only did he feel wanted again but Mexico City during the war had become an important capital, and the Bank of Mexico was a leading financial institution in the Americas with even closer links with the US Federal Reserve and international specialists. Moreover the lectures in Mexico meant that he would have an early opportunity to present the experiences and lessons he had gained during his tenure in the Argentine Central Bank.[21] The period in the wilderness was over.

On 2 January 1944, for the first time since October, Prebisch, with a spring in his step, returned to Buenos Aires and contacted his old friends in the banking and diplomatic communities for the most recent economic and political news. These were not good. He learned that his last two surviving initiatives from the 1940–41 visits to the US were being phased out. The Central Bank / Harvard University / Federal Reserve program would be terminated because such cooperative projects with US institutions were increasingly considered to be disloyal, and CAPI, the Argentine Trade Promotion Corporation set up with the private sector in 1941, was also being bypassed on its way to oblivion. To prosper (and as it turned out, even to survive), CAPI needed the leadership of the Central Bank, but it was now out of favour and humbled by the 18 October crackdown. Until then the New York office had held on despite the deepening US-Argentine tension, but now the Ramirez Government gave it the official cold shoulder. Instead Luis Colombo's UIA sought to replace CAPI by building its own relationships with the US Embassy. The Embassy wasn't interested. Not only did the UIA lack the resources and contacts for such an international role (it lacked the capacity even to translate letters into English), but this evident display of competition for access and power in the capital without a firm hand at the top doomed the CAPI experiment. It disappeared without a trace.

The news of Prebisch's trip to Mexico provoked commotion among friends and foes in the capital. Malaccorto helped prepare his travel documents; Raúl visited the faculty to renew acquaintances and make preparations for his spring seminar. Opponents were not pleased that Mexico had recognized him as Latin America's foremost economist and banking authority in a series that included internationally known economists such as Joseph A. Schumpeter; the invitation, so soon after his dismissal from the Central Bank, reflected badly on a military government too ideologically driven to tolerate excellence and unreasonable enough to condemn him as a lackey of Anglo-American imperialism. For Prebisch's supporters it was a welcome vindication of their friend and ex-colleague, and Ernesto Bosch congratulated him in a personal letter during his final preparations for Mexico: "The saying that 'no one is a prophet in his own land' does not necessarily hold," he wrote. "If it is true that our government has failed to recognize your leadership role in the Central Bank, public opinion in our own country and abroad has indeed understood the mistake of our imprudent rulers ... I miss you very much; although you left behind a strong element of your general staff, its commitment and hard work are not sufficient to be able to forget the presence of their Commander-in-Chief always at the helm."[22]

9 Discovery of Latin America

Disgraced officially in Buenos Aires, Prebisch was received as a visiting dignitary by Bank of Mexico Director-General Eduardo Villaseñor and his Deputy Rodrigo Gomez on his arrival in Mexico City on 5 January 1944. Apart from international conferences, he had not previously met senior Mexican Government officials; they also knew him only by reputation and the *Annual Reports* of the Argentine Central Bank. They would also have invited Adelita had they known Raúl was married. He was taken aback by the warmth of their welcome; even though he was not American or European they accepted him as a leading authority on money and banking. Raúl would always refer to these three months as a unique period of discovery and cultural learning during which his concept of "Latin America" began to form.[1]

Prebisch had never visited Mexico; he observed a magnificent city spreading out from its imperial heart and stately avenues to Chapultepec Forest toward the mountains ringing the old Aztec capital. Zocalo, the main plaza with the Presidential Palace and Cathedral, dwarfed the Plaza de Mayo in grandeur; housed in the nearby colonial Hotel de Cortes, Prebisch could use his first morning walks to visit the main sites of a capital built on an imperial scale. After a few days in the city Rodrigo Gomez took him into the Mexican interior; his hosts had decided that one week per month of Prebisch's stay should be devoted to travel inside the country so that he would see every region, and they proceeded without haste to Guadalajara via Queretero and San Miguel de Allende. The following month the trip continued to Morelia and Guanajuato, to San Luis Potosí, and then north toward Monterrey via the spectacular colonial silver town of Real de Catorce. Prebisch soon loosened up, and the relationship with Gomez and his colleagues became increasingly close as he explored the country. Taken aback at first by his Buenos Aires mannerisms, the Mexicans realized that under his formal surface lay a warm, generous, and humorous individual.

The discovery of a pre-European and colonial heritage with a cultural legacy he had never imagined, and with a richness of a entirely different order than Salta and Jujuy, transformed Prebisch's appreciation of Mexico – not just of its diversity, culture, wealth, and beauty but also of its potential. It was a different world than Argentina. His own country was immeasurably more developed economically, with the second highest per capita income in the world, socially integrated with a large middle class, and an improving but already high level of public education – a little bit of Europe in the Southern Cone. Argentine poverty, even that of the sugar workers of Tucumán, was not like in Mexico, where social exclusion retained a medieval aftertaste, where peasants had risen up in the 1910 Revolution to claim land on which many survived in subsistence. Argentina was a huge economic success, and Buenos Aires a New World treasure, but Argentina was a settler country still in search of itself: Mexico was a mass of contradictions whose wealth in colonial days had towered over that of North America until precipitous decline had left it vulnerable to amputation; and now its economy was only 2 percent that of the US. But Mexico was a civilization, not merely a country, and the Linares side of Raúl's personality recognized a strength and permanence in Mexico that did not exist in Argentina. Here the indigenous cultures had not been exterminated; although abused, they retained a historical bond with an ancient land transcending the ebb and flow of prosperity. His perspective on "Latin America" began to evolve from a geographic expression learned at school to a grouping of diverse states that could and should enrich each other, with Mexico and Argentina at the far ends of the great Latin American family.

Mexico in 1944 was alive with intellectual ferment and optimism. The Second World War was going well, and rapid industrialization was taking place. As an accepted destination for exiles from all continents, its most recent wave of migration from Spain following the 1939 victory of Franco had included a good percentage of the doomed Republic's intellectual class in the new Colegio de México. Other refugees had arrived from Europe after the outbreak of the larger war in September 1939, strengthening its cosmopolitan spirit and urban culture. This attraction, and its privileged geographic location in the Second World War, had transformed Mexico City into a priority destination by 1944. For the first time, it was linked in friendship and alliance with the United States.

War in Europe and Asia had led to a change in the traditionally poisonous US-Mexican relationship because it required Washington to promote a closer inter-American cooperation than the vague partnership envisioned in President Franklin D. Roosevelt's "Good Neighbor" policy announced after his election in 1932. Already on 1 December 1940 Roosevelt had sent

Henry Wallace, his vice-president elect, to Mexico to attend the inauguration of President Manuel Avila Camacho. Bilateral disagreements over Mexico's nationalization of oil in 1938 were patched up, and an agreement on defense and economic cooperation was signed in early 1941. Mexico promptly broke off diplomatic relations with Japan, Germany, and Italy after Pearl Harbor; and on 20 April 1943 the country was electrified by the historic visit of President Roosevelt himself. A permanent change in relations with the northern giant appeared certain and this widespread belief provoked a wave of pro-US sentiment throughout Mexico. Nor was it all one way. In Washington the "Western Hemisphere Idea" was rekindled in a wartime solidarity so noisy that it spread to US civil society. Before Pearl Harbor "Americas Day" on 14 April had been among the least known dates on the American calendar, but now it was dusted off and celebrated in a host of US cities with a week-long build-up of festivities. The US Marine Band was brought out; speeches invoked the special intimacy presumed to exist within the family of American states. In short the US and Mexico needed each other and by 1944 an entirely novel US-Mexican friendship and cooperation had been achieved.

More concretely for Mexico, the shared effort against the Nazi enemy and the closure of most of Europe and Asia provided an opening for new directions in economic development and US-Latin American relations. Even Canada was included. Trilateral negotiations for a US-Canada-Mexico North American free-trade agreement were initiated; and Washington funded programs of technical assistance. The US recognition of Mexico as an ally was such that its delegation to the 1944 Bretton Woods Conference, creating the World Bank and International Monetary Fund, co-chaired the proceedings with the US and Britain. Riding this wave of solidarity, the Bank of Mexico saw itself as a key national institution with the US Federal Reserve as its model.

United States universities and businesses also sought out Mexican partners for exchanges and investment with the Bank of Mexico program to which Prebisch had been invited, that invitation serving as an example of this opening. United States universities had professors eager to travel to Mexico if invited, and their graduate schools were important for training Mexican economists. No PhD programs in economics existed in Mexico, and there were only a handful of economists in the entire country. Moreover US universities had been strengthened by attracting economists from around the world, offering an unrivalled quality of teaching, research, and experience. Gottfried Haberler and Joseph Schumpeter were in this group, as well as Henry Wallich and Jacob Viner. These individuals were interested in Mexico and the Bank of Mexico, which by 1944 had become recognized as not only an elite institution in economic management but also a forum for debating new ideas and approaches in postwar monetary policy. Not only had it assembled a group of promising young Mexican economists in its Office of Economic Studies, but its president and senior staff, headed by Eduardo Villaseñor and Rodrigo Gomez, were committed to innovation and international dialogue. It had also attracted gifted young Mexican economists such as Victor L. Urquidi, a recent graduate of the London School of Economics. Daniel Cosío Villegas, the director of the Fondo de Cultura Económica, Latin America's largest publisher of scholarly texts, was also a member of the Bank of Mexico's research team. Outside the Bank a network of institutions including the new Colegio de México and the venerable UNAM (National Autonomous University, founded in 1551) amplified the circle of researchers.

The contrast with the growing political polarization and narrowing intellectual life in Buenos Aires left Prebisch anxious for the future of his country. Argentina was imposing religious instruction in universities, curtailing scholarly links, firing its best professors, and isolating itself from international networks and ideas; in Mexico there was no fear, no backbiting, and the quality of debate and atmosphere of scholarly freedom and commitment to dialogue was infectious. Mexico's overriding priority was national development; universities, business, and government were absorbed with this challenge, and a spirit of innovation was in the air. Despite its wealth and advantages Argentina was closing to the world, while Mexico with all its problems was opening to the future.

The two countries made for an interesting comparison. Mexico's population was somewhat larger at 20,393 versus Argentina's 14,169 million in the 1940 census; both towered over Chile (five million), although together they still did not match Brazil's expanding population of 41,523. Mexico, like Argentina, had responded to the Great Depression by abandoning the gold standard and introducing a broad policy of state intervention and expansion, but there were important differences. Mexico had defaulted on its debt and introduced more radical measures, including land reform, the nationalization of the oil industry in 1938 under a monopoly of the state oil company PEMEX, and the creation of other instruments such as a development corporation (Nacional Financiera) and a six-year plan.[2] Argentina was in the British trade orbit, while Mexico was in the US zone. For both countries the worst of the Depression was over by 1933, after which they again began to grow, with roughly similar results, until the outbreak of the European war in 1939. They differed most in the security and political areas. Mexico's security focus remained the US border, but this was no longer a military threat – in fact the US had implemented a program to attract migrant workers to cover a labour shortage during the war. Argentina in contrast faced armed rivals in Brazil to the North and Chile to the West. Both countries were governed by military men, General Avila Camacho in Mexico and General Ramirez in Buenos Aires. Indeed, both countries were authoritarian in their own way. But after the disasters of revolution and US aggression Mexico had constructed durable state institutions, with Cardenas enjoying widespread popular support and allowing the more conservative Avila Camacho after 1940 to adjust to a cooperative relationship with Washington, the old enemy. In Argentina the US was rapidly becoming the new enemy, perfectly out of sequence with Mexico, while its political institutions were disintegrating.

In so stimulating a climate Prebisch worked hard preparing his seminars, held between 24 January and the end of March, selecting as his main themes the background and creation of the Argentine Central Bank; foreign exchange controls – the Argentine experience; the history of monetary policy in Argentina, its guiding principles and linkage with the international system; the Central Bank as financial instrument of the national government; and lastly the issue of the gold standard and the financial vulnerability of Latin American countries. The atmosphere reminded Prebisch of the Argentine Central Bank before his dismissal, except that as general manager he had had little time to read and keep up with scholarly journals. The seminars were conducted in small groups twice a week, normally with only Villaseñor, Gomez, and a half-dozen other officials in attendance, in a relaxed give-and-take on topics including Mexican monetary and trade policy, its strategies in dealing with the US after the return of peace, and broader issues such as the forthcoming international conference being prepared by Keynes and Harry Dexter White for July 1944 at Bretton Woods in New Hampshire on global monetary and financial policy. In turn the Mexicans could learn from the Argentine experience. Mexico's Central Bank was created in 1925, earlier than Argentina's, because the private banking system had been nearly wiped out during the preceding years of revolution and civil war, but only in 1941 was it given the wide powers comparable to Argentina's Central Bank for managing the money supply and regulating exchange rates. This was true in theory – in practice Mexico had nothing comparable to Argentina's highly developed financial market and credit standing, and Villaseñor and Gomez were still feeling their way forward.[3]

Prebisch opened his seminar with a comprehensive analysis of the Central Bank experience in Argentina, providing a first-hand account of Central Bank operations during its first years and a forecast of the new challenges lying ahead for his country. The lectures and discussion also drew attention to the need for countries like Mexico and Argentina to be more assertive in steering their economies. Coming from the Southern Cone, Prebisch's experience had greater immediate relevance for his Mexican audience than that of US or European visiting scholars. They were captivated by his invocation of the "reality" Argentina faced after the Great Depression and his efforts at the Central Bank to moderate the international business cycle in its interests. Prebisch's confidence that smaller countries such as their own had the ability to understand and shape their destinies responded to Mexico's ambitions. Long extracts of his seminars were reprinted in the daily press. The combination of content and personality made these seminars significant events, extending their reach beyond the normal seminars given by foreign experts; Prebisch was evidently not just an academic but also a leading expert in his field in the Americas. Bankers in the US were notified of his arrival and invited him to New York as an old friend.[4]

Close friendships emerged from these weeks, from the president and his senior staff to Daniel Cosío Villegas, Victor Urquidi, and US economist Robert Triffin. Apart from his position as publisher, Daniel Cosío was a leading Mexican thinker and intellectual, and for Prebisch a bridge to understanding contemporary Mexican society and US-Mexican relations.[5] Prebisch recognized Urquidi as one of Mexico's foremost young economists and, despite the age difference, a friend who shared his interest in development theory. The Triffin encounter was different; although they were introduced in Mexico they had little time together. Triffin was on leave from Harvard University working in the US Federal Reserve, part of a generation of US economists committed to Latin American development and open to approaches beyond the prewar liberal orthodoxy. He invited Prebisch to work with him in some of the Fed's technical assistance projects on money and banking with Central Banks throughout Latin America and the Caribbean. This was an almost perfect match of interests. Few if any experts in either the US or Latin America possessed Prebisch's combination of language, practical expertise, and reputation; for him such consultancies would solve his financial dilemma while allowing him to write the book he had had to abandon in Mar del Plata.

The word spread quickly. Other Latin American governments, beginning with Venezuela and followed by the other Andean capitals, invited Prebisch to visit them on his return trip to Buenos Aires as soon as he completed the seminars. Mexico had also ignited his broader interest in understanding the other regions of Latin America, and he tried to accommodate these requests within the deadline set by the opening of his faculty course in Buenos Aires; while this meant declining an invitation from Venezuela, he was able to schedule short stops to the capital cities of Colombia, Peru, and Chile. His return trip from Mexico, therefore, was a ten-day procession of brief visits to Bogotá, Lima, and Santiago – none of which he had seen before. Everyone wanted to meet him, and each visit was a surprise.

He had hardly thought previously about Colombia, but it had almost twice Chile's population, with a growing economy and a capital city already spilling out from its colonial core. Lima was magnificent and even better preserved than Mexico City; even if smaller and depressed, it was a coastal museum piece set visually apart from the indigenous highlands. Although Chile and Peru were similar in size, Santiago was a competitor of Buenos Aires, with a governing elite determined to make Chile a leading country in South America. In every capital he met Latin Americans – such as Carlos Lleras Restrepo in Colombia, or Herman Max and Benjamin Cohen in Chile – who shared his own determination to promote economic development and who believed that Latin America had come out of the Great Depression with sufficient experience to succeed.

Prebisch returned home from his Mexican-Andean tour on Monday, 17 April with only one week to prepare for his seminar in the faculty. Adelita met him at the airport to welcome him home after more than three months away, the only time they had ever been apart. The rented house was now fully furnished, so that Raúl never had to spend one night in the Lobos garden house in San Isidro. He could, however, buy a small Citroen, so that Adelita would no longer have to rely solely on her bicycle. Professionally he was satisfied to have completed one of the tasks he had set for himself in his post-dismissal book project that had been rejected by publishers – to record his personal history of the creation and management of the Argentine Central Bank. His seminars in the Bank of Mexico had been recorded and transcribed by the Bank and would eventually be published as *Conversaciones en el Banco de Mexico*, even though the sessions were off the record and too highly personalized for immediate release.[6] But his memory was there for posterity, and he was satisfied that this part of his goal had been achieved.

Now he could move to the second challenge of articulating a new and coherent theory of development, as posed in his ill-fated *Money and the Rhythm of Economic Activity* proposal, but the immediate impact of Mexico left him feeling inadequate as a scholar. He confided to Triffin, "I have realized that I know far less than I thought."[7] Prebisch felt that his ad hoc introduction to economic theory left him at a disadvantage relative to Western scholars, and in fact his Mexican lectures had been largely descriptive, with hypothesis presented as fact in his repeated insistence on the "realities" of the business cycle. It was one thing to describe the disequilibrium faced by Argentina as an agricultural exporter far distant from the industrial centres (the term "periphery" did not enter his correspondence on a regular basis until 1945); it was quite another to challenge the prevailing worldwide economic establishment with a rival theoretical approach positing a permanent disequilibrium in the global system. He felt that he had more than enough personal and professional experience with monetary policy and central banking but that his theoretical training was inadequate. His seminars in Mexico had been successful, but Prebisch knew that his persuasiveness was related more to the immediacy of his policy experience during the 1930s than to theoretical sophistication. He therefore decided to deepen his research on business cycle theory by examining in detail the work of Keynes and probing its relevance for economic development in Argentina and Latin America. Titled *Money and Economic Cycles in Argentina*, the course therefore moved beyond his Mexican lectures.

The faculty to which he had returned provided few of the conditions required for serious work. It is true that he had his followers: he was awaited by his old staff and admirers such as Julio Gonzalez del Solar, who attended the seminars and assisted with the publication of several of them in the faculty journal. But unlike universities in most countries, Buenos Aires provided neither a living salary with the support of graduate students and well-equipped libraries nor access to the international research networks of economists working on monetary and trade policy. Prebisch had no money for research assistants nor access to the specialized studies and statistics required for his work. In Daniel Cosío Villegas he had a personal link to a prestigious publisher in the region, and scholars like Victor Urquidi and Robert Triffin partially ended his intellectual isolation and provided a contact with the US Federal Reserve. But these contacts could not compensate for the fact that Argentina was visibly closing to the outside world; economists abroad had access not only to each other but also to practitioners in the public and private banking systems, while the Faculty of Economics was increasingly destabilized by growing political scrutiny. There was little possibility of productive work or debate in these circumstances.

The political situation was more tense than before his departure for Mexico four months earlier, and Prebisch's return to teaching was denounced by a hostile press as a covert attempt to undermine the government.[8] The Ramirez Government was split when it broke diplomatic relations with Germany on 26 January 1944, leaving its future in doubt. On 17 February a friend wrote to Prebisch from Buenos Aires that "the situation in the country is very confusing after the latest developments. The impression here is that there are splits in the regime ... there is neither confidence in the leaders nor in the system."[9] Week by week the political uncertainty deepened. Supporters of Perón arrested the foreign minister on 26 February, and the president was forced into the background. A letter from one of Prebisch's friends in the Argentine Embassy in Washington noted on 7 March that "the political developments in our country discourage the most optimistic. It seems that our people have started to use blinkers, only seeing in one direction and then only at short distance."[10] By 10 March the political crisis finally came to a head with the formal resignation of Ramirez as president and his replacement by Vice-President Edelmiro Julian Farrell, who promptly annulled the anti-Nazi measures of his predecessor. Juan Perón, formerly undersecretary of war and minister of labour and welfare, was promoted to minister of war. From his position as labour minister he was reorganizing the CGT (General Confederation of Workers) into an instrument of power that incorporated the wave of poor migrants from the interior swelling the labour force in Buenos Aires. On 7 July 1944 President Farrell appointed him vice-president of the republic, and a month later he became chair of the newly appointed National Council on Post-War Planning, which assembled the leaders of business, labour, the military, agricultural producers, senior government officials, and the financial community to prepare the economy for a return to peace. Once again this new body included the private sector heavyweights of the country, including Luis Colombo and José Maria Bustillo, who saw a convergence of interests with Perón. President Farrell had still not lifted the state of siege, and the entire Central Committee of the Communist Party remained imprisoned in Patagonia. Internationally the Argentine reversal of policy on the German question further undermined relations with the US; on 4 March the US suspended relations with Farrell, and on 27 June Ambassador Norman Armour was recalled indefinitely to Washington.

Meanwhile final preparations were concluding for the Bretton Woods Conference, which was to open on 1 July; the Mount Washington Hotel in New Hampshire, spruced up for the occasion after being closed for two years, prepared to receive 730 delegates from forty-four countries. Shunned by the US, Argentina was the only major Latin country absent from the gathering, and Prebisch understood what this meant for its international standing. International events were moving quickly. By its close on 22 July the Bretton Woods Conference had agreed to create the IMF (International Monetary Fund) and the World Bank (International Bank for Reconstruction and Development), both to be set up in Washington. Remaining outside these vital multilateral institutions meant that Argentina lost all influence, while countries of similar economic size, like Canada, became respected middle powers with a voice at the table. Prebisch envied Victor

Urquidi, part of the Mexican delegation and the youngest representative at the Conference. Instead of helping to shape the postwar system and meeting Keynes and White, Prebisch was completely shut out of official networks and marooned without a secure institutional base in a political crisis that seemed permanent.

Triffin and Chris Ravndal, who had been posted to Sweden in October 1943 to monitor the war situation in Eastern Europe, both urged Prebisch to leave Argentina and move to the US, where research opportunities would be incomparably superior. Prebisch had long been attracted to the idea of teaching at Harvard, but his first priority remained Argentina; while his interest in economic theory was serious, he was committed to returning to public life in his country. He continued to believe that his dismissal was temporary and repeatedly referred to his new academic career as a pause, an interlude, which he would use for a book that would shake up the economics profession. Despite the arguments of his US friends, he therefore ruled out a move to the US, which he knew would sever links with Buenos Aires. Raúl and Adelita decided to buy a lot in San Isidro on a street numbered 563 Chile, with a good view of the surrounding hills. Alberto agreed to design another house for them – not grand like 134 Rivera Indarte but a solid building that could tide them over until they reoccupied their old home and serve as a stable investment in inflationary times.

Prebisch felt sidelined; he was frustrated, once again strapped for money, and at loose ends when his seminar closed in July. The war continued, and US-Argentine hostility intensified. The successful Normandy landing of Allied troops in June 1944 did not imply the imminent collapse of German forces, and an end to the Pacific conflict was even farther in the distance. Prebisch therefore was open for a temporary change of climate. When Robert Triffin arrived in Buenos Aires to visit Raúl in July he proposed consultancy work in Paraguay in cooperation with the US Federal Reserve. Triffin hoped that the mission would strengthen Prebisch's regional visibility and eventually draw him into a university appointment in the United States.

Paraguay, whose population had finally reached one million in 1940, had returned to a measure of political stability that year when General Higinio Morinigo succeeded General José Felix Estigarribia. The latter was a national hero whose unconventional tactics (learned while fighting with the French in World War I) had defeated Bolivia in the Chaco War but whose skills in managing the economy proved more limited. After Estigarribia's death in an airplane crash, Morinigo effectively put a lid on four years of turmoil and provided an opening to economic modernization. The US Federal Reserve had been requested to advise on the setting up of a central bank, and Presidential Decree 5130 on 8 September 1944 authorized its creation; Triffin suggested that Prebisch spend several months in the capital Asunción helping implement the legislation to launch the institution.[11] He was offered $2,000 per month plus expenses, and agreed with two conditions: that Adelita accompany him and that he be paid by the Paraguay Government rather than the US Federal Reserve. The strained wartime diplomacy between Argentina and the US together with the long history of close Argentine-Paraguayan relations counselled a payment arrangement between Latin Americans – excluding the evident hand of Washington – to mollify public reaction in Buenos Aires. On 17 September he received an official invitation from Carlos A. Pedretti, president of the Bank of the Republic of Paraguay, for a contract that would run from January to April 1945 with a return visit for ten days in July.

Triffin later apologized to Prebisch for "having pushed you into a job which certainly had many disadvantages," but he had actually accepted the Paraguay assignment with a certain eagerness.[12] First it was close to Buenos Aires, and while he wanted some respite from the political tension he also wanted to remain close to the capital to be able to return home quickly if necessary. It was not like working in the US, where he would have the double disadvantage of being completely out of touch and also being accused of selling out to the Americans. Second, Paraguay was an important country for Argentina in its rivalry with Brazil for dominance in the Southern Cone, almost like a province, and playing the role of consultant with the Central Bank was not inconsistent with the Argentine national interest. It had gained its independence from Spain in 1811; though clearly unwilling to accept annexation to Argentina, like Uruguay and Bolivia it could not help remaining in its orbit. In 1916 Paraguay and Argentina entered into a free-trade agreement, and Argentina had brokered the end of the Chaco War. Paraguay, an official Argentine memorandum noted in October 1943, "is not like any other country for us, but rather organically complementary to us economically and geographically."[13]

The outbreak of the Second World War, however, had threatened Argentine interests in Paraguay. In 1940 the US Export-Import Bank provided $3 million to General Morinigo to dilute Argentine influence. In October of that year Argentina countered by successfully promoting a four-power trade agreement in the Southern Cone, but this was nullified by the Pacific War after 7 December 1941. After Pearl Harbor, with Brazil part of the US alliance and Argentina neutral, Argentine-Brazil-US competition for influence in Paraguay deepened, with Argentina becoming increasingly worried by Brazil's growing strength and military power. When Argentina cancelled Paraguay's outstanding debts as a goodwill gesture, Brazil announced the same measure in May 1943. By 1944 Paraguay had the rare luxury of all three powers competing for its attention with commercial agreements. Although Prebisch went to Asunción as a consultant on money and banking, he was also an Argentine patriot committed to strengthening bilateral cooperation. Prior to his dismissal he had supported the formation of a joint commission and a customs union with Paraguay; before his departure he was briefed by the Central Bank on ongoing initiatives and assessments of Brazilian intentions and inroads in Paraguay, a buffer state that Argentines of all factions agreed was of vital importance.[14]

Beyond this strategic view of Paraguay as a pawn in the regional balance of power, Prebisch knew little about the history of the country when he and Adelita boarded a Uruguayan riverboat at the port in Buenos Aires to begin the three-day voyage to Asunción. Crossing the Plate River estuary they entered the shipping channel of the Parana River to sail high into Argentina's tropical province of Corrientes before crossing the border and entering Paraguay. After dining with heavy silver under swaying chandeliers they retired to equally well-appointed staterooms below and awoke the next morning to clouds of flamingos flying before the low steady beat of the boat's diesel engines.

As they moved deeper into the interior of untouched forests bordering the river, curious wildlife lined the shore to observe the intruders; by noon the tropical sun had driven the passengers into their deckchairs under awnings among hovering waiters circulating gin-tonics and canapés; only at 11:00 PM could dinner be served with a light breeze ventilating the dining room. Upriver at the town of Corrientes the big craft slowed, touched ground, and then backed off, finally moving forward again tentatively seeking a passage in the immense but shallow river for the final stage to Asunción. After an hour the captain admitted defeat; his two passengers for Asunción were notified, and their trunks off-loaded into a small and fast open boat. Adelita and Raúl then clambered onto their trunks, exchanging their riverboat luxury for a wild and wet ride to their destination in the geographic centre of South America. Asunción came into view as a mirage in the great heat, its tiny port inside a deep bay off the river, giving way to a plateau behind it with the Presidential Palace and Congress framed against a languid blue sky.[15]

For both Raúl and Adelita the months in Asunción proved involving and enriching; Paraguay was as much a discovery as Mexico, presenting another face of Latin America with a challenge in a different order of magnitude. They stayed at the Gran Hotel de Paraguay, now owned by a sedate Germany family, but made famous (they learned) by Madame Lynch, an Irish courtesan in the mid-nineteenth century who had made the capital a lively destination for the entire region. They were warmly received socially in the hot and humid capital; their host, Carlos Pedretti, and his colleagues were eager and attentive counterparts who were committed to building an autonomous Central Bank with an efficient exchange control division against the long odds of political interference and corruption. Without air-conditioning the work day of the city was organized around the climate. Out of bed at 6:00 AM for an early start at the Central Bank with Pedretti and his colleagues, lunch would be served at 11:00 AM, followed by siesta. Another round of office work would begin at 5:00 PM, and by the time a late dinner ended at midnight their hotel rooms would again be bearable for sleeping.

Asunción was clean and friendly; the people were poor but proud; and its tramways were efficient and punctual. Adelita in particular got to know the city and travelled throughout a diverse and interesting country that in Buenos Aires, Montevideo, or Rio was routinely dismissed as a backward and semi-civilized outpost. The language of the people was Guarani as much as Spanish; the culture was indigenous, therefore, and a dimension of Latin America that Raúl had ignored since Tucumán. He and Adelita began to understand the War of the Triple Alliance, as it was called, in which the three "European" countries – Argentina, Uruguay, and Brazil – joined forces against this comparatively minuscule landlocked neighbour and fought until Paraguay's population was reduced by two-thirds from an estimated prewar total of 450,000, with a catastrophic decimation of males – only one alive for four or five women – and the virtual disintegration of the state.[16] At last in the final stand at Cerro Cora only child soldiers and Paraguayan women were left, fighting with sticks and rocks against the Latin regiments attacking with rifles and cannon. The Archbishop of Asunción had given Adelita a tour of the Cathedral, which had been stripped of its silver altar and valuables by Argentine troops. In the peace treaty imposed on Paraguay, Argentina demanded 10 billion pesos in reparations, as did Brazil – in fact these were absurd debts cancelled by both powers in 1943, seventy years after the most catastrophic conflict in post-independence Latin America. The history books of Raúl's boyhood education in Tucumán blamed Paraguayan dictator Francisco Solano Lopez for foolishly declaring war on Brazil and Argentina, and he had never thought twice about it since. But from Asunción it had a different look. Whatever the origins, three powerful white neighbours (Brazil maintained slavery until 1890) fought a war of extermination against a proud indigenous society fighting literally to the last man. These troops had used the latest Gatling machine guns to wipe out whole units composed of young boys. Yet Paraguay had rebuilt after the catastrophe. Households of women with one man gradually rebuilt a male population, while quarrels among the victors and the subsequent arbitration award of US President Hayes left Paraguay half its previous size but still with less territorial loss than expected by its brutal neighbours. Normalcy gradually returned, but when the population again reached the 1865 level the Great Depression plunged the country into economic crisis. Then on 9 September 1932 Bolivia attacked from the east, with a much larger and better-equipped army, to detach the supposedly oil-rich Chaco region from Paraguay, igniting the second bloodiest war in modern Latin American history. Once again Paraguay was alone, fighting for its life. But this time it won against the invaders in a brilliant campaign. The powdery dust of the semi-desert bushlands jammed the weapons of the Bolivian troops, while the heat, drought, and distances of the Chaco overwhelmed their supply lines. Paraguayan irregulars commanded by General Estagarribia revived the fighting spirit of the 1865–70 war, falling on isolated Bolivian units with machetes and eventually driving them out of one of the world's most hostile regions. Saavedra Lamas brokered a peace agreement, and the war ended on 12 June 1935, leaving Paraguay with borders that enclosed three-quarters of the Chaco. For this the country had suffered more than 35,000 people killed, and even more wounded, or 10 percent of the population, and in the end there were no petroleum reserves in the region after all.

Prebisch's experience in Paraguay forced a rethinking of cultural stereotypes widely shared in his own society in Argentina and the West in general. How could the destruction of Paraguay between 1865–70 be understood, except in racial terms that extended to the entire New World? Even Augusto Bunge, he realized, an otherwise tireless critic of social injustice and a leader in the campaign against anti-semitism, had written a book, *El Culto de la Vida*, in 1915 that reflected prevailing assumptions regarding the racial inferiority of Indians and Blacks.[17] Raúl realized that Roca's "military" campaigns against the Indians, so proudly celebrated in Argentine school textbooks in the name of nation-building, had in fact been a campaign of extermination against the indigenous peoples within its own borders. He himself had been proud to discover letters from his uncle General Teodoro to Roca from one of the campaigns. The disgust sweeping the world over the Nazi Holocaust had to be viewed in a historical context that included the catastrophe inflicted on indigenous peoples by the European conquest – the original sin of the Americas and Africa for which these settler societies must ultimately accept responsibility. Paraguay had a tragic history, but its people were not defeated; and the other submerged indigenous peoples of the Americas would also revive: this was the lesson that Prebisch took from Paraguay.

Prebisch's advisory work in Paraguay was a departure from all his previous personal and professional experience. This was a truly underdeveloped country, unlike Argentina or Mexico, and lacked the human resources and infrastructure for economic modernization, including an adequate national statistical system. Persistent rumours of military coups (one was suppressed just before his arrival) complicated any effort to strengthen the state, and the country already faced an inflationary threat. Prebisch had few expectations that the Central Bank legislation he drafted would be effective even if passed into law. (Nor did Pedretti; not long after Prebisch's departure he would also find himself on a boat down the Paraguay River.) Despite these problems Prebisch helped strengthen bank administration, clean up the exchange control system, and create a research division to house a team of specialists to advise the government on economic policy and monitor public expenditures.[18] Prebisch had established a close rapport with his counterparts in Asunción, and three months of work had provided direction and strengthened the operations and morale of the Central Bank. He could do no more – the rest depended on political developments in Paraguay. Triffin was delighted with the results and wanted more of his time. "I have studied the project thoroughly," he wrote, "as I have studied also the regulations both of exchange control and of the central bank. I would like to have your permission to inspire myself from your work in any later mission that I may carry on."[19]

Raúl and Adelita's return to Buenos Aires was a blend of happiness to be home with the sober expectation of more political difficulties to come. The final stages of preparations for their new house at 563 Chile in San Isidro kept Adelita and her mother busy, while Raúl tried to concentrate on his research. Word came that Carlos Moll had not survived the war. On 23 April he was executed by Hitler's Croatian Guards at Plötzensee Prison in Berlin after helping to plan the 1944 assassination attempt against Hitler. At first his Argentine citizenship allowed him prison duties outside the cellblock, but, after helping forty prisoners escape when his jailors were drunk, he was placed in solitary confinement and targeted for elimination. On 22 April, when the Soviet Army was only a few kilometres from Plötzensee, Carlito advised a Dutch priest among the prisoners to give all remaining men the last rites, and the next evening they were taken out with the promise of release but instead were machine-gunned. Severely wounded, the priest was the sole survivor of the massacre, eventually recovering from his wounds in a Soviet field hospital to relate the story of Carlos Moll. His daughters in Buenos Aires were left with a Rolex watch, nineteen thousand Swiss francs, and the memory of a true Argentine hero whose vision had embraced all humanity.[20]

The political turbulence in Buenos Aires was as distracting as ever for Prebisch. The war was no longer a factor; as Germany's defeat loomed, even the Farrell Government had declared war on 27 March 1945 to align itself with the victorious Allies and share in the victory and property of German and Japanese nationals in Argentina, which it chose to confiscate. Convenient for all parties, the decision immediately improved relations with the US. Nelson Rockefeller was pleased. Argentina was invited to join the UN and sign the Treaty of Chapultepec; Washington restored relations and sent a new ambassador, Sproule Braden, previously US envoy to Cuba, to succeed Armour. Large, ruddy-faced, and determined to bring Argentina back into the inter-American fold, Braden was welcomed by the entire democratic opposition from oligarchs to socialists.

Buenos Aires faced serious anti-government protests as Allied victory neared in 1945. Political repression deepened; the university was in even greater turmoil. Demands for elections and an end to military rule were growing now that the war was no longer an excuse. A rift appeared in relations between the military regime and big business, unsettling political relations even more. Although Luis Colombo of the Argentine Industrial Union had originally welcomed Perón's postwar plans for industrialization, he now broke with him – and so did the SRA – when they realized that his political and economic plans undercut their power and interests. They now feared Perón's growing support in the working class and other excluded groups in both the capital and the interior; his surging popularity in the labour movement gave him a power base that could shut down the country's economy with strikes and that was demanding costly social reforms for its continued support. A populist revolt from below was brewing.

Triffin had revived his efforts to bring Prebisch to Harvard University, and the US State Department encouraged this move. In a letter on 20 March 1945, Triffin had again raised the prospect of a visiting professorship to assist Prebisch's "book in preparation," and a week later he wrote a longer letter outlining the practical alternatives for a US visit after Raúl finished teaching in 1945.[21] The Guggenheim Foundation was prepared to fund his visit, he reported, but there was a timing problem with Harvard. It was anxious to have him, as was Wassily Leontief, who had submitted a warm letter of invitation on his behalf for a visiting lectureship to both the Rockefeller and Guggenheim Foundations. However Harvard had already filled its position for 1945, and this would mean waiting for the next year. Instead Triffin advised Prebisch simply to come with a Guggenheim Award and gradually establish himself in the US research community. Not only would the Harvard position then be open but, he noted, "Once you are in the country there is no question that other arrangements can be made very easily. There are many organizations and universities which would be interested in obtaining your services for public lectures here in Washington, in New York and certainly at Harvard." Personal relations between the two men had strengthened during early 1945, with Triffin and his wife visiting Buenos Aires – "by far the happiest part of our whole trip South," he noted. He sent Raúl a copy of his proposals for new monetary and exchange control legislation in Costa Rica, viewing their combined work as a model for the Latin American region as a whole. "I have some hope," he confided to Prebisch, "that the type of exchange controls proposed in Costa Rica and Paraguay may be of interest to the IMF and provide some sort of pattern for the future policy of the Fund."[22]

Triffin also tried to enlist Prebisch for further advisory work with the US Federal Reserve in Latin America. "I would feel inordinately proud to associate you with this work," he wrote on 23 August.[23] Triffin was particularly enthusiastic about Prebisch working in Guatemala, although the options of the Dominican Republic and perhaps Cuba were also available. The Dominican Republic was interesting but laboured under the long-standing dictatorship of Generalissimo Rafael Leonidas Trujillo. In contrast, democracy had just been restored in Guatemala under President Juan José Arevalo, who assumed office on 15 March in a government committed to what Triffin called "path-breaking reform." The new government, he felt, was one of the most exciting developments in the Americas, and Washington was committed to its success. "Its members are all very young and inexperienced, but, on the whole, able and well-meaning," he reported. Not only were Guatemala's economic prospects excellent, but there was a regional dimension as well since the new government in Guatemala was committed to exploring the possibility of federation with El Salvador; if accepted, this development would change the political outlook beyond Central America. In effect the country stood at the opening of a new era, but it needed an effective Central Bank. The new minister of economy and labour, Manuel Noriega Morales, had the full confidence of his president and represented the new generation of Latin financial leaders emerging in the region. Triffin and Morales had been fellow students at Harvard, and Morales knew and respected Prebisch's work. Arevalo had spent years in Argentina at the La Plata University – they all wanted Raúl to lead the team.

Although Prebisch had earlier supported Triffin's efforts to open links for him with Harvard and the US foundations, he now declined both a trip to the US and consultancies that would take him out of Argentina. "I believe it better to abandon any idea of an early trip to the States," he replied. "I do appreciate your interest and time." He was once again giving his seminar at the faculty, focusing seriously on Keynes's work. "The truth is that

I am quite happy with my current situation forced on me by circumstances," Prebisch wrote to Triffin. "I missed study, reading and thinking." Once again he underlined his sense of theoretical inadequacy. "Before I pretend to teach anyone else I had better stay home until I catch up with the literature."[24] Prebisch noted a "surprising similarity" between his findings on the business cycle and those in US Professor Machlup's most recent publication, underlining the work under way on monetary policy at both the national and international level. Clapham's new book on the Bank of England showed how idiosyncratic Britain's experience had been compared with the US, for example. Such variations in country experiences, with a "confrontation between theory and fact," had persuaded him that a historical perspective was essential for developing postwar policies and institutions.

But research was not his main reason for staying home. Instead his decision reflected a new opportunity to re-enter public life in Argentina – Prebisch had his eye on the presidency of the Central Bank. Bosch, at eighty-two, was ill and nearing the end of his mandate, and he wanted Prebisch to return to the Central Bank; unlike the position of general manager, the presidency came with a guaranteed seven-year tenure and Dr Bosch had not been touched by Ramirez or Farrell. Prebisch was therefore not going to leave Argentina for any reason until the appointment had been decided. Tension began to build in late April when Bosch offered Raúl his former job as general manager in the belief that the regime understood its mistake in October 1943. Prebisch turned down this offer, however; after his experience in October 1943 he would not give the regime the satisfaction of seeing him return to a job that had no constitutionally defined tenure. Edmundo Gagneux was available and qualified, and in fact was named general manager on 22 May, after Prebisch declined. He wrote Triffin with his reason for declining the offer. "You know that I am against the current regime in the country. I therefore think that I should remain outside it, using my time well for reading and research."[25]

Prebisch's reluctance changed abruptly when Dr Bosch announced on 24 July that he was stepping down, along with Vice-President Evaristo Uriburu. The Farrell Government immediately sent a list of official candidates to the Central Bank Board of Directors from which they were to choose a successor. After some hesitation the directors rejected all the official candidates as unqualified and announced an independent search for a shortlist on the basis of merit and experience. Prebisch was approached and agreed to let his name stand for the position on condition that none of the other candidates be selected from the government's official list. Bosch agreed. The result was his selection by unanimous consent of the directors, including the BNA representative who had opposed him in 1943. According to Prebisch, "It was seen as a personal vindication with all the greater moral significance because it was absolutely spontaneous."[26]

President Farrell in turn refused to accept Prebisch as Central Bank president; a prolonged standoff between the government and the board of directors ensued. Neither side was willing to capitulate, with the Central Bank counting on enough support within the business community to stare down President Farrell and with the military regime preferring indefinite stalemate to accepting a candidate it disliked. The issue was critical and perceived as such by both sides. Either the Central Bank remained independent, in which case Prebisch was symbol and guarantor of its original mission – or it would be transformed into a docile instrument of government policy with a president chosen by the government. Prebisch tried again to meet Perón; Prebisch believed, as in 1943, that Perón's advisors were not telling him the truth about the Central Bank and that he would understand and support its role if the two could have a face-to-face discussion. This second attempt was no more successful than the first. Meanwhile press attacks against Prebisch and the "restoration of the 'brains trust' intensified.[27]

In the end political violence decided the impasse. Buenos Aires was wracked by demonstrations. José Maria Bustillo, the president of the SRA (Argentine Rural Society), who represented the big agricultural interests on the National Council for Post-war Planning, publicly criticized Perón at the annual SRA fair in Palermo Park and was promptly arrested, to the shock of the elite in Buenos Aires, who now realized that they had a very determined and tough opponent on their hands. If someone like Bustillo could be jailed with impunity for saying the wrong things, everyone was in danger. Then police stood by as a mob attacked the offices of *Critica* on 15 August, leaving four dead and over a hundred wounded. Argentine-US relations hit another low point, with Sproule Braden openly attacking the Farrell regime two weeks later on his departure for Washington to replace Nelson Rockefeller as assistant secretary of state for Latin America, and thereby provoking a wave of anti-US protest. By 21 September the Central Bank's board of directors had had enough and backed down with an acceptance of the government's list.[28]

That evening Prebisch wrote to Triffin, with apologies for his long silence, describing what had happened over the summer; he now accepted a one-year consultancy abroad.[29] He had changed his mind about a long stay outside Argentina, he told his friend, because there was no longer any reason to stay in Buenos Aires. His last hopes at the Central Bank had evaporated; he was locked out for good. Moreover conditions in the university were now so turbulent that regular classes could not be scheduled. In his earlier correspondence Triffin had suggested payment of $2,000 per month with living expenses; Prebisch agreed on condition that Adelita could be with him. As for preferred country, Guatemala and the Dominican Republic were each interesting in different ways, but he thought that Cuba offered greater scope for Central Bank innovation given its more advanced economy and educational development.

Before Triffin could respond, Prebisch's plans changed again; he reversed his decision to leave Argentina because a political crisis struck the capital unexpectedly and opened the prospect of political change: the future of the military regime was in question. It began unexpectedly after Farrell finally raised the state of siege on 4 August 1945, nearly four years after it had come into force, and thereby opened the prospect of democratic elections. Exiles streamed back, political prisoners were released, and political parties began to hold rallies. On 18 September Perón publicly complained on radio about this "combination of foreign elements, reactionary spirits, hopeless politicians, and selfish plutocrats."[30] The next day these parties held a march of constitution and liberty that turned into a demonstration estimated at one-half million people from across the political spectrum, the largest ever held in Argentina. Ex-President Rawson staged an abortive coup on 24 September, but Farrell and Perón struck back by arresting Luis Colombo, other leaders of the demonstration, and most senior journalists in the city, which in turn provoked a four-day battle at the university between armed police and students barricaded in the main buildings. On 5 October the students were defeated, with 1,629 arrested, and the police occupied the buildings. But fortunes were changing daily. On 9 October Perón was forced to resign the vice-presidency and all other positions after violent public demonstrations strengthened his opponents within the military and civilian groups increasingly alarmed by the radicalism of his movement. It appeared that Perón had overplayed his hand at last; imprisoned on the island of Martín García in the Plata River, he seemed to be finally out of the political game. In fact he was far from defeated, and the military allowed him an emotional public farewell on 10 October to fifteen thousand workers in front of his office, which was also broadcast on radio. Announcing that he had just signed into law a salary raise and a minimum wage, he ended with a challenge to the regime: "I ask you to respect public order so that we may follow our triumphant march; but, if one day, it becomes necessary, I will ask you to fight."[31]

Labour leaders mobilized to demand his return, with the CGT calling a general strike for 16 October. Perón had been transferred to a military hospital in Buenos Aires after four days on Martín García, and the day after the strike a working class mob heard he was at the hospital and crossed the Riachuela Bridge to liberate their hero. By noon a crowd began to gather for him in the Plaza de Mayo, the underclass of the city numbering in the hundreds of thousands by the time he appeared at the balcony of the Casa Rosada. Flaming torches lit the dark mass. "Where were you?" the crowd roared, over and over. They sang the national anthem. When Perón reached out with "Workers!" They responded, "Yes, the people are here, we are the people." The dialogue begun that night with Argentina's popular classes would last until his death. Many workers had waited since noon for him in the sticky heat and had taken off their shirts – the "shirtless" – or "*descamisados*" – instantly becoming part of Perónist lore. After 17 October the balance of power had shifted; Perón was the central personality of Argentine political life, much stronger than before his arrest. When national elections were set for 24 February 1946 to determine finally the political and economic future of the country, the political polarization was complete.

Prebisch could not leave Argentina at a dramatic time like this, and he finally ventured into the political world of rallies and meetings because the future seemed at stake. He apologized to Triffin for reversing his decision again but underlined the depth of the political crisis and his need as a citizen to see it through personally in Buenos Aires. "My dear friend,"he wrote, "the current moment in which we are living in Argentina is very somber. Violence is in the air and we have serious doubts that the electoral process will unfold correctly. In any event the next months will have profound significance for the future of our country. Let us hope that the times return in which we can work together."[32] Perón's movement confronted the opposition Union Democratica, which grouped together an uneasy alliance of Radicals, Socialists, Communists, Conservatives, Progressive Democrats, and the vast majority of students. Teaching had been cancelled; the entire university, including Prebisch's faculty, was now closed indefinitely after the 1–5 October battle between students and police. Morales wrote from Guatemala on 16 November, pleading with Prebisch to come and work in any capacity he wished, including Central Bank general manager if he wished, but he replied that "unavoidable commitments prevented me leaving the capital. The present moment in which the country finds itself counsels staying here until the political horizon clears with the triumph of the democratic forces during the present hard fight."[33] He hoped against hope that the Democratic Union would prevail after all.

But to Prebisch's frustration, he was ineffectual because he remained identified with the old regime of the Concordancia, without credibility in opposing Perón. The "infamous decade" was now gone for good and universally criticized. Although his name remained a symbol of rectitude in the financial and banking communities, he had absolutely no political allies. Instead the left caricatured him as a creature of the Concordancia while nationalists of all stamps dismissed him as a co-author of the Roca-Runciman pact. He could only counter that he had simply been a technocrat in the service of the state and that the Prebisch team had performed an essential service in the interest of all Argentines. He could also argue that without his leadership in the Central Bank things would have been worse. His only recourse was to oppose Perón's economic plans, warning against inflation. At the opening session of his lectures on 24 April he had answered the rhetorical question, "How do you control inflation?" with the terse response: "Prevention." On 8 August the Economic Research Division of the Central Bank published a report that he helped prepare: it sharply criticized government policy protecting inefficient war industries. Similarly he supported the Alejandro E. Bunge Institute's work, which condemned the regime's economic policies, such as the doubling of government spending and the number of public employees since 1943, with a military establishment that had doubled in size, with a budget share that had risen from 27.8 percent to 50.7 percent in these three years. But such dry condemnations of inflation could not stem the political tide; none of it counted in the political climate of the day.

Each side leased a train for the campaign, with the Perónists naming theirs the "No-Shirt" (*El Descamisado*) versus "Victory" for the Democratic Union. One novelty of the campaign was that Eva Maria Duarte, Perón's partner since January 1944 (and wife from 22 October 1945), accompanied him on his tours of the country, the first time a spouse had campaigned openly with her husband. From the beginning the political initiative lay with Perón's movement rather than the Democratic Union because he succeeded in uniting a large coalition of diverse elements: the Church's revolt against liberalism; the neglected farm workers and urban masses; sections of the military; nationalists worried about foreign control of the economy; and people with negative memories of the Concordancia. Spruille Braden in Washington and the US Embassy in Buenos Aires also assisted Perón by their open and clumsy intervention: their attempt to undermine him with a so-called Blue Book alleging Perón's role as a Nazi agent during the war created instead a national backlash in his favour. Anti-US flyers blanketed the city: "Cowboy Braden, Tamer of South American Governments" and "Unite Against Wall Street Imperialism."[34]

The outcome of the February elections could not have been more depressing for Prebisch. He had seen the approaching defeat and realized that he had not grasped the raw power swelling up from below. The energy in the streets favoured Juan and Eva Perón rather than the democratic parties, which seemed middle-aged, middle class, and very much whiter. Alfredo Palacios's invocation of solidarity with the working class recalled an earlier generation when three-quarters of the city's labourers were first-generation Europeans; with his neatly trimmed moustache and finely crafted speeches he seemed a cultural world away from the new underclass born in the interior. The well-known women leaders of the Socialist Party, such as Alicia Moreau de Justo, had fought for decades for women's rights from the safety of Buenos Aires society. Perónist slogans such as "WORK-BOOTS, YES! BOOKS, NO!" were literally from a different social world, but Perón was mobilizing the proletariat in an effectively organized and visceral mass politics not seen before in Argentina. On 24 February his movement won an absolute majority with 56 percent of the popular vote; although there were irregularities the election had been free and fair enough to reflect the will of Argentina. Although to external observers the margin of victory appeared low, he had swept the country, winning majorities in both houses of Congress and taking all but one of the provincial legislatures. It was clear beyond all question that Perón had won a mandate and that there was now nothing standing in his way to implementing the revolution he planned for Argentina.

Perón's first decision as president-elect, even before his inauguration on 4 June 1946, was to nationalize the Central Bank. On 28 March outgoing President Farrell yielded to the electoral results and cooperated with Perón in preparing the necessary legislation and formal decrees of 24 May. Notwithstanding Prebisch's dismissal in 1943, the authority of Bosch and the reputation of the Bank had allowed it to maintain its original mandate of anchor of the financial system, protecting the state internationally by shielding it from the business cycle, and guarding it nationally through its autonomy from governments. As the most modern and developed of the Latin American central banks, it was also a touchstone of Argentine credibility within the international banking community. Perón was determined to recast the bank from guardian to servant of the state. It would be "democratized" rather than dismantled; it would support his program, or else. It would print money. "A magnificent system," Prebisch wrote to a Mexican friend, "has been dismantled overnight."[35]

The dream was over. Members of Prebisch's old team now looked elsewhere for employment, and his half-brother Gonzalo decided to accept a position with the US Federal Reserve. Raúl struggled to accept that his life work in Argentina was going to be destroyed.

10 Solitary Scholar

Prebisch felt even more isolated after Perón's election but just as determined to remain in Argentina. Friends abroad worried about his future and offered jobs. Robert Triffin had urged him to work in Guatemala, where "path-breaking reform" was possible, after which the political situation in Cuba might be stable enough to allow them to visit Havana.[1] Leo Welch had now returned to New York. "I have thought of you often in the changing panorama of Argentina these recent months," he wrote, "especially as I read the developments in connection with the Banco Central, a great institution fashioned under your hand. As we used to say in those chats in the quiet of your office overlooking the patio, 'how much better things could be done if they would let you and me do them,' and that goes for the international scene in many phases. It is so regrettable that the larger the task now a days, the smaller seems to be the stature of the man appointed to handle it."[2] As in the autumn of 1943, Mexico too responded like a true friend with Eduardo Villaseñor offering him a full-time appointment in the Bank of Mexico "if you do not encounter a solution to your life in your own country."[3] In his reply Raúl thanked him, admitting that these months were indeed "problematic" and would soon reveal the reality of the new regime. But while he noted that work in Mexico would offer "a solution to a difficult personal problem," he concluded that he had decided not to leave Argentina. "I still have the hope of continuing to work in my country, which would be very painful for me to leave."[4] He would contact Villasenor if it didn't work out, he said. The Government of Venezuela also contacted him, offering him the presidency of either the Central Bank or its new Development Corporation, whichever he preferred. But Prebisch declined the Venezuela offer as well; he had decided to remain in his home base in Buenos Aires and concentrate on writing and research. "Four centuries of Argentine blood flows in my veins," he remarked. If before the Perónist victory he had remained to fight and try to regain office, he was even more determined now to show both friends and enemies that he would ride out this mad period as an engaged and loyal citizen – that he would not cut and run after defeat and give the regime the satisfaction of cheering his exile. Despite his gloom following the nationalization of the Central Bank he wanted to retain his credibility in the capital.

He also had a strong following among his students – wonderful students like Aldo Ferrer, Norberto Gonzalez, and Manuel Balboa – who were committed to the seminar he had developed since resuming teaching in 1944.[5] These young men and women represented the next generation of public servants in Argentina and galvanized Prebisch's long-standing commitment to professionalizing the training of economics in his country. Especially now after the triumph of Perón, when the government would likely isolate the Faculty of Economic Sciences while privileging the natural and physical sciences, it seemed all the more important for him to remain teaching and strengthen scholarly linkages with universities abroad.

Raúl therefore took refuge in his research and teaching. To make ends meet he agreed to a four-day per month consultancy with Enrique Frankel, a wealthy German-Argentine wool merchant who sought an unobtrusive way to support Prebisch's scholarship. Raúl noted to Villaseñor that, "although I have avoided until recently entering into private activities, I have had to accept certain advisory jobs in industry which leave me with sufficient time to continue the theoretical work which captivated me after my first trip to Mexico."[6] In fact he had little to do; Frankel was Prebisch's private sector patron – making the only offer he ever received in Argentina after 1943 – and the modest financial security allowed him to concentrate on his research. Meanwhile Adelita lowered their household bills by growing vegetables and cutting expenditures. For news of US developments he could now count on "Gonzalito" (his stepbrother Julio Gonzalez del Solar, the orphaned nephew of his mother adopted into the Prebisch household as a child) who was installed at the Federal Reserve Board in Washington, and Gonzalo's wife June Eckard. Gonzalo worked with Triffin, who headed the Latin America section of the Board's International Affairs Division and who was also in touch with Harvard Professors Williams and Hansen. In this way Raúl had a conduit for discussing work in progress and obtaining recent publications in the field unavailable in Buenos Aires. The early death of Keynes on Easter Sunday 1946, immediately after the inaugural meeting of the IMF Board of Governors in March, lent an additional somber note to Raúl's mood as the Perónist period opened: now he would never meet the economist he had so admired.

Ironically the long interlude between the election and Perón's inauguration on 4 June witnessed a return to civil peace, providing a cooling-off period in which the country put aside political warfare and awaited the Revolution. The very decisiveness of Perón's victory stunned industrialists, journalists, professors, and other potential opponents into coming to terms with the new regime. Students now regretted their wholesale commitment to the Democratic Union; university strikes ended, buildings were repaired and classes were rescheduled to resume on 16 May. The press remained as free as during the election. Jews were relieved when it became clear that the US Embassy had misread the movement; Perón had no intention of touching them. For business it was clear that he had control over both houses of Congress and could implement far-reaching reforms regardless of the attitudes of the UIA or Sociedad Rural; the private sector decided to accentuate the positive.

Raúl and Adelita, like everyone else in Buenos Aires, watched with fascination as Juan Perón prepared to take office and move with Eva into the Incue Palace. Every president since Uriburu had lived within the gold and ivory walls of its 283 rooms, but none compared with this couple who had emerged from the people. Perón was named general to mark his inauguration, and Eva, or "Evita," projected an indefinable charisma inside a daring silver gown that stunned high society. She was twenty-six, half his age, and together they were a force. The new government promised a five-year plan by November, leaving some additional months of uncertainty regarding the future of Argentina. Perón had indeed inherited a prize, because Argentina in 1946 had one of the strongest economies in the world and was ideally placed to prosper during postwar reconstruction. Gold and foreign-exchange reserves totalled 1,688 million pesos, and the foreign-trade surplus was larger than the entire import bill of 3,555 billion pesos. Perón was himself surprised by the wealth at his disposal. "We have the Central Bank full of gold," he said, "and we don't know where to put any more. The passages are full of piles of gold."[7] While Prebisch and others had complained about misuse of funds after 4 June 1943, Argentina was flush with income in a postwar economy that needed its products and for which it could charge premium prices.

In this political hiatus Prebisch's seminar from 16 May to 7 July was his most successful since leaving the Bank. Devoted to Keynes's *General Theory of Employment, Interest and Money*, it offered students an introduction and guide to the work of Keynes without attempting an alternative model for understanding development problems in Latin America. Prebisch's research had progressed far enough for him to appreciate the importance of Keynes's theoretical framework, but he was not convinced that it was adequate for what he had begun to call "the periphery," a term that had entered his correspondence with colleagues during 1945. These ten lectures, however, were more sought after than he had supposed, because Latin American students everywhere in the region still lacked a Spanish-language introduction to the work of this British scholar who had dominated the intellectual economic landscape for the past decade.

The Central Bank of Venezuela had been pursuing Prebisch since early 1944, repeatedly suggesting some form of collaboration. When he could not accept its invitation for a consultancy in mid-1946 the Venezuelans offered to publish his Keynes material in successive issues of the Central Bank Bulletin beginning in January 1947 for a lump-sum payment of 1,500 pesos. Daniel Cosío Villegas in Mexico, who was informed of this offer, invited Prebisch to prepare a revised manuscript for wider publication as *Introduction to Keynes.*[8]

The Keynes book would strengthen Prebisch's academic recognition beyond Argentina, and he agreed to a contract with the Fondo de Cultura Economica, but it was an additional obligation, which meant postponing the theoretical work he had set for himself in the *Money and the Rhythm of Economic Activity* proposal he had drafted more than two years earlier. Triffin was already asking in January 1946 when this book would be ready. But his research was proceeding well, with Gonzalo keeping him up to date on developments in Washington, and with a regular correspondence with colleagues such as Triffin and Victor Urquidi counteracting somewhat his isolation in Buenos Aires. A steady stream of research material reached him from journals and other sources unavailable in Argentina, and Prebisch became dependent on this interchange of ideas with his letters occasionally reaching article length. ("Would you like to chat about liquidity preferences?" he would begin, for example, with Urquidi.)[9]

Progress in his work made him reluctant to undertake external consultancies, but there was one trip that he could not turn down during summer 1946. The Bank of Mexico invited him to participate in an important event – the first Central Bank Conference of the Americas, a meeting of experts from most countries in the Western Hemisphere to deepen the wartime collaboration promoted since 1941 by the US Federal Reserve and the Bank of Mexico, among others. Mexico viewed itself as the interlocutor state between Latin America and the US. Urquidi was secretary of the conference, with a particular responsibility for editing the proceedings and guiding the work of a proposed "Permanent Committee" to ensure that Latin American and US central bankers remained active together despite the return of peace. Held from 15 to 30 August, the event featured key economists and experts in the field from the Americas and was therefore an opportunity for Prebisch to meet friends after a long period in the distant Southern Cone. In Buenos Aires *La Nacion* twitted the regime by noting Mexico's invitation to Prebisch and calling him "the most authoritative expert in issues of banking and finance in the American continent."[10]

The Mexico Conference was a success in convening for the first time a group of inter-American experts, including Canadians, on a technical subject of major importance. Prebisch's address at the meeting, "Panorama General de los Problemas de Regulación Monetaria y Crediticia en el Continente Americano," dealt with managing development and financial stability in the postwar business cycle and offered an opportunity to employ the terms "periphery" for Latin America, and "centro ciclico" for the US.[11] Apart from seeing his Mexican friends he met key Latin American economists from other countries, including José Antonio Mayobre and Manuel Perez Guerrero of Venezuela, Felipe Pazos of Cuba, and Jorge del Canto of Chile; they in turn recognized Prebisch's leadership abilities. But while interesting papers were presented within an agreeable networking environment, the Permanent Committee formed at the close of the meeting to develop permanent connections and regular events proved stillborn. By August 1946 inter-American cooperation, which had evolved during the Second World War, fell victim to the Cold War. The attention of the US was monopolized by the evident breakdown of relations with Moscow in Europe. Not only did Washington now focus its primary attention on Europe and Asia rather than strategically safe Latin America, but also whatever US interest did remain after the war was being recast along orthodox economic and security lines. Latin American hopes for regional multilateralism and cooperative development proved premature. One casualty in Washington was Americas Day; that celebration abruptly disappeared after 1945. In effect the US and Canada withdrew into the northern clubs of NATO and then GATT, leaving US-Latin American relations to develop in traditional bilateral "business-as-usual" terms.

The duration of the Mexican trip expanded as requests for side visits accumulated before his departure. En route to Mexico City he met Manuel Noriega Morales for thirty minutes in the Guatemala City airport and was persuaded to return immediately after the conference for ten days. He was also urged by the US Federal Reserve representatives (Woodlief Thomas and Henry Wallich attended in the absence of Triffin, who was on mission in Western Europe) to advise the Dominican banking authorities for several weeks beginning 13 September. While in Santo Domingo he devoted equal energy to the related goal of designing the new Faculty of Economics at the national university to train Dominican students to the MA level and link these young professionals with other Latin American colleagues. When he arrived there was not a single post-secondary institution for training economists in the entire country; Prebisch's plan sought to correct the inadequacies of his own faculty in Buenos Aires, such as its "lack of mental discipline and doctrinaire routines" with poorly paid and motivated professors regurgitating foreign texts. "That the Dominican Republic does not have an existing institution for Economic Studies represents a certain advantage," he noted. "It permits learning from the experience of other Latin American countries which have confronted this problem for a long time. The experience has been poor, as in Argentina, where despite a quarter century of a Faculty of Economics, it has not made a serious contribution to economic theory. Moreover it has not even achieved what one might have expected in laying the basis for knowledge: a systematic empirical description of the data and existing economic conditions in each country."[12] Between visiting Guatemala and the Dominican Republic, Raúl and Adelita had two days in Havana, where they relaxed at the magnificent Hotel Nacional on the Malécon seawall.

Raúl and Adelita arrived home in Buenos Aires on 15 October. Since their departure the initial glow marking Perón's inauguration had given way to polarization, and Prebisch faced a hostile political climate as the resumption of his seminar approached. Before he left the press still was independent; by now government controls had tightened. Already on 8 November he wrote to Urquidi, "I began my classes in the Faculty and had to stop after a few days. They are probably the last ... I guess that the ultimate purpose of the [Perónist] reforms is to get rid of all professors who do not agree with the regime. I believe that I will have to resign if the Government is successful in introducing its project." On 26 November Perón invited the workers of the city to the Colon Theatre, where he presented his five-year plan wearing an undershirt. He was, he declared, their first worker, and the new economy would be theirs. Prebisch knew and loathed the author of the plan, José M. Figuerola, a Spanish exile who had arrived in 1930 after the fall of the corporatist dictatorship of General Miguel Primo de Rivera. Prebisch thought the man was a blithering idiot. "My dear friend," Raúl confided to Daniel Cosío Villegas after he had read the plan, "I have nothing good to say about my country. Both the political orientation and Five Year Plan worry me, and without any positive sign on the horizon."[13] But Perón's political power continued to grow. On 27 January Evita announced on national radio that a law giving women the vote would soon be passed; earlier, in September 1946, she had installed herself in Perón's old office in the Ministry of Labour. Prebisch observed ruefully that the regime had succeeded in capturing important causes long neglected by the Concordancia to solidify its political base. Perón had also promised full employment at any cost. He would be hard to displace.

The 1946 five-year plan was Prebisch's nightmare. The Central Bank was now in the hands of Miguel Miranda, also head of the Industrial Credit Fund and appointed as Perón's chair of the Economic Council and president of the new IAPI (Institute for Production and Trade), which bore no relation to the CAPI – the export promotion body that Prebisch created in 1941. The son of a poor Spanish immigrant family who had made a fortune by supplying tin-plate to the burgeoning food-processing industry protected during the war, in Prebisch's view he would be a disaster as Perón's new economic czar, using the Central Bank as an instrument of industrialization without checks and balances. Henceforth no private banks could provide credit without Central Bank approval, while it undertook the financing of Perón's five-year plan. In effect it became Perón's vehicle for transforming the economy with easy credit to industry behind a labour-intensive, low-technology industrial strategy to promote full employment. High protective tariffs inherited from the war years were maintained to preserve internationally uncompetitive sectors; since any firm could now draw easy credit, bankruptcies plunged. Although politically popular on the short term, this policy rewarded inefficient firms and spelled long-term trouble.

Signs of trouble were already apparent in 1946. Money supply had doubled between 1943 and 1946; the military portion of the budget rose to 50.7 percent in 1946 from 27.8 percent four years earlier. Government spending and the number of public servants doubled. This was not "inward development" as Prebisch had envisaged it in his 1943 *Money and the Rhythm of Economic Activity*. He had endorsed liberal capitalism within a mixed economy, private sector leadership, and a balance between import protection and export promotion. Caution and prudent state management would be required to curb inflation and postwar instability, ensure the imports of essential goods, weed out inefficient war industries, and strengthen exports, beginning with neighbouring countries.

As Perón consolidated his power it became clear that the points of commonality with Prebisch were superficial; both were nationalists, but they were radically different in style and ideology. Both supported import substitution, but for Prebisch balance and caution ruled, while Perón was extreme. Perón's idea of all-out state-led industrialization, consisting of protective tariffs, subsidies, and low-interest loans through printing money, guaranteed a bloated public sector, heavy military spending, and an inflationary spiral. Prebisch endorsed an activist state using the full range of tariffs and other tools used by other trading countries, but only within a global and competitive liberal framework. Perón's model led to a corporatist and nationalist state with a command economy supported by the industrial masses and uncompetitive small industries created in the thousands throughout the country since the Great Depression. Prebisch's vision was of Argentina as a full participant in the international economy, including the IMF, and he thrived on international linkages with foreign banks and admired the US Federal Reserve. Perón boycotted the Bretton Woods Conference, denounced Anglo-American imperialism, and suppressed dissent. For Prebisch an arms-length, autonomous Central Bank was crucial because its mixed private-public structure gave it a source of power outside the control of the political executive; Perón's vision could not tolerate such a source of countervailing power and therefore required full control of the Argentine Central Bank. As he watched the dynamic of Perónism, Prebisch realized that his nightmare of Argentina becoming a "water-tight compartment" in isolation from the international community was becoming a reality.

Prebisch's worries prompted him to let down his guard with his Mexican publisher Daniel Cosío Villegas, a rare event that revealed the strength of their friendship. He was concerned about depression. "There are times when adversity finally gets the better of one," he confided. "You help me to fight against this tendency."[14] He was starved intellectually in Buenos Aires as Perónism undermined the rich cultural life of the city, although he remained active on the editorial board of a new publication, *Realidad.* Julio Gonzalez del Solar and his wife June were leaving Washington to work in Guatemala for a year with Manuel Noriega Morales as part of an ongoing technical assistance project with the US Federal Reserve. The prospect of publishing his *Introduction to Keynes* and preparing the final revisions of the manuscripts kept Raúl active and engaged despite the tense circumstances in Buenos Aires. Victor Urquidi helped also, with a generous dedication of time to a correspondence without which Prebisch would have been even more isolated. His letters at the opening of 1947 underlined his optimism that his research "on money and the business cycle from the perspective of countries in the economic periphery (as Argentina) and the circulation of income between them and the cyclical centres" was progressing well. He commented in January, for example, that "I hope to finish the fundamental part of my research during the present year." Prebisch felt increasingly confident that he was on the right track in pressing beyond Keynes.[15]

While he applauded Keynes for turning the free-market chain of causation on its head in his attack on the guardians of orthodoxy, Prebisch felt that Keynes had gone only half the distance in explaining the dilemma of countries outside the core economies. In fact, Keynes was not nearly as radical a thinker as many thought. "If Keynesian economics does not explain the reality of cycles, how does one explain the reality?"[16] Prebisch thought that Keynes, despite his elegance, did not break sufficiently from the premises of neoclassical work. In a sense he respected him more as a policymaker than an economist; from the perspective of developing countries, Keynes's contribution was important but not a qualitative step beyond the "Teutonic stubbornness" of mainstream US economists such as Gottfried von Haberler, whose fixation with equilibrium theory could not be dented. Victor Urquidi, who was in an argument with Haberler over a paper co-authored with one of his friends who was currently his student at Harvard, agreed sympathetically. For developing countries there was "always disequilibrium," he noted.[17] The focus of research by economists in the periphery, therefore, should not be on the problems facing developed economies like the US but rather on the nature and causes of the differential impact of business cycles on the centre and periphery. Urquidi was now the editor of Mexico's prestigious *Trimestre Economica*, published by the Fondo de Cultura Económica, and he detected a growing interest in Prebisch's area of study. Rutledge Vining's new article in *Econometrica* on the region as a concept in business cycle theory contained the seeds of a centre-periphery approach. Charles Kindleberger had written another suggestive article, "Planning for Foreign Investment," in the *American Economic Review*, which proposed that agricultural exporters were at a disadvantage compared with industrial exporters in international trade. The news of this new work both stimulated and worried Prebisch, who was concerned about falling behind competitors in the isolation of Buenos Aires and being pre-empted in his work.[18]

For this reason Prebisch perplexed his friends by his continuing refusal on principle to visit US universities; they were dumbfounded by his argument that such a visit would show weakness and undermine his credibility in Buenos Aires. Perón's relations with Washington were strained, to be sure, but Prebisch's prospects were sufficiently minimal that it seemed quixotic to mount a grand gesture of national loyalty at such high personal cost. Thus he declined an invitation from Princeton's Institute for Advanced Study to participate in a seminar on central banking built around the leading academic authorities in the field, as well as the Federal Reserve and Wall Street, such as Ragnar Nurske, Jacob Viner, Oscar Morgenstern, Friedrich Lutz, Woodlief-Thomas, and experts of similar quality. Princeton issued the invitation on the recommendation of the Americans who had attended the Bank of Mexico Conference in August, noting its disappointment that Prebisch's anticipated trip two years before had fallen through and "the hope of making up lost ground this time by making us your headquarters in the US. Because of your outstanding position you could visit the country, it seems to me, either as scholar, central banker, or man of affairs."[19] Prebisch was clearly tempted. He badly needed support, and therefore replied that he would very much enjoy the intellectual climate of

Princeton compared with Buenos Aires. "Here the possibilities are rather narrow, as very few people devote themselves to study and research ... But," he added, "this is not the proper time."[20]

In retrospect a research trip to Princeton was precisely what Prebisch needed, because he soon fell into a debilitating depression that lasted throughout most of the year. Everything seemed to go wrong although at first the outlook appeared positive. On 12 February he had described his upcoming lectures as "bringing together the results of his patient theoretical work for the first time."[21] A week later he was even more optimistic in a letter written from Mar del Plata to his employer, Frankel. "My theoretical work should now continue without interruption since I am persuaded that my conclusions differ substantially from conventional approaches to economic theory," he noted. "My work therefore has a certain significance and should progress rapidly without further delays."[22] He even bought land in Mar del Plata, a large lot at the end of a dead-end street, which compensated somewhat for the loss of his garden at 134 Rivera Indarte. Time was short; the next months would be decisive and he absolutely had to finish his writing project.

But his academic position became increasingly fragile, and pressures multiplied. He no longer published articles in the faculty journal and finally resigned on 26 June 1947, ostensibly for health reasons. Despite the friendly attitude of the government watchdogs Pedro José Arrighi and Dean Eugenio Blanco, the university had included his name on a list of Perónist supporters, and he resigned when it refused to remove it. The Faculty of Economic Sciences had been his last remaining institutional base, and he now faced a future in the capital as nothing more than a solitary scholar. Prebisch also became physically ill, unable to work for weeks as the depression deepened. He spent more time at Mar del Plata; his research lagged, and he felt old. Raúl's friends saw it simply as exhaustion, as the inevitable aftermath of his disappointment over the Central Bank and the intense period of writing and work on Keynes after his busy 1946 trip to Mexico, Central America, and the Caribbean.

The news from Urquidi in Mexico was also deflating. On 2 March 1947 he wrote Raúl that he would be out of Mexico for some time on a World Bank mission. In fact he was leaving the Bank of Mexico for a permanent job with this new and expanding international organization because work conditions in Mexico had deteriorated. A new president had been installed by the PRI, with Miguel Aleman Valdes replacing General Manuel Avila Camacho, and he had immediately replaced Eduardo Villaseñor with a party hack determined to curb the autonomy of the Central Bank. Urquidi was already well known despite his youth, and it was not surprising that the new World Bank would try to lure him to Washington. Urquidi had "long resisted the temptation" to move to the US capital, as he put it; he agreed with Prebisch on the need for Latin Americans to remain in their countries and develop strong and independent research centres without which Latin American priorities would not be addressed. The two had exchanged plans of study for such centres when Raúl was putting together his final recommendations for the design of the School of Economic Research in the Dominican Republic.[23] Urquidi for his part was active with UNAM (National Autonomous University) in modernizing its curriculum.

But now Urquidi was gone, another loss to Latin America as the UN, World Bank, and IMF extracted the best talent from the region. The attractions were obvious: as Urquidi noted, "It will be a valuable experience and a new stage of my education, plus an opportunity to realize in real life things which in Mexico we only discuss in theory." For Raúl his departure was a personal blow, because he felt Latin America was being denuded of the talent required to balance the power of industrial countries. Moreover Urquidi's move to Washington was seductive, pulling at him also. "I do not lose the hope," Victor had written, "that before long you will join us here – there is a place for you here. I have heard great praise of you in this bank from people, including those who do not know you personally, who would not hesitate to invite you if you would agree to come," and he reeled off the names of friends already in Washington – Felipe Pazos (Cuba), Javier Marquez (Mexico), Triffin, Grove and Wallich, Jorge del Canto, and others.[24]

In 1947, however, there were fewer requests and international invitations, and for the first time a fear of permanent marginalization took hold of Prebisch. Triffin had been assigned to European affairs, and now Prebisch's happy correspondence with Urquidi was likely to end. He was in the cursed position of being a solitary scholar on the shelf while younger colleagues were moving ahead quickly and doing interesting things: Urquidi's account of his "fantastic" trip around the world on a World Bank consultative mission left Raúl envious – bearing in mind that Victor lamented his absence in Singapore when his wife Marjorie bore their first child. But even in that department Prebisch was falling back: not a single baby had materialized in the fifteen years of his marriage with Adelita.

During this dead and lonely period of 1947 Prebisch's only new professional direction was provided by the Brazilian economist Eugenio Gudin, a former minister of finance and director-general of the Getulio Vargas Foundation in Rio de Janeiro. They met when Gudin visited Buenos Aires in May and felt an immediate mutual respect, thereby establishing for Prebisch a personal link with the emerging regional powerhouse that had overtaken Argentina as the economic leader of South America after the

Second World War. President Vargas had resigned on 29 October 1945 after fifteen years in power, the same year as Argentina's military government. But what a different legacy Vargas had left Brazil compared with the Concordancia in Argentina! In comparing notes on the fortunes of their countries and particularly the growing problem of inflation in Argentina, Prebisch commented that his government was "elaborating new themes which so far I cannot fathom," but "to judge by their results which we are experiencing it is highly improbable that the genial Miranda will achieve the stature in Argentine economic history which he has already claimed."[25] Cultured and humorous, Gudin was equally irreverent. Brazil had an equally poor minister, he said, but inflation was coming under control through the intervention of the Blessed Virgin Mary – or rather two Marys: Our Lady of [low] Imports, with the help of Our Lady of [tight] Credit.[26] Each spoke his own language while listening to the other's Spanish or Portuguese; they got along famously.

Despite the backdrop of long-standing Argentine-Brazil rivalry, Prebisch was remembered favourably in Rio from his Central Bank days; both Gudin and Brazil's other leading economist Otavio Gouvea de Bulhões, another self-taught economist and the powerful director of the Division of Economic and Financial Studies in the Ministry of Finance, solicited his advice as Brazil moved toward the creation of a central bank; Bulhões had already written Prebisch some months earlier for his comments on a provisional concept paper on this project. Prebisch had responded with the advice one could expect of a veteran banker: "I believe that the success of a Central Bank lies, in great measure, in knowing when it is prudent to take preventive measures ... to control the improper expansion of credit."[27] But while he gave Bulhões credit for clear, precise, and logical work, he also questioned his extreme orthodoxy, an excessively doctrinaire neoclassical orientation toward any interventionist policies such as import controls. He asked Bulhões why he ruled them out for Brazil on a priori grounds while admitting that they had worked in Argentina during the 1930s. Gudin, in contrast, was a typical representative of the old Brazilian governing class, with a strong dose of classical education and healthy pragmatism within an essentially conservative mindset not dissimilar from Prebisch's. Both men were stern, but they shared a willingness to listen; only later did their underlying differences come to the fore.

After meeting Prebisch in Buenos Aires, Gudin wrote on 2 July inviting him to spend two months at the Getulio Vargas Foundation as a guest participant in a seminar on banking and monetary policy. The seminar would analyse the government's proposal for its new Central Bank to ensure the most suitable legislation in the hope of submitting it to Congress at the end of the calendar year. Harvard's Gottfried von Haberler had also been invited and already confirmed his attendance at the seminar. Gudin mentioned that Haberler already knew of Gudin's invitation to Prebisch and that he was very keen to meet Raúl. In the interests of Argentine-US equity both foreign economists would be asked to complete a paper during the stay in Rio for publication in the Foundation's new *Brazilian Journal of Economics.* Both were invited to bring their spouses, both would receive the same honorarium, and both would have suitable quarters at the gracious Gloria Hotel.

If only for the sake of meeting Haberler, Prebisch should have leapt at the invitation. Haberler had worked with the League of Nations in Geneva between 1934 and 1936 as an expert in its Financial Section; then he joined Harvard's Economics Department and was appointed an expert to the board of governors of the Federal Reserve System during 1943–44. Altogether he was considered one of the most formidable authorities on international trade theory and the business cycle, particularly for his reformulation of the basic theory of comparative cost in terms of modern general equilibrium theory. Two months with Haberler would have afforded an ideal opportunity for Prebisch to debate head-on with one of the foremost scholars in the field and therefore to test and strengthen his emerging structuralist critique of equilibrium theory. Altogether it would have been an unusual confrontation between rivals with completely different background strengths: professional economist vs recognized practitioner; theoretical vs applied; deductive vs intuitive; industrialized vs developing country experience; refereed journals vs central bank reports; and prestige US universities vs Buenos Aires.

But again, as with Princeton, Prebisch declined the invitation. He acknowledged the unusual intellectual opportunity to work with Haberler, Bulhões, and Gudin; moreover Rio was close, a relatively easy flight, and a most agreeable city. But his health would not permit travel of any sort, he claimed.[28] Although he offered the prospect of coming for one month rather than two (to which Gudin responded favourably), he continued to postpone. "There is the risk of a relapse to stage one if I return prematurely to active work," he would explain, while complaining of lost time. "I have been afflicted, unfortunately, when I am in full theoretical flight."[29] Despite a lengthy correspondence, Prebisch never did visit Rio during the next two years, nor did Gudin – despite repeated attempts – succeed in including any work from Prebisch in the *Brazilian Journal of Economics.*

The nature of Prebisch's illness during 1947 remained obscure, although it was certainly debilitating and forced him on a strict regime of exercise and diet. His general pessimism was reinforced by the early death of his long-time friend Klein, while many others were now leaving Argentina. It is possible that he still felt too uncertain theoretically to test his findings against the certain attacks of Haberler and Bulhões. His judgement wavered. In a letter to his Venezuelan friend Xavier Lope Bello, he criticized Keynes's work with the fantastic prediction that "I believe that his contribution to economic theory will not be noteworthy on the long-term."[30] But what is certain is that he struggled with his health and work until November, when the University of Buenos Aires pleaded for his return and the minister of education asked him to head and edit a new *Journal of Economic Theory* for the newly created Academy of Economic Sciences. The minister, the prominent surgeon Dr Oscar Ivanisevich, wanted Prebisch back and refused to accept his resignation. "I want you to stay," he said. "This government will not retaliate against any professors who do not share its views unless they make politics in their classes."[31] Political repression was growing in Argentina, and Prebisch had been forced to cancel a public lecture a month earlier in October, but he accepted the academic opening immediately and got to work on the new journal with a call for papers. His mysterious illness vanished with the prospect of regaining a community of scholars: "I am returning after a long absence," he noted to his students on 16 March 1948, "having experienced what the Faculty means for my study and research."[32] Indeed he even toyed briefly with the idea of seeking the deanship of the faculty to introduce a series of reforms that in any case he had decided to discuss during his first lecture.

Prebisch's energy flooded back, and he now complained to Gudin about overwork rather than enforced idleness, but in a new tone of optimism and mounting excitement. On 10 February 1948 he underlined the "critical challenge" that he now faced in bringing out the *Journal of Economic Theory* – completing an article on what he called "a dynamic theory of the economy ... on which I have been working diligently during the last years." It was far from complete, he told Gudin. "I am therefore fully preoccupied with the task of synthesis and this requires an effort of analysis and clarity which is more time-consuming than simply writing. Despite my eight hours of work a day I am not even close to finishing."[33] While Prebisch struggled, Gudin was successful in launching his journal in Rio; the first issue was delivered from the Brazilian Embassy by courier on 5 November, and he deluged Prebisch with requests to write a piece for the second.

Although Prebisch continued to line up authors during the January-February 1948 summer holidays and prepared his lectures for his return seminar in the faculty, both tasks took time away from his research at a moment when he felt close to a breakthrough. "I am now very advanced in my work ... on the economic cycle and dynamic theory of the economy; I have dedicated almost all my time in the hope of soon initiating some preliminary publications," he wrote on 23 February in turning down a lecture tour in El Salvador. "The interruption of this work, therefore, is extremely concerning."[34] He also responded negatively to a request from Princeton asking for copies of his Bank of Mexico papers and recent seminar notes at the faculty. He wanted to avoid their circulation, he said. "The reason is simple," he explained. "In large part they represent initial points of view regarding money and the business cycle in countries like our own. This work has taken place over some four years. During this period I have continued my research in these areas and my views have evolved considerably, and for this reason I decided some time ago to bury these preliminary observations which no longer accurately reflect my thinking."[35] In fact this correspondence with Princeton only reminded him of how little progress he had made over the past year when he had assured his US colleagues there that "I hope to finish the fundamental part of my work during the present year." The anticipated breakthrough, however, did not occur during 1948 either as the roller-coaster ride of Perón's Argentina continued. Prebisch quickly found that his return to the university was short-lived as ministers changed and the political climate again deteriorated. Without Dr Ivanisevich in the Cabinet the universities were vulnerable, and a predictable economic downturn sharpened political tension in the capital.

By the end of 1948 the short-lived Perónist prosperity was over: inflation exceeded 50 percent, the trade balance had become negative, and foreign exchange was running low. Argentina's huge wartime foreign exchange reserves were also gone, sunk into the purchase of many worthless foreign companies, such as the deficit-ridden and worn-out British-owned railways and trolley lines. Widening corruption, including kickbacks to Miguel Miranda himself, contributed to dissent and polarization. So visible a figure as Prebisch was not likely to survive the accompanying crackdown as Perón moved to contain the opposition and prolong his regime by amending the Constitution, and although Raúl completed his seminar during the fall semester without incident, increasing Perónist intervention in university life augured poorly for his future. Arrighi demanded that he include the virtues of the five-year plan in his lectures; Prebisch flatly refused. The proposed new *Journal of Economic Theory* collapsed; the exile of Argentine professionals intensified.

This situation in Buenos Aires was a factor, along with financial need, that prompted Prebisch to accept the long-standing invitation of the Venezuelan Central Bank to visit Caracas and draft a report on banking policy.[36] It took him out of Buenos Aires during July 1948, giving him a rest from the growing worry over its economic decline, and a fabulous $4,000 honorarium provided a welcome cushion in inflationary and uncertain times. The trip also meant the companionship of his Venezuelan friends Manuel Perez Guerrero and José Antonio Mayobre, both of whom enjoyed the luxury of working in democratic Venezuela, which had become a destination for Argentines no longer able to work freely at home. En route Prebisch stopped off in Trinidad and Tobago, his first visit to the Anglophone Caribbean.

Completing his work in Caracas on 28 July, he returned to Buenos Aires to continue his research and prepare for the spring seminar. By October the situation in the University was so fragile that only the continuing presence of Arrighi stood between him and dismissal. But then Arrighi was replaced. On 15 November his successor advised Prebisch that on Perón's personal orders he had the choice of resigning or being fired; the next morning he submitted a letter of resignation ending twenty years of involvement with the University of Buenos Aires. This new disaster coincided with genuine advance in his research and therefore could not have occurred at a worse time. Prebisch's Venezuelan consultancy had already been costly in breaking the tempo of his work, and now he faced a more serious interruption in his career since he saw no early return to democracy in Argentina. He was extremely reluctant to leave Buenos Aires, which was not just his home but also a city with an incomparable urban culture. Adelita was recovering from surgery. He was also on the wrong side of forty-five, and though he was not immediately threatened personally by Perónism, that could not be ruled out in the future. However meagre, his four-day per month consultancy with Frankel remained as a first step in rebuilding a secure income. Eventually Perónism would end; when it collapsed he wanted to be available for the rebuilding of the Argentine state. But at the same time there was no place for him in public life under Perónism, and his research depended on some sort of audience and institutional base. "Never again do I want to find myself in the miserable position of the solitary scholar," he remarked four days after his resignation.[37] It therefore seemed inevitable that Prebisch would have to accept some sort of work outside Argentina.

He mused at the good fortune of US academics, who were able to work in predictable circumstances without the constant financial, political, and security worries that cannibalized time for research and writing. Nevertheless, unlike a year earlier, Prebisch was sufficiently confident of his work that he had faith in its eventual success. On 20 December he wrote to Gudin confident that he was close to completion and gave a brief synthesis of his approach and findings. "I believe that the cycle is the typical form of growth in the capitalist economy, and that it is subject to certain laws of movement quite different than the laws of equilibrium. In these laws of movement the disparity between the timing of the productive process on the one hand and the resulting circulation of money on the other plays a fundamental role." This had long been his central argument, but he had lacked a methodological approach powerful enough to critique general equilibrium theory. Now he felt on surer ground. "I have therefore tried to introduce systematically the concepts of time and space in economic theory ... It is precisely the concept of space which has allowed me to study the movement in the centre and periphery, not in the spirit of introducing formal deductions, but to signal functional differences of transcendental importance." Still he provided no details, and Gudin was understandably perplexed. While he accepted Prebisch as a gifted colleague, Raúl had given few clues so far regarding his much-proclaimed challenge to conventional economic theories. A certain credibility gap was appearing. Prebisch had not published in any major economic journal on this topic, and his book on Keynes did not lead far in this direction either. Would Prebisch limit his argument to business cycle theory, or would he include other areas such as the terms of trade between the industrial centres and primary resource exporters? Gudin didn't know. He did not have a copy of Prebisch's 1948 draft seminar texts and pleaded for his paper by 15 March 1949 to include in his journal.

In practice Prebisch found that there was little time for anything other than coping with day-to-day uncertainties in Buenos Aires, and Gudin once again was ignored. But Mexico was as loyal as ever. The National School of Economics at UNAM had developed an international seminar series featuring senior personalities including Haberler, Schumpeter, Hansen, and Ludwig Von Mises, and had invited Prebisch on 6 May for a possible July visit. He had not accepted, given his Venezuela commitment, but when UNAM heard of his resignation it renewed the invitation and this time Prebisch was delighted. He agreed to a series of lectures over a ten-day period beginning 16 February 1949, viewing the trip as an opportunity to concentrate fully on his research and finally deliver the elusive synthesis on the business cycle from the perspective of the Latin America periphery. "I am very pleased to have the opportunity of presenting my ideas in your country," he wrote to Jesus Silva Herzog. "In truth I carry an old and deep affection for Mexico, strengthened further now by your again extending a welcoming hand at a time of serious worry – just as you did several years back."[38] Of course success in Mexico would also complete his commitment to Gudin and yield a chapter for a festschrift in honour of John H. Williams being put together by the James Williams School of Economics at the University of Virginia and featuring an eclectic but stellar group of contributors ranging from Paul Baran, Robert Triffin, and Henry Wallich to

Paul Samuelson, Richard Musgrave, and Charles Kindleberger. Prebisch was the only economist approached from a developing country, and his proposed title ("Monetary Problems of the Peripheral Countries") obviously coincided with his forthcoming Mexican work.[39]

While the Mexican visit did not solve Prebisch's long-term problem it admirably met his immediate research needs: "After that, we'll see," he noted on 13 December, when the details had been finalized with UNAM.[40] Certain US friends also rallied. The US State Department invited him for a three-month lecture tour of business administration schools, presumably with the idea that the tour would yield a university appointment. This was arranged through the intercession of Chris Ravndal, who had now returned to Washington as director-general of the US Foreign Service. "It's the least we can do for him," he noted internally.[41] However the invitation carried a per diem of only $10, and with no itinerary arranged in advance Prebisch saw little real potential in joining a growing group of Latin Americans wandering like a mendicants from one US university to the next, taking whatever they could get. Within Latin America his options for permanent employment had also narrowed. Although in 1946 the Mexican Central Bank had made him a standing offer to join them any time he wished, this open invitation vanished with the advent that autumn of the Aleman presidency. More recently Venezuela had reiterated its offer for Prebisch to work in the institution of his choice – either the Central Bank or the Development Corporation. But that was with the democratic government of President Romulo Gallegas, and he was overthrown in a military coup on 24 November, sending Raúl's trusted friends Mayobre and Perez Guerrero fleeing Caracas in search of international jobs. Paraguay was also in flames, and Pedretti had been driven out of the country; it was as if everything Prebisch tried in Latin America was fated to fail. For the first time he resigned himself to working outside Argentina.

Fortunately he had two offers. First, the United Nations had been almost annoying in its attempts to enlist him in 1948. Already in February Ralph Bunche had surprised Prebisch by his invitation to join the three-person Preparatory Economic Group proposed by the UN Palestine Commission. Although flattered that anyone remembered him from his old League of Nations days, he had no interest in the position and turned it down. Later that year, with the creation of ECLA (Economic Commission for Latin America, or CEPAL [Comisión económica para América Latina]) on 15 February 1948, he was again approached by the UN to head the agency as its founding Executive Secretary.[42] Assistant Secretary-General for Economic Affairs David Owen and Assistant Secretary for Public Affairs Benjamin Cohen (whom Prebisch had met during their student years), considered Prebisch the logical candidate for executive secretary, and they persuaded UN Secretary-General Trygve Lie to approach him. In July, shortly before Raúl's trip to Venezuela, Trygvie Lie sent Cohen to Buenos Aires with a formal offer, while Owen spoke with him extensively on the telephone. A member of the French UN delegation approached him, seeking his consent for France to nominate him for the position. The tiny secretariat of ECLA in Santiago, Chile, was enthusiastic at the prospect; Acting Executive Secretary Eugenio Castillo was an Edward G. Robinson figure from Cuba, complete with wife Patricia Willis from the US South and widely believed in Latin America to have links with the US intelligence community, and he travelled to Buenos Aires in August urging Prebisch to accept. Even Perón agreed, no doubt hoping that he would soon be rid of a troublesome foe. But Prebisch had read about the creation of ECLA in the newspapers with indifference. He was not interested; he remembered the old blundering League of Nations from his Geneva days and the marginal role that developing countries such as Argentina had played in its deliberations. The title "Executive Secretary" also suggested a weak role in a subordinate agency far from power in New York with merely administrative responsibilities; he thought that ECLA would have neither power nor influence in an orbit dominated by Washington. "I am very disappointed," Castillo confided to UN headquarters in New York.[43] But he did not give up. As if to demonstrate its vulnerability, ECLA still had not rented a building or space of its own; its provisional quarters remained the fifteenth floor of the Hotel Carrera in downtown Santiago, and the new organization faced a vacuum of leadership. It was therefore not surprising that Castillo was soon knocking again on Prebisch's door; Raúl and Adelita found themselves entertaining Eugenio Castillo on 19 November in the midst of turmoil in the faculty, pleading with him to work with ECLA: if he couldn't come to Santiago on a permanent basis, could he at least give them some months of his time? Pestered interminably by Castillo, he agreed in late November to a four-month consultancy, but on two conditions: that ECLA would fly him home to Buenos Aires four times; and that even this agreement was dependent on the outcome of his ongoing negotiations with the IMF.[44]

For Prebisch was very interested in a job offer from the International Monetary Fund. The IMF had far greater clout and prestige than ECLA, and he was intrigued by the prospect of working in Washington. Compared with the IMF, ECLA was in the minor leagues; the IMF was a future global powerhouse of vital importance to Latin America and the global economy. He recalled Urquidi's letter in May 1947 urging him to strengthen the Latin American presence in Washington.[45] Moreover, the IMF clearly wanted him. After Prebisch responded favourably to initial informal soundings by

Javier Marquez, he received a visit at his home on 25 November from the IMF Managing Director Camille Gutt, accompanied by his deputy, Edward M. Bernstein. They offered him a permanent appointment as advisor to the managing director, without executive responsibilities, at a salary of $14,000. His telegram on 17 December accepting the offer welcomed the position as offering "sufficient time for essential theoretical work," and his follow-up letter to Bernstein noted, "You really tempted me in displaying the wide opportunities which the Fund provides for theoretical reflection and policy research. Since your departure I have reviewed your arguments again and have come to the conclusion that you are right; I am quite willing to join the Fund on the basis proposed by you through Mr. Gutt."[46]

The news spread. "You cannot believe how happy I am to get the news," Urquidi wrote on 3 December. The Ravndals repeated their welcome and offered lodging in their home until a house in Washington could be located; Adelita began preparations for their departure from Buenos Aires.[47] Only one month after the loss of his university appointment, Prebisch had resolved his career dilemma with a prestigious appointment on his own terms, with his forthcoming lectures in Mexico serving as an interesting interlude before beginning his IMF work in Washington. Castillo and the new ECLA in Santiago were forgotten.

11 Triumph in Havana

The managing director of the IMF had offered – and Prebisch had accepted – a senior position in Washington. But an actual contract had not been signed pending approval by the bank's executive board; Camille Gutt had dismissed this as a formality, but a disturbing silence from Washington after his visit suggested that Prebisch was being set up for a major humiliation.

A first sign of internal opposition appeared early, on 23 December, when Gutt cabled with an announcement that the terms of his appointment would have to be changed. "I have reviewed our recent talks with department heads. They feel that an advisor outside departmental lines is not feasible. Prepared to recommend appointment in Operations Department at proposed salary."[1] But Prebisch was reassured that the change was simply to avoid setting a precedent within the Fund and that the offer would soon be confirmed. M.L. Parsons of the Operations Department told him that the delay in approval was merely technical – the January flu in Washington had hollowed out the executive board; he expected a meeting before the end of January. "We are looking forward to having you here and taking advantage of your great experience, particularly in our dealings with Latin America."[2]

So, strongly reassured, Raúl and Adelita Prebisch continued preparations for their departure, with Urquidi and other friends combing the real-estate market in and around the US capital. Farewells were held, and Raúl prepared his lectures for Mexico to begin on 16 February. Martinez-Cabañas and Castillo continued to press him to arrange a special deal with the IMF, whereby Raúl would complete his four months with ECLA before starting full-time in Washington. Just before his departure Raúl received good news from the IMF; Parsons suggested that they meet in Mexico during his UNAM seminar to discuss a work plan. Executive-board approval was now imminent, he said. It was a busy month that augured well for the future, despite the emotional letdown of leaving Buenos Aires. However,

Adelita was confined to bed in Mar del Plata and unable to accompany him to Mexico when he left on 15 February; on his arrival at the Hotel Reforma he cabled his affection to her.

But when Prebisch opened his seminar on 16 February it became clear that the hold-up of his much-discussed appointment at the IMF had little to do with illness on the executive board. Parsons failed to arrive; he heard nothing from Washington. To his mortification, rumours of US Treasury opposition to his appointment became corridor gossip in Mexico. After the Mexican seminar ended, Prebisch decided to force the IMF issue with a cable to Gutt on 6 March demanding a definitive response. The managing director first procrastinated with a message asking for more time but then confirmed that the executive board had indeed rejected his appointment. Parsons wrote a personal letter of apology. "We have behaved intolerably ... I am not sure which is worse – to feel ashamed of oneself, or to feel ashamed of the organization for which one works. We shall pay heavily for our folly in losing your services and the prestige which you would have brought to the Fund in its relations with Latin America. I don't ask you to be tolerant with us because I think we have behaved intolerably, but I do ask that you pity us that we should add this kind of folly to what is already a heavy enough burden. Whom the gods wish to destroy they first make mad." He signed it with "Keenest regrets."[3] Raúl shared his disappointment by telephone with Adelita, who was now recovering. Adelita said that she was happy not to go to Washington and have to deal with such dishonourable people. Some day, she predicted, the tables would be turned.[4]

Robert Triffin and other friends in Washington provided the inside story of his rejection by the IMF, relayed by June Eckard to Prebisch in a long personal letter.[5] The issue had developed into an internal *cause célèbre* because the US had reversed its position and now opposed his candidacy even though the Treasury originally supported Prebisch. It was embarrassing and unpleasant; the Fund had sought him out rather than the other way around, and so firm a commitment would never have been given had the US not been on board. Moreover Prebisch was Latin America's best-known economist and central banker; there was no way the sudden rejection could be explained by questioning his competence. The fight over Prebisch in the Fund therefore was lengthy and bitter.

A complex set of factors lay behind Washington's refusal to accept Prebisch's appointment in early 1949, and it had nothing to do with a rumour that old Washington hands remembered his toughness during the 1930s in bilateral negotiations with the US and were getting back at him now for favouring Britain after the Roca-Runciman Treaty. Instead the US decision reflected the new opening in US-Argentine diplomatic relations,

Brazilian opposition to Prebisch's appointment, and the changing political climate in Washington. Perón vigorously opposed Prebisch for any influential position in the IMF even though Argentina was not a member of the Fund; while he had agreed six months earlier to support him for ECLA, presumably to ease him out of Buenos Aires into a marginal position in Santiago, the Argentine president did not want a domestic opponent in a key position in Washington. Considering the deep-freeze in US-Argentine relations since Pearl Harbor, however, such expected opposition should not have concerned Washington – quite the reverse. In 1946 the US Embassy had campaigned openly against Perón, who later had denounced the Marshall Plan as a scourge and disaster for Argentina.[6] However, on 19 January 1949, Perón fired the economic team led by Miguel Miranda, and Washington saw an opening to improve bilateral relations. A bilateral joint committee was established to review economic issues, including the potential opening of US petroleum investment; Washington sought to restore its prewar position in Argentina, then the most important market in Latin America, and "now threatened by European expansion of bilateral trade and the dollar shortage."[7] The Prebisch appointment was thus caught up in a bilateral diplomatic reorientation, with the State Department arguing that US support for Prebisch in the IMF could pre-empt this promising development with Perón. Thrown out of the Central Bank by the Perón-backed military government in 1943 against US protest, a man who had risked and lost his career for the Allied cause and who had continued to work closely with the Federal Reserve after 1945, Prebisch was sacrificed six years later on the altar of US rapprochement with Perón.

There was another less tangible factor at play in the US rejection of Prebisch. He not only lacked the support of his country, but he was also vulnerable in Washington's changing political climate, now unrecognizably different from the circumstances surrounding his exit from the Central Bank in 1943. He had worked with the US Federal Reserve throughout Latin America, and still knew some of its officials such as David Grove, chief of its Latin American Section in the Research Department. In those years he could also have picked his job among US banks: the Chase Manhattan Bank referred to him as "almost a member of the family"; Joseph C. Rovensky commented in his retirement letter to Raúl in 1945 that "you are so at home in the Chase that you will not miss me much."[8] But times had changed. Prebisch was no longer very well known in Washington, and the friends who still regarded him highly, such as Triffin and Wallich, were increasingly out of step with the gathering Cold War ideology in the Beltway. They represented the wartime generosity and innovation of US Latin American policy; a new and tougher approach rendered

Prebisch an outsider in Truman's Washington. The Berlin blockade continued; the division of Europe had crossed a point of no return; the communist victory in China was imminent. While not yet hysteria, a groundswell of anti-communism in the US capital demanded the greatest care in choosing senior people for the IMF and World Bank; while no one could possibly argue that Prebisch was pro-communist, he was a Latin American who used terms such as "core" and "periphery" and was therefore not automatically "safe." This new caution seeping into the IMF selection process was transmitted directly from the US Treasury but also internally by US officials who followed the flag. E.M. Bernstein, for example, who had made the approach to Prebisch in Buenos Aires and whose support might have made the difference in his approval, remained silent during the affair. Even Ravndal, who might also have influenced the State Department, chose to stand aside. In the end the IMF was an intergovernmental organization led by the Great Powers, and its politics could not escape the changing ideological alignment of the Washington foreign-policy community. Prebisch had been used by Washington while he was powerful and to their advantage; now that he was weak he could be discarded and made a laughingstock from one end of the Americas to the other. Recently hired Latins in the Fund, such as Felipe Pazos, could do nothing but watch the spectacle in frustration and anger.

Finally, Brazilian opposition to Prebisch fortified Washington's determination to press its veto on his appointment, and the diplomatic weight of Brazil in South America also made this a factor of considerable importance in the region. In this case, however, the issue was not so much politics as envy. Although on 5 February Otávio Bulhões had sent Prebisch a congratulatory letter from the Ministry of Finance on his IMF appointment, he also convinced the minister to veto it within the Fund's executive board.[9] Gudin, who genuinely respected and supported the Prebisch appointment, was away from Rio undergoing surgery in the United States and was therefore not in a position to prevent a betrayal that left a guilty feeling toward Prebisch for years in the Brazilian capital. Confronted by the US and Brazil, other members of the IMF executive board eventually fell into line.

As his alarm at losing everything grew in the last week of February, Prebisch finally accepted the long-standing ECLA offer for a four-month fixed-term appointment in Santiago to begin 10 March 1949. Martinez-Cabañas was enthusiastic, hailing Prebisch's decision as a victory for Latin America – and a coup for ECLA. Castillo was his usual overflowing self, cabling a message of welcome and sending a first-class air ticket. Raúl cabled Adelita to tell he what had happened and that he would be going to Chile in March. "You have to know best," she replied, wondering why the Fund was postponing a decision. Arriving in Santiago on Sunday 13 March, Raúl stayed a few nights in the Hotel Crillon before renting a small furnished apartment on Los Urbinos in Providencia near the ECLA offices. Adelita had to arrange renting out the house at 563 Chile but finally she flew in from Buenos Aires on the first Sunday of April. To Raúl's relief her health was almost completely restored, and they could be together as he concentrated on the challenge ahead.

Disappointments followed him as well. The Fondo de Cultura Económica in Mexico decided not to publish his lectures, and, in a nasty letter from his own faculty, the dean refused to pay Prebisch for his 1948 lectures since he had not officially received his letter of resignation. Raúl and Adelita celebrated his birthday on 17 April quietly at home, with a telegram of congratulations from Enrique Frankel and a long letter from Alfredo Moll detailing the latest political events in Argentina. More than ever *persona non grata* in Buenos Aires, he was cautioned by Eleodoro Lobos not to try to return. "They are seriously pursuing you," he warned on 20 March.[10] His Venezuelan friend Manuel Perez-Guerrero, in exile in the UN Division of Coordination and Liaison in New York, also noted that both of them were being watched by their respective dictators, with their mail intercepted where possible. His sister Maria Luisa wrote to him that she would be retiring on 31 May.

The stakes now were now very high. Since the beginning of his wanderings in 1943 Prebisch's options had progressively narrowed. In the first years after 1943 the best US universities had courted him openly, but this interest had dried up as well. Prebisch had met Henry Wallich during his Mexican seminar in February and had asked him about US university openings. Wallich was not optimistic. The US academic scene was changing as rapidly as Washington became increasingly preoccupied with the Cold War; New Deal economists were out of favour. Asia was also replacing Latin America as a priority region; Columbia University, for example, had changed its plans to establish a research centre on Latin America in favour of the Institute for Asian Studies, reflecting the broader post-1945 shift in overall US foreign policy as the Cold War spread to Asia-Pacific from Europe.[11] Having refused all opportunities to travel or teach in the US since 1943 or publish in the established refereed journals, Prebisch was now not at all well known in mainstream economic circles, with the exception of his old associates in the very narrow field of applied Latin American banking policy. He had lost every battle recently, and now he had only a four-month research consultancy without any other future plans or offers. Prebisch was not sure how, but he was determined to regain the initiative with an anger channelled and controlled by the need to confront the most difficult situation he had ever encountered. But he was down to the final card in Santiago.

The same atmosphere of apprehension pervaded ECLA in Santiago and UN officialdom in New York, because ECLA's future was as much on the line as Prebisch's. When he arrived at the office on 14 March 1949 the new organization was still only partially formed, its role and functions remaining in doubt, and nearly paralyzed with fear in the knowledge that Washington and some other governments preferred its early demise. The problem of ECLA's survival stemmed from its contested birth on 15 February 1947. What happened was that in 1946 the US had proposed the creation of two regional commissions within the United Nations Economic and Social Council (ECOSOC), the Economic Commission for Europe (ECE), with a secretariat in Geneva, and the Economic Commission for Asia and the Far East (ECAFE) to be located in Bangkok. Washington's objective was to enlist the UN in the reconstruction of these war-damaged regions, and both ECE and ECAFE were unanimously approved by ECOSOC. Latin Americans were not happy with the regional favouritism, and the Government of Chile, with the support of the other developing and Latin members of ECOSOC (Cuba, Peru, and Venezuela), introduced a resolution that the UN also create the Economic Commission for Latin America (ECLA), to match those in Geneva and Bangkok.[12] Hernan Santa Cruz, chief of the Chilean delegation, maintained that Latin American governments had both earned and needed a comparable vehicle within the UN to support accelerated growth. Not only was their principal goal economic development, but their region was also exhausted after the World War even if the actual fighting had taken place in Europe and Asia. Like these regions Latin America required economic stability and reconstruction, and (he argued) the Pan-American Union was a political rather than an economic body. Implicitly it was understood that ECLA's future secretariat, if approved, would be based in Chile rather than Washington; Chile was also making a bid for regional leadership since Argentina had voluntarily vacated this role after 1941.

The US, Britain, Canada, and other industrialized countries – as well as the USSR – balked, arguing that a UN regional organ was unnecessary because the Pan-American Union already existed, with its own Economic and Social Council (IA-ECOSOC). Why, US delegate William Thorpe asked, should the US, which was already the UN's principal paymaster, fund another new regional commission when one already existed to fulfill Latin America's postwar needs? In 1945 the Pan-American Conference at Chapultepec had agreed that the IA-ECOSOC should coordinate all official inter-American economic and social activities. Canada maintained that creating ECLA would promote "nationalism and anti-multilateralism."

The Soviets were more concerned that they would be frozen out, while the US (already a member of the ECE and ECAFE) would be included as full member.

The United Nations ECOSOC debated whether or not to accept the Chilean Resolution but was so split on North-South lines that a special committee was struck to study the merits of the case. When its eventual report supported the creation of ECLA, citing wartime overuse of capital equipment, the region's need for external assistance to strengthen development, and the high cost of repairing the economic losses incurred during World War II, Washington relented; ECOSOC therefore began assembling a staff in Santiago, searching for an executive director, and establishing June 1948 for ECLA's first session, at which the member governments would approve a work program, the membership including (besides Latin America) the US and the three remaining colonial powers in Europe – France, Britain, and Holland. Despite the logic of geography Canada chose to remain aloof. But it was a narrow, grudging, and ambiguous victory. The US only agreed to ECLA on a three-year trial basis, after which its final status would be decided. Meanwhile the new body would report to Harold Caustin in the UN's Division of Economic Stability and Development in New York, as well as to Wladek R. Malinowski in the Department of Social and Economic Affairs (DESA), which housed the small Regional Commissions secretariat.

The shallowness of US support for ECLA quickly became evident, and Washington did not try to disguise its robust diplomatic campaign for its termination after the three-year probationary period. Even before ECLA's founding session scheduled for 7–25 June 1948 in Santiago, the US used the Ninth Inter-American Conference in Bogotá in April 1948 to recast the old Pan-American Union as the new Organization of American States (OAS) and issue a direct challenge by increasing the IA-ECOSOC budget from $40,000 to $500,000 – or equivalent to ECLA's entire projected budget for 1949. Beyond official opposition, US academics also criticized the formation of ECLA. Simon G. Hanson, editor of a new journal, *Inter-American Economic Affairs,* launched his first attack even before the new regional organ was established.[13] "Life will be complicated," David Owen complained, "by the existence of two parallel economic commissions for Latin America with virtually identical terms of reference and equal budgets." He wondered if they should consider moving ECLA's headquarters from Santiago closer to Washington and New York; it was going to be difficult recruiting staff to a location so far from anywhere.[14]

Meanwhile ECLA existed mainly on paper. The first session of the Commission was held while the new secretariat remained in temporary quarters on the fifteenth floor of the Hotel Carrera in downtown Santiago. The meeting proceeded smoothly because little could be expected of a brand-new organization, but the main resolution of the Santiago session left the secretariat saddled with a huge problem by directing it to prepare a document called *Economic Survey of Latin America* for its second session, scheduled for Havana from 26 May to 14 June 1950. At first glance this seemed straightforward, requesting "a study of the movements of import and export prices, the determining factors of such movements, and the consequences thereof on the balance of payments." But nothing like this had been prepared previously for Latin America; and it was evident that it would exceed the capacity of the new secretariat in Santiago. Because ECLA's overall mandate was so general ("to initiate and participate in measures for ... raising the level of economic activity in Latin America and strengthening the economic relations of Latin American countries both among themselves and with other countries of the world"), the *Economic Survey* was also expected to provide a framework and direction for the new organization. "We are in agreement that to a very large extent ECLA's future is dependent upon the *Economic Survey*," Wladek Malinowski wrote to Harold Caustin. "I am not only concerned with the high standard of the publication (from a purely academic or professional respect), but I also think that as a result of the *Economic Survey*, we should be able to formulate the tasks, policy and organizational structure of ECLA."[15]

By the time Prebisch arrived in Santiago, the atmosphere was tense. There was, at least, an executive secretary – Gustavo Martinez-Cabañas, a thirty-nine-year-old Mexican economist whom Raúl had met during his trips in 1944 and 1946. But it was evident that he was a compromise choice with little experience, international recognition, or force of personality. After Prebisch declined, David Owen had tried Daniel Cosío Villegas without success and Victor Urquidi also disqualified himself as still too junior for the position. The secretary-general therefore accepted Owen's recommendation to hire Martinez-Cabañas effective 1 January 1949, but he did so reluctantly and refused the additional money requested by Martinez-Cabañas, which would have recognized him at the same level as Gunnar Myrdal, the famous Swedish economist who headed the ECE in Geneva. Unfortunately the new leadership lacked the credibility and management skills required for putting together the *Economic Survey of Latin America* in acceptable shape for the forthcoming Havana Conference. It would have been no easy task in the best of circumstances, and ECLA was also a new organization that lacked political recognition in the region: by 28 December not a single Latin American government had responded to a request for information sent out four months earlier. Yet regional data had to be pulled together quickly, or ECLA's reputation would collapse. Castillo and Martinez-Cabañas alternated between exuberance and gloom but were increasingly resigned to appeasing their critics and preventing overt failure. The tiny staff of UN professionals already hired in Santiago included individuals of quality, but they seemed uncertain of mandate and without leadership. Malinowski had already realized this in November before the new executive director had been appointed, complaining that ECLA lacked what he called "a central master brain."[16] Martinez-Cabañas, however, could not provide it either. In practice Castillo's main achievement in 1948 had been locating a pleasant two-storey house in Los Leones, Providencia (Pio Decimo 2475), away from the city centre, with sixteen rooms and good central heating. It was a warm and comfortable place, but pleasant surroundings could not compensate for a vacuum in leadership.

In New York the UN Department of Economic and Social Affairs was increasingly anxious about the future of ECLA, realizing that a failure in Havana would severely damage headquarters and ECOSOC as well; DESA had only three people in its Latin American Unit in 1948, with Argentinian Adolfo Dorfman the most senior, but he had other tasks besides assisting with the economic survey. Dorfman a year earlier had tried to assemble reliable economic series for Latin America but found such data elusive since, as he put it, "every country has a different system, and none of them is very thorough."[17] Owen therefore hired Francisco Croire, another former Prebisch employee in the Argentine Central Bank who had been sent to Harvard for graduate training, to provide a New York anchor for the economic survey. Arriving in December 1948, he found that little had been done during the preceding six months and that the two staff members he inherited were of doubtful quality and overly acculturated to paid holidays; UN morale and staff competence in New York contrasted badly with the old Central Bank in Buenos Aires, Croire sniffed.[18] The UN had to compete with the new big rivals – the IMF and World Bank – in Washington, and it was coming up short.

Croire poured out his concern to Prebisch in long personal letters.[19] He discovered that the *Economic Survey* had taken on a heavy symbolic value for Latin Americas within the UN system. There was, he reported, a growing *schadenfreude* among the skeptics in New York who doubted that Latin economists were competent enough to deliver good work unless supervised by US and European superiors. Since the *Economic Survey* was the single most important work of ECOSOC relating to Latin America, it therefore had become a test of Latin American economists themselves. The *Economic Survey* was unique in that Latin Americans themselves were in charge; it was the first major international report on the region to be directed and written by Latin Americans rather than foreign consultants – in the IMF or World Bank, Latin Americans were members of teams led by senior North American or European economists. Coire and other Latin Americans like himself in New York therefore felt on trial; failure in Havana would confirm a New York perception that they were second-raters. This situation made Prebisch's role doubly important. New York would mobilize all available resources to pull together the individual components for an acceptable document, including sending headquarters staff to Santiago on short assignments. A great deal of data was being collected; a more realistic work plan and *Economic Survey* outline were now accepted in Santiago. Other agencies such as the FAO and the IMF were being helpful, and the World Bank had just completed a study, *The Pattern of Latin American Trade Payments with ERP Europe and the US*, which was useful for ECLA's own report, entitled "Prospects for Trade Expansion," being prepared for Havana. Dorfman and Alfonso Santa Cruz were working overtime on it; Louis Shapiro from New York headquarters arrived in Santiago on 17 December to work with Cuban economist Regino Boti on regional foreign trade statistics.

The problem, however, was overall leadership: although the *Economic Survey* had to be a team effort, one person, finally, had to draft a framework document laying out its theoretical approach and rationale. Croire was relieved by Prebisch's acceptance of this role; had he not agreed to write the report, the UN would have gone outside Latin America, probably to Sweden's Gunnar Myrdal, thereby demonstrating to the world the bankruptcy of Latin economists and spelling the certain demise of ECLA.[20]

Even more, Havana was unexpectedly emerging as an important meeting in US-Latin American relations. In part this reflected the old theme of dashed expectations in US recognition and postwar cooperation. By 1949 and the beginning of Truman's second administration, a sense of injustice was boiling up again as Washington's priorities focused on Europe and Asia. During the Second World War, Latin countries had sold their commodities to the US at prices fixed by the Office of Price Administration and were unable to convert their dollar earnings into goods with consequent inflation, only to find that, when the time came that US goods were available for purchase, there were no price controls on these industrial exports while the prices for their primary and agricultural products declined. With the end of the war, single commodity countries such as Venezuela, Cuba, Chile, and Bolivia faced an inevitable downturn in trade and were on the verge of serious economic crisis. Yet the Truman Administration had vetoed every Latin attempt to implement its promises of economic partnership made during the war. Washington now opposed the creation of an inter-American development bank, continued to postpone the much-heralded Inter-American

Economic Conference, and rejected multilateral efforts to stabilize commodity prices. Worst of all, congressional opposition was building against US ratification of the ITO (International Trade Organization), which had been proposed in 1948 at a major international meeting, also in Havana, and this placed an additional strain on US-Latin American relations. Conceived during the Second World War, the ITO had been seen by Keynes as the trade counterpart to the IMF and World Bank; its failure left Latin Americans disappointed and frustrated. The sequence of Great Depression, war, and the postwar challenge of adjustment to Pax Americana had created an incipient regionalism in Latin America – a consciousness of shared experiences, and even greater needs, carried by a new generation of better-trained and travelled professionals. Young Latins ached for recognition, leadership, and definition all in one; there was an opening for new ideas and change. "*Does Latin America exist?*" Mexican author Luis Alberto Sanchez had asked a few years earlier in the 1940s. Latin America was a region ready to be created, and this idea and opportunity built on perceived grievances to give the 1949 ECLA Conference in Havana a symbolic significance out of all proportion to the actual agenda of the meeting.

The evident ECLA, UN, and Latin American anxiety and expectations added to Prebisch's agony as he began his work in an upstairs office at the end of the corridor somewhat apart from the rest of the ECLA staff, pausing only for his daily lunch with Adelita in Providencia. He needed a breakthrough, but he felt flat – as flat as his 1948 lectures or his Mexico seminar. He now understood fully the cost of his years in the wilderness; when he left the Central Bank in 1943 and drafted his outline for *Money and the Rhythm of Economic Activity*, he had been well ahead of the pack in his theoretical development. His central concept of a structural rift in the international economy between industrial and agricultural countries in which market forces tended to accentuate inequalities had been novel and exciting. But that was more than five years ago. He had seemed on the verge of major innovation, but he had not been able to deliver. The manuscript he had promised Triffin in 1945 still remained incomplete.

The truth was that he had largely stagnated. Why? Making a living, constant travel, personal and professional disappointments, the depression of daily life in Perónist Argentina, watching its growing isolations and cultural decline, the lack of resources for research, and above all the problem of working in isolation without a team of associates – all these factors had slowed down his work. He had certainly made progress; since 1945 he had grafted the "centre-periphery" terminology into his analysis to accentuate the dualism present in the international economy, and this was now a permanent fixture in his writing. His work on the business cycle had also advanced significantly. But the discipline was not standing still either, and younger economists were moving into development economics; the argument, for example, that agricultural exporters were at a disadvantage compared with industrialized exporters in international trade was appearing in the literature.[21] While no other scholar had yet presented an answer to Prebisch's hypothesis set out in his *Rhythm of Economic Activity* in 1943, it was only a matter of time before he would lose this race as well to scholars in Europe and North America.

Prebisch felt close to a new synthesis, but days went by in Santiago and his frustration grew as the Havana deadline approached. In early April he circulated some draft text to ECLA colleagues for comments. Celso Furtado, a young Brazilian economist who had recently arrived in Santiago to work in ECLA, read the manuscript and was disappointed. The style was academic and defensive, dealing with familiar topics – the declining US import coefficient, capital controls, foreign trade, savings and inflation, and the importance of industrialization. The paper seemed more a digest of his lectures in the faculty and Mexico than a policy document, and while it was enlivened by his "centre-periphery" terminology, his explanation for this lopsided capitalism was not complete, and, unlike his 1943 *Rhythm of Economic Activity*, it did not refer to declining terms of trade. Prebisch was clearly struggling as he faced the approaching deadline, aware that his work fell short of what he knew he could achieve.

What happened next has been masterfully related by Furtado in his autobiography, *A Fantasia Organizada*.[22] While Prebisch struggled in Santiago, Croire in New York received a copy of a draft report Hans Singer had written for the UN Sub-Commission on Economic Development, titled *Post-war Price Relations Between Under-developed and Industrialized Countries*.[23] Incredibly, Castillo had received an advance copy of Singer's document on 17 December, when UN statistician Louis Shapiro arrived from New York, but he had not shared it with Prebisch.[24] Croire noted a reluctance by senior staff for its circulation because Singer's report challenged conventional wisdom and would therefore likely be rejected by the UN Sub-Commission, but he sent it immediately to Raúl along with another IMF paper on foreign trade. Prebisch had never met Singer, a German-born scholar who had left Germany in 1933 and taken a PhD from Cambridge University. Recruited by David Owen to work at the UN, he arrived in New York in April 1947 on a two-year leave of absence from the University of Glasgow. Here he began his work in the trade section of DESA with an interesting group of economists who drew his attention to the terms of trade issue.[25] Singer argued that historical statistics demonstrated a decline in the terms of trade of developing countries. "[F]rom the latter part of the nineteenth century to the eve of the Second World War, a period of over half a century, there was a secular downward trend in the prices of primary goods relative to the prices of manufactured goods."[26] Such a decline provided an "added incentive toward industrialization" in developing countries, since they would otherwise lose resources for development relative to their industrialized counterparts.[27] The Singer piece also raised the issue of global equity, since, if his data was correct, the dynamic of international trade created a divide between rich and poor.

Singer's paper was the stimulus Prebisch needed to escape his mounting frustration and fear of failure. In his 1943 *Rhythm of Economic Activity* Raúl had already assumed a secular decline in international terms of trade for agricultural countries, and both Kindleberger and Samuelson had written articles based on this hypothesis.[28] But Singer not only demonstrated it statistically within a rigorous historical study, he also articulated the ethical implications of declining terms of trade in the global economy. Prebisch therefore recognized a kindred spirit in the British economist; Singer's work both corroborated his assumptions on trade and gave him the confidence to recast his work with a new structure and style. Raúl's energy returned, and he began writing from scratch, ensuring that all copies of his earlier text were discarded. Then in three days and nights he wrote *The Economic Development of Latin America and Its Principal Problems*, which came to be referred to as the *Manifesto* or the Havana *Manifesto*, in which the laboured prose of his earlier work disappeared in an essay that recalled the power and simplicity of Keynes. The fifty-page document may not have been scholarly as defined by refereed journals; nor was it replete with mathematical formulas, explicit hypotheses, or reams of footnotes. None of the individual components of his main argument was entirely novel – it is correct, for example, to identify the terms of trade breakthrough as the "Prebisch-Singer Theory" – but Prebisch's *Manifesto* served to mold these disparate components into a unique and compelling synthesis.[29] It succeeded in re-examining the determinants of economic activity in developing countries, and represents a key event that changed the vocabulary of international development and marked a new period in Latin America.

The 1949 *Manifesto* began by paraphrasing Aristotle's dictum: "The facts have not yet been sufficiently established. If ever they are, the credit must be given to observation rather than to theories, and to theories only in so far as they are confirmed by the observed facts." Latin Americans, he argued, must have the courage to confront their own reality to find solutions, and this meant subjecting inherited wisdom to the ultimate questions. Does it work? Who gains and loses? To understand is to be free and able to take control of one's destiny, the *Manifesto* implied, and Prebisch articulated an unforgettable, if deceptively simple, framework to explain why the system was not working in the mutual interests of rich and poor nations, why the industrial countries reaped the major gains, and what had to be done to restore equality for Latin America in the international economy; 1949's *The Economic Development of Latin America and Its Principal Problems* owes much to his 1943 *Rhythm of Economic Activity*. There is the same confident tone, the same stepping back from his data to highlight the key points, and the same assurance that the dilemma facing developing countries could be successfully overcome.

But the *Manifesto* was also different in its regional vision and call to action. The "centre-periphery" conception of the world economy was much more explicitly focused on the dynamics and structure of global inequality. It began with the claim of a unified world economy in which all states, industrial and developing, were linked in a single system of exchange and affected by a common business cycle. Within this system, however, he counterposed the quite different roles of the rich industrial versus developing agricultural countries: the latter produced primary products for industrial countries in return for manufactured goods, while the business cycle began in the core countries and spread to the periphery. Prebisch then argued that the distribution of benefits was unequal because the dynamics of foreign trade and the business cycle favoured the industrial countries. This was not ill-will of governments, but rather the inherent functioning of the system: that gains in productivity were greater in industrial than in primary goods could be documented by the declining terms of trade that he had assumed in 1943 and that Singer had now documented. This factor in turn was aggravated by an international trade cycle in which the agricultural countries were more vulnerable than the core economies during recessions because organized labour in Europe or North America was sufficiently strong to prevent an equivalent collapse of prices. The result of both factors – a secular decline in terms of trade and business cycle vulnerability – explained the fundamental flaw of neoclassical trade theory, which assumed equal benefits for industrial and agricultural exporters and which was assumed to have the same validity in Latin America as in the US or Britain. There was, in short, an inherent asymmetry in the system, the understanding of which was a necessary step toward understanding Latin America's insertion in the international system and thereby designing a new approach appropriate for its needs in the future.[30]

The attraction of the *Manifesto* lay in its dual thrust – not only did it offer a powerful diagnosis but it also contained a vision that promised agricultural countries a way out of their dilemma. To be peripheral was not necessarily to be dependent; as in his 1943 *Rhythm of Economic Activity* he proposed that industrialization, with due care to avoid inflation and distortions, offered Latin America the prospect of reversing the dynamic of unequal exchange that otherwise doomed it to constantly diminishing benefits in the global economy. Here was a non-revolutionary, non-communist prescription for change that all governments in the region, regardless of ideological orientation, could applaud. It was a call to action that Prebisch based directly on his experience in Argentina, where import substitution had already advanced considerably before 1914 and where the Central Bank had pursued precisely this role to the point where industrial production equalled that of agriculture in the national economy by 1943. From a regional perspective where most economies were less developed than Argentina, it was a bold departure. Moreover, once out of the bottle, his challenge to peripheral economies to move from commodity production to a more diversified industrial economy proved irresistible and durable – so that today it is so taken for granted that the originality of the Prebisch *Manifesto* has been obscured by its success.

Under its extraordinarily elegant and flowing prose, and for all its appeal to reason and measured argument, there was an almost imperceptible but unmistakable undertone of indignation, even suppressed anger, in the *Manifesto.* Development economics, he implied, meant taking a stand. The treatment he had just received in Washington may explain part of this edge, as well as the trade pessimism of 1949, in which the outlook for increasing Latin exports was gloomy. "Formerly, prior to the Great Depression," he argued, "the Latin American countries developed outwardly, stimulated by the constant increase in exports. There is no reason to suppose, at least at present, that this will occur again to the same extent, except in very particular cases."[31] Given this grim prospect, the international economic system was even less likely to stimulate development and technical progress in Latin America, and it was therefore urgent to get moving without delay.

On finishing the *Manifesto* Prebisch was more confident than at any time since 1943, and he was eager to leave for Havana. He recognized that the report would be controversial. In a copy that he sent to Ravndal, timed to coincide with his presentation in Havana, Prebisch indicated that "the ideas contained in the report do not follow conventional lines. With your wide knowledge of our reality you will be able to evaluate their true reach."[32] Martinez-Cabañas also did not circulate it to ECLA staff before the Havana Conference; only Furtado was given a copy to translate into Portuguese, since he would not be attending the Havana meeting. For all the others, as well as the delegates, it was to be a complete surprise. Prebisch telephoned Adelita from Havana after he arrived, and she cabled a note of good luck in return, "I have no doubt that it will receive the success it deserves."[33]

The conference opened on 29 May with fanfare in the Capitolio Nacional. It was ECLA's first big international test, and the national and regional press were mobilized to report the newest bureaucratic addition to the Americas, but the turnout of diplomats was uneven beginning with the Americans, who sent a message to ECLA by sending their low-ranking US ambassador to El Salvador as head of mission. Argentina matched Washington by sending its ambassador in Honduras to Havana. The Chileans as ever, led by Hernan Santa Cruz, were out in force. H.M. Phillips attended for Britain, diplomats Robert Buron and Philippe de Seynes for France. As if to compensate for the thin audience, the welcoming committee was most distinguished: UN Secretary-General Trygve Lie, Cuban President Carlos Prio Soccaras, and Chilean Minister of Economy and Commerce Alberto Baltra, who was chair of the session. President Prio delared that ECLA's mission was "driving the shadow of hunger from the American scene" and that "you are, gentlemen, the hope of the world."[34] Baltra added some realism, noting that Latin America was weak, dependent, and unstable and remained unable to surmount its semicolonial structures. The secretary-general was the most modest of all, duly noting the commission's dual role as a regional instrument within a body having global responsibilities, but finding little else of a concrete nature to add except that the *Economic Survey* was "ECLA's first great project."[35]

The *Economic Survey* was hardly the "great project" announced by the UN secretary-general, although it could be defended as the best possible document under the circumstances. It offered a regional panorama in 245 pages, addressing the "Trends in Production" in industry and agriculture over a ten-year period since 1937 (part A); with a part B summarizing "Other Economic Aspects," including population, transportation, foreign trade, inflation, balance of payments, and prospects for European recovery. The report offered considerable information otherwise not available – starting with basic population data. Ecuador had never had a census; Bolivia had last attempted one in 1900; Uruguay in 1910. By suggesting a total population of 146 million, with a 1.8 percent annual growth rate, the *Economic Survey* laid the basis for essential statistical data collection in the region – and it offered many other useful findings. It concluded that manufacturing in 1947 had grown 21 percent above the 1937 level, but that the per capita increase remained lower than the world average. In foreign trade, Latin America remained extremely sensitive to fluctuations in international markets. Exports of agricultural goods and livestock remained the same over the decade (52 percent), with a promising trend toward more processed raw materials balanced by a 45 percent increase in imports of foodstuffs. Nevertheless the region's share of global exports had expanded to 13 percent in 1946 from 9 percent in 1937, with the US having replaced Europe as its chief market. Latin America's challenge was to overcome the major obstacles to development, which the survey identified as low labour productivity in agriculture and industry, the shortage of savings for productive investment, a persistent housing crisis, and stagnation in the mining sector. The problem with the *Economic Survey* in Havana was its overly general and descriptive content. While the delegates saw enough value in it to recommend that ECLA build on its work and prepare another annual survey of the economic situation in Latin America for its next meeting in 1950, it lacked a framework and an action plan. This is what Croire had feared, and why he had welcomed Prebisch's short-term contract. Lacking a distinctive approach to development, the *Economic Survey* presented in Havana had too little bite to interest governments in ECLA's mission. They were bored; there was nothing here that other agencies like the World Bank or the IMF – or even the OAS – could not do just as well.

Prebisch's report filled this void. That his presentation in the lush Cuban capital electrified his audience understates the impact of his report. A bit of a mystery figure, he created an almost unbearable tension after rising to the podium in the hotel ballroom and extending a silence into anxiety, before beginning his address in hushed tone and deep voice. Dressed in a blue pin-striped suit, he spoke without prepared text or notes, and seemed to bond instantly with the delegates, who were caught up in an unexpected and mesmerizing collective experience. International trade was no longer the mere exchange of logs and rocks. Prebisch took them into his confidence, discussing complex economic concepts without a retreat into jargon, carrying the crowd along as the argument for regional self-reliance built. By the time he closed the delegates had no doubt that Latin Americans had to act immediately to share the benefits of economic progress with the industrial countries and also that they would be successful in changing their destiny among the world powers. No one was unmoved; it was a great show with a memorable response.

The *Manifesto* created a sensation in the media throughout Latin America, while creating consternation among senior UN and US officials in New York and Washington who understood its power. Prebisch's framework of structuralism offered a new approach to international development; he had declared for an activist state and industrialization in a new language that challenged the old doctrine of comparative advantage. The notion that agricultural countries in Latin America could thrive in the future by remaining commodity producers was undermined, and all development experts – whether from the industrial or developing countries – knew that a new debate had been launched.

The immediate and harsh reaction of mainstream economists, including Gottfried von Haberler, Gerald Baldwin, Charles Kindleberger, and Gerald Meier, to *The Economic Development of Latin America and Its Principal Problems* underlined the seriousness of Prebisch's challenge to traditional economic theory.[36] Jacob Viner of Princeton University set the tone by dismissing the *Manifesto* as a set of "malignant fantasies, distorted historical conjecture and simplistic hypotheses."[37] During a series of lectures in Brazil at the National University during July and August 1950, Viner's arrogance astonished his audience as much as his advice: stay with free trade; don't be wooed away from neoclassic verities by sirens promoting economic diversification; dedicate yourselves to agriculture and birth control. Prebisch was a heretic – even a "grand heretic"[38] – to be avoided at all costs. Other US economists were less ideological, with criticisms ranging from the empirical data underpinning the Prebisch-Singer terms of trade theory to the impact of technological innovation. But Prebisch's critics missed the point. The *Manifesto* never claimed to offer a fully developed theory of economic development; its text repeatedly appealed for more research. It was not anti-trade: "The more active Latin America's foreign trade, the greater the possibilities of increasing productivity by means of intensive capital formation." It was not anti-agriculture: "The industrialization of Latin America is not incompatible with the efficient development of primary production." Nor was it blindly pro-industrialization; chapter 6 of the report was titled "The Limits of Industrialization": "Industrialization is not an end in itself, but is the only means at their disposal of obtaining a share of the benefits of technical progress and of progressively raising the standard of living of the masses."[39] Viner, who called himself "an old-fashioned free trader," could only fall back on the old neoliberal rules of thumb, such as "strengthening the investment climate" or "pulling in one's belt." Prebisch also believed in the market and sound investment climates but demanded answers to another set of questions. "What else is required for development?" he asked. "What about asymmetry in the system?" He challenged the market itself as the great equalizer and called for purposeful state action so that weaker countries could share the benefits of the international economy.

This was the cognitive leap that identified Prebisch as the father of development: he had presented a new vision of underdevelopment in a fundamentally novel framework that challenged existing theories with an alternative approach including *both* industrial *and* peripheral countries. Indeed the most serious – and resented – of Prebisch's criticisms of neoclassical economists in American and European universities was their presumption of wisdom: "One of the conspicuous deficiencies of general economic theory, from the point of view of the periphery, is its false sense of universality."[40] Instead the *Manifesto* demanded the end of the prevailing absolutism in economic theory and pointed to the need to see development as a more complex process of change that depended as much on regional structures and characteristics as on neoliberal verities. The particular vulnerabilities of Latin America, which he had first articulated in his "Notes on the Money Supply" in 1921, had to be addressed if the region were to succeed and contribute fully to global prosperity; and since this part of the development equation depended on understanding the Latin American reality, economists from the region should concentrate on this task as much as on copying models from developed countries.

Raúl's personal metamorphosis after his triumph in Havana rivalled his professional breakthrough. Having stunned his audience, he abruptly left the conference and disappeared from the Hotel Nacional, remaining out of communication with everyone, including Adelita. This had never happened before. She didn't hear from him for days and read about the speech in the newspapers and cabled to him, evidently annoyed. "This was the first sign of life about you in the last three weeks," she wrote on 10 June. Evidently the strain and tensions of the past six years capped by the IMF rebuff, and now his sensational public success, had unleashed an unbridled sexuality heretofore contained by a life of disciplined work and family. Like his father's, Raúl's personality had harboured another side that broke free in lush Havana. Like his father he would keep this side of him completely isolated from his professional life. Another Raúl had made its unwanted appearance alongside his banker suits, and the irreversible character change was bewildering and saddening for Adelita and his friends who remained loyal to the "essential" Prebisch.

When he resurfaced from the Havana underground, Prebisch returned to the third session. No one could doubt that he had been the centrepiece of the Havana meeting, the big victor. Everyone, including he himself, realized that the *Manifesto* had launched him as a regional personality, and a formal resolution of appreciation was approved on 14 June at the close of the meeting. One year after his humiliating rejection by the IMF he had reversed his fortunes in dramatic fashion and emerged as a VIP. He was no longer Dr Prebisch: he was don Raúl.

12 Claiming ECLA

Before Havana, Prebisch had viewed ECLA as a secondary player in the inter-American game, and he went to Havana as a short-term consultant with one idea only: to present a report that would vindicate the years he had spent elaborating a new approach to Latin American economic development – after which his contract would expire, on 31 July.

Having experienced Havana, however, he was now convinced that under his leadership ECLA could be transformed into a powerful instrument for channelling the regionalism that his report had provoked. Santiago's apparent disadvantage of location could be transformed into advantage: the greater the distance from Washington and UN headquarters in New York, the greater its defense against their orthodoxy and pressure to conform; ECLA could prosper as a uniquely Latin American research centre outside the rigidities of the Atlantic Alliance. Since 1945, qualified Latin American economists had had few options other than the international organizations based in the US or Europe; ECLA could become an alternative location and intellectual counterweight to this bleeding of talent, offering an autonomous centre of ideas where indigenous approaches to development could be explored. Santiago could become a regional laboratory for linking theory with practice in the urgent and practical tasks of development. An ECLA with this purpose, and energized by his own leadership, could stem the exodus of talent from the region to Washington and New York, keeping young economists like Celso Furtado and Victor Urquidi in the region, enriching Santiago by bringing Latins from all the subregions together, profiting by their different experiences, and in general promoting the development of Latin American economists and research institutions rather than big international organizations such as the IMF and World Bank. Such an ECLA could be a magnet for economists in North America and Europe who were committed to development but sought insights and experience beyond the mainstream transatlantic alternatives. In short, Prebisch realized that with proper leadership ECLA could become a powerful centre of ideas and action rather than merely another small UN agency at the end of the world.

David Owen and other UN officials immediately understood Prebisch's value to the world body. They had heard him speak and saw what he could do with crowds. Here was a real leader, and the UN needed charisma to project internationalism. Prebisch was also from the South, rather than Europe or North America; and he was an original thinker as well as a charismatic personality. Owen knew that the United Nations should attract him into its ranks. There was, of course, the delicate issue of *The Economic Development of Latin America and Its Principal Problems* (the Prebisch *Manifesto*). It was obviously impossible for the UN to include it with the officially approved documents at Havana because the US and other Western missions disagreed with its central thesis; Hans Singer had experienced the same resistance earlier that year, and Prebisch had placed industrial countries even more on the defensive.[1] If the international economy represented a single interdependent global system, and if its dynamics favoured only one set of countries, then the responsibility for correcting the imbalance fell on both the vulnerable (agricultural) and the privileged (industrial) alike; only their combined action could create the right conditions for development. Martinez-Cabañas agreed with Owen on dissociating ECLA from Prebisch's *Manifesto*, and in the end Trygve Lie signed a preface stating that "the views expressed in this report are entirely those of the author" and that it was being published only because "the subject is of vital importance to the United Nations." Although contrary to UN policy and a unique exception, senior UN officials considered this route "very desirable."[2] This UN decision to insist that he take credit and responsibility for his report boosted Prebisch's visibility in New York and Latin America and gave him much greater recognition than if the *Manifesto* had been buried in the Havana documents.

Prebisch's future career plans were even more critical for ECLA, the principal beneficiary of his role in Havana. Martinez-Cabañas had a good instinct for survival and realized that Prebisch was vital to ECLA's continued success. Without him the Havana meeting might have failed, and the challenge of survival was not over by any means; ECLA had only two years left to prove itself. Prebisch's prestige and talents were necessary to maintain the momentum. Martinez-Cabañas's fears were realized in July when ECOSOC reviewed ECLA's performance; it was far from enthusiastic, warning against "bureaucratization," for example by creating the permanent Trade Committee much desired by the executive secretary.[3]

The implication of this lukewarm response was that nobody in Santiago or New York could relax.

Martinez-Cabañas therefore sought out Prebisch before the two men left Havana, but in these negotiations the beleaguered executive secretary must have felt distinctly like Dr Frankenstein: he had needed Prebisch even before Havana, and now had to pitch the offer much higher. At the same time he realized full well that since Raúl was more powerful than him in every way, he risked creating a potential monster likely to escape his control. Some early incidents had already lowered Prebisch's regard for his boss, such as his request that Raúl help him negotiate a better deal for him on a dining-room set purchased in Buenos Aires and destined for his Santiago residence – this in the midst of ECLA's struggle for survival and Raúl's own dismissal from the university. But a deal was struck, and on 16 June Prebisch agreed to a nine-month extension of his contract, to 30 April 1950. The negotiations over Prebisch's new terms of reference revealed how quickly the flow of power was ebbing away from Martinez-Cabañas: Prebisch agreed to stay on in Santiago, but only if he could create an autonomous research centre with himself as director, in effect taking full control of ECLA's entire research program including the preparation of the *Economic Survey* and limiting the scope of the executive secretary to "operational and policy activities." The agreement split the secretariat into two separate components: Prebisch would have "full authority over personnel assigned to the Centre," control his own budget, and be "solely responsible" for all studies and reports. Permanent staff appointed to the new Centre would "be made upon proposals by the Director." The executive secretary would be kept informed, "to enable him to express his views," but Prebisch himself would handle communications with outside persons and institutions. Since research comprised ECLA's primary mission this division of labour was in effect a *coup d'état* by a person who remained technically a "consultant" and who was not as yet a full-time UN civil servant. Prebisch further insisted on an additional clause stating that "should Mr. Prebisch become a member of the permanent staff of the UN ... he will have the same rank as the top-ranking Director." Martinez-Cabañas retained the title of executive secretary, but Prebisch would become ECLA's most visible personality in both Santiago and the region. New York agreed to this arrangement.

On 5 July 1949 Prebisch took his UN oath; it was the symbolic beginning of his new career. He cabled Adelita that "the next step in our lives has been definitively decided." In another letter he described the new arrangement in glowing terms: he finally had the research centre that he had been seeking for so long, and "under perfect conditions." True, it was not

Argentina, but a regional, Latin American, focus expanded the vision – and the challenge. They would be moving to Santiago. Because Adelita was to join him in Mexico on 15 July, she had little time to rent their house in San Isidro and prepare for the move. This time she arranged the shipment of all their furniture from 563 Chile, except the old Citroen, which remained in the garage for the new tenants – French banker friends of René Berger who accepted a one-year lease at 1,700 pesos a month. (Raúl took delivery of a big Chevrolet, which arrived in Santiago from New York on 9 October.) On her last night at 563 Chile, Adelita described her mixed feelings on leaving the country. It was, she said, "a nightmare to give up our little home in which I have lived so happily as your little secretary."[4] She sensed that they might never return to Buenos Aires.

Before returning to Santiago from Havana, Prebisch decided to shore up ECLA's diplomatic defenses in New York, Washington, and Mexico City, because the second session and the reaction to his report demonstrated that he would need far greater support in these capitals for survival. He therefore spent most of the summer in Washington and New York, returning to Santiago via Mexico City on 21 October. In New York Prebisch acquainted himself with the UN power structure, meeting Secretary-General Trygve Lie personally for the first time and visiting David Owen, H. Caustin, and Wladek Malinowski in the Departments of Economic and Social Affairs – to be merged into a unified DESA in 1954 – to discuss the future of ECLA and expand its scope of action within the system. Like Owen, Malinowski had attended the Havana Conference, and he and Prebisch immediately recognized each other as allies. Malinowski's father was one of the founders of the Polish Socialist Party, and he himself had been active in its Students' Independent Union before the Communist takeover and his expulsion from Poland. Aware that this background gave him no influence whatsoever in Washington or Western capitals, he became an adept UN insider, with a finger on the pulse of the organization, and a valuable ally in finding secret routes through the bureaucratic maze. The Latin American Unit under Caustin and Alfonso Santa Cruz was still understaffed; Croire's departure (he had returned to Argentina) made things even more difficult. But all agreed to avoid repeating the chaotic months before Havana and promised to improve liaison between DESA and Santiago in the preparation of ECLA's second *Economic Survey*, which would be presented at its third session, 5–21 June 1950, in Montevideo, Uruguay. Prebisch was now responsible for this task, and he was determined to avoid the confusion and near-failure of the first *Economic Survey*. Much of the data, information, and facilities for studying the Latin American economies were located in New York and Washington, and accessing these sources was essential in carrying out ECLA's work.

Washington presented a more difficult dilemma. The Truman Administration had abstained in the 1948 UN vote creating ECLA, and the US had already decided that it should be terminated when its three-year grace period ended in 1951. A month before Havana the OAS Inter-American ECOSOC had met in plenary session and recommended discussions with the UN to take over ECLA's budget while keeping "some of the more competent members of the ECLA Secretariat," and the State Department maintained its view after the meeting that ECLA and the OAS Inter-American ECOSOC should "merge."[5] This meant absorption; David Owen acidly noted that he would accept the US plan so long as the new "merged" organization reported to him in New York rather than to the OAS in Washington. A resolution at Havana requiring that ECLA improve its coordination with the OAS was universally seen as a procedural standoff while the future of ECLA was coming to a head. Prebisch therefore decided that the UN had to be proactive rather than passive in changing attitudes in Washington, and he recommended a small office as an essential window and listening post in the US capital. Several purposes would be served: it would pre-empt US criticism by promoting regular dialogue with US Government agencies, the Export-Import Bank, and the OAS; it would place ECLA in the inter-American diplomatic network of the Beltway; and it would also benefit Santiago directly by building a network of professional contacts in US agencies and major international organizations like the OAS and World Bank. Two Americans, Sidney Merlin (from the World Bank) and George Kalmanoff (from the US Commerce Department), were chosen to head the office. Prebisch even proposed that it be located in the OAS building, but the Inter-American ECOSOC was unwilling to share space with its new Santiago competitor.

Prebisch also decided to set up a small liaison office in Mexico as a visible toehold in the northern region of Latin America, and a key country to have on-side in the escalating struggle unfolding over ECLA's future. The Mexican Government was not considered an ECLA supporter, but it was also not likely to take any positive action in eliminating the organization because Martinez-Cabañas was a Mexican citizen. The tiny office – Prebisch placed it in the Mexican Central Bank with the support of Rodrigo Gomez, with only one junior official to save costs – would serve as a signal from Santiago that it intended to regionalize ECLA's work and thereby offer the northern countries a more direct role in its operations than did the OAS. Its first task was to ensure that data and reports from the Mexican-Caribbean Basin region were available for the *Second Survey*.

In Santiago, Prebisch was restored physically and mentally by the new challenge, regaining the energy of his Central Bank days and looking younger than before Havana. He returned to a daily eighteen-hour work regime, organizing the work of the Research Centre, selecting its staff, and seeking out new talent. The economists already in Santiago formed an eclectic but interesting group. Besides Martinez-Cabañas, who was constantly travelling, Eugenio Castillo and Louis (Speck) Swenson comprised the Office of the Executive Secretary in overall charge of the Secretariat. Swenson was the rare American both trusted by Latin Americans and also able to communicate effectively with UN and State Department officials, indispensable for ECLA, and vice versa. "We like Santiago," he wrote to a friend in New York after his arrival, "the Chileans are cordial and friendly."[6] Milic Kybal, half-Mexican although a citizen of both the US and Czechoslovakia, was another interesting international expert at ECLA. Originally hired in August 1948 on a six-month contract, and rapidly promoted to head of research before the Havana meeting, Kybal was a capable industry expert but more of a follower than leader. His constant reminiscences of unforgettable years at the Federal Reserve both irritated colleagues and called his commitment into question. Celso Furtado stood out as an outstanding economist and intellectual. He had fought with the Brazilian Brigade in Italy and remained in Europe for graduate work at the Sorbonne; Gudin and Bulhões recognized him as one of the leading minds in the country and encouraged him to try ECLA. Their interest, as well as the preference of his Argentine partner for a Spanish language milieu, had brought him to Santiago. Most of the other economists had been educated in the US or Britain. Regino Boti, a trade specialist was alternately brilliant, funny, and maddening in the Cuban way – a self-declared socialist obsessed with the US who had attended Harvard and boasted that he had never read a page of Marx and hired on the recommendations of senior UN headquarters staff for his statistical skills. Others stood out less prominently. Chilean Bruno Leuschener, a mining engineer, was the brother-in-law of founder Benjamin Cohen; the two Argentines Alizon Garcia and Raúl Rey Alvarez were ex-officials of the Central Bank in Prebisch's era; Bolivian Jorge Alcázar and Central American Francisco Aquino, both agriculture specialists, provided regional balance. Jorge Ahumada, a Chilean specialist in international trade research, joined the team soon after the Havana Conference.[7]

The appointment of Prebisch to head the new Research Centre marked the real birth of ECLA. Morale in Santiago improved; staff discovered a director who could actually draft his own texts and was a leader in ideas as well as management. His presence was commanding, and he was a stickler for literate prose. Some staff members had met Prebisch in December 1948, when Castillo had invited him to Santiago as part of the campaign to enlist him for the *Economic Survey*; the encounter had not been very successful. Meticulously dressed in a grey wool suit, with accompanying distinguished greying temples, he seemed aloof and from a different generation. Alizon Garcia and Rey Alvarez had prepared the staff for his visit with anecdotes, describing his iron control over all aspects of the Argentine Central Bank before 1943, including his insistence on special crockery for directors. But they found that he was not entirely humourless after all, even if demanding and ruthless when crossed. He himself set the standard of commitment and excellence, and he expected no less from his staff. Principally he was a listener, subjecting staff members to a barrage of questions that eventually left them drained and exhausted – but also exhilarated by engagement in the ECLA cause. Prebisch not only commanded the spotlight but also seemed to empower those around him. His leadership created a new enthusiasm within ECLA in Santiago, and it entered a period of intense activity and expectation. It was as if the continuing threat to its existence created a special bond within the small ECLA team. Visiting Santiago in 1950, Hans Singer was struck by an atmosphere of innovation and commitment so intense and rare that it recalled Cambridge in the 1930s.[8]

Between 1928 and 1943 Prebisch had supervised teams of researchers, and after his dismissal from the Central Bank he had felt isolated and bereft; now, finally, he had a team again, with a budget and the capacity to support the large-scale economic research required in the region. Latin America's needs were enormous, from reliable baseline data and policy development to human resource strengthening at all levels. An entire regional infrastructure had to be created. In November Prebisch was back in North America to recruit senior Latin Americans who were already employed in other agencies, such as Javier Marquez in the IMF. Bernstein agreed to release Marquez for work on the *Second Survey*, and Prebisch strengthened his ties with younger economists such as Victor Urquidi.

ECLA's immediate challenge was to prepare for its third session, in Montevideo, where success was essential for survival and would be measured by the quality of the second *Economic Survey*: it had to be demonstrably superior to Havana. Everyone from Prebisch to the secretaries was focused on a single date – 5 June 1950. By 27 February Raúl had sent a provisional agenda to headquarters encompassing long-term trends of economic development, the problem of productivity in industry, financing economic development, the role of trade in promoting economic development, and technical assistance for economic development. Latin governments were demanding an economic survey that would be sufficiently practical and policy-relevant to be interesting; they had used up their gold and foreign-exchange reserves accumulated during World War II and were experiencing economic difficulties. The report would therefore have to interpret the current situation with detailed sectoral analyses but also present case studies on individual regional economies in sufficient depth to show that ECLA could deliver useful research. Prebisch selected four countries for detailed study – Mexico, Brazil, Chile, and Argentina – but the preparation of such an ambitious economic survey threatened to overwhelm the Research Centre, even with staff working flat-out and Raúl's mobilization of additional resources in New York. He approached David Grove, chief of the Latin American Section in the US Federal Reserve Research Department, hoping that he could be seconded for special research assignments. But there was still a lack of staff strength, and Prebisch therefore went directly to Latin governments, requesting that their best Central Bank economists work with ECLA on short-term assignments – a concept with the double advantage of directly involving competent country specialists in the *Survey*, while also giving these economists the experience of working with other Latin Americans. Besides leading and coordinating his expanded research team, Prebisch prepared a theoretical paper ("Growth, Disequilibrium and Disparities") as an introduction to the *Economic Survey* to elaborate and deepen the theoretical framework of his Havana *Manifesto*.[9]

As Montevideo approached it became evident that ECLA had fallen behind in its work program and would not be able to circulate the *Economic Survey* and other important documents before the meeting. UN headquarters was unhappy, as were governments. In fact both New York and (even more) the staff in Santiago had been frustrated with the leadership skills of Martinez-Cabañas since his arrival. Although the Research Centre was generating draft research reports on schedule, the Executive Office was not supporting its work in the editing, production, printing, and circulation phase. As well as travelling too much and having little managerial experience, Martinez-Cabañas was not able to delegate effectively, and when he realized that ECLA would fail to circulate materials, he tried to placate the US State Department by sending a copy of the still confidential agenda well in advance of the Montevideo meeting.

All the Latin American capitals were watching Washington. The Truman Administration was still reviewing US policy toward the Americas after his reelection in autumn 1949; like virtually all US presidents before and since, Truman had opened his new administration by promising to revitalize relations with Latin America. From early 1949 Secretary of State Acheson talked up the priority of inter-American relations, insisting that US neglect since 1945 and the onset of the Cold War would be reversed. In a speech to the Pan-American Society on 19 September 1949, he announced a package of new initiatives that was widely praised in Latin capitals. The US Bureau of Inter-American Affairs was reorganized and strengthened around a mission promoting security, democracy, and economic development; and a full-time ambassador was assigned to the Inter-American ECOSOC to beef up regional multilateralism. President Truman reaffirmed Acheson's message in a reception on 12 October; Assistant Secretary of State Miller followed up with such flowery speeches invoking wartime solidarity that one of his ambassadors feared the consequences of overselling the new resolve in Washington. He grotesquely misquoted Milton's *Paradise Lost,* "With rain upon rain, rout on rout, confusion worse compounded," for the truth was that the Truman Administration still had made no decision on Latin American policy as internal disagreements continued over the final wording of "Objectives/Policies of the US regarding Latin America."[10]

Atlanticists like George Kennan downplayed the importance of a regional approach to Latin America, arguing that Washington should select a few significant allies like Brazil and Mexico rather that promote a geopolitical fiction like "the Western Hemisphere." Nelson Rockefeller in contrast underlined the need for long-term US economic engagement in Latin America. John C. Dreier argued that it was a mistake to give Latin Americans the impression that they had a right to be consulted before the US took important steps in the world. Louis B. Halle Jr championed solidarity, favouring consultation as the British did with "their Commonwealth," acknowledging that certain Latin American grievances against the US were justified, but nevertheless regretting the persistence of "old concepts" such as "the US exercises leadership in world affairs on behalf of the community of American states." Miller warned against "an excessive tendency to put on the hair shirt." Acheson tended toward the flowery. At a meeting of Latin American leaders he insisted, "we are a part, inescapably of the partnership of the free world," not, he said, "an alliance, like those which criss-crossed Europe in the last century," not as "a sphere of influence arrangement or a satellite system" but as "a spiritual confederation of peoples as well as nations" that are bound together by "their concern for freedom."[11]

But all these officials agreed that the Americas was a US zone, and therefore that the OAS represented the US "reserve security system." Halle confided that "the twenty other Republics are, largely by force of circumstances, our clients. That is the basis of our leadership."[12] The OAS served as the only exclusive US-Latin American link, and therefore was a worthwhile investment. The US paid most of the budget; its headquarters were in Washington; the US had control over appointments and programs; and, not least, Inter-American ECOSOC Executive Secretary Amos E. Taylor was an American. It followed that the OAS should remain as the unchallenged forum for US-Latin American relations, rather than having ECLA (funded by the United Nations) share this inter-American turf and duplicate responsibilities. The Truman Administration had already been stung by attacks earlier that year, gaining momentum after 9 February, by Joseph McCarthy, Republican Senator from Wisconsin, that the US State Department had been infiltrated by communists who were duping Truman into a policy of appeasement. The President's approval rating was eroding sharply. McCarthy's anti-communist crusade retrenched US foreign and domestic policy sharply toward the right and injected a harsher ideological orthodoxy into US-Latin American relations. Some experts on the UN payroll had been, or were still, leftists or communists; an ideological witch hunt within US agencies would certainly spread to the international civil service whether in New York or Santiago. Since Latin governments were themselves more anti-communist than the US – only in Guatemala were there rumblings against the United Fruit Company – the Truman Administration realized that the region was politically safe. But was it completely loyal? Whereas the OAS was safely headquartered in Washington, ECLA was potentially unpredictable in its hiring and activities. It was tiny now, but what if it hired leftists or even communists? What if it turned US-Latin American irritants into major confrontations – such as, for example, the creation of an Inter-American development bank, which Washington had just vetoed in Bogotá? From its very inception, tiny ECLA was a wild card and irritant in US-Latin American relations – not for what it was in 1948–49 but for what it might become in the future. Implicitly at least, it challenged the inter-American system represented by the OAS and the 1947 Rio Treaty of Reciprocal Assistance, outside the ideological conformity of Cold War anti-communism. Unlike the OAS, ECLA was not predictable or fully controllable, and there was no way to prevent the emergence of radical views on markets and the state or priorities different from those of Washington regarding the communist threat, security, and development. Latin Americans supported economic development, with the Cold War a secondary concern; in Washington it was the other way around. In this equation ECLA was clearly identified with development, and its survival had symbolic overtones in inter-American relations.

By early 1950 the Truman Administration was confident that the OAS would prevail over ECLA. At two inter-American meetings in April the termination of ECLA was openly supported by Mexico, Argentina, Colombia, El Salvador, and Panama, as well as the US. Chile, Brazil, Uruguay, Guatemala, and Cuba continued to back ECLA, while Peru objected to the presence of European governments in the Commission, and neither Venezuela nor Ecuador had strong opinions one way or the other. With this support Washington pressed its agenda forward. On 5 May, the OAS delivered a formal note to Trygve Lie announcing that it had created the Program of Technical Cooperation in direct competition with the UN.[13] Latin governments such as Chile, which supported ECLA, were frustrated by Washington's overt favouritism. A month before the Montevideo meeting, Hernan Santa Cruz, the Chilean UN permanent representative who had taken a lead role in ECLA's creation two years earlier, "literally collared" his US counterpart (according to a State Department account of the incident) to complain against this effort to liquidate ECLA. The US replied that there was "no justification to talk about a 'US Plan', but that there were a number of Latin American Republics which – with us, felt that the present duplication was paralyzing constructive action both in ECLA and Inter-American ECOSOC and which considered that the present situation was untenable." Santa Cruz "grew most plaintive over our attempt to 'scuttle ECLA.'" He considered the Inter-American ECOSOC useless ("how can you have duplication between something and nothing?") while ECLA was the only effective multilateral mechanism to deal with Latin America's economic problems.[14]

ECLA had only one more year to run before its three-year trial period was up, and it had to build support and momentum at Montevideo for its coming test. US strategy at the third session was the reverse – to undermine ECLA's credibility by a campaign of quiet diplomacy, letting Argentina and Colombia take the lead by promoting its merger with the OAS among hold-out governments in the region, while pre-empting any resolution that called for its continuation beyond 1951. But while the US delegation would play a largely passive role, hoping that ECLA's managerial disorder in preparing the Montevideo meeting would speak for itself, it would hold a series of dinners for each Latin delegation at its embassy to convince them that ECLA should be merged with the OAS Inter-American Economic and Social Council.

This strategy collided with loyalties from the past. Chris Ravndal had been appointed as US Ambassador in Montevideo, and in that position was named the Acting United States Representative for ECLA's third session. The Cold War had not been kind to his career: senior appointments in Washington and abroad had yielded only a modest diplomatic posting to close out his long service in the State Department. But at least Ravndal was back in the Southern Cone, his preferred part of the world, and could again work with Prebisch. He reported to Washington on 9 June, "I have known Dr Prebisch well since 1935 and I saw much of him both officially and privately during my six years' assignment in Buenos Aires. I have no hesitation in stating that, to my knowledge, Dr Prebisch not only is a gentleman of excellent character but also one of the most competent and revered economists in Latin America. Also, in my experience, he is a highly congenial person to work with." Alas, Ravndal's diplomatic task was to undermine both ECLA and his friend Prebisch.

The Montevideo meeting got off to a slow start as delegates gradually assembled from European and Western Hemisphere capitals. ECLA's preparations for the conference had been inadequate and confused, and since documents were not circulated to capitals before the meetings, governments were not able to give instruction to their delegations; some materials were not circulated until well into the event. The organization of the meeting fell apart altogether; it took ten days before the principal Committee on Economic Development began its detailed work, with the result that the other related agendas were lumped together. In the end four extra days had to be added to conclude the business. But there were other problems: standard procedures were not enforced by the chairs, so that new proposals would suddenly appear without notice, and it was never clear whether delegates were speaking in a personal capacity or as representatives of their governments. More worrisome for Martinez-Cabañas was the distinctly lower-level diplomatic representation in Montevideo compared with Havana a year earlier. The UN secretary-general did not come this time, sending David Owen, who only stayed for a few days. In Havana the Latin American delegations were not top-drawer, but at least they came; this time, as if ECLA's glamour had already diminished in the region, important countries such as Peru, Venezuela, and Costa Rica chose to remain absent altogether. Among the others Argentina, Colombia, Bolivia, Ecuador, the Dominican Republic, El Salvador, Honduras, Paraguay, Nicaragua, Panama, and Haiti were virtually invisible; Mexico took a low-key approach with a largely technical mission; and Brazil was represented by General Gomes, well liked because of his amiable personality and friendly attitude but not an appointment that signalled much interest in ECLA. This left four small countries – Chile, Cuba, Uruguay, and Guatemala – as the most vocal delegations at the conference. While representatives from the IMF, ILO, IRO, UNESCO, and the FAO showed up in Montevideo, the World Bank decided not to participate. The main interest of the three European members was in resettling refugees from Central Europe – Aide Suisse à l'Europe alone had plans to move 100,000 Europeans to Latin America – and therefore they requested that ECLA set up the Economic Development and Immigration Committee, to work with the IRO (the International Relief Organization, which was renamed the Office of the UN High Commissioner for Refugees a year later). The British delegation, led by H.M. Phillips, deferred to Washington or drank in the bar.

Despite all these problems ECLA's Montevideo session was surprisingly successful. US attempts to manage the ECLA-OAS issue almost succeeded, until General Gomes declared that Brazil "greatly admired the work of ECLA" and "that the Inter-American ECOSOC served no useful purpose." The Cuban delegation agreed, observing that "Certain Latin American countries feel that Latin American organizations are dominated by the US." Guatemala denounced the proposed merger in the most anti-American tones of all the delegations. Soon the unruly Latin family was on display: Chile in its role of apostle for the underdeveloped countries; the divided Cuban delegation introducing totally contradictory resolutions on its trade with the US, although united in praise for Prebisch and hostility to Martinez-Cabañas; and Marco Antonio Ramirez, the lone Guatemalan delegate, who was the "problem-child" of the meeting (according to the US delegation) in his relentless criticisms levelled against the United Fruit Company.[15] Amos E. Taylor attended, along with Jorge Mejia Palacio, the Colombian representative on the Inter-American Council, with the latter reading a bewilderingly disastrous speech (described by Hernan Santa Cruz as "the best argument he had yet heard for ECLA"). Overall the Santiago research team embarrassed its moribund OAS counterpart, but the reality on the OAS-ECLA standoff was continuing stalemate, since it was evident that, while the US was committed to getting rid of ECLA, a good number of Latin American governments had dug in their heels to support it. Ravndal reported this impasse to Washington noting that a merger might be acceptable in Latin America providing it "retained a single, strong, and independent Secretariat." In the same line he linked this condition with Raúl Prebisch remaining in ECLA. "Dr Prebisch is obviously held in the highest esteem by the Latin American governments and constitutes an unusually able champion of their economic views."[16]

As in Havana, Prebisch was ECLA's central figure at Montevideo. His presentation of the *Economic Survey* in the Economic Development Committee dominated the entire meeting; here was the same personality and charisma as at Havana, the same leadership in substance, and the same ability to communicate. Ravndal once again observed Raúl in action, seeing again the energy of the Argentine years, and in his confidential report of the Montevideo meeting he explained to Washington that Prebisch's new vocabulary of development had seeped into the meeting like osmosis, changing its dynamic subtly and profoundly. "It was interesting," he observed, "to note the manner in which many of the Latin American delegates, by the end of the session, had adopted as their own much of the thinking and even the technical phrases used by Dr Prebisch in his central thesis on Latin American economic development."[17] Prebisch was the magnet of attention – this was the undeniable reality – as the second *Economic Survey* was received with enthusiasm and reported favourably throughout the region. Work of this quality and depth on Latin America did not exist; the 650-page document and country studies represented frontier work. Prebisch gave voice to the overwhelming official and public interest in economic development in the region, spending days at the podium fielding both policy and theoretical questions on the four country studies produced for the meeting as well as global challenges confronting Latin America in the international economy. If Havana gave Prebisch visibility, Montevideo added credibility. "The research work produced under his direction," reported Ravndal, "is welcomed and endorsed by many who might be suspicious of facts and conclusions presented by economists in Washington."

The only resolution of substance presented at Montevideo, with the biblical sounding title of *Economic Decalogue,* comprised a set of principles to guide economic development in Latin America. It was drawn up by a working group in which US representatives had been absent. In essence the ten-point *Economic Decalogue* asserted that Latin American governments should adopt specific development goals, with an order of priorities for their realization, and that they should identify specific policies to intensify their growth rate and overcome obstacles.[18] It was evident that the resolution was linked with Prebisch's central thesis on development outlined in the *Economic Survey* – that Latin America had to overcome its external vulnerability and break a vicious cycle of low productivity, low income, and low savings by restructuring domestic production and imports (i.e., promote industrialization). The US delegation objected to being caught completely unawares and threatened to block the *Decalogue,* prompting the threat of a serious US-Latin American rift and even the failure of the entire conference.

This crisis was overcome through the efforts of Pierre Mendès-France, who led the French delegation and was also the UN *rapporteur* with the task of reporting its results to the ECOSOC meeting on 7 July in Geneva. Along with Prebisch he was the most visible participant at Montevideo, and the two became inseparable after meeting. Not only were they the only two persons at the meeting who had read every page of the vast documentation, but they were both dominant intellectuals who enjoyed each other's company and shared a common vision of the UN. If Mendès-France admired Prebisch's capacity and his fluent French, Raúl felt privileged to meet one of France's leading personalities. Both were prodigies and shared trajectories; Mendès-France had been elected as a Radical Socialist Deputy in 1932 and (like Raúl) was named undersecretary to the Treasury when he was twenty-nine years old. Both were outsiders, with Mendès-France born to Sephardic Jewish immigrants from Tunisia. Both were short and stocky; both were outstandingly endowed intellectually. But while Prebisch had been rejected by his country, Mendès-France was accepted and had become a key political figure with General de Gaulle during the war and then in Paris after 1945. He had led the French delegation to the Bretton Woods Conference, served on the World Bank board of governors and with the IMF, and had decided to serve on ECOSOC for the three-year period from 1947 to 1950. His arrival in Montevideo signalled definitive and full support for ECLA after France's initial reservations, and no person was better placed to broker agreements between the Latins and Americans. According to Ravndal, "Because of his remarkable intellect, his personal prestige, and his skill in negotiation and debate he had an unusual influence over the Latin American Delegations."[19] In return, Mendès-France urged his American colleagues not to oppose the *Decalogue* given its overwhelming endorsement within Latin America and the general nature of the wording, which avoided specific commitments from the US or other industrial countries. In the end the US accepted his advice with the insertion of "pending further study," and the meeting finally terminated with the adoption of the *Decalogue*. But the US remained unhappy. When Mendès-France presented his *Rapporteur* document to ECOSOC on 7 August in Geneva, its representative, Dr Walter M. Kotschnig, maintained that some of its conclusions were "debatable," and the Council merely "noted" ECLA's statement, rather than "noted with approval." Even then the US abstained from the otherwise 13–0 vote of appreciation for ECLA, which also set the date for its fourth session to open on 29 May 1951 in Mexico.[20]

Prebisch left for New York on 20 June immediately after the meeting to settle the question of his future with the UN, for his success at Montevideo forced the question of ECLA leadership into the open. During the meeting there had been a rumour that he would be leaving Santiago after the expiry of his one-year contract with ECLA to become deputy director of the newly created Technical Assistance Administration in New York – a powerful new UN instrument, grouping technical assistance and training, public sector management, scholarships and fellowships, and advisory social welfare services. Its director-general, Hugh L. Keenleyside, formerly deputy minister in Canada's Department of Resources and Development, had invited him to join, and Castillo also wanted to come as Raúl's assistant. Prebisch had himself confided his impending departure to Ravndal, who in turn reported it to Washington over a note hoping that Raúl could continue his work in the region rather than leave Latin America. This news enlivened the meeting with a sense of drama; Prebisch preferred the leadership of ECLA to moving to New York, but Martinez-Cabañas had only begun his term and showed no signs of leaving. Moreover, Mexico supported

Martinez-Cabañas as a native son, while Prebisch again was bedevilled by the absence of home government support.

In New York he met with David Owen, Keenleyside, Malinowski, and Secretary-General Trygve Lie; he also met with the Latin and US delegations to the United Nations, announcing that he had accepted the job of deputy to Keenleyside and would be leaving Santiago. When the Latin governments, particularly Chile, heard this news, they confronted UN headquarters and demanded that Prebisch be appointed executive secretary of ECLA instead. Trygve Lie faced a quandary, but after Montevideo he had little option. The other two regional commissions were struggling: the ECE under Gunnar Myrdal had started off well, as had the ECAFE, but the ECE confronted Cold War polarization while the Economic Commission for Asia and the Far East in Bangkok lacked identity and China. He needed at least one healthy commission, but Owen and the secretary-general knew that, while Martinez-Cabañas was not a leader, removing him could be messy. Prebisch was the one person who could pull ECLA together and give it a regional profile. Trygve Lie checked with Washington – and got a favourable US response. Acheson saw the State Department report on 26 June and scribbled on the margin, "Thanks for your note re: Dr Prebisch. I have heard good things about him." With this Trygve Lie appointed Prebisch executive secretary – at the price of promoting Martinez-Cabañas to the position Keenleyside had offered to Raúl. Leaving Santiago permanently on 26 July (without having received his furniture shipped from Buenos Aires), Martinez-Cabañas encountered Raúl returning from New York. They had little to say to one another.[21]

After Montevideo Prebisch's confidence and energy enveloped the organization. He redoubled efforts to keep his best staff and hire others, but the market for Latin American economists was extremely tight. Already in January 1950 he had approached the World Bank and International Monetary Fund for two American economists, noting the shortage of qualified Latin Americans and ECLA's determination not to poach. "I would not have dared to write to you as I know the scarcity in this field," he noted, only to have the problem confirmed by Leonard Rist at the Bank that, "with our growing activity in Latin America we are, in fact, in the same predicament as you, and we are competing for the same kind of training and abilities ... a scarcity which will only grow worse – or better for the economists."[22] The cost of living in Santiago went up 24 percent during 1950 while the value of the US dollar dropped 30 percent. Moreover the fact that ECLA's existence was at stake in the forthcoming Mexico fourth session also set a practical limit on ECLA's resources: the UN would not increase its budget until its future was secure. Prebisch needed people who were prepared to commit fully and permanently, and he therefore insisted with New York that ECLA increase salary levels to keep the best of his staff who were being offered better-paid jobs elsewhere. Swenson stayed on as executive assistant, from now on Prebisch's key right-hand man, and Castillo decided to stay in Santiago. Prebisch also convinced Javier Marquez to leave the IMF to become his successor as head of the Research Centre, but Marquez soon left Santiago to become Mexico's alternate executive director at the IMF. Furtado had two offers at higher salary levels from Brazil. So did Boti from the Cuban Central Bank. Prebisch hunted for other economists from Argentina, Brazil, Peru, and Colombia as well as Central America, where, he confided to First Secretary H. Gerald Smith from the US Embassy, "he had great difficulty in locating Central American economists who have not become tinged with the Marxist thinking of a considerable portion of Mexican economists."[23] He also fended off offers to extract Jorge Ahumada from ECLA; educated at Harvard in the same class as Manuel Noriega Morales of Guatemala and Regino Boti of Cuba, before beginning a series of jobs in Puerto Rico and the IMF (where he worked with Javier Marquez), the Guatemala Central Bank, and Chile, Ahumada's leadership potential made him a Prebisch favourite within the secretariat.

In spite of difficulties the ECLA team held and grew; while Prebisch could not match outside salaries, he offered two elements that other agencies could not and that proved irresistible for the best young Latin Americans. First they shared an awareness of participating in a unique experience – in the creation of Latin America. Economists from all parts of this region were working together and sharing experiences in the common overriding tasks: understanding Latin America's place in the international economic system and solving its economic, developmental and technological problems. They were beginning with their own experiences, not those of the industrial countries, in formulating theories of development. The very fact that ECLA might not survive heightened the awareness of personal risk and potential sacrifice; instead of the security of other less challenging jobs, they had chosen the solidarity accompanying life on the edge. Prebisch also captured the loyalty of ECLA staff by liberating them from the usual procedure at UN headquarters, where personnel files were automatically cleared with the US mission before approval. With this achievement, unique in the UN system, all staff, including Americans, became real colleagues rather than mere co-workers; none of the other regional commissions won this privilege, and as the McCarthy period deepened and its pressure on the UN grew, ECLA became an oasis of ideological calm relative to Washington. Alexander Ganz, for example, who had worked in Operation "Bootstrap" in Puerto Rico and had flirted with the US Communist

Party in the 1930s, was hired for his professional abilities by Prebisch in 1951 after a favourable recommendation by his conservative boss, Harvey Perloff. Adolfo Dorfman was a leftist from Argentina; he also would be hounded from New York, but could find shelter in Santiago so long as his work remained satisfactory. But ECLA's main attraction was Prebisch's accomplishment in creating a work environment without parallel, which both challenged his best staff and rewarded ideological pluralism. In the reorganization of the Secretariat, for example, Furtado became director of development (his team, which included Boti and Ganz, was known as the "Red Division"); but Prebisch chose Ahumada, a conservative Chilean Christian Democrat, to head the Training Program. Encouraging – but also balancing – these divergent views strengthened debate within the organization, with Prebisch retaining control over policy and publications.[24]

Prebisch also launched a diplomatic campaign to establish ECLA as a *fait accompli* in Washington and among international organizations. The US capital was in political flux, not so much after the outbreak of the Korean War on 25 June 1950 but rather after 26 November, when China sent US forces reeling in a ground attack that neutralized General McArthur's earlier military successes. Mobilization for a major Asian conflict deepened the latent conflict of priorities between the US and Latin America, and the combined impact of the Korean War and the irreversible division of Europe also strengthened Senator McCarthy. Prebisch opted for transparency in his relations with the US Embassy on the (correct) assumption that the CIA was tracking him in any case. But he was firm. When he briefed embassy officials in Santiago after Montevideo on his plans for the reorganization of ECLA he told them that he did not anticipate a one-year job. "There is apparently no doubt in Dr Prebisch's mind," they confirmed, "that the ECLA, including the secretariat, will be continued beyond 1951."[25]

Also, ECLA had to be effective within the cumbersome UN system, which alone could shelter Santiago from the storms in Washington but which also fed on its living parts. Leaving Swenson and Castillo in charge in Santiago, Prebisch attended the ECOSOC meetings in Geneva from 29 July to 1 September to make sure that ECLA was visible and represented. Mendès-France was magnificent, praising ECLA as the most efficient and least expensive of the regional commissions, making "an outstanding contribution to the understanding the region in the fields of economic development, domestic stability, foreign trade and balance of payments." He also lavished recognition on Prebisch for the "brilliant report" of the Research Centre and reassured his Western colleagues that ECLA was nothing if not moderate in its approach to economic development. Not only had it warned against inflation, but also it "had unanimously condemned autarky, on the grounds that economic development required, not self-sufficiency, but a greater volume of foreign trade." Canada found the *Economic Survey* "very useful"; Denmark was "greatly impressed"; and even the US delegate conceded (bearing in mind US reservations about the central thesis) that it was "a first-class study and a valuable contribution." Only Perón's delegate from Argentina condemned the "lack of balance in the secretariat." Prebisch also found, probably to his surprise, that the *Economic Decalogue* was not only praised by many members of ECOSOC but had also put ECLA on the development map globally. Sir A. Ramaswami Mudaliar (India) was impressed by the moderate and constructive tone of the resolution and by the similarities he saw in the problems and difficulties facing Latin American and Asian countries. Walker (Australia) acknowledged the parallels between Australian and Latin American experience, particularly regarding the linkage between industrialization and development. Taking the side of ECLA, he contradicted the British ECOSOC representative who warned Latin Americans against attaching too much importance to industrialization and advised a "wise middle course" to avoid the dangers of imposing high tariff barriers. In this way, he argued, Latin America would follow the experience of Canada and Australia, "whose economic development had been natural and had not been forced by undue industrialization, and which now enjoyed living standards among the highest in the world." No! Walker boomed. The British had it all wrong. So far from having followed a so-called "natural" or laissez-faire path, Australia (like Canada) "had attempted on several occasions to force the pace of its own economic development, with a considerable measure of success." Its steel industry, nonexistent before 1914, had been developed with state support during the interwar period, "with the result that by the time of the Second World War it had been possible to develop a large number of secondary industries on that basis." Mudaliar thereupon demanded greater understanding from the Western industrial countries of the aspirations of developing countries and their need to escape a reliance on commodity production. A richer developing world would also benefit them, he argued, and in any case they retained the upper hand by controlling foreign investment.[26]

But despite ECLA's expanding support within the UN, its survival at the fourth session could still not be taken in Mexico City for granted; this would depend partly on deepening its support within Latin America but mainly on the flow of US-Latin American relations during the Korean War. As in the Second World War, the US needed Latin America – or at least its strategic minerals – for the war effort and therefore courted governments in the region. For their part, Latin leaders became more assertive about linking the sudden wartime commodities boom with their longer-term economic development needs; while it provided a short-term economic stimulus, they feared the hidden costs, such as a shortage of industrial imports during the war and the certain collapse of prices when it ended. At a special foreign ministers meeting called by the US to discuss the crisis, Latin American representatives vowed not to repeat the negative experience of World War II. This time, they argued, a boom-and-bust cycle had to be avoided, and Latin strategic commodities should get a fair market price rather than subsidize the US war effort. Washington countered by invoking inter-American solidarity and burden-sharing in the face of a global threat to the West; the US was vocal at the level of principle, but silent in practice, careful to avoid specific commitments. The result was an undercurrent of discontent in Latin America where standing up to the Americans was tempting; and when the Truman Administration continued its campaign to merge ECLA with Inter-American ECOSOC, Santiago's survival became a symbol of maintaining Latin autonomy. Not surprisingly the US failed to win an endorsement of its plan by the Latin American foreign ministers before the Mexico meeting opened on 28 May.[27]

The US therefore arrived in Mexico City with fewer Latin or European allies than at Montevideo, and this time there were no organizational foul-ups; nothing at ECLA's fourth session was left to chance. Prebisch had narrowed the agenda and streamlined the structure, with four committees to guide the work of the conference, compressing the economic topics into Economic Development, Trade, Coordination and General Questions, and the Functions of ECLA. This time all the documents were circulated to governments well before the meeting and correctly labelled. He carefully selected the seven ECLA staff members who would accompany him, sent Castillo to Mexico months in advance, and arrived a week early himself to supervise the final preparations and liaise with the delegations. He also came armed with an expanded *Economic Survey*, which contained ten country studies (Argentina, Brazil, Chile, Colombia, Cuba, Venezuela, Mexico, Guatemala, El Salvador, and Uruguay), as well as special reports on the regional economic impact of the Korean War and trade between Latin America and Europe. To complement these immediate themes he also produced *Theoretical and Practical Problems of Economic Growth*, the final instalment of the theoretical essays initiated in Havana and continued in Montevideo, which together comprised the "ECLA Thesis." When Mexican Secretary of Economy Antonio Martinez Baez opened the third session, the delegations encountered a professional operation organized to the last detail and with clear future objectives, beginning with the ECLA-OAS issue. Prebisch's strategy was to force a decision on ECLA's status at the outset of the meeting, gambling that an ECLA victory would produce sufficient momentum to deepen its hold in the region and expand Santiago's mandate and budget; but this meant confronting the Americans on an issue everyone knew to be hazardous.

To Prebisch's amazement another American ghost from the past appeared in Mexico; Merwin Bohan had been named acting US representative for the fourth session. The old warhorse from Buenos Aires days, who had played such an important role in Prebisch's downfall in 1943, had earlier been appointed the US permanent representative to the OAS to strengthen it in its rivalry with ECLA. Like Chris Ravndal at Montevideo, Bohan was also struck by the irony of his newest confrontation with Prebisch; he was generally well-liked in Latin America and knew very well that this issue had become hot in US-Latin American relations. He realized, for example, that a blunt resolution to merge the two organizations would fail, and that Washington therefore had to come up with a more subtle option. Most important, the Americans were suspect and had to stay in the background; meanwhile, a solid Latin partner – Mexico – could take the lead role in luring other countries into acceptance. Bohan came up with the idea of proposing that ECLA continue for another two years, conditional on coordinating its activities with the OAS, and hold its meetings concurrently with Inter-American ECOSOC, and for a while the outlook appeared promising; the US convinced Mexico to play the role of stalking-horse while the US delegation flooded the meeting with materials condemning the evils of duplication. But the plan had to be abandoned in the face of overwhelming Latin American opposition to yet another US manoeuvre to abolish ECLA. The French delegation also came to ECLA's defense. Philippe de Seynes, a protégé of Pierre Mendès-France, and no less attracted to Prebisch, told the meeting that, while France did not want to intervene in so sensitive an issue, he nevertheless felt compelled to stress that "ECLA was the only specialized UN organization which worked without ideological quarrels and the tiresome division into ideological blocs which affected its other agencies." This oblique criticism of McCarthyism in Washington left the Latins howling. Bohan groaned but was stumped. Even Mexico's head of delegation, Carillo Flores, broke with his government by openly backing ECLA.[28] "Debate in plenary and all committees has demonstrated unanimous support for continuance and independence of ECLA," Bohan cabled to Washington. The Americans then worked for three days to find a face-saving formula that would at least leave the issue open for future decisions; they finally came up with a new approach that attracted quite broad Latin – particularly Mexican – support. In this plan the Commission would accept the permanence of ECLA, but agree to a permanent ECLA-OAS Working Group to be established in Washington. Prebisch was concerned that this compromise was dangerous for Santiago because decision-making would inevitably drift north toward the power concentrated in the US capital, but he agreed to work with Bohan on a wording that would limit the damage to ECLA.

By 10 June Bohan thought he had achieved consensus, but Miguel Osorio de Almeida, the Brazilian delegate, suddenly threw his carefully laid plans into disarray by communicating his government's objection to any resolution that undermined ECLA's future independence. Bohan's compromise was irrelevant, he argued, because there was no problem of duplication with the OAS. Bohan complained that Miguel Osorio had exceeded his instructions and that he had not in fact received personal instructions from President Vargas to block the US initiative. But Brazil wouldn't budge, and the US was stuck. Brazil was the bright spot in Latin America for Washington, and it was unwilling to create further divisions over an already controversial issue. "In Latin American eyes the whole history of ECLA is one of [US] non-cooperation," Bohan reported after the debacle. Washington had consistently misjudged the regional mood, and Bohan requested authority to capitulate – to align the US with the Latin Americans and Europeans in endorsing a permanent secretariat in Santiago: "USDEL believes ECLA question must be decided on policy and not position basis," he concluded. Acheson agreed.[29] Bohan immediately changed course and trumpeted that the "US Government is profoundly impressed by the high quality of work being performed by ECLA, and wishes to see the work continued and will give it whole-hearted support." Prebisch sent a telegram to his staff celebrating the good news: "We would like to share our sense of profound satisfaction with all our comrades in work in Santiago." It was "Auld Lang Syne" all around. Raúl responded warmly to Bohan, praising "our work together in earlier times," and thanked him for his support in Mexico. The Mexican Government lavished praise on ECLA; OAS and ECLA delegates embraced and heaped superlatives on each other. Americans applauded the farewell message that "the time has come for Latin America to find its own path," and Bohan became Prebisch's main ally in Washington until the Truman Administration tottered to a close the next year.[30]

The OAS victory was only the beginning of Prebisch's success at Mexico City; everything fell into place as the session evolved. ECLA was not only confirmed as a permanent UN regional commission, but it was expanded and strengthened. Instead of merely producing research reports, it moved to practical activities and concrete policy work with the addition of two functions to the secretariat's terms of reference. First Ahumada's new Training Centre for Latin economists was officially approved to begin operations in 1952, converting ECLA into an important regional educational instrument; and second, ECLA's operational capacity and advisory services in the region were strengthened by a new technical assistance mandate and budgetary resources from New York. Santiago would now be more visible and assertive in its development role. The Mexico Office was upgraded from liaison to branch office responsible for activities in Mexico, Central America, and the Caribbean; ECLA was also requested to lead a novel project to support Central American economic integration, to be overseen by a committee of economic cooperation comprised of the economic ministers from the five countries involved. To assert its importance, ECLA would direct it from the Mexican Office. Castillo moved up from Santiago to become its director, while Prebisch was finally successful in attracting Victor Urquidi as Castillo's research director, to take charge of the new Central American initiative. This vote of confidence in Santiago was symbolized by a resolution that further ECLA sessions be held every two years, rather than annually (with the much smaller Committee of the Whole between meetings). This gave Prebisch the necessary breathing space to complete ECLA's expanded work program, and he could now focus its strategy for the fifth session, scheduled for Rio in April 1953, with due calm and deliberation. Prebisch and ECLA shifted into high gear.

13 The Creation of Latin America

Happy the person who has a second chance in life, and ECLA's Mexico conference had delivered it to Raúl. The Central Bank – the concept, creation, team, and accomplishment – had been a historic moment for Prebisch. Everything had fit; he was at the centre of the Argentine state leading an administrative elite that provided a firm anchor for the national economy in the turbulent years after the Great Depression. Prebisch's team of Central Bank professionals was a modernizing elite united behind a coherent vision of national development in which competence was the sole criterion for advancement. The bank was not just another bureaucracy; he had created instead an island of rationality that maintained the economy despite political chaos. In 1943 he had suddenly lost everything – his job, his influence, and eventually his country. Cast into the wilderness, he could only watch as his beloved Central Bank was destroyed and his team dispersed, while Argentina floundered economically.

Unexpectedly the United Nations, beginning with ECLA's Havana Conference, opened a second coming. Raúl's years in the wilderness had this benefit: he could now view the scene from a regional perspective, having visited every part of Latin America and changed his understanding of development. Before 1943 his teaching and thinking had focused on Argentina; six years later his Havana *Manifesto* (*The Development of Latin America and Its Principal Problems*) represented a breakthrough that justified the struggles after his dismissal, while ECLA provided the vehicle to recreate his earlier Central Bank synthesis of theory, institutions, and policy. The doctrine was the ECLA Thesis developed between 1949 and 1951; the ECLA office in Santiago was his institutional base for animating regional development; and his team formed another modernizing elite under his guidance to provide an autonomous development policy for Latin America. Prebisch had created structuralism, and by the 1951 Mexico

City Conference he had brought together a formidable group of young economists. Every member of this small band felt privileged to work within ECLA; its fierce and reciprocal loyalty was reminiscent of the mood at the Central Bank under Prebisch. Santiago became a movement – almost a church – under the firm guidance of the "great heretic."

Where would all this lead? At Mexico City no one could possibly know. As head of the Argentine Central Bank, Prebisch had wielded real power; he now depended on cumbersome UN agencies, and these in turn were controlled by governments. Would either the Latin Americans or Washington retain faith in ECLA? The outlook in Washington was unpromising. McCarthyism had paralyzed the Truman Administration since 1950, and Truman's defeat in the forthcoming 1952 presidential elections looked certain. A Republican victory would sweep away the last of ECLA's supporters in the capital. As for the big international financial institutions, such as the IMF and World Bank, they could be expected to align themselves with US policy, whatever its stamp. Where would Prebisch find new allies if he became *persona non grata* in Washington?

The future of ECLA, it appeared, lay with Latin America itself. While the prevailing instability of the region ruled out the certainty of durable governmental allies, a new and educated generation across the region yearned to give substance to the concept of "Latin America." The challenge was to tap this latent energy, becoming both symbol and instrument of self-reliance. Prebisch's visits to Cuba, Brazil, and Central America after the Mexico City Conference were astounding successes – even national events. The gospel was there to be spread; the hearers were there to be reached.

And what of Raúl himself? Personally the new Prebisch bore little resemblance to the Buenos Aires central banker. Then he was socially invisible, a workaholic who spent the few hours away from work with family and friends. In the UN he was a striking public personality, elegantly clothed and coiffed, polished and pressed, charismatic. Now he was at the centre of crowds, quick and devastating in debate, and utterly commanding with large audiences, which he steered with effortless skill – writing his own speeches with care, memorizing them until he spoke without notes, and using all his energy to connect with the cheering crowds before him. Prebisch was an international celebrity, sweeping in with his entourage of ECLA acolytes like an archbishop with his priests, projecting the arrogance of brilliance. He pressed life hard and people flocked to him. Completing the aura was his reputation as a rake, discussed within his entourage in embarrassed undertones. But beneath this urbane, dynamic exterior lay the old self-deprecating, reserved, devoted, and ethically driven Prebisch of Tucumán, ready to emerge in the company of Adelita and close friends in El Maqui, their cliffside retreat outside Santiago overlooking the Maipo River.

Raúl's dream of returning to Argentina also simmered; ECLA was exciting, and Santiago was pleasant, but Buenos Aires retained its allure. Raúl and Adelita still owned two houses in Buenos Aires, including the mansion in San Isidro and country house in Mar del Plata, and Raúl kept abreast of political developments in Perónist Argentina through regular correspondence with Alfredo Moll and other friends in the capital. Reports confirmed a growing political opposition, which Raúl might have taken some satisfaction for predicting but which also confirmed his fears for the future of Argentina. Alfredo Moll wrote that Perón had realized his mistake in excluding Raúl from public life and that members of his inner circle wanted him back. He had made a decision not to return as long as Perón was in power; but would he go back after the dictatorship fell? All this lay in the future. Raúl's first life was over; the ECLA adventure of building Latin America was about to begin. There was no time to lose.

Prebisch left Mexico for Cuba to a glittering reception on 3 July 1951. President Carlos Prio Socarras insisted on long private discussions; the national press followed every word, printing the texts of his many speeches and press interviews, and he was overwhelmed with dinners and receptions and late nights at the Tropicana. Havana was in high excitement over a Latin American who had become an international celebrity. Raúl's earlier trips to the island were lovingly recalled, and he was again installed in the Hotel Nacional on the Malecón. Only two years had passed since he had presented his *Manifesto*; Cuba had loyally supported ECLA from the beginning through its most difficult years, and it was now rewarded with the first Prebisch visit to a Latin capital after beating back the US challenge in Mexico.

Technically he had been invited by Cuba's Agricultural and Industrial Development Bank (BANFAIC), but Prebisch was received with protocol and honours associated with heads of state. Filipe Pazos, formerly at the IMF, had returned to create the Cuban Central Bank (Banco Nacional) and was now its president. Eugenio Castillo, despite his known dislike of President Prio and friendship with Fulgencia Batista, accompanied Prebisch everywhere in Havana with his wife Patricia Willis.

President Prio sought a loosening of the US embrace, and ECLA's message of transformation through trade and industrial diversification was understandably compelling: in all Latin America, Cuba was the most firmly integrated within the US economy, a virtual satellite and extension of southern Florida and Texas. Trade unions and students at the University of Havana yearned for change, but the audience that came out to hear Prebisch also included businessmen and bankers. He had been, after all, a highly respected central banker himself, and in his impeccable blue pinstripe suits and with his confident presence he looked the part.

Prebisch's central message was change; Latin America had to think in new ways, he began. "The forced march of the first countries in the Industrial Revolution has created an economic firmament with a sun composed of the developed economies at the centre," he noted, "around which the peripheral countries rotate in their disorganized orbits."[1] Now Latin American countries needed the will to transform this relationship between centre and periphery. Latin Americans were caught up in a new global human drama – a historic struggle – which they could either win or lose. "Would they rise to the occasion?" he asked his hosts. If they lost faith they were doomed, because the fundamental requirement for success was moral – the *desire* for development.

Cuba, he noted, required a "radical change" in its economy away from dependence on the sugar sector. And Cuba, he insisted, *could* succeed. It possessed the resources and human talent for the transition, and President Prio's government had demonstrated its commitment to the new path advocated by ECLA by introducing protective tariffs to develop its infant textile industry. Cuba now had tools for protecting its economy, such as a professionally led Central Bank and BANFAIC to finance economic development and "substantially refashion the Cuban economy." The word "industrialization" was everywhere. "A country can only advance by industrial transformation," blared the typical headline during Prebisch's Havana visit.

The Cubans were spellbound by his rhetoric, and most saw only this side of his carefully crafted performances. But beneath the show there was another Prebisch evident to those who listened closely. While his broad message of regional revival appealed to Latin American pride and nationalism, Raúl was typically cautious when it came to specific measures for the promotion of economic development. While the overall regional goal must be the economic transformation of Latin America, he cautioned that the process would be lengthy and complex, requiring planning, accelerated industrialization, taxation and agrarian reform, technical cooperation, foreign investment, and the growth of trade. Cuba, he argued, should not fall into the trap of such extreme measures as abandoning the sugar sector; instead the Prio Government should strengthen it as a source of foreign exchange. While he strongly supported import substitution, he counselled against inflation and approved of Pazos's careful handling of monetary policy in the Central Bank. Repeatedly pressed by Cuban journalists, he offered few specific ideas about industrialization. Kenaf, he thought, offered a good opportunity for diversification, as did textiles, but of course the Cubans had already thought of that themselves. He emphasized the need for a strong private sector and the need for government flexibility. "A subsidy is simply a prescription for the retraining of workers," he noted, a transitional measure in the process of industrialization.[2] This other Prebisch – the technocrat – appeared to stress the limits of industrialization as much as his commitment to it as a central tool for development. And he was careful not to raise expectations about material help from ECLA. It would take several years to develop its full capacity; a training program was being set up, but miracles should not be expected.

The two Prebischs – the inspirational and the pragmatic – were as different in tone as they were in message. As a preacher his eloquence accentuated the message of hope and promise, pressing the mundane caution of Prebisch the policy advisor into the background. His Cuban hosts, journalists, workers, and students heard only the inspirational Prebisch.

Only once did the magic fail. A journalist asked a direct question: did Prebisch think that Washington had cut Cuba's sugar quota as a reprisal for tariffs on US textile imports? If so, how could Cuba ever hope to change its satellite status vis-à-vis the US? There was a sharp intake of breath and a pause, before Raúl responded sharply, firmly rejecting such a linkage, and wondering how anyone could possibly think along these lines. The Truman Administration, he noted, was supportive of industrialization in Latin America; Brazil continued to import US goods even though it was now practically self-sufficient in a textile industry built behind protective tariffs. The Americans, he insisted, finally understood the new reality of mutual benefits: expanding markets and Latin American development benefited both sides.[3] Prebisch even worried aloud, in a hurt tone of voice, that such negative thinking might weaken the commitment to economic development in Latin America.

For a moment, the reality of US power cast a cloud over the gathering. Everyone in Havana knew that Cuba faced only the illusion of choice – that it was the heart of the US empire. Many suspected that Prebisch's deputy, Castillo, was helping Batista prepare the military coup that would remove the overly independent President Prío from office in March 1952. But the stab of truth passed as the Prebisch charm revived the glow, and he left the island after a visit that from arrival to departure had been a complete success.

Returning to Santiago, Prebisch enjoyed a month of pure joy – and not all work. On an excursion twenty-five kilometres out of the city to the Maipo River, he and Adelita came across a modest cottage hidden on a cliff overlooking the river, with the Andean cordillera framed in the background. They purchased it at once as a weekend retreat. El Maqui – the hideaway, they called it, and it became a special destination when they were together in Santiago. While Adelita began fixing the house, Raúl planned a garden on the hectare-sized sliver of land that perched precariously over the Maipo.

Internationally there was again reason for optimism: an unexpected turn of events in the Korean War had raised the prospect of peace in the Far East. All parties seemed fed up with a costly war that was stalemated at the thirty-eighth parallel, and a ceasefire was announced on 27 July with apparent Soviet support. The timing of the news seemed almost miraculous: the Cold War fever in Washington might subside; Senator McCarthy's bubble would burst; and balance would return to US foreign policy. Peace would finally bring the long-awaited return of US attention to the development problems of Latin America, and ECLA would gain more breathing space in Washington. This was the view of Merwin Bohan, now converted by ECLA's Mexico City meeting into a Prebisch ally. ECLA still had friends in Washington, he argued, and he campaigned within the Truman Administration after his return from Brazil for greater financial support in the UN budget. "It is hard for me to oppose any reasonable increase in the ECLA budget for two reasons," he argued in an internal State Department Memorandum, "a) the fact that the other regional organizations get much more than ECLA; and b) my feeling that ECLA is doing a job that is by and large in the interests of the United States."[4]

When Prebisch returned to ECLA headquarters after his long absence in Mexico and Cuba he was greeted as a hero. His staff knew that only Raúl could have stared down Washington in Mexico and saved ECLA. But he was in no mood for self-congratulation; he assured his team that their work was only beginning and that the work plan adopted in Mexico would require even greater effort than before. His immediate task was reorganizing and expanding ECLA. Since the future of the organization had remained uncertain for its first three years, until the Mexico meeting, the UN had confined it to a temporary status; now that it was finally permanent Prebisch had to reshape the secretariat, adding staff and refining its structure. He therefore recast ECLA on the model of the German Army after World War I, creating a skeletal organization of small units headed by existing officers, which could be expanded rapidly with new recruits as new opportunities and resources were secured. In this way an office with fewer than fifty full-time professionals would eventually form the nucleus of the powerful research organization Prebisch had in mind.

At the top he set up an executive group of four economists and five secretaries headed by his deputy Louis Swenson to maintain overall policy direction within ECLA – his general staff so to speak. "Lucho," as Swenson was called affectionately by his Latin colleagues, was a skillful interlocutor between ECLA, Washington, and the UN; deceptively mild, with a thin gangster moustache that gave his face instead a teddy-bear quality, he spoke rarely but forcefully, and with authority. Five divisions (along with a statistical unit) reported through Swenson to Prebisch: Development, Training, Economic Survey, Agriculture, and Industry and Mining. In Mexico, ECLA's northern outpost was housed in the Social Security Building, paid for by the Bank of Mexico as a sign of its continuing support for Prebisch, but with the mission of leading the Central America integration project rather than doing work on Mexico itself. The Washington Office, with its four officers, completed the team. Prebisch personally supervised and approved ECLA publications and all appointments, and he managed external relations with the Secretariat in New York, governments, and international agencies. The Mexico and Washington offices were kept on a short leash; neither had separate budgets or hiring privileges.

The most powerful of the ECLA units were the Development Division, headed by Celso Furtado, and the Training Division, directed by Jorge Ahumada. Furtado had a nine-person staff including Regino Boti and Mexican Juan Noyola, who was recruited after the 1951 ECLA conference. His division was the centre of thinking on development theory and planning in the organization. One specific goal was the preparation of country studies, but the broader focus was to take up the challenge that ECLA explored between 1949 and 1951 culminating in its *Theoretical and Practical Problems of Economic Growth* presented at Mexico City – how could Latin America develop a planning model of its own? – examining the three existing systems that had emerged after the Second World War: US liberal capitalism, Soviet communism, and the hybrid French/European approach.[5] Ahumada had nearly left ECLA after initial disagreements with Martinez-Cabañas, but Prebisch convinced him to stay and lead a unique centre for professional training in Latin America. Promising young economists from governments throughout the region would come for twenty-four weeks of basic training in economic analysis, social accounting, sociology, economic development theory, and project planning. Sixteen additional weeks of work in small groups followed, focusing on special topics such as public sector management, budgetary planning, and human resource development. Along with this annual "basic course," Ahumada's division provided intensive courses and special seminars throughout the region at the petition of governments and in collaboration with universities and institutes. International scholars were invited to teach in Santiago.[6] Ahumada and Furtado were de facto rivals: one communicated new ideas, while the other created them. But they were also ideologically distinct: Furtado's group was known as the "Red Division"; Chilean Ahumada was a Christian Democrat closely involved in local politics in Chile. They balanced each other, and Prebisch was careful to maintain this ideological pluralism in the secretariat.

At the head was the perfectly dressed Prebisch, listener and leader, allocating work and worrying about the immediate future. He had solved the problem of survival in Mexico City, but now ECLA faced the challenge of meeting expectations. Prebisch felt trapped. Unless he doubled or tripled his staff, he would not be able to prepare for the next ECLA Commission meeting set for Brazil in May 1953; unless he deepened his support in the region, he could not hope to win the budgetary wars in New York required for expanding his staff. In practice this meant, as a first priority, consolidating and broadening Brazil's backing for ECLA. While the other countries were also important – Chile could always be counted on; Colombia remained indifferent but could eventually be brought on board – Brazil was indispensable and had to be Prebisch's key ally. Its economy was now larger than Argentina's; starting from a much poorer base, and still far poorer in per capita terms, Brazil had grown rapidly while Perón's economy was inflationary and stagnant.

Prebisch set off on a two-week trip to Rio de Janeiro and São Paulo on 19 August, accompanied by Celso Furtado, to explain ECLA to business, government, the media, and academics and students. It was an unusual trip for Prebisch. The stakes were high – he was from Argentina, the traditional competitor; he had little personal knowledge of Brazil and did not speak Portuguese. Still, he felt a kinship with Brazil after the negotiation of the short-lived, if visionary, bilateral trade agreement with Argentina in October 1940. But that was a long time ago, and he had not been back since the Rio Conference of January 1942. Apart from Furtado he personally knew few Brazilian economists, the exceptions being Eugenio Gudin and Otavio Bulhões, with whom he had corresponded since 1947, and the young Alexandre Kafka, working in the IMF, who returned to Brazil for Raúl's visit. Gudin had also invited Prebisch three years earlier to lecture at the Getulio Vargas Foundation, but this had not worked out, and Bulhões's betrayal of Prebisch in the IMF affair a year later had left a sour taste. On the other hand the Havana *Manifesto* was available in Portuguese and well known in Brazil, so that the announcement of Raúl's visit had aroused widespread curiosity. But ECLA as an organization was hardly known in Brazil, beginning with President Vargas himself. He had supported its continuation in Mexico primarily to confound the Americans; when Prebisch met him on 27 August, he found that Vargas had only the vaguest ideas about ECLA and little memory of Brazil's decisive intervention in 1951. When he began the interview by explaining ECLA's objectives, Vargas interrupted to ask if this indeed was the international organization he had decided to support in Mexico City. When assured on this point the president wanted to know the composition of the Commission, its headquarters, and its cost to the countries of the region.[7] The knowledge gap elsewhere in Brazil about ECLA was huge since Portuguese was not yet an official language in ECLA – unlike Spanish, English, and even French; its documents were circulated in Spanish. Prebisch had only two weeks to establish its credibility and prestige.

Prebisch's visit to Brazil was therefore entirely different from the trip to Cuba earlier that year. The two societies shared educated cosmopolitan elites and acute inequality in income distribution, but while Cuba was an extreme case of a depressed monoculture economy absorbed into the United States, Brazil was a country of optimism and energy. Its rapid growth was most evident in the industrialization of São Paulo; sprawling and dynamic, it was the new powerhouse of South America. Cuba's relationship with the US was obsessive and conflicted. In contrast Brazil's war effort with the Allies against Nazi Germany had created a strong friendship with the US, and it was the only country in South America to have a permanent military agreement with the US, putting it in the company of Mexico and Canada. A Brazil-United States Joint Economic Commission was helping Brazil lay the foundations of a modern industrial state. Cuba was small and dependent; Brazil's culture, size, and resources gave it a confidence lacking in Hispanic America. Prebisch had had an easy task in Havana, with few qualified critics in his audiences, and he could get away with proclaiming the inspirational side of the ECLA gospel. In Rio and São Paulo he faced informed and engaged officials, industrialists, and experts who had observed twenty years of industrial change since the Great Depression and had tough questions about the relevance of the ECLA doctrine for Brazil, and he was (as in Cuba) careful to avoid raising expectations: ECLA was "an institution strictly economic in nature, with UN social affairs in another department"; it did not pay special attention to problems of social legislation, "although there were obvious points of intersection."[8]

Interest in the Prebisch visit in all sectors grew as it got under way in Rio and continued in São Paulo. He had interviews with the ministers of foreign affairs (Itamaraty), finance, and agriculture, the president and officials of the Bank of Brazil, and virtually every senior minister and official involved in monetary and economic policymaking. Sessions were set up with Brazil's National Economic Council, the Brazilian Technical Assistance Commission, and private-sector leaders such as the head of the National Iron and Steel Company and the president of the National Federation of Industries, who arranged site visits to industrial plants, the stock market, and the Institute of Technical Studies. Sure enough, there was Bohan again! Called in only a few days earlier as US director of the new Brazil-US Joint Economic Commission when Truslow Adams, Truman's choice for the position, died en route to Rio, Bohan wanted to cooperate with Prebisch after "we made peace with ECLA."[9] Virtually every economist of standing came to the meetings in Rio or São Paulo. At the Getulio Vargas Foundation, where Gudin organized four roundtables with thirty of Brazil's most prominent economists, five to six times more visitors attended Prebisch's events than those of any previous guest – including the celebrated Jacob Viner lectures the year before. Prebisch's roundtables in 1951 became, in effect, a counterpoint to Viner's advice that Brazil follow classical theory and observe the laws of comparative advantage in trade policy.

Prebisch met practically the entire next generation of Brazil's leaders: Cleanto de Paiva Leite, personal advisor to Vargas, Alexandre Kafka from the IMF and Roberto de Oliveira Campos from the Bank of Brazil. Kafka was the president's choice for director of the imminent BNDES (Brazilian Development Bank), and Campos was a Gudin protegé who caught Prebisch's eye as a person marked for swift advancement. Born in 1917, three years older than Furtado, Campos had spent eleven years studying for the priesthood before leaving the seminary and joining Itamaraty. His first appointment was in the commercial section of the Brazilian Embassy in Washington, where he arrived in 1942 with a reputation as a radical. In 1944 Gudin invited him to join the Brazilian delegation to the Bretton Woods Conference, after which he enrolled in the Graduate Program in Economics at George Washington University, and then returned to work in the Bank of Brazil. Certainly no Marxist in 1951, his political orientation remained uncertain, but in his manner Campos stood out as a natural competitor of Celso Furtado. Prebisch found him interesting and began a friendship with him to ensure that he always had two views of Brazil; during Campos's visit to Santiago a year later they formed a joint ECLA-BNDES program in Rio to which Furtado was seconded as director.[10]

Prebisch began with his trademark "war of ideas" theme: that "new" countries like Brazil must regain their intellectual autonomy and shake off the dead hand of US and European theorists like Viner. Their version of the international division of labour and the "laws" of comparative advantage condemned Brazil and Latin America to remain suppliers of commodities under declining terms of trade.[11] Ideas mattered. Economists like Viner created a "psychological environment" that limited the will to industrialize and change commercial relationships between the old industrial powers and Latin America; ECLA offered instead, he argued, an indigenous theory of development based in the actual conditions and history of the region, which challenged orthodox liberal theory. Viner had missed the point; Brazil could not return to its agricultural roots, avoid industrialization, and solve its employment problem with birth control.[12] And since there was no going back – the economic modernization of Brazil was already firmly established, and industrialization was already a fact – the issue was not *whether* it should industrialize but rather *how*. Prebisch congratulated Brazil for its successes in building heavy industries such as the Volta Redonda steel complex, but São Paulo was nevertheless an object lesson in the need to soak up surplus labour pouring in from the countryside with accelerated industrialization.

There were dissenters. Gudin criticized Prebisch for "abandoning old theory to construct entirely new theories of purely indigenous origin without having even one Indian grandfather among its authors."[13] Why couldn't he stay with the established and proven laws of classical economics? As he put it, ECLA's "myth of planning" was incompatible with private sector initiative and free markets, and once intervention began it would lead irresistibly to state control. The essential role for the state should be limited to building infrastructure and above all to controlling inflation with a strict monetary policy; the combination of a minimalist state and private-sector initiative would be sufficient for industrialization and growth.[14] Prebisch agreed about inflation but insisted on a more activist state to accelerate industrialization. "Programming" or "planning" as understood by ECLA, he told the Federation of Industries of São Paulo on 31 August, did not mean a Soviet-style takeover of the private sector. "It is not a complete intervention in business or production," he said, "but instead it assists with specific instruments to ensure that they achieve specific objectives and volumes." Business decisions should be taken by the private sector, and he underlined that the private sector needed to be strengthened in Brazil and Latin America. There was absolutely no incompatibility between state planning and a strong private sector; ECLA's doctrine merely sought to raise the volume of investment to accelerate growth and "to avoid the all too visible disequilibrium in Latin American economic development." In short the public sector was merely playing its primordial role of promoting public welfare. As for import substitution, international trade under the GATT could be reconciled with protectionism since industrialization changed the commercial relations between developed and developing countries but did not prejudice the growth of trade itself.[15]

In the end most Brazilians who came to hear Prebisch were interested in specific development issues. What should Brazil do to strengthen industrialization? President Vargas was creating the Brazilian Development Bank in 1952: was this a sound approach, and what should be its role? (Prebisch saw it as an essential step forward but warned against Perón's excesses in promoting inefficient industries.) What were the special roles of monetary and exchange policy at this stage of development? How far should import substitution go? What was the correct level of government intervention in the market? How could Santiago assist Brazil in dealing with all its problems at this stage of industrialization? Prebisch cited cases and examples: ECLA's creation of regional industrial associations, for one the forthcoming First Meeting of Experts on the Iron and Steel Industry in November; the major study on the Brazilian economy being done under the direction of Furtado; Ahumada's forthcoming training program; and, above all, ECLA's pioneering work in economic programming techniques.

Here is where ECLA came in, Prebisch pointed out. It was the only truly independent economic research centre run by Latin Americans; it was a vital think-tank for new initiatives to build a new Latin America. A hundred businessmen cheered him at the Federation of Industries in a standing ovation; the media and academics applauded. The establishment newspaper *O Estado do São Paulo* called him "a living symbol of Latin American industrialization."[16] President Vargas himself and officials in his administration were enthusiastic about Prebisch's vision of an activist state. Gudin and Roberto Campos still disagreed, their liberalism reflecting one side of a widening fault line in Brazilian society. But as long as Vargas was in power Prebisch could count on his government, and Santiago now had many powerful and well-connected supporters in Brazil. He made sure that Portuguese became an official language of ECLA the next year.

The success of Prebisch's Brazil visit shored up his position in Latin America, but relations with the US remained difficult. Hope for peace in the Korean War had evaporated, and the conflict dragged on. The deepening of the Cold War in Asia and Europe concentrated US political and economic attention on these regions, to the neglect of Latin America. Containment in Asia required massive US economic aid to friendly governments as a bulwark against communism. Latin America, within the US defense perimeter, was safe and forgettable, and its share of development aid from Washington had fallen to 1 percent. Within the Truman Administration there was diminishing support for Latin America, which translated into less energy for improving relations.

The prestige accumulated by the United States in Latin America under the Good Neighbor policy dissipated during 1952 as the Truman Administration battled political criticism at home and abroad. Its recognition of Cuban dictator Fulgencia Batista, who took power in a coup in March, was not popular in Latin America. The US appeared to be falling behind in the promotion of human rights, as racial segregation in the US became an international issue, and US civilian saturation bombing of North Korea reached irrational levels. On 23 June 1952, five hundred US bombers destroyed the Suiko hydro-electric and irrigation dams on the Yalu River, the largest in Asia and fourth largest in the world, supplying water for 75 percent of North Korea's food production. It was an undefended civilian installation, like the dikes of Holland. The next morning another five hundred bombed the remains, and a US Air Force officer noted that the collapse of the one hundred-metre dam unleashed a flood that "scooped clean 27 miles of the valley below, and the plunging flood wiped out rice paddies, railroad lines, bridges and highways." It was a greater catastrophe than the Nazi destruction of Holland's dikes – which the US then had declared a war crime. "The Westerner can little conceive the awesome meaning which the loss of rice has for the Asian – starvation and slow death," said the US Air Force spokesman.[17]

The United States seemed to have narrowed in spirit. Prebisch found that the US media had regressed since the war years in attitudes and knowledge of US-Latin American relations. In June 1952 a US journalist asked Prebisch at a press conference why Latins supported industrialization; he explained that it was necessary to find jobs for the rural migrants to cities being displaced by advances in agriculture similar to those in the US. "Isn't that a little unhealthy to start an industry just to keep people fed, if there is no absolutely moral reason to do it?" Why couldn't Latin America instead relocate peasants to unused land in the tropical regions? Why were they so "selfish"? Prebisch's patient explanation that Latin America had to develop balanced economies – like Asia, Europe, or North America – was met by Cold War taunts: did Latin Americans prefer communist or free-market economies?[18] Curiously, the Cold War revived old stereotypes of Latin America, while Asia and Europe were assumed to be normal, advancing, and industrializing regions in the international economy.

Prebisch hoped that the 1952 presidential elections would clear the air. When the Republican Party recruited General Eisenhower as its candidate, its choice was widely admired throughout Latin America, and the prospect of a change of administration in Washington revived expectations. Eisenhower made the deterioration in US-Latin American relations a major election issue. In a speech on 3 October, he promised a new approach after Truman's "stop-and-go, zig and zag" policy. The Good Neighbor policy had failed, he claimed, because the US had been inconsistent and unable to deliver on its promises of support to Latin America. In a clear reference to Truman's failure to hold a promised US-Latin American Economic Conference, he said: "With the coming of the war we frantically wooed Latin America. Then came the end of the war, and the Administration proceeded to forget these countries just as fast. Terrible disillusionment set in throughout Latin America. There was no mutual working out of long-term economic problems. This good neighbor policy has become by drift and neglect a poor-neighbor policy."[19] Eisenhower called instead for a "Good Partner" approach to US-Latin American relations, less intimate than "Good Neighbor" but based in solid performance rather than rhetoric. What this meant in practice was unclear.

Eisenhower won easily, and in Santiago ECLA awaited news of his Cabinet choices with apprehension. On 23 November Raúl's brother Julio, who had had a promising career as a surgeon, died – the first of his siblings to pass away, a victim of depression and drug abuse. It was a melancholy family funeral in Tucumán. Alberto, now a society star in Buenos Aires, was on vacation in Europe and could not be located. The moment was gloomy; Adelita's mother, who lived with them in Santiago, was also declining rapidly. Raúl needed some good news. The future directions of the Eisenhower Administration toward Latin America were not, at first, unpromising. Career officials like Bohan remained, and Dr Milton Eisenhower (president of Princeton University and brother of the US president), who was known for his commitment to Latin America, was asked to travel to the region and report the outlines of a new policy by 20 November 1953.

President Eisenhower's choice for secretary of state, John Foster Dulles, was an enigmatic figure at best. The first assistant secretary of state for Latin America, John Moors Cabot, was sympathetic to Latin American concerns,[20] but he was soon replaced by Henry Holland, a former US ambassador to Venezuela, who shared Dulles's narrower geopolitical and orthodox liberal approach to Latin America. State Department officials preparing the new policy suggested that it should be based on "maturity, self-reliance and self-respect." Latin Americans must "face up realistically to their own problems," and the US should "make them feel that they are our partners ... [but] avoid actions and statements which emphasize their inferior economic and social status."[21] Holland extolled the virtues of private investment as the motor of growth and ignored appeals from US businessmen such as Peter Grace to promote economic development. In fact, Treasury Secretary George Humphrey, rather than Holland in the State Department, ran US-Latin American relations, dominating this issue from the outset of the Eisenhower Administration. Even the president admitted that "When George speaks, we all listen."[22]

Senator Wayne Morse accused the president of "putting reactionaries in complete control" when he heard of Humphrey's appointment.[23] The benchmark for US policy in the region became an almost religious commitment to the sanctity of private enterprise "as the essential foundation stone of a free and democratic society." Humphrey championed free-market orthodoxy, tax cuts, and private investment as the motor of growth, insisting that all the conditions for global development were already in place and warning Latin Americans against socialistic practices such as planning. They already had access to the World Bank, the IMF, and commercial banks; they certainly did not need foreign aid at the expense of US taxpayers. Humphrey decided to curtail Export-Import Bank operations in 1953, leaving the financing for Latin American development entirely in the hands of the World Bank and private capital. Brazil was informed through a press conference that the popular US Ambassador Hershel Johnson had been fired, and Washington confirmed on 2 June that it would dissolve the Brazil-US Joint Economic Commission set up only two years earlier. Bohan chose to leave the scene. "The Secretary of State," he noted, "had no interest in Latin America, and policy in the economic area was dominated by Secretary of the Treasury Humphrey, who thought only in terms of big business; and that may sound socialistic but it happens to be the absolute truth."[24]

Inter-American relations worsened on 26 May 1953, when the Eisenhower Administration set up the International Organizations Employees Loyalty Board to weed out officials considered undesirable by Senator Joseph McCarthy. "A fifth column of Americans and other non-communist countries existed within the UN and some specialized agencies," the Senate Internal Security subcommittee reported.[25] Not only US nationals but also Latin Americans and other foreigners within the UN were suspect, and the administration agreed to "press for a thorough review of the entire UN personnel from non-communist countries." Even 1950 Nobel Prize winner Ralph Bunche had to appear, as did 1,700 others by mid-1954. Many were hounded and driven out.

If the UN was under close scrutiny, so was ECLA, which the FBI and CIA considered subversive. As the McCarthy campaign deepened in Washington, so did FBI surveillance of its Santiago and Washington offices. Ten years earlier J. Edgar Hoover listed Prebisch as a dangerous Nazi supporter; now he had apparently switched to the communists. While Hoover's agents intimidated the Washington office with unannounced visits, Prebisch simply assumed that his offices in Santiago were wired, and therefore had Swenson brief the US Embassy regularly to ensure that it got the story right.

Prebisch, alone among heads of UN agencies, succeeded in protecting ECLA from the McCarthy threat. Despite pressure and warnings, he hired economists of his choice on the criteria of merit and need rather than ideology. Adolfo Dorfman, an Argentine expert in industrial development, was driven from the UN Secretariat in New York because of his previous membership in the Argentine Communist Party; Prebisch asked him to come instead to Santiago, hiring him in ECLA for his acknowledged professional qualifications. Alex Ganz was similarly politically unacceptable in the US or at the UN for having flirted with the US Communist Party as a student, even though his work with the US Department of Commerce from 1946–50 in its National Economic Analysis Division was successful enough to earn him a tenure-track appointment at the University of Chicago. Ganz's training and experience in national accounts and projection techniques were needed in Santiago, particularly by Furtado in his Development Division. When UN Headquarters refused to approve a permanent contract, Prebisch hired him on a renewable short-term contract that did not need approval from New York. Raúl was revered for standing firm in defense of his team, confounding the fears of some, like Noyola, who predicted that he would be fired. The intellectual and moral desert left behind by Senator McCarthy magnified Santiago's attractions; ECLA shone all the brighter as a centre of new ideas, and its magnetic pull brought scholars from around the world to work or teach. Academic pilgrims converged on Santiago because it was an island of ideological pluralism where new approaches to the region could be debated without fear, where a new language of development could be constructed. Women were hired and accepted as equals: in 1951 ECLA unilaterally lifted UN restrictions on their promotion to directors. If Prebisch was the "great heretic," his disciples were proud to share the heresy, daring to be different and innovative.

With freedom to hire came independence of thought, and Santiago maintained complete intellectual autonomy within the UN system. Equally important, Prebisch won budgetary battles that allowed him to hire qualified economists at a rate to maintain a heavy work program and produce consistently excellent work. By October 1953 he had 130 full-time staff, augmented by joint projects with other UN agencies to widen ECLA's operational reach. So long as it remained independent and produced high-quality and relevant materials, Prebisch could count on official support from Latin American governments. The OAS did not have autonomy or comparable staff, and it therefore lacked respect. Even friendly observers joked about its meetings in Washington "where the Latins sat like poor nephews at their rich uncle's table whining for special deals." Bohan agreed that it "just never seemed to get any place."[26]

Although ECLA's direct bargaining strength in New York was small relative to larger agencies, Prebisch had certain advantages in the peculiar world of UN diplomacy. First, it was a rare UN success story, and the Secretariat, up to the secretary-general himself, needed it. The other two regional commissions set up after 1945 were trapped by Cold War pressures. In Europe the EEC (European Economic Commission) could survive the Cold War and Stalinism only as an empty shell, with Gunnar Myrdal soon departing in frustration and disappointment. The Asian Commission, ECAFE (Economic Commission for Asia and the Far East), faced similar obstacles as the Cold War spread to Asia. In contrast ECLA had a clear paradigm, an agenda, and programs, with its global recognition extending to the General Assembly. Prebisch, in short, had carved out a place as a key Third World figure with strong internal and external allies; ECLA had a visibility out of proportion to its size and sufficient respect to safeguard its independence.

In addition, Latin America formed the single largest bloc of members in the UN, Africa and the Caribbean still being under colonial rule. Washington was of course the global centre of power, and the US Treasury was not coincidentally near the IMF and World Bank. But Latin America remained a key economic area for the US, with investment twice that in Asia and larger than in Western Europe or Canada, and a significant trading relationship.[27] US sentiment against the UN and ECLA was hardening, but there were also limits to US influence at the UN. The UN Economic and Social Council (ECOSOC), to which Prebisch reported through DESA (UN Department of Economic Affairs), was a consistent source of support. Unlike the Security Council, ECOSOC did not have permanent members with veto power, and its meetings were rarely at the ministerial level. Nevertheless it had sufficient legitimacy to provide countervailing opinions that mattered, and Prebisch never missed its meetings in Geneva and New York; ECOSOC's membership comprised both industrial and developing countries and its resolutions always endorsed ECLA's work, with France and India as particularly valuable supporters. India provided the perspective of a developing country of giant size. France was a valuable ally because it nominated the assistant secretary-general in charge of DESA, because it was a member government of ECLA, and because John Foster Dulles's closest personal friend on either side of the Atlantic was Jean Monnet, whom he had met during the 1919 Paris Peace Treaty negotiations.

Finally the very complexity and arcane politics of the UN provided unexpected opportunities for locating partners and widening Prebisch's scope of action; DESA, ECLA's New York interlocutor, was huge but amorphous, with an unclear balance of forces operating within it. Guillaume Georges-Picot from France was its formal director, but Jacob Mosak, his number two, was the US enforcer with close links to Washington and the US

Mission to the UN. As secretary for the regional commissions, Wladek Malinowski had been a valued friend and supporter since 1949, skilled in identifying potential allies and adversaries – a window into New York's Who's Who of agencies and secretariats. Many officials within DESA respected Prebisch and carried weight in decision-making because of their professional expertise. Within the UN Secretariat as a whole Prebisch had a network of contacts throughout the organization extending to the office of Secretary-General Dag Hammarskjöld and Andrew Cordier, his US executive assistant. His strength lay in using interdepartmental diplomacy to forge these contacts into unusual coalitions to build a flow of energy and idealism behind the ECLA vision.

The Eisenhower-Dulles stalemate in US-Latin American relations broke with the Guatemala crisis in June 1954, when a CIA-led insurgency overthrew the government of President Jacobo Arbenz Guzman. Arbenz was a modernizer who made the mistake of introducing land reform. Dulles saw him as an entry point for Soviet influence. For ten days after the US protested the arrival of an alleged shipment of arms from Poland on 17 May the fate of Arbenz was uncertain; then a clandestine force put together by the CIA and headed by Colonel Carlos Castillo Armas entered Guatemala from Honduras. Arbenz hung on until 27 June, when he resigned; Castillo Armas replaced him formally as president on 8 July with a purge that drove one thousand refugees into Latin American embassies, five hundred alone in the Mexican compound where Arbenz himself sought safety. The intervention introduced one of the bloodiest dictatorships in Latin America and destroyed democracy in the country for generations.

Prebisch was in New York when the Guatemala crisis broke, receiving an honorary doctorate from Columbia University on 1 June – along with John Foster Dulles. Dulles did not refer to the coup, and Prebisch did not raise it with him. Nor did Guatemala come up during their elegant lunch celebrating the bicentennial of the university's founding. But it was big news all around them. Not only was this the first direct US intervention since the Second World War, but it also signalled a new era in US foreign policy of using CIA-led proxy forces. US recognition of Batista in 1952 had annoyed Latin Americans, but it was old-fashioned; Guatemala announced a form of US penetration that could destabilize any country in the region. Against international protests the United States UN mission warned Security Council members off the Guatemala issue and began lining up endorsements from friendly countries in the region. But not all Latins were pliant. Mexico and Venezuela openly refused, and most countries scorned it in private. Even the OAS failed to deliver for Washington. Its first and respected secretary-general, Alberto Lleras Camargo, resigned with a much-applauded farewell speech of restrained betrayal, leaving Washington in the company of the worst little Latin despots – the Batistas, Trujillos, Somozas, and Stroessners.[28]

So unexpected a display of Latin assertiveness put Washington on the defensive regarding a special OAS meeting of ministers of finance or economy scheduled for 22 November in Quintandinha, Brazil, on the invitation of President Getulio Vargas.[29] Dulles had reluctantly accepted the proposal in March before the Guatemalan crisis broke, as a way to deflect persistent Latin pressure to hold the so-called Inter-American Economic Conference promised by Truman in 1949. The Eisenhower Administration was even less willing than Truman to budge on familiar Latin grievances; agreeing to the Quintandinha meeting was a face-saving concession to let them blow off steam and get a few more years of peace and quiet. But the impact of the coup in Guatemala was to reopen the perennial wounds of US-Latin American relations and stiffen the backs of the Latin delegates in demanding action from the Americans. While Dulles came to see the importance of improving relations with Latin America, Treasury and State ruled out a change in policy: the outlook for the conference was uncertain and unpredictable.[30]

The OAS had to turn to ECLA to help prepare the Quintandinha meeting because of its staff inadequacies. Prebisch agreed, and the governments of the commission, the US included, agreed that Santiago staff should set aside their regular work and prepare a background document titled *International Co-operation for a Latin American Development Policy*.[31] It was unclear, however, what it would include or recommend.

Since taking over ECLA in 1950 Prebisch had been invariably cautious in dealing with his sponsoring governments, always working to build consensus rather than provoking confrontation. He personally reviewed all reports prior to publication; he would warn Furtado not to be impetuous; and he was scrupulous in trying to be objective and neutral with governments even to the point of opposing general recommendations in ECLA reports.[32] Unlike some of his younger colleagues in Santiago, he was not anti-American. Britain and the insufferable Pickwick Club in Buenos Aires, festooned with Oxbridge college crests, had been the imperial bores in his experience, after which Americans like Triffin and Williams and the US Federal Reserve had been a welcome change. Prebisch knew the US better than his Santiago team, and he had experienced a benign phase of US-Latin American relations that suggested the pendulum would eventually swing back to restore ideological balance in Washington.

The Guatemala coup was so outrageous, however – with a generation of reformers and friends now dead, jailed, or in exile – that Prebisch decided to abandon his customary caution. Normally a conference document like *International Cooperation for a Latin American Development Policy* would be developed in consultation with Washington, but Prebisch decided to confront the Americans with a completely unexpected *fait accompli,* in effect setting up the US for a certain diplomatic embarrassment. This alone went well beyond accepted diplomatic norms in the UN. Beyond his exceeding the normal procedural rules of the game, however, Prebisch decided as well to propose an agenda for development that he knew the Americans would reject but that they would have to reject publicly without retreating into patronizing pleasantries. He knew that such a humiliation would provoke anger or even possibly retaliation in Washington, but it was worth the risk. Quintandinha was a unique opportunity to propose a new agenda that could break through the established clichés surrounding "development." Everyone – the US, Europeans, Soviets – supported "development" in principle. In the abstract it had become a consensus term and universally accepted goal. But if everyone could agree on the word, the actual dynamics of development provoked discord and were normally ignored.[33] At Quintandinha, Prebisch decided to accept this common discourse of development as a point of departure and focused mainly on the international as well as national conditions for its success. In so doing he made the structures of interdependence and governance the primary focus of analysis, forcing the debate away from meaningless generalities and to the reciprocal responsibilities of industrial as well as developing countries, projecting an action plan and policy framework for such a common agenda. This was new and subversive ground. In a sense Prebisch's *International Cooperation for a Latin American Development Strategy* became the operational counterpoint to the Havana *Manifesto.*

To give his initiative maximum legitimacy he created a support group of six internationally distinguished Latin Americans: Eduardo Frei of Chile; Carlos Lleras Restrepo of Colombia; Evaristo Araiza from the Bank of Mexico; President Rodrigo Facio of the National University of Costa Rica; Director Cleante de Paiva Leite of the Brazilian National Development Bank; and Francisco Garcia Olano from Argentina. The six represented all the subregions of Latin America, and their involvement widened ECLA's support base; Frei and Lleras Restrepo were future presidents. Moreover Prebisch ensured that governments and UN headquarters received their copies of *International Cooperation in a Latin American Development Policy* just four days before the opening of the conference – too late to allow a veto. Dag Hammarskjöld, the new secretary-general, held conservative views on international development and might also have intervened to block the report. The US State Department, immediately aware of the significance of the document, was taken aback and enraged by the surprise. Holland dismissed it as "anti-US."[34] State sent the Quintandinha package over to the Treasury Department with a warning message: "This document has attracted an unusual amount of interest and will undoubtedly provide the theme for much of the argumentation which will be used by Latin delegations in pressing their views on the economic problems in their areas."[35] But the delegations were already arriving in Quintandinha, and there was nothing to be done about it.

Quintandinha lived up to its billing for liveliness. Short of Dag Hammarskjöld, who could not attend and asked Prebisch to represent him, the attendance was blue-chip, including the World Bank and IMF teams. The Latin American media covered it in detail. Most delegates had been here the year before, enjoying the luxurious old hotel with its oversized cast-iron bathtubs on bronzed lion paws, but this time they anticipated a grand confrontation between Raúl Prebisch and George Humphrey. The mood in Brazil contributed to the sense of drama surrounding the conference: President Vargas had committed suicide on 24 August, and his emotional suicide message had unleashed a wave of sympathy across the country; his self-identification as defender of ordinary Brazilians and their national patrimony against big interests and foreign companies provoked anti-American demonstrations in the period after his death.

Prebisch introduced his *International Cooperation in a Latin American Development Policy* on 24 November with a challenge to the assembled governments to vindicate the promise of liberal capitalism. "The validity of the private enterprise system in countries such as ours, with strong development possibilities," he said, "primarily depends on its dynamic capacity – on its capacity to ensure a high rate of growth." Washington could hardly disagree. Prebisch had simply paraphrased a memo by industrialist Peter Grace a month earlier to John Foster Dulles.[36] Prebisch noted that growth was stalling, and social unrest growing. He welcomed the present occasion "when for the first time the basic development problems of the Latin American countries are to be discussed in their entirety and at high level of responsibility." But he then presented the joint responsibilities stemming from interdependence, stating very clearly that, while the report was directed "primarily to Latin America itself" and domestic obstacles to development, "Latin American statesmen should not be criticized for measures which are only feasible with the support of international credit." The improvement in investment levels cannot be achieved by domestic resources alone without international financial collaboration, "not only to meet the pressing demands of external disequilibrium, but also to aid a rapid increase in production and to guide it toward exports and the substitution of imports to prevent future disequilibrium." There was, of course, no simple answer. The Latin American entrepreneur had to be strengthened with technical assistance and government action as well as finance. This was not Canada, where its private sector could develop side by side with the United States without the disparities in techniques and capital density so familiar in Latin America. *International Cooperation for a Latin American Development Policy* therefore proposed "a combination of national and international measures" to be applied "simultaneously and on a coordinated basis" to open a new era of US-Latin American cooperation. These included the creation of a regional development bank; the strengthening of economic planning to avoid turbulence; stability for commodity exports; technical cooperation and training; taxation and agrarian reform; financing for development with a minimum target of one billion dollars a year in development assistance to accelerate industrialization; and the holding of the long-promised Inter-American Economic Conference in 1956. Individually all these items had been raised before, but the process of cooperation he suggested would be radically different. Prebisch proposed that such a new vision of US-Latin American relations also required a new mechanism – evaluation groups composed of distinguished experts to evaluate the development plans of Latin governments and thereby ensure a suitable framework to permit economic growth. The concept, in short, suggested a new approach to governance and region-building based on cooperation and long-term mutual interest.

Humphrey rejected all the key recommendations. An inter-American development bank was unnecessary, he argued, because Latin America already had "more than adequate" access to capital; a $1 billion target for development financing was unacceptable to the US, as were ideas put forward for commodity stabilization. The result was a familiar polarization in which Cuba (Batista), Dominican Republic (Trujillo), Guatemala (Castillo Armas), and Venezuela (Jimenez) supported the US. Ortiz Mena, Mexico's finance minister, humiliated himself by thanking Humphrey for US generosity toward Latin America. The US delegation was sufficiently angry to raise anew the threat to incorporate ECLA within the OAS, but Brazil, in the spirit of the newly deceased Vargas, squashed this outburst. The State Department resented Prebisch's tactics in parceling out his recommendations to supporting governments, so that Chile, for example, proposed the creation of the regional development bank. Mainly it disliked being put on the spot to the point where even US legislators attending the conference jeered at Humphrey's "empty briefcase." Few inter-American conferences were such obvious failures, but it had succeeded in projecting a durable regional agenda, particularly the future regional development bank, which was the most-discussed item at Quintandinha. Nevertheless when the delegates left Brazil on 2 December, US-Latin American relations were in worse shape than ever.

On the other hand, ECLA's prestige in the region reached new levels after Quintandinha, and its next session, in Bogotá from 29 August to 17 September 1955, was a celebration of its success since 1948. Relations with UN headquarters in New York had never been better. Not only had ECLA easily weathered yet another UN internal performance review, but Philippe de Seynes replaced Guillaume Georges-Picot as UN undersecretary in charge of DESA on 1 January 1955. This position was particularly sensitive for ECLA, and now Prebisch had a key ally in the New York office. De Seynes was a skillful bureaucratic infighter, committed to international development but also to building coalitions that diluted US negativism. In his letter of congratulation, appreciatively written in French, Raúl remembered de Seynes's participation in earlier ECLA sessions and the consistent support of France.[37] His arrival meant that New York would now be an even friendlier city, augmenting the existing network of allies such as Malinowski, Hans Singer, and others who included favourable comments about ECLA's work in their internal memos.[38]

Colombia had been one of the last Latin countries to line up behind ECLA, and its invitation to host the sixth session was itself a breakthrough for Prebisch, a recognition of its work in the country since 1953 supported by his good friend Carlos Lleras Restrepo. The only disappointment at Bogotá was the recent military coup led by Gustavo Rojas Pinilla. When delegates to the sixth session arrived at the Hotel Tequendama in downtown Bogotá, the capital city was in a state of siege: Pinilla had outlawed all "communist" activities on 4 March, with five-year jail sentences for offenders. Both leading newspapers in the city, *El Tiempo* and *El Espectador*, were closed, and on 31 August *Time Vision*, a US publication, was also banned. As armed police and troops roamed Bogotá and press riots and arrests multiplied, Prebisch learned that Raúl Mendes, a Colombian economist who had been a consultant with ECLA, was in jail; he intervened directly with President Pinilla for his immediate release – successfully, to the astonishment of Mendes, who was out of prison before the day was over.

Confined to the Hotel Tequendama for the duration of their sixth session, ECLA delegates had little option but work, and Prebisch felt a surge of success and new possibility as events conspired in his direction. At its close Prebisch cabled a long message to de Seynes claiming it to be "most successfully completed." And given the achievements Raúl had a certain right to crow: full Latin American support for its country studies of Brazil and Colombia – with requests for more country studies, given their evident usefulness for governments; a consensus on the need for economic programming reflected in the growing number of National Planning Offices throughout the region; and support for further technical work on the energy and agricultural sectors. Prebisch could also report another important accomplishment: the decision to create a Trade Committee to help remove obstacles to inter-American trade. This meant that ECLA was being invited into the most important policy area facing governments, and it foreshadowed a changing emphasis in its work; he noted to de Seynes that Latin American governments wanted action as well as studies, "feeling that Secretariat studies had reached the stage where practical steps forward were necessary."[39] All the decisions had been unanimous; it was evident that the Quintandinha consensus had unified the major Latin American governments behind an agenda of international economic cooperation, which Washington would sooner or later welcome rather than reject. The Bogotá meeting reviewed the progress of regional producer associations and the steady advance of more autonomous economies as they matured. An evident sense of regional identity seemed to be advancing. A Mexican journalist provoked a commotion in the US State Department by arguing that Latin America needed a "common policy and common front" to offset the US's "penetrating and sweeping influence" and that this could only be achieved by combining industrialization and regional integration. These were small but telling signs.

Prebisch had done it; ECLA was an astonishing achievement, a permanent and valued regional voice, calling a region into being. Of course it was a collective achievement in which ECLA both led and responded to ideas or concepts of others. But it was more than anyone could have expected, and undeniably it was his creation, forged by tenacity and diplomacy in the tough world of the UN system and Latin American politics.

It was a moment of deep satisfaction, and Raúl should have had time to relax and enjoy. But after sending his telegram to de Seynes on 16 September he was informed that General Lonardi had risen against Juan Perón in Argentina and that the dictator had fallen. Should he return? He felt dizzy before a fatal attraction against which he seemed defenseless, drawn irresistibly to a crossroads that might lead equally to spectacular victory or disastrous defeat.

14 Paradise Lost

Of course Prebisch should not have gone back to Argentina. Malaccorto had lived through the Perón years in Buenos Aires and pleaded with him: the Argentina he had left in 1948 was now, in 1955, a changed country he would hardly recognize and in which he would not be effective. Croire tried to explain the wild ride of the Perón Revolution, which had swept away the old regime, including the Central Bank, without creating a political centre on which to build in the future. Frankel documented the demoralization of the Argentine private sector, and this was in manufacturing, not to speak of the neglected agricultural sector. What did Prebisch hope to gain, Malaccorto asked? Who would listen to him after all these years? In Santiago he had the best job in Latin America. Why not keep it and put the Argentine dream to one side? He would never be accepted in Buenos Aires, and returning would be the most serious mistake of his life. Prebisch should not let excitement and emotion overcome his trademark qualities of intellect and rationalism; he had to remember that his name was identified with the oligarchy and that this public stigma was entrenched and could not be erased by years of service abroad with the United Nations.

Yet, in retrospect, Prebisch's disastrous return to Buenos Aires had an irresistible momentum from the moment he received the news in Bogotá. The siren call of his years of achievement called him back to his greatest defeat.

For more than a week a moody and anxious Prebisch had remained in Colombia, weighing the news coming out of Buenos Aires, unable to believe that the Perónist era was over. For many months there had been violence on the streets of Buenos Aires along with rumours of military plots; nothing had come of them and Perón had crushed a serious military uprising on 12 June. Raúl remembered his previous false hopes then and remained cautious. Contradictory claims of victory and defeat were reported in the Bogotá press as the ECLA conference dispersed, but it was impossible to verify their accuracy until 19 September, when Perón resigned and boarded the *SS Paraguay*, a Paraguayan gunboat docked for repairs in Buenos Aires harbour, bound for Asunción, where he had chosen exile. Lonardi was sworn in as provisional president on 23 September to a crowd of half a million, the largest ever reported in the Plaza de Mayo. Even so pockets of resistance remained; as late as 26 September the situation in Buenos Aires remained unclear, but Lonardi's press conference the next day restored political calm, and governments around the world recognized the new regime: the Revolución Libertadora (Liberating Revolution) was indeed a reality.

General Lonardi called: would Prebisch return to serve his country in this time of need? More urgently, could he come immediately to consult with the new government? Without consulting the UN, Prebisch agreed to arrive in Buenos Aires on 1 October for exploratory talks with the president and to undertake a one-week mission to lead an intensive interdepartmental review of Argentina's economic prospects.

How could he refuse? In his years of exile after 1948 Prebisch had never abandoned his dream of returning to Argentina. Raúl and Adelita had kept their big house in San Isidro, and from Santiago he had followed events in Buenos Aires more closely than he was prepared to admit, with regular personal visits, calls, and letters from Alfredo Moll and the "Prebisch band" in and outside government agencies, although he had rebuffed at least one emissary from Perón who had approached him in Santiago for a rapprochement. Nevertheless Prebisch had maintained a studiously correct approach to the Perón Government – which was also, of course, a member of ECLA. Not only had he never used his position to isolate Argentina, he had also ensured that key ECLA meetings were held in Buenos Aires. But in mid-1955 there had been a thaw in Perón's relations with the UN, and on 8 August the Government of Argentina had submitted a formal request to New York for technical assistance to help resolve the impasse of Argentine economic stagnation. Prebisch had openly refused to return as long as Perón was president, and his fall removed the dilemma of responding to Argentina's request.

It was now an altogether new game because General Lonardi was a new species of military leader – not a typical power-hungry Latin dictator but rather a loyal officer committed to constitutional government who would restore democracy as soon as the electoral rolls could be put in order. For Prebisch, who had always insisted in Santiago that he would never again serve a military government, the Revolución Libertadora was a special case in which the military were acting as a constitutional bulwark for the Argentine people. In his first and hugely successful press conference on 27 September, Lonardi vowed to govern by the principles of liberty, rule of law, justice, and full employment: he was no more than a servant of the people of Argentina – a soldier, a Catholic democrat, and a friend of social justice in service to his country. There would be national reconciliation instead of revenge, he promised, and the former supporters of Perón were reassured that they were also welcomed for the task of reconstruction. "The deposed dictator unquestionably had at one time a great part of the Argentine people on his side," he stated. "It is not possible to apply the epithets 'unpatriotic' and 'partisans of tyranny' to all who supported the dictator disinterestedly or in good faith. The great majority of the Argentine people should be allowed to participate in the country's civil life unrestricted, even though some, often against their will, supported the deposed regime."[1] Just as Lonardi had earned his credibility by breaking with Perón in 1951 and refusing a military command under his leadership, so his appointment of the similarly incorruptible lawyer Eduardo Busso as his new minister of the interior reassured Argentines of all backgrounds. And if Lonardi felt compelled to dismiss both Perónist-dominated houses of Congress until new and free elections could be called, he filled the political vacuum with a new national advisory group of political leaders from all parties, except the Perónists and Communists. It would be a true Liberating Revolution rather than a typical seizure of power for political ends. Even Lonardi's title of "Provisional President" underlined that he had no interest in overstaying a strictly transitional role.

Adelita was in Holland visiting her sister during the military coup against Perón, and Prebisch asked Carlos Echegoyen, an Argentine economist who had worked with him in Santiago since 1950, to get in touch with her and keep her informed on events unfolding in Buenos Aires.[2] Adelita's sister did not have telephone service, and it took several days to reach her by cable, but her response was immediate and unequivocal: not only did she want to return to the city of her family, friends, and memories, she also decided to fly directly to Buenos Aires from Europe to see for herself what was going on in the capital and at their house in San Isidro and to arrange temporary accommodations in the event of their early return. In this she was unsuccessful; her flight from Holland was routed away from Buenos Aires to Santiago, and she stayed there until prospects were clearer. In the end Raúl and Adelita arrived in Buenos Aires together in the afternoon of 1 October to flowers and a crowd of dignitaries.

Prebisch's first week in Buenos Aires was magical. He was welcomed home as a hero, and the university immediately restored his professorship. His first meeting with President Lonardi confirmed his belief in the seriousness of the Revolución Libertadora, and he spent the next day with

Cabinet ministers discussing the general economic and political situation in the country. The press, which had generally been hostile to him in his earlier career, was now enthusiastic, even referring to him as a "symbol," since it was almost exactly twelve years since he had been forced from the Central Bank, initiating the decline of this great institution and with it the national economy.[3] With a full amnesty declared and the state of internal war in place since 1951 annulled, Buenos Aires basked in the pleasure of freedom restored. Statuary of Juan and Eva Perón in the capital was pulled down to delirious cheering; ships, provinces, and streets bearing signs of the now unpopular couple were renamed. The traditional national oath ("Before God, the country and the Holy Gospels") reappeared for the swearing in of the new Cabinet. And just as Prebisch arrived in Buenos Aires the *SS Paraguay* finally completed its repairs and crept out of the harbour with Perón aboard to close out his era for better times.

Prebisch began work early on 3 October with an inaugural meeting of the undersecretaries of all the national economy and industry portfolios as well as external experts and consultants during which working groups were set up, followed by a working lunch well into the afternoon.[4] They continued around the clock, with Raúl directing the working groups and drafting the outlines of the preliminary assessment he had promised Lonardi. The atmosphere and loyalty of the staff, many from the old days like Roberto Verrier, reminded him of his Central Bank days. Prebisch's large office in the Ministry of Commerce hummed with activity; the media extolled his "loyalty, efficiency and patriotism."[5] Spring was beautiful in the capital, and the grace and civility of Buenos Aires captivating. Raúl and Adelita went out to inspect their still-leased but well-maintained old house in San Isidro and longed for it all the more, particularly its garden, now overgrown and needing care but altogether wonderful in its colours and trees. It was easy to forget that twelve years had passed, and he fell immediately into a familiar routine of work little different from earlier days. By 7 October he was able to present his findings to the new government assembled in the president's office at 5:00 in the afternoon and gave a press conference himself the next day, where he discussed the preliminary report at considerable length, concluding that "the situation of the country is not a question of optimism or pessimism; it is simply a question of beginning the work."[6] He was cautious: "The situation is serious, but not critical." He was also careful to avoid controversy, given his dual role of national advisor and head of ECLA, but he did indicate that he would be requesting a leave of absence from the UN to continue his work in Argentina.[7] But his voice betrayed him when he spoke of "this second career which circumstances oblige me to undertake in which I can serve the grand interests of the community." In the press conference Prebisch almost choked when he spoke of Argentina's underlying potential. He was hooked.[8] ECLA and the UN and seemed far away. So complete was this sense of return that his preliminary report and press conference of 8 October began where he had left off in 1943: he made no references to ECLA or the UN.

Malinowski, who had been with Prebisch in Bogotá and was his closest friend in the UN, learned that he was in Buenos Aires from a *New York Times* article reporting on his first press conference on 2 October; personally hurt that Raúl had not even bothered to inform them – much less to request permission from de Seynes and Hammarskjöld – his note of 3 October enclosed the *Times* article and cautioned Prebisch not to strain the UN link gratuitously. "Although we are fully reassured regarding your intentions," he wrote, "we would like to obtain as soon as practicable an indication from you regarding your possible mission."[9] In fact Prebisch was struggling with the dilemma of leaving the security of Santiago and the UN for the turbulence of Buenos Aires. Adelita understood that Raúl was preparing the groundwork for a permanent return to public service in Argentina, but Malaccorto's warnings were so dire that he held back from a full commitment to the Lonardi Government. In his 2 October press conference he explained that he remained a UN civil servant and would have to return to Santiago on ECLA business after his assessment had been completed, and the subsequent announcement on 8 October that he would be seeking a longer leave of absence rather than resigning from the UN underlined his continuing indecision.

Lonardi was not happy. He had offered to create a super-ministry for Prebisch to guide the recovery program so that he could enter the government as a full minister. Since Perón had effectively destroyed the Central Bank, a Cabinet position was now the place to be for moving along a reform agenda, with real political power. It would also be the simplest and cleanest solution, allowing Raúl to take direct responsibility for economic leadership, but it also meant resigning from ECLA and committing himself fully to a future within Argentina. Malaccorto objected to Prebisch returning in any capacity but insisted that if he persisted in such a rash and likely disastrous course of action, he should at least keep a fallback position by negotiating a leave of absence, rather than leaving the UN. Prebisch thereupon convinced Lonardi to appoint him as special economic advisor to the president, rather than minister, on three-month leave from the UN, and without salary from the government since he had ample accumulated holiday pay to cover this period. This less risky alternative had the advantage of allowing him to postpone a final decision to move to Buenos Aires until he had a better sense of his prospects in the capital. If things went sour he would have an exit. The danger in returning to volatile Buenos Aires in the safe role of UN advisor, however, was being seen as unpatriotic – unwilling to take the full plunge in a moment of national need – and therefore endangering his credibility from the outset. There was no good option, Malaccorto grumbled: Raúl should have stayed out of Buenos Aires altogether.

Prebisch argued that he would have significant power with the position of advisor, since a resignation threat from so senior an international figure would carry a special weight in the circumstances. Argentina needed international support, particularly in New York and Washington, and the new government would be unwilling to compromise Prebisch's connections in these circles. Second, he argued, Lonardi would realize that Argentina's international standing and leverage would be enhanced by Prebisch maintaining his UN position and travelling to New York and Washington as a special type of emissary for his country. Argentina would certainly need a major UN-led technical assistance program in which ECLA would play a lead role – even Perón had realized this when he had contacted New York on 8 August; Prebisch would be better able to do this from within the UN system. Finally, by not accepting a salary for his work in Buenos Aires, he thought he would definitively pre-empt any charge of enriching himself at public expense.[10]

Supported by Malinowski and de Seynes, Hammarskjöld approved a three-month leave of absence, with the understanding that as part of his advisory work Prebisch would prepare a long-term UN technical assistance program for Argentina. Returning briefly to Santiago for household items, he met with his ECLA staff to announce his decision and appoint Swenson as acting executive secretary in his absence. Raúl and Adelita then departed for Buenos Aires in expectation of reoccupying their house in San Isidro after the tenants departed. Meanwhile they would stay with Alfredo Moll. Although the formal decree setting out the terms of Prebisch's appointment as special economic advisor to the president responsible for "the formulation of a program of economic recovery as well as the measures necessary for its achievement" was not signed until 25 October, he plunged immediately into the next stage of his work: preparing a national recovery plan.

With Lonardi under public pressure to announce the national recovery plan – Argentines from every sector feared for the future and foreign investors worried about their prospects – a special presidential address to the nation was set for the evening of 25 October, leaving Prebisch only two weeks to draft a report. Minister of Trade Cesar Bunge assisted him where possible and set up a special working group for this purpose, but it was a tough challenge. Prebisch had been out of the country for most of the Perón period; national statistics were unreliable. Unlike Brazil, Argentina did not have a comprehensive country analysis by ECLA to help define priorities. He therefore relied heavily on interviews with some one hundred major figures in the public and private sectors, as well as the cooperation of former colleagues from the Central Bank days, such as Roberto Verrier, now the deputy minister of finance, and former students Aldo Ferrer, Norberto Gonzalez, and Ricardo Cibotti, now recognized as young and promising economists of the new generation. Notwithstanding the work Prebisch had initiated during his first week in Buenos Aires the most that could be expected for 25 October was a report – certainly nothing like a finished plan. The result was a decision to split the work into three parts. A first document (labelled the *Plan Prebisch* due to its enormous public and media exposure) formed the basis for Lonardi's *Address to the Nation* on 25 October, containing the diagnosis and immediate emergency measures. However two additional reports dealing with longer-term policy were to follow in early January 1956: *Sound Money or Uncontrolled Inflation* and the *Plan for Economic Restoration.* The first report was rushed out so quickly that it risked miscalculation. To dramatize the national crisis, Prebisch deliberately focused on domestic failures, downplaying trademark ECLA themes such as declining terms of trade, which addressed the international economic context; nor did he evaluate the economic impact of natural disasters – flooding and earthquakes – which had afflicted Argentina since 1951.

"Argentina is in the worst economic crisis of its history," the *Plan Prebisch* began, worse than the 1890s, the civil wars of the nineteenth century or the Great Depression "because in those times the country retained its productive forces intact."[11] In fact the crisis after Perón was even worse than Germany's in 1945 because the damage to Argentina was invisible while Germany amidst the ruins retained the dynamism to rebuild. "Ten years of irresponsibility and corruption" had left the nation's infrastructure run down, its private sector decapitalized, and its economy indebted and in an inflationary spiral. In Germany only cities and factories were destroyed, but the industrial spirit of the country was intact and lacked only resources to restore growth. Argentina, Prebisch noted, faced a worse threat, which he called "a crisis of production." Exports had collapsed; industrial productivity had fallen; inflation was entrenched; the agricultural sector was mired in decline; external liabilities totaled $757 million; and petroleum imports gobbled up scarce foreign exchange despite Argentina's rich energy resources. In ten years the economy had grown by 4 percent compared with

40 percent in Brazil and Mexico. Even Colombia, not to mention Chile, Brazil, and Mexico, had steel industries; but Argentina, once the leader in South America, had failed to invest in heavy industry. The remedy was to construct a sound basis for restoring growth and prosperity through structural adjustment to reduce the deficit and inflation: reduction and devaluation; price increases; tax increases; export promotion; and joining the IMF to attract foreign credits. Agricultural production must become a priority for expanding exports and earning foreign exchange. Pipelines and infrastructure were critical bottlenecks, but Prebisch advised the Lonardi Government to reverse Perón's late conversion to Standard Oil before his fall: instead of opening the sector to US investment, Argentina should maintain national control since the country had ample expertise on its own. He exhorted all Argentines, particularly the wealthy, to sacrifice for the common good and promised that such pulling together would be rewarded with a rapid economic recovery. Whether they liked it or not Argentines had to take action, and income tax reform for social equity was necessary in the forthcoming period of austerity. Lonardi promptly decreed a series of measures recommended in the *Plan Prebisch*, beginning with a devaluation (which made imports more expensive and complicated middle-class travel plans), exchange-rate reform, measures to stimulate exports, and a national reconstruction fund.

The *Plan Prebisch* was welcomed in the foreign press. "The outlook has changed from nightmare to morning," Norman Crump of the *Sunday Times* reported from Argentina. "I am confident that London and New York will regard a Government advised by Dr Prebisch as credit worthy, and I am equally confident that a Government advised by him will justify this view."[12] Disastrously, the Sociedad Rural complimented Prebisch, reviving memories of his presumed links with the oligarchy; and the ultra-conservative English-language *Review of the River Plate* similarly called it a "masterly analysis."[13] But Prebisch's bleak diagnosis also met with widespread public skepticism. The cafés of Buenos Aires flourished as usual; Argentina's per capita wealth was higher than that of Brazil, Mexico, or Chile, or for that matter of Japan, France, or Italy. Argentines consumed more beef per capita than Americans; its restaurants served the thickest steaks in the world. The accumulated wealth of Argentina remained intact; its growing isolation from world markets and international networks or the collapse of standards in economic faculties or public administration had been so gradual as to be imperceptible. The public read, instead, of continuing progress – that Latin America's first modern automobile assembly plant producing 150,000 cars a year was opening in Cordoba, for example, or that their science, engineering, and medical schools continued to attract students from all over Latin

America. Few Argentines could believe Prebisch's characterization of the post-Perónist situation as the "worst crisis in history," serious as it was, or the melodramatic comparison of proud Buenos Aires with the wasteland of bombed-out Berlin. The *Sunday Times* of London agreed, noting that Argentina's debt problems were only $757 million over four years, "low in comparison with her potentialities once her economic affairs have been restored to an even keel."[14] The US Embassy suggested that he had deliberately exaggerated Argentina's current problems to discredit Perónism and had gone too far in dramatizing the severity of the economic crisis.[15]

Prebisch's report unleashed the first wave of media attacks on his motives and credibility. *Politica y Politicos* resurrected all the old themes: Prebisch as past and present servant of the oligarchy during the *decada infama*; Prebisch as general manager of a central bank dictated to by Britain; Prebisch as behind-the-scenes éminence grise insinuating his team of followers into leading positions in the Revolución Libertadora; Prebisch as disloyal German from Tucumán; Prebisch as an opportunist with no formal position in the new government.[16] *El Clarin* immediately took up these themes.[17] Old enemies in Buenos Aires revived allegations against the pre-1943 Prebisch "brains trust" – which had sold out the country – and Lisandro de la Torre's taunt about his claiming to have a doctorate when in fact he was only a public accountant. Questions were raised about his current loyalty to Argentina. Was he not, after all, a "foreigner" and the agent of outside interests – the Americans, the British, and now the IMF?

Stunned though he was by the violence of the media assault, Prebisch himself had no doubts about his grim diagnosis of the Argentine economic crisis, and he was not alone. José Ortega y Gasset, Spanish philosopher and author of *Revolt of the Masses,* who had found refuge in Buenos Aires after the Spanish Civil War, also wrote of the deep malaise afflicting this otherwise favoured country and his pessimistic diagnosis was reprinted after his death a week before the release of the *Plan Prebisch.*[18] So far from joining Australia, Canada, and the Scandinavian countries as developed countries, Argentina was sinking into underdevelopment compared, even, with southern Brazil. Something vital had been lost, according to Ortega y Gasset; a sullen mediocrity pervaded public life; individually accomplished in every pursuit, Argentines seemed incapable of the collective purpose required for a modern economy. They consumed, but production was stagnant. No traditional theories such as liberalism, Marxism, or corporatism seemed to fit this unique case: the old political class had disintegrated as Perónism swept the country, and now with its demise all the contending political forces were fragmented but highly mobilized, trapped so to speak in a frenetic and destructive equilibrium. But unlike the deceased Spanish writer, Prebisch was in Buenos Aires and part of this struggle.

The immediate assault disappointed Prebisch, but so long as he had the full support of Lonardi his position was unassailable. Many critics could be dismissed as predictable old enemies from the 1930s of little consequence; *La Nacion* and the quality press in Buenos Aires supported his emergency measures, as did the leader of the Radical Party, Ricardo Balbin, a key ally with a majority in the National Advisory Group, and widely expected to become president when the Revolución Libertadora held national elections. In fact the overall political outlook remained generally optimistic. Most of the key public figures in Argentine political life had rallied to Lonardi's call for a new era, including many of Perón's supporters, particularly the core of his party – the six-million strong CGT (General Confederation of Workers) – which had accepted the provisional president's conciliatory approach with little protest: the union leadership had asked their members to continue working rather than strike, in exchange for a promise that their social rights and collective bargaining agreements would be respected. Perón was in exile and marginalized, stripped of his uniform forever by a military tribunal, and discredited by the revelation of a tawdry hoard of love letters, money, and jewellery to Nelida Rivas, a fourteen-year-old mistress. The CGT did not call for work action when Péron broadcast a speech from Asunción blaming the economic crisis and ensuing military coup on "the parasitic class" with "the oligarchy contributing their money, and the clergy their sermons," against the will of "the producing class."[19]

Buoyed by the calm returning to Buenos Aires, Prebisch accepted an invitation to visit Montevideo, was warmly received on 11 November by his many friends in Uruguay, and was swept up in a round of meetings, press conferences, receptions, and official dinners. Repeating the diagnosis he had presented in the *Plan Prebisch*, he explained that his worst nightmares were realized when he returned to his home country: "I thought it was bad, but the reality was worse than the most pessimistic conjecture ... Only austerity and sacrifice can save Argentina."[20]

But, as Prebisch enjoyed the tranquility of Montevideo, the Lonardi regime was under mortal attack in Buenos Aires. Within weeks of the his overthrow of Perón he had already antagonized supporters; anti-Perónists within the military and the Radical Party criticized him for his leniency toward supporters of the dictator; others worried about the growing influence of ultra-Catholic nationalists in the new government. When Lonardi dismissed Eduardo Busso as interior minister, the National Advisory Board and all five newly appointed Supreme Court justices resigned, triggering a successful palace coup on the night of 12–13 November led by Pedro

Eugenio Aramburu, chief of the General Staff. Aramburu immediately restored Busso and regained the confidence of the National Advisory Board and justices of the Supreme Court, and to this extent the coup was a bloodless change of leadership within the Revolución Libertadora. But the advent of Aramburu marked the end of Lonardi's policy of national reconciliation, which had appealed to Perón's followers. In its place was war against the CGT. Aramburu sent marines to occupy its offices and dissolved the Perónist Party with a campaign of repression against both party and union members. The CGT retaliated by calling a general strike, to which Aramburu responded that he would "in no way tolerate certain sectors using workers to achieve political ends." Predictably labour strife exploded: working days lost rose from 114,000 in 1955 to 5.2 million in 1956.[21] If before 12 November Lonardi's policy of national reconciliation offered some hope of recasting Argentine politics along new lines, Aramburu's attempted repression of six million workers – in effect disenfranchising a majority of Argentine voters – condemned the country to renewed political polarization. After just two months, the Revolución Libertadora had entered a new and uncertain phase.

Appalled at the Aramburu coup and its dangers for political stability, Prebisch cabled his resignation as advisor from the Montevideo airport to Buenos Aires, only to be informed that the new provisional president refused to accept it and insisted on seeing him immediately after his return. Malaccorto advised him to stay clear of the Casa Rosada and to leave the government while he could still depart with dignity: the coup had terminated the idealistic phase of the Revolución Libertadora, and Aramburu's repression of Perónism and the CGT would reopen wounds and condemn Argentina to continuing turmoil. But again Prebisch chose to ignore his friend's advice; a journalist saw him in the palace and learned that he had agreed to rescind his resignation. Too much was at stake to leave now, he felt. As an incentive for him to stay, Aramburu made two appointments that reinforced Prebisch's support in the Cabinet: Alizon Garcia was named minister of finance and Eugenio Blanco minister of economics. Blanco was a key figure in the Radical Party, close to party leader Ricardo Balbin, and therefore a bridge to the person most likely to emerge as future president. In a personal letter to General Lonardi, Prebisch underlined his sorrow at the turn of events and his fears for the future of a divided nation. Lonardi replied in kind, thanking Raúl for his service and for staying with the Revolución Libertadora despite the Aramburu coup. Argentina, he said, needed him more than ever.

Aramburu's arrival and Prebisch's decision to remain further emboldened the critics. After a particularly venomous piece in *Noticias Graficas* on

15 November imputing that he was more influenced by British than Argentine interests, Prebisch called a press conference without consulting the president's office or members of his Cabinet. "I have decided to end this once and for all," he stated. "I am more than tired to hear them," he said, particularly when they were raised "only in my own country and always vague and nebulous." His record of public service was available; "everything about me is on file in the Central Bank archives." Even Perón had not been able to discredit him during his years in power; all journalists had to do was verify the facts because these records were now accessible. It was nonsense to claim that he had been a tool of British interests or that he had opposed industrialization. Find one scrap of evidence for corruption, he challenged his tormentors. The worst was the attack on his patriotism; he was proud of his "old Spanish blood and good German blood."[22] He, Prebisch, rather than Perón, stood for national interests such as keeping national control of the petroleum sector. As for the so-called *Plan Prebisch* of 24 October, it was just "a structural report; there is no plan." All it contained were simply facts of life; any government would have to implement an austerity program; a loan to help stabilize the economy was not selling Argentina out to imperialism. Joining the IMF was essential because "whether we like it or not we must have external credit." He pleaded for restraint: "We must all collaborate to overcome our difficulties, supporting all unavoidable burdens. I believe in the capacity of the people, the understanding of all our citizens and the spirit of solidarity of the country in this difficult hour. Moreover, I have confidence in the potentialities of the country and its enormous sources of production. I am confident that all difficulties will be overcome in the near future."[23]

A Chilean journalist at the press conference was amazed at the anti-Prebisch campaign he saw in the press. In the US and Latin America he was considered a dangerous leftist. "How could it be that you are criticized here for your alleged support for special interests against the Argentine people, when our criticism in Chile is precisely the reverse?" Prebisch answered with a comment that further complicated his relations with the Argentine press: "The entire United Nations think one way; Argentina in another. Here there reigns a towering superficiality. Journalists do not analyze or consult; rather they offer their personal opinions. In all other Latin American countries I have serious interviews, or conferences, with journalists who wish to clarify their doubts regarding various problems. But in our country it is different: they start with their own interpretation, which they insist be accepted regardless of evidence. As Hitler said 'if you repeat a lie often enough it becomes the truth,' and we simply must change this absurd system if we are to achieve any approximation of the truth in Argentina."[24]

Such bluntness only deepened the hostility; already the next day he felt it necessary to call another meeting with journalists to answer his critics, leading to almost daily press events raising the same doubts about his integrity, which he would patiently clarify over and over again, pleading with journalists to read the record for themselves. He went to the offices of *La Nacion* himself to help get the message across, but the campaign against him was too deeply ingrained for any tactic to be effective. Even Pinedo mocked him in the press for bragging about his Central Bank heyday so long past.

At this stage Prebisch decided to ignore the media and retreat into work on the three big issues confronting Argentine recovery. The first was the policy framework that Prebisch and his staff were busy completing in the two final reports, *Sound Money or Uncontrolled Inflation* and the *Plan for Economic Restoration.* The second task was repairing the Argentine state to implement the new reform package. "The best minds were eliminated," he observed to a journalist, "and no others were trained to replace them."[25] Prebisch therefore was preparing the largest UN technical assistance program in Latin America to enable international experts to train some 150 Argentine economists and officials to upgrade financial management and public administration in Buenos Aires. The third challenge was preparing for the upcoming visit of a US delegation headed by Henry Holland and Samuel Waugh, president of the Export-Import Bank. The US alone had the means for the national recovery plan to succeed: industrial credit, foreign investment, and speeding up Argentine entry into the IMF. Prebisch hoped to replicate his experience of 1940, when his special intervention with the US Embassy had prepared the groundwork for success in Washington.

Swenson visited Prebisch in late November and reported to de Seynes that Raúl remained deeply commited to his proposed measures as "necessary and correct. I found him relaxed and calm in mind and spirit – in fact I have seldom seen him so tranquil. He is completely oblivious to any pressure and is clear in his mind that the present government must take unpopular measures involving sacrifices and the elimination of special privilege."[26] The last two reports were near completion; the ECLA team headed by Adolfo Dorfman and Alex Ganz was finalizing the UN technical assistance submission for the government, shuttling back and forth between Santiago and Buenos Aires, and would finish its work by January. The November Holland-Waugh visit had been cordial; while they had not agreed to speed up negotiations by sending a special technical mission to Buenos Aires in advance of Prebisch's planned trip to Washington in January, the positive atmosphere had established a solid working relationship.

December, therefore, was a month of preparation. Prebisch put the finishing touches on the final reports and gave a private briefing to the senior officers of the armed forces on 21 December just as government offices closed for the holiday. Raúl and Adelita were still living with Alfredo Moll and went to Mar del Plata after Christmas for a few days of sun. On 4 January he submitted *Sound Money or Uncontrolled Inflation* and the *Plan for Economic Restoration* to President Aramburu at the Casa Rosada.

Aramburu responded the next day by creating a special Honorary Economic and Financial Commission to work with Prebisch. This was a good sign. The group had a broader political and social base than the National Advisory Group of political party representatives, drawing its larger membership from delegates selected from all the main economic sectors including labour as well as business, and with an energetic, competent secretary in Adelberto Krieger Vasena. The president also hosted a special lunch for Prebisch on 6 January. The money markets watched anxiously, and there was a sense of expectation in the capital. But it became apparent that Aramburu had not yet decided what to do with the final reports.

Prebisch was scheduled to leave Buenos Aires on 8 January for two weeks in New York meeting with UN and US officials on future plans for Argentina; he could hardly hold these talks without the release of his reports and an official letter from the Argentine Government formally requesting UN technical assistance. Complicating matters further was a scheduled trip to Bangkok, Prebisch's first to Asia, to meet with the other heads of the UN regional commissions, which extended his absence from Buenos Aires at this critical moment. By late afternoon on 7 January he could wait no longer: Prebisch called a press conference and outlined his main conclusions, in effect forcing Aramburu to release his reports, which were published on 12 and 13 January, when Prebisch was in New York. The president also made good on his promise to send an official request for the UN mission.

The last two reports were softer in tone than the October *Plan Prebisch.* They supported a wage increase of 10 percent but, consistent with the earlier report, proposed an austerity program with liberal reforms: cutting staff and budgets; privatizing inefficient state companies like Aerolineas Argentinas; reducing public expenditures; reducing the deficit; removing price controls; devaluing and freeing the exchange rate to weed out inefficient firms; reforming taxation to increase revenues and prevent evasion; lowering inflation; promoting agricultural production and exports, including the establishment of the National Institute of Agrarian Technology; investing immediately in the petroleum sector, particularly pipelines and heavy industry such as steel; attracting foreign capital except in the strategic oil sector; and joining the IMF.[27] While Prebisch called for sacrifices across classes, with the wealthy leading the way, his *Economic Recovery Plan* boiled down to an orthodox IMF structural adjustment package to move Argentina away from Perón's version of state capitalism, which had been biased against capital formation and competitive industries and had resulted in a bloated state, inefficient private sector, acute inflation and overconsumption.[28]

Questioned in New York about Argentina, Prebisch used a medical metaphor: "Argentina has a strong body in basically good health, but it has been abused. Get rid of the poison and its health will be restored."[29] After a week of heavy negotiation Prebisch realized that arriving at a formal agreement on the UN mission in Argentina would require additional time: an announcement could not be expected before 21 March, with a start-up date of 4 May 1956. Even then Prebisch would have to return to Washington and New York to ensure its launch. Since his three-month UN leave of absence was expiring, journalists asked him to clarify his intentions: Raúl replied that he expected to continue his advisory work "in some form," hoping to incorporate an ECLA advisory team within "his group" in Buenos Aires. This may have been a slip of the tongue, but it underlined his continuing dilemma: he wanted to head the proposed UN mission while also directing the *Economic Recovery Plan* out of Aramburu's Office. On 18 January, en route from New York to Bangkok, Prebisch announced that the UN had agreed to these terms: he would be returning to ECLA in Santiago but would also continue his work in Argentina.[30] And in his brief visit in Bangkok, he exuded confidence about Argentina's recovery, while again dramatizing the challenge with comparisons between Berlin after 1945 and Buenos Aires after Perón.[31]

Returning to Buenos Aires on 23 January, Raúl realized that his *Plan for Economic Restoration* had unleashed an ever-greater wave of national fury and that the government had still not fully endorsed it. The Argentine peso had lost 10 percent of its value during the week of 9–13 January, when the Prebisch reports were released, one of the sharpest declines since 1950. Consumed by high-level bargaining at Cabinet level, Prebisch had grown accustomed to press attacks, dismissing them as the sour grapes of disappointed Perónists, on a par with the familiar anti-patria diatribes in the gutter press, which he now simply ignored. But this new wave united both right and left against him. Established writers and critics in Buenos Aires condemned Prebisch's *Reports* as both factually wrong and damaging to the Argentine economy. It was one thing for the Trotskyist *Lucha Obrero* to proclaim "Down with the Plan Prebisch: the Oligarchy and Imperialism Will Not Win the Final Battle"; it was quite different when a national figure such as Raúl Scalabrini Ortiz published "The Imaginary Crisis of Dr Raúl Prebisch."[32] Scalabrini alleged that Prebisch had distorted statistics and fabricated government obligations; it was a "false report" and written with "an absolute lack of sincerity and seriousness" to slander Perón's policy of industrialization and minimize the damage and costs of the floods and earthquakes of 1952. Argentina did not owe anyone one cent; Prebisch's allegation of a $757 million external debt was rubbish – the main culprit was the worsening terms of trade during the past year, which magnified the trade deficit. The economy was actually improving. In short the *Plan Prebisch* was "capricious and confused," worse than irrelevant; the only explanation for such distortion was his selling out to foreign investors, opposing industrialization, and returning Argentina to the agrarian days of the oligarchy, which Perón had tried to break. The *Plan Prebisch*, derided as the *Flan Prebisch*, was wrong-headed and reactionary, its welcoming of foreign investment a return to colonialism. "Behind the Economic Advisor is the Very Same John Bull," Scalabrini insisted.[33]

A swelling national chorus of opposition demanded its rejection by the government, and the Aramburu regime was clearly split. Open revolt had flared within the new Honorary Commission when Radical Oscar Alende broke with the Plan. "Sound money, yes," he complained on 18 January, "but sound money must not become the final objective achieved at the expense of the suffering, misery and toil of the lower income groups."[34] But Prebisch still had sufficient momentum to press forward. After a difficult week of negotiations Alicia Moreau de Justo, the symbol of socialism in Argentina, agreed to support the Plan with qualifications regarding social issues and price increases. At this Oscar Alende relented and the *Plan for Economic Restoration* finally gained Cabinet approval on 28 January. It seemed like a major victory: Raúl's Personal Advisor's Office in the presidency would continue its work, and it formally replaced Perón's old Office of Economic Affairs.[35] Institutionally Prebisch's position had apparently been strengthened in Argentina, and the president circulated a twenty-page synthesis of his January reports, noting that their implementation required "without exception, patriotism, honor and hard work."[36]

With this, Raúl and Adelita could finally leave for Santiago, but with a noticeably lower-key send-off (only Alfredo Moll and Malaccorto) than their triumphant public welcome to Buenos Aires on 1 October. Pedro Orradre had accompanied Raúl to Buenos Aires as personal secretary for Argentine Affairs, and neither he nor Adelita thought that their dream of returning to Argentina was over. However when Raúl returned to Buenos Aires two weeks later the political scene was even more uncertain, the polarization around his plan had continued to mount, and Aramburu's Cabinet was not prepared to follow through on his recommendations. The economic situation had also deteriorated. Inflation fuelled public anger and wage demands of 30 percent. Prebisch insisted that the president hold firm, but

Aramburu's announcement on 17 February that wage increases would have to be linked to productivity provoked a new round of labour discontent and strikes. Perónists were no longer cowed; the military could lock up trade union leaders, but Perón in exile had recovered his leadership, power base, and eventual hope of return. More, the Radical Party was ever more split between, on the one hand, Balbin and his supporters and, on the other, a dissident wing led by Arturo Frondizi, who was reaching out to disaffected Perónists to build a winning coalition for the next national elections. Frondizi – rather than Balbin – was the coming power in Argentina; determined and skillful, he had established his reputation by denouncing Perón's decision to open the petroleum sector to Standard Oil. Though his views on foreign investment in oil matched Prebisch's, Frondizi broke completely with the *Plan Prebisch*, using it as a whipping boy for discrediting Aramburu's government and courting a broad coalition of Radicals, Perónists and nationalists of all kinds in his bid for the presidency.[37]

Prebisch's position in the country was now increasingly fragile. On 20 February he suffered a major setback when his Personal Advisor's Office in the President's Office was terminated and merged in the newly created Economic and Social Cabinet with a membership restricted to ministers and their officials. He was now shut out of direct access to Aramburu and the Cabinet, with the last two supporting ministers (Alizon Garcia and Eugenio Blanco) finally turning against him as well, suspicious that Prebisch was interfering in their areas of competence and resenting his impromptu press conferences to influence public opinion over their heads to compensate for his lack of support within the regime. Prebisch's old Central Bank team had lost its edge, and Verrier was gone.

It was a difficult moment. Vulnerable from every side, he could only hope that his countrymen and -women would eventually understand the gravity of the crisis; he decided to plead his case again at a special conference organized by the University of Cordoba on 27 February. Cordoba had grown into a big industrial city, a symbol of Argentina's industrialization and a Perónist stronghold, and the conference offered a national forum for denouncing the *Plan Prebisch*. Raúl himself was unaware of the trap laid for him until he arrived with his entourage of Giner de los Rios, Oscar Bardeci, Julio Silva, and Benjamin Cornejo to an angry mob of demonstrators prepared with anti-Prebisch posters before a fully mobilized national press. "What did you do with the money from the Central Bank?" the students shouted. "What did you do with our British pound sterling?" It was evident that the event had been set up to destroy him. The jammed lecture hall was hot and unruly, the taunting crowd nearly out of control before he spoke. Facing this mob Raúl realized that he would be shouted down and humiliated if he stuck to his dry and narrow ECLA text; instead he surprised the audience by advocating land reform, controlling US investment in the oil sector, and deepening industrialization with a national strategy for heavy industry. The crowd wavered. When interrupted by Rudolfo Irazusta, president of the Union Republica, Prebisch suggested to the chair that he come to the podium and present his question. "Why," Irazusta asked, "did Prebisch recommend new international loans when Argentina had a fortune of pounds sterling – 900 million to be exact – deposited in England?" Since Britain owed at least 800 million dollars, Argentina could resolve its problems without an austerity program by simply demanding prompt repayment.

Prebisch asked him where he had obtained these statistics. Irazusta explained that they had calculated export and import data, demonstrating that Argentina had a favourable trade balance with Britain in this amount. "Has this figure included everything?" Prebisch continued, "all Argentine exports and imports?" When Irazusta answered yes, Prebisch wondered aloud to him how Argentina paid for its petroleum and other imports. Did he know? No, he didn't know. "With pounds sterling, sir," Prebisch barked. "Do you really think that we would advocate loans if we had £900 million in Britain? It is inconceivable that in these moments of national calamity there are irresponsible people who produce information of this kind. Don't use statistics from irresponsible types, use instead those from young unsullied people like yourself, since I associate you as a young person with purity of soul, and don't put yourself in the hands of sons of bitches."[38]

With this Prebisch swept out of the hall to his car bound for Ezeiza airport in Buenos Aires, where he changed planes for Venezuela. But the audience inside the lecture hall cheered Prebisch: expecting a reactionary they were won over with his impromptu speech and dramatic humiliation of an evidently ignorant and abusive opponent. It was a minor victory, but not enough to make a difference: "I understood finally the political atmosphere in Argentina and used the tone and content which I should have used in my *Report* if I had properly perceived the Argentine reality," Prebisch later concluded.

Arriving in Caracas, Prebisch learned on 2 March that his Argentine troubles had followed him to Venezuela, that Irazusta had challenged him to a duel by pistols to reclaim his honour offended in Cordoba. The absurd had become bizarre, and Raúl was happy to be out of the country. But he had to respond or be vilified as a coward, and the national press duly noted that he had selected Julio Silva and Estaquio A. Mendez Delfino, chair of the Honorary Economic and Financial Commission, as his seconds to negotiate the terms of the challenge. Adelita was amazed when contacted, and UN headquarters had never seen anything like it. Friends feared for Prebisch's life, given his acute lack of physical coordination – he might even shoot himself. Julio Silva decided to try a peaceful settlement; with the help of the authoritative Spanish Royal Academy dictionary he persuaded Irazusta's seconds that the word "irresponsible" used by Prebisch in Cordoba was purely descriptive and should in no way be construed as a personal insult. Irazusta agreed and decided on 6 March that Prebisch had not trampled on his honour and that trial by duel was unnecessary.

By this time Prebisch was assailed from another quarter – his own staff – who were appalled by his visit to the Perez Jimenez dictatorship in Venezuela. Even though Venezuela was a member of ECLA Raúl had resisted all previous overtures to avoid shoring up the legitimacy of this regime; now, despite his vow never again to support generals, here he was, as head of the organization, side by side with General Jimenez, praising his achievements – even the so-called freedom of the press in Venezuela. For his ECLA colleagues the Caracas trip was a bit much, quite different from Raúl's argument that the Argentine Revolución Libertadora was a necessary and special case justifying his return to work with General Aramburu. Actually the *Plan Prebisch* itself had left Furtado perplexed and disappointed, its IMF orthodoxy fitting badly with the Prebisch he had known in the brilliant years. Furtado, temporarily posted in Mexico, was following events in Argentina closely (his wife was Argentine) and had expected a more nuanced approach from Prebisch – including lessons to be drawn (for example) from more relevant comparisons such as postwar France, which had successfully restored its economy after years of political demoralization and economic decline. One explanation could be that Prebisch was in Caracas to fund the new ECLA building planned in Santiago: flush with oil wealth, Perez Jimenez was the only president in the region with lots of cash.

Hounded everywhere by critics, Prebisch flew to what he thought would be the relative sanity and warmth of UN headquarters in New York and Washington for follow-up talks with Henry Holland, Samuel Waugh, and other officials in the IMF and World Bank. But Washington had turned cold, in a reaction that had been building gradually since the *Plan Prebisch* in October 1955. John Foster Dulles particularly disliked the recommendation to block foreign investment in the oil sector after Perón had finally granted concessions to Standard Oil. Dulles frankly distrusted Prebisch. While careful not to oppose the proposed UN technical assistance mission for Argentina on principle, he viewed Prebisch's dual position as presidential advisor in Argentina while remaining executive secretary of ECLA as "strange." He and Holland objected strongly to the participation of Adolfo Dorfman and Alex Ganz, who were both high on the US hit list of suspected communists. Dorfman and Ganz "will occupy a particularly strategic position," and such persons "with an economic ideology at odds with that of this government would create a particularly serious problem in US-Argentine relations."[39] Dulles agreed. The petroleum sector was particularly sensitive; the UN mission might even lead to Soviet consultants or equipment. Dulles instructed Lodge in New York to make sure that competent and recognized economists would be hired to balance Prebisch's "socialistic advice" on restricting investment by US oil majors.[40]

But the underlying dislike of Prebisch in Washington, shared by Dulles and his officials like Henry Holland, was fuelled by their sense that he had outwitted them – again. Quintandinha had left a permanent bad taste in their mouths: Prebisch had constructed a diplomatic trap behind Washington's back exposing them to ridicule and forcing them to endure a public loss of face while he expanded his role at their expense. Now he was doing it again. The huge UN mission to Argentina was a Prebisch initiative right, left, and centre, announced as a *fait accompli* that Washington could hardly oppose. Once again the US was stuck in an embarrassing situation, this time having to endorse a UN program with a team including Dorfman and Ganz, not to mention Prebisch himself who had just scuttled Standard Oil's expansion into Argentina. Washington was not willing to compromise relations with the Revolución Libertadora by blocking it altogether, since it also desired a stable post-Perón Argentina. Worse, this UN mission went way beyond ECLA's mandate, having expanded from its limited research and think-tank role into becoming a major provider of technical advisory services. Prebisch was trying another end run, and his empire building had to be stopped.[41] From Dulles on down, the State Department was determined henceforth to police ECLA's work program, holding Prebisch to the letter of government agreements at the commission meetings and preventing another case of mission-creep on the pattern of Quintandinha and Argentina. Never again would they get taken to the cleaners.

The result was a rough reception for Prebisch in Washington; he was forced to bargain from a position of weakness and confronted a US demand that he load up the Argentine mission with reliable Americans. "Since he desires US economic aid for Argentina," Holland crowed, "it is likely that he will be responsive to Department's desires."[42] US leverage was pervasive, not just in Washington but also in New York headquarters where US Ambassador Lodge had the UN bigwigs leaping to attention. In the end Dulles got his US petroleum experts, as well as an acceptable Argentine team of ex-government officials and technocrats, many trained in US universities, and generally (such as Raúl's brother Alberto) staunch members of the elite. However Prebisch held firm, and eventually prevailed, on keeping Dorfman and Ganz.

Prebisch called a press conference on his return to Buenos Aires on 11 March to state that the UN Mission would be announced by UN boss Hugh Keenleyside in Buenos Aires on 21 March and that it would open officially on 4 May under Prebisch's direction. He had made up his mind about the future, almost shouting, "I, however, will not remain permanently in my country." The dream of returning home was over for the foreseeable future; Santiago, not Buenos Aires, would be his home base. Prebisch really had no choice; the thinly attended press conference told the sad story: his own influence in Argentina had evaporated. He had angered everyone, it seemed, and was left with no allies. Support for devaluation and linking wages to productivity offended the working class; his promotion of agriculture was seen as a sell-out to the oligarchy; joining the IMF was a sell-out to imperialism. Meanwhile Argentine financial interests resisted tax reform; the agriculturalists vetoed land reform; and the private sector wanted less government but more protection. Neither the military nor the Radical Party would accept the political costs of structural adjustment. Nobody wanted taxes. Increasingly, he became a scapegoat for all aggrieved parties and malcontents. Hostility – to him, the IMF, foreign investment, the *Plan Prebisch* – had become religious.[43] Argentines did not want a saviour because they did not believe that they had to be saved.

But Prebisch was still too committed to free himself of his Argentine fixation. He again travelled to Washington on 21 April to negotiate credits and Argentina's entry into the IMF, defending entry as essential and with absolutely no impact on sovereignty, while in Buenos Aires it was so widely condemned as a national betrayal that Aramburu himself barely confirmed the decision. A week later he sent a stern report to the government, as ex-advisor, to hold firm on its anti-inflation line, expressing alarm over the public resistance to price stabilization. (He told a Brazilian journalist that he was not advocating "tightening the belt" so much as "just not to open it too wide."[44]) Instead Prebisch's 10 percent wage increase became 30 percent; price controls were intensified, Aerolineas Argentinas was not privatized; taxation reform was postponed; and Aramburu was unable to reform the state, which consumed 42 percent of GDP.

The UN mission (or "Prebisch Commission" as it came to be known) began its work on 4 May as planned, just as the downward spiral of the Revolución Libertadora was gathering momentum.[45] The many experts arrived; teams were duly formed, and studies commissioned; the statistics gathered and research conducted were impressive. But it was entirely academic, overwhelmed by the political dynamic sweeping the country. The dozens of UN experts, with their Argentine colleagues, operated in the deep shadows waiting for the return of political will: none came their way. They were "an army of economists," a visiting Brazilian noted, "but an army fighting a hopeless war."[46]

Prebisch instead devoted May to writing an analysis of the Argentine crisis, his way of coping with the shock of a defeat that sharply affected his thinking as well as his personality and that threatened to become a permanent fixation. At ECLA, for example, he could talk of nothing else. During its plenary meeting in Santiago on 15 April he projected this preoccupation with Buenos Aires as if the experience had become the new benchmark for its work. Whatever the sacrifice, monetary stability had to be maintained in the region. "Chile is fighting inflation with great decision and firmness," he approved; governments must stand firm against wage demands. He had been concerned about the danger that Latin American protectionism could become excessive in the past, but his experience of failed import substitution under Perón turned him into an active proponent of export-capable economies. "The necessity of Latin America adopting a vigorous policy of export promotion is becoming more obvious by the day," he noted in his plenary address. "Without it we cannot intensify the industrialization process."[47] But to free himself from Argentina Prebisch had to revisit the experience; the occasion of a ceremony inducting him as honorary member of the Faculty of Economic Sciences at the University of Chile on 8 June provided the opportunity to reflect on this chapter of his life – in his personal capacity rather than as UN functionary.

The paper was a bitter denunciation of import substitution gone wrong. Perón's objective of industrialization was correct, but his strategy was wrong. Without industrialization Latin America could not absorb the masses and increase its standard of living, but Perón had used protectionism to stifle productivity. All countries used some form of protectionism in the early stages of industrialization – the US, Europe, Canada, Asia, and so forth, and Argentina's needs were no different. But import-substitution industrialization could be purposefully or disastrously applied. The right way depended on domestic political choices regarding the respective roles of the state and market: in successful countries the state pursued a limited and intelligent interventionist policy that supported rather than stifled the private sector; instead Perón had sapped the lifeblood of the productive sector in a populist cult of mediocrity, in playing to the mob, leading "the revolt of the masses" with a bloated state instead of leading a healthy and disciplined political economy. Instead of aligning industrial and agricultural growth and using import substitution to build a sound economy, the regime had deliberately fostered inflation to conceal imbalances and growing disorder.[48]

Argentines should not blame "external strangulation," outside powers and events, terms of trade, national disasters, or "imperialism" for the failures of the Perónist model. Of course Argentina now needed assistance from the IMF, Washington, and the UN – as well as private investment – to regain stability and relaunch the economy; but the main problems were homegrown, and the hard decisions that now could not be avoided were Argentina's own responsibility and therefore had to be taken in Buenos Aires. Leaders had to begin by being honest – by convincing the public that the country truly faced a long-term crisis and that the future could only be secured through sacrifice and deep political changes. A national psychology of complaining had to be replaced by rejoining the world, opening local monopolies to competition, beginning serious land reform, and fundamentally shaking up the tax system. Disaster could still be prevented, but only Argentines could reverse a momentum taking the country in a wrong direction.

The day following Prebisch's Santiago address, Aramburu crushed a rebellion provoked by a particularly outlandish anti-Perónist government decree, declared a state of siege, and summarily executed twenty-seven men with hundreds others wounded and imprisoned.[49] If political reconciliation had ever been possible in post-1955 Argentina, the 9 June massacre terminated this potential opening. The dynamic of the Revolución Libertadora changed for good; the mobilization of disenfranchised Perónists against the regime was now complete, with personal vengeance sworn against Aramburu when his turn came. The *Plan Prebisch* was now history, an epitaph to a moment passed, as contending forces struggled for power. Superseded as policy, it entered Argentina's lore of political devil-myths along with the Roca-Runciman Pact or Lisandro de la Torre's Great Beef Debate from the 1930s. Symbolic of national betrayal, it became a catchword for politicians, and after the 9 June massacre Arturo Frondizi was the most skillful in condemning it to his advantage. His overture to Perón supporters, capped with a formal agreement with Perón himself, produced an unstoppable momentum for electoral victory on 23 February 1958, when he captured the presidency by easily defeating Ricardo Balbín's wing of the now-bifurcated Radical Party.

As for Prebisch, now the most hated man in Argentina, he was haunted by a searing sense of failure. He lost interest in the Prebisch Commission, leaving Dorfman and Ganz in charge, and rarely visited Buenos Aires; when he did come, he slipped in and out of the capital like a refugee, avoiding the press. In December 1956 he unwisely agreed to a ghastly press conference beside Federico Pinedo and Ernesto Hueyo, recognized stalwarts of the *ancien régime.* Even the normally enterprising Alfredo Moll, who could run businesses and make money without apparent effort, had sunk into alcoholic stupor. It was a metaphor for the times.

He felt truly alone, the only person in Argentina who had ever succeeded in mobilizing both right and left against himself. He had antagonized Washington, which would now watch him even more closely, he had disappointed his UN colleagues, and he had thrown ECLA into confusion after a glorious five-year run. Adelita and Raúl put their house at 134 Rivera Indarte up for sale, and Raúl signed a new five-year contract as ECLA's executive secretary to take him to the retirement age of 60 in 1961. Francisco Bustelo, a wine merchant in Mendoza, sent him six cases of Pere Grau sherry in recognition "for all you have done for our country." It seemed precious little reward for a year so totally lost.[50]

15 Return to Santiago

His exile from Argentina reconfirmed, Prebisch settled into Santiago for the long haul. The big house at 134 Rivera Indarte in Buenos Aires was sold; El Maqui, their little weekend dwelling on the Maipo cliff, thirty miles outside Santiago, was now refurbished into a year-round residence – a rambling, hidden house that preserved a cottage-like intimacy. From a centre hall, the left wing of the low-ceilinged cottage housed the bedrooms and his small study; in the drawing room to the right his uncle's panelled desk comprised an entire wall, facing which deep French windows framed the Maipo Canyon. The family portrait of his great-grandfather given by his mother hung over the fireplace mantle. A music room off the drawing room, also overlooking the Maipo, held Adelita's Bechstein with a pair of wing chairs for listeners beside the grand piano. The dining room followed, seating ten around a mahogany table and sideboard. Outside Prebisch built a terraced garden radiating bursts of colour against the bright Andean peaks, while Adelita worked with the local settlement of Los Vertientes to build a first community public school. El Maqui was a secluded world of understated elegance, an island of warmth and peace, and here he could relax.

And there was now ECLA for another five years. Since the fall of Perón, Prebisch had been consumed by the Revolución Libertadora; he had barely been in Santiago, Swenson had been in charge, and the organization needed attention. As he resumed chairing the weekly administrative meetings he saw signs of flabbiness throughout the organization, from senior researchers to janitors. Economists were showing up late for work, or not at all, unheard-of in earlier days when they willingly worked late into the night. Membership on the Car Committee had become a valued prize; Raúl learned that ECLA staff – senior as well as junior – were importing duty-free vehicles to be resold for profit in the local market, and their parking lot was a classy affair compared with the first years, when no one had talked about money or cars or mail-order catalogues. This Prebisch could never accept, and a reign of terror promptly restored discipline.

But discipline could not restore mood. Their leader seemed not himself, different after the Argentine fiasco; he had changed and the question was where he would lead the organization. In fact even before Prebisch's departure for Argentina a debate over future directions had started, a sign of intellectual dynamism in which areas of disagreement had been evident. Furtado and Noyola diagnosed Latin American inflation as a symptom of institutional and political backwardness, with every country quite different and requiring more complex solutions than simple monetarist stabilization.[1] Prebisch had a narrower focus. "I am so convinced of the considerable harm that inflation is doing to Latin American countries," he wrote to New York in April 1954, "that, as a matter of principle, I am little inclined to discuss measures for correcting certain consequences of the inflationary process. I would prefer to devote all our attention to the elaboration of a policy for curbing inflation and for stabilizing economies, without injury to incentives for economic growth."[2] Younger staff saw the 1955 *Plan Prebisch* as overly beholden to the old incorrigible pre-1943 elite that had recently triumphed over Perón and lacking an understanding of the social forces on which the success of any recovery depended. They saw him acting too much like General Ibanez in Chile, who had brought in a US consulting firm in 1954 to lead a similarly simplistic anti-inflation package.[3] Everyone from Prebisch down was frustrated by ECLA's crushing workload of projects and reports, which prevented scholarly research while economists in North America and Europe behind their endowed university walls were steadily advancing in development studies. They all wanted to publish. Furtado actually printed his *Economy of Brazil* with his own money, to the annoyance of UN Headquarters and a stern letter from Santiago laying out the conditions for ECLA staff to publish under their own names. For Prebisch the appearance of Sir Arthur Lewis's immediately famous article "Development with Unlimited Supplies of Labour" was particularly frustrating, since it effectively scooped his own research – simply because he had never had time after his Havana *Manifesto* in 1949 to rework his material for academic journals. He thereupon vowed to take a book leave and finally complete his magnum opus on centre-periphery relations. But then Perón had fallen, and he had been drawn back to Buenos Aires. And when Raúl returned to Santiago he was too crushed in spirit to undertake the book project.

Memory of the Argentine disappointment was not easily dispelled even as the *Plan Prebisch* fiasco faded: withdrawn and newly intolerant, Prebisch was ever more reckless in his personal life, including unconcealed flings with his own secretaries. Occasionally he would leave for Buenos Aires with Jacobo Timerman, editor of *Primera Plana*, describing his fleeting visits "like a foreigner in his own country." In Santiago he hunkered down with the Argentine economists recently hired from that city. Staff tiptoed around the corridors, missing Furtado, who could always reason with their boss: he had left Santiago in fall 1955, while Prebisch was in Argentina, to undertake a major country study of Mexico.[4]

Finally in June, after Aramburu's massacre of workers had terminated his engagement with Argentina, Prebisch roused himself to look to the future: a new burst of leadership at the head of a new ECLA mission was urgently required to reverse a diminishing enthusiasm among his followers and to revive his own spirits. They waited for new directions: where, they wondered, would Raúl take them? The deadline for recasting the organization was the next commission meeting set for May 1957 in La Paz, Bolivia, leaving less than a year – really little more than summer and fall – for fashioning a new ECLA mission, and staff were relieved when Prebisch's sullen depression of earlier months gave way to preparing what he called "a new stage in ECLA's productive existence."[5]

The first period, which had begun in 1950, Raúl argued, was over. These years had been successful in creating a framework for action; the common denominator uniting the diverse ECLA team, from the orthodox Ahumada to the Marxist Noyola, had been creating Latin America – exploring the concept of Latin America in its many dimensions, the internal and external features that gave this region its identity among the powers, and consolidating ECLA's Santiago secretariat as the unique regional centre for this intellectual work. "We have completed our theoretical analysis," he concluded, "and are now ready to devote ourselves fully to the practical measures for resolving our problems." New thinking would be replaced by "concrete action." It would be nice to do both things at the same time, he stressed, but this was impossible. Choices had to be made; ECLA had to focus on solutions rather than problems; day-to-day challenges facing governments had to replace theory-building and grand designs.[6]

Prebisch complained that ECLA staff forgot that the secretariat was not a university but rather part of a UN commission accountable to governments; ECLA had to keep the lines open to governments who were tiring of studies that had been compelling in 1949, still interesting in 1951, but dismissed as academic in 1956. They were impatient with the interminable internal debate about inflation, for example, and whether it was "structural" or not. Prebisch sensed a growing problem of legitimacy: that Latin American countries were not supporting ECLA as they had in the past and that they were preoccupied by a slowdown in economic growth as the post-Korean War boom ended. Under Prebisch's leadership ECLA had won and maintained a unique level of intellectual autonomy, but it could not ignore its governing body at a time when governments in the region faced growing challenges. Even at the height of its popularity in 1955 ECLA's work was more highly praised abroad than by Latin governments in ECOSOC. Georges-Picot, who had represented France at ECLA's sixth meeting, in Bogotá, journeyed to Geneva from Paris for the December 1955 meetings specifically to pay tribute to "Dr Prebisch's leadership of the secretariat and to the able assistance given by his staff." Pakistan saw it as a model for its own region; the Yugoslav representative thought the quality of ECLA's Brazil and Colombia studies "transcended in usefulness the countries concerned." Even the US representative, Dr Kotschnig, expressed satisfaction. De Seynes concluded that comments by all speakers at the session were invariably couched in laudatory terms, stressing the importance of ECLA studies for the Latin American region as well as for other parts of the world, their quality, and the methodological approach adopted in pursuing the work program. But delegates from the Latin American countries were silent or non-committal. More important, and despite all the praise in ECOSOC, Prebisch was not able to persuade the UN to increase ECLA's budget, a sign that Latin governments were not supporting him strongly enough in New York. Brazil after Vargas was cooler to ECLA; Mexico was typically distant. Prebisch saw a warning sign: ECLA had to adopt a more practical agenda to regain the Latin American governments' interest, and this meant attacking immediate economic problems.[7]

Regional integration towered above all other "immediate economic problems" facing Latin governments in 1956, and Prebisch seized it as the defining activity for his second term. The issue had already been identified as a priority in ECLA's early years and indeed formed part of the 1950 "Decalogue" adopted in Montevideo. But then the timing had been wrong. Countries were only beginning industrialization, whereas now Brazil (for example) had a substantial economic base poised for even more rapid expansion ("Fifty years in five," blared President J. Kubitschek, Vargas's successor, not to mention his epic project of building a new capital in the wild middle of nowhere). The European Common Market, now taking shape across the Atlantic, was a galvanizing interest for a region so closely tied culturally and historically to the Old World. While ECLA had pioneered Central American integration in 1951, the European Coal and Steel Community had been set up the same year to replace Europe's rigid national boundaries in the war-making industries. The experiment had prospered amid doubts, and in Messina in June 1955 the six member states endorsed the creation of the EEC (European Economic Community) with a common market, common institutions, and a progressive fusion of national economies to be enshrined in the Treaty of Rome in 1957. Such success in Western Europe called attention to Latin America, where industrialization was being pursued in twenty small and isolated national markets – "water-tight compartments," in Prebisch's words. No great genius was required to understand the significance for Latin America. If the industrial states of Western Europe, a pillar of the global economy, felt it necessary to pool their strengths to compete internationally, how much more so the incipient economies of the Latin periphery, which were only beginning to industrialize! Compared with Europe, Latin America was only beginning its industrialization: it had to plan for the future.

The creation of ECLA's new Trade Committee in September 1955 at Bogotá was a first indication of the region's growing interest in international trade, but its terms of reference had not included "regional integration" at all. The Santiago secretariat was simply requested to prepare a document called *Preliminary Study of Inter-American Trade*, which would help "resolve practical problems which limit or undermine the growth of intraregional trade."[8] But events built rapidly in support of regional integration, and in July 1956 Prebisch sent Ivovich, Eusebio Campos, José Garrido Torres, and Santiago Macario to canvass government opinion throughout the region. They found more support than expected. The key supporters included all the Southern Cone countries – Brazil, Argentina, Chile, Uruguay, and Paraguay – and in fact the overall degree of commitment was startling. While acknowledging the many challenges confronting regional integration, and that only gradual solutions were possible since countries faced balance of payments and credit difficulties, Latin governments unanimously supported an exploratory trade conference in Santiago 19–29 November 1956 to exchange views and assess the feasibility of a major ECLA-led initiative.

The Meeting of Experts on Iron and Steel in São Paulo, 15–18 October, co-sponsored by ECLA, drummed up additional interest for the new trade initiative. The Brazilian private sector registered in force, the first time it had rallied so evidently behind ECLA (provoking a congratulatory message from New York), and São Paulo's new smokestacks advertised the city's industrial dynamism. Its new Technology Research Centre and Aeronautical Research Institute were engaged in advanced sectors of metalworking, engineering, and automobile and aircraft production; a sense of opportunity pervaded the meeting, and attendance was strong. European delegates set the tone by underlining the advantages of a single market. "There are no longer borders in this sector," they said. "Europe is on the march – don't you forget it," and they urged Latin Americans to persevere toward full industrial integration rather than settle for well-meaning promises of regional cooperation. The lesson of Europe in the iron and steel industries was that small national markets were passé; if Latin America failed to match the Europeans, or the US with its continental market, or the giants of the developing world like India and China, it would lose out. Latin America had to take the leap or be left behind.[9]

By the opening of ECLA's Trade Conference in Santiago on 19 November 1956 most Latin American governments had identified regional integration as their number one priority, and with 120 delegates it became as large a gathering as a regular Commission meeting. Apart from the twenty-four member governments, Japan, Italy, Poland, Canada, Russia, Czechoslovakia, Rumania, and Yugoslavia sent observers, along with representatives from the GATT, the IMF, and other international organizations. It was the first major international conference since the twin disasters of autumn 1956 – the Middle East War launched by Anglo-French-Israeli forces on 29 October, followed by their subsequent humiliation by President Eisenhower, who denounced the invasion and demanded their withdrawal, and the subsequent Soviet intervention in Hungary on 3 November to crush a popular revolution. Even the weather at the trade meeting – the glorious spring in Santiago compared with the bleak November fog in London and Paris – underscored the contrast between the violent Old and the genial New World. (Latin America had supported the UN against both the England/France alliance and the USSR.) Far away from Hungary and the Middle East, and after some initial glaring, the various delegations from Europe, the East Bloc, and the US decided to put aside their awkwardness in a productive session marked by the complete absence of rhetoric. Arturo Maschke, conference chair and president of Chile's Central Bank, underlined the need to put aside the frustrated dreams and rhetoric of Bolivar in favour of dealing frankly with the practical domestic and external barriers to a regional market. Prebisch also urged realism considering "the diversity of economic structures within the region," the lack of infrastructure, the fact that interregional trade was virtually nonexistent – mainly agricultural products worth only $350 million comprising a mere 7 percent of total trade. Precisely these obstacles demanded action now.

In a careful speech Prebisch outlined the vision as well as the implications of regional integration for Latin America. In Europe the common fear bringing the six nations together in the EEC had been security against the Soviet threat and the resurgence of a united Germany. Since a return to prosperity in Western Europe both depended on and enhanced security, integration across borders in a common market had a strategic logic to overcome inevitable local special interests and ensure US support. Such was the happy coincidence of the approaching Treaty of Rome. Latin America was an entirely different case: the Soviets were not about to invade, and there was no threat like Germany. Instead Latin America was a periphery caught in the backwaters of time. Twenty economies had emerged as a series of appendages of the colonial powers, and twenty isolated economies they remained, still selling traditional commodities – beef, wheat, coffee, bananas, and sugar – to the same industrial countries as if it were still the nineteenth century, when they had gained formal political independence. Ports, roads, railways – the entire infrastructure of Latin America – had been built around these markets, reinforcing the twenty water-tight compartments; it was an anachronism: something from the nineteenth century surviving into the twentieth.

Industrialization since 1945 had not broken this pattern of segmentation in Latin America, Prebisch said, because the first and easy stage of import-substitution industrialization in consumer goods such as textiles and shoes had merely replaced imports for the local market. This phase was nearly complete. Latin America was now entering the second and more complex stage, involving dynamic sectors: durable goods, steel, heavy engineering, mass automobile assembly, engines, chemical plants, and so forth – new and dynamic industries requiring the economies of scale of a regional market for attracting investment, new technology and high productivity to soak up an expanding labour force. Brazil, Mexico, and Argentina were beginning limited production of jeeps and tractors, for example, and were now poised for automobiles: now was the time to make the leap from small national markets toward the region, as in Europe, with preferences that would lower and finally abolish trade duties. The first task, Prebisch maintained, was "to develop new forms of reciprocal trade and above all in industrial products that practically didn't exist before."[10] Industries already established would require a more gradual approach to expand the range of competitive industries and sectors and force businesses to look beyond their borders.

"Without the common market," Prebisch maintained, "there will be a tendency by each country to try to produce everything – say from autos to machinery – under the sheltering wing of high protection which means splitting the industrializing process without the benefit of specialization and economies of scale." As in Argentina under Perón the cost of such a choice would be uncompetitive industries, limited participation in international trade, and the relative decline of Latin America in the global economy. Separate, truncated markets were no longer adequate for competitive, export-capable, production: the common market was a step on the road to international export growth. In fact, Latin America's pattern of "import substitution in water-tight compartments" since the Great Depression had led to a new form of vulnerability rather than giving it greater autonomy; it had not broken free from the nineteenth-century trade pattern of exchanging commodities for manufactured products from the same industrial countries, with high tariffs and restrictions toward the rest of the world as well as within the region. Now Latin America needed costly capital goods for the new industries of the second phase of industrialization, 90 percent of which had to be imported and paid for with the same low-value exports forecast to grow by only 1 percent per year to the US during the 1960s. The result was a permanent trade deficit that threatened the supply of essential imports and therefore the means for further industrial growth. The solution was regional specialization to overcome this "trade squeeze": to create Latin America's own competitive capital goods industries – "to break with this anachronistic pattern by the gradual and progressive creation of a common market and the consequent diversification of imports and exports."[11]

"What does the common market concept imply for trade with the rest of the world?" he asked his audience in Santiago. "That we are going to exchange the 20 autarchic markets of Latin America with one large autarchic zone *vis-à-vis* the rest of the world? Such an idea would be an error of incalculable dimensions. Latin America has to export more and more ... there is a perfect compatibility between the idea of a progressive integration of our economies and the equally meritorious idea of the most intense export thrust." The private sector in Western Europe proved the point: it supported integration, with domestic and foreign companies strengthening their operations by region-wide investments, and thereby realizing the vision of regional growth with greater productivity conceived by early European visionaries like Monnet.[12]

In a letter to de Seynes, Prebisch reported that the Trade Committee meeting had been "highly satisfactory and exceeded what might have been expected for a meeting designed to put the work into operation." Four resolutions were approved authorizing ECLA to continue work on a gradual system of multilateral payments, an inventory of existing industries, a Latin American regional market in manufactures, and measures to stabilize traditional markets in intra-regional trade. Latin governments, particularly those in South America, were highly motivated. The US position was carefully watched, given its central role in the region. Before the meeting Swenson had cautioned Prebisch against claiming that the Western industrial centres wanted to keep Latin America to the production of raw materials: maybe "some circles," yes, but "in fact considerable progress has been made in recent years to change the view not only of economists but also of government officials and industrialists in the US and the West European countries."[13]

Was ECLA becoming paranoid? At Santiago this advice appeared correct: Prebisch reported to de Seynes that the US delegation accepted the Common Market idea under two conditions (that any new arrangements take into account international commitments under the GATT; and that they not prejudice the expansion of international trade). And even though, when it came to actual voting, the US (along with Cuba and the UK) abstained, he felt that the positive US attitude "went a long way towards meeting the aspirations of the Latin American countries."[14] It was known that the US strongly supported the evolution of Western Europe, and that while John Foster Dulles supported European integration for strategic reasons, his long friendship with Jean Monnet had also convinced him of its intrinsic value.[15] The most serious problem at the Trade Conference had been the IMF delegation's open contempt for ECLA's "emotional idealism" and "lack of clear thinking," and its insistence on the need for "the non-Latin American representation to prevent the worst absurdities from happening." Prebisch's group based its work "on the principle of maintaining full employment in international institutions ... Being true Latins they unanimously and happily decided not to have meetings over the weekend, but to relax in the balmy climate of Santiago." Cadaverous Edgar Jones of the Fund scoured the meeting for willing Latins (Peru's dictatorship seemed a promising candidate at first) to play "some of the traditional conference tricks" on its behalf to ensure IMF "keeping a watch on ECLA."[16] But even Peru failed to play, Jones claimed to have been misunderstood in his opposition to the common-market idea, and despite the embarrassing clash Prebisch concluded that the conference "had initiated a new period for ECLA," where – repeating his now familiar admonition – "practical action had replaced theory." Organizationally the work of the new Trade Committee was allocated to two working groups – one on central banks to devise a regional payments system, and another on the regional market to recommend structure and principles.[17]

Thus Prebisch could go forward to the decisive encounter at ECLA's seventh meeting, in La Paz in May 1957, with the blessing of New York as well as the Latin governments. The meeting was heavily attended despite the cramped facilities of romantic but impractical La Paz, with just two modest hotels, the Sucre and the Copacabana, the desolate classrooms of nearby San Andres University for meeting rooms, and all paper, office supplies, and copying equipment having to be brought from Santiago. De Seynes and Malinowski, enchanted by the vertical streets, exotic central market and brightly costumed, impoverished indigenous children, wondered if it was politic to announce UN approval of ECLA's splendid new multimillion dollar compound in archrival Santiago. President Hernan Siles, caught between hyperinflation rivalling that in Weimar Germany and a catastrophic IMF-induced recession about to descend on his country, opened the meeting lamenting the economic downturn throughout the entire region, where per capita growth had fallen from 3 percent to 0.1 percent in 1956.

Siles's sober message set the stage for Prebisch's upbeat call to action, reworked from the Trade Conference into an almost personal appeal from Simón Bolivar himself. The Common Market idea was vital for Latin America; there was no other way to incorporate the masses from the countryside. Previous dreams of integration had been as ephemeral as the past attempts to give it substance. All had failed. But now Latin America could not afford to fail again when its future prosperity and place in the international system depended on solving the integration riddle. The audience applauded. "I believe ECLA succeeded in awakening the interest of Latin America in the subject at the first meeting of the Trade Committee and La Paz," Prebisch later volunteered, and the issue dominated the subsequent sessions of the meeting.

Prebisch got what he wanted at La Paz: regional integration was confirmed as ECLA's flagship project, in a class by itself. "The regional market has become the new thing in Latin America," Raúl concluded in a letter to de Seynes, describing the results of the La Paz meeting as "highly successful from the point of view of practical accomplishments and the future role of the Commission in Latin America." New York agreed; Philippe de Seynes, recently arrived from Paris, was enthusiastic about Prebisch's initiative – a bold assertion of regional leadership that revived ECLA's visibility after the depressed Argentine interlude. In a letter to New York Prebisch urged de Seynes to see regional integration as "a very big project for the UN." New York had also been pressing him to be more relevant. "Maybe this is the proper time for you, and perhaps for the Secretary General, to give a step forward that may have great impact not only in Latin America but also in the US and Europe whose understanding and support of the idea may be of considerable value."[18]

But the new period after Prebisch's success in La Paz also began with a surprise: staff were shocked when Celso Furtado resigned. Only thirty-seven and a founding member of ECLA who had arrived even before Prebisch, he was a bridge between Brazil and Hispanic America. Personally magnetic and fearless in debate, already established as a leading author and a presence second only to Prebisch in the organization, Furtado constantly challenged ECLA to grow and adapt to the emerging reality of Latin America. His range of personal experience, beginning with the Brazilian Expeditionary Brigade in World War II, gave him a personal credibility in Europe shared by few in the secretariat. A large and generous personality, popular in Santiago at every level, Furtado seemed to be Prebisch's logical heir.

The dispute appeared trivial: Prebisch called Furtado into his office before leaving for La Paz to tell him that he had decided not to publish his two-year study on the Mexican economy. Furtado was staggered. This was a major project approved by the organization in 1955. In fact the opportunity was so extraordinary – the Mexican Government had previously been suspicious of ECLA researchers – that he had moved with his wife to Mexico City to lead the study out of Urquidi's ECLA Office. There he put together a team including Mexicans Juan Noyola and Oscar Soberon, and Osvaldo Sunkel, Ahumada's favorite Chilean protegé recently returned from the London School of Economics with an established recognition for innovative work. With Soberon's inside work they had pried open and gained access to Mexico's secretive national statistics and put together a comprehensive and independent – if unorthodox – analysis of Mexican development and its prospects.[19]

Furtado's conclusions did not conform strictly to Prebisch's thesis in the Havana *Manifesto*. Unlike in Argentina, import substitution in Mexico had delivered strong economic growth and in this respect was closer to the Brazilian experience. But, as in Argentina, import-substitution industrialization had come with a high (if different) price – growing inequality. Furtado and his team found that Mexico had the advantage of a permanently dynamic external sector thanks to its high interdependence with the US economy but that more effective government regulatory policies were required to prevent a persistent tendency to concentrate income in the upper classes.[20] It was a potentially groundbreaking report, pressing forward into new terrain to renew and expand ECLA's earlier thought and work, calling for a new look at the changing economic realities in the region. While important as a case study, not least given the size and role of Mexico in Latin America, it also demonstrated the need for ECLA to understand the more complex phase of development now under way in the region. Import substitution was well-established in the region, but was it the answer? The Argentine debacle suggested otherwise, and contradictions (such as regional disparities between the north and south in Brazil, and inflation in Chile) were emerging in other countries.

In a sense it was a generational challenge, Furtado versus Prebisch, and this was clearly understood on both sides. Instead of having completed the theoretical phase, ECLA (according to Furtado) needed new thinking more than ever for guiding development policy. The Mexico study was a test for Santiago, a test for the "great heretic" to accept that his was not a rigid school of thought but rather one that fed on debate. The Government of Mexico was not happy with the report and demanded that it be quashed; for Furtado its publication became an issue of principle.[21] He pleaded with Prebisch, but to no effect; it was the first staff report that Prebisch had censored. Furtado finally broke down and wept in frustration.

Prebisch deepened the wound by asking Roberto Campos to be rapporteur of the La Paz meeting and funded his trip to Geneva to present its findings to ECOSOC. The departure of Furtado and the arrival of Roberto Campos, now president of the Brazilian BNDE and the most sophisticated conservative advisor to President Kubitschek – no message could be more clear that Prebisch meant business. Urquidi was next. While he accompanied Prebisch to La Paz and continued their argument over the Mexico study as they walked the winding cobblestone streets of the Bolivian capital, he was as deeply hurt as Furtado and resigned a year later on 26 June 1958 with a symbolic act of defiance: he authorized a limited publication of Furtado's Mexico study in his own capacity as director of ECLA's Mexico Office.

But Prebisch went further. After the La Paz meeting Prebisch invited Alex Ganz to resign by asking if he had ever belonged to an "outlawed organization." Ganz idolized Prebisch for his defiance of McCarthy in hiring him; he had worked as a valued member of the ECLA team for six years, most recently in Argentina, during which time his loyalty or political beliefs had never been questioned or confronted; his exceptional gentleness and warmth, poorly masked by gruff Bronx mannerisms, had made him (with Swenson) the best-liked American in Santiago. Prebisch already knew every detail of Ganz's file following years of fighting with US State Department security personnel after he joined ECLA. In 1956 the US International Employees Loyalty Board again notified the UN that it had denied clearance to Ganz for a permanent UN appointment – until then he had been kept on a temporary contract so that ECLA and the UN could avoid directives from the US Board. However in November 1957 the UN Secretary-General's Advisory Committee decided to set aside the US finding and offered him a contract, which Ganz accepted. But now Prebisch insisted that he leave ECLA – when the threat was long since over and McCarthy was dying of alcoholism. "Why?" staff asked.

With Furtado and Ganz gone, Juan Noyola in Mexico, and Regino Boti having returned to the University of Havana in Cuba, the Development Division – the old so-called "Red Division" – was no more. Venezuelan José Antonio Mayobre, who replaced Furtado as its director, was a regional personality recognized for his personal and administrative skills within ECLA and the UN, but he had come a long way since his youthful membership in the Venezuelan Communist Party. He was not a thinker like Furtado; Mayobre would follow – not challenge – Prebisch's lead. Although resident in Santiago, he had his eye on the presidency of Venezuela once the tottering Perez Jimenez dictatorship should finally end, and his exuberant but conflicted loyalties complicated his future with ECLA.

Overall, Prebisch's staff changes before and after La Paz clarified the ECLA succession. Chilean Jorge Ahumada, director of the Training Division, seemed poised to receive the baton, but Mayobre was in the wings just in case. Ahumada was of orthodox views and had close ties with Eduardo Frei, leader of the Christian Democratic Party of Chile. When Mayobre returned to Venezuela as minister of finance in 1958 after Perez Jimenez fell, Prebisch appointed Ahumada as head of the Development Division, so that his eventual succession appeared even more secure. But the Furtado-Ganz affair cast a certain chill even as it strengthened the orthodox wing of the secretariat. Until then the ECLA team had seen itself as a *petite troupe* with shared loyalties, enthusiasm for exploring new ideas in an atmosphere of complete intellectual freedom, and a sense of family. Now it was clear that innovation was welcome only so long as it was consistent with the "practical results" to be achieved in the new period. It was no longer the golden period for ECLA after 1956. It was as if autumn had succeeded spring in Santiago without an intervening summer after Prebisch's disastrous year in Buenos Aires.

After La Paz, Prebisch moved quickly to take advantage of the favourable regional momentum to launch his project – the creation of the "Latin American Common Market." Coinciding with the Treaty of Rome in Europe, it was immediately recognized as a major experiment in its vision and boldness and was followed closely in the media with economists from Europe and North America (as well as Latin America) such as Nicholas Kaldor, Dudley Seers, and Raymond Mikesell converging on Santiago.[22] Sidney Dell came from New York headquarters for special assignments; EEC consultants arrived to share their experience in negotiating regional trade pacts. Such renewed visibility softened the downdraft in Santiago from the Furtado and Ganz departures and restored morale in the secretariat; ECLA's new Inter-Latin American Trade Division became the main hub of activity, with additional staff allocated from other sections. Nearly all travel funds were tapped for the Common Market project, the balance scarcely sufficient for essential travel on other work. Prebisch himself was invited by the American Economics Association to give a lead paper at its January 1958 annual meeting and otherwise inundated with requests for public appearances and lectures in the US.

No design or blueprint existed anywhere to guide Prebisch's Latin American Common Market initiative, and the problems confronting its success were obvious from the outset, beginning with weak to nonexistent foundations for trade cooperation. "Latin America" had a residual cultural and geographical meaning, but region-building was only beginning and the distance and difference among the twenty republics were more impressive than the commonalities. Roads and railroads between countries scarcely existed, reflecting geopolitical rivalries and ongoing border disputes, and there was little trade or cultural interchange. There were three Latin Americas – Caucasian, Indigenous, and Black – at different levels of development and exhibiting major differences in size and endowment.[23] The EEC, with just six members, started with such great advantages as to make it an inspiration – but not a model – for Latin America. Before 1914 Europe already had free trade, which had collapsed with the outbreak of the First World War; Latin America had no such history. The EEC's challenge was postwar reconstruction and accelerated growth among highly developed economies, against the Cold War backdrop of powerful external institutional and financial support from the Bank of International Settlements, the Organization for European Economic Cooperation, the Marshall Plan, and NATO. Latin America had only the hapless OAS – nothing, in short – thus increasing its dependence on the IMF, the World Bank, and Washington. While US official support for Europe during the Cold War emergency was unequivocal, its endorsement of a Latin American Common Market was distinctly uncertain, since no comparable external threat existed to leverage attention in Washington.

However, ECLA's first post-La Paz results were promising. The two working groups – on Central Banks and the Regional Market – got off to a quick start, holding meetings of experts in Montevideo and Santiago in early 1958. An eminent persons' group was established on the Quintandinha model to support the Common Market work, including Galo Plaza (Ecuador), Rodrigo Gomez (Mexico), and Colombian Carlos Lleras Restrepo. Leading consultants from Latin America, the US, and Europe were engaged as experts to broaden the ECLA research team and reassure the US; the IMF was invited to join the Central Bank Working Group; and discussions were opened with Eric Wyndham-White at the GATT. The objective of this first phase, which lasted into early 1958, was to identify the key problems and prepare the background work required for their solution.

The second phase would culminate in ECLA's next Commission meeting scheduled for May 1959 in Panama City, where (it was hoped) regional agreement could be achieved for a formal treaty establishing the Latin American Common Market.[24]

Early positive news buoyed spirits. On 29 May 1957 Chile and Argentina signed a bilateral trade accord with a unique feature: it included ECLA's approach to liberalizing trade and transferring accounts to third parties; and officials from these two countries plus Brazil and Uruguay scheduled meetings in Santiago to discuss a coordinated trade policy and to begin preparing a Latin American position for the GATT. Evidently the Southern Cone retained the historical interest in a regional market demonstrated during Prebisch's 1940–41 MERCOSUR initiatives and other failed attempts over the years. Uruguay had proposed the formation of ECLA's Trade Committee in 1955; by inheriting the Perón mess, Arumburu's Revolución Libertadora got a lesson in the folly of closed markets. There, in the region's richest country, import-substitution policy had advanced the furthest, but had left Argentina with a vicious cycle of declining trade, falling productivity, stagnation, and inflation; there could be no better case for the regional market, weeding out inefficient local monopolies and plants protected from competition in the long-term interest of Latin American development as a whole. Of course the results of the upcoming elections on 23 February 1958 were uncertain, and the Buenos Aires political situation was highly charged, but for Prebisch this parallel Southern Cone track offered a nucleus for regional integration that could expand as other countries agreed to join – like the example of BENELUX in Western Europe anticipating the Treaty of Rome. The reality of different levels of development in Latin America suggested that such clusters of countries would be the building blocks of an eventual common market. Along with Brazil and the Southern Cone, the Andean countries of Colombia (industrializing rapidly), Ecuador (small but interested), and Venezuela (about to eject Perez Jimenez) formed another potential subgroup. Looking ahead, a Common Market project comprising these countries, along with Mexico, added up to a perfectly respectable initial membership, including most of the population and economic activity in Latin America, and leaving Central American integration to proceed at its own speed, as it had since 1951.

By February 1958 the US State Department was clamouring for membership on the working groups, an indicator of success and seriousness. The IMF was also coming on board. There were still snide comments and smirks. "The idea is beset with so many practical difficulties that it will hardly have any chance of being seriously considered. I suppose that the

ECLA experts have just hit upon this fancy idea but have not given the problem adequate analysis and scrutiny," Gordon Williams opined. The IMF should be cautious in its dealings with Prebisch: "We should not allow ourselves to become a servant of the ECLA Secretariat."[25] But this hostile attitude changed to caution when regional political interest in a common market continued to build. "There are no reasons to belittle the efforts that are being undertaken," an official mused on 15 January 1957, which are "genuine and backed by strong feelings of prestige and political expediency"; IMF aloofness, he noted, would only "egg on the ECLA countries." Behind this sensitivity lay a dark secret: the IMF had failed to assist Western European governments in the embryonic stage of the EEC; it had been asked to serve as the agent of the "Six" in organizing a payments system to resolve the credit problems of member countries but had declined by default when unable to make up its mind one way or the other. Instead the Europeans formed the Organization for European Economic Cooperation in 1948, which oversaw the European Payments Union supported by the Bank for International Settlements. First the European Coal and Steel Commission in 1951, and then the EEC created by the Treaty of Rome in 1957, gave birth to European integration with extraordinary success. Ever since, the IMF had had to live down its initial snubbing of the EEC.[26] Given this historical miscalculation, the Fund thought it wiser now not to snub Prebisch altogether, and at one point thought it might end up fighting for a role in Latin American integration[27] "It would be better for it to be on the inside," one official noted, guiding it in the right direction and avoiding what he termed "the repetition of past mistakes." When another counselled a do-nothing approach, Per Jacobsson and his deputy Merle Cochran were less certain, and Jacobsson scribbled hard in the margin: MUST NOT GET OFF WRONG. EPU [European Payments Union] – TURNED OUT RIGHT. WE DID NOT KNOW!

The result was that the IMF agreed to join the Central Banks Working Group and prepare a paper for its first Meeting of Experts in mid-1957 in Montevideo, a decision that produced guarded optimism in Santiago and New York. De Seynes followed the unfolding negotiations closely and supported Prebisch with quiet diplomacy, squashing UN reports that might damage relations with the Fund.[28] Prebisch was also extremely careful, knowing the importance – but also the fragility – of the IMF link.[29] The integration project for Latin America required IMF support; there was no option since ECLA had few resources other than persuasion – more like the role of Jean Monnet's Action Committee for the United States of Europe in mobilizing public opinion behind the Treaty of Rome. But the initial response of the IMF was encouraging, and Prebisch felt that the pieces were starting to come together as serious bargaining loomed.[30]

US Vice-President Richard Nixon's visit to Latin America two months later, from 28 April to 15 May 1958, completely changed the future of US-Latin American relations, and therefore the prospects for a common market. Strained since Eisenhower's arrival in Washington six years earlier, relations had deteriorated further with the failure of the Inter-American Economic Conference in Buenos Aires during August 1957. This event, the origins of which few remembered, stemmed from an overhasty US commitment in 1948 to strengthen US-Latin American economic relations; coinciding with the Marshall Plan in Europe, the promised Economic Conference was viewed by Latin Americans as a similar major departure in which finally they would become privileged postwar recipients of major American largesse. Embarrassed by having no such intentions, Washington under Democrats and Republicans kept finding excuses for postponing the conference – until finally, after the fall of Perón, Argentina revived the idea, successfully as it turned out, by pinning the US down to a date. Convened by the OAS with soaring rhetoric and customary ineptitude, the meeting in Buenos Aires brought together all the finance ministers and most journalists from the entire region. It should not have been held at all. George Humphrey's approach was so cold – he repeated that the Eisenhower Administration had no intention of altering any established policies – that the US delegation was itself mortified. Two of its members were strong personalities. Core Republican C. Douglas Dillon, US Ambassador to France from 1953–57 and son of a powerful Wall Street investment banker, had returned to Washington as deputy undersecretary for Economic Affairs in the State Department; Ambassador Thomas Clifton Mann, a capable career diplomat and Southern Baptist with a righteous high forehead and pursed, full, well-defined red lips, had just returned from El Salvador. Both understood that the conference had revived high expectations, that its failure would ignite a predictable anti-American outpouring in the regional media, and that US-Latin American relations seemed stuck in the Cold War years, with the OAS once again humiliated as Washington's doormat. Prebisch's update on the Common Market project was one of the Economic Conference's few non-polarizing moments, its contrast with the OAS debacle reinforcing ECLA's prestige in the region as a centre of ideas and energy. "I complain many times about our organization," he confided to de Seynes, "but when I heard the reports about how the Economic Conference was handled I do not think it is so bad."[31]

Nixon's trip was a spectacular disaster. The US recession had spread to Latin America; on 7 April Prebisch warned of stagnation and social problems ahead as young people faced unemployment. "Latin America is again displaying its usual high level of vulnerability," he noted, with a 6 percent deterioration in the terms of trade for the region. "We are again facing an emergency without the means of taking emergency action."[32] Spreading economic problems in the sprawling new urban centres brought latent frustration with US policy and multinational corporations to a head.

Signs of trouble were ignored in Washington, however, because of the *Sputnik* factor: on 4 October 1957, the Soviet Union launched the first artificial satellite into orbit. Only 22 inches in diameter and weighing 184 pounds, it nevertheless opened the space age ahead of US engineers. "The new socialist society had turned the boldest dreams of mankind into reality," Khrushchev noted. In contrast, US news headlines that week focused on Arkansas: three hundred Army troops had to escort nine small and terrified black children to Central High School in Little Rock on 25 September after Governor Orval Faubus refused to end racial segregation.[33] This coincidence of vivid Soviet space success and US social failure rattled the self-confidence of the Eisenhower Administration; not just US education but also the security of its backyard, Latin America, could no longer be taken for granted. Even John Foster Dulles suggested on 14 April, two weeks before Nixon's departure, that US trade policy toward Latin America should be reviewed, a hint that something really had to be done to improve relations after six years of drift.[34]

But no one in Washington realized the depth of anti-US feeling in the streets of Latin America. Nixon's visit was billed as a goodwill tour of regional capitals at a time when democracy was returning to Venezuela and Argentina, and his itinerary centred on the inauguration of Arturo Frondizi in Buenos Aires. But from the start the entire trip was a nightmare. Violence in Caracas on 13 May reached a level of verbal and physical abuse sufficient for Washington to send four companies of marines and paratroopers to the Caribbean ready to assist the Venezuelan authorities if needed. Nixon explained, "It is certainly not pleasant to be covered from head to foot with spit and to have a man spit directly into the face of my wife."[35]

A day after Nixon returned to Washington the Senate Foreign Relations Committee launched an investigation into the background of the evident anti-US feeling in Latin America. Nixon blamed the violence on a small minority of communist-inspired students and hooligans, but others in the Eisenhower Administration, such as Deputy Undersecretary of State for Economic Affairs Douglas Dillon, who had been with the US delegation at the Buenos Aires Economic Conference ("It was a revelation to me," he noted), supported a change of policy toward the region.[36] Sensing this opening, Brazil's President Juschelino Kubitschek wrote to President Eisenhower. "We must search our consciences to find out if we are following the right path in regard to Pan-Americanism," he confided. "Something must be done to restore composure to the continental unity." US-Latin American relations required what he termed "a firmer basis."[37] The US reply was delivered personally three days later by Assistant Secretary of State for Inter-American Affairs Roy R. Rubottom Jr; John Foster Dulles would welcome being invited to Rio de Janeiro on 4–5 August for a bilateral dialogue. In Rio the two powers agreed to convene a meeting of presidents at which new programs of economic development would be discussed; and in August Kubitschek proposed that the Americas launch "Operation Pan America," reviving the Quintandinhna agenda from 1954.[38]

The pace of change was startling. Not to be outdone by Brazil, Washington moved quickly on the most visible Latin priority – an inter-American development bank – so long a dream and so recently denied. On 11 August President Eisenhower gave approval for the initiative, after the State Department and the US Treasury supported its creation, and an announcement was rushed out the next day.[39] By April 1959 – when "I Like Fidel" bumper stickers could still be found on North American cars – the Inter-American Development Bank (IDB) was a reality. Other changes followed in Washington. After Milton Eisenhower toured the region looking for sensitive areas where action could be taken immediately, he noted "the appeal of Latin American nations for stable relationships between raw commodity prices and the prices of manufactured goods."[40] Washington heretofore had invariably opposed international commodity agreements during the 1950s. Now, after the Nixon shock, the US hurriedly agreed to an International Coffee Agreement – particularly important to Brazil and Colombia – which was in fact concluded under UN auspices in 1962. It was another signal of the new era in US-Latin American relations.[41]

A few months earlier, in January 1958, the US State Department had fulminated mightily against Prebisch for advocating "progressive capitalism," or a "third alternative" in which US relations with Latin America would more nearly approximate US domestic policy and support equitable growth. "Misrepresentations and fallacies," it roared, and US missions abroad were instructed to denounce them if the opportunity arose. Six months later Washington had quietly adopted a good portion of Prebisch's "progressive capitalism."[42] Senior US officials decided that he was not so bad after all. Dour Assistant Secretary for Inter-American Affairs Roy Rubottom, from New England, actually apologized for past behaviour, noting for the record that "he would like to dispel any possible misunderstandings that may have arisen in the past with respect to the attitude of the US Government toward ECLA" and his appreciation for "the work done by ECLA and of the leadership provided by Dr Prebisch himself." He reassured Raúl of "our friendship toward ECLA and of our desire to work closely with it," notwithstanding "differences on specific questions in which problems could be discussed, if not resolved, on a friendly basis as to be expected among men of intelligence and good faith." To which Prebisch, for the record as well, gave what State described as "a gracious acknowledgement."[43]

But how far did this change go in Washington? For Prebisch the key test of the new spirit in US-Latin American relations was the Latin American Common Market project, now reaching a decisive point as his two working groups prepared to meet prior to ECLA's Panama session in 1959. The US role was vital in every area: the financing of development and trade; its diplomatic support in the GATT and IMF; but also its private sector role since US transnational corporations were entering Latin America in large numbers. Washington supported its firms, advocating open markets to foreign investment in the region. Kubitschek, for example, welcomed US multinationals in his drive for rapid industrialization, particularly in the more dynamic technologically advanced sectors; their lobbying would drive US policy toward the proposed Common Market. Prebisch had confronted Standard Oil in the *Plan Prebisch,* and his version of regional integration implied a planning role for the state as opposed to unfettered foreign investment. Now, with Eisenhower's unexpected opening to Latin America in 1958, he felt on uncertain ground.

On 18 November 1958 Dillon clarified the US position, noting that "we are also prepared to do what we can to help interested Latin American countries in framing arrangements for economic integration which are economically sound."[44] Assistant Secretary of State for Economic Affairs Thomas Mann and Deputy Director of the Office of International Trade Policy Isaiah Frank gave this same impression. The US would support any Latin American initiative of economic integration, but with a condition: that it not reduce the volume of foreign trade or contribute to domestic monopolies by reducing competition. It must be GATT-consistent, Frank stressed, and he advised all the Latin countries to join (so far only six were members). Other than that, Washington had no dogmatic attitude, and in fact would prefer starting with groups of countries (Mann mentioned his hope of an economic union between Argentina and Chile) rather than all of Latin America. The "new" position was not new at all, merely a repetition of its "approval in principle" in Santiago at the first meeting of the Trade Committee: the US supported regional integration "without reservation" subject to the GATT qualifier.[45] There were pleasantries: Mann said that he recognized ECLA's pioneering work in the field of economic integration; Frank, with whom Prebisch had developed a friendly personal relationship, reminded him that the US had stood up for ECLA in the OAS, defending its lead role in regional integration. He hoped to organize a staff conference the next time Prebisch visited Washington to meet other officials in the State Department.[46]

On the negative side, and despite the new language in Washington, most of the senior Eisenhower people drawn to his policies didn't like Prebisch personally. He was frozen out of any role to do with the new Inter-American Development Bank, pointedly not being invited to an OAS meeting of foreign ministers on 23–24 September to discuss the new Bank project in the context of regional integration. "Of course I am willing to go to Washington on a moment's notice to participate in this discussion," he wrote to his Washington chief, Milic Kybal, "but until now we have not received any indication about it."[47] When the twenty-one foreign ministers of the US-Latin American region struck a group of experts for work to begin on the new Bank, the US insisted on a blanket prohibition of observers – with the express purpose of keeping Prebisch out, despite his credentials as former head of the Argentine Central Bank and his earlier work with the US Federal Reserve throughout Latin America. Since the Bank would become the most important inter-American institution, US officials wanted Prebisch as far away as possible from the key issues of policy, location, and leadership. US Treasury official T. Graydon Upton, set to become the first US executive vice-president in the new IDB, called him "a left-wing economist with ideas about Latin American economic development that would be costly to the US."[48] Thomas Mann and Douglas Dillon, the top two US officials in inter-American affairs, distrusted Prebisch intensely – all the more because they had ended up adopting the ECLA agenda they had previously rejected. Mann, a talented administrator, reflected attitudes characteristic of the early 1950s: "Latin Americans," he once said, "like a buck in their pocket and a kick in the ass ... They don't think like us. Their thought processes are different. You have to be firm with them."[49] Confident in the special prerogatives of a senior US Government official in dealings with the South, he enjoyed the exercise of power: smiling at Latin officials while insulting them to their faces. Prebisch, an even tougher negotiator and more experienced and more knowledgeable than Mann, fit poorly into this Latin stereotype: his toughness was "arrogance." Dillon and Mann made sure that Prebisch was not invited to the opening ceremonies of the IDB board of governors in El Salvador on 5 February 1960.[50]

When Prebisch visited Washington in late 1958 to discuss the project, Mann told him to his face that he did not believe his claim that the Latin Common Market would be (like Europe) consistent with Article XXIV of the GATT (i.e., not trade-distorting). Prebisch maintained that it would be "open" rather than "closed," but (as with Europe) there had to be safeguards. Moreover as a developmental model it would also require a "dynamic" policy of protectionism that would be "rational," "orderly," and "selective" in order to create an automobile sector and other new industries. The EEC had been granted huge exceptions in the Common Agricultural Policy and privileged trade with old colonies; why would the US refuse similar treatment for Latin America? As in Western Europe, so also in Latin America trade with the rest of the world would grow rather than decline, and regional integration would benefit all.

Mann ruled out a development model for regional integration in Latin America that amounted to "special, monopoly-favouring provisions for the protected expansion of new products."[51] No matter how much Prebisch repeated his commitment to a GATT-consistent process, he was considered either wrong or deliberately misleading: ECLA's regional integration project was state-led – a classic model of "closed regionalism" behind tariff walls, which would take Latin America in exactly the wrong protectionist and anti-business direction. The future of Latin American growth depended on foreign investment, and US multinationals would only be attracted by a business climate that guaranteed the free movement of capital. It followed that the best strategy for regional integration was to combine open markets and minimal government regulation, so that the private sector – multinational and domestic – would invest rationally within and across borders. Mann bridled over Prebisch's talk of automobile production; Latins could not make complex products like cars or airplanes. "It would be wrong to create an artificial or uneconomic industry in automobiles or any other product that could never compete." Mann appeared to know already what products Latins could or could not make. He seemed to be referring to existing products – since "soundly conceived ones" would require time to demonstrate that they were "outward-looking and based on the idea of competition." In the meantime they should be content to grow coffee, bottle soft drinks, make textiles, and continue shipping minerals – which accounted for 80 percent of its imports from the region – to the US.[52] For Mann there was no budging from this position. His constituency – the US multinationals in the region – were hostile to trade liberalization and full supporters of ISI (import-substitution industrialization), in order to expand in the small but lucrative national markets where high profits could be assured with existing technology from the US parents. In Western Europe multinationals had endorsed the EEC; in Latin America they opposed it, and only a core threat to national security would have convinced Mann and his associates to deviate from their position.

In lock step, Eric Wyndham-White's GATT, the gate-keeper for regional free-trade agreements, which had just placed its stamp of approval on the EEC, rejected the Latin American Common Market as a legitimate accord, using Mann's argument word for word that it contravened Article XXIV[53] – GATT insisted that any trade arrangement resulting from the ECLA initiative be termed a "free trade area" rather than "common market." Urquidi railed against Wyndham-White's hypocrisy: are not safeguards normal fare in international agreements? he asked. Are there none in the GATT, in US commercial policy legislation, or in the EEC's notorious protectionism in agricultural products? "These are time-honoured devices," he concluded, "economic facts of life … which are worked out over time. One cannot demand of Latin Americans that they be the last perfect free-traders on the planet."[54]

The IMF joined the US and Wyndham-White in rejecting Prebisch's Common Market project. Its new quantitative model, finalized in 1957 and applied to the Bolivian stabilization package that year, effectively terminated the more flexible ideological approach of previous years, and Per Jacobsson's arrival as managing director, with Merle Cochran, Jacques J. Polak, and Irving Friedman at his side, further cemented the new line: Jacobssen viewed the dividing line between civilization and the jungle as being close to the English Channel, definitely excluding Latin America, in which he had neither interest nor knowledge.[55] Jacobsson's head of the Western Hemisphere Department, Jorge del Canto, symbolized the new line. A Chilean and the first Latin appointed to the Fund after its creation, not known for a penetrating mind, he lived his life with one unwavering conviction: monetary orthodoxy. Del Canto's position on Latin integration was rigid: the Fund should assist as long as it did not compromise the strict application of the four golden principles: removal of discrimination, convertibility, bilateralism (direct dealings between the IMF and member governments), and simplified exchange rates. The Fund's best contribution to regional integration was ensuring sound money – period.

The good soldier, Jorge del Canto, was ordered to contain Prebisch at ECLA's eighth session held in May 1959 in Panama City, at which the fate of the Latin American Common Market would be decided.[56] Prebisch tried to pre-empt his many adversaries by answering, line by line, Mann's earlier criticisms about "closed regionalism."[57] But del Canto took the offensive against the Common Market proposal and became openly abusive toward the "so-called ECLA consultants" or "Prebisch's stormtroopers."[58] "The futility of the whole exercise was evident," he reported to Washington, while complimenting himself on the "dignity and courage with which [the IMF observers] defended the Fund's point of view."[59]

The IMF need not have worried; the Latin American Common Market had a new enemy – Arturo Frondizi, who effectively killed the project. Combined with external resistance from Washington, the GATT, and the IMF, Argentina's opposition to effective regional integration ensured at best a minimalist, face-saving compromise.[60] Winning the general elections on 23 February 1958 over Ricardo Balbin under the banner of the UCRI (Intransigent Radicals), Frondizi assumed power on 1 May, facing high expectations for economic recovery.[61] By January 1959 he had reversed direction, terminating his electoral alliance with Perón, turning tanks on striking Perónist workers, and adopting an IMF structural adjustment package that made him del Canto's star performer in Latin America. He also sharply reversed direction in US relations, jettisoning his earlier nationalism and opening the economy to US multinationals and other foreign investors at any price in a bid to replicate neighbouring Brazil's growth under Kubitschek. In effect Frondizi gambled on bargaining directly with the IMF and the US, and this meant restoring Argentina's standing in Washington with an active pro-US diplomacy.[62] An immediate burst of economic activity that rallied public opinion seemed to prove his point; and with Standard Oil back the petroleum sector was headed for national self-sufficiency within four years, just as the US Embassy had predicted.

Frondizi opposed Prebisch's approach to the Latin American Common Market; "integration" for him meant building an Argentine identity rather than sharing sovereignty in a regional trade pact. In any case he loathed ECLA; Prebisch's talk of Latin America having to compete with the new global giants, China and India, as well as with Western Europe and North America, left Frondizi uninterested.[63] At an IMF luncheon in honour of Prebisch on 18 November 1959, Merle Cochran and his senior staff agreed, holding up Frondizi's stabilization program as one of Latin America's finest achievements, confirming del Canto's position at Panama that the IMF would stick with existing policy of sound money in one-to-one dealings with individual governments.[64] Prebisch could not expect anything more from the IMF. Nor from Frondizi. Raúl completely understood the old Argentine saying that in Argentine politics the predominant law is the law of hate.

The compromise solution – so much investment in the Latin American Common Market had to result in the creation of something – was LAFTA

(Latin American Free Trade Association). All of Prebisch's opponents, from Frondizi to the GATT, Washington and the IMF, could tolerate the Treaty of Montevideo signed on 18 February 1960 by (initially) Brazil, Uruguay, Argentina, Brazil, Colombia, Mexico, and Ecuador. A modest step, with numerous loopholes and exceptions, and explicitly not a customs union or common market, LAFTA set up a mechanism for a free-trade zone as understood under Article XXIV of GATT, to be implemented gradually and progressively over twelve years with 75 percent of reciprocal trade in value to become free after nine years, and "substantially all" thereafter. The Conference of Member States, with an executive committee, formed the highest organ of the association and its chief decision- and policymaking body. The secretariat would be located in neutral Montevideo, headed by an executive secretary, with officers and a budget. The reductions of tariffs and other barriers were negotiated on the basis of product lists, with countries exchanging preferences. But governments retained a veto – LAFTA was not a supranational entity – and there were numerous safeguards for member governments, and no provisions for commercial credit.[65]

The Montevideo Treaty was an anti-climax. Few agreements on industrial rationalization had less chance of success: leaders like Frondizi were enthusiastic about free trade in their benefit but balked at concessions in difficult sectors (agriculture, automobiles, textiles, consumer goods, etc.) as soon as jobs were at stake. Meanwhile the private sector and workers in each country – domestic and foreign multinational companies alike – clamoured successfully for high trade barriers to restrict imports. Dag Hammarskjöld and de Seynes cabled their congratulations: "Highly pleased with outcome of Montevideo Meeting. Consider agreement reached a major achievement in which the United Nations have been able to take an essential part thanks to your relentless efforts and enlightened leadership."[66] The regional press proclaimed LAFTA to be a "historic" achievement. But Prebisch knew better. Both Washington and the IMF scoffed at it; the IDB was welcomed into the major league, but no one stood up for LAFTA.[67] It was a thin beginning to regional integration considering the expectations of its launch in 1956; ECLA, in fact, was denied the leadership of LAFTA in the Treaty of Montevideo, and Prebisch dismissed out of hand the suggestion that he serve as its first executive secretary.[68]

The Treaty of Montevideo behind him, nearing sixty, and disappointed, Prebisch finally took a vacation at El Maqui to reflect on his successes and failures since 1956. There was little enough to show for it – the costs of his single-minded fight for the Common Market dream were all too evident. There had been mainly setbacks in the second period of ECLA since 1956; the new mission of "concrete action" had come up short. Of course staff had proposed big ideas – the creation of a Latin American tropical institute, for example – but they were dropped to pursue the Common Market. He had pushed hard – maybe too hard; ECLA had lost its special cachet. It had succeeded in carving out a niche for itself in the UN and Latin American landscape; its divisions ground out their reports in four languages for the big commission meetings every two years. Its statistics were now the most reliable in the region. It had even spawned new additions, like CELADE (Centre for Economic Projections), with its own board. But it no longer had a monopoly on new thinking in Latin America as other well-funded national institutes appeared throughout the region.[69] Nor, after the Nixon visit and the evident thaw in US-Latin American relations, could Santiago maintain its image as embattled outpost in the American Empire. If Prebisch and his small band had flourished on US hostility during the 1950s, could they survive a suddenly friendly Washington?

Worse, ECLA was becoming fully ensnared in bureaucracy. Having carved out its regional niche, its work program threatened to become predictable; ECLA reports had even developed a recognizable, deadening style. The other UN regional commissions were caught in the same vise of pressures from centralizing New York headquarters and controlling member governments. A weariness was evident in Santiago; a sense of nostalgia for the old days haunted the corridors; ECLA would never go away, but it was in danger of degenerating into another dispirited UN organization.

Prebisch was tiring of the administrative burden after ten years of ceaseless work and felt personally stale after the long Common Market slog; and the meagre results at the 1959 Panama meeting and then the LAFTA compromise re-ignited his desire to get back into the intellectual mainstream. Invited to the 1958 meeting of the American Economics Association, he realized that his paper had been an embarrassment, a rehash of his Havana *Manifesto*, showing that new international trade and development scholarship was moving well beyond his earlier work. It wasn't just Arthur Lewis; younger scholars were moving ahead – building on his "pioneering" work – as he and ECLA colleagues knocked themselves out with tedious reports. Creative work, Prebisch acknowledged, "had to be subordinated to the claims of practical action, in compliance with the requests of governments." The result was that "for the last few years, ECLA has been living on a previously accumulated fund of theoretical interpretation which has not been progressively renewed or increased." And in fact he had written to UN Personnel a year earlier about taking early retirement in 1961.[70] But there was no push from New York for him to leave ECLA. In 1958 Dag Hammarskjöld had extended Raúl's second five-year appointment to 1963, two years beyond the normal retirement age, and Malinowski told him that he would likely get a third term if he wanted it – so great was his prestige in New York.[71]

Instead, to recast the early doctrine, which was now inadequate, Prebisch craved a more autonomous body than ECLA had become. He had grown increasingly critical of Latin governments and the elites they represented; he could no longer bear their posturing – their complaining about the US, or the world, or the "system" – while they refused domestic reform themselves. A dynamism was lacking in Latin America; the region was now more marginalized in the global economy than at the birth of ECLA, and comparisons with East Asian countries were embarrassing. Although poorer – Japan still had fewer automobiles per capita than Peru, not to mention comparisons with Argentina's enviable standard of living – these countries were moving forward. They were spending no more on education and training than Latin America, but their work forces were superior in quality. Their import-substitution industrialization strategies were broadly similar, but unlike Latin America they were creating globally competitive industries. Latin Americans had to rethink their model of development, and Prebisch wanted to lead this next stage of creative adjustment. In La Paz in 1957 he had proposed ECLA-led "advisory groups" to work at the request of governments on development planning and project evaluation, with teams of experts inside ministries to attract capital and steer it toward productive investment behind a realistic development plan. Where possible they would work with sister UN agencies such as the FAO or TAA, and Bolivia was the first to volunteer for a mission in 1959. But the concept was under attack from the beginning; ECLA was too rigid for successful advisory-group missions, which required autonomy to be effective.[72] Prebisch needed a new centre, sheltered from management and budgetary struggles, to become an advocate for new economic thought and planning in the region.

The unexpected solution for Prebisch's dilemma came from Paul G. Hoffman, visiting Santiago after his appointment as manager of the newly created UN Special Fund. Hoffman was a senior US corporate personality and confidante of President Franklin Roosevelt who had led the Marshall Plan 1948–50, served as president of the Ford Foundation 1950–53, and had been appointed US delegate to the UN in 1956. In March 1960 Hoffman visited Prebisch to explain his new operation; they had dinner at El Maqui, and Adelita played his favourite Goldberg Variations. Hoffman explained that the Special Fund Consultative Board would be meeting later that year in September, and he needed a respectable stable of projects for a clean launch. What did Prebisch think of creating a new Latin American research centre – the Latin American Institute for Social and Economic Planning (ILPES) – to build on ECLA's early work?

With a separate governing council for his Special Fund, Hoffman was a powerful figure on the New York UN scene, heading a new agency with the potential to grow into the single largest technical assistance agency in the international development game. The Special Fund was the remnant of a much larger General Assembly proposal for the creation of SUNFED (Special UN Fund for Economic Development), recommended in 1951 by a UN group of experts to provide development capital on the basis of need rather than the approval of Western banks, including the World Bank.[73] Supported by UN officials such as Hans Singer, the concept had had no chance of success. That the banks, the World Bank, and developed economies would fight back was inevitable, and since they controlled the funds they were bound to be successful. Yet they were shamed into two concessions: the IDA (International Development Association), a soft-loan facility that the World Bank would manage; and the Special Fund, directed by the silver-haired patrician Hoffman, which would finance large "pre-investment" projects such as research centres, surveys, or extension projects, rather than investment capital as originally intended.[74]

The Special Fund, with its own governing council, operated outside the regular UN budget; if it funded the new ILPES, Prebisch would have the necessary autonomy. Moreover, once the Special Fund was on board, the much larger Inter-American Development Bank would surely match it with counterpart funding for the institute. Prebisch could envisage an ideal scenario: the new ILPES would be in but not of ECLA – sharing the same building but with a separate board of directors and administration to free it from outside controls. Raúl could hand-pick the economists he wanted and could give higher pay because the institute could bypass the strict UN categories for classification and salaries: with him would come his Argentine circle – Benjamin Hopenhayn, Norberto Gonzalez, Ricardo Cibotti, and Oscar Bardeci – and his favourite Chileans like Oswaldo Sunkel. Unable to leave Swenson behind, Raúl would attach him to the institute as his "Special Consultant." Prebisch himself would retain his UN undersecretary status as director-general; and now that he was out of the secretariat he could continue beyond the normal UN retirement age.

De Seynes and Malinowski, who had briefed Hoffman before his trip to Santiago, also endorsed the ILPES concept: not only did they want Prebisch to remain in the UN after his retirement, but regional institutes modelled on ILPES and linked to the four Commissions would add a creative element currently missing in the system while also satisfying the perennial demand for greater UN decentralization. If successful in Santiago, ILPES would become a model for the other regions. Prebisch sent a short proposal to Hoffman and was rewarded with immediate approval-in-principle. Malinowski and de Seynes drafted a General Assembly resolution for the creation of regional planning institutes linked closely to the commissions.[75] IDB head Filipe Herrera agreed to co-fund the institute with Hoffman. In such a new environment Santiago could reclaim its leadership in training, research, and advisory services for development. It was a neat package and a dignified exit from ECLA when his term would expire in 1963.

But as the new ILPES was born, US-Latin American relations were veering out of control. And Senator John F. Kennedy defeated Richard M. Nixon to become the new president of the United States.

16 The Kennedy Offensive

Prebisch and Latin Americans in general awaited the US presidential elections on 4 November 1960 with anticipation, sensing change. Eisenhower had been the venerated military leader in World War II; Democratic candidate John F. Kennedy heralded the arrival of a new generation should he prevail against the dour Vice-President Richard M. Nixon. He was not much known in Latin America – unlike Nixon, who carried the baggage of April 1958 as an unsympathetic knee-jerk anti-communist cold fish who had defended the destruction of democracy in Guatemala in 1954. ("This is the first instance in history where a Communist government has been replaced by a free one.")[1] Kennedy was handsome, well-married, and rich; surrounded by intellectuals, writers, and artists, he and his young team radiated an excitement that contrasted dramatically with the ambience in the tired Eisenhower-Nixon entourage. He symbolized a confident US projecting vigorous international leadership; Kennedy could, it seemed, make Washington the fascination of the entire world. His campaign promised the "Alliance for Progress" – a new US policy toward Latin America in fact rather than mere promise.[2] For Latin Americans Senator Kennedy seemed different: he appeared to value international development as a human objective in itself rather than merely a tool to fight communism.

But was this image of Kennedy substance or mirage? Or was he himself, Prebisch wondered, imagining things, indulging in hero-worship in his advancing years, wanting to believe that the ideal of North-South development he had fought for these many years had finally become a genuine foreign-policy priority in Washington? If US-Latin American relations could indeed be recast in this vision under Kennedy, Prebisch wanted to be part of this new Washington-led awakening. But during autumn 1960, as the US presidential campaign entered its final stage, the tension mounted between Kennedy the humanist of the Alliance for Progress and Kennedy the Cold Warrior obsessed with the "missile gap," the Soviet lead in the space race, and the "loss of Cuba."

Fidel Castro, the spectre of communism incarnate, hovered over the presidential succession. In the two years since his victory in Havana on 1 January 1959, Cuba had exercised an influence in Washington altogether out of proportion to its size, and on 4 January 1961, three weeks before John F. Kennedy and his family moved into the White House, Eisenhower severed diplomatic ties with the island. The US had engineered the downfall of President Arbenz in Guatemala in 1954; Latin Americans awaited Kennedy's policy toward Cuba, hoping for his victory over hardliner Nixon, whose enthusiasm for military intervention was not in doubt.

Many at ECLA rejoiced over the Cuban Revolution when the Batista regime fell on New Year's Day in 1959. Regino Boti became minister of economy in charge of Cuba's National Economic Council; Juan Noyola pleaded with Raúl to begin a special program for Cuba and to appoint him head of mission; Filipe Pazos left the IMF to resume the presidency of the Cuban Central Bank after a forced absence of seven years. All believed that they could serve the new Cuban Revolution. A sense of renewal flooded the region at the prospect of genuine social change in this inner redoubt of the US empire; Batista fled to the Dominican Republic and the disgraced Eugenio Castillo found himself in Baltimore for good with his wife's family.

Prebisch feared from the first that the Cuban Revolution would come to a bad end. He understood Boti and Pazos and their reasons for returning; he also was an exile and yearned to return home some day. He also felt the emotional impact of the Cuban Revolution, and he agreed with Noyola that Cuba could not be denied technical assistance from Santiago, since it was a founding member country of ECLA that had always been loyal in difficult times. Boti requested that Noyola come with a group of experts to help modernize the sugar industry; and Prebisch supported a small ECLA mission, notwithstanding immediate evidence of US displeasure.[3] He was fascinated by the young men and women of the revolution led by Fidel and his fellow Argentine Che Guevara – their zeal and seriousness of purpose, their determination to do away with the venality and corruption of the Batista dictatorship. He did not doubt their commitment to social change for the poor and dispossessed and the submerged black Cubans, or their instinctive support for social movements elsewhere in Latin America. But he feared fanaticism, a reflex from his student days in Buenos Aires, when he rejected Marxism-Leninism, and the mob psychology of Perónism, which had driven him from Argentina. He worried about what the revolution would do to Cuba and how Washington's fury with Fidel would poison US-Latin American relations.

Despite initial caution in Washington, Cuban-US relations deteriorated when Castro tried and executed police and military officials and then announced sweeping reform plans in February. Fidel's first visit to the US capital in April 1959 was not a success. "Boti is here with Fidel Castro," Kybal wrote from Washington on 17 April, "and I saw him yesterday; I hope that together with Pazos they will carry some weight in their nation's affairs."[4] At ECLA's May 1959 session in Panama, Boti headed the Cuban delegation and reassured Prebisch "that Cuba needed to undertake a series of domestic reforms (agrarian reform, tax reform, etc.) which might appear revolutionary to the outside world, but that the financial policies of the government were as conservative as those the fund (IMF) would recommend to any country: no credit expansion; budget surplus; and the government was holding a firm line with labour." He warned, however, "as to how far these present conservative financial policies could be maintained, depended on the cooperation they could get from abroad."[5] But US doubts were already solidifying into animosity: Dudley Seers, a British economist on leave in Santiago, was detained by the FBI on entering Panama because he wore a beard. Polarization quickly replaced farce as it became clear that this was not a typical Latin American coup d'état, that Fidel was fully in charge, and that his vision of Cuba was unacceptable to the Eisenhower Administration. In mid-May 1959, the Cuban Government enacted the Agrarian Reform Act, raising the prospect of nationalizing US-owned property, and prompting a sharp official warning from Washington rejecting Cuba's compensation offer (long-term interest bearing bonds) and demanding immediate cash payment on its terms. The situation between Cuba and the US now became tense, with congressional demands to send in the marines and terrorist attacks launched from the growing community of Cuban middle-class refugees from the island. By mid-November the US threatened to cut Cuba's sugar quota – its economic lifeline. In response Havana proceeded on 15 January 1960 with a symbolic expropriation of uncultivated US-owned land, clearly challenging Washington to react, but the Eisenhower Administration stepped back from so drastic a reprisal against the island economy.

Soviet-US relations now complicated the Cuban picture. On the eve of Eisenhower's long-awaited talks with the Soviet leader, Khrushchev announced another success: on 14 September a Soviet rocket had hit the moon, the first object sent from one cosmic body to another, carrying the hammer-and-sickle emblem to the lunar surface; previous US attempts had failed. Moscow went a step further: on 5 February 1960 Soviet Deputy Premier Anastas Mikoyan arrived in Cuba to announce the purchase of five million tons of Cuban sugar over five years, a $100 million credit, and supplies of oil and petroleum products. This seemed to challenge Washington in its own region, and Moscow also offered Cuba military supplies when Western countries, under US pressure, refused. Eisenhower thereupon cut sugar purchases by 700,000 tons, leaving only a token shipment of 39,752, and when US oil companies refused to supply Cuba, Moscow announced that it would fill this gap. After US-Soviet tensions mounted when a US U-2 spy plane was shot down over Soviet territory and its pilot, Francis Gary Powers, captured, Khrushchev announced that "the US would have to deal with Soviet rockets if it chose to intervene militarily in Cuba." On 6–7 August the Cuban Government nationalized all US property on the island, breaking the pre-1959 integration with the US that Washington (and many Cubans) had long taken for granted.[6]

By mid-1960 a dynamic of reciprocal accusation and radicalization had led to a new political icon in the Caribbean: a proud Cuban revolutionary outpost, surviving against US military, political, and economic siege, welcoming Soviet economic and military support against the blockade while insisting on an independent diplomatic voice in the UN, reeling under mass emigration of the Cuban middle class but remaining a unique regional symbol – magnified by US hostility and intervention – of building a new society in an unjust continent. For every US denunciation of Castro's human-rights violations Fidel countered with reminders of US atrocities drawn from a century of US intervention. In his July 26 1960 Address, which marked the anniversary of his first rising in 1953, he speculated that the Andes would become the next Sierra Maestra of Latin America. By January 1961, when Eisenhower severed diplomatic relations, preparation for the US Bay of Pigs intervention to topple the Cuban Revolution was in full swing.

The Cuban example was infectious; Latins of all persuasions were more assertive, less fearful of offending Washington. Conservative President Jorge Alessandri of Chile visited Havana in April 1960, ignoring protests from Washington. Writers throughout the region mocked US fears of Cuba. "How small this great United States has become! How it has grown and grown only to become smaller," Mexican poet Jaime Sabines jeered on 8 July 1960, hearing of US efforts to curb Mexico's continuing relations with Cuba.[7] The usual ingratiating Latin deference to Washington at regional encounters evaporated. "The US and three other non-Latin American Members of the Commission were victims of a concerted power play," sniffed a US official in a hurt tone, reporting to the secretary of state from a special ECLA meeting in New York on 2 July 1960, complaining of a "seemingly deliberate rudeness to US in particular."[8]

While ECLA was heavily criticized in Washington for its alleged "socialist" tendencies and particularly its mission to Cuba, Prebisch was increasingly preoccupied by the course of the revolution. In November 1959 Che Guevara, who had been posted to the National Institute of Agrarian Reform, replaced Felipe Pazos as president of the Cuban Central Bank. Pazos had lasted less than a year in Havana before returning to Washington.[9] "Neither revolutionary, nor radical,"[10] Che complained of him, while insisting that Salvador Vilaseca join him as deputy despite protests that he knew nothing about banking: "Listen, when the revolution assigns you a job you have to do it and do it well."[11] Prebisch respected Pazos; if such top economists who had left everything to return to Cuba could no longer work with Castro and his group, something was seriously wrong. In April 1960 he shared with the US ambassador in Santiago his own concern that radicalization and increasing state control in Cuba could lead to a Soviet-style command economy, assuring him that ECLA would not allow itself to become a pawn in the unfolding US-Cuban chess game. He was fully aware of what was going on, he said, and was determined that ECLA personnel stay clear of political activities. Castro's invitation to ECLA to send experts had been "accepted in good faith in the early days of Castro's regime"; but now he felt that "some ECLA officers had become too deeply involved with Guevara and other Cuban officials" and he was "seeking some graceful way of withdrawing them."[12] Prebisch and Washington had become strange allies in a touchy area.

Tension between Prebisch and Noyola grew as the crisis built toward the nationalization of all US property. On 9 August 1960, in a personal note to David Pollock, Noyola referred to "certain problems" he was having with Prebisch but added that these were of little consequence. "I am working intensely on something which I consider the most important and decisive in my career, and I am fortunate to be able to participate in a project which is the most important event in Latin America since its independence."[13] The following months grew more tense as Noyola's partisanship strayed far outside UN rules. On 20 September 1960, he gave a press conference in Havana as ECLA chief, in which he maintained that, because it had a new economy based in social revolution, Cuba had advanced more in the last ten months than many other countries in ten years. "The Cuban revolution," he declared, "is example and guide for Latin America." Unemployment had fallen more in ten months than in the last twenty-five years, and Cuba had delivered a "heavy blow to relations between imperialism and dependent countries." Commercial and credit relations with the Communist Bloc were preferable to those with capitalist countries because they were not based in an ethic of accumulation – unlike the US, for example, which "demands political conditions, both international and national."

Prebisch exploded and had him out of Cuba within a month on an order from the secretary-general; Noyola resigned from ECLA in protest, returning to Mexico, and attacking Prebisch for intolerance.[14] To cool tempers on all sides Raúl sent Jorge Ahumada, his most reliable of lieutenants, to Havana to oversee the ECLA office in the wake of Noyola's departure: orthodox enough to satisfy Washington, his many years directing the Santiago Training Division had also earned him the respect of Fidel Castro. But Ahumada found Havana no less irresistible than Noyola; he promptly threw over wife, family, country, the Chilean Christian Democrats, and the ECLA succession for a woman half his age. Rejected in turn, he died prematurely in exile in Caracas, slumped over an empty metal desk. The defection cut Prebisch hard and complicated the ECLA succession, leaving his second choice, Antonio Mayobre, to inherit his office in Santiago – if, that is, Raúl could persuade him back, since he had just been named Venezuelan ambassador to the White House.

As the US presidential election approached, and as the Cuban revolution became an ever graver crisis in Washington, the Eisenhower administration increased its attention to Latin America, which could no longer could it be taken for granted as a "safe" region. Building on the positive steps taken after *Sputnik* and Nixon's 1958 visit, it accepted Latin demands for greater development support in lock step with the unfolding Cuban drama. After the Kubitschek-Eisenhower discussions of Operation Pan America, the US had accepted the creation of the IDB, but it had held back from a major bilateral program beyond the normal commercial trade and banking channels. However as the Cuban-US dynamic veered out of control, a "Committee of 21" – or Special Presidential Committee of Representatives to Examine New Mechanisms of Economic Cooperation – was created to move from dialogue among the twenty-one Latin and US presidents to a regional plan of action. In February 1960, President Kubitschek revised his Operation Pan America as the blueprint for this new era of inter-American cooperation and sent it to Eisenhower, who then visited Brazil for the inauguration of the new capital, Brasilia, the second time a US president had visited the country. Finally, in July 1960, when Eisenhower eliminated Cuba's sugar quota and plunged the island economy into chaos, he announced a $500 million Social Progress Trust Fund for Latin America. This was indeed the change of US attitude for which Latin Americans had long been waiting, and a special meeting of the "Committee of 21" was called for Bogotá in September 1960, to which the heads of international organizations, including Prebisch, were also invited.[15] The location – Bogotá – symbolized the renewal of the inter-American system, twelve years after the adoption there of the OAS

Charter in 1948, by extending US-Latin cooperation to the social and economic dimension of the Western Hemisphere.

But agreement was not easy. Latin Americans, led by Kubitschek, had different expectations – a vision more like US policy toward Europe after 1945; the $500 million commitment to the Social Progress Fund seemed a timid, limited, and belated response. They expected a multi-year and multi-billion-dollar US bilateral assistance program for the region; and they also insisted on a new secretariat, rather than the Washington-dominated OAS, to run the new Operation Pan America.[16] But the Eisenhower Administration had reached its limits; Mann and Dillon, representing State and the US Treasury, refused to go beyond the US initiatives already announced and made it absolutely clear that Washington would accept only the OAS to head a new inter-American program. Congressional support for the Social Progress Fund was far from certain in any case, and the OAS at least reassured US lawmakers that decisions on US money would be made in Washington rather than Latin America. In fact Dillon had to intervene with Senator John F. Kennedy during the Bogotá conference to get the legislation through congress.[17]

The compromise eventually achieved featured the *Act of Bogotá*, to which all twenty countries could agree, outlining a new set of principles to pursue justice and equity in inter-American cooperation. To these joint commitments in principle was added US support for Operation Pan America, although suitably amended to meet its demands on the OAS and the Social Progress Fund. Fidel Castro denounced the agreement as unworthy. "What is understood by this?" he asked. "How can there be a solution to the social problems without a plan for economic development? Do they want to make fools of the Latin American countries?"[18] But for most Latin leaders, Prebisch among them, the *Act of Bogotá* marked a change in US thinking, even if he was less enthusiastic regarding its prospects should Richard Nixon be elected to succeed Eisenhower in the elections only two months away.

However, the *Act of Bogotá*, with its commitment to the OAS as lead development agency in the Americas, had complicated ECLA's future within the "Big Three" organizations in the Americas led by Mora, Prebisch, and Felipe Herrera for the IDB. Duplication was a first problem. But if, as now seemed certain, the OAS would be given an overall leadership role, its budget would be multiplied for an expanded program. ECLA's role, in contrast, could correspondingly shrink or be squeezed out altogether because it was a UN agency in an era of expanding regionalism. Only ECLA faced the possibility of marginalization: the OAS had US funding, while the IDB as regional development bank had the inherent leverage of dispensing money. Of course, ECLA had far deeper analytic capacity than the fledgling

IDB and much greater organizational capacity than the OAS, not to mention credibility; in practice, the "Big Three" needed one another more than ever in this period of change in Washington, and on this Mora, Prebisch, and Herrera were in full agreement. Following the Bogotá meeting Prebisch proposed a new coordinating mechanism, the OAS-IDB-ECLA Tripartite Committee on Cooperation, with a new division of labour to reflect their different strengths and improve coordination. To gain full partnership, Prebisch gave up the *Annual Survey* (now to be jointly produced with the OAS in Washington) but kept the advisory groups as a special ECLA niche. His colleagues agreed, so that the birth of the Tripartite Committee coincided with the arrival of the Alliance for Progress.

John F. Kennedy's victory over Richard Nixon was narrow, but the enormous promise of his arrival as president was confirmed the moment Nixon conceded defeat, and the expectations of his presidency further escalated as his inauguration approached. The new president decided to pursue the Alliance for Progress as promised during the campaign, and a task force chaired by Adolph Berle worked up a background paper on the Americas with the assistance of Lincoln Gordon from the Harvard Business School. On 19 December they called together a group of influential US academics including Albert O. Hirshman, Paul Rosenstein-Rodan, Frederico G. Gil, and Walter W. Rostow, along with private sector representatives, to review a draft entitled "Alliance for Progress: A Program of Inter-American Partnership."[19] "The election of Senator Kennedy has excited expectations and hopes throughout Latin America," they warned, "but this new opportunity may be the last. Without a prompt and drastic reorientation of United States foreign policy, the opportunity will be lost." Latin America was not only the richest of the developing regions but also the most vulnerable to communism, they concluded, and, with public expectations peaking, the regional crisis was now at the breaking point. The Alliance would feature the unique challenge of using foreign aid to promote a peaceful social revolution in Latin America in which communism would lose its long-term appeal, combining it with immediate initiatives of unprecedented scale to meet Latin expectations in the areas of economic and trade policy, regional integration, and land reform.

The new element for Prebisch was the attitude of Kennedy's task force in immediately reaching out to Latin Americans – the US as donors actually asking recipients for advice about what to do with their money – and thereby giving meaning to the overused language of partnership and multilateralism. Prebisch was amazed to be called by Richard Goodwin, wondering if he, along with Filipe Herrera, José Antonio Mora, and several other prominent regional personalities, would help with ideas for the new Alliance for Progress. Mayobre's embassy in Washington served as a meeting place for this small ad hoc group of Latin experts who met with the task force. When, therefore, Kennedy announced the Alliance for Progress in his January Inaugural Address, Prebisch and his colleagues felt involved and listened carefully for the president's exact wording. What they heard was better than expected: Kennedy committed his administration to support international development as a first priority "because it is right." Prebisch heard that phrase on the radio and felt it signalled a new era – or rather the definitive end of the 1950s in US foreign policy.

Belief became conviction when Prebisch and the Latin group were again approached after the inauguration to prepare more detailed comments for President Kennedy's formal launch of the Alliance for Progress on 13 March at a special White House reception and press conference for members of congress and the Latin American diplomatic corps. Prebisch's situation in Washington was unique; he was at the centre of the Alliance, and no one would or could deny that he was its intellectual godfather. Five days before Kennedy's 13 March event Raúl drafted a joint letter to him from the heads of ECLA, the IDB, and the OAS on a new approach to US-Latin American relations. Writing it out in longhand, he circulated the memorandum to his colleagues for comments, then sent the original draft containing the marginal notes to Adelita as a souvenir. The memorandum, it turned out, discussed eight of the ten main points in Kennedy's Address on 13 March, including one key feature that the Kennedy speechwriters incorporated wholesale from Prebisch's memorandum.[20] On the implementation of economic reforms, he had recommended that "each country could draw up its own program of social and economic development, perhaps in a preliminary form, establishing realistic goals and setting forth the financial contributions and the social and administrative reforms that the country will undertake." Rephrased by the White House, this section became "each country must formulate long-range plans for its own development ... These plans will be the foundation of our development effort, and the basis for the allocation of outside resources." This was a gigantic victory for Prebisch and ECLA, a vindication of their work over the last decade: there would be more outside assistance, but on condition that Latin governments were serious enough about development to undertake the required reforms.[21]

President Kennedy's 13 March reception at the White House was an unforgettable *coup de théâtre*, with Prebisch at the centre of a cluster of senior Latin diplomats around Kennedy, to whom the announcement was addressed: nothing like this had been seen before, and the expectations it aroused in Latin America were enormous. It was wonderful and gripping, combining details, drama, and impact with flowing terms and stirring commitment. "I propose that the American Republics begin on a vast new Ten Year Plan for the Americas," Kennedy began, "a plan to transform the 1960s into an historic decade of democratic progress." The "majestic concept of Kubitschek's Operation Pan America" was only mentioned as a precursor, as if to further dramatize the new Alliance for Progress, a "vast cooperative effort, unparalleled in magnitude and nobility of purpose, to satisfy the basic needs of the American people for homes, work and land, health and schools – *techo, trabajo y tierra, salud y escuela*." There would be $1 billion annually for the ten-year period and another $500 million as a first step in implementing the *Act of Bogotá*. A special ministerial meeting of the OAS Inter-American Economic and Social Council would be convened 5–17 August in Punta del Este to draw up the new Charter and "begin the massive planning effort which will be at the heart of the Alliance for Progress." "We have not heard such words since Franklin Roosevelt," Mayobre exclaimed.[22] After the press conference Prebisch was invited to help prepare the Punta del Este meeting, and *Foreign Policy* invited him to write a pre-conference article on US-Latin American relations, titled "Joint Responsibilities for Latin American Progress."[23] ECLA's office staff was strengthened as a base for Prebisch's increasingly long and frequent visits to the US capital.

Prebisch felt accepted in Washington in a way that recalled Ravndal and the years preceding Pearl Harbor, or his later work with Robert Triffin and the US Federal Reserve. During the twenty years that had passed since then US-Latin American relations had sharply regressed. He had been shunned during the Eisenhower years, and although civilly tolerated, Mann and others had kept him at arm's length in the reshaping of inter-American economic relations after 1958. Now it was different; he was no longer an object of suspicion. While not many members of Kennedy inner team accepted Prebisch's economic ideas, they were attracted by his social policy, the coherence of his ideas, his knowledge and contacts in the region, and his force of personality. In April Prebisch was invited to a gathering with the top Kennedy people, including Douglas Dillon, W.W. Rostow, Richard Goodwin, Adolf Berle, Senators William Fulbright and Hickenlooper, and Lincoln Gordon. Gordon recounted Prebisch saying ("emotionally and with tears in his eyes"), "I've headed ECLA for over a decade now and this is a wonderful experience for me because for the first time a high-level US delegate has talked to me as an equal."[24] The Alliance for Progress seemed like a dream come true: a version of "progressive capitalism" based in a spirit of mutual interest and respect, in which Latin ideas were once again welcomed, rather than spurned or at best, as a way to placate the unruly Southern neighbours, barely tolerated.

Days later Prebisch's euphoric sense of a new beginning, and indeed the entire Alliance for Progress, were swept away. World news turned to Moscow on 12 April, when Premier Nikita Khrushchev proclaimed "the genius of the Soviet people and the powerful force of socialism" as Major Yuri Gagarin orbited the Earth for 108 minutes in his Vostok space capsule and became the first astronaut in space. Khrushchev compared the smiling, quiet Gagarin with Christopher Colombus; once again the Soviets had beaten the US in space. But the US easily matched Moscow for headlines three days later by launching the Bay of Pigs operation against Cuba. US B-26 bombers struck airfields on the island, followed by the landing of Cuban exile Brigade 2506 to overthrow the Government of Fidel Castro. Bogged down in swampy terrain, unable to link up with rebels operating in the Oriente, denied decisive US air and ground support, and above all unable to rally Cubans against their leaders, the armed intervention stalled. On 19 April the 1,189 remaining members of the Cuban exile Brigade surrendered in defeat and ridicule.

Several aspects of this debacle were highly damaging to Kennedy: his overt violation of international law; the obviousness of US intervention, clearly planned for months under Eisenhower and reaffirmed by the new administration, despite official denials; the use of napalm against lightly armed Cuban militia; but mostly the overwhelming incompetence of the botched operation. It revealed the animating anti-communist instinct of the Kennedy Administration underneath the language of development, and recalled vividly the US intervention in Guatemala in 1954 using CIA dirty tricks and Latin turncoats. For the already suspicious in Latin America the Bay of Pigs was unforgivable; for Prebisch and fellow Latins at the White House reception it raised the first doubts about Kennedy. In Cuba it was the point of no return.

Yet the remarkable feature of the Bay of Pigs fiasco was the rapid recovery of Kennedy's credibility and the popularity of the Alliance for Progress: most Latins wanted to believe that a new period had begun, and they were prepared to give him a second chance. They (like Prebisch) saw the new president's faux pas as an error of inexperience, compromised by a flawed operation inherited from the Eisenhower years in a state of advanced design. The president's acceptance of personal responsibility, combined with the deepening glamour of his new administration, restored confidence and diminished the smell of deceit and failure. By 5 May, when President Kennedy sent a personal message of congratulation to Prebisch at ECLA's

May 1961 session in Santiago, memories of the Bay of Pigs rout had been replaced with anticipation for the approaching Alliance for Progress Conference at Punta del Este, where a charter would be proclaimed and its structure established.

Off-season, the coastal resort town of Punta del Este was deserted except for the OAS delegates, the media, and security people, but the weather was brilliant in this Argentine enclave of Uruguay stretching out over the white sand dunes of the Plate estuary 110 kilometres east of Montevideo. A polo tournament was in full swing. With so much at stake – nothing like the Alliance for Progress in scope or money had been tried before anywhere in North-South relations, or with such expectations of a new era in the Americas – it was the premier US-Latin meeting since the founding of the OAS in 1948. The Alliance was essentially political, and the political backdrop of the Conference was the containment of the Cuban revolution, on everyone's mind with the arrival of Che Guevara and the stir he created. Douglas Dillon headed the US delegation, intimidating wine-conscious Latins less by his Harvard credentials, his seat on the New York Stock Exchange at twenty-three, his family wealth, his decorated war-service as Lt Commander in the US Navy, or his personal friendship with Eisenhower than by owning the *grand cru* Chateau Haut-Brion estate in Bordeaux, founded in 1550 by Jean de Pontiac, and bought by his father for 2.3 million francs in 1935. Everyone waited for President Kennedy, but in the end he failed to appear.

The US and Cuban delegations watched each other and were watched by everyone else, to see whether they would talk – finally Richard Goodwin and Che Guevara met on 22 August.[25] President Frondizi invited his famous countryman across the Plate River to Buenos Aires for a secret four-hour visit – provoking a crisis with his generals and the Washington security establishment; CIA hacks hovered, their new Operation Mongoose ready for another attempt to eliminate Castro. Felipe Pazos ostentatiously refused to acknowledge Richard Bissel, co-organizer of the Bay of Pigs fiasco and ex-MIT professor.[26] But Che was the star, passionately applauded, willfully insulted as "spinach-bearded," and infuriatingly courteous.

Prebisch maintained as low a profile as possible, bemused at the unfolding scene at Punta del Este. The issue was not whether Cuba would be excluded from the Alliance, since this was the US objective at the conference: Fidel Castro himself thought it a clever US strategy to pre-empt revolution in the region, but Che was not authorized to sign the *Declaration to the Peoples of the Americas*, which specifically excluded Cuba by insisting on "the institutions of representative democracy." Instead the main question at Punta del Este was the actual meaning of Kennedy's 13 March commitment to partnership with Latin America. The dilemma was that the Kennedy intellectuals backing the Alliance, and omnipresent at Punta del Este, had little or no prior experience in Latin America apart from holidays in Acapulco and pre-1959 Havana. Worse, prior long-term thinking on Latin American development had been absent in the US State Department since World War II. Suddenly the US needed a model of development to combat Fidel Castro; whatever its problems ECLA had the only program, based on the lessons of the 1950s, which also underlay Operation Pan America and the *Act of Bogotá,* on which it could draw. Thus the US delegation at Punta del Este came to incorporate virtually the entire ECLA program in the Charter, including many ideas that Washington had fought with very strong language since its creation. It approved, for example, the mutually supporting roles of developed and developing countries in development and the need for foreign capital on concessional terms; social change as in land and tax reform; long-term economic planning within mixed economies (Latin America); and a new regime for trade in commodities. No fewer than ninety-seven recommendations covering the sectors from housing to infrastructure were included in the Alliance program. The US pledged to "provide a major part of the minimum of $20 billion, principally in public funds, which Latin America will require over the next ten years from all external sources, in order to supplement its own efforts."[27]

Prebisch was alarmed by this unreality. Taking basic ideas from a think-tank like ECLA and using them for a speech was one thing; trying to turn them into a vast blueprint for action apparently conceived in the US was quite another. "I am really concerned about this trend," he noted, because "its political implications are highly detrimental to the Alliance itself and to the broad popular support it requires in Latin America."[28] Grandiose rhetoric was not necessarily a negative tactic in promoting a historic cause, but it could prove counterproductive if practice conflicted violently with reality. The US Congress, for example, did not share the mixed economy language of the Punta del Este Charter; even as the latter was being signed, Congress only narrowly approved the president's Act for International Development, and only then with the addition of pro-business restrictive conditions. Prebisch did not doubt the sincerity of Kennedy and his advisors or their commitment to the reform goals of the Alliance; he simply wondered whether and how they could be achieved.

The unreality at Punta del Este was equally evident among Latin American delegations, which solemnly agreed to undertake the structural reforms required for peaceful democratic revolution. Some, like the new Brazilian Government of Janio Quadros, who succeeded Kubitschek, were too weak to undertake anything. Others confronted vested interests and embedded resistance to change, which the Alliance for Progress mystique could not reverse. In endorsing the *Act of Bogotá* a year earlier, Prebisch was not optimistic that Latin American countries would be able to profit from US aid. "Greater assistance," he underlined, "is not enough ... there will be greater international cooperation, but will Latin America be able to use it?" In a sombre tone, at sharp variance with the otherwise upbeat mood at Bogotá, Prebisch noted the internal obstacles to development – inequality, unreformed land tenure, poor education, and lack of social mobility – that had to be addressed if development funding was to be effective. "Are we prepared," he asked, "not only from the point of view of technology – which is certainly not an insuperable obstacle – but also from the political point of view, to introduce into our countries all the structural and social reforms required for the application of an effective economic policy ... Let us not turn a blind eye to the facts. It is obvious, even notorious, that disparities in income distribution in Latin America are growing, and that inflation, that monstrous evil, is not being checked … food production lags far behind the population's requirements … Latin America has not been able to introduce the changes in its economic structure and pattern of production which are the essential requisites for development."[29] The Cuban revolution had unleashed two waves: one was directed from Washington to regain control of the region using all the economic, political, and military tools in its armoury and pre-empt further revolutionary change on the Cuban model; but the other wave from Havana threatened the unreformed Latin American elites with social and economic change. Beneath the *Act of Bogotá* and new promises sweeping Latin America lay polarized societies with suspicious and narrowly based governments preoccupied by internal challenges from below. But because Latin elites refused manual work and insisted on cheap domestic labour, a key incentive for basic reforms was missing. "The higher-income groups usually have a much higher standard of living than equivalent groups in more advanced centers, because they enjoy both the benefits of the traditional ways of living and all the advantages offered by modern technology." Prebisch warned that major US resources could have the perverse effect of giving Latin governments the means to delay the hard but essential reforms required for healthy long-term development.

The combination of superlatives and idealistic clichés at Punta del Este left Prebisch determined to concentrate on the structure and mechanics of the Alliance for Progress, for these decisions would determine its actual implementation. President Kennedy had promised a multilateral US-Latin American program, "a vast new cooperative effort," with OAS leadership – "a greatly strengthened Inter-American Economic and Social Council to assemble the leading economists and experts of the hemisphere to help each county develop its own development plan." The OAS budget (it was agreed) would be doubled to $6 million and its staff increased to five hundred. Progress was also made on the issue of coordination: the OAS-ECLA-IDB Tripartite Committee was reaffirmed as the senior coordinating mechanism within the inter-American system, subject to Frondizi's insistence that Prebisch not be named its executive director.[30] Kennedy's 13 March press conference had mentioned the importance of ECLA and the IDB; the Tripartite Committee was a sensible mechanism to support the Alliance.

But the key issue facing the Alliance for Progress was approving or rejecting government requests for economic assistance, and the delegates at Punta del Este kept postponing this part of the agenda, as if wanting to avoid the question of actually running the Alliance. Eventually, however, some committee would have to say yes or no to funding requests, and this issue finally became the most controversial. Prebisch had come to the meeting with a proposal: to create, within the overall OAS system, an inter-American review mechanism for national development plans based on a conditionality principle, namely that funds from the US and other donors would be linked to the performance of specified goals. The challenge was to implement the Alliance from within the OAS with sufficient autonomy to be effective in a weak parent organization and oversee the Alliance goals of development, democracy, and social change. Prebisch's proposed mechanism would therefore comprise a committee of seven experts with its own executive director located in Washington, with the responsibility for evaluating national plans, working with the OAS-IDB-ECLA Tripartite Committee where necessary. Alliance funding would be directed to those countries that could demonstrate progress toward social reform, self-help, and sound economic policy. A minimum annual growth rate of 2.5 percent was prescribed as a target for each country. Convinced that only a strong multilateral body with executive powers could discipline Latin governments into accepting structural and social reforms and thereby ensure consistency with the social and economic goals of the Alliance for Progress, Prebisch had aimed at a permanent committee with internationally recognized members who would evaluate development plans and issue a binding report to the OAS, the IDB, and the member country. It would review the implementation of development plans each year, with appraisals, and recommend improvements in both plans and execution. With such a membership and purpose, and led by its own executive director, governments would find it in their interests to cooperate with the committee.

In its closing hours the Punta del Este Conference rejected Prebisch's recommendation for a strong "Committee of Seven" within the Alliance for Progress. Frondizi took the lead, supported by Brazil, in watering down Prebisch's proposed review process into a new "Panel of Nine" with a purely advisory role. While it would have a separate existence, the panel would not have the status of a permanent OAS standing committee, and it was denied executive authority. Instead its task would be to strike ad hoc committees to review country development plans, with three panel members and three experts appointed by the government in question. With nine members, rather than seven, the new Panel of Experts (as it became known) would be larger and more unwieldy, but it reassured Latin governments by maintaining the established norm for setting up regional bodies, with two representatives from the US, one each from the five largest countries (Argentina, Brazil, Chile, Colombia, and Mexico), and two rotating members from the smaller members of the region.

Disappointed, Prebisch worried that these changes undermined the goal of a permanent, effective, and politically powerful review committee and therefore failed to create the necessary element required for the success of the Alliance. But he also realized that the Panel of Experts was a significant innovation, and that only time and experience would tell if and how the mechanism would work. He was also heartened by support for the OAS-IDB-ECLA Tripartite Committee: the three executives, Mora, Herrera, and Prebisch, were asked to nominate the members of the future panel. Best of all, the Kennedy people at Punta del Este approached Prebisch to head it.[31]

Prebisch could be excused for a certain self-satisfaction after Punta del Este. The Alliance for Progress was moving ahead; his personal role and that of ECLA had been confirmed; and its early success contributed to Kennedy's proposal to the UN General Assembly on 25 September that international development be "expanded and coordinated" and that the 1960s be designated the "UN Development Decade." The new Panel of Experts drew Prebisch logically to Washington, the centre of ideas and decisions under the Kennedy Administration, which had welcomed him since its inauguration. Much of 1961 had already been spent there; although sixty years old, he was ready for a new challenge. Rumours had circulated during the conference of Prebisch's impending resignation – that he would be leaving ECLA before the end of his contract in 1963, with Alfonso Santa Cruz acting as deputy until Antonio Mayobre's return to Santiago – and US newspapers reported that Raúl would be moving to Washington immediately to set up the Panel of Experts in the OAS. Arriving on 9 September, he rented a suite in the Sheraton-Plaza Hotel for $500 a month and arranged for essential household effects to be sent from Chile in April.[32]

That Eliana Diaz lived in Washington, and that this relationship was special for Raúl, only confirmed the near-perfect alignment of stars over the New World in the glow of Punta del Este. Ms Diaz was Chilean, and they had met in Santiago. Now working as Librarian in the IMF, she had become a permanent factor in Prebisch's already complicated life as he planned the beginning of a new development era in US-Latin relations.

Prebisch knew what he wanted in Washington. Before his departure on 2 September, he discussed his ideas with colleagues, and these plans quickly made their way to Washington via the US Embassy from its mole in ECLA headquarters. He left convinced that he would be named director-general and that he would have the lead role in shaping the new OAS Panel of Experts. In terms of overall Alliance architecture, Prebisch foresaw three bodies working together: the new OAS Panel to oversee the evaluation of national development plans presented by Latin governments; the OAS-IDB-ECLA Tripartite Committee to coordinate the implementation of the Alliance; and the USAID (Agency for International Development) to provide most of its funding. Since the three proposed structures were in the formative stage he wanted to get to Washington as soon as possible after Punta del Este. Avoiding early mistakes with the Panel of Experts was particularly important because the quality of its membership would determine its success: lacking executive power, it could only persuade by respect. Prebisch made no secret of his determination to attract the foremost personalities in the Americas comprising four senior generalists (including himself as director-general), along with five high-level specialists in the fields of industry and power, agriculture, transportation, housing and urbanization, and education. Such a combination would combine macroeconomic and sectoral competence, speed up the screening of the national development plans, and instil sufficient regional trust in the panel to establish its credibility.

But Prebisch arrived to a frenetic Washington where little could be done in the dense and confusing cloud of briefings, meetings, and bargaining sessions surrounding US-Latin American relations. The Kennedy Administration's appointments were slow in coming; finally Teodoro Moscoso was chosen as US Coordinator of the Alliance, the number two position in USAID, the most important funder for Latin American development over the next ten years. This was welcome news for the panel: Moscoso's earlier leadership role in Operation Bootstrap in Puerto Rico and his strong support for the Alliance Charter made him a popular choice throughout Latin America. But there were other delays: the new offices for the Panel of Experts on the fourth floor of the Premium Building were not yet ready, so that Prebisch worked out of ECLA's cramped offices with appointments secretary Bodil Royem and Benjamin Hopenhayn, whom he had chosen as secretary for the Panel of Experts.

The Argentine Government, meanwhile, was lobbying hard in the OAS and White House against Prebisch, with Frondizi objecting to his reviewing confidential national plans in the Panel of Experts, and in general complaining that the Alliance unduly extended ECLA's role and influence in Washington. This vendetta reflected Frondizi's political trouble at home; the economic model pursued with the support of the IMF and Washington after 1958 had collapsed in red ink, unemployment and business bankruptcies after its initial success.[33] Apart from privileged sectors such as petroleum or auto assembly, the economy was now floundering: the national deficit for 1960 set an all-time record; 75,000 railway workers were dismissed; and strikes spread across the country. Increasingly vulnerable to a military coup, and dependent on Washington for financial support, the mortally crippled Frondizi took theatrical refuge in attacking his old foe from *Plan Prebisch* days. However infantile in substance, the attack came from a senior member-country of the OAS, and it was effective. Frondizi's opposition meant that Prebisch lost his bid to lead the Panel of Experts as director-general; while Mora insisted that he had declined, citing other commitments, this was patently false. Snubbed, Raúl refused simple membership, creating deadlock as he was the obvious candidate. A solution had to be found. In the end the position of director-general was dropped, and he was named "coordinator" on a part-time basis: this Frondizi would accept as long as the nine members would be approved by governments as well as the Tripartite Committee. Prebisch reluctantly concurred, but the early row was a warning over the future of the panel.

Despite this setback, Prebisch began his work convinced that the Panel could be a major departure in the Americas.[34] He had the advantage of starting fresh; his terms of reference were broad (convening and directing the panel, supervising its working groups, and leading its liaison work in Washington and Latin America); and US support was strong. On 29 November, in a special ceremony at the OAS, President Kennedy officially announced the panel, declaring that "today marks another milestone in the Alliance for Progress, for today we begin to select the Panel of Experts by the Charter of Punta del Este. This Panel is an historic innovation – not only in inter-American affairs – but in the effort to develop the economies of half the world. Not since the Marshall Plan has a group of allied nations embarked on a program of regional development guided by a regional body largely selected by the developing countries themselves." The panel members, seven Latin and two Americans, did not reflect Prebisch's proposed mix of generalists and specialists, but they were undoubtedly distinguished persons from across the region, and all committed to the Alliance goals. The two US members, Paul Rosenstein-Rodan and Harvey Perloff, were Prebisch allies, and he had close relations with Ernesto Malaccorto (Argentina), Ary Torres (Brazil), Raúl Saez (Chile), Hernando Agudelo Villa (Colombia), Gonzalo Robles (Mexico), Filipe Pazos (Cuba), and Manuel Noriego Morales (Guatemala). Douglas Dillon, appointed secretary of the Treasury by President Kennedy, reaffirmed the US commitment of $1 billion for the first year of the Alliance ending 13 March 1962 and stressed the "primordial significance" of the panel in "evaluating development plans [and] ... strengthening project selection," as well as assisting the US Government "in providing and channeling external capital."[35] In a show of particular recognition, the OAS asked Prebisch to close its session.

Determined on a quick start in the new year, Prebisch called an organizational meeting of the panel in December before the start of their official appointments on 1 January 1962 to decide on priorities. The Punta del Este Charter spoke confidently of "the plan as the principal instrument of the Alliance," but Latin American countries had very different understandings about "planning" and "plans," and they were at very different stages of development. Brazil's approach to the Alliance was to set up a national coordinating committee for emergency projects.[36] Bolivia, lacking comparable expertise, did have a national "plan" based on the work of an ECLA advisory group since 1959, but it only set out broad goals and was nowhere near a blueprint for a coherent public and private investment program. Detailed and operational development plans would take years to complete in many countries. Before the Punta del Este Conference, Prebisch had said that only "medium-term" plans were feasible, but he now faced the danger of governments running to him with emergency requests without a plan at all.

The Panel of Experts needed a test case to prove its work, an early Alliance for Progress success story from a major country to set an example for the region by submitting its national plan to the panel as a condition for development funding. Chile (as usual) was ready. Unlike Argentina (ill-disposed), Brazil (reluctant), or Mexico (secretive), President Allesandri was both committed to the panel process and keen to be leading the first country to have a national plan approved under the Alliance for Progress. With a strong Central Bank and national institutions, along with economists who had long experience with public sector planning, Chile was delighted to be chosen first by the panel and welcomed its help in finalizing a long-term investment plan. Felipe Pazos, Hernando Agudelo, and Rodrigo

Gomez were selected by the Panel of Experts to serve on the Chile Ad Hoc Group assisted by the outside experts chosen in consultation with Chile.[37] With this decision made, the panel settled into its new offices, Hopenhayn came over from ECLA as secretary, and the nine experts began their work plied with requests for talks and papers, given the interest aroused everywhere, in the Americas and globally, by the experiment.

Since success depended so much on Chile, the Ad Hoc Group worked with intensity and commitment, with promising first results. But events in Argentina soon overshadowed its work. On 29 March 1962, Arturo Frondizi was seized by the Army and imprisoned on the island of Martín Garcia in the Plate River in a set piece Buenos Aires melodrama. Grenadiers came for him in the middle of the night; as they approached the Casa Rosada Frondizi dismissed his personal guard to prevent bloodshed; reluctantly it agreed to stand down rather than resist but remained in the palace with the entire civilian staff cheering their president. When at last the grenadiers arrived and led him away, the entire assemblage – soldiers, staff, and Frondizi himself – broke into the national anthem amidst a wave of tears, jailors included. The military coup had been building for some time and was not unexpected, but what concerned Prebisch in Washington and Alessandri in Santiago was that the new regime of José Maria Guido, installed by the military until elections could be held the next year, appealed to the Kennedy Administration for immediate economic assistance to head off "another Cuba," in the parlance of the day.

The post-Frondizi US-Argentine crisis went to the heart of the Alliance for Progress. Argentina had so far submitted nothing to the panel, not even the outline of a national plan; Guido's bid for half a billion dollars from Washington therefore made a mockery of the Charter and the machinery set up for its implementation. Alessandri was outraged when Washington agreed to the Argentine request on grounds of security; "I have opened my books for nothing," he roared. For the Panel of Experts and its Ad Hoc Group on Chile, the US-Argentine deal was doubly demoralizing in showing them to be both redundant in Washington and irrelevant in Latin America. For Prebisch the tragedy of the military coup also affected him as a citizen; but as an Alliance protagonist it was devastating to be undercut before office renovations were complete. If Latin generals could get easy US money by waving "communist threats" at the Kennedy Administration, why would any government take his Panel of Experts seriously? Like a leaking airship accelerating earthward, its deflation was all the more striking for the apparent vigour of the Alliance's launch only six months earlier.

If the post-Frondizi decision also revealed the weight of the security establishment in Washington, the overall atmosphere in the US capital was also hardening against the Alliance for Progress. Compounding the damage of Argentina, President Kennedy backed down from the other key US Punta del Este commitment to a so-called "new era" in the trade of basic commodities, the most important exports of Latin America, by extending the International Coffee Agreement negotiated by Eisenhower to other products for greater market access and price stability. Price fluctuations, and the consequent unreliability of export earnings, undermined consistent financing for development: a new US-Latin American agreement would promote the trade agenda in parallel with Alliance commitments for greater aid. But time had run out at Punta del Este and negotiations for a deal could not be completed. Instead the Joint Working Group on the Stabilization of Export Earnings resumed negotiations in January 1962, with US officials apologizing for past US intransigence, blaming the departed George Humphrey for previous ill will and assuring their Latin American colleagues that things would now be quite different and that President Kennedy was personally committed to a regional export stabilization policy. The only question was the choice of policies and mechanisms. By March it was obvious that US officials had raised unrealistic expectations; a protectionist US congress preoccupied by a growing deficit and unemployment would not accept what it saw as a program of so-called "disguised aid." For all the Kennedy bombast, he could not deliver: the Democrats did not control the congress and no solutions could be found – neither policies nor mechanisms – and the US-Latin American talks terminated in failure.

The entire political atmosphere in Washington was evolving rapidly in a new direction. A surge of renewed optimism and confidence was sweeping the country. In space rivalry the post-*Sputnik* trauma ended with a successful US manned flight on 20 February 1962, when astronaut John Glenn orbited Earth in *Friendship 7*. It turned out that the feared "missile gap" with the Soviet Union was incorrect: the US was in the lead. For its part the US corporate sector had taken the offensive against the Alliance for Progress and Prebisch himself as anti-business. An influential article, "Latin America: Bureaucracy and the Market," came out in *Fortune* magazine in February 1962 describing Prebisch (of Yugoslav background now) as anti-business: "doctrinaire ... perhaps the most influential – but not necessarily the soundest – political economist in the hemisphere, with an engaging, volatile personality and a mind as agile as it is capricious ... one of those politically minded economists who tailor their economics to fit their objectives."[38] John D. Rockefeller was forming the Council of the Americas in New York as a corporate counterthrust against the "statist" approach of the Alliance, and in May Kennedy set up the Commerce Committee for the

Alliance for Progress composed of twenty-five business leaders led by himself. Senator Bourke Hickenlooper's amendment to the US Foreign Aid Bill mandated an automatic termination of assistance where US investors were subject to discriminatory taxation or nationalization.[39] US foreign direct investment was only $85 million in 1960 and $144 million in 1961, while profit and interest remittances for these two years were at a postwar high – an astonishing $632 million and $675 million.[40] The outlook for 1962 was no better. Although Kennedy had arm-twisted congress into a 20 percent increase in economic aid to $1.3 billion in 1962, the administration faced a decrease for fiscal year 1963 and a dramatic cut in 1964, which would reduce the aid package to little more than $500 million. Both public- and private-sector funding for development in Latin America was therefore in trouble with mid-term congressional elections approaching in fall.

During 1962 the Washington community as a whole shifted against the governance model represented by the Panel of Experts, as a new and harder cohort of the Kennedy team took over: Richard Goodwin was replaced by Edwin Martin; Thomas Mann (who would soon be recalled from Mexico City), Douglas Dillon, and W.W. Rostow were ascendant. A new counterinsurgency policy adopted by the Kennedy team in August 1962 to combat the communist threat in Latin America accelerated the rising imperative of national-security thinking in the US capital. The opposition lined up against Prebisch was deep: the US Treasury resisted planning (fiscal and monetary discipline solved everything); the US private sector agreed; Thomas Mann opposed Prebisch strongly on everything; the CIA saw the Alliance as a communist trap; the IMF, World Bank, and IDB worried for their turf; and State Department bureaucrats dismissed Latins as too flabby and corrupt to handle anything.

But if US officials could not accept multilateralism, dismissing the Panel of Experts as irrelevant, most Latin governments understood it all too well and resisted the model because it might be effective. The defeat of the Alliance therefore was mutual. Latins criticized Kennedy's failure to deliver but were relieved as Washington's impulse for tax and land reform relaxed. Neither the US nor Latin America was prepared for the commitments they accepted when signing the Punta del Este Charter. A year earlier, in the excitement following Kennedy's 13 March Address, Prebisch had thought a new period was beginning; he now realized that his sense of vindication had been premature. Underlying US-Latin suspicions remained; the Alliance shell in the OAS would remain, but people were no longer caught up in its spirit – neither in Washington nor in Latin America. The "Year of Latin America" was now over in Washington; the Kennedy team was moving on. On 13 June Prebisch resigned; it was his shortest job ever, in which he shared the defeat of the Panel of Experts. "I have arrived at the conclusion," he said, "that it is not possible to correct the grave error, in my judgment, committed at Punta del Este when it rejected the original proposal of a Chair forming part of group of seven experts."[41] Without leverage or executive power of any kind the panel was simply unworkable and the position of the coordinator untenable.

With the panel unexpectedly behind him Prebisch gave up his Sheraton Plaza suite and returned to Santiago. Antonio Mayobre had now left Venezuela and was heading a UN assignment exploring the creation of a new centre on industrial development; he could not return to Santiago until August 1963, and Raúl therefore agreed to stay on as ECLA executive secretary until the transition was complete. But Prebisch's career was veering toward ILPES, the new Latin American Institute for Social and Economic Planning, which had been gradually taking shape since Paul Hoffman's visit to Santiago two years earlier. The alliance of Hoffman, Herrera, and de Seynes was unstoppable: the UN Special Fund approved a $3 million funding package on 11 January 1962; Felipe Herrera contributed another $1 million from the Bank to complete a five-year funding package; and de Seynes shepherded the appropriate resolution through the General Assembly approving the creation of autonomous regional institutes.[42] As the Panel of Experts began to fail Prebisch became increasingly interested in the institute; in May 1962, the UN named him the institute's director-general for a five-year term, and finally, on 8 June, he secured ECLA's commitment allowing him to resign from the Panel of Experts and return definitively to Santiago with a new title and challenge.

It was a coveted honour to be invited by don Raúl to join this new autonomous centre of research and training, and he staffed at choice from the ranks of ECLA. Hopenhayn, who left the Panel of Experts with Prebisch to become secretary of the institute, reflected staff expectations. "I have no doubt that the Institute embodies the highest hopes for Latin America."[43] No team was more eager to begin operations, and the institute celebrated its official opening in July 1962. But much had occurred during its two-year gestation. There was now serious competition. Unlike the IDB, the World Bank decided to create its own Economic Development Institute, "a very substantial expansion of our technical assistance activities, primarily through creation of an elite corps of development officers available for field assignments."[44] Presented as the World Bank's offering to the Alliance for

Progress, it was acknowledged to be directly competitive with the ILPES project, offering a better-financed and sounder option for facilitating USAID programs in Latin America. Richard H. Demuth, the director of Technical Assistance and Planning Staff for the World Bank, noted that the proposal had "put us back in touch with the whole US foreign aid program formulation," and condescended, "Informally, I think we should use our influence to keep the ECLA program within reasonable grounds so that if, as I suspect may be the case, it is not wholly successful, it will not be a great white elephant."[45]

Hoffman and Prebisch felt pre-empted and unhappy, but there was nothing to be done; Latin governments wondered what the institute was to accomplish now that the new World Bank institute was created and other research institutes such as the United Nations Research Institute for Social Development were being established. Two years earlier, when Hoffman visited Santiago, the concept of a regional UN institute in Santiago had seemed visionary; by late 1962 the international development landscape was becoming cluttered. There was also increasing resistance by Latin governments, which called the institute's mandate into question: ECLA already existed; Prebisch was asked at its eighth plenary meeting in February 1962, why should the institute weaken ECLA by extracting the best people? CELADE, the new Latin American Centre for Demographic Studies, had been created as a separate but not autonomous unit and was working perfectly well; why should the institute be privileged with a separate organization when ECLA's entire professional staff numbered only eighty-five, and why should it try to claim a status in the UN system comparable with the big UN specialized agencies?

Prebisch explained that the institute was to take over ECLA's role on the Tripartite Committee and therefore needed "an autonomous character similar to that of the Special Fund and UNICEF," led by a director-general with UN undersecretary rank. The institute also needed autonomy to reignite the creative impulse of the early 1950s; its governing council must comprise members acting in their individual capacity (rather than as government representatives, as in ECLA) to uphold the purpose of its creation. "If economists spend too much time on practical problems, without being able to step back from them in order to engage in theoretical and scientific study directed to their solution, they run the risk of becoming mere empiricists, excessively pragmatic in their approach. If, on the other hand, they devote all their energies to the scientific interpretation of facts and the formulation of theories, without coming down to earth from time to time, the danger is that they will become enmeshed in abstractions that increasingly removed from real-life problems in Latin America."[46] ILPES and ECLA would be sister organizations, expanding training and research for development while maintaining the applied work of the Santiago Secretariat across the corridor.

Frondizi flatly opposed Prebisch's plans, and, without the military coup that forced his exit, ILPES would not have been approved at all. Even so it required a special session of ECLA on 2 June in New York, where Raúl narrowly beat back a challenge to replace his list of directors for the institute's governing council, but only with the support of Celso Furtado, now a power in Brazil, who (despite 1957) could not refuse the call of his old friend. In the end the IDB and ECLA were both given full voting powers on a governing council expanded to eight Latin members to ease anxieties.[47]

The institute's breech birth was a portent. "Listening to the proceedings surrounding the establishment of the new Institute," the World Bank observer to the New York meeting noted, "one could not help but gather the impression that the Institute is likely to be faced with more than the usual share of problems associated with the launching of any new organization. The additional difficulties may be expected to stem from the deep cleavage among the States' members regarding the nature, purposes and scope of the organization. These differences will probably exert a debilitating influence on the staffing, curriculum and activities of the Institute and will limit its practical contributions to the economic development of Latin countries for some time to come."[48] ILPES could begin with the training program pioneered by Ahumada. These courses, long competently taught and administered by ECLA, were definitely in demand and could be expanded – and ILPES's July 1962 opening event featured the standard basic course for eighty Latin American junior professionals from across the region. Shorter training seminars in education and health were being planned. But training alone was not enough to justify or carry the institute, and staff looked to Prebisch for new roles: anchoring the Santiago end of the OAS-IDB-ECLA Tripartite Committee, and turning ILPES into the leading development think tank in Latin America.

Prebisch found ECLA unrecognizably changed on his return from Washington. The Alliance for Progress had absorbed its agenda. Santiago headquarters, although proud of its historical achievements, felt bereft and somewhat out of place before the irresistible attraction of Kennedy's Washington. ECLA's situation was not unlike that of a minority political party in a coalition facing elections after its dominant partner had adopted its platform and now claimed it as its own. In fact the almost embarrassing bows to ECLA as "pioneer" and "missionary" at Punta del Este only deepened a sense of malaise. All the praise from Americans, the UN, and so forth seemed too much like funeral eulogies: the centre of creativity and action in development was moving to Washington, with Latin Americans attracted into this orbit of light and power. Outlying stars like Santiago were diminishing, their days of glitter numbered. The political impulse, the agencies, the money, lay in the North. ECLA had peaked; the region needed a new generation to retool the organization.

Prebisch was happy to be stepping down; the institute was his new hope for reversing ECLA's decline. Colleagues at ECLA were more doctrinaire, arrogant, and ideological, and a new militancy was growing even as its prestige waned. Prebisch remarked to Mayobre, "Beware of the ECLA horse. You must ride it hard or it will buck you off."[49] The new dogmatism in ECLA was a road that led to certain irrelevance at a time when Latin America faced growing challenges: a declining share of global trade and production, and a loss of its privileged position in the UN and international organizations as dozens of new countries gained independence. When asked by US officials about the future of ECLA after his departure, Prebisch noted "the need for ECLA to rebuild its stock of intellectual capital."[50] Instead of repeating old slogans from the past, it should focus on areas where it had a particular competence: social policy (housing, education, and migrant workers) and microeconomic research in industry and agriculture to reconnect with the actual realities of the region. But it would not be easy, with the new ECLA reflex of blaming the outside world for the failures of the region; the violence of its attacks on the IMF, for example, provoked even its usual critics, such as Nicholas Kaldor or Joseph Grunwald, into compassionate support for the beleaguered del Canto.

His farewell speech from ECLA revealed the new direction in Prebisch's thinking: he now went much farther in criticizing Latin elites and linking external support with domestic change – land tenure, public education, and income distribution. Expanding markets, technology, and secure access to assistance and development capital were necessary ingredients of modernization, but political and social reforms were the fundamental preconditions for development – without which such foreign assistance would fail.[51] It was a stark, even gloomy, assessment as polarization between Latin capitals and Kennedy's Washington mirrored the internal polarization in Santiago. It seemed doubly important, therefore, to try to reverse the negative dialogue and bitterness that had crept back into US-Latin American relations during 1962, and Prebisch supported the OAS calling a foreign ministers meeting to dramatize the problem and seek new directions for revitalizing the Alliance for Progress. The Kennedy administration supported the idea, and Mexico agreed to host the high-level event in October 1962.

The conference opened on 22 October with a recorded message from President Kennedy praising the Alliance as "the most valuable contribution to the strengthening of the social and political stability in the American community," and urging US-Latin American cooperation for its renewal. It was too valuable to let go, he added, and despite accomplishments the twenty-one governments faced the challenge of revisiting the Charter. But the delegates, Prebisch included, were not listening to this taped statement; the real, live Kennedy in Washington had just ordered a US naval blockade of Cuba and demanded the withdrawal of Soviet intermediate-range missiles from the island. With the world facing nuclear peril, US officials and foreign ministers rushed home in a mood of nervous excitement to confront a crisis against which the Alliance for Progress seemed minor fare. The meeting stalled; Prebisch waited out the standoff in Mexico City. Three days later Khrushchev backed down to end the crisis, and the OAS meeting in Mexico City was recalled in a transformed atmosphere. The US delegation entered to a packed hall and prolonged standing ovation. Latins realized that Kennedy's victory was shared – Soviet nuclear weapons in Cuba threatened all countries in the Americas, not just the US. But a profound déjà vu accompanied the cheering; a genuine Latin sense of relief in the Soviet defeat was shared by recognition of the new power equation facing them in the Americas.

Prebisch left Mexico City on 27 October knowing that the magnitude of Kennedy's triumph had unleashed a new Napoleonic instinct in US-Latin American relations that left little room for creativity in regional development. For five years, since 1957, Latin America had been a priority in Washington because it was not fully secure; and the Punta del Este Charter symbolized a new partnership born of necessity. The October 1962 Cuban Missile Crisis was a dramatic US Cold War triumph, obliterating the 1961 Bay of Pigs humiliation and restoring a US confidence rattled by *Sputnik* and the loss of control of Cuba. US self-satisfaction and the natural order of the Americas returned; lingering self-doubts and hand-wringing toward Latin America in Washington were over. With Cuba neutralized as a direct national security threat, Washington turned to counterinsurgency everywhere in the region, toughening relations with non-docile Latin governments, while strengthening conservative elites throughout Latin America resisting social change as "communism." Brazil had already emerged as a top US concern, with President João Goulart identified as a particular threat to US interests.[52] Lincoln Gordon was named ambassador to Brazil, assisted by Colonel Vernon Walters as military attaché, to deal firmly with him. Latin America was returning to its traditional status of safe US backyard in which the competing tendencies of US foreign policy mirrored the power struggles playing out in the capital, a playground for an oversized and overconfident US national security establishment. The momentum of change had shifted decisively to Washington as Latin America was being reincorporated in a special embrace; that much was certain, and, while a revival of the Alliance for Progress could not be ruled out, the rules of the game would be set in Washington alone.

The fate of the OAS-IDB-ECLA Tripartite Committee, Prebisch's last link with Washington, underscored ECLA's increasing marginalization. Before leaving the Alliance for Progress he had agreed to head the new Advisory Committee on Planning of the Tripartite Committee; after resigning from the Panel of Nine in June 1962, he had shuttled back and forth between Santiago and Washington for meetings with Filipe Herrera and Mora, hoping that the combined strength of these organizations would yield greater success and leverage with governments. But now he found that the major countries – 90 percent of Latin America – were no longer interested; they managed their own plans, seeking consultants where they chose, dealing with USAID and the banks and funding agencies on their own. The ECLA advisory-group missions sent by the Tripartite Committee were outmoded: even the small countries thar accepted them, like Uruguay, complained about cost and quality. The turf-conscious IMF and World Bank had no interest in the Tripartite Committee either, which meddled in their areas of competence, so to speak; and USAID similarly played its own game. The IDB was respected: no Latin American government large or small could afford to ignore it since it was part of the big league with the World Bank and the IMF. But ECLA did not lend money; although Filipe Herrera treated them with respect and courtesy, Prebisch and Mora were being reduced to play actors without resources, pleading for money and attention. Only three years old, their Tripartite Committee had run its course. As Prebisch listened to the many reports of the many meetings, recalled the many letters he had promised to write, and reflected on the littleness of it all, he understood that a period was over, even though the committee would not be officially disbanded until 1967.

Prebisch's friends in New York were urging him to look beyond the region to the global development agenda. When he resigned from the Panel of Experts Raúl had no intention of leaving the Americas; now he was open to offers.

17 Global Gamble

Friends in New York doubted that Prebisch wanted to return for good to Santiago. The unravelling of the Alliance for Progress in early 1962 dismayed him all the more because it was, after the Common Market, his second setback in as many years. But Malinowski knew that he was not resigned. On 14 May, after Raúl was finally officially appointed secretary-general of ILPES, they walked from the Secretariat up First Avenue to 69th Street and over to Central Park, northward to the Conservatory Garden, where the azaleas, columbines, and peonies were ready to bloom. Prebisch wondered if he always aimed too high and set himself up for disappointment or whether there was a natural perversity in US-Latin American relations in which hostility and friendship bred contradictory results. The idea of Latin America had advanced under ECLA's leadership during a period of US hostility in the 1950s; led by governments, it was true, and not yet widely shared by society, a regional identity was slowly forming. But Washington's reaching out to Latin America under Kennedy's Alliance for Progress was killing it amidst special deals, counterinsurgency, and mutual recrimination. Instead of "good neighbors" sharing strengths, they were Abel and Cain feeding on differences, or simply a bad marriage that magnified only their latent defects and weaknesses. Certainly nothing seemed to go right in the New World – the fate of the Panel of Experts the most maddening of all, since it had embodied a genuinely fresh start, replacing power and envy with a practical system of development cooperation. But it hadn't worked out, chopped down only months after its launch, exposing the ancient geopolitical frustrations of US-Latin American coexistence.

Malinowski realized that in two hours of conversation Prebisch had not mentioned the institute once: withdrawal to Santiago and the contemplative life was evidently not a first choice for Latin America's foremost development celebrity. Prebisch's frustration was too visceral to accept defeat; at sixty-one, with so much to be done, he sought engagement rather than a secure retirement niche in the periphery. Malinowski therefore pressed Prebisch to refocus toward a global rather than Latin American perspective and urged him to attend the upcoming Cairo Conference on the Problems of Economic Development in July 1962 as Secretary-General U Thant's representative. Thirty-six non-aligned countries from Asia, Africa, and Latin America were meeting to discuss a common approach and future program on international trade policy. It would be an interesting pause from the present stalemate in US-Latin American relations; it would be his first meeting in Africa; and he might find surprises and opportunities.

Prebisch was skeptical. He had heard it all many times before – the perennial Third World demand for a new international trade policy, which never went anywhere beyond the familiar diagnosis that he already knew as a policymaker from Argentine days. Everybody could reel off the main points, beginning with the failure to create the International Trade Organization (ITO) as a complement to the IMF and World Bank – the so-called "three pillars" of a stable postwar order. It had nearly happened. Proposed at the founding of the United Nations in San Francisco in 1945, the ITO promised fair and equitable global rules for trade to avoid the dangers of unregulated international markets, which had contributed to the Great Depression. Eric Wyndham-White was selected as its first executive secretary to prepare a special conference in March 1948 in Havana, and developing countries, with their special vulnerability in commodities trade, were particularly looking forward to the ITO as a foundation for growth and development.[1] By 1948, however, the initial enthusiasm for the ITO had cooled in the US, UK, and other industrial economies, and although a draft charter was adopted in Havana, signed by fifty-three of the fifty-six participating countries, ratification by the US Congress failed, setting off a negative cascade and shelving the project: only Liberia ratified the Charter.

Meanwhile, in a parallel initiative beginning in 1946 (also led by the US, with the approval of Britain and the other Atlantic allies), a much smaller group of twenty-three Northern "like-minded" countries began tariff-cutting meetings in Geneva. By 1947 these partners created a new organization named the GATT (General Agreement on Tariffs and Trade). Although technically subordinate to the ongoing ITO process, with Eric Wyndham-White as the GATT's executive secretary (while keeping his original ITO title), it flourished while the Havana Charter collapsed. The reason was simple: the twenty-three industrialized members were rebuilding after World War II, and they needed an organization to promote trade and settle disputes. They were not concerned with the needs of developing countries, and still controlled Asia, Africa, and Latin America.[2] Instead of the universal membership foreseen for the ITO, the GATT addressed the interests of the advanced powers: lowering trade barriers in industrial goods and services where they had a comparative advantage, while ignoring agriculture and textiles where developing countries had an advantage.

With the ITO definitively dead, the balding, double-breasted Wyndham-White personified GATT's narrowness and Atlantic focus. But he was effective, presiding in 1949 over a successful tariff-reducing conference in France; others followed. By 1956 Germany and Japan had become members, and the GATT's small but highly competent secretariat was firmly and permanently established in Geneva. Instead of a single global trade organization as envisaged in 1945, a fissure had opened up in the international community between the GATT and the rest. Virtually all developing, primarily non-Western countries, agreed that GATT served the interests of the industrial powers very well indeed; here they were in agreement with the satisfied founders of the GATT. The problem was that it lacked a broader framework linking trade and development, including stable and acceptable prices for agricultural exports as well as measures to support industrialization. It was not meant to be "fair": Wyndham-White rejected Prebisch's Latin American Common Market as "closed" regionalism while welcoming the EEC despite its protectionist Common Agricultural Policy; and he suggested that developing countries join the GATT, so long as they accepted the priorities and rules of the founding members.

As the GATT became a core feature of the Atlantic community and Japan, deepening postwar cooperation among the Western industrial powers, it increasingly became a target of Third World criticism. As the 1950s progressed, these countries were convinced that systematic constraints undermined their economic progress even when they followed sound development policies – declining terms of trade; lack of investment capital as compared with developed countries; steadily declining aid disbursements; rising debt; rising trade barriers in rich countries to curb competition from Third World producers; shipping and insurance services outside their control. In other words, the international economic institutional structure set up after World War II and managed by the advanced Western states operated primarily in their interests; and to maintain this state of affairs they controlled the key agencies, particularly the IMF, the World Bank, regional banks, and the GATT. This image of skewed power relations and structural unfairness – of "them" versus "us" – was denied by the industrial countries, which viewed the prevailing GATT-based system as sound.[3] To them the chief obstacles to Third World development were internal; once a favourable business climate was restored by their own governments there was nothing stopping economic modernization, certainly not Wyndham-White's

GATT or the other big agencies. The market worked; the cry for so-called "structural" changes was frankly misguided and played into the hands of Soviet leader Nikita Khrushchev, busy currying influence with developing countries with repeated calls for reviving the ITO.

Prebisch asked Malinowski why the 1962 Cairo Conference should produce results when previous efforts had failed so predictably. Latin Americans had had a particularly bitter experience since 1945: given their experience of the collapse of wheat, coffee, sugar, and metal prices during the 1930s, they had been the region most committed to the success of ITO; after the failure of the Havana Conference, Latins used their voting power in the UN (twenty out of fifty-one seats in the General Assembly) to advance trade and development. Throughout the 1950s they were strong enough to strike new committees with impressive names but never able to make them effective against the opposition of the developed countries satisfied with the GATT.[4] Latin governments also tried a regional US-Latin American approach – the proposed Inter-American Council on Trade and Production, for example – but that also failed. And Prebisch himself had a ringside seat earlier in 1962 when Washington flatly rejected the trade agreement it had promised at Punta del Este.[5] Looking back, Prebisch mused, this huge effort in international trade policy had only yielded more UN bureaucracy and frayed nerves. Malinowski was adamant: Prebisch needed a break from US-Latin American relations and should go to Cairo; he was too consumed by Washington to note important changes building in the global system and getting out would do him no harm. "See for yourself," he advised.

After resigning from the Panel of Experts in early June, Prebisch agreed finally to attend the conference, and it was quite a revelation. Impressively prepared, attended, and organized, without inflamed North-South rhetoric, it resulted in a declaration that set out the main features of a common program dealing with both internal and external obstacles to development and endorsed a UN conference to deal with important questions relating to international trade, primary commodity trade, and economic relations between developing and industrial countries.

The Cairo Conference, in fact, was more than stimulating – apart from introducing new faces and ideas, it heralded a change in power relations. Since 1945 the developed countries had controlled the global economic agenda, and they had every intention of keeping things this way. From the US Treasury in Washington, francophile Douglas Dillon had further strengthened US-European-Japanese cohesion by leading the creation of the OECD (Organization for Economic Cooperation and Development), with a secretariat in Paris as an instrument for caucusing and research, and opening the "Dillon Round" of the GATT, in which the EEC for the first time voted with one voice.[6] On the other side of the North-South divide, the 1962 Cairo meeting brought together another group of countries around a common agenda; while still much weaker than the OECD, collectively these thirty-six developing countries of Asia, Africa, and Latin America had the potential to influence – if not yet shape – the trade and development debate. It was a key test of coalition-building: the failure of all previous UN trade initiatives during the 1950s had resulted from an inequality of bargaining power. Cooperation among Third World countries across the three continents, still in its infancy to be sure, therefore had immense potential. At its meeting in Belgrade in 1959 the Non-Aligned Movement (NAM), which had been founded in 1955, had agreed that trade and development required international action and that the discipline and organization at Cairo was a major step forward in reshaping global politics. Dozens of new countries were joining the international community with the end of colonial empires; and trade and development re-emerged after 1959 to become the biggest issue in North-South relations, fuelled by the declining share of the South in world trade.[7] The Cold War standoff between NATO and the Warsaw Pact was of secondary importance to the Third World. President Kennedy's 1961 Address to the General Assembly was infectious, catalyzing international interest in Third World progress and elevating the UN "Decade of Development" into an international priority for the 1960s.[8]

Two weeks after Prebisch returned from Cairo, ECOSOC agreed on 3 August to recommend the convening of an international trade and development conference, virtually guaranteeing General Assembly approval for UNCTAD in fall 1962. Malinowski had correctly diagnosed the new international dynamic: Cairo demonstrated that developing countries could have an impact if they worked together. From his key positions as secretary of ECOSOC and the Economic and Finance Committee of the General Assembly he had become an influential lobbyist, urging delegates to unite on votes and resolutions aimed at global income redistribution and to caucus as a group in order to offset the power of the developed countries. Faced by determined Third World resistance, Washington reversed its opposition to an international trade conference in order, at least, to influence what it could not prevent. With that the remaining global holdouts also acquiesced.[9]

But Malinowski wanted more: UNCTAD would require strong leadership, and he urged Prebisch to consider taking on this new global challenge. He called Prebisch repeatedly in Santiago and Washington and lobbied delegates from Asia, Africa, and Latin America; UNCTAD is a top priority, he argued, with Prebisch the ideal head. During his thirteen years as executive secretary of ECLA his global reputation and network of supporters were unrivalled by any other Third World figure; UNCTAD presented an extraordinary opportunity to project his concept of the North-South Dialogue to the international level and to forge a new organization just as he had molded ECLA into a powerful regional secretariat. In fact the parallels between region-building in Latin America after 1949 and this new challenge were intriguing: under Prebisch's direction UNCTAD could be a global version of ECLA in its diagnosis of structural inequity and global transformation, the need for planning and proposed remedies. Prebisch acknowledged that ECLA had paved the way for the creation of UNCTAD. "It was an idea," he said, "gradually being deployed through the United Nations on the basis of activities of ECLA."[10] Theoretically UNCTAD drew on and extended ECLA's core concepts of unequal exchange and asymmetry to North-South relations. Tactically it offered a global alliance for progress, which focused on trade stability and access, ODA, and regional integration. Would Prebisch, Malinowsi continued, agree at least to receive a Third World delegation?

After the Cuban Missile Crisis and the failure of the Tripartite Committee Prebisch notified Malinowski that he was open to an UNCTAD offer, and representatives from Brazil, Argentina, and Yugoslavia were soon in Santiago with a formal request to nominate him to head the UNCTAD Preparatory Committee.[11] Furtado flew in from Rio; Alfonso and Hernan Santa Cruz mobilized the Chileans. After listening and speaking again with Malinowski, Prebisch decided to gamble. "I'm not asking for this post. But if it is offered to me, I will consider it." Prebisch then visited New York for an on-the-spot assessment and further discussions with friends after the UN formally approved UNCTAD on 8 December – the Feast of the Immaculate Conception in Latin America and the best of omens.[12] The mood at UN headquarters was encouraging. It was a tantalizing challenge to turn this mouthful of acronym, UNCTAD, into a major showdown for equity within the global community. Without lobbying personally ("I did not move a finger," he later insisted), Prebisch left no doubt with Malinowski and his friends that he wanted the position.

But his nomination was contested. The UN search for a secretary-general to head UNCTAD underlined a deep split between the Western industrial countries on the one hand and the developing world with the Socialist Bloc on the other. The position was potentially significant, but only Australia, Canada, and New Zealand among the developed countries had voted in favour of the UNCTAD initiative, against the opposition of the US, Britain, France, Italy, Spain, Ireland, and South Africa. Japan, the Netherlands, the Scandinavian countries, and the French ex-colonial states in Africa had abstained. After caucusing the Western countries decided on Australian Sir

John Crawford as their nominee; Malinowski was so detested in Washington that his vocal campaigning for Prebisch stiffened US resistance.

U Thant stalled, and opposition to Prebisch's candidacy mounted in the first weeks of 1963. Developed countries claimed that Wyndham-White's earlier refusal to support the Latin American Common Market had embittered Prebisch toward the GATT, deepening suspicions that he was too much his own man, unwilling to compromise, and a critic of free trade. Prebisch waited anxiously in Santiago as silence from New York continued into the third week of January 1963. Since UNCTAD's first Preparatory Committee meeting had been called for 23 January, the deadline was acute. Only that morning, at the very last moment, could U Thant call Prebisch by telephone to offer the position of secretary-general on a fixed-term contract until 1 July 1964, since there was no assurance that a permanent institution would be created. Later that day U Thant cabled to apologize for "this lack of formality," in not sending a formal written offer in advance outlining the terms and conditions of his appointment. The decision had to be made "in a great rush," he noted, "in order to meet the impatience of many delegates." The note expressed his "pleasure and gratitude" at Raúl's acceptance of the offer: "I am convinced that your presence in this strategic position will be a most important factor in the success of the Conference."[13] To which Prebisch responded with "my full appreciation for this new responsibility," and to de Seynes that "your continuous support and guidance [will be] more necessary than ever." Wladek Malinowski circulated an enthusiastic announcement to his associates everywhere in the UN system.

"I hope your health is improving," U Thant had noted, "and I look forward to seeing you soon in New York when we can discuss some administrative and material arrangements." Prebisch had been bothered by arthritis during December and responded, "Expect to be normal again in March." But he was already on the telephone and settling affairs in Santiago for a much earlier appearance in New York, surprising the First Preparatory Committee by attending its closing session on 31 January.

Malinowski had urged Prebisch to come to New York as soon as possible to prevent UNCTAD's opponents from gaining the initial advantage. Arthritis or not, Prebisch could not risk delay; he had to assert his leadership immediately by taking control of the Preparatory Committee at its first New York session. This body of thirty country representatives from the industrial powers, developing countries and the Socialist Bloc was one of two bureaucratic devices created to slow down and micromanage the new initiative (the other was a separate group of experts to study the creation – or not – of a permanent trade secretariat after UNCTAD). The meeting had started out well enough with friendly cooperation among the three camps, only to witness a sudden cooling off to the point of deadlock as their divergence in expectations surfaced. Leading developing country proponents like Brazil and India proposed nothing short of a new approach to North-South relations; the US and its allies were very reluctant participants in any case and doubly annoyed with Moscow's loud and opportunistic backing of the Third World. All of the disparate forces in the global economy quickly surfaced, magnifying the dilemma of compromise toward mutually acceptable decisions. Appointing Mexican Cristóbal Lara as his deputy in ILPES, Prebisch rushed to New York to prevent an initial failure that could undermine the entire initiative. In fact his unannounced arrival to a tense scene of hostile glares and ironic asides was providentially timed: Raúl's impromptu address as their new secretary-general calmed the encounter, hailing the historic moment, appealing for cooperation, and lightening the ambience from approaching disaster to an auspicious, if fragile, beginning.

But while the UNCTAD initiative looked more serious with Prebisch in New York, the challenge was immense. In 1950, when he assumed the leadership of ECLA, he had arrived to an existing, if threatened, organization; so far not even the location of UNCTAD had been decided. Before leaving Santiago Prebisch had cabled ahead to David H. Pollock, chief of ECLA's Washington office, to meet him in Idyllwild Airport and accompany him for the next year as personal assistant. "Be where I am," he requested simply, for he needed Pollock's skills and unqualified loyalty to pull off UNCTAD. A genial and articulate Canadian and Washington insider, he could recall and summarize conversations and meetings with startling accuracy; his role was to ensure an accurate record of meetings in New York and to monitor developments during the weeks Prebisch would be absent in Santiago.[14] Other than Pollock, he had neither staff nor office – not even a desk or a telephone: four thousand square feet of office space would be available on the twenty-fourth floor starting 1 March, when UNICEF moved out. The UN had set aside only $1.5 million for financing the Conference during 1963–64, with Secretary-General Prebisch and his immediate staff limited to $64,400 in 1963 – six to ten persons with up to a dozen consultants for nine months – and $16,000 in 1964. He had just over a year to hold the biggest event in UN history, which developing countries considered the most important international gathering since San Francisco in 1945 and which Western countries wanted to bury!

Prebisch had the formal position of UNCTAD secretary-general, but his actual authority was unclear within the New York hierarchy. The two top UN power-brokers in the Department of Economic and Social Affairs (DESA) were Philippe de Seynes and his deputy Jacob (Jack) L. Mosak, director of General Economic Research and Policies. Mosak and de Seynes were very different: American versus French (equally convinced that their countries approached perfection, with past errors both minor and committed in good faith); Mosak suspicious of Prebisch, de Seynes a personal friend; Mosak workaholic and earnest, de Seynes relaxed and worldly; Mosak square, de Seynes sophisticated; Mosak hands-on manager, de Seynes cerebral tactician; Mosak heterosexual, de Seynes gay; with Mosak's unselfconscious superiority of manner balancing de Seynes's irritating arrogance of tone. But on one point they agreed: maintaining their power in the UN Secretariat in New York.

Just as Prebisch was known as an advocate of decentralization in the UN system, Mosak and de Seynes blocked any attempt to reduce their (DESA's) role. Prebisch's persistent attempts to wring greater autonomy for ECLA from New York had been resisted on grounds of "accountability," and Mosak and de Seynes knew that UNCTAD would provoke another challenge.[15] Neither they nor their governments in Washington and Paris had supported it, but now that it had been approved they were determined to control it. In practice this meant subordinate status for the new UNCTAD within DESA, reporting to ECOSOC. Otherwise Prebisch could emerge as a rival power within the UN system.

Just as certainly Prebisch knew that UNCTAD had to escape the clutches of Mosak and de Seynes to be considered legitimate by developing countries, that it had to be autonomous from DESA, and that the title of secretary-general – the only other official in the UN system apart from U Thant to be granted this special recognition – had to be matched by genuine authority. In fact developing countries had specifically demanded the title of secretary-general for the new UNCTAD chief to keep it at arm's length from DESA's control and ensure that Prebisch not become a figurehead for a Mosak-de Seynes operation. They also insisted on equitable staff appointments: only two of seventeen officials in DESA's International Trade Relations and Commodities Studies sections were from developing countries (one each from India and Indonesia), with no representation at all from either Africa or Latin America.

This internal war began Monday morning, 6 February, when Prebisch and Mosak met for a first round of negotiations. Mosak was confident and expansive, and very much in command, controlling staff and research appointments in trade and development within the secretariat.[16] Even if Prebisch wanted senior people like Sidney Dell and Wladek Malinowski – the two persons he knew Prebisch most needed – he would have to talk to Mosak and de Seynes for their secondment from DESA. Mosak had been in charge of UNCTAD preparations since its UN approval on 8 December, and he wanted to remain so. "This Bureau," he informed UN staff on 9 January, "has responsibility for the United Nations Conference on Trade and Development." Having organized the first session of the Preparatory Committee in New York, he was already deep into preparations for its next meeting in Geneva, 21 May-29 June, contacting staff and experts and requesting support from other agencies. The new Group of Experts was scheduled to meet on 18 February, again under Mosak's direction.[17] His expectations for UNCTAD were modest and well known: he anticipated "declarations of principles" and a "pious statement of intent" but no new international trade organization – at best a compromise committee or body reporting to ECOSOC.[18] Such a solution – essentially a UN headquarters-controlled initiative – would strengthen DESA and gain the backing of the US, France, and the other industrial countries. "The one thing the US did not want was a creation of new machinery," he noted. The US, like the other industrial nations, was satisfied with GATT ("its rules are well-known; it has developed a substantial background of experience; and most important of all, policy control is dominated by the developed western countries"). He compared UNCTAD with the objections to the SUNFED debate (Special UN Fund for Economic Development) of the 1950s, where the developing countries finally had to content themselves with Paul Hoffman's Special Fund pre-investment facility. "If there was such tough in-fighting about $100 million being channelled through an aid agency without weighted voting, imagine the opposition to an organization in which over $100 billion will be involved."[19] In fact Washington's first priority, according to Mosak, was preparing a new round of GATT negotiations to begin in 1964 to pre-empt EEC protectionism.

So far Mosak had the momentum; he promised Prebisch most of the staff required for the Trade Conference; he advised economies: Prebisch should limit travel to a few "key" countries ("perhaps half a dozen"). He had matters well in hand; Prebisch should feel comfortable returning to Santiago to prepare for the arrival of José Antonio Mayobre as the executive secretary.[20] By 8 February, when Raúl left for South America via Washington, nothing of substance had been decided. Prebisch realized that Mosak's "compromise" position on UNCTAD was de facto as unacceptable to developing countries as to himself. But he also realized that Mosak was in over his head and that events would soon work in Prebisch's favour; he therefore avoided a direct confrontation in the interest of maintaining an essential working relationship.

Mosak's bid for leadership rapidly dissolved when he could not recruit leading economists and experts to UNCTAD from developing countries. At first overly optimistic ("the bigger the net, the more fish can be caught," he had joked), the results were embarrassing: Salant Myint from Burma and Nigerian economist Okigbo, among others, declined his invitation. The eleven-country Group of Experts assembled by Mosak in late February was deadlocked between the OECD (US, UK, Netherlands, and Denmark) and the rest (Brazil, India, Lebanon, and Mauritania for the developing countries; and the USSR and Romania for the Socialist Bloc). A second meeting from 25 March to 5 April with the same groups but different economists ended in the same stalemate.

With Prebisch away, Mosak realized he could not fill the leadership vacuum in New York. He was a capable and respected official, his class at the University of Chicago producing four Nobel Prize winners; while a graduate student he had worked with the Cowles Commission, which pioneered the linkage of economic theory and mathematics; and Mosak's 1944 book, *General Equilibrium Theory in International Trade*, was favourably reviewed as a workman-like contribution. Although an orthodox economist and unsympathetic to the structuralism of Prebisch, Mosak was not in the rigid neoclassical mould of what the Chicago School would become in the 1960s. But his tentative professional credibility was additionally handicapped by overly intimate relations with controversial agencies of the US Government during the McCarthy period.

By early April Prebisch was full-time in New York and had taken charge of the UNCTAD Preparatory Committee. The drift was over. He rented a small suite in the Beekman Towers Hotel within walking distance of UN headquarters, and the new offices were ready. The legitimacy of UNCTAD would depend on the quality of its work and the international perception of Prebisch's fairness as secretary-general, and he therefore began by assembling the nucleus of a future staff – a trusted inner core that could direct his work plans, free his time for the lengthy consultations required to locate areas of consensus, prepare the preconditions for compromise on key points, plan the agenda, and organize the tactical activities of the conference. In February he had requested Sidney Dell, one of the UN's most capable economists. The two had become close friends when Dell spent three months in Santiago in 1958 working with him on regional integration. Dell had entered the UN in 1948 on David Owen's encouragement, with qualities of intellect and ethics heralded by a brilliant first at Oxford in 1939 and subsequent wartime service in the British Army. Tall and handsome, incisive and decisive, Dell's commitment to global equity was unwavering, and he had risked his career by defending UN victims of McCarthy. But in addition he was one of DESA's senior economists who could also direct major projects and had risen rapidly within the Secretariat in New York. For Prebisch Dell was as vital on the substantive side as Malinowski was on strategy, both serving as first among equals in the UNCTAD team. Although Dell's relations with Mosak were correct, if not cordial (unlike those of Malinowski, whom Mosak detested), winning Mosak's consent for his release from other duties in DESA proved difficult, and Prebisch was finally forced to appeal directly to de Seynes, who agreed to a one-year leave on 5 April.[21]

Malinowski's situation was more complicated. Prebisch needed a deputy to absorb some of the administrative work and travel pressures; he wanted Malinowski for this key position, given his Third World contacts. But neither the US nor senior UN officials would agree.[22] Seymour Finger from the US delegation warned that if Malinowski was formally nominated the other two camps (developed countries and Socialist) would put forward their own candidates and veto the others unless Prebisch accepted all three. Faced with this hostility, he dropped the idea of a deputy and instead named eight "Executive Assistants" on 25 April to function as UNCTAD's informal steering committee. With this number an acceptable geographic and professional balance could be found for a heterogeneous group that included Malinowski (Poland) and Sidney Dell (UK), but also J. Mosak and S. Shevchenko (to reassure the US and the USSR), Perce Judd (Australia), R. Krishnamurti (India), Samuel Lurie (Belgium), and A.H. Abdel-Ghani (Egypt). Prebisch as an Argentine national represented Latin America. Krishnamurti had arrived in April; as with Dell, Prebisch had asked that he be seconded, in this case from ECAFE in Bangkok, given his proven abilities and accomplishments in Asia. Perce Judd was one of the most knowledgeable specialists in international commodity markets and was named secretary of the Conference. To these key secondments Prebisch added consultants Alfred Maizels (UK), Lal Jayawardena (Sri Lanka), Paul Berthaud (Switzerland), Christopher Eckenstein (West Germany), and others in a balance reflecting the subtle nuances of North-South and East-West divides as well as functional expertise.

Prebisch's own office had a four-person executive committee comprised of Jack Mosak (in charge of Research and Policies) and S. Shevchenko (Special Policy Problems), while Sidney Dell (Final Act and Report) and Malinowski (Coordination) reassured developing countries. While this lineup suggested the dominance of Western delegates, Prebisch ensured that developing country experts held key substantive positions. Krishnamurti, for example, was in charge of the central issue of UNCTAD – the creation of a new institution – and his choice of upward-bound Diego Cordovez (Ecuador) as expert was applauded in Latin America. Prebisch reached back to ECLA for David Pollock and Jorge Viteri de la Huerta (Ecuador) as special assistants in charge of political and general conference organization, and Bodil Royem from ECLA's Washington office managed the office as administrative assistant. This was the initial core staff, thirty in all by the end of 1963, including secretarial and administrative staff. None were permanent appointments.[23]

The non-New York residents stayed at the Gorham or (more modest but convenient) Tudor hotels, and worked ten-to-twelve-hour days in a spirit of growing camaraderie. Twice a week they fled the UN cafeteria for city restaurants: La Cabana and Brazilian Pavilion (Latin favourites) or Tandoori and Madras (Krishnamurti's choices), alternating with the pricier Russian Tea House and Tobeus, or the Kitchko, Ramanyana, Grove Street Café and the ever-popular Stage Deli on Broadway for variety. Prebisch would arrive at his office before his staff and still be there when they left, a hard but fair boss who wrote his own reports in longhand, retained a code of formality, never mentioned his personal life, and showed no indication of stress.

There was now a sense of urgency. The date and location of the conference (to be known as UNCTAD I) was finally secured: Geneva at the Palais des Nations, 23 March-16 June 1964.[24] But the Preparatory Committee would meet again in late May and for a final session before UNCTAD I on 2–15 February, and they also required a mountain of documentation. With its identity established, the UNCTAD team developed momentum, and progress was rapid. The timing was right; the best minds around the world mobilized for this new focus of international development. Leading consultants and academics took note and clamoured to be involved.[25] Special international workshops and research enriched the Groups of Experts meetings scheduled for Geneva in early July and New York on 19–24. The World Bank, IMF, GATT, UN headquarters staff, the UN regional commissions, UN specialized agencies, government departments, and research centres cooperated in a deepening sense that UNCTAD was a serious new international initiative.[26]

This tide of public and media support for UNCTAD provided a positive backdrop for cooperation across camps when Prebisch summoned the Preparatory Committee in Geneva for its second meeting on 21 May–9 June 1963. Unlike the first of these sessions in New York, it was marked by consensus from beginning to end. Industrial country delegates were pleased by the "business-like" conduct of the session; the background work of Prebisch's team was noted approvingly; and agreement was reached on the five substantive themes for UNCTAD I: trade in commodities; trade in manufactures; financing and invisibles (shipping and insurance) related to trade; new institutions; and regional problems. What had previously been seen as impossible – high-quality conference documents in all the UN languages by January 1964 in this vast area where many newly independent states lacked adequate documentation – no longer appeared an insurmountable task.

The meeting's main achievement, however, was the birth of the G-77 (Group of 77), referring to the developing countries that voted for the General Assembly resolution authorizing UNCTAD in 1962.[27] At Geneva delegates from Asia, Africa, and Latin America adopted a resolution pledging cooperation in the common cause of a new world order. "From that very first moment," Prebisch noted, "I came to the conclusion that the similarity of concerns, of problems, and of ways of tackling them called for a uniting of wills and search for common methods of action to strengthen certain trends which had for some time been taking shape in the United Nations General Assembly." The insight "gave me enormous encouragement" and "opened new perspectives," he added, for it meant that a group identity – the G-77 – was becoming a reality. A historic opening for institutional innovation was taking place, it seemed, with the glimmer of an emerging counterweight to "the geocentric approach of industrial countries."[28]

Although still embryonic compared with the political and security underpinnings of the OECD, the emergence of the G-77 heralded the formation of a group system of negotiation within UNCTAD: Group A (Asia and Africa) together with Group C (Latin America) comprised the G-77, while Group B included the Western industrial powers in the OECD. The Moscow-led countries of the Socialist Bloc became Group D. There were anomalies: Yugoslavia and Israel needed a home and were taken in by the Asian group, for example, and New Zealand was uncertain for a while about whether it belonged in Group B or the G-77.[29] But it seemed that developing countries from Asia, Africa, and Latin America were serious about a permanent negotiating instrument. Having come into independence in single file without such a caucusing device, they were collectively vulnerable; now with the G-77 as a forum to prepare negotiations, the developed countries would no longer hold all the cards in international trade and development.

A political breakthrough in US-USSR relations complemented these positive developments in international development. On 5 August 1963 the superpowers signed the historic Nuclear Test Ban Treaty in Moscow and opened a new period of détente. Reduced fears of nuclear war would allow greater attention to poverty reduction and open more possibilities for developing countries to focus on development. Kennedy and Khrushchev had stepped back from the brush with nuclear war during the Cuban Missile Crisis: there were rumours of a Cuban-US rapprochement as Operation Mongoose fizzled out and signs that Kennedy would control the escalation under way in Vietnam. It was a blessed summer when idealism and support for international development had peaked; Prebisch was surely not alone in referring to this first phase of UNCTAD as a "great adventure."[30]

Prebisch's next task was selling UNCTAD: finding areas of agreement and building a coalition of supporters in every continent, especially outside of Latin America. In the end he chose thirteen essential capitals for a "40 days around the world" tour between 1 September and 9 October to be followed by visits to Washington and Ottawa.[31] Dell and Pollock prepared the trip with introduction and questions for governments sent in advance from New York, and both men accompanied Prebisch as he departed for Australia; Krishnamurti joined them for the Asian leg of the tour. In each capital meetings with senior officials would begin at 9:00 AM and continue in the afternoon until 5:00 PM. Formal lunches and dinners with ministers, vice-presidents, and presidents lasted late into the evening. Prebisch never took notes during the interviews or carried a briefcase, and a pattern emerged in the interviews where Raúl opened the discussion with general analysis and statesmanlike questions, while Dell would take up the direct, probing, or embarrassing follow-on topics. Back in their hotel Dell and Pollock would summarize the discussion and highlight key policy or procedural points, dictating onto the green plastic discs (then used instead of tapes) that were mailed to headquarters for transcribing prior to their return. Lumbering DC-7s flying between capitals contributed to an exhausting trip, but Prebisch could sleep on airplanes and was in fine fettle as they reassembled in New York to evaluate their findings.

Hosts seemed confused on protocol. No minister in Australia met Prebisch (as back payment for defeating Sir John Crawford's bid for UNCTAD leadership), but in India he was regally received and driven from New Delhi to the Taj Mahal for a midnight viewing under a full moon. Moscow sent out a big black Chylka in the most elaborate reception of all the fifteen countries, complete with side visits to the Hermitage in Leningrad and (for Dell and Pollock) the Bolshoi Ballet. Warsaw displayed its Old Town, rebuilt from the war, with a procession of vodka toasts and heavy food, which finally provoked Prebisch's normally iron-clad stomach. When a local doctor who treated him refused payment, Raúl presented him with the two bottles of French cognac he had received earlier in the day as a welcoming gift from his hosts. He then returned to the classics that he always read before sleep. Yugoslavia was all business; Cairo strictly ceremonial, intent on securing Deputy Premier Abdul El Khaisani as president of the Geneva Conference. In London, Edward Heath and Harold Wilson, Tory chancellor of the exchequer and leader of the Labour Opposition respectively, both offered Prebisch his most hated food: steak and kidney pie. Japan refused any individual initiative, invariably siding with the US, UK, or Germany, while India insisted on a visible leadership role.

Prebisch's tour underlined the polarization of views between the G-77 and industrial countries; the developing countries were spearheading the creation of a comprehensive and highly visible trade policy initiative under the UN banner against a deep and broad opposition. Prebisch addressed this issue frankly when he met informally with the Second Committee of the UN General Assembly for a debriefing after returning to New York. Although there were certain differences among Group B countries (particularly between the UK, France, and the US), the industrial countries were in general agreement on main issues such as commodity agreements, supplementary financing, and new machinery; and they all supported GATT. The developing countries were not nearly as organized as the OECD, but they were in broad accord on the prevailing unfair rules of the game in international trade, and all viewed the IMF, the World Bank, and the GATT as "rich men's clubs."[32]

There was, Prebisch noted, a growing anxiety among developing countries as their earnings from trade continued to fall relative to the industrial countries and the need was felt for long-term changes to create "a new order in the international economy."[33] The existing machinery centred on GATT lacked universality of membership and scope, and while it benefited the industrial countries it was deficient for the G-77. Instead the general framework – the long-term relationship of trade and development – had to be changed "so that the market functions properly not only for the big countries but also for the developing countries in their relations with the developed." Presently, Prebisch noted, "there is a conspiracy against the laws of the market" that cannot be met by short-term gimmicks. UNCTAD's challenge would be to produce an international economic policy that had no historical parallel "but which the world needs today and which is possible for both the big and developing countries."[34]

Prebisch reassured the industrial countries that any new institutional structure for achieving this "new order" would have to be a compromise position between Moscow's ITO concept, which Group B would clearly veto, and staying with the GATT, which the G-77 would find equally objectionable. Such a compromise could take many forms, but after his trip

Prebisch was thinking about a permanent UNCTAD as a unique and autonomous agency within the UN. Periodic trade conferences like UNCTAD I in Geneva every 2–3 years would serve as a global forum, and a permanent secretariat with a standing committee would set targets, develop and promote policies, and evaluate results. The GATT, Prebisch suggested, would continue as an essential part of such machinery "without losing its autonomy or role, adapting itself to the problems of developing countries."[35]

This update, frank and provocative in its call for a "new order," was more favourably received than Prebisch had anticipated, and other good news followed a week later in early November. The acerbic, plain-talking George Ball, US undersecretary of state, praised his work as "extremely valuable and thought-provoking" and noted the "obligation on the part of the developed western world to find solutions in a sympathetic and constructive manner," and his agreement that "developing countries must increase their share of world trade."[36] George Woods, president of the World Bank, was even more supportive. In a cordial welcome at a lunch given for Prebisch in Washington, he stressed the importance of UNCTAD for the World Bank itself. "Something is basically wrong when the annual gross lending by our Bank can be wiped out by commodity price reductions."[37] Such a counterproductive situation should be tackled, and he hoped for UNCTAD's success in Geneva. After all, although aid could facilitate trade, the reverse was also true: unless World Bank customers could export, their credit worthiness would decline and constrain future lending. Protecting developing countries against sharp reductions in trade earnings simply made good economic sense. To Prebisch's question about repeating his argument to the Geneva conference, Woods not only committed himself to attending but said that "I would hope to make an even more positive contribution."[38]

Encouraged by positive news and widespread support Prebisch's UNCTAD team turned to the completion of a report of the secretary-general, "Towards a New Trade Policy for Development." "Document overload" was already a corridor complaint: a digestible focus had to be created out of the myriad background papers and technical data. Prebisch's Report would therefore shape the debate in Geneva as the one paper every delegation would read. It had to be relatively short, offering a statement of the problem, a framework, and a general summary of G-77 demands. It had to articulate the demands of the G-77, while at the same time outlining a realistic agenda acceptable to the Western and Soviet Bloc countries. The first draft was ready by mid-December, to be celebrated with two bottles of champagne waiting under Prebisch's desk for the event. Approaching midnight, as the last pages were completed and an early blizzard swirled around New York headquarters, Prebisch asked, "Jovenes, where can we chill these two bottles at this late hour?" The cafeteria was closed, and a search located no ice anywhere in the building. But the ever-resourceful Pollock-Viteri duo found an empty office on the 39th floor and chilled the champagne by hanging the bottles from a window with cords from Venetian blinds. The driving snow soon accomplished its task, and they returned triumphantly – "ingenuity at midnight," Prebisch exclaimed.

Prebisch felt he had hit the right notes in his report. "I was able," he later reflected, "to submit to the First Conference a report, perhaps the sole virtue of which was that it expressed in systematic form those common concerns of the three regions of the developing world and served as the basis for the organization of action which was both urgent and unavoidable." He followed the same working style in UNCTAD as in ECLA or the Argentine Central Bank: every sentence and topic in the report was fought through by Dell and his staff. Prebisch called special staff meetings to finalize a common secretariat outline for each chapter; he requested written memoranda from staff members and consultants to debate different theoretical and regional perspectives; and he invited both staff members and external persons from all sectors ranging from UN ambassadors and public or private sector officials to NGO, academic, and media representatives. But at the end he sat down and wrote the text in a longhand that only Bodil Royem could decipher.[39]

The core concept of the report was the "trade gap" impeding the economic prospects of developing countries. Prebisch developed his argument by endorsing the 5 percent minimum real economic growth rate accepted for the First UN Development Decade and demonstrating that success required an annual export increase of at least 6 percent per annum. G-77 countries were, however, far from this goal. In real terms, he continued, the effective purchasing power of Third World exports had grown only 2 percent a year since 1950. If export and import trends resembled those in the past, they would face a large and growing "trade gap," estimated to reach a figure of $20 billion by the end of the decade. Here was the dilemma: the developing countries would either have to obtain $20 billion per annum in financial flows during the remainder of the 1960s or else increase their share of exports in commodities, manufactures, or services to fill this gap. The body of the report therefore presented policy alternatives, or what Prebisch termed "a coordinated international strategy of converging measures," for UNCTAD I to debate (and hopefully) approve.

One cloud, however, remained. The shock and consequences of President Kennedy's assassination on 22 November 1963 had undermined the previous optimism about international development and North-South relations. Kennedy's assassination elevated Vice-President Lyndon B. Johnson to the presidency, and Johnson had been skeptical about the Alliance for Progress with its rhetoric of land reform and social policy. Personnel changes also suggested a harder line: Dillon left the US Treasury for Wall Street; Isaiah Frank left the State Department for Johns Hopkins University; and Thomas Mann succeeded Edwin Martin as assistant secretary of state and coordinator of the Alliance. When he received a cable asking whether the US should support Prebisch as the new secretary-general of UNCTAD, Mann rolled his eyes. "Prebisch ruined Latin America. But who cares about UNCTAD? It doesn't matter in the slightest what is going on in the UN."[40] From his first visit to Washington as UNCTAD secretary-general in February 1963, Prebisch's reception had been mixed; since the US had only reluctantly accepted the initiative in the first place he had no illusions about its enthusiasm for the new organization. But during Kennedy's tenure there was an opening for new initiatives reflected in a range of views on UNCTAD within Washington's foreign-policy community. If some US officials were consistently negative, such as Lincoln Gordon, US ambassador to Brazil since 1961, maintaining that domestic policies in developing countries were the entire source of the problem, there were others, such as Isaiah Frank, who agreed that the industrial countries could not "immunize themselves against what is happening in developing countries" and that a protracted polarization between rich and poor was a long-term threat to global and US security.[41] Most important, Kennedy possessed the charisma to lead global change: with his violent departure his underlying commitment to international development no longer animated the US capital quite as much. Spurred by anti-US rioting in Panama, Mann called all the Latin ambassadors together to redraw US policy toward the region: there was no mention of the Alliance for Progress, democracy, or social reform. Washington tightened its pressure on President João Goulart in Brazil. The hopes of a Cuban-US rapprochement prevalent in the months before the assassination faded. Instead of de-escalation in Southeast Asia the first US bombing raids on North Vietnam had just begun, with the first combat troops about to arrive in March.

Prebisch's unsuccessful meeting with Walter W. Rostow, chair of Johnson's Policy Planning Council, was symptomatic of the uncertain but changing atmosphere in post-Kennedy Washington. Rostow, whose *Stages of Economic Growth: A Non-Communist Manifesto* made him the resident White House intellectual, had formed a "Modernization Institute" in Special Group CI (Counter-Insurgency) and was now a key Johnson advisor on Vietnam, "nation-building," and North-South relations in general. The interview was an important opportunity for Raúl to introduce his UNCTAD I report and to listen and respond to US concerns. Instead Rostow declared that UNCTAD was on the wrong track altogether – that Latin America countries, for example, should rely more on import-substitution industrialization than trying to export manufactured goods to foreign markets.[42] Prebisch thought he was joking – import substitution within the closed markets after the Great Depression had produced Latin America's current dilemma of protected and inefficient industries for local markets – and asked whether this was US trade strategy in the current Kennedy Round of the GATT. Challenged and unable to respond, Rostow transformed into Mr Hyde, and his earlier professorial tone turned to threats. The best advice for developing countries was "remedying their own internal deficiencies" and helping the United States develop new technologies with faster growth. In this way "old industries like textiles will gradually wither away on their own" and transfer production to the Third World. In any case the US administration was unable to do much for UNCTAD since "protectionist lobbies are protected by Congress and fiats established by the State Department can do little about it."

The final meeting of UNCTAD's Preparatory Committee met on 2–15 February in a curious humour. On the one hand the interest was extremely high: all thirty-two members attended with observers from practically all UN members and international organizations. Tempers, on the other hand, were short: it looked like the General Assembly in the poorest of moods. Intended to deal with strictly procedural issues for the conference, which would open on 23 March, the thirty-two delegates could not resist jocular asides as they sorted out the general committee, main committees, committee chairs, and so forth – no fewer than twenty-eight vice-presidents had to be selected – and lightly barbed comments quickly intensified into a full display of global rhetoric.

Despite – or because of – this tension, UNCTAD I had momentum and was eagerly awaited. Expectations were high; the World Bank viewed it as too important to be allowed to fail, and George Woods was a bellwether figure in international development in the US capital. On 14 March Prebisch and his entourage arrived in Geneva to set up his office, and Adelita came the next day giving her a week to organize their apartment in the Parc de Budé building across the road from the Palais des Nations. She had accompanied Raúl to the League of Nations meeting thirty years before, and for him her presence provided the emotional anchor he needed to survive the three-month orgy of work that now awaited him.

Geneva's UN headquarters, and more particularly Georges Palthey, director of conference services, were in charge of opening ceremonies for

UNCTAD I. Protocol was supposed to be his strong point, and Prebisch had not bothered with it during the months of work before the meeting. But on the morning of 22 March, just to make sure that everything was in order, he decided to review preparations for the inaugural plenary the next day featuring U Thant and dignitaries from around the world. What he saw exceeded any bureaucratic snag previously encountered in his UN or Argentine careers. Instead of an appropriate auditorium with suitable translation and media facilities, the Geneva staff had signalled the lowest priority for UNCTAD: a small third-rate room with military-style metallic tables and ancient, beaten-up folding chairs, in one of the oldest of its buildings dotted throughout Geneva. The podium looked like a small theatre stage, separated from the delegates by a limp cloth curtain along an improvised wire, with the overall effect of a wartime Gilbert and Sullivan production.

Prebisch stared, then turned without a word and drove back to the Palais with Pollock and Viteri, the three marching abreast into Palthey's office past a startled secretarial staff who had never before witnessed such an invasion from the colonies. Palthey retreated before the stony-faced trio, backing step by step to the large windows behind his desk. As he cowered against the glass, a peacock cried raucously from the courtyard below. "I will crush you like a bug and feed you to the peacocks," Prebisch growled. Later Prebisch chanced on Palthey in the neighbouring stall of the Palais's marbled urinals: "I will piss all over you," he warned. The UN worked overnight, and the conference opened the next day in dramatically improved conditions to a growing drumbeat of excitement and tension.

Prebisch's UNCTAD was the international event of 1964, not to be missed, and the largest international event ever held. More than four thousand official delegates from 119 countries, the media, international organizations, and nongovernmental bodies were in Geneva; hotels were long since booked, forcing authorities to billet visitors in private homes. UN translators were unable to accommodate five official languages for three months without assistance from private firms across Europe. Che Guevara in a well-tailored pin-striped suit was the social sensation of the event, and Pope John XXIII detailed five robed monsignores from the Vatican and sang a special Papal Mass for the success of the conference.

Prebisch's inaugural address was theatrical. U Thant's ponderous welcoming message, read from a prepared text, created no more than a sense of expectation; Prebisch rose slowly, evidently without notes, to the vast and silent audience in the Palais and gazed over the assembled delegates with patrician ceremony. In a voice so low that people strained to hear he requested their attention: the global community faced a turning point in history and their actions here in Geneva would be measured against the challenge of their times. History would be made – for good or ill. Even participants who had previously experienced Prebisch before a crowd marveled at the sense of moment that swept the Palais. "Old hands at such international conferences are unanimous in saying that they had never seen such a thing before," a hardened World Bank observer admitted.

He then skirted melodrama by abruptly switching from solemnity to humour, lacing his speech with irreverent asides and comments. He criticized his own report as bland (he would have preferred to be much more radical than the conference's secretary-general was allowed to be), dramatized the crisis of development (failure of the conference would be a world calamity), praised the efforts made so far by the developed countries (while avoiding specific commitments that might limit his freedom of action during the conference itself), and challenged Third World countries to hold up their end: "a policy of international cooperation is only complementary. It cannot be a substitute for development." In his closing remarks Prebisch urged a new partnership between rich and poor nations that would benefit all. Boy-scout or missionary motivations were irrelevant to the drama of development, he insisted; all countries, rich and poor, shared a long-term self-interest in overcoming poverty. "Converging measures" were required, as identified in his report, to manage the "trade gap." With a last warning that growth in recent years had slowed, he brought the audience to a standing ovation by returning to the opening challenge: they must succeed, and they could succeed; overcoming global inequity was not a utopian goal if the world community worked together for the common good.

Skeptical delegates agreed that it was quite a show. "Its start was well-planned," one noted. "Where it will end is anyone's guess." Two weeks later much of this initial cohesion had dissipated in an unwieldy and numbingly boring format. Instead of a narrow and more structured agenda, Prebisch had deliberately chosen an inclusive format in which all 119 governments (not to mention the heads of international organizations) were invited to present an opening statement to the conference. The intention was admirable – to focus attention on Third World development to a global audience and enlist the broadest political support for UNCTAD – but this protocol was risky in practical terms. Most delegations came with long formal statements and insisted on reading them in full. Attendance flagged between the appearance of major figures, and journalists complained that nothing was happening. Che Guevara received a standing ovation (the only one besides Prebisch), but Cuba was not far down the speaker's list and the audience was still patient.

Prebisch sat through each daily eight-hour session with stoic patience and apparent full attention. Pollock asked him how he could stand it. "Nonsense, David," he responded. "I flick back and forth on simultaneous translation to practice my languages." George Woods, however, was as good as his word and gave a strong official message of World Bank support for UNCTAD, for which Prebisch called him the "Pope John XXIII of international development." And Eric Wyndham-White acknowledged a clear difference of mandate between the GATT and UNCTAD: his organization had a narrow and focused purpose – to lower tariffs; it would not negotiate commodity arrangements, for example, "a field which has been entrusted by the United Nations to its own organs." There would not be, therefore, competition or duplication of purpose between the GATT and UNCTAD, and this forthright statement was hugely welcomed by the conference as a vote of confidence by its principal presumed opponent.[43]

But everyone was waiting for US Undersecretary George Ball, the key personality at the conference, who spoke on 25 March, following French Finance Minister Valéry Giscard d'Estaing. "I was aware that the delegates expected the United States to offer similarly generous-sounding promises," he recalled, "but I held to my commitment to candour." Ball's bluntness was exceptional at a major international event where pleasantries and ingratiating intentions of solidarity were the norm, and "the speech fell like cold rain." He warned that Prebisch's report was idealistic, ethically uplifting and inherently reasonable – but not, unfortunately, realistic; he wanted to be clear that the US would not confuse this point with insincere flattery.[44] He rejected virtually all Prebisch's recommendations for a new system of international cooperation. Ball challenged the statistical underpinnings of his projections for a $20 billion "trade gap," the central element of the report, which he dismissed as nothing more than a "figure of speech." Prebisch's call for $20 billion financial or trade concessions from Group B countries without adequate controls risked the G-77 using UNCTAD as "an escape from their own domestic responsibilities." Prebisch had only concentrated on international deficiencies and responsibilities; he should have been equally tough on the shortcomings of developing countries. "This gives excessive emphasis to only one side of the coin." Richard Gardner, Ball's lead negotiator in the US delegation, scurried about after the speech insisting that Washington took the conference very seriously and was indeed interested in promoting the trade and development of the South. But Ball's pit bull attack so early in the game spelled trouble ahead, just as the five committees (Commodities, Manufactures, Finance, Institutions, and Regional Problems) started their work.

These five committees were responsible for shaping the conference recommendations; their work over the next three months was therefore the key to the success or failure of UNCTAD. But all five committees were too large to be effective because all the 119 delegations insisted on representation; they became as large as the plenary meetings, and just as prone to speeches. Although T. Swaminathan (India) and Stanovnik (Yugoslavia) were accomplished chairs, not all the committees were well-managed – for example, Commodities, over which Bernardo Grinspun of Argentina presided. Economic advisor to President Arturo Illia, who was elected in 1963 a year after the military coup against Frondizi, he represented an Argentine Government that supported Prebisch – an amazing about-face from previous experience – and that was determined to match Brazil in UNCTAD zeal. Grinspun, alas, could never stop talking. Urged by Prebisch to limit interventions to five minutes, he spent twenty minutes announcing the proposed strategy to his colleagues. Subcommittees and working groups proliferated in a complicated undergrowth of North-South activity; the conference began to resemble, according to one participant, "a curious mixture of political intrigues and seminars on economic development."[45]

Prebisch and his team faced the challenge of monitoring – preferably guiding – this activity to locate areas of potential consensus. Staff fanned out to observe as many meetings as possible, and each day would begin with a staff meeting at 8:30 chaired by Prebisch to review developments in the five committees. Delegate speeches would be analysed line by line, summarizing views on the main agenda items. How did the US, UK, France, Canada, and others approach commodity agreements, for example? Or preferences? These would be compared with the developing countries. By 10.00 AM, when the official sessions resumed, staff were back at their assigned posts. Staff also prepared backgrounders for Prebisch before his daily private meetings with delegations, a personal diplomacy that continued into the social events crowding each evening. Although sixty-three years old, Prebisch absorbed this regime of seventeen-hour days without evident stress. Nevertheless he insisted on three ground-rules when he celebrated his birthday on 19 April with a dinner for the Latin delegates: no discussion of UNCTAD, Fidel, or the Brazilian coup that had brought a military regime to power three weeks earlier and sent Furtado and other associates into exile. Prebisch and Che sat together, exchanging Argentine jokes. Adelita found Che's eyes captivating. "Dangerous eyes," Raúl commented. To his surprise Che sent Prebisch a photograph with his note of thanks, which Raúl kept on his desk in Santiago until his death.

As May approached, Prebisch's team noticed some room for manoeuvre as the much-anticipated East-West confrontation at UNCTAD I failed to materialize. East European countries, led by Hungary and Romania, openly refused to accept Moscow's leadership in international trade: it no longer even headed a "bloc." Worse, few developing countries beyond India saw "East-South" trade as a priority compared with Western markets, and even the East Europeans focused on future trade opportunities with OECD countries. Moscow itself seemed as uncomfortable with the G-77 as Group B, and the lavish banquets thrown for Prebisch during his tour only magnified Moscow's international parsimony: it would give "moral" support to the G-77 but had no intention of offering additional financial or commercial resources to compensate for centuries of Western colonialism. The Soviet Union had been in effect marginalized from the very outset of UNCTAD preparations, with progressively waning influence and now was reduced to sporadic eruptions of temper or routine demands for a new ITO to replace GATT.

With superpower rivalry no longer a serious factor, attention shifted to flexibility within the OECD and G-77 groups. Although the US and West Germany were implacably firm, other countries appeared more flexible. The UK and Sweden – like George Woods – were prepared to consider supplementary financing mechanisms and even trade preferences for developing countries: Prebisch looked to Edward Heath, shuttling between London and Geneva, as his main interlocutor within Group B, but both Belgium and the Netherlands were also committed to finding common ground.[46] In Asia, Australia was noticeably more open to G-77 positions than Japan – the single greatest disappointment for the developing countries – which sided with the US on every major point (except for its endorsement of the creation of an Asian development bank). Agricultural trade (commodities) was more sensitive, with Paris and Washington disagreeing fundamentally on approach. France's "Organization of Markets," the so-called Baumgartner-Pisani Plan, proposed that primary producers in developing countries should be treated like the agricultural sector in the developed world, with prices set higher than long-term levels. In effect, consumers in developed countries would be paying to stabilize Third World export earnings as France was already doing for Madagascar and several other African countries. The French plan proposed a global extension of its farm-income parity scheme for these ex-colonies. The US opposed this indirect price-support system in favour of directly subsidizing its own agricultural producers, and Washington's skepticism about international commodity agreements was so virulent as to rule out major advances in this area in Geneva. A major new international accord on, say, cocoa or sugar was simply impossible, although the deliberations of Committee 1 did provide a basis for negotiations in future years.

And so the five committees plodded on. Certain areas of agreement were identified and resolutions adopted by the end of May, but they tended mostly to be of secondary interest, or useful only in setting the agenda for future negotiations. Some recommendations were noteworthy: explicit endorsement of "South-South" trade (among developing countries), shipping conference reforms, provisions to assist land-locked countries, Western countries' support of regional integration, and so forth. But these results fell far short of expectations. The Prebisch Report had listed specific policies of international economic cooperation to close the trade gap: international commodity agreements, tariff preferences for Third World exports of manufactures, greater market access for primary products, expanded intra-Third World trade, new trade initiatives with Soviet Bloc countries, and new supplementary financing mechanisms to compensate for unexpected export shortfalls. All were too radical for Group B. No formula for international commodity market organization was acceptable: the common denominator for Group B was a case-by-case approach, with minimum government interference in the workings of each individual commodity market. Regarding exports of manufactured goods, the lowering of tariff barriers would also have to be negotiated on a case-by-case basis, and only within GATT – not in a UN forum like UNCTAD. As for the proposed GSP (Generalized System of Preferences), it was considered broadly acceptable in concept but "more study" would be required before any implementation, even partial, could be envisaged. The concepts of new complementary or supplementary financing mechanisms would have to await post-conference "study" before anything concrete could be considered. Even changes in terms and conditions of international loans, whether public or private, would have to await such "further study" by the IMF and World Bank. There were no new initiatives to emerge on the financing of intra-Third World trade, nor on G-77 trade with COMECON countries. There was total stalemate on every important substantive issue. Interlocutor states – Belgium and Switzerland for Group B, and Yugoslavia for the G-77 – had made no headway in such an arena of confrontation. A corridor joke was that, for developed countries in both West and East, "UNCTAD" was understood to mean "Under No Circumstances Take Any Decisions."

Instead the Conference was polarizing between Group B and the G-77 as each group realized that its common interests outweighed short-term internal disagreements. This was easier for the industrialized countries. Despite certain differences of opinion on whether Prebisch's proposed trade policy for development was unduly dirigiste or market-unfriendly, Group B countries agreed to disagree over their differences and accept the US lead. They were clearly very worried that the projected $20 billion trade gap would be used to justify Third World demands after the Conference ended. Likewise, for all the internal whining, there was simply too much to lose by breaking ranks: in the end they shared a partnership of proven value, forged since 1945 and symbolized by their OECD Secretariat in Paris. Trade irritants could be managed; they were no threat to the underlying unity of purpose shared in the success story of the Atlantic Alliance and postwar US-European-Japan trade and economic relations. Agreement on the new Kennedy Round in the GATT to be officially launched on 4 May 1964 was all they needed for the expansion of world trade. Nor were the much-discussed US-French differences all that obvious in practice. The French "organization of markets," when broken down into understandable terms, looked surprisingly like US policy toward Central America, with the French ex-colonial African dictators at Geneva playing the part of US clients like Anastasio Somoza of Nicaragua.

The situation confronting the G-77 was much more challenging because these countries came to Geneva with no more than rhetorical solidarity. Valuable as this had been in the UN General Assembly in getting UNCTAD approved, Geneva required actual coordination and cooperation to maintain this unity, and differences within the G-77 went far deeper than among the industrialized countries: size, culture, levels of development, security interests, political ideologies and so forth. Despite the Declaration of Algiers a year earlier the odds for success were low. Some animosities were predictable. To snub Israel for its invasion during the 1956 Middle East War, Conference President El Khaissani of UAR (Egypt) refused to invite its delegation for the opening G-77 dinner in Geneva, a move that cost Cairo the entire bill since UN-funded events did not permit the exclusion of any member state. (In practice Israel played an active role at the conference.) Latin America and Africa faced different challenges and were in some respects rivals. The countries of the former were more developed, with diversified economies requiring markets for manufactured goods and a legacy of autonomy in central bank and monetary policy. The African sub-Saharan states were newly independent and mainly agricultural producers with large subsistence sectors: industrialization lay in the future. The ex-colonial francophone states in Africa, with the exception of Guinea and Mali, were Paris-centric to the point of retaining the franc and refusing separate national currencies.[47] If these differences were not enough, eighteen African states and Madagascar had a special link with Europe – the Yaoundé Convention of July 1963 providing them with a mixture of aid and trade concessions to maintain close ties with Europe. Africa (and Europe) could therefore pursue a two-track trade policy at UNCTAD, while Latin America lacked such privileged ties with either the US or Europe.[48]

But unity was achieved, the most valuable outcome of the Geneva Conference, with the three UN Regional Commissions ECA, ECAFE, and ECLA playing essential support roles.[49] During the first month of the conference the developing countries gradually began to consult regularly though their separate regional groupings – Africa, Asia, and Latin America. As these talks matured, mechanisms for regular consultation became formalized; conflict resolution procedures to harmonize differences and permit unified proposals to the developed countries were approved. And once the G-77 had developed a pattern of collaboration, its members realized that solidarity was their main weapon in these negotiations. "The unity of the developing countries has now been more or less institutionalised," Krishnamurti wrote on 29 May as the conference entered its final stages, "and they are fully alive to the imperative need for preserving and strengthening this unity in the interest of economic development."[50]

Unfortunately this growing unity within the G-77 and Group B aggravated the impasse for Prebisch and his team because growing internal cohesion in both camps made them increasingly unwilling to compromise.[51] Prebisch and his team watched the evolving paralysis and the diminishing possibilities of success. Would it end in nothing more than a flowery communiqué? The mammoth meetings droned on and on; frustration mounted on all sides as deadlock emerged everywhere. By now the conference was nearly chaotic with private caucuses taking control of its activities. A newly arrived Indian diplomat tried to make conversation with Prebisch in a crowded elevator of the Palais. "Are you part of this zoo?" he asked. "Yes," Raúl replied, "I am the ring-master."

Prebisch had to achieve something concrete, not just a string of resolutions requesting "further study," and the one area where significant movement was possible involved the institutional question. Proposals from the Afro-Asians, Latin Americans, and the Western powers had been debated to a standstill. Meanwhile the developing countries had produced a unified document, while the Western countries were revising their previous paper. Deadlock meant that Committee 4 faced failure. The crux of the matter was whether UNCTAD would remain a mere single event (with existing UN organizations and GATT responsible for implementing its recommendations); or whether an entirely new and autonomous UN body should be created, geared specifically to the link between trade and development. It was clear, both within and outside the conference, that "success" or "failure " would depend on how this issue would be resolved.

By this time Group B's position on UNCTAD had evolved: they no longer opposed the creation of a new international trade entity under UN auspices and were willing to consider a new "Centre" or "Institute" that would report to ECOSOC and be managed by DESA in New York. Mosak had suggested this option to Prebisch back in February 1963 at the beginning of the Preparatory Committee, and it was really no surprise that it should emerge as the Group B "final offer." ECOSOC was tame; DESA was directed by a Frenchman and managed by an American; and Washington was close to New York for appropriate monitoring. This was clearly not enough for the G-77. Criticism of GATT was their rallying cry: they demanded a far more independent body with its own staff and budget, and not located in New York.

On 2 June the G-77 countries brought the central problem of the conference – the implacable adversarial relationship with Group B – into the open by sponsoring a resolution in Committee 4 and thereby forcing a vote that passed easily, given their greater numbers. In response the Western countries warned them that the issue of institutional machinery had to be negotiated rather than forced through by a majority vote, that they would oppose it in plenary and refuse to support or participate in any new body even if the secretary-general decided to establish it. Only two weeks remained before the end of the conference, and disaster loomed for UNCTAD.[52]

Media attention, dormant for weeks, suddenly revived with the scent of crisis in the air. Journalists flooded back to Geneva in waves reminiscent of the conference opening. In a last-ditch effort Prebisch inviting selected representatives of both developed and developing countries to his Parc de Budé apartment on 3 June for private discussions. For ten days straight they met all day, from morning to late night, to find a workable compromise. Adelita organized food and refreshments. The marathon negotiation resembled the last stages of a bitter management-labour dispute, with the same strategy of exhausting both sides until they would finally accept a compromise position. The eight delegations were the US, the UK, and France as the key Group B countries, with Pakistan and Nigeria from the G-77. Yugoslavia was represented by Stanovnik, the able chair of Committee 4, and Belgium and Switzerland played a similar interlocutor role. From time to time Prebisch invited delegates from India, Uruguay, and Ethiopia, but the Soviet Union was not part of this delicate negotiation. Not even Dell and Malinowski were present: Prebisch selected only one advisor, the infinitely discreet Krishnamurti, master of UN institutional intricacies, to remain at his side for the marathon session. Krishnamurti had worked at ECAFE with C.V. Narisiham, U Thant's capable *chef de cabinet*; ultimately U Thant would have to approve the arrangement worked out in the Parc du Budé negotiations, and Philippe de Seynes was increasingly concerned about G-77 insistence on an UNCTAD separate from, and with greater powers than, his DESA. De Seynes lurked and Narisiham mediated.

The protagonists were Richard Gardner, Washington's amiable and capable US negotiator, squaring off against the equally agile and agreeable

Amjad Ali, Pakistani delegate and chair of the G-77 at this stage, who worked from the diplomatic advantage of requiring a deal that he could sell to his mobilized constituency in a ratification vote. Washington wanted an agreement, Gardner insisted, but a fair one where the great trading nations of Group B would not be at the mercy of the G-77 as in voting in the UN General Assembly. The top six or seven countries accounted for 70 percent of global trade; they could hardly be expected to accept a majority vote in a "one country, one vote" system demanded by the developing countries. Acceptable governing body models like the IMF and World Bank would go a long way to allay Group B fears of a possible "tyranny by majority"; Gardner therefore suggested a "dual vote" system where issues of substantial importance would require majorities of both Group B and the G-77. Ali could only respond that the G-77 viewed the issue of "one country, one vote" as vital to their national sovereignty, and the "dual vote" of Gardner was no more than the proverbial velvet glove over an iron fist: the IMF and World Bank were precisely the models most opposed by the G-77. Nor would developing countries settle for another ineffective ECOSOC body of the Mosak-de Seynes variety. Watching and listening, with Adelita catering meal after meal, at one point draining the nearby supermarket of its soda water and tonic, Prebisch wondered what on Earth would come of it all and realized after a week that he would have to break the deadlock to avoid collapse.

Prebisch and Krishnamurti therefore drafted a new and unofficial working document for the Parc du Budé group, the so-called "Prebisch Paper" (as opposed to his *Report of the Secretary General*). The key points built on the formula he had been considering ever since his September 1963 around-the-world trip with Dell and Pollock; only a compromise formula would bridge the gap between the G-77 and the developed market economies, and it would have to include three elements: regular conferences every three or four years like UNCTAD I, where the entire global trading community could assemble; the creation of a trade and development board as a standing committee drawn from the groups on a representative basis and to meet regularly between conferences; and a new and separate secretariat, located outside DESA (preferably outside New York) and reporting directly to the UN secretary-general. Prebisch had endured a confrontation with de Seynes at a secret meeting in Paris, brokered by U Thant, to finalize a compromise on the relative hierarchical relationship between the proposed new trade secretariat and DESA. The agreement reflected Prebisch's demand that the secretariat have "a separate budget and full autonomy" subject to the condition that UNCTAD would be "an integral part of the entire United Nations Secretariat." Its secretary-general would "make arrangements as appropriate, in consultation with all the officials concerned, to integrate the work of the continuing secretariat with the total work of the United Nations in this field" but would be appointed directly by the UN secretary-general and responsible to him rather than to DESA or ECOSOC. U Thant sent de Seynes a copy of his letter to Raúl via Narisiham: "My dear Philippe," it began, "I hope you will find it satisfactory." De Seynes fumed over the accord negotiated behind his back, which accepted Prebisch's demand for autonomy, but Raúl could not have gone back to the G-77 with anything less.[53]

To bridge the Gardner-Ali divide, Prebisch recommended that the group system of negotiations be established on a permanent basis, together with a special form of conflict resolution: a conciliation process could be invoked by any group before voting on any action that might "substantially affect" the economic or financial interests of particular countries. Gardner could live with this, but the G-77 would have to accept a watering-down of their insistence on "one country, one vote" decision-making. On the other hand the developing countries would get an independent secretariat with a privileged position in the UN hierarchy. Ali realized this was the best the G-77 could get; like Prebisch he saw that it was the only realistic alternative. Negotiations now centred on the details of the conciliation process and the role and composition of the new UNCTAD Trade and Development Board. Edward Heath arrived from London at the last moment and told Gardner that he was much less pessimistic than the US delegation. The entire Parc du Budé group thereupon endorsed a package over final dinner, tired but jubilant, with only days remaining. Group B and the socialist countries (Group D) accepted the plan, and Prebisch requested Ali to call a plenary meeting of the developing countries in Groups A and C, where he could report proudly on the "successful compromise" achieved in the final negotiations and receive their ratification.

Prebisch was in a triumphant mood when he met the G-77: the enormous effort of his staff and his consultations and proddings over countless meetings and dinners, had delivered. But instead of congratulations he was confronted by an overflowing and hostile audience. For the first time Prebisch faced open resistance from important segments of the G-77 in a tumultuous meeting. Third World countries had come to UNCTAD I with high expectations. Many, especially from Africa, had just emerged from decades of bitter political and military fighting against colonialism, and they would face bleak economic prospects unless major international assistance was forthcoming from UNCTAD. Many G-77 delegates had little international conference experience and did not have an OECD-type secretariat to help them prepare for such complex and give-and-take negotiations. For some newly emerging nations there was still a strong belief in revolutionary experiments, and the word "compromise" was not in their political lexicon. Many very poor countries had invested a great deal of scarce money in expensive Geneva during the three months of UNCTAD I and expected something concrete in return. "They were," as one staff member recounted, "like a group of tired soldiers under the leadership of a seasoned general, being asked to storm a heavily fortified hill. Halfway up the hill however, the general suddenly orders his troops to stop. Why? Because they had achieved a successful compromise."[54]

Given the force of his personality and with the conference deadline looming, Prebisch carried the day against the more radical G-77 elements. He rejected charges that the compromise was undemocratic, that it restored a de facto Group B veto over UNCTAD. He insisted that consensus, rather than confrontation, was the only viable approach to the reform of global trade and development policy. The Latin American group accepted this explanation and voted with him in a bloc. Egypt and Nigeria, together with India and Pakistan, rallied most of the countries in Africa and Asia to him. Even so the fragility of the G-77 was obvious and worrying: it could only counterbalance the superior resources of the OECD if it remained united. But on the last day the divisions apparent in the ratification meeting were healed by a final declaration of the entire G-77, drafted by Gamani Corea and adopted unanimously in a dramatic show of cohesion as UNCTAD I ended in success.

It was an unusual and paradoxical finale. If the conference was a "success," it was because of Prebisch's skill as a negotiator. Whereas at the beginning of UNCTAD I, Prebisch had appeared to Group B as a radical ideologue, at the end of the conference he had emerged as a pragmatic compromiser. It was, after all, Prebisch who almost single-handedly forced the radical G-77 elements into a compromise with Group B on the central issue of UNCTAD's future organizational structure. His global image, although resting on a precarious base, had been substantially strengthened.

"For all its frustrations, the Geneva exercise could still be of historic significance," the skeptical *Economist* noted in an unusually positive follow-up editorial on 6 June 1964. "Prebisch and the countries he represents are no longer outsiders. A new force is the emerging leadership of the poor. Some delegates from the developing countries, and Dr Prebisch himself, are a match for the best the industrial countries can put up ... As the likely head of the new UN trade secretariat, Dr Prebisch will have his foot in the door and he is not one to take it out again."

18 The Gospel of don Raúl

After the triumph, the closing of the conference meant packing and farewells. Staff dispersed recounting the bittersweet memories of UNCTAD I. Dell, Malinowski and Cordovez returned to DESA at UN headquarters, Krishnamurti to Bangkok, Pollock to Washington. As yet UNCTAD was only a UN proposal, without a budget or organization, and therefore without personnel. Most of the Prebisch team hoped to return after UNCTAD received General Assembly approval in autumn 1964 as expected, but for now they were going back to the their regular jobs, with some – like Malinowski with Mosak in New York – particularly unhappy. Prebisch would obviously be named UNCTAD's first secretary-general, and there was so little doubt that the new organization would be in Geneva that he was offered, and accepted, Villa La Pelouse on the Palais grounds in Geneva as an official residence. Adelita prepared the move from Chile.

Prebisch walked the long shoreline road of Lake Geneva to the vineyards of La Cote to break the UNCTAD routine, but disengagement from the last fifteen months of intensive work – despite its undoubted success – brought little peace or comfort. An urgent, personal, agenda loomed: nothing less than a new family with Eliana Diaz and a son (Raúl Jr) born in December 1963 as Raúl was completing his UNCTAD *Report to the Secretary General.* Prebisch's new situation provoked dismay in New York, and only his closest intimates were informed. U Thant and de Seynes, who was furious, advised that the UN could not tolerate a scandal at this delicate stage of UNCTAD; if it became public knowledge UNCTAD would not survive. To be openly (if discreetly) gay, like de Seynes, was tolerable; to conceive a child outside of a highly popular marriage was not. Despite the success of the Geneva Conference, the UN insisted that Prebisch's divided loyalties remain hidden to protect the evolution of UNCTAD in its formative years.

Raúl's secret life had finally caught up with him. Strictly monogamous until 1949, the Havana Conference, which launched his UN career, had ignited an insistent sexual appetite that became known, lamented, or tolerated during the subsequent Santiago years. Adelita's loyalty never wavered; "I became aware that what Raúl was doing was so important that I could not help but dedicate all my energy to assist him," she observed.[1] To his friends this side of Prebisch's personality seemed inconsistent and inexplicable, but the behaviour itself was a fact and it never interfered with his work. Yet in all these years there was no hint of pregnancies with sexual partners, just as Adelita had remained childless. Prebisch had come to know Eliana in Santiago, and the relationship had continued in Washington. When she became pregnant and moved to New York, some people questioned the paternity, but Prebisch had no doubts, thanking good fortune for the gift of a healthy son at age sixty-two. Bodil Royem, his secretary in Washington, agreed to assist Eliana in New York; the secret was maintained, while Raúl galvanized his team for Geneva.

The problem was what to do now, after Geneva, since the new UNCTAD was intended for Europe rather than New York. Adelita had seen him through the conference and would reside with him in the Villa La Pelouse, while Eliana and the baby would be in the apartment at 340 64th Street in New York. Maintaining these two households would require a transatlantic shuttle with the constant threat of discovery and scandal; Washington would come to know, certainly, since the CIA was certain to (and did) insert a highly placed source in UNCTAD. It also required funds beyond his UN salary, and therefore he took a $25,000 mortgage on El Maqui, for which Adelita had to sign. Only the inner core – Malinowski, Dell, Krishnamurti, Pollock, Jorge Viteri – understood the logistical complexity: bringing Raúlito to Geneva would resemble an intelligence operation. Altogether it was a humiliating situation, maintaining a secret family existence of unknown duration – very much like his father's, he might have mused. Nor was it clear how long so determined and capable a woman as Eliana Diaz would put up with this covert parentage in a foreign land. Above all, one part of Prebisch's life would remain concealed and potentially turbulent as he returned to New York to establish UNCTAD – a cause, he believed, of generational significance and one to which he was fully committed.

Turning to UNCTAD, Prebisch knew that success depended on moving forward quickly, exploiting the momentum of UNCTAD I to build a strong secretariat from the deliberately vague wording of the Geneva Final Act. But now a completely unexpected and different crisis intervened: ILPES, his Santiago institute, was under threat – indeed its very existence was suddenly in question. The new military government of Brazil notified him that it was blocking IDB funding for ILPES; without that funding his staff in Santiago could not be paid. Prebisch left at once for Brasilia to meet Roberto Campos, Goulart's ex-ambassador in Washington promoted by the military coup to Castelo Branco's minister of planning, to defuse the emergency. Uncontrollably pro-US even before the coup, his immediate defection and endorsement of the dictatorship, and now his key appointment in Brasilia, made Campos an even more formidable favourite and insider in Washington. The threat to cut IDB funding for ILPES was therefore credible: Brazil could count on US support. And much more was at stake than the institute: Brazil was a critical G-77 leader in UNCTAD whose support before and after Geneva had been essential for its approval – and for its continuing progress. Brazil, under military rule or not, was a global and regional power, and Prebisch would need its active support more than ever in building UNCTAD. Campos knew this as well.

Campos explained why he would oppose the institute with all the means at his disposal. During the Geneva Conference, while Prebisch was struggling for the survival of UNCTAD, ILPES had given refuge to Celso Furtado, Fernando Henrique Cardoso, Francisco Weffort, and other prominent exiles from the Brazilian military coup. This was bad enough, but ILPES's management in Santiago went further by approving a development seminar beginning 3 June in which the Brazilians – particularly Furtado and Fernando Henrique – had leadership roles and were directly criticizing Castelo Branco's new model of capitalism.[2] They were leftists and partisan, and such activities were out of order for a UN organization, Campos insisted, particularly one with a mandate to give advice on planning to Latin governments. ILPES, in short, had insulted Brazil.

The actual events surrounding the ILPES Development Seminar were more complex. Furtado was, with José Medina, co-organizer of the weekly initiative on succeeding Wednesdays, but it went far beyond a response to the Brazilian military coup. Instead the seminar featured a long overdue review of ECLA's original texts in light of recent experience throughout Latin America as a whole. The fact that the participants were younger and not from the founding generation gave the initiative additional importance, and it was a stellar group of young economists indeed. On his first appearance at the seminar after his arrival from Geneva, and listening to the quality of debate – the Brazilian contingent having added both scholarly strength and personal commitment – Prebisch beamed with satisfaction: here was the core of a first-rate institute indeed.

It was readily apparent that the old ECLA doctrine required revision. Profound changes in the region had occurred since the 1949 Havana *Manifesto*, not least the growing importance of multinational corporations.

Although the term itself had not yet been invented, their role in production, technology, and trade in Latin America was increasingly apparent. MNCs also challenged Prebisch's original concept of centre-periphery relations: for sociologist Fernando Henrique Cardoso, this powerful corporate presence meant that the "centre" had moved directly into the "periphery," but Latin America was more dependent than ever and even less capable of incorporating the marginalized inside a democratic system. The 1964 Brazilian coup was key to understanding this so-called "internationalization of the internal market," he argued, because the new "national security" state introduced by General Castelo Branco and Roberto Campos demonstrated the new combination of open markets, repression, and a minimal state. It was not just another military takeover: instead it heralded many similar authoritarian experiments in Latin America. In light of these developments ECLA's early faith in industrialization as the answer to development should be critically reviewed, and Santiago researchers should expand their disciplinary tool-kit in exploring Latin dependency on the centres: MNCs were redefining and expanding international economic relations, profoundly affecting consumer choices, class formation, political parties, and civil society, not to mention the role of Washington evident in the Brazil coup.

The crisis was touchy and took time to resolve. Campos understood very well that ILPES was supposed to be autonomous rather than a creature of governments, but he also knew where the Development Seminar was headed and was determined to terminate research on multinational corporations, which would examine corporate-elite underpinnings of the new Latin military dictatorships. He proposed a deal. Explaining to Prebisch that the institute's relations with the Brazilian exiles had been "an error of judgement" committed by Cristóbal Lara, he put the blame on Prebisch's absence during the final climactic phase of UNCTAD 1. "When you were at the helm of the Institute such issues would never have occurred," he noted. "I will give instructions to my representative at the IDB that he support the Institute, but with one condition: that you promise to return to the Institute."[3]

Eventually a solution was found. Prebisch agreed to remain secretary-general of ILPES during UNCTAD and to return after he completed his term, and Furtado's edited papers from the Development Seminar were quietly shelved. Campos knew perfectly well that Prebisch would hire whom he wished, but he also knew that he would henceforth keep a close watch on institute activities. Brazil restored its support for ILPES in the IDB; Furtado left for Yale; Fernando Henrique Cardoso remained in the institute working with Chilean Enzo Faletto; and Prebisch detailed

Benjamin Hopenhayn to inform him blow-by-blow of institute activities.[4] Overall the decision to remain director general of ILPES was problematic: the UNCTAD challenge alone exceeded even Prebisch's enormous capacity for work; and the fragile institute needed the full-time and dedicated direction of a resident director to establish its identity without the additional political baggage of Geneva.

De Seynes was frosty when Prebisch returned from Santiago. Neither he nor Mosak was happy that he had out-bargained them at UNCTAD I, and every detail of the new organization would have to be negotiated under their scrutiny. Progress was bound to be slow, and summer holidays were approaching. On 29 July de Seynes wrote and complained to the secretary-general that "discussions with Raúl on setting up his secretariat – its functions, staff and location – remain hazy." He then left to spend the entire summer in France, so that Prebisch was not able to present the draft of his proposed new organization to U Thant until late October 1964.

While they were personal friends, de Seynes and Prebisch were also professional adversaries in this UN war; an inevitable confrontation was approaching. The secretariat Prebisch had in mind would be larger and more independent than DESA and its Group B allies had envisaged at Geneva; he rejected dependence or any kind of subordination to DESA. UNCTAD had to be "independent in the sense of being able to take full responsibility, under the UN Secretary General [not under DESA], for servicing the conference, the TDB [Trade and Development Board]and subsidiary bodies," requiring a separate budget and "full autonomy, subject to the usual financial rules and procedures of the United Nations," together with its own Research and Projections Office and Trade Policy Division. In practical terms this meant transferring positions and budget from DESA to the new UNCTAD.

De Seynes rejected this conception of UNCTAD and fought back when he returned to New York on 31 October. Taking the offensive, he complained to U Thant of "lack of consultation," accusing Prebisch of threatening "a *de facto* situation of apartheid." He charged that a "structure such as the one proposed by Dr Prebisch ... will have a depressing, perhaps even devastating effect in other parts of the Secretariat working in closely related fields and requiring comparable skills and assistance." The UNCTAD Secretariat must be "an *integral part* of a single United Nations Secretariat and its work as an *integral component* of the total work of the United Nations in the economic and social field." Raising the familiar spectre of "duplication of services in the UN system," he demanded that UNCTAD should be smaller and use DESA's existing programs.[5] Prebisch countered de Seynes, appealing to the secretary-general that, yes, the "integration" of UNCTAD into the UN Secretariat was vital, but this did not go beyond consultation and coordination: "it means interdependence but not dependence or any kind of subordination ... the intellectual monopoly implied in Mr De Seynes's memorandum is not admissible."[6]

U Thant agreed; so far Prebisch was winning. But de Seynes counterattacked by stacking the UN budget committee with allies to slash Prebisch's budget; Raúl rallied delegates from twenty-five key developing country allies in New York to intervene directly with the secretary-general over the heads of de Seynes and Mosak. Led by Brazil and India the G-77 delegation was successful in restoring the budget, and with this victory Prebisch succeeded in wrenching trade and development out of DESA.[7]

Celebrations, however, were premature. Key staff selected by Prebisch were under existing contracts in DESA, and de Seynes and Mosak weakened UNCTAD by refusing or delaying transfers. Here they had a clear advantage since Prebisch had to get UNCTAD under way while DESA could stall forever. Raúl needed Dell urgently to anchor the new secretariat, but Mosak and de Seynes procrastinated in a new war of attrition, refusing to release him from his work on the new Centre of Industrial Development. Prebisch finally had to go directly to U Thant, but even then DESA kept Dell for another six months, to mid-1965. Prebisch had assumed that all the existing staff would be transferred together with their posts, but Mosak refused, insisting that DESA had the right to pick and choose. The International Trade Relations Section headed by Percival Judd and Commodity Studies Section directed by Reginald Smith of South Africa were clearly units within UNCTAD's mandate, but Mosak disbanded the Commodities Studies Section to keep its senior staff, arguing that they formed "something of a task force" for him to deal with general purposes. He tried to unload two particularly unqualified political appointees from Britain and the Soviet Union. "If they [DESA] had the right to select I have the same right and I refuse to accept G and K," Raúl bellowed.[8]

While generally prevailing in the struggle to protect his autonomy within the UN system, he had accepted compromises on key provisions rather than risk derailing the whole project. Agreeing to two meetings each year of the unwieldy fifty-four-member country Trade and Development Board (in New York and Geneva respectively) implied a huge burden for the new secretariat when combined with its already huge work program and preparing a massive conference on the scale of UNCTAD I every four years.[9]

UN politics intruded at every turn. Regional balance was essential, but difficult to achieve in practice, particularly from newly independent African states, which were entering the United Nations at the rate of ten a year with few professional economists available to fill the many offers from international organizations.[10] Moscow insisted that Prebisch hire a Soviet nominee to balance the (somewhat more qualified) CIA informer from West Germany already under contract. Prebisch, with U Thant's support, proposed Malinowski for the position of director of coordination, given the size and complexity of UNCTAD. Everyone seemed to agree at first – the G-77 and the UN budget committee – until Washington demanded another deputy secretary-general for Group B, preferably from Europe, on grounds of North-South balance. Britain concurred. It was, in fact, a good idea since Malinowski was identified with the G-77, and UNCTAD required a bridge to the OECD countries. Prebisch agreed and promptly identified two suitable Scandinavian candidates, but, in one of its rare initiatives, Moscow demanded a third deputy secretary-general from Eastern Europe for East-West balance. The USSR was adamant: either scrap the US-British proposal or appoint Czechoslovakia's deputy minister of foreign trade as Prebisch's deputy; the appointment of a West European, it argued, would be "unjust and contrary to the principle of equal treatment of various groups of countries." Not even Finland could be considered a "neutral" country. Confronting the certainty of an unmanageable troika in his office, Prebisch dropped the position altogether, weakening UNCTAD's future effectiveness. No matter how many hours he worked, Prebisch simply could not manage the large and complex UNCTAD agenda without a permanent deputy like Malinowski, with his G-77 linkages and infectious energy.[11]

A final and unexpected obstacle surfaced in May 1965 over the location of UNCTAD's permanent headquarters, assumed from the beginning to be Geneva, with the finance division remaining in New York under Dell's direction, since that subject needed constant contact with Washington. But on May 10 Director P. Spinelli of the UN's European Office reported that the Canton of Geneva opposed another international organization in their city because outsiders were driving up the price of land and housing. Additional foreigners, it appeared, would aggravate the "psychological and social problems" faced daily by its hard-pressed inhabitants.[12] Dumbfounded, Prebisch cast about for alternative sites and set up a committee to evaluate offers: Addis, Accra, Rome, Mexico City, Lagos, and London immediately lobbied New York to host the secretariat. When Britain offered a new building in central London, the Swiss Federal Council became alarmed and sent a letter to U Thant on 13 October welcoming the UNCTAD Secretariat to Geneva after all.[13]

At last UNCTAD was in place. For months Prebisch had been virtually alone, rushing back and forth between New York and Geneva, where a skeletal staff worked out of UN headquarters. But progress was made, key positions were filled, and the divisions of UNCTAD began to take shape. Krishnamurti's departure from ECAFE was approved on 22 November 1964. Pollock soon followed from Washington; Malinowski came over as director for international shipping. With a rapidly growing core staff, to reach 175 by 1968, UNCTAD moved into high gear. The teething problems were largely over; complaints about inadequate secretariat work in preparing meetings diminished with adequate staffing.[14] Morale in Geneva was high. Although UNCTAD was unable to match the salaries of the World Bank and IMF, the international response from economists was strong as UNCTAD became a principal cause for an idealistic generation. When Adelita arrived in Geneva, and the official residence at La Pelouse opened to guests, UNCTAD had become the most exciting international experiment since World War II.

Prebisch and de Seynes put the bureaucratic struggle behind them and renewed their close personal friendship over dinner at Au Pied du Cochon. De Seynes worried that UNCTAD's relationship with GATT was still undefined; Wyndham-White had publicly endorsed a division of labour between their two organizations at Geneva, clearly stating (for example) that Prebisch had responsibility for commodity agreements. But this commitment was not in writing, he warned. Bull-necked Wyndham-White was English, but he was definitely not a gentleman.

Prebisch believed UNCTAD had to lead; he rejected from the outset UNCTAD as merely a sounding board or "forum for discussion." Instead he wanted an organization with substance, one that could undertake negotiations to arrive at practical solutions. UNCTAD was set up to rethink and recast the rules-of-the-game in international trade, leading the campaign for a world economic order with less unequal power relationships. Prebisch was not neutral, just as the IMF, World Bank, and the GATT were not neutral. If these established bodies defended the interests of developed countries, UNCTAD would be unapologetic in promoting new rules to benefit the Third World.

The problem was that Prebisch lacked power. His permanent secretariat in Geneva could lead with vision, ideas, and proposals for change, but he could not command the compliance of governments. International agreements could only be reached if North and South, the G-77, and Group B kept lines open and worked together. But if UNCTAD could only succeed by persuasion and moral pressure, Prebisch believed that people everywhere, including the developed countries where governments remained skeptical, would support his vision once they were correctly informed of the facts – once they understood the huge stakes involved and the minimal sacrifices needed today to achieve global equity, compared with the future economic and security benefits of a more equitable and peaceful world. Prebisch sensed a surge of support after UNCTAD I, and he was not alone in noticing that the language of international development was already subtly changing: the "trade gap" of Prebisch's report to UNCTAD I, widely rejected at the conference as vague nonsense, was already entering the day-to-day vocabulary in Washington as a cornerstone of mainstream analysis.[15]

But the G-77 was impatient for actual results rather than a new vocabulary; expectations were high, and Prebisch had to deliver concrete accomplishments from the UNCTAD I agenda to maintain its support, and nearly eighteen months had gone by since Geneva. But there were, in fact, few possibilities for early and dramatic success. At UNCTAD I, the four big categories for action had been identified: commodities; manufactures; financing related to trade; and invisibles and international shipping. No agreements had been reached in any of these areas at Geneva, given their complexity once it became clear that lengthy negotiations would be required, and the main committees of the new UNCTAD secretariat were set up to continue work on them after 1964. But the only candidates for immediate action were in commodities and financing, more specifically negotiating an international commodity agreement (ICA) for cocoa; and a supplementary financing mechanism (SFM) led by the World Bank to stabilize export revenues of developing countries. Both concepts had been raised for years in the General Assembly and the GATT with limited success. Commodity agreements regulating markets in agricultural products and metals to ensure fair and stable prices would protect producers against boom-and-bust cycles; since these products dominated the trade of Third World countries they were of overwhelming concern. In supplementary financing, the World Bank also aimed at reducing trade vulnerability by compensating developing countries for unexpected shortfalls in export earnings. Without such a scheme the best development plans supported by the most dedicated and non-corrupt government would still be destroyed by sudden price instability entirely outside their control. "The scheme," a senior World Bank official explained, "in fact tries to help countries to carry out their medium-term plans and to avoid a downward revision of targets."[16] The obstacles facing developing countries, which both proposals addressed, were so central that success would demonstrate that UNCTAD could deliver, changing its prospects from a debating shop to a global decision-centre and shoring up G-77 unity behind the secretariat.

As soon the 1964 conference ended, and within the limitations of the secretariat's growing pains, Prebisch began to explore the prospects for an international commodity agreement in cocoa. Initial research turned up favourable prospects, beginning with jurisdictional clarity – the fact that trade negotiations in commodities had long been recognized as a UN (rather than GATT) mandate. Moreover, cocoa more than all other major commodities in world trade such as tin, copper, sugar, coffee, etc., presented the fewest obstacles to early negotiation of an agreement. Unlike sugar, for example, all the major cocoa producers were in the G-77; and there was no competition from producers in developed countries. There was also no Cuban factor to arouse a US political veto; overproduction was not a serious problem; and the demand for cocoa was steadily growing in world markets including the Soviet Bloc countries. Moreover there were relatively few cocoa producers, primarily in Africa, the poorest region, which had the greatest moral claim on priority action in UNCTAD. Within Africa, there were large producers such as Ivory Coast and Ghana, but no one country controlled the market. Finally the G-77 including Latin America was in agreement on proceeding with a cocoa agreement, avoiding intraregional rivalry and the ever-present suspicion of a Prebisch bias toward the Americas.

Prebisch asked David Pollock to work with Perce Judd, director of the new commodities division, in designing an international cocoa buffer stock under UNCTAD auspices. "I assume you've read the Old Testament?" he asked. "Do you remember the story of Joseph and the seven lean years and fat? I'd like UNCTAD to be able to carry out buffer stock activities like those of Joseph. But with one difference – we'll need to buy and sell information that doesn't come from God."[17] Alfred Maizels, a UK specialist on buffer stocks, at home in London with his leg in a plaster cast, agreed to join the Geneva team. Together they hired Jan Tinbergen, then an economic consultant in the Netherlands, to construct a simulation model for a cocoa ICA and prepare a cost estimate for the buffer stock pre-financing. Lever Brothers in London had recently solved its own cocoa storage problem by using new kinds of air-conditioned warehouses and had also developed an inexpensive process for converting surplus cocoa beans into margarine. With these pre-negotiation issues resolved, the commodities division set up an expert working group to prepare a cocoa commodity conference in August 1966 to approve in principle the UNCTAD-brokered Cocoa Authority.[18]

But the cocoa conference failed before the implacable opposition of the US and West Germany; instead of victory, Prebisch had to admit defeat in managing primary commodity markets. Washington objected on familiar ideological grounds (global supply management, which it did not control), as well as for financial reasons (Washington rejected UNCTAD's formula for stock financing).[19] Direct private sector interests were also at stake as New York cocoa dealers lobbied hard to maintain this market. Prebisch protested what he saw as the unreasonable positions of Group B countries and their lack of openness to change. He even criticized Washington and Bonn in the UN General Assembly. ("If, in spite of these advantages," Prebisch warned, "it is not possible to reach an agreement on cocoa, I wonder what can be done to fulfil the hopes of the developing countries with regard to other primary commodities?") That, surely, was the main point of Group B resistance to change. A major UNCTAD success would only serve to consolidate its G-77 constituency, leading to other demands, certainly for more international commodity agreements under UNCTAD. Jointly, the Group B countries announced to Prebisch in mid-1966 that they would only accept sugar negotiations under the GATT umbrella.

The initial optimism over a cocoa agreement, and then the dashed hopes, sparked bitter G-77 criticism, particularly from Africa, and increased the stakes for success in negotiating an SFM with the World Bank.[20] The odds here seemed more favourable because in this case, unlike with cocoa, Prebisch had a Washington champion in George D. Woods, the World Bank president. Britain and Sweden had also supported the concept at UNCTAD I, and the Final Act instructed the World Bank to prepare a "draft proposal on supplementary finance measures" for post-conference consideration. Staff began work immediately; by late 1965 the draft report was ready for circulation and George Woods sent the study to UNCTAD as the "basis for a feasible solution to a problem of major importance." He underlined, however, that it was only a staff report. "This study does not purport to represent the views of the Executive Directors of the Bank, or of their governments which appointed or elected them."[21]

The Woods Report was favourably received by both developed and developing countries at the first meeting of UNCTAD's Committee on Financing in December 1965, "evidence," Prebisch remarked, "that the ideas of the first UNCTAD conference were making headway."[22] The World Bank concept linked supplementary financing to performance; there was little criticism from developing countries. Indeed, progress was so rapid that Prebisch opened its next meeting in April 1966 by stating that the proposed World Bank scheme "was an adequate and feasible solution" toward solving the serious problems facing developing countries due to fluctuations in their export earnings. It marked "an important transition of UNCTAD from a forum for discussions to an instrument of action."[23] Delegates overwhelmingly agreed. Only the Soviet Union dissented, but it was completely isolated since all the other Soviet Bloc countries on the committee were interested in participating. Indeed the developing and developed countries found themselves in such agreement that the meeting concluded in three rather than seven days. There was consensus that unexpected export shortfalls should and could be measured by export projections, and the IMF representatives also agreed that it was an interesting and practical solution.[24]

As 1966 ended Prebisch was hopeful that a solution was close. The Trade and Development Board endorsed the proposed supplementary finance agreement; an international agreement seemed assured. Only the work of a joint Group B-G-77 Technical Working Group of the Committee remained to iron out details. Relations between UNCTAD and the World Bank were deepening. Irving Friedman sent Prebisch a New Year's card with personal good wishes.[25] From Santiago Raúl cabled his "warmest regards," adding, "Let me, in light of your excellent report on supplementary finance, express to you my conviction on the important role the International Bank is bound to have in the positive work of UNCTAD."

It was inevitable that Eric Wyndham-White would counterattack, and Prebisch observed his sudden passion for developing countries after 1963 with increasing frustration. It was, however, a compliment to Prebisch. The convening of UNCTAD I and its related mobilization of world opinion had a profound effect on GATT. Already in 1963, anticipating the Geneva conference, Wyndham-White had rushed through a number of first steps to mollify Third World frustration over GATT's exclusive focus on OECD countries, and then attempted to undermine the new competitor by duplicating UNCTAD's mandate. On 4 May 1964, in the midst of UNCTAD I, GATT opened the new "Kennedy Round" of trade negotiations with an elaborate ceremony of sixty-six countries, making the point that G-77 countries formed a majority of members for the first time. On 19 March it followed up with another announcement for a long-promised trade promotion program to woo G-77 leaders from developing countries.[26] In a symbolic gesture, he had his title upgraded from executive director to secretary-general.

After Geneva the GATT intensified its effort to undermine UNCTAD's effectiveness and future evolution. Largely indifferent to trade problems of developing countries in the past, Wyndham-White added a fourth part to GATT's mandate, titled "Trade and Development" – essentially the Final Act of UNCTAD I. Adopted in early 1965 the new Part IV (flush with a committee on trade and development and working groups on commodities, preferences, and the expansion of trade among developing countries) permitted him to move aggressively into UNCTAD's territory. At UNCTAD I Wyndham-White had declared that GATT had no mandate in the field of commodities and no intention of entering it; by 1966 it was heading negotiations on cereals and sugar. European leaders informed Prebisch that they had decided GATT should handle international sugar negotiations; UNCTAD should "avoid duplication" by withdrawing voluntarily from its internationally recognized area of responsibility in favour of GATT.

Wyndham-White's target was not the existence of UNCTAD but rather Prebisch's goal of a negotiating instrument. In general Group B's position on UNCTAD was consistent: it would accept a UN agency for trade policy debates and research; but GATT should wield decision-making authority on international trade and development matters. Using UN imagery, UNCTAD would be the equivalent of the General Assembly whereas GATT would function as the Security Council. In this conception UNCTAD would merely play a supportive and deliberative role, leaving multilateral negotiations to be carried out through a pre-eminent GATT. Tactically Wyndham-White sought alliances with key G-77 states such as India and Brazil, which would determine the success or failure of UNCTAD, exploiting the deep internal fissures among developing countries on international trade policy. Brazil, poised uneasily between North and South, was particularly ripe for wooing after the 1964 military coup. Brazil was turning inward toward a more nationalist conception of its future as a regional leader, like India or China, a continent on its own so to speak. A growing tension with Argentina over the Plate Basin and hydroelectric dams deepened this tendency toward Brazilian exceptionalism rather than regional integration with Hispanic America. As a reflex Itamaraty had never fully accepted the language of G-77 solidarity or considered Brazil as more "South" than "North" after twenty years of rapid economic development. As Azeredo da Silveira, chosen to head the Brazilian mission to UNCTAD II, put it: "We must invade GATT, or UNCTADize GATT, before it GATTizes UNCTAD."[27] While this could mean simply linking trade and development in both forums, it might also imply Brazil using UNCTAD as a global soapbox to achieve its own goals in the GATT. Prebisch called it "playing on two pianos."

"We are witnessing," Prebisch wrote U Thant in March 1967, "a general trend towards enlargement of the field of competence of GATT, in clear duplication of the functions, mandate and activities of UNCTAD ... GATT's competence in the field of policies and practices regarding tariff and non-tariff trade restrictions is quite clear," he argued, but "it is equally clear that UNCTAD is the central organ on all matters of trade in relation to development. This fact should be fully recognized within the United Nations family so that GATT may not present itself as an equal or more competent partner in this field."[28] The issue for Prebisch was not merely territorial – a turf war between two international agencies fighting for recognition and budget. He had always recognized GATT's role in trade negotiations and its efficient secretariat, and he had never tried to undermine it, or criticize the entry of developing countries that were able to profit from trade liberalization focused on the OECD. Prebisch objected to Wyndham-White's approach because of its cynical opportunism, designed to destroy UNCTAD's credibility and bargaining power without a new approach to development or regional integration at all. He was simply picking off selected G-77 countries with targeted concessions, leaving Group B's power and priorities intact. A "new international economic order" would never emerge from GATT; only in 2001 would its successor, the World Trade Organization, mount the so-called Doha Development Round in recognition of developing country issues – and even then to the continuing indifference of northern negotiators and to failure in 2008.

Wyndham-White further strengthened GATT's international standing with the successful conclusion of the Kennedy Round in May 1967. Prebisch congratulated him in a gracious interview published in the *New York Times* on 16 May 1967, noting that, while its trade benefits were marginal for the G-77, it was nevertheless "a considerable step forward in the achievement of a world policy of trade liberalization." Signed by sixty-two governments, as opposed to only twenty-six in the earlier 1962 Dillon Round, it provided for across-the-board tariff reductions of 35–40 percent; it included an anti-dumping agreement (tarnished by its immediate rejection by the US Congress); and it contained an international wheat agreement providing for 4.5 million tons of wheat available to the most needy countries. It also introduced the concept of "special and differential treatment" for developing countries, an important step in international trade agreements. All the major G-77 countries were included (such as Brazil, India and Egypt), and even Yugoslavia had been accepted a year earlier as a "market economy." Not to be outdone, Poland became the first country to accede to GATT as a non-market economy. A rush of applications from the remaining G-77 countries ensued: the next round (Tokyo) of the GATT would comprise 102 members – not far off UNCTAD's membership.

U Thant and Philippe de Seynes agreed to mount a campaign from New York to help shore up UNCTAD's authority within the UN system. All agencies were reminded to recognize its mandate and Prebisch met with Paul Hoffman and de Seynes on 7 April 1967 to draft a letter from the secretary-general that recognized it as the "focal point" for all UN trade-related activities. Hoffman also provided Prebisch with new ammunition: UNDP funding for technical assistance in support of trade promotion. And while Prebisch rejected an imperious invitation from Wyndham-White to form a "joint programming committee" to prepare the UNCTAD II agenda, he demonstrated that UNCTAD sought a mutually beneficial relationship with the GATT by proposing a joint international trade centre in Geneva. Here the two organizations should cooperate as equals rather than fight to avoid duplication of effort; neither GATT nor UNCTAD would have to give up their trade and development prerogatives, and neither had much of an existing program to lose. For once the two rivals agreed. Operational on 1 January 1968, with joint funding by the UN and GATT and in equal partnership, the ITC became by far their most important cooperative achievement and an undeniable success.[29]

Alas for Prebisch, supplementary financing went the way of the cocoa failure in a similar trajectory of initial enthusiasm, stalemate, and defeat. A change of tone from World Bank staff took hold early in the year, picked up by veteran bank economists like Bela Belassa, who noticed deliberate misinformation on supplementary financing in internal memos along with disparaging and dismissive references to UNCTAD.[30] Senior staff also began to distance themselves from UNCTAD using the oldest ruse – claims of superior efficiency. "My concern, frankly," Michael L. Hoffman noted to Burke Knapp on 7 April 1967, "is the number of occasions on which we undertake to make expert staff available to UN or UNCTAD committees and then, because of sloppy chairmanship or some other reason, they sit around wasting their time while the delegates waffle along." Invitations to co-sponsor meetings were routinely turned down.[31] Prebisch had to intervene personally with George Woods to receive World Bank documents previously shared as a matter of course after UNCTAD I. This gradual freezing-out of UNCTAD reflected the more hostile tone of Group B governments and the IMF. France flatly rejected supplementary financing; Washington never liked the scheme; and Britain could no longer be counted on for support. A forceful speech by Prebisch in August 1967, in which he claimed that the IMF, rather than the World Bank or divisions between Group B and the G-77, was the main obstacle to an agreement, gave George Woods an opening to disengage. "An effort must still be made to reconcile the policy of the World Bank with that of the IMF," Prebisch had noted publicly.[32] Stung by what he felt was an embarrassing and unnecessary airing of well-known World Bank-IMF differences in his final months as

World Bank president, and about to be replaced by Robert McNamara at the end of the year, George Woods turned cold; his officials were given clear instructions on future relations with UNCTAD: continuing "moral support," and amicable conversations limited to promises of "further study."[33] All future staff dealings on the subject were to be cleared with Managing Director Burke Knapp. Prebisch's final appeal to Woods two weeks before his departure was unsuccessful; UNCTAD had been frozen out on another key issue, and there was a new coldness in the air.[34] Sidney Dell put his finger on it when he referred to the "strange taint of bilateralism" that was reappearing in world politics. "What has happened," he wondered, "to the economic philosophy of multilateralism which we were always told was an indispensable feature of a rational world?"[35]

The World Bank failure accentuated G-77 complaints about UNCTAD's lack of progress. Over two years had passed since Geneva, with the next conference not too far off; India, which would host UNCTAD II, had surveyed governments to confirm its opening in New Delhi on 5 September 1967. Prebisch was heavily criticized during a mid-term review of UNCTAD's record.[36] Africans attacked him for alleged discrimination in selecting staff; there were sneers of his alleged campaigning to replace U Thant as UN secretary-general and complaints that some recommendations in the 1964 Final Act (such as an economic and social survey of depressed areas within developing countries) had still not been tackled by his overworked secretariat.[37] "The Trade and Development Board is more depressing that ever," a delegate mused, "the LDC's [less developed countries] complain of the lack of accomplishments ... Prebisch is on the defensive ... and the "haves" simply refuse to react."[38] The mood was surly and UNCTAD no longer looked fresh and new. To rally the G-77 and restore confidence Prebisch promised that the "New Delhi Round" would be about actions rather than more talk, not a general conference like UNCTAD I but "a negotiating forum" on development cooperation with representatives coming as plenipotentiaries with authority from their governments to make decisions rather than mere delegates.[39] Only those issues where concrete results could be achieved would be brought to the meeting, with a much leaner agenda than four years earlier in Geneva, and with some agreements either ready for signature or nearly in hand; UNCTAD II, in short, would showcase "a global strategy of development."[40] Privately Group B scorned Prebisch's notion of delegates coming to UNCTAD II as plenipotentiaries and objected to the term "New Delhi Round" for its implicit equation of UNCTAD and the GATT: the Kennedy Round was a true negotiation, while New Delhi would be a mere trade conference.[41] Publicly the OECD countries (despite originally voting for 5 September) demanded that UNCTAD II be postponed until 1 February 1968 to avoid a conflict with the annual meeting of the World Bank and IMF – a poor omen of diminished ranking in the international family.

Group B's tepid acceptance of UNCTAD in 1964 had since declined. Important political changes had taken place; four years earlier in Geneva the superpowers were competitors in North-South relations; now the US was at war in Vietnam with a growing anti-war movement as well as having to cope with inflation, jobs losses, civil rights protests, and approaching presidential elections. The British economy was flagging with unsteady financial markets; French society was rapidly polarizing toward student revolt; and Tokyo was beset with governmental paralysis. How different from 1964, when optimism was running high and the international economy was buoyant! It was as if the easing of the Cold War had been offset by a proliferation of internal woes in the OECD countries. The G-77 was hardly in better shape as UNCTAD II approached.[42] The June 1967 Middle East war was a shock to G-77 unity, with Egypt's humiliating defeat in the brief six-day conflict knocking out a key UNCTAD supporter; Israel's evident superiority of arms and occupation of Arab territories strained international relations as a whole. Unresolved tensions kept flaring up on both sides as the Group system revealed its weakness: a tendency to adopt the positions of their most extreme members to paper over internal disunity.

Nevertheless, all was not gloom as UNCTAD II approached. At Geneva in 1964 Prebisch had proposed a group on preferences at Geneva within the Manufactures Committee to research and design a GSP for developing countries. This concept, unlike international commodity agreements, which sought to regulate the production and trade of basic products to guarantee access and stability of earnings, sought to promote the exports of manufactured and semi-manufactured products through non-reciprocal preferential treatment. Such preferences required Group B countries to recognize the special need of relatively weak infant industries in the Third World by waiving demands for reciprocal rights to market access – in effect giving them an advantage in international trade. The GSP was particularly attractive for the more advanced developing countries like Latin America, and some industrialized countries like Britain and Australia accepted the concept of preferences. But the GATT had long resisted, and as late as August 1966 the UNCTAD secretariat considered it unrealistic to put it on the agenda of the next conference. But as the isolation of the Lyndon Johnson Administration in Washington grew, so did pressure for a change of policy, and Group A (Latin America) scored an unexpected success at the (otherwise disastrous) 12–14 April 1967 Presidents of America Summit at Punta del Este, where Johnson was persuaded to endorse a GSP scheme in international trade negotiations.[43] Thereafter OECD opinion (and with it that of the GATT), evolved during 1967 into agreement in principle to discuss the GSP proposal at New Delhi.

Armed with this new possibility, Prebisch and the UNCTAD team persuaded the G-77 into a unified negotiating position at a ministerial meeting in Algiers in October 1967. Named the *Algiers Charter* and described by the World Bank as "restrained and responsible," it focused on a short agenda headed by commodity trade agreements and supplementary financing; the GSP for trade in manufactured products; recognition of a 1 percent ODA target; and a package of international shipping reforms that the surprisingly effective Wladek Malinowski had prepared for New Delhi.[44] A delegation headed by Brazil left for Western capitals, the World Bank, and the IMF to brief officials on the main features of the package before the opening of UNCTAD II. And in New Delhi preparations were completed on time for a conference much awaited by a government eager to demonstrate its leadership in global affairs.

Opened by Prime Minister Indira Gandhi on 1 February 1968, the elegant inauguration of UNCTAD II in New Delhi could not conceal the sombre mood of the 1,600 delegates from 131 countries and forty-four international organizations. It was the first time ever that a really major UN meeting would be held in the capital of a developing country, and India was determined to host a success. But despite the lavish hospitality in the new Conference Hall on the Curzon Road, built specifically for the event, the gathering lacked the spirit of guarded optimism and commitment of UNCTAD I. Gandhi invoked the promise of Geneva four years earlier, the need for change and the urgency of the global development agenda, and the symbolic importance of meeting in the Third World rather than in the familiar European or North American gathering places. Geneva had been the beginning, she said, but UNCTAD II would mark a watershed in North-South relations. But both superpowers were in poor moods. Moscow faced a serious challenge after Alexander Dubcek took control of the Communist Party in Czechoslovakia on 5 January, threatening its control of Eastern Europe. Only two days before, North Vietnamese forces had launched the Tet Offensive, which ended the Johnson Administration's illusions of military victory in Southeast Asia and galvanized domestic opposition to the war. W.W. Rostow headed a much smaller US delegation than for UNCTAD I (less than a dozen, down from thirty-five). A principal architect of the Vietnam War, he was alternately truculent and withdrawn, both anticipating and sensitive to criticism. Gandhi's appeal for international solidarity was diminished with a media captured by images of blood and bombs rather than economic development.

Prebisch's address to the conference the next day opened with an analogy to the "bad weather" of international problems so evidently on delegates' mind in New Delhi, and therefore the need for both perspective and action. "Optimistic arguments" he noted "have vanished into thin air ... Four years ago there were those who thought the radiation of prosperity from the centres, and the good behavior of the periphery, provided the key to the problem of development. The terms of trade had improved, primary exports were increasing at satisfactory rates, and it was said that the Kennedy Round would offer the peripheral countries great opportunities for the expansion of their trade." Now those hopes were gone, he noted. Financial transfers to developing countries were falling fast, industrialized countries were making increasing use of non-tariff barriers, G-77 export earnings were declining and creating a "savings gap," and their overall economic growth was now barely 4 percent. The so-called "Decade of Development," according to Prebisch, had become a "Decade of Frustration." Both sides – the G-77 and industrialized countries – were understandably cautious. "When things are going well," he said, "attention is diverted away from the fundamental transformations that must be carried out to prepare for a higher rate of development. And when times are bad, these transformations, which are difficult enough in themselves, are usually postponed until some more propitious future date." But that could not be allowed to happen. "This Conference is not just an excursion liable to be spoiled by bad weather," he noted; "we are preparing a long and difficult expedition which, while it has to cope with vicissitudes of weather, must not be diverted from its final objective. Circumstances of the moment must not make us forget that we are faced with basic problems which demand long-range solutions. If this is accomplished, the Conference will have left a definite mark on the history of international cooperation."[45]

Prebisch's friends wondered where he was leading: this windy opening was difficult to square with his magisterial address in Geneva four years earlier and his phobia toward clichés. As usual in international meetings he had written his own speech, and although he spoke in Spanish without notes, he always carefully prepared and memorized his texts. As he proceeded it became clear that this was a special effort with a different purpose. He did not centre his address on a main concept – it offered no new theoretical equivalent to the "trade gap" of 1964.[46] And while he enumerated the short list of items on the conference agenda ("It is only natural that the Second Conference should try to arrive at productive solutions," he noted), he surprised everyone with a deliberately low-key but solemn appeal for a new international economic order. In Geneva he had invoked a new ethic of international development, insisting that an unjust world of North and South was morally repugnant and politically unsustainable and that their fates were joined in this enormous but inescapable challenge of the twentieth century. He now repeated the urgency of this new "global compact": only a durable ethic of cooperation would safeguard the international community in the long term. But UNCTAD II must advance beyond moral appeal to the next step of identifying a "global strategy of development." Linking economic prosperity with global governance, not revolution, was the way to reform the international economic system; only a program of "convergent, simultaneous and properly concerted measures" involving trade and financial cooperation (illustrated by the UNCTAD II agenda) could address the structural obstacles facing developing countries while maintaining the benefits of expanding markets. Indeed multilateral action was the only option to avoid polarization or revolutionary change. It was also feasible. Five years after beginning his UNCTAD quest in New York, he told his audience, the first hurdle of moving the debate from vision to implementation had been achieved.[47]

Prebisch had used the term "new international economic order" for the first time in October 1963 before UNCTAD I, and it gained clarity and precision as he spread the gospel in every forum, stumping boards of trade, universities, and civic and international organizations around the world. It went without saying that a global strategy required the combined effort of Group B and the G-77; and for success their members had to accept joint responsibility and a long-term "discipline of development." Developing countries, in particular, could no longer shelter behind Third World rhetoric; no matter how generous, international assistance "will be largely wasted" unless developing countries themselves initiated internal reforms. "This policy makes it absolutely necessary for developing countries to undertake a series of internal transformations of their structures and attitudes where this has not already been done. It also requires them to adhere to the reasonable discipline of a development plan, to spur reciprocal trade by means of regional and sub-regional groupings aimed at economic integration, and to promote inter-regional measures for the expansion of trade."

If the G-77 had to accept difficult reforms and discipline their national economies for growth, the developed countries and financial institutions were being asked to underwrite stable financing, market access, and transfer of technology; a global strategy therefore had to link resources and performance. This was not charity or woolly headed idealism, Prebisch repeated, but rather a long-term investment in the mutual interest. Governments of developing countries needed the backing of the international community to reform their societies, while donors had to justify development transfers to their electorates and therefore had an understandable stake in the results of the funding they provided – meaning that G-77 recipients of assistance could not expect automatic support. He was not, however, supporting IMF conditionality, which developing countries would reject as a model. Instead the global compact required a credible *mechanism* for determining which countries were eligible for support, and he proposed two golden rules: that only those countries actually committed to development should qualify for financing; and that independent and politically neutral experts from both donor and recipient countries review national development plans. In practice such sensitive evaluations could not be undertaken credibly by the IMF or World Bank, given their lack of transparency and the fact that their staffs not only evaluated but also took part in loan negotiations – they were both judges and executors, so to speak.[48] Instead a separate agency would be required, either in UNCTAD or outside, but in any case with the autonomy to serve this role.

Fortunately, there was relevant international experience to demonstrate that such innovative evaluation mechanisms were feasible in practice. While the OAS Panel of Experts created at Punta del Este, and on which Prebisch had served, proved deficient in structure, the work of the panel was strengthened in December 1963 with the creation of the new and more autonomous Inter-American Committee for the Alliance for Progress (CIAP),[49] in which seven experts from the US and Latin America reviewed the development plans of member countries prior to submission to lending agencies. Chaired by ex-Colombian Finance Minister Carlos Sanz de Santamaria, these country reviews offered a non-coercive forum for comparing ideas, improving plans, and helping countries develop their economic and social agendas. There were even three country review studies of the US economy. This "CIAP model" arrived too late to save the already blighted Alliance for Progress, but it was the one part of the OAS where American and Latin experts worked together effectively outside the normal political constraints to strengthen the planning capacity of governments. Prebisch saw it as readily applicable in general terms to UNCTAD with its much larger membership and shifting coalitions. The essential point at UNCTAD II, therefore, was the recognition of "mutual commitments for mutual benefits." As the many difficulties since 1964 had already shown, implementing the global strategy for development would be arduous, but at least they now had a roadmap. A great deal had been accomplished, Prebisch concluded, even if the hard part was only beginning, starting with the measures before them as delegates began their deliberations in New Delhi, and he urged them to set aside differences for a successful conference.

The applause was sustained, but not like at Geneva. After Prebisch, delegates from 131 countries and forty-four international organizations rose, talked, and sat down. U Thant's address to the conference, delayed until 9 February, proved controversial. Noting the "danger of assuming that problems of security could be dealt with by purely military means," he commented that "the most important ingredient of international security is economic and social development, and not armaments and armed forces, however powerful the latter may seem to be," Rostow took it as a reference to the Vietnam War and as a serious slight to the US.[50] Most speeches were predictable. The G-77 endorsed the *Algiers Charter*, elaborating its main themes; Group B delegates complimented themselves on their past records in aid and trade and refused to go into details. The socialist countries condemned Group B policies and the Vietnam War but rejected responsibility for redressing the evils of imperialism unless they got the same benefits as the developing countries. The mood was noticeably worse than at UNCTAD I, in Group B as well as the G-77. Delegates from the developed countries were fewer in number and less senior; those from the G-77 were bitter and aggressive.[51] It was a routine of merciless boredom; as with UNCTAD I, Prebisch once again sat Buddha-like at the podium as days passed. After the first week UNCTAD II was barely mentioned in the global media, which remained focused on the Tet Offensive and the "Prague Spring."

The interminable plenary statements lasted through the end of February when, in bad temper, the Conference split into committees to debate specific agenda items and report back when and if agreements were reached. With this, morale picked up because the actual working phase was finally under way and there was a rush to join the five conference committees: commodities, manufactures, financing, invisibles including shipping insurance and tourism, and trade with socialist countries. It seemed, momentarily, that UNCTAD II had found a second wind, but optimism was quickly dispelled. Procedurally, the committees simply replicated the plenary, both in size (since at least one member from each delegation felt compelled to attend all meetings) and format (the long obligatory statements defeated virtually every chairperson). There was little real chance of success on commodity agreements and supplementary financing as Group B dug in and refused further action; the G-77 quickly realized that "further study" was the most they could get in these categories.[52] Attention then shifted to the other committees, particularly manufactures, where easier market access for exports of developing countries under a GSP became the most lively and promising conference topic. Three working groups (world food problems and transfer of technology; economic integration among developing countries; and landlocked countries) were also under way.

The GSP was particularly closely watched, but by 15 February these talks were floundering as Group B and G-77 countries faced deadlock on key points: while the former accepted non-reciprocal preferences in theory, they differed with developing country delegates about the products to be selected, safeguards for their own producers, and the point of "graduation" out of GSP-eligibility when industries of G-77 countries had matured. Safeguards were a particularly serious problem. Listening to the widening demands of Group B countries, the World Bank delegate reported, "if this continues, the only manufactures eligible for preferences will be jet planes."[53] Prebisch worried that "the benefits would be limited to a small number of the more advanced among the developing nations."[54] African-Latin American relations became tense, with the former viewing the GSP as a Latin American issue especially favoured by Prebisch, while the Latins resented Africa's demand to keep its special links with Europe in the Lomé Convention. The prospect of agreement and the unity of the G-77 on this issue were imperilled until a draft resolution was approved creating a special committee on trade preferences to continue work after New Delhi for final approval of a GST in early 1969, with actual implementation forecast to begin in 1971.[55]

Chaos succeeded boredom lightened by frequent interruptions: Americans walked out on Cubans; the French walked out when supplementary financing was raised; Arab delegates walked out on Israel; and everyone walked out on apartheid South Africa until the conference expelled it altogether from New Delhi. Soon the Indian press was openly critical of the lack of progress, with repeated articles about deadlocks in the main committees. It became clear that there would be no agreement on any of the main agenda items, and hence that smaller negotiating units – or "contact groups" – would be necessary to consider individual items and report back to the committees. Since UNCTAD maintained a democratic "open committee" rule, the membership of each contact group inflated to full committee size as soon as its existence was known, mirroring the parent committees they were supposed to simplify.

Critical of this proliferation, Prebisch lamented, "I don't know what's going on." Nor did anyone. One staff member estimated a total of 965 meetings took place during the eight-week conference, adding together the plenaries, the main committees, and the related "contact," "sub-contact," and "mini-contact" groups. By early March, ninety-six in-house meetings were taking place simultaneously and teams of interpreters were flying to New Delhi from all parts of the world. All this required far more monitoring and coordination than Prebisch and his small team could manage; "it was impossible to deal with all of them seriously and in an orderly fashion," he noted.[56] On 12 March Prebisch called a special plenary meeting, warning delegates that UNCTAD II was on the verge of failure. Some Group B countries were refusing all compromise, indeed were moving back from previously agreed positions, and Prebisch met individually with them to restore diplomatic momentum.

Two schools of thought were coalescing within the G-77 – an "agreement at any price group" versus a "failure group" demanding the disbanding of the deadlocked conference. Silveira led the second group and demanded that Prebisch listen to him since Brazil had been selected as G-77 coordinator for New Delhi; many developing countries suspected him as a Trojan horse in their midst for the GATT. In fact, prone to emotional outbursts in any case, Silveira was overwhelmed by the violent deaths of both his daughters immediately prior to UNCTAD II. During a dinner for Latin American delegates called at this stage of the conference to demonstrate Group A solidarity, he called Prebisch a "traitor to the Third World," to which Raúl responded, "You son of a bitch!" and the group disbanded.[57] After this disaster Prebisch, in a replay of Geneva, used his personal authority to rescue whatever might be salvageable before the closing date of 25 March. On 12 March he created a summit group comprising the chairs of the committees and working groups to prepare a unified text for submission to the plenary, with points of disagreement to be marked by square brackets. The result was a blanket of square brackets covering all or most of the text, but at least there was now some possibility of progress. But the conference was still deadlocked by the third week of March, and the summit group had swelled into another unwieldy committee of more than fifty delegates. Meanwhile Group B delegates were distracted by student barricades in Paris, as the 1968 rising began on 22 March, and the rush on gold in London's financial markets. As 25 March approached, a World Bank observer reported back to his headquarters in Washington that "I'm sorry I cannot give you a more optimistic report about this conference, but this is how I see the situation to the best of my knowledge. It is a pity that so much time and effort had to be spent for so little achievement. I am doubtful whether we can still hope for a miracle in the course of the last six days."[58]

Prebisch's suite at the Oberoi Hotel now became the focal point for last-ditch negotiations. Even more than in Geneva in 1964, where a package deal was finally achieved at the Parc de Bude, UNCTAD II depended on a small band of insiders – the "Himalayan Group," complete with its inevitable "sherpas" – which Raúl assembled in his suite. Observers assumed that a last-minute breakthrough was emerging when the conference president announced a twenty-four-hour extension until midnight, 26 March, but the extension expired without result and delegates expected the worst. However, Prebisch requested a second delay, this time of three days, and a compromise formula was achieved at the last minute on 29 March. The main achievements were the GSP commitment, although success in the latter depended on follow-on negotiations, and a specific international shipping resolution. The UNCTAD secretariat would continue its work on commodities and supplementary financing, as well as numerous other interesting proposals that had emerged during the conference and were included in the Final Act.[59]

Prebisch could finally declare UNCTAD II closed, but the conference ended in pessimism despite the accord. In contrast with 1964, when the creation of the organization in Geneva had made headlines around the world, there was no dramatic announcement and both Group B and G-77 countries immediately pronounced UNCTAD II a failure. Silveira denounced it as falling far short of expectations, amounting to "no more than a few hesitant steps in the right direction."[60] Irving Friedman of the World Bank underlined "the failure of the Conference to produce positive results."[61] The *London Times*, the Manchester *Guardian*, and the *New York Times* all concluded that the conference "at best was not a success and at worst was virtually a total failure" ... "Conference a failure – we got nothing," read one cable from a developing country, versus "Conference a success – we gave away nothing," from a Group B country. The *Washington Post* concluded that no important agreements had emerged from New Delhi. The attitude of the wealthier nations could be summarized as "We don't need them – they need us."[62] Once untouchable, Prebisch himself was the object of irreverent conversation by journalists speculating on the need for UNCTAD to enter "a new era."

In a sober evaluation of the Conference for U Thant, Prebisch declared the results to be "positive, though extremely limited" and that, although the results did not match expectations, they were "more promising than the impressions one would draw from the press or the statements of the LDCs."[63] However he could not hide his disappointment; the last-minute package deal at New Delhi had left Prebisch acutely upset. "A global strategy without concrete measures is just another document of pious declarations without any practical consequences." Privately, especially to his Latin American friends, Prebisch could not hide his bitterness at the meagre results of all his work: New Delhi had not been a "negotiating conference" at all. Just as the cocoa conference and World Bank supplementary financing scheme had failed, so too the results of UNCTAD II were largely symbolic and the results showed that UNCTAD was never likely to advance decisively toward the goals of commodity market organization, trade liberalization, supplementary financing, or the 1 percent aid target, let alone the broader issues of multilateralism and a global strategy.

U Thant, de Seynes, and other close UN friends disagreed that New Delhi was a failure and urged Prebisch to be more positive. The surprise of the conference was not what it failed to accomplish, but rather the modest advances that it actually achieved. There were no "breakthroughs," of course, as many had hoped for, but such expectations were not realistic in complex international trade negotiations. But this did not mean defeat, and reforming the international shipping conferences in the interests of the Third World was remarkable, however un-newsworthy. UNCTAD faced the long-term uphill slog of incremental change, fighting inch by inch and issue by issue to reform the international trade system. It had been a mistake to raise the stakes for UNCTAD II so dramatically when an incremental approach was both more likely and appropriate, they argued. Prebisch expected too much too soon. By UN performance criteria, such as the gradual inculcation of new concepts and standards, the educative function through quality reports and expert meetings, and the adoption of important substantive measures, UNCTAD's results since its birth in 1964 were more than impressive. It was now established as an important new member of the international development community; even Wyndham-White's conversion to trade and development with Part IV in the GATT and the creation of the IMF Special Drawing Right on a universal rather than restricted basis had to be seen as UNCTAD successes similar to the 1 percent ODA target in the General Assembly and other Group B concessions in the World Bank and other agencies.[64] Although ahead of its time, Prebisch's "new international economic order" was a permanent vision against which progress in the North-South Dialogue could be measured. That a GSP was now in sight marked an impressive shift in Group B thinking. The G-77 was now a permanent reality, with "chapters" formed in the FAO, UNIDO, UNEP, and the Group of 21 in the IMF and World Bank.[65] UNCTAD had already introduced many new development concepts such as "least developed countries" to address differences within the G-77, or the plight of "land-locked countries." Adding everything together, Prebisch had no reason to be discouraged with his years of work since 1963.

Immediately after New Delhi, Prebisch was back in Geneva and New York to deal with the unresolved issues from the conference, particularly moving forward with the GSP proposal. There was traction, he found, the actual design of such a system was now possible, and the UNCTAD Trade and

Development Board would complete the negotiations in 1969 as planned. By 1990, $70billion worth of G-77 trade would be GSP related. And there was movement in other areas. It was possible to finalize a compromise international sugar agreement in October 1968, although tarnished by an EEC boycott and a botched ceremony when the US walked out to protest Cuban participation. There were even hints of reviving the cocoa talks. Prebisch scored another success in streamlining the clumsy UNCTAD machinery. "After twenty years of international bureaucracy, the question had to be asked: was the present system of proliferating organizations and meetings the best?" Prebisch asked ECOSOC on 10 July 1968. He was able to reduce the number of Trade and Development Board meetings to one a year from two and discussed with U Thant the possible hiring of a compromise candidate from Scandinavia for the much-needed position of a deputy secretary-general.[66] He was also reconsidering the harsh criticisms of New Delhi; "many of the judgments passed on the UNCTAD II were exaggerated," he noted in his report to ECOSOC at its forty-fifth session in July 1968. "Seeds had been sown which could prove important if they received the care that would enable them to germinate and bear fruit."[67]

Prebisch's more optimistic mood disappeared as autumn approached. On the night of 20–21 August Dubcek's "Prague Spring" was crushed by five thousand Soviet tanks and more than 200,000 invading East Bloc troops. He had visited Prague only days before at the invitation of Foreign Minister Jiri Hajek because Czechoslovakia had been elected to preside over the next Trade and Development Board meeting on 2 September in Geneva; the revival of democracy in Czechoslovakia, accented by Dubcek's bold "Action Program" in April, had been the one bright spot of a violent year marked by student uprisings in Paris, civil rights protests in the US, and the assassinations of Martin Luther King and Robert Kennedy. Meeting under the venomous cloud of Prague, delegates from the fifty-four countries were negative and confrontational and took out their bad humour by again criticizing Prebisch for the meagre results at New Delhi. His response to G-77 criticism was unusually direct, condemning their resistance to domestic reforms while demanding foreign assistance, and on 14 September he went so far as to urge the board to rank developing countries seeking Group B support according to their acceptance of structural reforms and realistic development plans. A negative dynamic had developed, with the OECD retrenching and the G-77 radicalizing; both seemed to be moving away from the convergence advocated by Prebisch. From Geneva to New Delhi he had struggled to avoid votes in favour of decisions by consensus: compromise produced decisions, votes paralyzed. If one of the G-77 opposed something the whole machinery was paralyzed; the same applied to most of the West. "Dr Prebisch has always favored an agreement by consensus," an observer concluded, "and if that is not possible he has urged the application of the 'conciliation' procedure."[68] But how much further could he go? The group system had become so entrenched as to be untouchable. It could not be changed "without damaging the 'soul' of the institution," an internal review concluded.[69]

The Pearson Commission, commissioned by Robert McNamara when he assumed the presidency of the World Bank in early 1968, was the final disillusionment. Determined to shake off his Vietnam bomber image, McNamara sought a softer North-South face, and he adopted his predecessor's call for a "Grand Assize" of international development. In a speech to the Swedish Bankers' Association on 27 October 1967, George Woods proposed that an eminent persons group examine the declining interest of developed countries in international development and recommend measures to "launch a movement … for exceptional action" to recapture momentum behind a second and more successful UN Development Decade.[70] Prebisch strongly supported this initiative, endorsing it in a letter on 13 December and inviting Woods to repeat his message in New Delhi.[71] Who better than George Woods to lead this review after his retirement, Raúl had urged, since he knew what did and didn't work and had the confidence of Group B countries – a senior statesman who believed in the new international economic order and the need for a new burst of leadership to match resources and reform. "Your own vast experience and wise counsel," he repeated, "will continue to be invaluable."

But when McNamara established his Commission on International Development in August 1968, he chose former Prime Minister of Canada Lester B. Pearson rather than George Woods to lead it, a blow to Prebisch's expectations. However admirable in personality and diplomatic accomplishment, and a deserved recipient of the Nobel Peace Prize for his work after the 1956 Middle East war, Mr Pearson lacked comparable North-South experience. At first glance his commission colleagues were well chosen, primarily from the North as expected, since the industrial countries shaped the international architecture of trade, technology, finance, and cooperation either bilaterally, or multilaterally through decisions taken in the GATT and the OECD: Douglas Dillon (US), Sir Edward Boyle (Britain), Saburo Okita (Japan), Wilfried Guth (West Germany), and Robert E. Margolin (France). Only two members were from developing countries: Sir Arthur Lewis, expatriate St. Lucian and long-time Economics professor at Manchester University, and Brazilian Roberto Campos, the most polarizing figure in Latin America. McNamara offered his World Bank staff to support the Pearson Commission, which issued its report, *Partners in*

Development, on 15 September 1969. Ironically, World Bank economists who had resisted supplementary financing before UNCTAD II formed Pearson's back-up team.[72]

Decent and committed, Pearson began his appointment as a listener, and it became clear immediately that his goal differed from Woods's earlier intention. It was certainly different from Prebisch's expectations. When McNamara met Prebisch for the first time after New Delhi on 12 April 1968, the North American insisted that he was just as committed to international development as Woods; Raúl consequently assumed that the eminent persons group would strengthen his own *Global Strategy of Development* presented at New Delhi by mobilizing the political coalition necessary to underpin its implementation, broadening UNCTAD's support beyond the G-77 base, and nailing down the responsibilities of both G-77 and industrial countries. If the 1960s had been so far "a Development Decade without a development policy," Prebisch explained to U Thant in May, their main goal now had to be "a great effort at persuading public opinion and thus creating political will" for the success of the *Global Strategy of Development.* "This is a matter of the highest priority."[73] New approaches had to be found to locate and mobilize new constituencies for rallying civil society support for North-South relations.

Instead the Pearson Commission offered nothing more than another diagnosis of a familiar problem with a set of sixty-eight predictable recommendations. This seemed going backward to Prebisch; the problem was implementation – not the agenda. It was as if UNCTAD didn't exist – as if the intellectual advance since 1963 in understanding trade and development problems meant nothing. UNCTAD had just spent five years and held two global conferences studying the problem and identifying the agenda; numerous specific proposals for action, from supplementary financing on down, were ready for implementation if governments so chose. The Pearson Commission was a lost opportunity to mobilize support within and beyond governments; instead of supporting Prebisch's *Global Strategy of Development*, it broke its fragile momentum by providing a convenient excuse for delay and inaction. UNCTAD was marginalized as simply another defensive and weak "South-identified" agency instead of the lead organization on trade and development within the UN system, the bridge where North and South met for policy development and new approaches. No new knowledge could be expected from such an exercise – or (in the event) was gained: *Partners in Development* was filed away as the first of many such proposals for international commissions.[74] The evident fact that both McNamara and Pearson meant well, and thought they were doing the right thing, made it all even worse.

Prebisch believed that his vision of a new international economic order was checkmated, at least for the time being. The dual concepts of planning and a global strategy, so dear to his Cartesian dreams of an orderly world where developed and developing countries took converging measures for their common long-term benefit, were buried by the Pearson Commission. He felt blocked, more and more out of place – either dinosaur or visionary, conservative or radical – losing his constituency in the G-77 as well as the industrial North, spreading the gospel of a new international economic order that few wanted to hear. His underlying support for market capitalism while demanding deep reforms left him without support in either camp. Group B distrusted him; the G-77 feared his insistence on conditionality and reform. Wyndham-White had retired in triumph in summer 1968: like de Seynes he had been ahead of the game compared with Prebisch. Clever de Seynes had been right at the beginning in 1963 when they had fought over the design of UNCTAD, trying to lower expectations, while Prebisch had been carried away by his vision – trapped by its logic at the expense of political realism. Other friends, like Hans Singer, who was heading for Sussex University, were leaving the UN while Prebisch remained on the frontline. Continuing on only made sense if UNCTAD had genuine clout; while Prebisch understood that it could never be the World Bank or the IMF, it should be the world's leading centre of research and ideas on trade and development and a forum for global negotiations within its UN mandate. He was not interested in another expensive consultative body; if this is what it was to become, as now seemed inevitable, he was not interested in its leadership.

After 700,000 air miles since 1964, with worsening arthritis, Prebisch was worn out and disillusioned, beset with a growing malaise. His personal dilemma had worsened; the toll of living in Geneva while dividing his time with Eliana in New York was rising. A Raúlito visit to Geneva had to be clandestine, like something out of John le Carré; Eliana was impatient, and Adelita lonesome in La Pelouse. The British were complaining about his many transatlantic flights and time away; the Africans accused him of never visiting their region. Prebisch became testy and provocative; Dell and Krishnamurti were vigilant in revising his dictations and helping him maintain his trademark balance after New Delhi.

The first rumours of Prebisch's resignation swirled up during UNCTAD II, but U Thant moved quickly to quash the gossip by renewing his contract to 1 July 1971, persuading him to remain in Geneva for another three years to implement the resolutions from New Delhi.[75] Both men would then be seventy and could end their UN careers together; U Thant needed Prebisch to consolidate UNCTAD in these difficult times of war and financial uncertainty. But only months later, on 15 June, Prebisch met Filipe Herrera in Washington for confidential discussions on a major new project outside UNCTAD. In April 1968, during the annual meeting of the Inter-American Development Bank's board of governors, Colombia's President Carlos Lleras Restrepo had proposed that the IDB fund a major study on the financing of economic development in Latin America, a key problem for the region, which was experiencing low domestic savings, declining international assistance, disappointing export values, and therefore inadequate growth. Latin America needed a parallel analysis to that of the Pearson Commission to highlight its own needs; and Herrera wanted to leave the bank on a creative note as his ten-year presidency drew to a close. Prebisch was the only Latin American personality with the international prestige to give its findings the required legitimacy, and he asked him to consider an offer. Their first meeting produced a first draft of a study that bank staff elaborated and sent to Prebisch for his comments. A month later, on 24 July, Herrera sent a revised draft incorporating Raúl's suggestions and looked forward to continuing their discussions on his next trip to Washington or New York. Herrera was already discussing possible completion dates – he wanted a report by May 1969 for the next meeting of the bank's governing board, clearly too early for Prebisch. Nevertheless Herrera continued to move the project forward, completing the budget and plan of operations on 21 October on the assumption that Raúl would direct it.[76] Prebisch had not yet consulted anyone on this new career track, not even Dell or Krishnamurti, and he had not yet made a decision to leave UNCTAD, implying to Herrera that a short-term assignment would be covered by a leave-of-absence and refusing any salary beyond travel and per diem expenses.[77]

But Prebisch's mood changed in mid-November as the global discontent of 1968 enveloped Latin America. On 2 October the Mexican Army and police killed and wounded hundreds of students in the Plaza de las Tres Culturas immediately prior to the Summer Olympics. The massacre shocked the region: the Mexican "miracle" was suddenly suspect, its stability now in question. The following day a military coup replaced the elected president of Peru, Fernando Belaunde Terry, with General Juan Velasco Alvarado. "Che" Guevara's capture in Bolivia on 8 October 1967 and his execution a day later by military dictator René Barrientos had unleashed a wave of sympathy that deepened anti-government insurgencies throughout the region. When Felipe Herrera invited Raúl again for talks in Washington, he was more interested in new approaches to Latin American development, and events accelerated. Prebisch was also visibly ill. On 18 November he openly speculated on an early departure from UNCTAD, commenting that he had not yet made up his mind about the IDB offer; but five days later, after consulting with U Thant about a replacement, he tendered his resignation effective 1 March 1969 on grounds of poor health. Manuel Perez Guerrero, Venezuela's ambassador and permanent delegate to the UN, a friend since 1944, would take his place at UNCTAD. In addition to returning full time to ILPES, he agreed to remain an advisor to U Thant and de Seynes in preparing the UN Second Development Decade.[78] News of Prebisch's abrupt resignation was leaked before the official announcement and stunned friends and colleagues. But the decision was final: he would be returning to the Americas. UNCTAD's heroic phase was over.[79]

19 Trials in Washington

Prebisch returned to Santiago, Chile, on 27 November 1968, five days after submitting his resignation to Secretary-General U Thant. The UNCTAD years had aged him; his arthritis had worsened. Ashen, he had fainted twice en route to South America and craved the peace of El Maqui for physical and emotional renewal. But undisturbed in his garden over the Maipo River, Prebisch quickly revived. His arthritis subsided; colour, confidence, and his familiar energy returned. El Maqui was again full of guests, and it was evident that he had no plans for retirement. Within a week he held a press conference denying rumours that he was physically ill and urging Latin American leaders to engage the newly elected US President Richard M. Nixon: it was essential that the twenty governments put aside their differences and agree on a regional Latin American agenda. Confusion deepened when he announced that he would be resuming full-time duties as secretary-general of ILPES and would reside permanently in Santiago.[1] But when he left on 8 December for Washington via Mexico to finalize the terms of his new IDB Commission on Latin American Development rumours were swirling of his remaining abroad and a journalist reported that "Despite the wishes of the *dama de la casa* that don Raúl remain in Santiago ... it is clear enough that he will be away for some time yet."[2]

After New Year's, Prebisch left for New York to attend a special meeting of the UN Regional Commissions Executive Secretaries on 13–14 January 1969, en route to Geneva and his last address, on 22 January, to the UNCTAD Trade and Development Board. Tanned, commanding, and youthful in a new wool pinstriped suit, Raúl declared that he had resigned on grounds of poor health. "I am not leaving UNCTAD because I am frustrated or disillusioned, but because the executive and diplomatic burden is too heavy for me ... I am leaving UNCTAD in order not to fail ... This is the reason for my resignation. I do not wish to fail."[3] On 1 March 1969,

Manuel Perez-Guerrero, with his low-key style, attention to bureaucratic detail, and negotiating patience, formally assumed office. Prebisch gave his final press interviews and attended the last farewells with UNCTAD staff and friends in Geneva's diplomatic community.

Raúl divorced and remarried; Eliana Diaz Prebisch emerged effortlessly from the shadows as his official spouse at a New York reception hosted by Robert McNamara. This decision could no longer be avoided: Raúl Jr was six years old; he needed his father and a stable household. But the break with Adelita, who accepted his decision with typical stoicism after thirty-five years together, was not – and would never be – complete or final. She never felt that the bond was broken, or that his feelings toward her had changed. Raúl would continue to spend as much time as possible at El Maqui, still without telephone service, and would call her on Tuesdays when she took her weekly piano lesson in downtown Santiago. He sent fresh flowers. Friends everywhere, however, divided into warring camps with loyalties to respective wives in Santiago and Washington.

On 10 March 1969 Prebisch flew to Washington: there really was no other possible location for a residence. Eliana reclaimed her position with the IMF; there was no reason to keep the New York apartment at 340, 64th Street. Santiago was out of the question after his divorce from Adelita, and he was politically more unwelcome than ever in Buenos Aires after President Arturo Illia was removed by General Juan Carlos Ongania in 1966. In any case his IDB Commission on Latin American Development, to result in a document titled *Change and Development: Latin America's Great Task*, had to be directed from the bank's headquarters in Washington.

The US capital was, in fact, the perfect address for the "global elder statesman" part of Prebisch's post-UNCTAD life. He was one of the most recognized Latin American personalities in the world, he was a member of the leading international networks, and he had an unparalleled insider's knowledge of international organizations after his twenty years of UN experience. New York was close to Washington for consultations with U Thant and de Seynes, while Washington was the ideal perch for heading eminent persons panels such as the IDB Commission on Development or responding to UN or Latin requests for special or emergency assignments. Prebisch also had a special cachet in Washington as unofficial envoy for the region. His spacious house at 6804 Tulip Hill Terrace in Bethesda, Maryland, became a gathering place for Latin and US leaders and scholars, a destination for off-the-record talks and social gatherings. Welcomed by his many friends in the city, Prebisch made himself available; he was keen to listen and lead, and he joined the International Club at 1800 K Street, where he lunched daily when not entertaining at home or in his favourite restaurants: Jean-Pierre, Chez Camille, Sans Souci, Toque Blanc, and the Boston. Prebisch flourished in the constant flow of people and power of the US capital, the unchallenged centre of ideas and innovation in the Americas, happy to call it "my centre of operations."

The dilemma for Prebisch, however, was that Washington was a poor location for the other half of his professional life – as director-general of ILPES based in Santiago. The institute was his first responsibility: in 1964 he had committed himself to retaining the position during UNCTAD, and now on leaving Geneva he saw it as his vehicle for leading an increasingly urgent debate on the future of Latin American development.[4] But Prebisch also needed the institute because he was chronically short of money and could not subsist on a UN pension. With ILPES he maintained his UNCTAD salary, but it could barely cover two households, mortgages, and a passion for cars (he bought a white Mercedes 230 for his time in El Maqui) and left him scrambling to pay the bills with extra income from speaking engagements and travel per diems. He would split these proceeds with Adelita's account, but on occasion a slim balance resulted in dishonoured cheques. Entertainment expenses (up to ten lunches or dinners per month, including events in Europe when he was not in Washington) could be clawed back, and he even kept a detailed record of his tips for reimbursement. Diplomatic privileges held down expenses: his maid, Maria Luci Loudrono de Arenas, was brought in on a G-4 visa; not just Argentine wines but liberal consignments of spirits, champagne, caviar, and sherry arrived without tax and import duties for his private lunches and dinners. In distant Chile, Adelita grew a vegetable garden and watched every penny, eking out a small profit from their rented house in Buenos Aires. On her trips there she policed Raúl's tailor Amadeo Maiolino on 570 Esmeralda for the highest quality at lowest cost. Caught in the trap of needing ILPES but having to live in Washington, Prebisch convinced U Thant to approve a joint ECLA-ILPES office in the small Washington branch of ECLA on the argument that the institute would benefit from the IDB commission and his new base in the US capital. But the "joint office" was little more than a celebrity perch; no additional staff were hired beyond his ever-loyal personal secretary, Bodil Royem, who coordinated a heavy schedule of lunches and dinners, funded by a representation allowance of $3,500 per year, and arranged his travels to and from Santiago.

Raúl's dual careers of global elder statesman and director-general of a regionally based UN institute were bound to conflict: the former was post-retirement, where he was really free to do and say what he wanted, while ILPES required the support of Latin governments, which limited his independence. Despite its "autonomous status," even one powerful challenge (as Campos had demonstrated in 1964) could paralyse the institute; directing it, therefore, required hands-on management and constant negotiation with regional stakeholders. Here Prebisch was at a disadvantage: he had not lived in Latin America for years, and his generation was being replaced though retirements and changes of government; his international visibility did not necessarily translate into advantages in Santiago. Above all ILPES required strong leadership to safeguard its independence; living in Washington, at the other end of the Americas, magnified Prebisch's challenge of managing two careers: his institute staff wondered how much time he would have for them and how he would resist the temptations of special offers for speaking, teaching, or consulting in the North when they needed him so badly in Santiago. Meanwhile younger leaders, to whom Prebisch seemed a member of the venerable old guard, had ideas and ambitions of their own.

This underlying generational tension awaiting Prebisch as he returned from UNCTAD surfaced immediately after the inauguration of President Richard Nixon in January 1969. After the disappointing years of Lyndon Johnson, Latin Americans were willing to reach out to Nixon despite the old negative images, preferring his old-fashioned realism to the ideological paranoia of W.W. Rostow, banished forever to a harmless professorship at the University of Texas, or Lincoln Gordon, whose warnings of the communist hordes in Brazil turned out to be a *fantasma* of his fertile Harvard Business School imagination. Even the appointment of Henry Kissinger as National Security Advisor seemed reassuring at first, although his last known reference to Hispanic America was to the War of the Spanish Succession of 1821: he seemed a principled and intelligent conservative who understood the concept of enlightened self-interest in US foreign policy – someone to talk to after the unreliable Great Society do-gooders of the chaotic Johnson years. On 19 January 1969, the heads of Latin America's three main Washington bureaucracies – Felipe Herrera, Secretary-General Galo Plaza of the OAS, and Carlos Sanz de Santamaria of CIAP – asked Prebisch to prepare a letter to President Richard Nixon with recommendations for the new period approaching in US-Latin American relations. He agreed, keen to lay the political groundwork for *Change and Development: Latin America's Great Task*. The assignment fit perfectly with his role as elder statesman, an economist with international perspective, close ties with the UN and inter-American networks, and a Washington insider. His carefully crafted note stressed the need for reviving cooperation in the diplomatic vocabulary of mutual interest and reciprocal benefits. Nixon announced the appointment of Nelson Rockefeller to head a new commission on US-Latin American relations; Prebisch looked forward to its work in charting a new path.

However, the governments of Latin America sought a more direct approach to President Nixon and looked to Chile's multi-talented Foreign Minister Gabriel Valdes to prepare a regional foreign ministers meeting. The imposing and aristocratic Valdes, riding the coattails of President Eduardo Frei, had emerged as the most dynamic foreign minister in Latin America after 1964, and this new initiative solidified his visibility in the region. His idea was to create a new Latin American Forum, including Cuba, but without the US – in short an authentically regional voice – by recasting CECLA (Special Coordinating Committee of Latin America), which had been born in late 1963 as UNCTAD took shape (with Prebisch as midwife) to serve as a Latin branch of the G-77. Instead of a caucusing mechanism for Latin American governments in global trade negotiations, the new forum would become a permanent foreign ministers group, and its first task would be to develop and send a message to Richard Nixon on US-Latin American relations. At its meeting from 31 March to 7 April at Viña del Mar in Chile, with Patricio Silva (Chilean ambassador in Washington) as his lieutenant, he challenged his fellow foreign ministers to be frank with Nixon about their "profound dissatisfaction" with US policies and to assert what they actually thought and wanted rather than retreat in fear behind the customary pleasantries on inter-American relations.[5] "We agree," he noted, "that we have to be realists, but not timid, compromised, small, timid or cowards," and he proposed the nineteen-page *Consensus of Viña del Mar*, which the assembled foreign ministers requested him to deliver personally to the White House on their behalf.[6] The subsequent meeting in Washington confirmed his fame in Latin America: "You come here speaking of Latin America," Kissinger sneered, "but that is not important. Nothing important can come from the South. History has never been produced in the South. The axis of history starts in Moscow, goes to Bonn, crosses over to Washington, and then goes to Tokyo. What happens in the South is of no importance. You're wasting your time."[7] Valdes stood his ground; he was now an acknowledged regional personality and a rising power in the region.

Prebisch and Valdes were on a collision course, although not on ideological grounds. Raúl attended the Viña del Mar meetings and was unimpressed with the *Consensus*, which he saw as a wordy cocktail of old recipes and tired exhortations, all over the map and with a superior tone. Its many pages of good advice for Washington and US companies on everything from tariffs to transportation were bound to be rejected by any US administration, especially one facing a serious war and its first deficits since 1945. But its overall conclusions were not in conflict with his own. Moreover President Eduardo Frei and his government were Prebisch's closest political allies in Latin America, representing his ideal of developmentalism; and Valdes himself had played a key role in supporting UNCTAD. Instead the issue dividing Prebisch and Valdes was ILPES. Valdes loathed it as a nest of socialists interfering in Chilean politics who had strayed very far indeed from the institute's original purpose. Presidential elections loomed in September 1970: as a senior Christian Democrat, he was furious with institute staff for promoting Salvador Allende and his Popular Unity Front coalition and demanded that Prebisch do something about it. For Prebisch such criticism from a leading member of the host government was cause enough for concern – Valdes was likely to succeed Frei as leader of the Christian Democrats – but his regional stature made it even worse. He would be a formidable opponent whether his party won or lost the approaching elections: if the Christian Democrats lost Valdes would have sufficient political backing to come forward as automatic regional nominee for the next big UN job, the most likely opening to be in the rapidly expanding United Nations Development Program – the institute's main funder.

Prebisch agreed that the institute had become politicized but argued that Valdes was wrong in focusing his anger on Allende supporters: there were as many activist Christian Democrats as socialists in ILPES, and the line between research and advocacy was increasingly being crossed by both camps. But the larger challenge facing the institute, of which Valdes's complaints were merely the most visible symptom, was that it had been floundering since Prebisch left for Geneva and had to be fixed – urgently. The leadership issue had remained unresolved. Furtado had left Santiago; Chileans Osvaldo Sunkel and Anibal Pinto had the intellectual credentials to lead ILPES but lacked executive ambition, the reverse of the Argentine contingent. The result had been the continuing compromise of Mexican Cristóbal Lara as Raúl's deputy, but he was unable to assert control over the factions. Raúl's visits to Santiago since 1964 had been too few and too brief: sometimes ILPES officials would go to the airport for briefings and instructions while he changed planes. Benjamin Hopenhayn, his trusted lieutenant and troubleshooter, was disliked for his tight control over ILPES's operations and the executive group.

As early as February 1965, José Medina Echavarria lamented to Prebisch, "Your continuing absence here is painful."[8] The work atmosphere became poisonous; morale and productivity were low. Prebisch was informed that only half of his staff arrived on time for work.[9] By 1966, resignations began. Osvaldo Sunkel departed, on leave to Cambridge. Fernando Henrique Cardoso left ILPES for the University of Paris-Nanterre. By 1967 the lack of leadership in ILPES was a common topic in Santiago.

But the deeper problem facing the institute was its failure of innovation since 1964, which made nonsense of its ambition to be a regional leader in ideas and research, an autonomous think-tank freed from immediate government pressures and UN bureaucratic politics. The arrival of Celso Furtado and Fernando Enrique Cardoso could have launched frontier work on multinational corporations in the region, but Prebisch had pointedly curbed this area of research in 1964 after Campos had threatened the institute. The same fate awaited an ambitious project on marginalization, approved by the institute's executive group and directed by the precocious Argentine scholar José Nun. No research area was more important in Latin America given the rise of chaotic urban slum settlements fed by mass migration from rural areas. Following the 1965 US invasion of the Dominican Republic, this topic became politically controversial at a time when Prebisch needed US support for UNCTAD; he instructed Nun to scale it back and halt fieldwork, and the project collapsed.[10] These messages did not encourage new thinking, and ILPES had few published works to show for itself after eight years of existence. Fernando Henrique Cardoso and Enzo Faleto had developed an internal study examining the new networks and forms of relationships emerging between Latin America and the industrial powers, but Prebisch had vetoed its publication. It appeared instead as *Dependency and Development in Latin America.*[11] If Prebisch rather wistfully compared the leadership role of the early ECLA ("We didn't know much, but we knew more than the others.") with what he called the present "isolation" of ILPES, he had to take considerable responsibility for the malaise. The same problems had dogged its planning activities as Latin American governments no longer needed the institute's traditional offerings: they wanted fundable development projects, not more general studies. Before he had left Santiago in 1966 José Antonio Mayobre asked, rhetorically, "Why are the most successful countries in the region precisely those which have NOT received ILPES/ECLA planning missions?"[12] Attempts since 1963 to develop a niche market in consulting services had also failed. Various governments (Venezuela, Dominican Republic, Central America) had tried ILPES, but staff were not equipped for this role; "another weak point in our work," Prebisch admitted. Meanwhile the OAS-IDB-ECLA Tripartite Committee had folded officially in 1967. In training as well, ILPES had worked itself out of a job. More than five thousand professionals had passed through Santiago – a whole generation of Latin Americans – since the first ECLA courses began in 1953. But now there were other training institutes; Latin American educational establishments had matured, and if ILPES wanted to stay in the training game it would require a new approach with more specialized and creative initiatives.

In short, ILPES needed a fundamental overhaul and was dying from neglect. After a painful administrative scandal in June 1968, Prebisch promised his staff that he would give them more attention. "Now that the great intensity of work for New Delhi is over," he wrote, "I intend to devote a substantial part of my time to the Institute."[13] When Prebisch suddenly resigned from UNCTAD, they were delighted with the imminent prospect of his return. The US Embassy also welcomed his return to restore the institute's capacity and prestige. Everyone waited. But Prebisch bought a house in Washington and, in 1969, would lead the IDB Commission on Latin American Development, which would postpone his attention to the institute for another year.

Nevertheless Prebisch brought together his board of directors in August 1969 and convinced them that his original vision of ILPES – as the foremost policy research centre and networking hub on Latin American development – was more important than ever and that the institute would regain the initiative with a brand-new mandate after the completion of his IDB commission. He insisted that the IDB commission was actually an ILPES contract with himself only its executive director.[14] In the meantime he proposed, and the board accepted, a set of interim measures to restore momentum: a special seminar composed of planning ministers in the region, a dialogue of practitioners comparing concrete planning experiences and practical lessons rather than mere theoretical discussion, and a new program of resident senior Latin American practitioners.[15] To stiffen staff morale during his continuing absence, he held out the prospect of creating a new research journal and raised the possibility of a special project called *The Volume*: a definitive multi-disciplinary analysis of Latin American development embodying the collective experience of ILPES and ECLA – a "vulgate," Raúl called it, for development specialists, and a landmark work upon which the institute could reclaim the intellectual high ground in Latin America. To tighten internal procedures, Prebisch designated Argentine Oscar Bardeci as his new lieutenant and point man within the institute. To shore up external confidence, he hired a "good American" – William Lowenthal – to work within ILPES as his special advisor in Santiago, very much on the early ECLA model of Lewis Swenson. These measures, behind a convincing show of leadership, resolved the immediate crisis, revived a favourable working atmosphere in the institute, and liberated Prebisch for the final phase of the IDB Commission on Latin American Development.

Unlike Lester Pearson, with his gold-plated World Bank Commission on International Development, Prebisch worked with a small budget of $206,680 (reduced from $240,000), with his own salary already covered by the UN. Most of his staff were to be seconded from the IDB, ECLA, or ILPES; and the small project office of five full-time economists was housed in the IDB in Washington. He therefore started with a serious staff disadvantage in numbers, quality, and international experience, particularly the absence of top UN officials like Sidney Dell or Krishnamurti, who had helped shape ideas with their severe but loyal criticism. Unlike at UNCTAD, where he could attract the best minds available for short-term assignments, he lacked a budget for mobilizing international talent. Enrique Iglesias, full-time coordinator of the project, was his key collaborator. President of Uruguay's Central Bank between 1966 and 1968 and currently the chair of ILPES's board of directors, Iglesias was marked for rapid advancement in inter-American politics. He had admired Prebisch since they first met in 1951 at ECLA's third commission meeting, in Montevideo, while Raúl saw him as the next executive secretary of ECLA to reverse its declining fortunes.

Prebisch had a deadline of 20 April 1970, when *Change and Development: Latin America's Great Task* would be presented to the eleventh annual meeting of the IDB governing council in Punta del Este. The question facing him from the outset was his terms of reference. The original idea when the concept was proposed in early 1968 was a narrow examination of the problems of financing development in Latin America. The advantages of such a tightly focused commission on financing would be clarity, depth, and operational recommendations; the potential disadvantage would be missing the key obstacles to growth and therefore the irrelevance of the entire effort. After a first fact-finding tour of the region in early 1969, Prebisch decided that it was essential to expand the terms of reference. Wherever he looked, from the crisis in US-Latin American relations, to Latin American domestic politics, which were polarizing before a tidal wave of political anxiety, or to the bankruptcy of the OAS, the region was at a crossroads; a broader analysis was required. The growing anti-Americanism in Latin America became evident when the Rockefeller Commission tried to hold regional hearings in May and June 1969 and confronted a repeat of Vice-President Nixon's disastrous 1958 visit. Opposition groups, students, and workers dismissed it as a public relations stunt from the beginning, and, while Latin leaders acknowledged that Rockefeller was a moderate in US-Latin American relations, he was sufficiently identified with the US oil majors to be pilloried throughout the region when Peru announced it would nationalize a subsidiary of Occidental Petroleum on 23 August 1969 and signed a first trade accord with the Soviet Union. Student and union protests in Venezuela forced the commission to cancel its hearings altogether; it quickly retreated to the airport before mobs in downtown La Paz; and President Frei cancelled the planned Rockefeller visit to pre-empt hostile demonstrations in Santiago. Only the right-wing military dictatorships of Brazil and Argentina unconditionally welcomed the US delegation.[16] Mirroring the decline in inter-American relations, the OAS was in eclipse as regional interlocutor, discredited by endorsing the US invasion of the Dominican Republic in April 1965 in which Johnson sent 25,000 marines to defend the US against yet another "communist" threat. Even the Brazilian generals, who played the role of loyal subaltern in the Dominican affair in a bow to Johnson's support of their conspiracy in the 1964 coup, distanced themselves from Washington thereafter.

When Prebisch had left ECLA in 1963 most countries were constitutional democracies; after the 1964 Brazilian coup, military dictatorships had spread to Bolivia, Argentina, and Peru with escalating violence, guerrilla warfare, and counter-insurgency operations. The instability of 1968 had carried over into the new year. In July 1969 war broke out between Honduras and El Salvador, and Bolivia suffered yet another military coup on 29 September. Terrorism and kidnappings were on the ascent in early 1970. The US ambassador to Brazil and a US military officer were kidnapped in Rio; on 6 March another US Embassy official, this time in Guatemala, was abducted. The Japanese consul-general in São Paulo was kidnapped a few days later on 11 March, followed by a US air force attaché in Santo Domingo on 24 March. During the following week in Argentina, a Paraguay consul and a Soviet Embassy official were kidnapped by left- and right-wing groups respectively, and the German ambassador to Guatemala was assassinated on 31 March 1970 as delegates assembled for the IDB annual meeting.

Latin America was growing apart rather than integrating: Brazil and Argentina were rattling sabres, their borders practically closed to trade, fatally undermining LAFTA (Latin America Free Trade Agreement), and the Honduras-El Salvador conflict destroyed the Central American Common Market. While the Cartegena Accord of May 1969 created the Andean Pact – a regional integration project for the five Andean countries, including Chile – Peru's new military ruler, General Juan Velasco Alvarado, was pioneering a particularly unsustainable brand of "Peruvian socialism." Venezuela and Colombia appeared to be stable democracies, but both political systems remained elite-driven and conflict-prone. Virtually every country faced new and complex prospects. Brazil's GDP was growing at over 11 percent a year as its 1968–73 "economic miracle" took hold, with Campos boasting that the Latin countries doing best had the worst distribution of incomes, behind a strategy of open multinational corporation investment, macroeconomic stability, and social discipline.[17] But press censorship and political repression aside, the future of the "economic miracle" was linked to the millions of migrants arriving in cities without prospects of education. Mexico, where two decades of high growth had produced sufficient confidence to print the official peso-dollar exchange rate in school textbooks, no longer looked so stable after the 1968 student massacre. Argentina was trapped in an escalating cycle of economic stagnation and political violence, and an abortive military mutiny on 21 October underlined the political fragility of Chile.

Prebisch therefore convinced the Bank to expand his terms of reference for a full-scale political economy analysis of the region. The region confronted a "supremely significant turning-point in Latin America's history" and needed new thinking on development rather than ideas that "have been left behind by the demands of an increasingly complicated set of circumstances."[18] ECLA's doctrine of the 1950s, for example, needed renewal. The challenge was transformation rather than a technical fix – in short, *Change and Development: Latin America's Great Task* would return to first principles rather than repeat the backward-looking approach of Pearson's *Partners in Development.* Additional funds of $98,200 were required, but Prebisch convinced Filipe Herrera that no other approach was realistic. The result of such a spectacular expansion in scope, however, guaranteed that *Change and Development: Latin America's Great Task* would be vulnerable to familiar criticisms of projects with impossible deadlines. It was an achievement to rush out a draft in Spanish for the April 1970 deadline, the translation to English not yet available. But it was overly long and repetitive and lacked editing, and there were evident and inexplicable gaps.[19] Sections were leaked. The tone of the report was reported to be sombre, but Prebisch denied that it was "fatalistic" – "only realistic," he argued. "Take note, brother Sancho," he quoted from *Don Quixote* in the preface, "that this adventure and those like it are not adventures on islands, but at crossways."[20]

Uruguay itself was on edge for the IDB's tenth anniversary annual meeting; violence was intensifying and security at Punta del Este was tight. The

Tupamaros, a national liberation movement formed in 1965 among sugar workers in the north of Uruguay, had evolved into a highly effective clandestine urban terrorist organization, destabilizing one of Latin America's most solid and wealthy democracies. A spectacular prison escape on 8 March contributed to the prevailing sense of urgency, and the meeting was therefore as guarded as a military headquarters, creating a Hitchcock scene of Army trucks against moonlight seascapes.[21] It was off-season, and except for the 1,600 delegates and military police, the enclave was deserted. Treasury Secretary David M. Kennedy led the large US delegation, which included eleven wives of assorted congressmen and staff and its own secret service contingent and which occupied an entire apartment building at the tip of the narrow peninsula jutting out from Punta del Este. Jack Daniels was selling for $4 a bottle. Although not to be compared with Douglas Dillon in August 1961, with his fine French wines and elegant soirées, Kennedy's old-fashioned hospitality offered delegates a much-needed refuge from a dreary gathering. But the deteriorating situation providing the backdrop to Prebisch's *Change and Development: Latin America's Great Task* could not be ignored.

Latin America, Prebisch told the assembled delegates, was doomed to political extremes unless it accelerated economic growth. Rapid population growth, "alarming unemployment," and increasing migration to hard-pressed cities accentuated social exclusion; soaking up this surplus labour and limiting poverty and inequality were essential to head off violence and social conflict, which were polarizing the region. The political turbulence throughout Latin America was increasing in cities and among the rural masses. Time was running out; revolution was on the horizon. "The gradual aggravation of the ills besetting the Latin American economy is, of course, creating a propitious moment for ideologies which advocate transforming the system, root and branch," Prebisch warned.[22] Populism was not the answer: as a menace to sound regional development it equalled Marxism-Leninism; "in the absence of strong convictions, and in default of a well-knit system of ideas, populism resorts to the unfailing device of using emotion in order to exalt the charismatic figures ... Populism is therefore not an acceptable alternative to a development discipline."

The root cause of the crisis was the exhaustion of the model of inward-looking development and the onset of "dynamic insufficiency." "The cost of import substitution," Prebisch noted, "must count for much in economic calculations"; it had long since served its purpose and was now generating another "crisis of developmentalism" in which Latin America was declining in trade and production in global terms while Asian economies were advancing.[23] He warned that simply for the absorption of the labour force coming into the market Latin America required an 8 percent annual growth rate, 2 percent higher than the level set for the UN Second Development Decade, and well above the region's 5.2 percent growth rate since 1945. Such an increase required stepping up the investment rate from 18 percent in Latin America to the Japanese level of 27 percent and progress on eliminating "the waste of Latin America's considerable intra-regional trade potential." An overall "rational approach" to avoid excessive protectionism was essential including the promotion of foreign trade (especially industrial exports), the elimination of protectionist structures and greater international competition to improve productivity, the promotion of private foreign investment, and urgent taxation reform to increase domestic savings.[24]

Prebisch had made these points before, particularly during the last years of UNCTAD. The innovation of this Prebisch report was bringing them together into one systematic analysis with explicit links among economic reforms, social change, and development in Latin America. From UNCTAD he had seen South Korea, for example, apply the ECLA doctrine much more successfully than Latin American countries. Like Prebisch's pre-1943 work in Argentina, that doctrine sought a combination of "inward" and "outward" orientation, but South Korea had been able to link success in exporting with companies producing for the home market. The difference with Latin America was not doctrine but rather government policy – and South Korea's policymaking reflected its more equitable social structure with accessible public education and successful land reform. Latin American governments remained elite-driven and weak, less able to resist the special interests that undermined national purpose and priorities in development. The causes of the difference in performance were less technical, or related to resource deficiencies, than institutional.[25] Restoring dynamism in Latin America therefore implied structural reforms: social mobility and education, agricultural reform, redistribution of income from the upper classes, and above all the need for what he termed "the discipline of development" – honest governments mobilizing support for rational development strategies to foreclose both populism and socialist command economies.

It followed that *Change and Development: Latin America's Great Task* was highly critical of existing governments in the region: Latin Americans, Prebisch argued, had to recognize "hard facts," "inescapable realities," and the need for "changes in structures and mental attitudes," with governments taking "conscious and deliberate steps to influence them." They should look first to their own failings rather than those of outsiders or the international system. The chief effort in development must be internal; Latins must discard their "ingenuous and irresponsible optimism" that development was synonymous with external cooperation. "The time has come," he said,

> to shake off the all-too-common habit of attributing the inadequacy of Latin America's rate of development to external factors alone, as if there were no major internal stumbling blocks in the way. We must fully recognize our own responsibility … It is inconceivable that an 8% growth rate can be reached in Latin America in the absence of profound changes in the economic and social structure and in attitudes towards the development process. And without these big changes even the best policy of international cooperation is bound to fail. If the developed countries, as is often said, must have the political will to cooperate, the developing countries, too, must have the political will to introduce fundamental reforms into their societies.[26]

"Richard Nixon ought to be Raúl Prebisch's most ardent admirer," Stephen Rosenfeld of the *Washington Post* reported from Punta del Este; "it is apparent that the report is awfully good news for the United States."[27] But Prebisch also based *Change and Development: Latin America's Great Task* on his New Delhi *Global Strategy* of "converging measures," underlining the need for greater US and OECD commitment to Latin American development: strengthening international trade, increasing ODA to 1 percent GDP from developed economies, and greater private sector investment. Although foreign aid was secondary to domestic efforts, it remained a critical support for governments trying to increase production while facing growing political demands from the masses. These "national majorities," as he called them, had to be given a greater share in economic and political power; an increasing level of international cooperation could ease the pressure on governments and help them maintain stability. Prebisch was sombre on the prospects of such assistance materializing since there had been a significant *outward* flow of resources from Latin America to the developed world during the 1960s.

Felipe Herrera thanked Prebisch on behalf of the assembled delegates, calling *Change and Development: Latin America's Great Task* "a document of great importance" and appealing to governments for increased lending capacity to meet the proposed growth target of 8 percent. David M. Kennedy agreed, announcing that Washington would underwrite $1.8 billion of the projected $3.5 billion capital infusion required for the Bank to increase its lending capacity by 50 percent.[28] With that Herrera declared the annual meeting – his last before retirement – a success. Still, as the last delegates packed up to leave Punta del Este, armed Perónists reminded them of regional realities: General Pedro Arumburu was captured and executed, a settling of accounts as promised for the 9 June 1956 massacre of workers in Buenos Aires.

The institute staff in Santiago were delighted to see the end of the IDB commission. Not only would Prebisch return to full-time duties, but *Change and Development: Latin America's Great Task* strengthened their mandate and future opportunities. Manuel Balboa, Benjamin Hopenhayn, Ricardo Cibotti, Norberto Gonzales, Oscar Bardeci, and Giner de los Rios had worked overtime deep into the night for months to complete the report and recognized that it could restore a leadership role to ILPES. Prebisch had demanded new thinking for a new period of Latin American development and challenged both the dependency theory prevalent on the Latin left since the mid-1960s, as well as the neoliberal authoritarian model being applied in Brazil and supported by economists at the University of Chicago and followers in Latin America and elsewhere. His new "developmentalism" endorsing international trade, market capitalism, and reform of the state, along with liberal democracy, planning, and international governance, positioned Prebisch in the theoretical middle where he wanted to be, and the timing was perfect: with ISI modernized after twenty-five years, Latin America needed a completely new debate on development models, and ILPES/ECLA had a comparative advantage in leading it. Santiago had research strength in key areas such as informal markets and marginalization. Its turn, finally, seemed to have arrived.[29]

But this opportunity could not be realized without Prebisch himself leading the effort to retool ILPES, and he had less time than ever after April 1970. A first wave of briefings, speeches, and special events accompanied the release of *Change and Development: Latin America's Great Task* – the inevitable by-product of any major international commission, but of particular intensity given its controversial findings. The IDB struck a special task force to work with Prebisch on distilling specific recommendations from the massive tome, uncertain what to do with it since its academic structure gave little actual policy direction. Then a special emergency mission was set up to coordinate a relief strategy after the 31 May earthquake in Peru: U Thant asked him to lead it on 22 June, and he felt unable to refuse. Nor could he refuse joining the secretary-general and other members of the UN top echelon for the celebrations marking the opening of the Second UN Development Decade. He did pass through Santiago in July but left after two days for Lima, promising to return soon to follow up on *Change and*

Development: Latin America's Great Task. But when Prebisch did return for ten days on 8 August, Santiago, ILPES, ECLA, and the entire country were caught up in the approaching presidential elections. Polls showed that Salvador Allende, the Christian Democrat Radomiro Tomic, and Conservative Jorgi Alessandri were roughly equal in public opinion support, but all could agree that this was one of the most important elections in Chilean history. Eduardo Frei was denounced by the left because his Chileanization of copper, land reform, and educational programs were too timid, while the right criticized him as a radical. Washington (which under President Johnson had provided Chile with the highest US aid per capita in Latin America) disliked his independent foreign policy and the reopening of diplomatic relations with Moscow. Chile's sluggish growth and inflation, meanwhile, undermined the chances of re-election for the Christian Democrats. But the possibility of Allende's victory had polarized the country, and the heavily Chileanized ILPES and ECLA were split into four hostile camps: the largely middle-class Latin economists were equally divided between Allende's UP and Frei's Christian Democrats; the secretaries, women from the Chilean upper class, solidly supported the anti-Allende Conservative opposition; clerks, waiters, and casual help from the lower-middle class were determined Allende supporters; and the non-Latin international professionals stayed out of the national political struggle, content with buying farms and vineyards with their hard-currency salaries. The national ideological struggle pervaded the entire UN compound with active campaigning for the rival political parties. Not much, it was agreed, could be done before the political situation cleared, and Prebisch left Santiago for Washington and New York, where he was invited to join U Thant on the podium in formally introducing the UN Second Development Decade on 24 October. Ten days before this event, however, he was called urgently to Buenos Aires, where his brother Alberto, recently appointed director of the National Academy of Fine Art and Urbanism, had died suddenly. The two had been inseparable on arriving in Buenos Aires; destined for different careers and social trajectories, they were eventually estranged by conflicting politics; Alberto's abrupt death pre-empted the reconciliation for which both had hoped.

Meanwhile Salvador Allende's election victory on 4 September 1970 stunned Chile and the region, but his Popular Unity Front had taken only 36.3 percent of the vote against 34.9 percent for Jorge Alessandri and 27.8 percent for the Christian Democrats, and so close a result required the Chilean Congress to decide the winner. Since the non-socialist parties outpolled Allende's coalition by far, it seemed probable that Allende would be blocked by a Tomic-Allessandri deal. But Allende promised to respect

Chile's democratic process; Chile had a long tradition of party alliances; Tomic and Alessandri could not cooperate; and Congress endorsed Allende to take office on 4 November. Thereupon the new president, with one-third of the popular vote, opened a campaign to transform Chilean society by breaking the power of the elite. "The central objective," he declared, "is to replace the present economic structure, ending the power of monopolistic national and foreign capital in order to begin the construction of socialism."[30] Kissinger snorted, "I don't see why we need to stand by and watch a country go communist due the irresponsibility of its own people." The Chilean elite agreed. Nixon and Kissinger detested Allende even more than Frei. Already in March 1970 a so-called "41 Committee" chaired by Kissinger had approved funding for anti-Allende electoral propaganda. Livid at failing to prevent his victory, Washington placed Chile on its geopolitical hit list as a pawn in the Cold War and outpost for Cuban-Soviet expansionism, determined to destabilize its economy and government by fair means or foul.

Allende's victory was a turning point for Prebisch, ILPES, and ECLA headquarters as a whole. Prebisch did not trust the UP, worrying that Allende would lose control of the movement. Both Allende and Frei were friends and regular visitors at El Maqui. During a dinner with the two politicians, just the three of them, he twitted Allende on class experience and his socialist credentials: "You have never put one foot inside a *callampa* (squatter shack)."[31] Chile was for him a country of fundamental importance in Latin America, and now he saw the end of its leadership role for "developmentalism" in Latin America. Allende's victory also completed the politicization of ILPES/ECLA, with Pedro Vuskovic becoming minister of economy and Gonzalo Martner the new minister of planning. Allende said, only half in jest, "If I fail it will be ECLA's fault."[32] A bad work environment became even more poisonous after November 1970. Lowenthal, who arrived in Santiago full of energy, wrote Prebisch, "My desire for your return ... is personal in the sense of wanting to discuss with you ways in which I can be of service to the Institute. I consider my present position to be much on the periphery. There are no regular meetings of the staff in which division heads and the executive officers can learn about what is going on or discuss ideas of mutual concern. I have not been invited to any of the meetings which take place on the problems facing the Institute."[33]

It was the worst moment for Prebisch to announce that he would be directing a thirteen-week graduate seminar at Columbia University beginning in January, with weekly commuting to New York from Washington, and therefore would have no time for the institute until mid-1971. Andrew

Cordier, former UN undersecretary, Hammarskjöld's special representative, and outgoing president of the university, personally invited him and he again could not refuse. "It fits very well with my wish to open my Institute to winds from the North,"[34] he responded, but it was a serious error of judgment. "I should have been at ILPES when they needed me," he later lamented.[35] Staff were further demoralized: Cristobal Lara and the institute lived in confusion, worry, and private despair. Recruiting international staff became impossible: the dreams of attracting scholars like Yale economist Carlos Diaz Alejandro faded when he turned down their offer on 20 February 1971. Even qualified Latin Americans had other jobs; only Chileans and Argentines, it seemed, were available in abundance to distort even more an already geographically lopsided staff. The financial outlook was perilous: Latin American governments, most pointedly Brazil and Argentina, were not interested in providing financial support; fundraising from Canada, Western Europe, and the Ford Foundation was uncertain. The UNDP (United Nations Development Programme) had been its primary supporter since its creation in 1962, and its contribution to the institute had been renewed in 1965 without opposition; but at the UNDP governing council meeting in January 1971 only a three-year phase was approved, worth \$3.9 million. Ortiz Mena, the new president of the IDB, was not sympathetic and cut its support from \$1,050,000 to \$437,500; this left a 40 percent shortfall and did not even cover staff costs, requiring drastic cuts in all six divisions and the shortening of staff contracts from three to two years.[36] Lowenthal, who had emerged as ILPES financial advisor, reported to Prebisch on 23 April, "I hope, Don Raúl, that this letter doesn't give you indigestion. It is a sad reality that we cannot maintain our staff without all kinds of financial gymnastics and constant worry."

Paul Hoffman had retired as managing director of the UNDP, and Prebisch barely knew his successor, US banker Rudolf Petersen, who was reorganizing his New York headquarters. Now the largest funder of technical assistance in the world, the UNDP had become a powerful international agency, and an advisory committee on its future proposed that four regional directors be appointed to oversee all UN-related work in their regions and report directly to Petersen. Approved during the 24 January-2 February 1971 meeting of its governing council, the new UNDP structure required a Latin American regional director, and Gabriel Valdes was appointed immediately. He, in turn, lost no time in hiring Patricio Silva as his assistant. With Chilean Christian Democrats in the political wilderness after losing to Allende, they took aim at ILPES as a badly managed UN organization that had allowed "leftist" elements to distort its mandate and interfere in Chilean internal politics. The danger was suddenly obvious: Prebisch's last base in the UN system was under hostile fire and he committed himself to ILPES at last.

After his Columbia lectures Prebisch spent an uninterrupted six weeks in Santiago with his ILPES team, re-establishing administrative control over the institute and preparing a new plan for future operations.[37] He turned down another teaching offer (this time by Rosenstein-Rodan at Boston University); he vetted internal documents and demanded weekly reports; he set up an editorial board for the proposed journal and allocated articles for the first issue; and he tried to pre-empt Valdes's criticism of professional standards with an internal review committee for curricula and publications. To improve morale within ILPES he promoted all six directors (four Argentines and two Chileans) to L6 – over the opposition of Quintana, who had denied a similar request by the ECLA directors on budgetary grounds. Prebisch worked on US ambassador to Chile, Edmund M. Korry, a dove and potential UN ally in the Nixon Administration, to reverse his negative attitude toward ILPES. Most of all he sought a secure, independent funding base for the institute to limit its dependence on the UNDP.

The inevitable result was hustling for external contracts to cover the immediate shortfall while convincing the UNDP and IDB to maintain their long-term commitments. There were successes. Money was obtained from Canada and Holland, but neither was likely to continue if Latin governments refused to contribute financial support. However the Ford Foundation was interested in developing a multi-year program of "resident practitioners" from Latin America to spend a year at ILPES for advanced professional training. This was a sound concept, and it proposed funding an immediate pilot project for 1971 to get it under way. But to the anger of the Ford Foundation, Prebisch appointed Sergio Molina, Frei's ex-minister of finance, as the first "resident-practitioner" before selection procedures had been approved and despite his membership on ILPES's board of directors. Not only was the appointment of a senior unemployed Chilean Christian Democrat questionable under these circumstances, but Molina was given the top salary scale in hard-currency dollars. In August 1971, Prebisch saw another major opening when Nixon abandoned the gold standard and terminated the postwar Bretton Woods era. He proposed an ILPES-led continuing seminar in Washington for development bank and USAID officials to examine these implications for US-Latin American relations, involving senior economists in the study, including Gottfried Haberler, who had retired from Harvard and moved to Washington. The initial response was favourable, and a multi-agency working group was set up draw up a funding proposal. Haberler noted that "I find myself in agreement with most of what you are saying."[38]

The attempt to diversify funding sources failed, however, so that the UNDP ultimately controlled the fate of ILPES. Valdes could not see the potential of the institute and made no secret of his low regard for certain ILPES economists: courses and reports were scrutinized for ideological acceptability. Silva, acting as Valdes's lieutenant, policed ILPES's operations, demanding time sheets to control attendance in a pervasive criticism that demoralized staff. Giner de los Rios felt personally betrayed "for the first time in 20 years with ECLA and the Institute." Lines of authority became blurred, and the discovery of plagiarism by a senior staff member humiliated and angered colleagues. Nothing that Prebisch or the staff did was ever good enough for Valdes or Silva. José Medina Echevarria prepared to return to Spain, which he had left in 1939. Even notoriously placid Norberto Gonzalez, the director of research, was disheartened. On 25 February 1972 Valdes finally made clear to Quintana, on the eve of the latter's departure as executive secretary of ECLA, that he had "frank doubts regarding the duplication of tasks in various areas, and the inadequate capacity of ILPES personnel." UN finances were in trouble, with a continuing freeze that had begun in the 1970–71 fiscal year. Cuts had to be made, and he proposed that ILPES should re-enter the ECLA fold with a more limited training mandate.

Prebisch fought hard during 1972 to save ILPES, because he knew that "integration in ECLA" meant the end of the institute as an independent centre of research and ideas in Latin America. Only the shell would remain. But the battle was hopeless and disappointments accumulated. His Washington seminar proposal failed, as did the Ford Foundation project. The IDB under its new leadership turned cold in general toward the institute. Canada and Holland did not renew their funding, and since these two OECD donors were the easiest touches there were no other ODA fish to be caught. The journal concept had to be shelved for lack of resources; *El Volumen* was quietly abandoned. Despite Prebisch's reassurances in November 1971 that "the atmosphere has been changing over the past year," the US Embassy remained unimpressed.

By this time the struggle in Santiago was not merely for the institute but for saving the parent ECLA, increasingly the target of anti-Allende critics as political polarization in Chile deepened. ECLA had long ceased to play the leadership role that it had exercised in previous times: Mayobre had left Santiago in 1966 after only three years as executive secretary, unable to tear himself away from Venezuela and the Caribbean; under his Mexican successor, Carlos Quintana, a feudal structure had descended on the institution, where no one knew what was going on outside the "watertight compartments" of their dispirited divisions; innovation seemed to be limited to building the gardens for its magnificent new compound.[39] "Much deteriorated," Prebisch had sniffed at its thirteenth session conference in Lima, March 1969. Departures for service to Allende cut deeply into the staffing and morale of the secretariat; when Quintana left Santiago to become general manager of *Nacional Financiera* in Mexico, Prebisch devoted his attention to locating a successor. There was not much time: U Thant was completing his last term, after which Prebisch's influence would certainly decline. After his return to North America in 1971 Raúl invoked his accumulated years of work with the secretary-general to ensure that Enrique Iglesias would inherit his old office. No other colleague approached his potential for regional leadership, he wrote to U Thant in January 1972. He was "a brilliant man, with great driving power. People expect that he will give ECLA a sense of mission." Iglesias's appointment, to begin 1 April 1972, constituted Prebich's only major victory during the ILPES fiasco.[40]

On 24 January Prebisch had had enough and resigned before the end of his term, tired of wasting his time in wearying bureaucratic infighting, he wrote to a friend, rather than working to resolve Latin American problems.[41] ILPES as originally conceived was history. Before leaving he ordered a final consignment on diplomatic privileges: eight cases of whiskey; fifty cases of wine; a case each of Pieper Heidseck champagne and Tio Pepe sherry; and twelve jars of Serraga Black Russian caviar. Valdes did nothing to ease Raúl's pain, refusing to pay the ECLA Washington Office for what Prebisch called the *piltrafa* (scrap) of $6,600 rent for 1973, thereby immediately disbanding the joint ILPES-ECLA operation in Washington. "They will only pay, no doubt, if Patricio Silva moves into my office," Prebisch complained. Bodil Royem was also out of a job, her position as his secretary eliminated, and there was no work available for her in Santiago either. "Is it possible to believe that a UN agency would treat someone like this after 20 years of devoted service?" he asked.[42] He intervened with Enrique Iglesias; together they found a job for her in Nairobi with the new United Nations Environment Program.

What a way to close out a distinguished career! The founder of structuralism and creator of UNCTAD had been reduced to fighting over the least of the acronyms, ILPES. It was like an ex-archbishop squabbling over a side-chapel in a remote country church. He reflected on his old foe and friend, Jorge del Canto, who left the IMF announcing to all that he was available for work, only to find himself roaming the streets of Washington with an empty briefcase. It was all wrong. He had hosted a marvellous farewell dinner party for

Filipe Herrera on 6 February 1971; but Herrera didn't even hear of Raúl's UN retirement cocktail party in Santiago for weeks.[43] The baton had passed to a new and tougher generation: with the exception of de Seynes his old friends, such as Herrera, Paul Hoffman, and U Thant, were retired or on their way out. "I have passed into the category of "international day-labourer," he wrote to his old UNCTAD colleague Christopher Eckenstein, "which is to say, working for profit."[44] Nearly seventy-two years old, Raúl still needed extra income, and with Eliana working as IMF law librarian he had to stay in Washington. Stopping work wasn't an option.

Prebisch remained advisor on development to the UN secretary-general; de Seynes, Iglesias, and the UN offered to pick up his remaining ILPES contract worth $32,812.47 for the period 1 February 1973 to 30 June 1974. In fact, he had already lined up multiple and overlapping commitments for 1973–74 even though this agenda came with as heavy a travel schedule as with UNCTAD – 104 days between 8 March and 14 October 1973 – meaning an almost complete absence from his family in Washington. He also agreed to direct a seminar at the School of Advanced International Studies at Johns Hopkins University for a stipend of $10,000. There was also, embarrassingly, a contract with the OAS, the ugly duckling of the Washington circuit, its beautiful official building off Pennsylvania Avenue hiding the tatty, overstaffed and incompetent secretariat at 1889 F Street. When he resigned from ILPES in January he agreed to a twenty-three-month contract to the end of 1974 to serve as principal advisor to ILPES Secretary-General Galo Plaza.[45]

It was a depressing year, after an already hard landing in the Americas after returning from UNCTAD. The OAS wanted him to come up with a new plan for CIAP: the obvious answer was "nothing." All major governments in the Americas, starting with the White House, wanted it terminated. But a report was necessary, and in September Prebisch presented a visionary concept of transforming CIAP into an OECD-type body with Canada, Japan, and Western Europe as full members. "It could contribute to a new phase of cooperation between Europe and Latin America," he wrote to the foreign minister of Spain; and by adding Canada it would also expand the concept of the Americas and thereby strengthen the Western Hemisphere community "from Alaska to Patagonia."[46] Not surprisingly the governments were not interested and rejected it without discussion: from Watergate in Washington to corruption and violence in Latin America, they had weightier things on their minds. Carlos Sanz resigned, and the whole OAS system lay prostrate for another generation. Prebisch instructed David Pollock to cover off further OAS responsibilities, and Pollock ended up teaching most of Raúl's summer course as well.

Kurt Waldheim, the new UN secretary-general, invited Prebisch to act as an external consultant to the newly created UN Panel of Eminent Persons on MNCs (Multinational Corporations) comprising twenty experts – nine from developing regions, ten from industrial countries along with one Soviet Bloc delegate – to examine a possible code of conduct and the setting up of a special UN centre to monitor MNC role and impact.[47] It was one of the most important and controversial subjects on the international agenda: the UN secretariat was caught between, on the one hand, the demands of developing countries demanding the regulation of Western-dominated MNCs, given their powerful role in trade and technology, and, on the other, the equally insistent "hands-off" approach of OECD governments.

This new UN assignment, however, coincided with increased political tension in Santiago, and events in Chile would cast a heavy cloud over Prebisch's life and work during 1973. Even as the MNC panel assembled for its first meeting on 4 September 1973 in New York, his mind was on Chile as rumours spread of an imminent military coup. Exactly one week later, on 11 September, the panel was interrupted by news that rebel forces under General Augusto Pinochet had seized areas of the capital and were attacking the Moneda Palace. President Allende was trapped inside and resisting against hopeless odds. News gradually replaced rumour: Salvador Allende was dead, and Pinochet's forces controlled the country. Iglesias assured Prebisch that Adelita was safe, and Raúl arranged a visit to Santiago as soon as he could, to arrive on 24 September for three weeks.

The violence of the coup overwhelmed Prebisch; he had assumed that Chile's well-established democratic tradition would rule out gross human rights violations on this scale. Mass arrests, executions, and torture were in progress as Pinochet decapitated civil society along with the Chilean left; a flood of refugees, beginning with Allende's wife Hortensia and children en route to Mexico via Havana, clogged embassies and airports. Internationally respected Orlando Letellier, Chile's ambassador to the United States in 1972 and a regular visitor to Prebisch's house in Washington, was missing, along with Carlos Matus and many other friends and colleagues. ECLA was now marooned in a hostile capital, with some of its staff declared *persona non grata* by the military. Allende's reforms were rolled back; the estates of the oligarchy were restored. Beyond its violence, the Pinochet coup enlisted a small but zealous group of economists at the Catholic University associated with Milton Friedman's "Chicago School" to introduce a strict neoliberal ideology regardless of social cost or unemployment.[48] Even more than Brazil's in 1964, this was therefore no ordinary coup. The main debate in Chile over economic policy before and after 1970 had pitted Allende's UP against the Christian Democrats, but both had rejected the Chicago School;

Pinochet, in contrast, would impose shock treatment – a brutal regime of supply-side economics, with democratic institutions and elementary human rights in Chile destroyed. Without prompting from the IMF Pinochet's team privatized the nationalized industries, drastically cut public expenditures, and threw open the economy to global trade and investment.

Raúl's letter of condolence to Hortensia Allende was brief and anguished. Not knowing her address in exile in Mexico City, he had it delivered by the local ECLA office. "My dear friend," he wrote on 24 September, "Salvador Allende will live in history as a shining symbol to encourage and energize movements of social transformation. I have always had a great respect and admiration for the force of his convictions and his extraordinary fighting spirit, feelings which deepened in the long years in which he honoured me with his friendship and which have cut deeply now with this tragedy. I think that if he had lived he would have offered us profound reflections on his political life, the events of these years as well as the enormous obstacles confronting his efforts to realize his ideas – including some obstacles from those who had no business being there." His characterization of post-Allende Chile as "a long night, cruel and dark," referred to his own gloom as well as Pinochet's prisons.[49] Before 11 September he had criticized Allende's program; now Chile lay under a barbaric regime – and with the Chicago School in full swing. Of course he had not anticipated this outcome, but he also had no answers: his own brand of developmentalism associated with Eduardo Frei had failed in Chile – a true case of tilting at windmills while history passed him by. The truth was that Prebisch was an Argentine citizen and UN civil servant; however deeply his attachment and gratitude to Chile for its support since 1949 he could not become personally involved in the political drama unfolding before him. But at the human level the gathering crisis was a constant and growing worry: Adelita lived in isolated El Maqui; Eliana's family was Chilean; ECLA was engulfed by the crisis; and Allende and many senior Chileans across party lines were personal friends. Allende's policies after his November 1970 inauguration had increasingly worried Prebisch, and three years later he witnessed the looming debacle as an unavoidable and disastrous tragedy.

For several years, Prebisch had been having serious misgivings about the direction Allende's regime was taking. When Allende had announced his intention in July 1971 to nationalize the copper mines and undertake a deep land reform, Prebisch criticized the decision. "Populism is the negation of genuine transformation," he argued. "A populist redistribution of income is unacceptable. Cutting the income of minorities for redistribution frustrates development." He had feared the "masses" since his first days in Buenos Aires in 1918, citing Marx regarding "the danger of social mobilization in a capitalist society because it destroys its leaders."[50] Prebisch's dilemma was that his own report, *Change and Development: Latin American's Great Task*, had advocated precisely the deep land and social reforms that Allende was undertaking in Chile, and he constantly repeated his belief that the concentration of wealth and power into few hands were obstacles to development. But Allende's strategy was wrong; Raúl felt that the marginalized were being radicalized into "masses," while stable development required democracy and material incentives through the market. Allende, he said, was "sincere but misguided."[51]

Eduardo Frei, rather than the UP, had had the right approach by working with the elites to achieve consensus: "the new consciousness of the marginalized classes," he insisted, "requires leaders who have been absorbed by the establishment."[52] Frei embodied Prebisch's ideals of developmentalism, regional integration, and liberal democracy – an enlightened leader from the middle class who sought a "third way" between the spreading military dictatorships and the Cuban Revolution – and this contest had made Chile the epicentre of the ideological hurricane sweeping the Americas. Frei's Chilean experiment had gained additional support in the Western capitals as well as financial institutions such as the World Bank and IMF during the 1960s; Chile had by far the largest US aid program in Latin America, totalling more than $1 billion between 1962 and 1969. Instead UP leaders such as Pedro Vuscovic, minister of economy until mid-1972, when he was replaced by Carlos Matus, another long-time ECLA official, had seemed intent on radicalizing Chilean politics, deepening an already alarming polarization and provoking US support for a military coup. Nixon had identified even Frei as anti-American and pro-communist, cutting aid, and striking his name from a list of foreign leaders to be received at the White House.[53] If Frei and Valdes, both members of the National Falange in Chile before the creation of the Christian Democratic Party, had been considered unreliable in Washington, it was evident that Salvador Allende would face US destabilization. By October 1971 Secretary of State William P. Rogers had threatened to cut off US aid – "a slap in the face," he admitted, but the "only language they understand."[54] In fact, CIA Director Richard Helms was instructed to "make the economy scream." With Chile isolated and beset with inflation and growing scarcities, the opposition to Allende had accelerated. The initial growth and then precarious stability that had held for a year and a half after his 1970 election had evaporated, giving way to a vicious cycle of inflation, paralyzing transport stikes, GDP decline, and rumours of military coups.[55]

Chile had increasingly become an international issue during 1972, mobilizing left and right in campus events and public protests. By the end of 1972, Prebisch felt that the situation was getting out of hand. Boo Royem had reported after a trip to Santiago in November that "things are not just bad, they are terrible."[56] In a letter to Galo Plaza on 15 January 1973, after the OAS secretary-general had visited Chile, Raúl remarked, "I agree completely with your views regarding President Allende. Unfortunately, factors beyond his power and convictions have led him, especially as regards the copper sector, into unadvisable policy directions." Prebisch disliked disorder, and the escalating tension and accelerating inflation had finally convinced him that the president was losing control. Leaving the Moneda Palace earlier that year for another meeting in the president's car, with mobs clashing with the police, Prebisch had asked Allende if he worried about the loyalty of the police. Turning toward him, Allende had confided, "Yes, I do worry, but they are not as worrisome as my own people,"[57] and he waved at his supporters. Senior UP members were leading demonstrations, supporting land seizures, refusing compromise in the copper negotiations, and unnecessarily baiting the opposition. On 29 June Colonel Roberto Souper had surrounded the Moneda with tanks, but the military remained loyal and the coup attempt collapsed.

On the other hand, Chile under Allende remained a constructive international partner. Despite the overt US campaign to isolate and undermine its economy, the UP had tried to defuse tension and heal divisions with Washington in international forums, including ECLA's Quito session in March 1973; the OAS general assembly the next month in Washington, 4–14 April; and most notably in repeated calls for dialogue between North and South at UNCTAD III in Santiago in 1972.[58] Chile did not respond in kind to US provocation, maintaining its traditional diplomatic balance and penchant for dialogue with Washington. Allende also remained an undeniable constitutional democrat as he had promised in 1970, forging a unique "Chilean Way" toward a "progressive construction of a new power structure."[59] In fact free and fair elections in March 1973 had increased UP support in the Congress to 43 percent from 36.2 percent in 1970.[60]

In April 1973, *El Mercurio* had attacked Prebisch in a lead article entitled "ECLA: Doctrine and Failure." This had set the tone for a debate in the Chilean Senate, where he was held personally responsible for Allende's economic policies – a departure for a national press that had previously held back from such finger-pointing. He had responded with a letter titled

"Unjust Attacks on Raúl Prebisch," identifying himself as "Argentine Passport number 339621." Argentine critics picked up the theme. When Argentine journalist Eudocio Ravines repeated *El Mercurio's* line in *La Prensa,* Raúl lost his temper: "the son of a bitch was a communist; now he's jumped into bed with the reactionaries."[61] But Prebisch did acknowledge his concern about Allende's choice of advisors. "Some ECLA seeds may have fallen on fallow ground," he admitted, "but this was not ECLA's fault."[62]

The political polarization deepened in Chile during 1973 against a background of growing isolation and destabilization. So far from reassuring his opponents, Allende's electoral gains in 1973 terrified them all the more by suggesting his eventual success. In June the Uruguayan military seized power in a bloody crackdown, signalling a shift to the right in the Southern Cone; and a coup attempt the next month unnerved a deadlocked Chile. Visiting Santiago in mid-August after a week in São Paulo, Prebisch was increasingly worried about the menace to Adelita, living alone in El Maqui in the isolated mountains surrounding the Maipo Valley. Over thirty kilometres deep in the Andes outside Santiago, trapped on a cliff three hundred feet above the Maipo River, and with no means of communication (not even a telephone), the narrow access road to El Maqui was vulnerable to seizure and occupation by militant groups such as MIR (Revolutionary Movement of the Left) that threatened the area. Illegal land seizures had already occurred around El Maqui, and the police had done nothing. A rumour spread that El Maqui itself would be next. Raúl purchased a revolver for Adelita to fire warning shots over the heads of would-be intruders, but in early August 1973 while he was in still in São Paulo this feeble defense proved inadequate; Adelita was driven from El Maqui by a mob and narrowly escaped capture as her car broke through their barricades, which had closed the road to Santiago. The Army had reopened the road, and Adelita returned, but the situation remained tense as Prebisch left for Washington en route to New York for the first meeting of the UN Panel of Eminent Persons on MNCs on 4 September.

It was an excruciating dilemma for Prebisch. He had foreseen the crisis engulfing Allende but had felt helpless to avert the looming disaster. Allende was unfailingly a generous friend; despite all his troubles, for example, he had found time to send a letter of appreciation to Kurt Waldheim on Raúl's departure from ILPES, recognizing his efforts for Latin America, and wishing him well in future work. Against Allende were ranged thuggish elements like paramiliary leader León Vilarín, head of the National

Truckers Union. As in 1956, depression invaded Prebisch's life as the military coup of 11 September approached.

The period following the Pinochet coup was a bleak time, the worst year for Prebisch since 1943. Alliance for Progress economists like Paul Rosenstein-Rodan hailed Pinochet as Chile's Jean Monnet, but Prebisch wrote little and rarely spoke about the coup, instead following the political prisoners he knew, encouraging them to be patient, congratulating them on their eventual release, and helping to find them jobs.[63] Orlando Letellier's release in September 1974 for exile to Venezuela and then Washington raised Raúl's spirits. Carlos Matus reappeared in 1975. But the succession of failures – ILPES, the OAS, and the Allende debacle – drained Prebisch of intellectual and physical energy. He had resigned from UNCTAD to make a difference in Latin America, but these five years had been undoubtedly his least creative, and even *Change and Development: Latin America's Great Task* had been shelved. Since then he had merely witnessed the gathering political crisis in the region without producing a single article of consequence. Once again he withdrew to El Maqui to recuperate. As usual his complicated finances were in trouble: a cheque was returned NSF after he prematurely transferred $577 into Adelita's account; and he was reduced to the indignity of submitting a travel claim for $5.53.

In December 1973, five years after resigning from UNCTAD, Prebisch called together a small group of associates led by Enrique Iglesias for a week-long retreat at El Maqui. They met day after day, with walks in the garden, the atmosphere of the city heavy with worry and fear. Latin America was in turmoil. What had gone wrong? Where was it heading? The coup deepened Prebisch's post-coup catastrophism, an intimation of impending confrontation and social violence. He warned that many Che Guevaras would appear in Latin America if socioeconomic disparities were not corrected. The rural and urban masses, he argued, had new expectations because of the mass media; new Che Guevaras might have more success than Allende. He remembered the 1961 Punta del Este meeting where Che had had a door slammed in his face. "Slamming the doors of history might be harder this time around," he predicted.[64]

Frustrated and depressed, Prebisch decided to retire as international consultant. Life as a "day-labourer" had not been easy. Between 1 February and 6 April 1974 he had logged 154 days for the UN alone, not to mention the OAS work – full-time, in short, mostly away from home on assignments of secondary interest. He had been as busy since leaving ILPES as during UNCTAD – but to what purpose? Even the UN Panel of Eminent Persons on MNCs, the most interesting of his UN assignments, no longer engaged his full commitment, and he attended its follow-on sessions in Geneva and Rome in early 1974 more as bystander than participant; his friends were alarmed at his passivity. Prebisch realized that he was outside the power networks, that a new generation saw him as elder statesman rather than a decision-maker, and therefore that his proper role was to shape ideas rather than work within the system. He had to change course – to begin a new stage free from the big international bureaucracies he had conceived and shaped, but where he no longer fit. And there was never a more urgent need for analysis and new ideas, given the changes sweeping Latin America and the international system. It was essential, he decided, to join the global dialogue with an independent voice.

As if to demonstrate the proverb that good fortune follows a return to virtue, a pleasant surprise rewarded Raúl's decision to retire. On 7 May 1974 Kurt Waldheim asked him to return to New York for a special one-year assignment as his special representative to head the UN Emergency Operation (UNEO) on behalf of the so-called MSA (most seriously affected countries). Developing countries dependent on oil imports were struggling with OPEC's four-fold increase in the price of petroleum following the 1973 war in the Middle East, which threatened international economic stability for rich and poor nations alike. The developed countries faced a serious, unexpected downturn depending on their exposure to petroleum imports; developing countries without oil – the majority – faced an additional huge burden and increasing trade deficits; and the OPEC-led oil exporters, which had pulled off this upset, confronted the prospect of lopsided profits. A sixth special session of the UN General Assembly had been called by the developing countries for 9 April-2 May 1974 to discuss changes in the international economic system advanced at the NAM Summit held in Algiers during the previous September. Two days before the special session closed, the gathering turned its attention to the immediate emergency facing the "fourth world" – the MSA countries after the oil shock – and a short-term emergency operation was approved, with a longer-term possible special fund to be discussed later.[65]

Waldheim's call to Prebisch engaged him immediately, and his depression lifted. It was just what he needed – a final mission that combined North-South idealism with high international priority. This is "a new adventure which has come rather late for my years but which I have accepted with enthusiasm," he noted to Aldo Solari on 24 May. On the same day he wrote to Enrique Iglesias, "The adventure has begun! Tomorrow I leave for a trip starting with the European Community, and continuing on to Algeria, Rome, Libya, Kuwait, Abu Dhabi, Lebanon, Saudi Arabia and Iran." He felt morally compelled to accept the Waldheim mission, not just on the merits of assisting needy peoples and nations in the present emergency but also out of loyalty to the UN, which he had served for twenty-five years. All the secretaries-general since 1949 "have treated me very well." But there was another reason. "The mission will help me forget some unfortunate episodes."

Prebisch plunged into his job with an almost youthful energy, but his mandate was narrow. Although the UN response dealt with both the short and medium term – an emergency operation to help the hardest-hit countries cushion the immediate shock; and the creation of a special fund to help countries develop policies for balancing imports and exports in this new topsy-turvy world – he was only in charge of the emergency operation. Having been snubbed for two years by the likes of Patricio Silva and OAS underlings, Prebisch was back in the circuit. Robert McNamara (World Bank) and his IMF counterpart, Johannes Witteveen, invited him for discussions. President Carlos Andres Perez of Venezuela invited him to Caracas – and over dinner Minister of Finance Hector Hurtado, the continent's most powerful financial figure, presented him with a $50 million cheque for the emergency operation.

He reassembled some of his old teammates – Sidney Dell as his deputy, David Pollock as personal assistant, and Diego Cordovez, now secretary of ECOSOC, complemented by secondments from other UN and outside agencies; the tiny group, the Inter-Agency Committee (with never more than a dozen members), guided the emergency operation between June 1974 and July 1975. The goal was $3 billion in money, grain, and fertilizers to help the MSA countries cushion the immediate oil shock. Detailed background studies regarding contributions, allocations, coordination and follow-up were woven into Prebisch's visits to foreign capitals. Targets were discussed; formal requests for donations followed; and an informal group of UN ambassadors from the US, Algeria, Iran, France, Japan, Sweden, Venezuela, and Saudi Arabia succeeded in achieving consensus rather than conflict between OPEC and the oil-importing Western countries.

To general surprise Prebisch and his team managed to exceed the original target at a donor's meeting in September, collecting nearly $5 billion for the forty-two hardest hit countries, of which $290 million was in cash with no strings attached. Oil exporters had committed $2.736 billion, while the US and the EEC had contributed $926 and $500 million respectively in food aid, with Europe committing the first $150 million on 18 October. Canada, Japan, and a number of European countries rounded out what Prebisch called "an extremely impressive sum." In his final report on 15 September 1975, Prebisch added "with some satisfaction," that the administrative cost to the United Nations of running this entire $5 billion program had been less than $300,000. Washington, in a rare compliment to the UN, noted "the excellent use he had made of limited staff resources."[66]

He was frustrated by the unwillingness of the Arab OPEC countries to take his emergency operation seriously. "They acted like *nouveaux riches*," he complained, "much worse than the old rich."[67] And he was disappointed at the fate of a newly created UN special fund to continue his work on a permanent basis. A board of governors was selected and met on 31 March, but only Venezuela and Norway were prepared to make commitments ($11.6 million and $10 million respectively). The vicious circle of OPEC and the industrial countries pointing fingers at each other could not be resolved, and follow-up to the emergency operation at the global level therefore failed.[68] Venezuela (alone again) assisted hard-pressed neighbours by selling oil at a discounted price and lending at long-term concessional rates.

Kurt Waldheim wrote expressing "my sincere gratitude for your most energetic and effective accomplishments as my Special Representative for the UN Emergency Operation … Yet another achievement … of characteristic loyalty, dedication and competence."[69] Bidding farewell to the emergency operation, Prebisch's earlier pessimism vanished; the difficult post-UNCTAD years were behind him, and he could now start afresh – yet again – at the age of seventy-four.

20 Prophet

The gospel of don Raúl, dormant since New Delhi, became the fashion of 1975: the power of oil brought the New International Economic Order (NIEO) to the top of the global agenda. The South now had bargaining power: small countries had raised oil prices dramatically without retaliation from the industrial powers; for all its military might, the US had lost the war in Vietnam; and Cuban forces had sent the powerful South African Army packing from Angola, back to its apartheid heartland. Diplomacy between East and West had given way, it seemed, to the other chessboard – North-South relations. Action moved from the Security Council of the great powers to the UN General Assembly of the heretofore disenfranchised.

The NIEO, pioneered by Prebisch in the UNCTAD years – the package of proposed changes in international trade, finance, and cooperation required for southern countries to break a cycle of dependence and poverty – was suddenly in high demand.[1] Brought forward to a sixth special session of the UN General Assembly in April 1974, it was accepted in principle in the *Declaration and Program of Action of the New International Order*. Momentum built quickly. The *Charter of Economic Rights and Duties of States* was approved later that year, and in September 1975 the Northern countries endorsed the demands for a NIEO in a UN resolution considered a breakthrough for developing countries.[2] So stunning a change of prospects for global governance rebounded to its author's credit: Prebisch was rediscovered after his slog in Washington and was honoured as a global visionary with awards, invitations, and numerous honorary doctorates from around the world. Among these, the Nehru Prize for International Understanding received 10 November 1975 and the first Dag Hammarskjöld Medal awarded on 24 October 1977 had special significance.

The election of Jimmy Carter in November 1976 confirmed Prebisch's recognition in the US capital as well, as the new administration promised to support the NIEO, restore the North-South dialogue, and promote human rights rather than geopolitical confrontation. US funding for international aid had fallen by more than 50 percent in real terms during the 1960s and was now down from 2 percent during the Marshall Plan to 0.23 percent GDP, well below European and Canadian levels. Kissinger gave good speeches, and he could herald the NIEO as a "collective decision to elevate our concern for man's elementary well-being to the highest level," but his instinct was geopolitical: the US $1.5 billion aid package for Israel and Egypt to support the 1975 Sinai Agreement equalled the entire AID budget for development.[3] "When the Marshall Plan was announced there were 100 people in the bureaucracy waiting to move on it," noted Professor Gardner, who covered US negotiations for the NIEO. "Here there are 100 powerful interests who would like to sabotage it."[4] With Carter's election these interests seemed to cast a shorter shadow over the NIEO.

Cyrus Vance, the new secretary of state, called for "a positive, long-term strategy toward the Third World," and Andrew Young's appointment as US ambassador to the UN was a particularly promising sign of Carter's sensitivity to North-South relations. President Carter's first address to the UN General Assembly stated his country's readiness "to promote a new system of international economic progress and cooperation. We will contribute our own ideas and ask that you examine them as we examine yours. The time seems ripe for this manner of exchange. New ideas – ideas that grow out of a common concern and out of new experience – are usually generated in an atmosphere of common search rather than one of mutual distrust. It is that lesson that the nations of north and south are learning again today." Prebisch, in fact, could have written Andrew Young's statement to the UN Economic and Social Council on 8 July 1977, which identified US policy with the achievement of the NIEO: "The aspirations of the developing countries – the Third World – for achieving economic justice," he noted, "have come to be symbolized in the phrase 'New International Economic Order.' We support this concept, whatever particular phrase is used to express it."

"How times have changed since we started to work at ECLA," Prebisch wrote to Alfonso Santa Cruz. "Remember in those days how they would not stoop to receive me at the State Department."[5] He felt vindicated; for twenty-five years he had been setting an agenda, and his ideas might become reality in the NIEO. The magnitude of his achievements – creating UNCTAD from scratch, attracting so many of the best people, and willing it into so powerful a presence that it set the international agenda for fifteen years – was recognized. He was again an international celebrity, in demand everywhere, praised by Washington and the G-77 as the father of the NIEO. During his first years in Washington after UNCTAD, he had felt somewhat on the shelf. All this was now gone; international cynicism seemed to wilt under the Carter-Young offensive: perhaps a breakthrough between North and South really was possible.[6]

The practical complexities of Prebisch's life were resolved, and his financial worries settled, by finding the secure anchor of a major journal. Raúl needed a base: he was not a solitary scholar and dreaded retiring to his study on Tulip House Terrace. Latin exiles could not find shelter in major universities or research institutions; creating and editing a journal was, in fact, his only option for obtaining the voice and independence he required. He had tried unsuccessfully to found one in 1948 in the University of Buenos Aires before his abrupt departure from Argentina. In the early ECLA years he had set up a bulletin, but nothing more. After leaving UNCTAD, he had floated the idea of an ECLA journal with Quintana, but *Change and Development: Latin America's Great Task* intervened. Then he raised it as a potential project of ILPES, only to see it cut for lack of funds as the institute entered its downward cycle. But in the gloom following Pinochet's military coup Enrique Iglesias invited Prebisch to edit the new *CEPAL Review* (so named to reflect ECLA's Spanish acronym) to "help elevate ECLA's diminished prestige." While it had to be postponed until after the UN emergency operation, by August 1975 Prebisch could devote full attention to the journal, charging forward with the energy of earlier times, hiring Argentinean sociologist Adolfo Guerrieri as secretary in charge of production and planning the format and layout of the new publication.[7] He faced the challenge of writing the opening lead article; he had broken his right hand in a fall, but nothing could hold him back now. The prospect of the *CEPAL Review* lifted staff spirits, and Raúl set about soliciting articles; letters went out everywhere, and he blocked out prospective issues. In September 1976, Prebisch announced that the first number of the journal was in press. De Seynes, recently retired from the UN, urged him on.[8] When it appeared the following month, it was immediately apparent that the *CEPAL Review* filled a gap in the development literature, giving staff in Santiago as well as external economists an outlet for their work. ECLA was back in the work of ideas and debate, with the worst period of the Pinochet dictatorship behind them. It was also Prebisch's best possible reintegration within ECLA. At the far end of the long corridor from the desk of Iglesias, his warm and dignified corner office, with his old antique desk and leather couch, symbolized permanence and memory. In Washington David Pollock supported the journal by restoring funding for the secretarial position Raúl has lost when ILPES was disbanded; in Santiago his ever-closer friend Iglesias assured long-term support for his latest venture.

Liberated for good from multiple careers, Prebisch left the world of organizations with a sense of mission completed and the luxury of unencumbered freedom to criticize and reform the system he had so long served. Whether official or consultant, he had never been entirely free to speak his mind. "I could not," he explained, "present a report to governments preaching the need for drastic internal measures because they would have responded drastically by going after my head rather than accepting my ideas."[9] During his long professional life he had accepted these limits as the price of engagement, but in this final stage Prebisch sharpened his criticism well beyond his centre-periphery framework from the 1950s and *Change and Development: Latin America's Great Task* toward a new formulation of dependency theory.

As late as December 1973, after the Allende debacle, he had rejected dependency theory; now, in the first issue of the *CEPAL Review*, he returned to the more critical tone of his 1924 talk to the Lloyd George Club in Melbourne, Australia, when he had condemned the Argentine elites and demanded land reform. "Peripheral capitalism," he claimed, was increasingly exclusive and conflictual because it was based in social inequality; the model developed by the industrial countries and projected into Latin America was incapable of raising lower-class living standards in the periphery. Whereas capitalism succeeded in distributing benefits throughout society in rich countries, the "imitative capitalism" of developing countries benefited only the "haves" because the "structural surplus" extracted by the elites in Latin America and their transnational corporate allies was used for consumption rather than productive investment. In effect the penetration of a US ethic of consumption brought with it capital-intensive technology that reinforced the class-based structure of these societies: the result was high consumption, low savings, and growing unemployment, with undynamic economies prone to featherbedding, cyclical crises, and the embedded poverty of migrants in urban centres. In contrast, the core industrial states had more equitable societies in which all groups had social power and could demand a share in the benefits of technology. To put it another way, US social relations mediated a US ethic of consumption and reinforced productivity, while the extreme inequality characterizing Latin American societies – which was, alas, its distinguishing feature when compared with any other region of the world – was incompatible with development. Attacking social exclusion implied transforming the elite system and political power, and such a revolution required new thinking. "It is not enough to proclaim the well-known formula of neither capitalism nor socialism," Prebisch wrote in 1977, "it is the unshirkable duty of the development economists, or rather the developmentalists, to offer a socially and politically valid way of solving the crisis of the system on the basis of political consensus."[10]

The new stage also freed Prebisch to take up topics beyond international development and the Latin American economy, returning to the breadth of interests that had characterized his work much earlier, before he had become a senior official in Argentina. These included the environment, human rights, ethics, history, economic theory, food security, social policy, and regional integration – in a vast educational campaign of writing, media interviews, and public lectures. Recurring themes – or warnings – dominated his work. Latin Americans had to become serious: regional integration was essential if a strong, democratic, and prosperous Latin America was ever to take its rightful place among the regions of the world; and they had to end their uncritical fascination with foreign fads and models in economic theory and produce their own approaches to sustainable development. Development implied social and political change, not just economic growth, and was a difficult, ethical challenge; without a global strategy and governance it would not succeed. Finally, in the search for a model, extremes had to be avoided despite temptations. A strong state was as important as open markets in economic development, and a regression to Friedman neoliberalism on the grounds that import substitution had been abused by Latin governments was dangerous and counterproductive.

The new stage of Prebisch's life restored his youth, and his striking features displayed serenity and command – "a sculptor's dream," an observer noted.[11] His enthusiasm and conviction were undimmed after seventy-five years. "Life is too short," he would say. "I would like to have another 40 years to see the changes that must come." Prebisch now had a regular schedule, with three months in Santiago; he rented a small apartment near the UN compound on Vitacura, which became a favourite after-work destination for colleagues and friends, and spent weekends at El Maqui. Both houses, one in each continent, were busy with guests. He travelled widely with Eliana, lecturing in Spain, Japan, India, Europe, the Middle East, the US, Canada, and Latin America. His speeches became more playful and personal; everyone had an anecdote about don Raúl. Drawn more often to Europe and Asia, where his thinking had greater impact, Prebisch received a recognition often denied in the Americas. He was a frequent guest of former colleagues in Europe or of Dudley Seers and Hans Singer at the University of Sussex; and he took a special interest in rebuilding the cultural ties between Spain and Latin America curtailed during the long Franco dictatorship.[12] No session of UNCTAD or ECLA was complete without Prebisch's opening call to arms.

The Carter team brought an entirely new face to US relations with Latin America. Nixon's self-proclaimed "non-paternalistic," low-profile policy toward Latin America had turned out to be no policy at all. After Allende's removal, US interest in the region lapsed in favour of other agendas: East-West relations, Africa, and the Middle East; the Ford years closed out with the assassination of Orlando Letelier in Washington on 21 September 1976 by agents of Pinochet, revelations by the Church Committee of CIA covert activities in Chile and Latin America, and calls on all sides for a revived US engagement in the region.[13] Carter's agenda in Latin America marked a sharp break from that of the previous administration: a new regional dialogue on development, negotiations for a Panama Canal treaty to end the US enclave, human rights, and rapprochement with Cuba. Beyond his Cabinet, Carter's choice of officials looked promising, with Sol Linowitz attracted back to head the negotiations for the Panama Canal Treaty, and senior officials like Viron P. Vaky who preferred dialogue to confrontation.

Carter identified Prebisch personally as a leader in North-South relations and singled out ECLA for special attention, referring to "the urgent need to mould together the concepts of social justice and economic development so that the poorest people of the region may share in the fruits of Latin America's impressive economic growth." This was astonishing. "Despite what they so often say," Alfonso Santa Cruz wrote to Prebisch, "there is no doubt that there are differences between the Democrats and Republicans toward Latin America and the attitude of Carter reminds me of the early Kennedy years when I travelled with you to Washington to influence policy."[14]

Abraham Lowenthal, normally an astute observer of US-Latin American relations, declared the end of Washington's "hegemonic presumption" in Latin America and the Caribbean. "I hope you agree that the new US Administration and the statements of its leaders represent the best hopes for a favourable change in the near future," Cordovez noted to Prebisch shortly before Carter's inauguration.[15] ECLA's meeting in Guatemala City on 6 May 1977 marked the recovery of its prestige in Washington. Since its decline after 1963 its primacy as regional think-tank had been challenged by CECLA under Valdes, the new Latin-only Latin American Economic System (SELA) based in Caracas, and even the OAS. But the Carter Administration decided that ECLA should be the region's most influential policymaking forum. The *Financial Times* underlined this change. "Mr Young threw his weight behind ECLA as an intellectually impeccable body given to creative thinking about the future, managed by economists and not, like the OAS, by often less than respectable politicians."[16] Waldheim arrived in Guatemala for the event, and Iglesias's electrifying opening speech marked his arrival as a major figure in inter-American relations. "A microcosm of world diplomacy," a journalist gushed, "a UN in miniature." Andrew Young was the undoubted star, however, unleashing wild applause for his comment that "'trickle down' as a social theory is increasingly a cruel joke."[17]

Prebisch immediately backed the Carter approach to human rights in Latin America. Young defined development as "a process by which full human rights and dignity are achieved rather than just an economic process," and he attacked the skewed income distribution and repression in Latin America as key obstacles to be corrected. But even the US State Department acknowledged that Prebisch drew the longest applause for his personal statement. "The more I study Latin American development," he began, "the greater is my concern."[18] Prebisch appealed to Latin governments to support Young, to understand US human-rights policy as "an expression of moral solidarity from the northern hemisphere that we are not used to," and to support conditionality on this broader human-rights dimension rather than the narrow IMF formula. As one observer who heard Raúl's speech noted, "he rejected the belief that the New International Economic Order – which all governments supported publicly – could ever be achieved without a domestic ethical impulse."[19] Critical poverty was the result of maldistribution of income; it could not be resolved only by economic growth. The issue had to be faced squarely, without blaming Latin America's "wasteful imitative consumption patterns" on multinational corporations ("although they encourage it and profit from it") or other influences. "Latin America had chosen the pattern itself and must accept the responsibility."[20]

The result was an unexpected realignment in inter-American relations. If the Carter-Prebisch position on linking the promotion of human rights and economic development gathered supporters throughout the Americas, the Southern Cone military dictatorships fell back on the doctrine of non-intervention, insisting that social issues not be linked with economic questions. In fact the "North-South" and human-rights rhetoric of the Guatemala meeting tended to obscure a lack of substance in Carter's new agenda for Latin America: caught up in domestic issues like inflation, unemployment, and energy, the new administration lacked, so far, a development strategy for the Western Hemisphere. In any case it faced a protectionist congress skeptical about resource transfers to the Third World, and labour unions worried about trade concessions that threatened US jobs.

Excessive Latin expectations of US largesse were matched by naiveté in Washington about the so-called "economic tigers" of the region, undermining Prebisch's early enthusiasm for the Carter Administration. Economists from all parts designated Latin America as having the greatest potential of any Third World region. Assistant Secretary of State for International Affairs C. Fred Bergsten claimed that "Latin America has become a central actor in the world economy."[21] The *Latin America Economic Report* predicted that its per capita income would rise to the level of Italy by the year 2000, giving the region the same GDP as Japan.[22] It would outpace Asia; one-half of all industrial production in developing countries would be Latin American; it would enjoy a projected growth rate to 2000 of 7–8 percent. "In many respects, Latin America seems closer to the advanced industrial countries than to the developing world," it noted. During the 1970s the region's growth rate was 6 percent a year, the second fastest in the world after the "miracle" East Asia countries. Even the exports of manufactured goods, which Prebisch had called for in 1970, had expanded rapidly – at a rate of 20–25 percent a year compared with 27 percent for East Asia. W.W. Rostow maintained that Latin America was moving rapidly in the right direction, with great strides since the Alliance for Progress in 1961. The region was now "far along" in its drive toward "technological maturity," which is the "post take-off stage," in which countries develop diversified industries, applying to them, in both the agricultural and industrial sectors, increasingly sophisticated technologies and levels of real output per capita. Mexico, Brazil, Venezuela, Colombia, Chile, and Argentina could now be classified as "upper middle-income countries."[23]

Prebisch swam against the prevailing tide of public and professional opinion; he knew his region as they did not, and he warned that Mexico and other economies were heading for serious trouble. Already in *Change and Development* (1970) he had identified the danger of foreign lending as a short-term expedient for a style of growth that hid an underlying fragility. The international banks needed customers after the oil boom in October 1973 and urged Latin Americans to take advantage of petrodollars at cheap rates; with the US in recession they were looking for other markets and Latin governments were eager. Endorsed by the IMF as sound development policy, the debt-led growth converted Latin governments into the best customers of international bankers. Already by the end of 1975 the US banks had $59.5 billion in outstanding foreign credits, of which $23.9 billion were in Latin America, more than twice as much as all of the

EEC; 90 percent were short-term loans. "In the 1970s," a senior Latin American banker later regretted, "the private initiative of the international banks turned into a kind of blank check that, regrettably, underwrote many of the whims and policy errors of the period."[24]

By 1976 Prebisch was lambasting debt-led growth as a distortion of sound development that was reversing the gains of the postwar decades by underwriting bloated state enterprises and bureaucracies using borrowed dollars – or what he called "elephantiasis of the state."[25] During the 1960s public investment and budgetary management in most countries of Latin America had been prudent, devoted to priority infrastructure and social projects rather than expanding inefficient and protected state enterprises; now with easy money governments and bankers channelled a large part of their borrowing to state and para-statal enterprises. "The state structures in Latin America have not known how to adapt, modify, or transform themselves to respond to the needs of development," he noted, and he predicted a crisis when interest rates rose and borrowed money could no longer paper over the growing cracks of corruption in Latin America. Public-sector spending almost doubled during the single decade of the 1970s from 25 percent to 42 percent GDP, with the foreign debt rising from $10 billion in 1965 to reach $150 billion in 1980. But income distribution, public education, and agriculture had not improved for the bottom 40 percent. "Thirty years of industrialization, accompanied by high rates of growth, have left 40 percent of the population lagging far behind. For them there has been no progress," Prebisch noted. "Inadequacies of state enterprises have not only contributed to leaving the masses behind, but are also affecting the middle sectors of the social structure." This of course did not exonerate the international banks "for acting like judges," he continued, but Latin American state enterprises were frankly unsustainable and the region lacked "a healthy and legitimate social sector."[26] Prebisch was particularly concerned about Mexico, where President Luis Echevarria (1970–76) broke with a cautious style of economic management and a low-key foreign policy to project his country as a major Third World leader, and business leaders and ministers from around the world lined up in front of the presidential palace to share in the miracle. No one in Mexico was interested in Prebisch's warnings; his audiences yawned.

Instead of an era of progress and leadership, the 1970s would stand out as a lost decade for Latin America, Prebisch argued. In 1975 Mexico had a deficit for the first time, obscured by the discovery of a major oil deposit the next year; there was already a balance of payments crisis in the region, and low internal savings ensured that the model could not be sustained.[27] The state was failing. "Twenty years of economic plans haven't worked,"

Prebisch concluded, urging the region to regroup behind a revived integration framework before it was too late, and repeating his fears about the short-sightedness of the oil boom in Mexico. "For the first time in human history we have the means to accumulate capital, in physical as well as in human terms, to change the face of the Earth. And the danger is that we may allow this opportunity to be frittered away through greed and conflicts."[28] Prebisch's analysis of "peripheral capitalism" and prediction of an approaching debt bubble were widely criticized in Washington and Latin America. He was denounced as a doomsayer, generalizing from the narrow experience of stagnant Argentina and Uruguay and ignoring the success stories like Mexico and Brazil, which were growing at 7 percent a year with strong manufacturing sectors. Since these countries were now substantial powers, what was the "crisis of peripheral capitalism," and what was wrong with the current model?[29]

By mid-1978 internal tensions stalled the Carter Administration. Prebisch admired Carter's commitment to the Panama Canal Treaty and his success in steering it through powerful congressional opposition until its ratification by one vote. But this enormous effort seemed to exhaust the Carter team, and from now on it gave confusing signals about policy toward the region.[30] The human-rights language of the administration was undermined by contradictory messages from State Department officials and the National Security Council. Viron P. Vaky, the new assistant secretary of state for Latin America, spoke the language of human rights, but his deputy, John Bushnell, supported dictatorships in the region. Vaky spoke of reform and social change and promoted US citizens of Latin origin to his team, while Bushnell openly praised the governments of Chile and El Salvador and lobbied for World Bank loans to Argentina to prop up General Jorge Rafael Videla, "one of the world's most flagrant violators of human rights since the mad dictator of Uganda, Idi Amin, was driven out of power," as columnist Jack Anderson put it.[31]

Within two years the Carter team had fractured; Vance and Young departed; the early promise of détente diminished as US-Soviet rivalry intensified after 1978 – from the Horn of Africa to Grenada and Central America; and the Islamic Revolution in Iran in January 1979 was a severe setback to US foreign policy in the Gulf.[32] Carter encouraged the fall of Nicaraguan dictator Anastasia Somoza in July 1979 and even prepared an aid package to the FSLN (Sandinista National Liberation Front), but he panicked in October after the outbreak of civil war in El Salvador. Cuban-US relations chilled. Meanwhile the G-77 was increasingly confrontational; and the Non-Aligned Movement summit in Havana in September 1979 was aggressively anti-American and morally indignant. Lacking power, and profoundly and increasingly divided below a shallow rhetorical unity, the G-77 depended on the industrial countries if the NIEO was ever to be more than a rallying cry for the South. In fact its implementation was going nowhere.[33] Prebisch warned the G-77 at UNCTAD's fifth global conference at Manila in May 1979 that self-righteous confrontation would fail: only reasoned and constructive cooperation would resolve the problems of developing countries. He urged self-help measures among the nations of the South – OPEC oil producers should invest more of their revenues in developing countries, for example – and exhorted poor countries to stop blaming their own mismanagement on the North. Many G-77 countries such as India and Brazil were pragmatic in private but went along with G-77 rhetoric to avoid the appearance of breaking ranks; it was evident that the North-South dialogue was in trouble, with the NIEO as its likely first casualty.

The geopolitical shock of the Soviet invasion of Afghanistan in December 1979 brought US-Soviet relations to a level of tension not seen since the Cuban Missile Crisis and shifted international development to the margin of global politics. The fraying of North-South relations prompted another commission on international development, again funded by the World Bank and headed by former West German chancellor Willi Brandt, to find new directions; another special summit of twenty-two leaders – fourteen from developing countries and eight from the OECD – was called for Cancun in early 1981 to revive the stalled NIEO negotiations.[34] When the Cancun meeting assembled, however, it was Ronald Reagan rather than Carter who attended for the US. With the Carter Administration floundering at home and abroad, unable to rescue US hostages held in Iran, unable to revive the economy or restore national morale, Americans looked to Ronald Reagan for leadership. His landslide presidential victory also showed the force of the New Right, a militant movement of social conservatives swelling in Washington against the Democratic liberal consensus.[35] The second Cold War was under way; Reagan's victory in November 1980 opened a new period, sweeping away New Deal liberalism and Carter's foreign policy of dialogue to reassert US primacy, in which the "Third World" was cast more as enemy than friend and there was no room for the NIEO or its supporters.

The eruption of Ronald Reagan onto the US national political scene bewildered Prebisch, who, at eighty, was an old-timer in Washington. Looking back, he recalled all his experiences with Americans – his first trips to Washington as a young man, his meeting with President Roosevelt, his work with Triffin, Ravndal, and many others he had admired for their dedication and social commitment. He recalled Urquidi's amazement at established US professors doing without maids, in fact not imagining having domestic help. This vision of an open and inclusive society, sustained through the McCarthy period and with added momentum during the civil-rights movement, had made US civilization the central attraction of Latin Americans seeking the reform of their own polarized societies. New Deal liberalism, which the Republicans under Richard Nixon had maintained, was considered the domestic reflection of an overwhelmingly admired US foreign policy. Even when tracked by the FBI during the McCarthy years, Prebisch had never lost his positive vision of the US; whatever his criticisms, and during the 1950s there were many, Washington had led a stable multilateral framework for the post-1945 world. Dulles might have destroyed democracy in Guatemala, but at least he supported postwar recovery and European integration.

The US under Reagan seemed a different and hostile place. President Carter had attempted a new approach toward Latin America based on shared values that looked beyond US hegemony. But in the Manichean world of the Reagan Administration, divided into good and evil, there were also good and evil Latins: the "Cuban-Soviet threat" was entrenched in Nicaragua, El Salvador, and Grenada and had to be rooted out. Cutting the tentacles of the Soviet beast in such Third World outposts in Latin America, Angola, Afghanistan, and so forth would force the "evil empire" to contract. US rearmament would rally the world in a crusade for freedom. Cuba braced for an attack; instead the US escalated intervention in Central America with a war of destabilization using proxy forces. In the Southern Cone the dictators were welcomed as ideological allies, along with P.W. Botha of apartheid South Africa. Argentine General Roberto Viola was welcomed to the White House and decorated as a hero. In return he agreed to train Reagan's Nicaraguan contras.

Prebisch had no friends or admirers in the new administration. "My existence continues to be very confused," he confided on 12 January 1981, resigning from the International Club that afternoon ("one last good lunch before Reagan's inauguration"). As an Argentine patriot he was shamed by Reagan's reception for Viola: appointed president in March 1981, after Videla's failure to avert a banking crisis, Viola had maintained his predecessor's human-rights violations while overseeing an even worse economic meltdown and had finally reduced his once-proud country to training US-backed terrorists. The new US administration was almost violently anti-UN, the appointment of Jean Kirkpatrick as US permanent representative sending the appropriate message, and particularly hostile to the Third

World-dominated General Assembly. Multilateralism was out, in favour of unilateral US power. Americans could be unashamed nationalists again, free to retaliate against the Third World, which had voted against the US during the 1970s and then demanded more aid into the bargain. They could tell the UN to get lost; they finally had a leader who would rearm, challenge the enemy, and (whatever liberals might say) reward anti-communist friends, whatever their background.

No one felt more out of touch in the new Washington than Prebisch. If the OPEC oil shocks of 1973 and 1979 had been the first blow to the post-1945 consensus on North- South cooperation, the supply-side economics of the "Reagan Revolution" completed the rout. Tax cuts of $749 billion over five years, combined with increased defense spending and a restrictive monetary policy, produced interest rates of 20 percent, which beggared Third World countries and sucked global capital to the US. But Reagan pulled the US out of recession, whatever the future costs of ever greater deficits and federal debt, and the tax cuts were wildly popular within the Republican Party. Multilateralism, however, was out of favour in Washington; power and the market replaced governance and equity; and the NIEO and North-South dialogue were dismissed as anti-Western relics. The very principle of development assistance was questioned in the US capital as the Reagan Revolution put the welfare state behind it both at home and abroad.

Even as he felt so acutely unwelcome in the twilight of internationalism in Reagan's Washington, Prebisch received his highest distinction – the $100,000 Third World Prize presented in New York on 2 April 1981 at the Hilton Hotel. Led by the UN secretary-general, seven hundred of Prebisch's closest friends and associates gathered to honour him in a swan song for North-South relations as a whole, accentuated by the title of his acceptance address: "The Crisis of Advanced Capitalism." Even the language of the media, describing him as "patron saint" and "grandfather," gave him the feeling of being passé. The *New York Times* referred to him playfully as "the scourge of industrial nations for thirty years" and "the grand old man of Third World economists."[36] A US friend wrote to him, objecting to his being characterized as the "grandfather" and "patron saint" in the mainstream press. "It makes me suspicious that the capitalist world is about to take you into their establishment and go so far as to award you a Nobel prize."[37] This was a sore point. Prebisch had been nominated for the 1977 Nobel Prize in Economics by a group of economists and international personalities led by Victor Urquidi and Jan Tinbergen, the first winner in 1969, and supported by fellow recipients Paul Samuelson (1970), Gunnar Myrdal (1974), and Wassily Leontief (1974). As Tinbergen and others wrote, Prebisch's contribution was multidimensional and unique, comprising theory, institution-building, and policy – no other development economist of his generation could match his record of achievement.[38] But the nomination was rejected in favour of Sir Arthur Lewis.[39] Tinbergen resubmitted Prebisch's nomination for 1978, but it was equally unsuccessful, confirming that Prebisch lay outside the circle of economists with acceptable northern credentials.

Prebisch watched the predictable unravelling of the Latin American economy from Washington; it was poor comfort for him to cry "I told you so" after his warnings throughout the 1970s that easy money was not a sound basis for growth. The crisis came to a head in August 1982: as US interest rates rose, servicing the debt became onerous, until investment flows reversed and repayments exceeded new money. Latin America became a net exporter of capital to banks in the developed countries, and growth fell from 5.8 percent in 1980 to 1.2 percent in 1981, collapsing altogether the next year. Neither trade deficits nor interest payments could be financed. When Mexico announced its inability to service its foreign debt in August 1982, a crisis enveloped all of Latin America and plunged the region into its worst decade since the Great Depression.[40] The collapse of growth and access to credit sent poverty and capital flight skyrocketing, and the Latin self-confidence of the Carter years disintegrated. Chile did not escape: Pinochet's so-called economic miracle evaporated into deep recession.[41] From a region of global promise Latin America became synonymous with problems – debt, dictatorship, depression, and drugs – and its leverage became the humiliating threat of international financial insolvency. A fundamental restructuring could no longer be avoided: the Latin American state had to be reformed; the lush undergrowth of protected state enterprises had to be curbed; stability had to be restored; and the Latin private sector had to be modernized and made more productive. It was the worst possible moment for overhauling the state: Latin America had never been more vulnerable, and the IMF and Western banks were not going to be lenient. All of the region's gains since the Second World War were at risk as Latin America began adjusting to the new globalization taking place under the leadership of a resurgent Washington.

Prebisch felt completely isolated, completely outside the triumphant Reagan mainstream. The centre-periphery concept became hopelessly old-fashioned – almost an embarrassment. After 1981 the notion that development cooperation was an ethical imperative seemed quaint in Washington, the euphemisms of North-South relations such as "converging measures," "reciprocal interests," and the like out of favour. While American universities were narrowing their analysis and focusing increasingly on mathematical techniques, Prebisch stressed the multidisciplinary origins of the study of economics and the ethics of development. He noted the "fundamental problem of the ECLA years (common to all economists in centre-periphery relations but also in domestic affairs): focus was narrowly economic, rather than technology, culture and politics. These are not marginal," he insisted, "but form part of economic theory, or the ethic of development." He referred to economist Adam Smith's tenure as the chair of Moral Philosophy at Glasgow University and quoted Pope John Paul II: "Property is burdened by a social mortgage."[42]

When he was not forgotten altogether, Prebisch was vilified for leading the region in the wrong direction – pigeonholed as the author of Latin America's downfall for promoting an import-substitution model. For this reason he was also made responsible for the 1970s bubble, as well as the ensuing crash-and-debt crisis. No one remembered *Change and Development*, his term "elephantiasis of the state," or his warning that the 1970s would be seen as the lost decade. But no matter; an enemy was needed, and his attempts to set the record straight were drowned out in a wave of misrepresentation.[43] The popular identification of Prebisch with "the failure of the model" and debt crisis meant that ECLA's work of the 1950s was distorted and consigned to a remote historical corner for the next generation.[44]

Under attack in Washington's policy circles, Prebisch also faced criticism from theorists of all schools for his last work, *Peripheral Capitalism, Crisis and Change,* published in 1981 to faint applause. Chilean Marxist Heraldo Muñoz took him to task severely for his theoretical failings, quoting chapter and verse from Marx, Lenin, and Rosa Luxemburg. Osvaldo Sunkel found that Prebisch's analysis had strayed into his dependency-theory turf, that it lacked a theory of the state and left too many loose ends. Even Dell, although increasingly deferential to Prebisch as years passed, volunteered a five-page critique; and reverential ECLA colleagues like Octavio Rodriquez were perplexed by his imprecise definition of terms such as "structural surplus" in the text.[45] Meanwhile supply-side economists, now in the mainstream and supporting the existing global power networks, were miles distant from Prebisch's commitment to ethics and multilateralism. Post-Marxists such as his countryman Ernesto Laclau and other postmodern theorists were developing a "discursive" vocabulary foreign to Prebisch, who used language simply as an instrument to talk about the real world. Here also he appeared inadequate and old-fashioned.

But Prebisch held his ground. In his final years he was writing from his immense experience as a great intuitive economist turned prophet – he was not writing for academic journals. In this final phase of his thinking he enlarged his approach to development, discussing poverty, capital formation, consumption patterns, multinational enterprises, human rights, and institutional change alongside regional integration and international trade obstacles. In a return to the radicalism of his student days in Buenos Aires and traces of his thinking in the 1943–48 years, he directed discussion to social exclusion as the primordial obstacle to development in Latin America.[46] Confronted by the Reagan challenge, his task was to help focus the debate on development in Latin America. "Equitable distribution, vigorous economic growth and new institutional patterns in a genuinely participatory democracy: these are the major objectives," he underlined. Prebisch was certain that communism didn't work because it eliminated political freedom (and moreover didn't work in practice), while unrestricted liberalism was economically efficient but socially unsustainable. The challenge in building a new order was to bring together the advantages of both systems while avoiding the pitfalls. "I ask you what are your other solutions?" he demanded. "The free market and authoritarian governments have not solved the problem. I'm not dogmatic; I am just trying to provoke discussion."[47]

Of course life went on in Washington, and Prebisch refused to regret or despair. When Sidney Weintraub worried in April 1981 about the fallout from Reagan's victory, Raúl chose to describe it as a transition period in which "a few more years are necessary to see the light in another long and tortuous tunnel."[48] Old friends were dying and leaving. José Medina Echevarria had returned to Santiago to die in 1978, rejected by the Spain he had longed for since exile in 1939 and to which he had returned in 1973; José Antonio Mayobre passed away in September 1980; Alizon Garcia was terminally ill. David Pollock was returning to Canada to teach at Carleton University. Raúlito was grown up and would soon be off to Boston University. Raúl's health was still strong but not many more good years could be assumed. Unexpected disasters struck: in July 1982 surging floods on the Maipo undermined the cliff under his house, and one-third of his garden broke off into the canyon. Even the weather seemed to be turning against him. He renewed his US driver's license on 2 February 1981 to settle in for the longer haul and even became interested in his own history as long as this could be kept to his early Argentine years and the UN period.[49]

But increasingly Prebisch yearned to return to Buenos Aires, the city of his boyhood dreams and now those of his final years. Indeed his greatest joy was involving Argentine colleagues in the *CEPAL Review*, or joining them in special events such as the Oxford Conference in July 1981 on Argentina's political economy, 1920–60, which included leading scholars such as Guido di Tella, Arturo O'Connell, Tullo Halperin, Peter Alhadeff, and Javier Villaneuva. But returning to live was another matter. His departure in 1948 was an age away, and the only friendly government since the disaster of 1955–56 had been the brief Illia presidency, 1963–66, snuffed out by General Juan Carlos Ongania, after which Prebisch's name remained toxic in Argentina. A press rumour in February 1972 that General Alejandro Lanusse, Ongania's second successor, had invited Prebisch to lead another economic recovery program provoked protests in the capital, with Perónists denouncing him as an ultra-IMF liberal and business groups labelling him an ECLA socialist. Facing this outburst Lanusse immediately denied any offer to Prebisch, who sent cables swearing that he would never – drunk or sleeping – work for the Argentine military.[50] Since then the situation in Argentina had become increasingly violent and chaotic, the return of Juan Perón on 20 June 1973 and his death a year later on 1 July failing to stem a virtual civil war. The so-called "National Reorganization Process," led by Army Chief of Staff Jorge Videla after deposing Isabel Perón in March 1976, witnessed a descent into barbarism worse than Chile's under Pinochet and deepened Raúl's despondency. Videla was the twenty-first president since Prebisch had been named undersecretary of finance in 1930, and Argentina was approaching Bolivia in Latin America as a special study in political instability and decline. But he kept an eye on Argentina nonetheless, hoping for a break in news. In 1980 he visited Tucumán with Eliana to meet his sisters, Rosa, Elvira, and Lucia Piossek, and found it sullen and neglected; moreover, their old family home had been pulled down to widen a street. It used to be like Burgos in Spain, he lamented, but no more.[51] He envied Celso Furtado, Gabriel Valdes, and others who had returned to their countries as the dictatorships eased and civil society was gradually rebuilt. Valdes was now president of Chile's Christian Democrats, organizing a "Democratic Alliance" to prepare for a restoration of constitutional government. But while there were signs of progress in Brazil and Chile, Prebisch saw only steps backward in Argentina. The Ongania dictatorship had followed up its military coup against President Arturo Illia in 1966 with a self-destructive assault on Argentine scientists, the "Night of the Long Police Clubs," which sent 309 specialists into exile and terminated its regional leadership in computer technology, medicine, and agricultural research; and the 1976 "Process" had resumed the witch-hunt against Argentine intellectuals.

The 1982 Falklands/Malvinas war unexpectedly interrupted the military regime in Buenos Aires. General Leopoldo Galtieri, successor to Videla as the newest strongman, decided to reclaim the Falklands/Malvinas and Georgia/San Pedro Islands by force, invading and occupying these undefended British territories on 2 April in open violation of international law. Sovereignty over the islands was a popular theme at a time of growing shortages, and Galtieri believed that his training of Nicaraguan contras in Honduras counted more in Washington than two centuries of historic ties and shared interests with Britain – a fantastic dream that vanished on 30 April when the US formally supported Britain and declared economic sanctions against him. Argentina was therefore isolated before an approaching British naval group prepared to recapture the Falklands/Malvinas, with his lightly equipped soldiers stranded far from the mainland without adequate supplies. Trained to fight urban guerrillas, they were no match for Margaret Thatcher's Royal Marines, and while the Argentine Air Force proved plucky and skilful, Galtieri was forced to surrender and resign after seventy-two days. Even before the war inflation was running at 600 percent, and the economy had contracted 11.4 percent the previous year; defeat and 655 casualties, added to economic isolation and gross economic mismanagement, left the military unable to govern the country, and the junta was humbled into calling elections for 30 October 1983. "I am intensely attracted by the restoration of the democratic process after years of disaster," Prebisch remarked after hearing the news. The long exile, it appeared, might finally be ending.[52]

With democracy in the air after dictatorship and terror, Buenos Aires was transformed once more into an exciting world capital. Argentines everywhere shared the exhilaration of a definitive break from the long cycle of political futility and repression, and Prebisch used every opportunity to visit Buenos Aires. A G-77 meeting there from 28 March to 2 April 1983 followed a major all-party conference convened at the Faculty of Economic Sciences, and he was back again in July for a seminar on Latin American integration sponsored by INTAL (Institute for the Integration of Latin America). Both speeches emphasized the link between development and democracy and were widely reported in the media. Prebisch returned 23–26 August to attend a major conference, The Construction of Democracy in Argentina, organized by Aldo Ferrer, an unusual pre-electoral event that rallied old foes from across the political spectrum and with representatives from both the corporate world and labour. The leaders of all the political parties were present, including Perónist labour leader Saul Ubaldini, pledging to work together and build a new future for the country. Celso Furtado and Gabriel Valdes were also invited as symbolically essential representatives of Brazil and Chile as they also prepared their return to democracy. Prebisch gave the opening address, in which he laid out an agenda for restoring sound economic growth by ending the "vicious cycle" of deficits, inflation, and decline. He participated in a special closed meeting of the core group at Aldo Ferrer's home after the conference with Radical Party candidate Raúl Alfonsín. Chosen party leader in July, Alfonsin was a veteran party militant and human-rights activist whose criticism of the military regime in *The Argentine Question* had made him a national figure. Alfonsín and Prebisch had only briefly met over dinner in Washington five years earlier with Bernardo Grinspun, but Raúl knew ex-President Illia and many Radical Party members close to Alfonsín had been his students before 1948 or had worked with him at ECLA, ILPES, UNCTAD, or elsewhere in the UN. It was logical, therefore, that he should be perceived as a valuable link with the past.

When Alfonsín arrived in Washington in September for a pre-election briefing with US Congressional leaders, he met with Prebisch again to discuss the difficult economic options for an Argentina mired in debt and recession. Practically the entire future Alfonsín Cabinet was with him, including Bernardo Grinspun, Juan Sourrouille, and Enrique Garcia Vasquez. Whoever won the elections – Alfonsín or the Perónist Party – would inherit a miserable legacy from the Argentine generals. The new government would face the double challenge of reviving the country politically, while coping with 400 percent annual inflation, a $46 billion debt, and an annual economic contraction of 4.3 percent since 1980. In addition, capital flight by wealthy Argentines had to be reversed. The ten largest US banks had about 20 percent of their capital invested in Argentina, interest rates were rising, and Argentina's debts could no longer be serviced without rescheduling. After years of encouraging borrowing, the IMF and the banks had changed their tune: they were now insisting on "belt tightening" in exchange for new credits. During Alfonsín's visit to Washington a national rage against the IMF swept Argentina to the point where a judge froze negotiations between the Central Bank and foreign bankers and imprisoned Central Bank President Julio Gonzalez del Solar for ignoring domestic interests. Although he was released within a week, del Solar's experience frightened foreign bankers, and there was widespread speculation of a debt default with serious damage to the US banks holding most of the debt.[53]

After his election victory on 30 October, Alfonsín called Prebisch immediately to ask him to assist the new government. No other Argentine national could articulate Argentina's needs more forcefully with international agencies, and the range of Prebisch's experience made him an ideal senior advisor, given the economic challenges facing the country. For his part Raúl was overjoyed by Alfonsín's prompt invitation, yearning to leave Reagan's Washington and be part of the rebuilding of Argentine economic and political life. "I had to accept the kind invitation of President Alfonsín," he stated later; "The President is an excellent person, but the difficulties ahead are enormous ... I came with the emotion of an Argentine to see the country return to normality under such a great man."[54] They discussed options for Prebisch in the new government: there was no Council of Economic Advisors, and Raúl wanted more than the title of "roving ambassador," preferring something closer to the president and actual political power. Alfonsín therefore suggested "Advisor to the President with the rank of Secretary of State," immediately below ministerial rank in the new Cabinet – an "advisor at large," so to speak, on domestic and international economic matters facing the new government. It would be a unique position: Prebisch would work out of the Central Bank and report directly to the president, but he was to assist the four economic ministers: Minister of Economy Bernardo Grinspun, Minister of Foreign Affairs Dante Caputo, President of the Central Bank Enrique Garcia Vasquez, and Minister of Finance Juan Sourrouille. As in 1955, he insisted on working pro bono to pre-empt criticism of his motives; unlike in 1955 he had decided to return for good no matter what happened. By mid-1984 Eliana and Raúl had sold their property in Washington and purchased a spacious apartment in the centre of Buenos Aires on Galileo 2425.

Appointed before the inauguration, Prebisch started work immediately after President Alfonsín took office on 10 December 1983. It was a delicious moment: he was installed in a small suite across from the Church of the Merced, down the corridor from his grand old office in the Central Bank inhabited by Enrique Garcia Vasquez, who clearly valued his presence. He rehired Pedro Orradre, his secretary before October 1943 and again in 1955–56, who was now approaching seventy. He was lionized by the younger bank staff and adopted as éminence grise, given his international reputation and strong personality. But it was not clear whether Alfonsín or his ministers saw him as an "ideas person" or (as Raúl assumed) a hands-on advisor on government policy.

His first assignment, an analysis of the economic crisis facing the new government, monopolized his time until 19 January, when he submitted his report to President Alfonsín. The *Preliminary Plan for the Immediate Reactivation of the Economy* began by repeating the grim diagnosis set out in the president's address to the nation on 16 December: a per capita income less than in 1970, a disorganized banking and financial sector, declining productivity, and entrenched inflation – and all this in an international climate of falling terms of trade, low commodity prices, and high interest rates. It was, Prebisch acknowledged, an "extremely serious crisis," indeed, a "second depression," which was more difficult for Argentina than the first Great Depression.[55] Argentina had to return to stable growth, job creation, and higher productivity to increase real incomes.

The dilemma facing Alfonsín was fighting inflation while simultaneously reigniting growth and employment, with the Radical Party deeply split on policy. Prebisch had no doubt that the first and overwhelming priority had to be deficit reduction and the control of inflation, even though such measures were politically difficult for the new government. "The great economic and social objectives of the Government – as a point of departure for a long-term policy of development – will fail if public expenditures are not reduced and if the necessary resources for a planned reduction of the deficit are not located." Alfonsín's entire plan – lower interest rates, higher return on capital, increased investment, and a return of prosperity – rested on liquidating the inflationary spiral. The government, therefore, had to be prudent on wage increases and expenditures while cleaning up the disastrous mess left by the military and reactivating productive investment to expand exports of manufactured goods within a rational policy of import substitution. Once sound growth was restored, high prices and interest rates would gradually decline, and Prebisch urged that Alfonsín adopt an approach of "sacrifice with equity," or what he called "a rational sequence of measures" to deal with the crisis. But the starting point had to be controlling inflation.

Garcia Vasquez supported Prebisch, but Grinspun opposed him and the Cabinet was split. Alfonsín faced strong public sector demands for wage increases after the fall of the military; resisting these pressures in favour of deficit reduction ensured a challenge from the Perónist labour movement. The president had already agreed to a big public sector salary increase after taking office, to Prebisch's sharp disapproval. "The substantial adjustments granted in the second half of 1983 impose a heavy burden in the current year since wages account for an important share of government expenditure," he noted. "I am not arguing against wages, which are notoriously low. It all depends on how and when this is done." He concluded, "It is a difficult choice, but it must be made."[56]

Grinspun and Alfonsín decided to disregard Prebisch's advice, choosing a path of so-called "moderate inflation" to spread the adjustment process over a two- to three-year period. It was a difference, Grinspun, claimed, of tactics rather than strategy. Confronting many challenges and strong constituencies, they decided that a slower, consensual approach would placate the opposition and allow time for a still very fragile democracy to coalesce. Circumstances were difficult: the Radical Party victory had raised expectations, threats of a military coup remained, and so forth. Instead of decisive action, therefore, they preferred timid steps and were surprised when they proved ineffective: the first wage increase produced immediate demands for another, while their joint committees of labour, management, and government created in each economic sector to agree on wage and price guidelines collapsed in deadlock.

Grinspun explained his dilemma on inflation to Prebisch using a homely analogy of the family kitchen. "Like pepper and gefilte fish," he explained:

"It needs pepper," my father would always complain.

"How much?" mother would ask.

"Just right."

"How much is that?"

"Just enough."

"Just enough which way?"

"Not too much, and not too little."

"No, Bernardo," Prebisch differed. "No pepper at all!"[57] Successful stabilization was the central challenge, and decisive action at the outset would be accepted by the Argentine public, he argued; in fact it was the only way to maintain the prestige of the Radical Party. Internationally, Alfonsín also had strong support if he acted quickly, with his victory endorsed by leaders in France, Spain, and Italy. Bold action meant short-term, but nevertheless major, sacrifices from all the sectors – business, labour, and government – and Prebisch felt that any delay would undermine the sense of solidarity restored to Argentina after the return of democracy in 1983. The mood of the country in December was still positive, but the post-military euphoria was fragile. Once the glow faded, Argentine political life might return to its chronic paralysis, and governments in Argentina did not have a history of extended honeymoons. He openly condemned the government's wage increases. "Bad policy," he commented to the press.[58] Grinspun and other members of Alfonsín's team saw his criticism as disloyal and damaging, but Prebisch felt it his duty to warn the public against taking the wrong path in the forked road that lay ahead of his country. As inflation resumed and the earlier favourable public opinion toward the government began to reverse, his fears seemed justified.

Alfonsín's next assignment for Prebisch was leading a delegation to Washington to find a way out of the Argentine debt impasse. The near-satanic public image of the IMF in Argentina made this mission practically impossible. Much of the foreign debt contracted by the military regime and previous governments had been lost, squandered, or siphoned off to personal accounts, and pressure to default had initially persuaded Alfonsín to suspend interest payments.[59] But pressure also mounted for ending Argentina's international isolation, and in March 1984 Prebisch was sent to negotiate an IMF agreement. Grinspun's erratic behaviour, at times conciliatory and at times bellicose, but always arrogant and ignorant of the rules of the game, had brought relations with the IMF to a standstill. Like the inflation issue Washington could not be avoided, and Prebisch agreed to travel to Washington as a personal delegate of the president with all the bargaining power of an empty treasury. The negotiations were complex, involving the US Treasury as well as Mexico, Brazil, Colombia, and Venezuela, but an agreement-in-principle was reached on 29 March, which ended Argentina's exclusion from global capital markets on surprisingly favourable terms. Argentina's access to IMF lines of credit was restored, with a more generous servicing and repayment schedule on its $46 billion foreign debt than normal IMF practices. In addition, instead of Argentina resuming payments without regard to economic growth, the preliminary agreement signed by Prebisch and IMF Managing Director Jacques de Larosière linked debt payments to import needs; servicing the foreign debt would kick in only after these were satisfied. But although the agreement was a major achievement, it only gave breathing space until 30 June.

As news emerged of the IMF agreement, a public furore led by the opposition Perónist Party enveloped the Alfonsín Government. Argentine ambassador Julio Garcia del Solar, an incorruptible who had spent seventeen years in the UN during the dictatorship, gave a black-tie dinner for Prebisch in Washington the night of the IMF agreement, during which news arrived that someone in the Foreign Ministry had leaked the top-secret cable to *La Prensa,* the extreme right-wing newspaper of Buenos Aires. Next morning a front-page story titled "The Yellow Canaries" carried the full text of the agreement.[60] Returning home Prebisch held a press conference in the Casa Rosada, introduced by Alfonsín himself, in which he tried to explain what he had signed in Washington (a preliminary agreement), and why a formal agreement would take much more work. The journalists were interested only in taunts and personal insults.[61] Prebisch found himself celebrating his eighty-third birthday in an atmosphere reminiscent of the Roca-Runciman Pact or the 1955–56 syndrome, hounded on all sides by an ignorant and abusive press. Prebisch was condemned as IMF-friendly in his insistence on sound money as the prerequisite of healthy economic recovery. He was denounced for duping Alfonsín and Grinspun, for selling out Argentina to Western imperialism, and for negotiating an important state agreement as an unelected advisor behind the back of the Argentine congress. "Behind the structural adjustment favoured by Presidential Adviser Prebisch lurks the ghost of orthodoxy," *Clarin* warned.[62] The apparently inexhaustible undercurrent of Prebisch-phobia in Argentina was easily activated in academic circles as well. In 1983 the University of

Tucumán had approached him to accept an honorary doctorate, but professors in the Economics Department protested until the invitation was withdrawn.

Grinspun tried to defuse the growing opposition with a special visit to the Senate. Accompanied by his wife Eva, two children, and forty-one officials (to give a majority, one Senator noted), he spent eleven hours on 16 May 1984 answering questions about the IMF negotiation in Washington. When he mentioned Prebisch's name, Vicente Saadi, the Perónist majority leader from Catamarca, rudely interrupted: "I would like to say that the Perónist bloc does not share the Minister's views regarding the prestige of Doctor Prebisch, who has only served to deepen the colonialism and slavery of nations. The memory of his Central Bank work is still fresh."[63] Grinspun went over the IMF agreement word for word, trying to clarify the difference between the role of an advisor on the one hand, and that of a negotiator on the other. Prebisch had not "negotiated" the memorandum of understanding – Alfonsín and he, Grinspun, had made the political decisions. He insisted that the IMF austerity plan was not forced on Argentina but instead was freely agreed to as necessary public policy. "The new wage policy has nothing to do with the IMF discussions," he said, "with or without the IMF it has to be done."

By this time Grinspun and Alfonsín realized that they badly needed Prebisch in regional diplomacy on the debt crisis. In early 1984 ECLA had organized a foreign ministers' meeting to coordinate inter-American economic policies on interest rates; all Latin American countries were faced by a credit squeeze and virtually all Latin American and Caribbean countries supported a new regional initiative.[64] But in practice it was left for the "Big Four" – Brazil, Mexico, Argentina, and Colombia – to take the lead. Prebisch prepared the Argentine position with Foreign Minister Dante Caputo, and the "Four" met in May 1984, immediately before the G-7 Summit, issuing a joint statement that the debt was both a political and economic issue, implying joint responsibility of debtors and lenders in finding a solution. The "Four" then convened another foreign ministers' meeting in Colombia a month later and signed the Cartagena Consensus, whereby Latin American central banks would discuss and coordinate regional debt negotiations with creditor governments and institutions. The IMF, the World Bank, the US Treasury, and Western banking consortia worried that it was a first step toward forming a debtors' cartel. In fact, Prebisch and the Cartegena Group were not opposing negotiations with debtor countries but rather insisting that they take place within a regional framework linked to trade and development policy, which recognized the principle of "co-responsibility" of debtors and creditors in resolving the problem. Step by step Prebisch observed a revival of Latin confidence after the disaster of the debt crisis, a precondition for the so-called Baker Plan of 5 October 1985, which transformed the Third World debt crisis into a manageable problem.[65]

Grinspun asked Prebisch to return to Washington in summer 1984 for a second round of negotiations with Jacques de Larosière, and another provisional agreement was signed on 25 September. Paul Volcker, chair of the US Federal Reserve, commented, "Raúl is a man of great prestige," and suggested that he be named Argentina's permanent negotiator in Washington.[66] But Grinspun's own support in the Cabinet was undermined as the austerity program failed and the inflationary spiral continued – from Alfonsin's inauguration where it stood at 402 percent, it climbed to 449 percent by March and reached 713.4 percent by the end of the year. "I do not yet see a clear decision for a good emergency plan," he wrote on 10 September, "I am persuaded that it is absolutely possible to attack very vigorously the problem of inflation but regret to say that ideas exist different to mine, that interfere with the formulation of a good plan."[67] Government policy was not successful in reversing a deepening malaise; the early glow and sense of common effort surrounding the return to democracy dissipated during 1984, sapping the credibility of the Alfonsín Government; and Grinspun, the wild man of Argentine politics, was replaced by Juan Sourrouille in February 1985.

Prebisch's usefulness as advisor to the president diminished as differences with the new minister proved unbridgeable and inflation climbed to four digits. As Prebisch left Buenos Aires for eye surgery on 14 May, the US Embassy reported that he had resigned.[68] Subsequent efforts to stabilize the economy with a new currency, the Austral, were no more successful: hyper-inflation would reach a record level by Alfonsin's exit in 1989, and the Argentine public finally endorsed stability under his Perónist successor, Carlos Saúl Menem, when all other options had been explored and had failed.

21 House of the Spirits

If the practical outcome of Prebisch's advisory work for Alfonsín was similar to that with Lonardi and Arumburu in 1955–56, his reaction to failure was very different. This time he took his fate as advisor in stride: if disappointed, he was not wounded or depressed and had no intention of leaving Buenos Aires. He moved from the Central Bank to a modest desk in the local offices of ECLA and became a public fixture with his daily long march, head high and shoulders back, between Galileo and Corrientes. There was no bitterness in his relations with Alfonsín, Grinspun, or Vasquez: when the president made a state visit to India, Raúl accompanied him (given his many personal contacts and friends) and worked to rebuild Argentine ties with this global giant after its long diplomatic isolation. In fact Alfonsín refused to accept Raúl's resignation and proposed his appointment as "Ambassador-at-Large."[1]

In fact he was gripped by a curious, infectious excitement at a structure appearing in his own long life – that he was seeing the end of the twentieth century, just as he had arrived in Buenos Aires in 1918 as that terrible new century was taking shape. Then the situation of the world – militarily, politically, and economically – was unrecognizably different from the safety and prosperity before 1914. Empires had fallen, free trade had ended, and the Soviet Revolution had opened an East-West ideological divide. Now Gorbachev was in power, and the end of that defining rivalry between Soviet communism and market capitalism was playing out – in triumph for the West, with Washington poised to become the sole superpower. The Soviet Empire would fail, incapable of maintaining control of Eastern Europe or its own republics. Along with this geopolitical transformation, a new period of globalization in international trade, finance, and technology was about to sweep the entire world of developed and developing countries, changing their status and future, some like China and India to emerge as great powers. One could hope that this post-Cold War transformation would see democratic change, a winding down of regional conflicts, and a peace dividend to be invested in the great remaining agenda area of international development.

From Buenos Aires Prebisch saw important prospects, if not yet secure hopes, for a better century. He had arrived there sixty-eight years earlier to begin university; Argentina and Latin America had now changed in every way. For his homeland the comparison was unhappy: when he arrived from Tucumán on his birthday in 1918, Argentina was the second wealthiest country in the world; by 1986 it had been reduced to developing country status with an uncertain future. For Latin America as a whole the balance was also uncertain. The region had looked so promising in 1945 relative to Asia or Europe; now it was stuck in recession and debt and had fallen behind in the global system. However, the worst of the Latin American debt crisis was over with the Cartagena Consensus and the Baker Plan: governments were shaking off the "lost decade" of the 1970s and the great shock of 1982 and were again thinking as a region, as if to enter the new century with profile and energy, slowly regaining a political personality. In Central America, the Contadora Group was challenging US intervention in the region and actively launching a peace process with their own stamp.[2] Latins were discussing the launching of a new round of GATT negotiations; Uruguay was re-emerging as a regional interlocutor with the return of Enrique Iglesias from ECLA as foreign minister. A new impulse in regional integration was visible. Politically, the Rio Group Annual Summit of Presidents was emerging in Latin America from the habit of consultation that had been taking shape over debt, trade, and the Contadora peace process since 1982.[3] In regional trade within the Southern Cone, Prebisch also witnessed the change he had longed for since the 1930s, as Brazil and Argentina agreed to end their competition in 1985. Picking up where they left off in 1941, they began negotiations for MERCOSUR,[4] initially with Uruguay and Paraguay, in a bid to anchor regional free trade and terminate a dangerous nuclear and military rivalry.

Some salutary lessons had been learned in Latin America from the turmoil of the twentieth century. Democracy was returning to the continent as a generally recognized human right; military rule had ended in Argentina, Brazil, and Uruguay, and in Chile Pinochet was under pressure from an innovative left and the Christian Democratic Party who were building a more enduring and flexible democratic consensus. If Gabriel Valdes was reaching out to his erstwhile opponents, Heraldo Muñoz was abandoning Marxism for political pluralism and tolerance. The shock of the 1982 debt crisis had also yielded some lessons for economic policy in the region – the folly of closed markets, for example, or bloated state bureaucracies with high deficits and inflation, or the high cost of corruption. If macroeconomic stability did not guarantee growth, at least it was now seen as its prerequisite. If the twentieth century could be described as the "Age of Extremes,"[5] Argentina and Latin America had suffered sufficiently to enter the post-Cold War era with the knowledge – learned the hard way – of what to avoid.

But had Latin America learned enough, Prebisch wondered in his final year, and in his final essay he turned to this worry. Globalization was emerging as the new cliché in Washington, a new consensus was forming about measures appropriate for developing countries, and Latin economists were now as enthusiastic in importing North American models as they had been in 1918, when they devoured the English classics wearing their waistcoats and smoking briar pipes. Prebisch titled his paper "Absolute Imperative: New Economic Thinking in Latin America," to warn against accepting ideas uncritically.[6] He had survived too much of the twentieth century to believe in magic: the new religion of open markets could lead to extreme measures after the Cold War as easily as the previous abuse of ISI in the 1970s. If this happened after the Cold War, Latin America would find itself twenty years later in another period of disenchantment and sense of failure. He was not sure where Latin America was headed; this task belonged to the new generation. But eventually – perhaps not before another round of extremes – Latin Americans would find their own way out of the periphery to growth and equity. His own legacy to future generations was less policy than a distinctive style of thought, action, and ethics: whatever the fashion of the day, globalization must, and could, be guided by purposeful and rational policies, but success also required a new spirit of international cooperation to motivate societies and their governments.

Prebisch remained in flattering international demand with as much travel as he wished. He still directed the *CEPAL Review* in Santiago; visits to Santiago were always events, memorable to the junior staff he would invite for conversations. But most of all Prebisch was home: this was it – he would move no more. In Buenos Aires Eliana's infectious energy and quick wit quickly turned their attractive large apartment at 2425 Galileo into a meeting place for friends and the political debates he enjoyed so much. Already there was talk of designating a Raúl Prebisch Library in the Central Bank. Times were changing: a Prebisch revival in Buenos Aires was slowly but unmistakeably building. His popularity rose to the point where he and Eliana couldn't eat in restaurants without being disturbed. They deepened ties with Tucumán and family. Each day produced a greater calm and acceptance; after a life of stiff formality he began to *tutear* everyone. He rejoiced in the company of his disciples: don Benja (Hopenhayn) and his owl collection, mi querido Vasquito (Bardeci), Nun's great size ("What, Pepé, are you still growing?"), Pollock's hypochondria, Ciboti's engineer jokes, Aldo Ferrer's excessive earnestness ("*por favor,* Aldito"). He was at peace. He had coffee in all his old haunts, lamenting the decline of Buenos Aires while extolling its indestructible charm and compelling civic culture. Having returned, he realized how much he had missed this great city. How had so much survived so well? Buenos Aires, for all its scars, potholes, calamitous telephone service, and decaying subways, had retained an urbanism without parallel in the Americas. If the country seemed ungovernable, the capital was worthy of its great promise.

And of course, across the Andes above Santiago, he had El Maqui, his refuge and house of dreams, with its view of canyon, peaks, and skies embodying the majesty and mystery of Latin America, where Adelita was always ready to welcome him "home." Here alone Prebisch could ask the hardest questions. What was the balance of so long a life? Had he done his best? With all his gifts and talents, Prebisch had seen most of his great projects fail or not meet his expectations: the Central Bank, ECLA, UNCTAD, and ILPES. Was he marked by birth, his father's son so to speak, denied that singularity of purpose for the final hurdle? Could he have steered the Argentine Central Bank through the war intact? Or could his return in 1955–56 have worked out differently if he had not become personally involved? Why had he turned on Furtado and Ganz? Why had he not spoken out in defense of Allende? Why had he never written the "big book" on development theory after Havana, when it was crying to be completed? Why was he driven to treat Adelita the way he did, or to live like a millionaire while condemning "imitative capitalism"? A thousand failings and more – notwithstanding the odds against him in his work at every stage.

The historical verdict is different. Greatness, Prebisch would have remembered from his Jesuit teachers in Tucumán, is not the absence of vice so much as the achievement of good works; and his harsh self-criticism itself illustrates the deep and complex humanity that touched the lives of those around him. Prebisch was never neutral; he was a driving force in development thought and diplomacy who changed the vocabulary of international politics and cast a long shadow over the twentieth century. Theorist, humanist, and builder, he insisted on excellence, with his innovation withstanding the ebb and flow of fashion in development theory and current debates on Latin America and international governance. Without wielding state power, Raúl's vision and leadership achieved an extraordinary hold over those who knew and worked with him in Argentina, Latin America, and the global system. Prebisch's idealism carried him into the top international group of people who make history rather than endure it and continues to animate his followers in the struggle for global equity and justice.

On 6 April 1986, Prebisch left Buenos Aires for a conference in Ottawa organized by David Pollock. The students heard his attack on imitative capitalism; they marvelled at the time he spent with them and at his uncommon consumption of red wine at lunch and dinner. He then left to attend ECLAC's conference in Mexico City and delivered a lively address to the delegates. But the April chill of Ottawa and Mexico gave him a cold, and he returned to El Maqui on Sunday, 17 April, looking tired. But he drove to ECLA next morning in his white Mercedes for a full day's work on the journal, returning for dinner at 5:30, strolling with Adelita in the garden, enjoying an aperitif – whisky for Raúl, sherry for Adelita – as the sun fell behind the pines. He retired early to read Isabel Allende's new novel, *House of the Spirits*: a multigenerational family saga of great crimes and generosity, love of the land, and fortunes made and lost, where those who struggled hardest were the first betrayed – a portrait of a Latin America of power and vitality, beauty and forgiveness.

Turning off the light Raúl looked at Adelita: "That is a great book," he smiled, before going to eternal rest at 2:15 AM.

Acronyms

ABC Argentina, Brazil, Chile

BANFAIC Banco de Fomento Agricola e Industrial de Cuba (Cuban Agricultural and Industrial Development Bank)

BEW Board of Economic Warfare (US)

BNA Banco de la Nacion Argentina (Argentine National Bank)

BNDES Banco Nacional de Desenvolvimento Econômico e Social (National Economic Development and Social Development Bank) (Brazil)

CAPI Corporación Argentina para la Promoción de Intercambio (Argentine Trade Promotion Corporation) (1941)

CEBRAP Centro Brasileiro de Análise e Planejamento (Brazilian Centre of Analysis and Planning)

CECLA Special Coordinating Committee of Latin America

CGT Confederación General del Trabajo (General Confederation of Workers or National Labour Federation) (Argentina)

CIAP Comité Interamericano de la Alianza para el Progreso (Inter-American Committee for the Alliance for Progress)

COMECON Council for Mutual Economic Assistance (Soviet Bloc)

CSN Companhia Siderúrgica Nacional (National Steel Company) (Brazil)

DESA Department of Economic and Social Affairs (UN)

ECAFE Economic Commission for Asia and the Far East (UN)

ECE Economic Commission for Europe (UN)

ECLA Economic Commission for Latin America; in Spanish, CEPAL: Commissión Económica para America Latina. The name was changed in 1984 to ECLAC to highlight the inclusion of the Caribbean region

ECOSOC Economic and Social Council (UN)

EEC European Economic Community

FAO Food and Agriculture Organization (UN)
FM Fabricaciones Militares (General Agency for Military Industries) (Argentina)
FSLN Frente Sandinista de Liberación Nacional (Sandinista National Liberation Front) (Nicaragua)
G-77 Group of 77
GATT General Agreement on Tariffs and Trade
GOU Grupo de Oficiales Unidos (Group of United Officers) (Argentina)
GSP Generalized System of Preferences
IA-ECOSOC Inter-American Economic and Social Council
IAPI Instituto Argentino Para la Promoción de Intercambio (Argentine Institute for Trade Promotion) (1946–56)
ICA International Commodity Agreement
IDA International Development Association
IDB Inter-American Development Bank
IFI International Financial Institutions
ILO International Labour Organization (UN)
ILPES Instituto Latinoamericano de Planificación Económica y Social (Latin American Institute for Social and Economic Planning)
IMF International Monetary Fund
INTAL Instituto para la Integración de América Latina (Institute for the Integration of Latin America)
IRO International Relief Organization, later renamed the Office of the UN High Commissioner for Refugees
ITO International Trade Organization (UN)
LAFTA Latin American Free Trade Association
LDC Less Developed Country
MNC Multinational Corporation
MSA Most Seriously Affected Countries
NAM Non-Aligned Movement
NATO North American Treaty Organization
NIEO New International Economic Order
OAS Organization of American States
OECD Organization for Economic Cooperation and Development
PRI Partido Revolucionario Institucional (Institutional Revolutionary Party) (Mexico)
SELA Sistema Económico Latinoamericano (Latin American Economic System)
SFM Supplementary Financing Mechanism
SRA Sociedad Rural Argentina (Argentine Rural Society)

SUNFED Special UN Fund for Economic Development
TDB Trade and Development Board (UNCTAD)
UBA University of Buenos Aires
UCR Unión Cívica Radical (Radical Party) (Argentina)
UCRI Unión Cívica Radical Intransigente (Radical Party – Intransigent) (Argentina)
UIA Unión Industrial Argentina (Union of Argentine Industrialists)
UNAM Universidad Nacional Autónoma de México (National Autonomous University of Mexico)
UNCTAD United Nations Committee on Trade and Development
UNDP United Nations Development Programme
UNEP United Nations Environment Programme
UNESCO United Nations Educational, Scientific and Cultural Organization
UNIDO United Nations Industrial Development Organization
UNLP Universidad Nacional de La Plata (Argentina)
USAID United States Agency for International Development

Notes

CHAPTER ONE

1 Magariños, unpublished part of an interview with Raúl Prebisch that was edited and published as *Diálogos*, 12. Future references are to the published *Diálogos*.

2 In a vast bibliography, see Walter, *Politics and Growth in Buenos Aires*; Abós, ed., *El libro de Buenos Aires*; Keeling, *Global Dreams, Local Crises*; Ruggiero, *Modernity in the Flesh*; Bailey, *Immigrants in the Land of Promise* Press; Scobie, *Buenos Aires: From Plaza to Suburb.*

3 Lalanne, *Los Uriburu.* The following pages rely on interviews with Raúl Prebisch before his death in 1986, particularly Pollock, *Conversations with Raúl Prebisch*, subsequently edited and published in sections by Pollock, Love and Kerner; Magariños, *Diálogos*; and Gonzalez del Solar, "Conversaciones."

4 Scobie, *Argentina: A City and a Nation*, 143.

5 Magariños, *Diálogos*, 30–3, in particular.

6 *La Prensa*, 21 November 1903, quoted in Korzeniewicz, "Labour Unrest in Argentina," 71–98.

7 Magariños, *Diálogos*, 31. According to Prebisch, his grandmother would say, "Hijo, no te juntés con lomos negros." ["Boy, don't mix with these dark ragamuffins."]

8 Magariños, *Diálogos*, 36. "She was the one who protected us."

9 Ibid., 38.

10 Pollock, *Conversations with Raúl Prebisch*, 6. Adela Moll de Prebisch, interviews with the author between 1989 and 2001.

CHAPTER TWO

1 The best account of Prebisch's experiences during this period is found in Magariños, *Diálogos*.

2 For the history of political parties in Argentina, see Pasos, *Historica del Origen de los Partidos*; Canton, *Elecciones y Partidos*; Manzetti, *Institutions, Parties and Coalitions*; Gibson, *Class and Conservative Parties.*
3 Lewis, *Crisis of Argentine Capitalism,* 34ff, 84, 112.
4 Scobie, *Argentina: A City and a Nation,* 134, 191.
5 Lalanne, *Los Uriburu,* 396–9, 407–9.
6 See Magariños, *Diálogos,* 39–46, on Prebisch and the intellectual life of Buenos Aires after the Soviet Revolution. See also Kay, *Latin American Theories of Development,* 16.
7 Gonzalez del Solar, "Conversaciones," 3–4, 10.
8 Love, "Economic Ideas and Ideologies in Latin America."
9 Lewis, *Crisis of Argentine Capitalism,* 62; Dorfman, *Historia de la industria argentina,* 207.
10 Ibid.; Lewis, *Crisis of Argentine Capitalism,* 87. See also della Paolera and Taylor, eds, *New Economic History of Argentina.*
11 Pollock, *Conversations with Raúl Prebisch,* 7. Quoted in Gonzalez and Pollock, "Del orthodoxo al conservador ilustrádo," 455–86.
12 Lopez, "Hugo Broggi," 303–28.
13 Magariños, *Dialogos,* 20; Gonzalez del Solar, "Conversaciones," 8; Pollock, "*Conversations,*" tape 1B 1, 21 May 1985.
14 Prebisch, "La cuestión social," 11–12.
15 The first eight articles in Prebisch, *Obras,* vol. 1 are examples of these.
16 Magariños, *Diálogos,* 47.
17 Malaccorto, interview with the author.
18 Magariños, *Diálogos,* 50–1.
19 Ibid.
20 Ibid., 50.
21 Gonzalez del Solar, "Conversaciones," 8.
22 Magariños, *Diálogos,* 50.
23 Prebisch, *Obras,* vol. 1 pp. 6–7. For Prebisch's defense of the conventional view of the international division of labour during the 1920s, see "De cómo discurre el profesor Olariaga," 466–80.
24 I am indebted to Dr Mario Bunge for his insights and assistance, particularly in this section.
25 Lalanne, *Los Uriburu,* 387–8, 394.
26 Palacios, *Dos años de acción socialista*; cited in Lalanne, *Los Uriburu,* 387–91. Justo was sufficiently prominent in the Second International to have been invited at its annual meeting in 1914 to address the socialist gathering on the subject of worker wage parity.
27 Mario Bunge, interview with the author.
28 Gonzalez del Solar, "Conversaciones," 4–5.

29 Malaccorto, interview with the author; See also Pollock, Kerner, and Love, "Aquelles viejos tiempos," 164.
30 Prebisch, "La Conferencia de Bruselas," 43–54.
31 Prebisch, "Anotaciones sobre nuestro medio circulante," 93–175.
32 Ibid., 95.
33 Ibid., 149.
34 Ibid., 126.
35 Prebisch, "Planes para estabilizar el poder adquisitivo," 176–216.
36 Barone, "Studi di economia finanziaria." In Magariños, *Diálogos* (unpublished version), Prebisch says that Pareto "had a great influence on my intellectual formation" (35).
37 Prebisch, "La sociología de Vilfredo Pareto," 365–74.

CHAPTER THREE

1 See Gurrieri, "Las ideas del joven Prebisch," 69–82; Gonzales and Pollock, "Del ortodoxo al conservador ilustrado," 455–86; and Lewis, *Crisis of Argentine Capitalism*, 21–2.
2 Magariños, *"Diálogos,"* 52.
3 Lewis, *Crisis of Argentine Capitalism*, 52. Also see Thorp, *Progress, Poverty and Exclusion*.
4 Thorp, *Progress, Poverty and Exclusion*, 102.
5 Prebisch, "Información estadística sobre el comercio de carne vacuna," 236–303; Mowat, *Britain between the Wars*, 257.
6 Prebisch, "Sobre la degradación del marco," 234; Mowat, *Britain between the Wars*, 257.
7 Prebisch, "Comercio de carne vacuna," 259.
8 Lewis, *Crisis of Argentine Capitalism*, 52; Gonzalez del Solar, "Conversaciones," 6.
9 Prebisch, "Anotaciones sobre la crisis ganadera," 304–49.
10 Eleodoro Lobos, "Prologo" to Cercano, "*Evolucion historica del regimen*," 32–3.
11 Gonzalez del Solar, "Conversaciones," 6.
12 Quoted in Prebisch, "Primer informe del Doctor Raúl Prebisch," 403.
13 Prebisch, "El problema de la tierra," 376–80.
14 Prebisch, "Determinacion de la capacidad impossible," 381–92; "Primer informe," 401–3.
15 Gonzalez del Solar, "Conversaciones," 7.
16 Lewis, *Crisis of Argentine Capitalism*, 72.
17 Prebisch, "Aclaraciones al Proyecto de colonización del Poder ejecutivo," 393–409; also Gonzalez del Solar, "Conversaciones," 9–10.
18 Magariños, *Diálogos*, 57.

19 I am indebted to Ernesto Malaccorto for this section.
20 Gonzalez del Solar, "Conversaciones," 11.
21 Prebisch, "Anotaciones a la estadística nacional," 404–20.
22 Prebisch, "Anotaciones demográficas," 421–65.
23 Prebisch, "Anotaciones demograficos," addresses the neo-Malthusian controversy, 460–3.
24 Gonzalez del Solar, "Conversaciones," 13.
25 Thorp, *Progress, Poverty and Exclusion,* 112.
26 Ibid., 101.
27 Malaccorto, interview with the author; Meltzer, *A History of the Federal Reserve, 1913–51.*
28 Gonzalez del Solar, "Conversaciones," 12.
29 Followed by Prebisch organizing Argentina's First National Statistical Conference in Cordoba, bringing together statisticians from all over the country and representing every sector. Gonzalez del Solar, "Conversaciones," 13.
30 Correspondence between Albin Prebisch and Raúl Prebisch, 20 September 1926, Prebisch Papers. See also Margarinos, *Diálogos,* 50–1, for Prebisch's description of father-son relations.
31 Prebisch, "El régimen de pool," 481–97.
32 De la Torre was also a wealthy landlord, but he belonged to the cattle-breeders supplying calves to the SRA ranchers who sold mature animals to the Buenos Aires stockyards.
33 Prebisch, "De cómo discurre el profesor Olariaga," 466–80.
34 Prebisch, "El movimiento internacional del oro," 553.

CHAPTER FOUR

1 Bunge, interview with the author.
2 *Revista Economica* 1, no. 1 (1928): 3–5.
3 Magariños, *Diálogos,* 63.
4 Scobie, *Argentina: A City and a Nation,* 219.
5 Lalanne, *Los Uriburu,* 446–7.
6 Lewis, *Crisis of Argentine Capitalism,* 89–91.
7 Magariños, *Diálogos,* 30–1.
8 Ibid., 65. Bunge, interview with the author.
9 Lalanne, *Los Uriburu,* 445–54.
10 Gonzalez del Solar, "Conversaciones," 14.
11 Ibid., 15.
12 Gonzalez and Pollock, "Del ortodoxo al conservador ilustrádo," 460–1; Louro de Ortiz, *El Grupo Pinedo-Prebisch,* 28–9.
13 Lewis, *Crisis of Argentine Capitalism,* 117.

14 Mowat, *Britain between the Wars*, 441.

15 Ibid., 417–18; Love, "International Intellectual Environment," 59–66.

16 Mattera, *Argentine Commercial Banking*, 65–6; Gonzalez del Solar, "Conversaciones," 14–20.

17 Gonzalez and Pollock, "Del ortodoxo al conservador"; Gonzalez del Solar, "Conversaciones," 15.

18 Magariños, *Diálogos*, 69–70.

19 Lewis, *Crisis of Argentine Capitalism*, 86; Lalanne, *Los Uriburu*, 476.

20 Gonzalez del Solar, "Conversaciones," 20.

21 Adela Moll de Prebisch, interviews with the author.

22 Adelita Prebisch to Rosa Linares, 10 October 1932, Prebisch Papers.

23 Adela Moll de Prebisch, interview with the author.

24 When Argentina rejoined the League, Saavedra Lamas became president of the League Assembly in 1936.

25 Printed in *The Times* (London), June 1933.

26 Adelita Prebisch to Rosa Linares, 6 January 1933.

27 Cassel, "Recent Monopolistic Tendencies," 43–4. Noted in Love, "International Intellectual Environment," 59–66.

28 Manoilesco's book, *The Theory of Protection and International Trade.* Love has written extensively on Manoilesco and Prebisch in the history of economic thought in the 1930s. See, for example, his "Manoilescu, Prebisch, and Unequal Exchange."

29 Mallorquín, "Un texto de Raúl Prebisch," quoted in Eichengreen, *Golden Fetters*, 320–1.

30 Prebisch, "La Conferencia Económica y la crisis mundial," 86–101.

31 Mowat, *Britain between the Wars*, 417–18.

32 Lewis, *Crisis of Argentine Capitalism*, 86.

33 Gonzalez and Pollock, "Del orthodoxo al conservador," 10–16; Lewis, *Crisis of Argentine Capitalism*, 90. See, among others, Di Tella and Platt, eds, *Political Economy of Argentina*; Villanueva, "Economic Development"; Di Tella and Halperin, eds, *Los Fragmentos del poder*; Fordor and O'Connell, "La Argentina y la economia Atlántica"; Escudé, *The Argentine Eclipse.*

34 Keynes, *The Means to Prosperity.*

35 Quoted in Mowat, *Britain between the Wars*, 414.

CHAPTER FIVE

1 Lewis, *Crisis of Argentine Capitalism*, 81–3, 88; Diaz Alejandro, *History of the Argentine Republic*, 11.

2 Malaccorto, interview with the author. Prebisch, "La producción rural y el mercado de cambios," in *Obras*, vol. 2, 146–57. For further discussion, see Gurrieri, "Las ideas del joven Prebisch," 78–9.

3 Lewis, *Crisis of Argentine Capitalism*, 50, 91.
4 Gonzalez and Pollock, "Del orthodoxo al conservador ilustrádo," 470–2.
5 *La Nacion*, 29–30 November 1933; 29 January 1934. Enrique S. Perez directed the National Mortgage Bank.
6 Adela Moll de Prebisch, interviews with the author. See, for example, *La Nacion*, 13 November 1933; 27 December 1933; 30 January 1934. All of the newspaper articles Prebisch wrote during this period are in the Prebisch Papers.
7 Love, "Economic ideas and ideologies," 214.
8 *Deutsche la Plata Zeitung*, 9 February 1934.
9 *Critica* was owned by Natalio Botana.
10 Bunge, interview with the author.
11 *La Nacion*, 19 July 1934.
12 *La Prensa*, 18 July 1934; *La Nacion*, 16 June 1934.
13 Prebisch, "Anotaciones sobre el Cambio y los Emprestitos," *La Nacion*, 28 June 1933.
14 *La Nacion*, 3 August 1934.
15 *La Nacion*, 18 November 1934.
16 Mattera, "Argentine Commercial Banking," 40–1.
17 Triffin, "Central Banking and Monetary Management," Prebisch Papers, 10.
18 *La Nacion*, 7 June 1935.
19 *La Nacion*, 16 July 1935; Mattera, "Argentine Commercial Banking," 58.
20 *La Nacion*, 2 September 1935.
21 Gonzalez del Solar, "Conversaciones," 22–3.
22 Adela Moll de Prebisch, interview with the author. The original typewritten draft of the speech is in the Prebisch Papers.
23 *La Nacion*, 20 December 1934.
24 *La Nacion*, 9 January 1935.
25 *La Fronde*, 20 February 1935.
26 For Prebisch's thoughts on Lisandro de la Torre's banking activities in this period, see Magariños, *Diálogos*, 117.
27 *El Hogar*, 28 June 1935.
28 *Caras y Caretas*, 13 July 1935.
29 Magariños, *Diálogos*, 49.
30 Triffin, "Central Banking and Monetary Management," 11.
31 Love, "Economic Ideas and Ideologies," 212.
32 For example, 6 March 1938, regarding exchange-rate policy of the Central Bank.
33 Berger to Prebisch, 23 September 1938. All correspondence referred to in this chapter can be found in the Prebisch Papers.
34 Mattera, "Argentine Commercial Banking," 67.
35 Berger to Prebisch, 21 November 1938.
36 Prebisch to Brebbia, 15 July 1939.

37 Mannheimer to Brebbia, 16 July 1939.

38 *La Nacion*, 22 August 1939.

CHAPTER SIX

1 The official Nazi agency Deutsche Dienst announced the news, indicating that a diplomatic breach had opened between the two countries; US Embassy (Berlin) to Secretary of State Cordell Hull, 9 January 1940.

2 US consul-general (Buenos Aires) to State Department, 28 October 1940. *The Cumulated Index to the US Department of State Papers 1939–45*, volume II, 481.

3 For example, in a letter of 12 January 1940, the California Deciduous Growers' Group, representing 75 percent of all deciduous and grape growers, underlined the "desperate condition" of its members to Cordell Hull and their urgent need for a quota on Argentine imports.

4 Armour to Hull, 17 June 1940.

5 Armour to Hull, 17 June 1940. This was the second telegram that day to the secretary of state; Armour used the phrase in the second.

6 *La Nacion*, "Tomara el P.E. una Serie de Medidas para Promover un Desarrollo Industrial Sano," 28 June 1940. Llach, "El Plan Pinedo de 1940"; Baldinelli, *Comercio Exterior Argentina;* Diaz Alejandro, *Essays on the History of the Argentine Republic*; Di Tella, "Policy Changes in Argentina"; Alhedeff, "The Economic Formulas."

7 Porcile, "The Challenge of Cooperation 1939–55," 129–59.

8 Llach, "El Plan Pinedo de 1940," 524–5.

9 Ibid., 533; Rapaport, *Clases dirigentes argentinas*, 1976.

10 Alfonso Sanjuan, "Camino al MERCOSUR," 50–5.

11 *La Nacion*, "La conferencia económica Argentino-Brasileña fué inaugurada ayer en Rio," 10 October 1940.

12 John W. White, "Argentina Seeks Trade Concessions," Washington *Post*, 17 November 1940.

13 John W. White, "Customs Union with the United States Real Goal of Argentine Economic Mission," *Boston Herald*, 17 November 1940.

14 *The Times Herald*, 20 November 1940.

15 Gonzalez del Solar, "Conversaciones," 33.

16 The CAPI is not to be confused with IAPI, the Argentine Institute for Production and Trade, set up in the time of Perón.

17 Ibid., 31.

18 Ravndal to Lawrence Duggan, 9 August 1941.

19 US State Department memorandum, "The Pinedo Plan to Stimulate the Export of New Articles from Argentina," 29 November 1940.

20 Adelita Prebisch, interview with the author.

21 Henry Frantz, "US, Argentina sign $50 m Economic Pact," *The Times Herald*, 28 December 1940; *Wall Street Journal*, 28 December 1940.

22 *Journal of Commerce*, New York, 26 and 28 December 1940; "Agreement Signed to Help Argentina," *New York Times*, 2 January 1941.

23 Gonzalez del Solar, "Conversaciones," 33.

24 Ibid., 36.

25 Hull to Armour, 8 January 1941.

26 *La Prensa*, 25 January 1941.

27 Lewis, *Crisis of Argentine Capitalism*, 192–3.

28 Llach, "El Plan Pinedo de 1940," 529–30.

29 Hull to Roosevelt, 6 February 1941.

30 For example, articles praising the state of US-Argentine relations appeared in the New York *Journal of Commerce*, 26 December 1940, the *New York Times*, 2 January 1941, and the *Times Herald*, 24 December 1940.

31 Norbert A. Bogden, J. Henry Schroeder Banking Corporation, New York, to Laurence Duggan, advisor to the secretary on political relations, US State Department, 8 July 1941.

32 US State Department, *Memorandum*, 5 and 18 August 1941; Llach, "El Plan Pinedo de 1940," 528.

33 L. Duggan to Welles, 31 July 1941; Welch to Welles, 31 July 1941; Welles to Welch, 5 August 1941; Ravndal to Duggan, 9 August 1941.

34 US Embassy to State Department, 23 May 1941.

35 Armour to Hull, 5 July 1941; Llach, "El Plan Pinedo de 1940," 522.

36 Gonzalez del Solar, "Conversaciones," 35.

37 *Washington Post*, 17 September 1941.

38 Newton, *The Nazi Menace in Argentina*, 219. Gonzalez del Solar, "Conversaciones, 48–9.

39 Llach, "El Plan Pinedo de 1940," 530.

40 Ibid., 539.

41 Prebisch to Armour, 9 May 1941.

42 Brebbia to Prebisch, 24 January 1940.

CHAPTER SEVEN

1 Cordell Hull to Norman Armour, 7 January 1942.

2 Armour to Hull, 19 December 1941.

3 Rapaport, *Gran Bretaña, Estados Unidos y las clases dirigentes Argentinas*, particularly chapter 2.

4 US State Department memorandum, "Argentine Delegation to the Rio Conference," 2 January 1942. Quoted in Scobie, *Argentina: A City and a Nation*, 221.

5 Armour to Hull, 2 January 1942.

6 Hull to US Embassy, 4 January 1942.
7 Welles to Hull, 19 January 1942.
8 Welles to Hull, 22 January 1942.
9 Armour to Welles, 11 June 1942.
10 Armour to Hull, 15 June 1942.
11 Bohan, *Oral Interview*, 9.
12 Gonzalez del Solar to Prebisch, 10 February 1942.
13 Armour to Hull, 14 October 1941.
14 US State Department, *Foreign Relations of the US, 1939–45*, II, 435.
15 US secretary of state to US ambassador, 8 October 1941.
16 Hoover to Assistant Secretary Of State Berle, 22 January 1942.
17 Armour to Hull, 2 January 1942.
18 Armour to Hull, 2 January 1942. Adolphe Berle has less patience with J. Edgar Hoover. In a letter of 25 April 1942 to US Attorney General Francis Biddle, he emphasized that "Dr Prebisch has been very cooperative with the American Ambassador in Argentina" and added that Alfredo Moll, at Raúl's insistence, had visited the US Embassy specifically to discuss his previous work with German-owned firms. US Department of State, Adolfe A. Berle to Frances Biddle, 25 April 1942.
19 Gonzalez del Solar, *Conversaciones*, 34.
20 US Treasury Department memorandum, 12 May 1942.
21 US State Department memorandum of conversation with Raúl Prebisch, 5 August 1942.
22 Merwin Bohan, US State Department memorandum, 17 April 1942.
23 US State Department, memorandum of conversation, 5 August 1942.
24 Ravndal to Prebisch, 7 January 1943.
25 Rapaport, *Clases Dirigentes Argentinas*, 135–7.
26 Merwin Bohan, US State Department memorandum, 24 May 1943.
27 Newton, *Nazi Menace in Argentina*, 219.
28 Ibid. Indeed, Britain demanded that Argentina continue its beef exports to support the war effort; US State Department, "Economic Policy toward Argentina," 23 September 1942.
29 Hull to Armour, 14 December 1942.
30 Bohan, Conversation of Visit to Raúl Prebisch in the Central Bank, 27 March 1943.
31 Bohan, *Memorandum*, 26 April 1943.
32 Bohan, 12 April 1943.
33 Bohan, 26 April 1943.
34 Malaccorto to Prebisch, 27 May 1943.
35 Ravndal to Prebisch, 31 August 1943.
36 Bohan, memorandum of conversation, 24 May 1943.
37 Ibid.
38 Argentine Central Bank, *Annual Report*, Buenos Aires, 1943.

39 *Revista de la economia Argentina,* 22 May 1943; Lucchini, 42, 44–58; Central Bank Annual Reports, 1942, 1943.
40 Lewis, *Crisis of Argentine Capitalism,* 124; Llach, "El Plan Pinedo de 1940."
41 *La Nacion,* 20 April 1943.
42 Rapaport, *Clases Dirigentes Argentinas,* 137–40.
43 Ibid., 142.
44 British Chamber of Commerce, Buenos Aires, 22 November 1942.
45 Rapaport, *Clases Dirigentes Argentinas,* 133, 148–51.
46 Bunge, *Una nueva Argentina.*
47 US State Department, Armour to Hull, 5 June 1943.
48 *New York Times,* 5 June 1943.
49 Gonzalez del Solar, *Conversaciones,* 34.
50 Bunge, interview with the author; FBI records for this period, its 23 July and 2 August 1943 reports in particular, have been totally blacked out.

CHAPTER EIGHT

1 The author's interviews with Adela Moll de Prebisch are a key source for this section of the book.
2 *La Nacion,* 23 August 1943.
3 *La Nacion,* 1 and 3 September 1943.
4 *La Nacion,* 1 September 1943.
5 *La Nacion,* 17 September 1943.
6 Pollock, *Conversations with Raúl Prebisch.*
7 US Embassy to US State Department, 15 October 1943.
8 The Prebisch Papers contain a full record of media coverage of his dismissal.
9 Armour to Hull, 25 October 1943.
10 Bohan to Associate Advisor on Economic Affairs Emilio G. Callado, marked "Strictly Confidential."
11 *Time* Magazine, "The Harm Is Done: Argentine Military Fascism Is Well Established," 31 January 1944.
12 Allan Dawson to US State Department, 12 January 1944.
13 Silva to Prebisch, 23 October 1943.
14 Adelita bequeathed the family estate in Plön on the Baltic Sea to the Lutheran Church, which converted it into a youth centre and school.
15 Prebisch, "La moneda y el ritmo de la actividad economica." Subsequent quotations in the text are taken from this important document which was never published (located in the Prebisch Papers, Reel 2, 1944–47).
16 For details, see Dosman, "Markets and the State," 90–4.
17 Gonzalez del Solar to Prebisch, 28 December 1943; also M.A. Martinez to Prebisch, 27 December 1943. Prebisch met the dean on 2 January 1944; he had not given his seminar for the previous six years.

18 Ambassor Carlos Dario Ojeda to Prebisch, 22 December 1943.
19 Manuel Monteverde to Prebisch, 6 November 1943.
20 Prebisch to Dario Ojeda, 25 December 1943. In fact, the Bank of Mexico's invitation had been sent 1 December 1943 by air mail and had not yet reached Argentina. Banco de Mexico, "Memorandum para don Raúl Prebisch en relacion con su viaje a México," Banco de Mexico, Mexico, 1 December 1943.
21 Prebisch had not given up the prospect of eventual return to the Central Bank: he was therefore cautious about publication. "They invited me to explain the experience of the Central Bank of Argentina. It is the best explanation and the best criticism of what I did. I spoke openly, on the condition that they would not publish it immediately, but only after a couple of years." Pollock, conversations, tape 3A 1, 21 May 1985.
22 Bosch to Prebisch, 5 January 1944.

CHAPTER NINE

1 Prebisch often spoke with great affection about this first trip to Mexico. Margariños, *Diálogos,* 131–3.
2 Thorp, *Progress, Poverty and Exclusion,* 114, 313.
3 Robert Triffin, "Central Banking and Monetary Management in Latin America," 11–12. This manuscript is included in the Prebisch Papers.
4 For example, R.H. Thomson of the National City Bank of New York, 20 January 1944, and G. Butler Sherman, Manufacturers' Trust Co., 5 April 1944.
5 Daniel Cosío Villegas would be offered the position of founding executive secretary of ECLA in 1948, which he declined; he would later serve as Mexico's ambassador to UN ECOSOC from 1957 to 1968.
6 Prebisch, "Conversaciones en el Banco de México." During the same period Prebisch also gave a seminar at the Colegio de México, "El patrón oro y la vulnerabilidad económica de nuestros países."
7 Prebisch to Triffin, 17 June 1945.
8 *El Federal,* "The AntiPatria is trying to conceal its financial leaders like Prebisch to control the country," 5 May 1944.
9 M.A. Martinez to Prebisch, 17 March 1944.
10 Roberto Hurtiacavq, Argentine Embassy in Washington, to Prebisch, 7 March 1944.
11 Republic of Paraguay, Presidential Decree 5130, *Que Crea y Organiza el Banco del Paraguay,* Asuncion, 8 September 1944.
12 Triffin to Prebisch, 28 March 1945.
13 Coll Benegas, "Anotaciones sobre las negociaciónes comerciales con el Paraguay," Argentine Ministry of Foreign Affairs, October 1943.
14 Needless to say, J. Edgar Hoover took a different view of the Paraguay mission, reporting "possible subversive activities," to the US secretary of state; US National Archives, Diplomatic Branch, 27 June 1944 894.20210 (FOIA).

15 The preceding section describing the river voyage to Asunción relies on the detailed accounts of Adelita Prebisch, particularly the many interviews conducted between 1989 and 1995.

16 Whigham and Potthast, in "The Paraguayan Rosetta Stone," 174–86, estimate the pre-1864 population at between 420,000 and 450,000. The authors reply to critiques of their work in *LARR* 37:3 (2002). See also Scheina, *Latin America's Wars*; Leuchars, *To the Bitter End*; Maestri, "Guerra contra o Paraguai."

17 Bunge, *El Culto de la Vida*.

18 Prebisch, *Informe sobre la organization y el programa de tareas de la Division de Investigaciones Economicas*.

19 Triffin to Prebisch, 23 July 1945.

20 Family of Carlos Moll, interview with the author, Santiago, 16 March 1998.

21 Triffin to Prebisch, 28 March 1945.

22 Ibid.

23 Triffin to Prebisch, 23 August 1945.

24 Prebisch to Triffin, 17 June 1945.

25 Ibid.

26 Prebisch to Triffin, 21 September 1945.

27 For example, *La Epoca*, "The Failure of the Plan to Re-insert Prebisch in the Central Bank," 19 September 1945; and again on 30 August 1945, "The Snipers of the Central Bank." *Semana Financiera* (1 September) and *La Nacion* (14 September) carried long reports on the case and the US Embassy in Buenos Aires followed the Central Bank crisis closely (US National Archives on 17 August 1945; and 835, 26 September 1945).

28 *La Prensa*, 22 September 1945. Emilio F. Cardenas and Faustino Infante were appointed Central Bank president and vice-president respectively.

29 Prebisch to Triffin, 21 September 1945.

30 For the rise of Perón, see Murmis and Portantiero, *Estudios sobre los origins del Peronismo*; Alexander, *Juan Domingo Perón: A History*; Brennan, *Peronism and Argentina*.

31 Crawley, *A House Divided*, 95–8.

32 Prebisch to Triffin, 10 December 1945.

33 Prebisch to Manuel Noriega Morales, 10 December 1945.

34 The infamous US State Department Blue Book was titled *Consultation among the American Republics with Respect to the Argentine Situation*. Spruille Braden, briefly US ambassador to Argentina, had returned to Washington as undersecretary of state for Latin American Affairs. Crawley, *A House Divided*, 103–5 provides a spirited account of the incident.

35 Prebisch to Luis Montes de Oca, 2 November 1946.

CHAPTER TEN

1 Triffin to Prebisch, 30 October 1945.

2 Welch to Prebisch, 23 April 1946.
3 Villaseñor to Prebisch, 23 April 1946.
4 Prebisch to Villaseñor, 14 May 1946.
5 Margariños, Conversaciones, 137, for explicit mention of these students and his commitment to their future as professional economists.
6 Ibid.
7 Quoted in Lewis, *Crisis of Argentine Capitalism*, 177.
8 Prebisch, *Introduction to Keynes*. Cosío Villegas to Prebisch, 16 December 1946; 13 October 1947. The correspondence between Prebisch and the Venezuelan Central Bank in 1946 regarding the Keynes project is contained in the Prebisch Papers. See particularly J.M. Herrera Mendoza to Prebisch, 30 July 1946.
9 Urquidi to Prebisch, 28 November 1946.
10 *La Nacion*, 16 August 1946.
11 Prebisch, *Panorama General de los problemas de regulación y credito.*
12 Prebisch, *Proyecto de Ley Organica*; Prebisch, "Bases para la creacion de una Escuela de Economia." For Prebisch's views on the inadequacies of his faculty, see Prebisch, "Introducción al curso de dinámica económica," *Revista de la Facultad de Ciencias Económicas*, Ano I (2), March 1948.
13 Prebisch to Cosío Villegas, 8 November 1946.
14 Ibid.
15 Prebisch to Urquidi, 28 January 1947.
16 Prebisch to Urquidi, 28 November 1946.
17 Urquidi to Prebisch, 6 December 1946.
18 "You can imagine the anxiety I have regarding the early announcement of Mitchell's book," he noted to Urquidi on 8 November 1946.
19 E.A. Goldenweiser to Prebisch, 10 October 1946.
20 Prebisch to Goldenweiser, 18 October 1946.
21 Prebisch to Urquidi, 12 February 1946.
22 Prebisch to Enrique Frankel, 19 February 1946.
23 For example, Urquidi to Prebisch, 12 April 1946; see also Prebisch's "Anotaciones acerca de la reforma del plan de estudios de la facultad de ciencias económicas," Prebisch Papers, 1946.
24 Urquidi to Prebisch, 10 December 1947.
25 Prebisch to Eugenio Gudin, 31 July 1947.
26 Gudin to Prebisch, 5 May 1947.
27 Prebisch to Otavio Gouvea de Bulhões, 4 November 1946.
28 Prebisch to Gudin, 31 July 1947.
29 Prebisch to Eugenio Gudin, 17 July 1947.
30 Prebisch to Lope Bello, 4 November 1947.
31 Magariños, *Diálogos*, 127–8.
32 Raúl Prebisch, *Apuntes de Economica Politica*, 1.
33 Prebisch to Eugenio Gudin, 10 February 1948.

34 Prebisch to Gilberto Lara, 23 February 1948.
35 Prebisch to Jacques Appelmans, 23 February 1948.
36 Manuel Perez Guerrero to Prebisch, 30 July 1948. Perez Guerrero was Venezuelan minister of finance.
37 Prebisch to Eugenio Castillo, 23 November 1948.
38 Prebisch to Jésus Silva Herzog, 13 December 1948.
39 David McCord Wright to Prebisch, 12 November 1948.
40 Prebisch to Jésus Silva Herzog, 13 December 1948.
41 Ravndal to Prebisch, 21 October 1948. The letter makes clear that Prebisch seriously considered visiting the US in early 1949.
42 Hernan Santa Cruz to UN secretary-general, 12 July 1947, for the document that launched the creation of ECLA.
43 Eugenio Castillo to H. Caustin, 13 August 1948. "After I explain in detail the work of the Commission he might show a deeper interest," he noted.
44 Prebisch to Castillo, 23 November 1948.
45 Urquidi wrote, "I hope to see you one day in Washington. You could do much for Latin America [here] where the region is poorly represented."
46 For a detailed discussion of this event see Dosman, "Los mercados y el estado," 94–5.
47 Urquidi to Prebisch, 3 December 1948; Ravndal to Prebisch, 9 December 1948.

CHAPTER ELEVEN

1 Gutt to Prebisch, 23 December 1948. This and the following correspondence is found in the Prebisch Papers, unless otherwise noted.
2 Maurice L. Parsons to Prebisch, 19 January 1949.
3 M.L. Parsons to Prebisch, 11 March 1949.
4 Adelita Prebisch to Raúl Prebisch, 13 and 30 March 1949.
5 Eckard to Prebisch, 22 March 1949.
6 Lewis, *Crisis of Argentine Capitalism*, 191–2.
7 US State Department, Internal Memorandum 835.5151/7–149, 1949.
8 Rovensky to Prebisch, 28 December 1945.
9 Bulhões to Prebisch, 11 February 1949.
10 Lobos to Prebisch, 20 March 1949.
11 Wallich to Prebisch, 3 June 1949.
12 Hernan Santa Cruz to Secretary-General Trygve Lie, 12 June 1947. E. Cuesta provides an in-house report on the formation of ECLA in "The Background to the 'Terms of Trade' Controversy," Santiago, 12 December 1971.
13 Hanson, "Preliminary Report to the United Nations."
14 Owen to R.G.A Jackson, 19 May 1948.
15 *Memorandum*, Malinowski to Caustin, New York, 12 November 1948.
16 Ibid.

17 Dorfman to Eugenio Castillo, New York, 23 July 1948.
18 Croire to Prebisch, 24 December 1948.
19 Croire to Prebisch, 28 February and 8 April 1949.
20 Croire to Prebisch, 24 December 1948.
21 Love, "Doctrine of Unequal Exchange," especially 60–5, for the classic treatment of this issue.
22 Furtado, *A Fantasia Organizada*, 60.
23 Later renamed *Relative Prices of Exports and Imports of Under-Developed Countries* (United Nations, 1949).
24 Gustavo Martínez Cabañas to Prebisch, 5 March 1949, and Croire to Prebisch, 8 April 1949. See Toye and Toye, "The Origins and Interpretation of the Prebisch-Singer Thesis," for a valuable account of the transmission of Singer's findings to Santiago. See Shaw, *Sir Hans Singer*, for the authoritative biography of Hans Singer.
25 H. Singer, "The Terms of Trade Controversy," 275–311.
26 Toye and Toye, "The Origins and Interpretation of the Prebisch-Singer Thesis," 25.
27 United Nations, *Relative Prices of Exports and Imports of Under-Developed Countries*, 16–17.
28 Kindleberger, "Planning for Foreign Investment"; Samuelson, "International Trade and Equalization of Factor Prices." The Prebisch Papers (in particular Prebisch's correspondence with Victor Urquidi, such as on 2 June 1944, which dealt with the work of Kindleberger) shed light on the evolution of Prebisch's theorizing during the period 1943–49.
29 Sir Hans Singer, when questioned on the Prebisch-Singer thesis, and whose name should come first, responded in 1990: "All I can say now is: a) it seems natural that Prebisch should come first in due alphabetical order; and b) it terms of UN hierarchy Prebisch was the senior man … However all this is probably secondary – in my own mind I always thought of Prebisch as a senior man and in fact his views, with more emphasis on factoral terms of trade rather than barter terms of trade, were better integrated into general development thinking than my own original emphasis which was more on barter terms of trade (although pretty soon afterward, and under the influence of my first meeting with Prebisch in Santiago which must have been 1948 or early 1949 I quickly came round to accepting his emphasis.)" Singer to David Pollock, 22 October 1990 (Pollock Papers, Box 8).
30 Within the vast literature on this subject, note the particular contributions of Love, *Crafting the Third World: Theorizing Underdevelopment in Rumania and Brazil*; Mallorquín, "Raúl Prebisch before the Ice Age"; Rodríguez, "Aprendizaje, acumulación, pleno empleo"; Gurrieri, "Technical Progress and Its Fruits"; Mallorquín, "Un breve recuento de la deconstrucción del estructuralismo latinoamericano"; and Sprout, "The Ideas of Prebisch." Also useful are all the articles in Iglesias, ed., *The Legacy of Raúl Prebisch*; Spraos, "The Statistical Debate on the Net Barter"; and Tanzi and Chu, *Fiscal Policy for Stable and Equitable Growth in Latin America.*

31 Prebisch, *The Economic Development of Latin America and Its Principal Problems,* 11 and 48–50.
32 Prebisch to Ravndal, 10 May 1949.
33 Adelita Prebisch to Raúl Prebisch, 25 May 1949.
34 President Carlos Prio Socarros, "Address to the Second ECLA Session," Havana, 29 May 1949.
35 Secretary-General Trygve Lie, "Address to the Second ECLA Session," Havana, 29 May 1949.
36 See Solís, "Raúl Prebisch at ECLA," for a preliminary examination of the scholarly controversies surrounding the Prebisch thesis.
37 Viner, *International Trade and Economic Development,* 44. Alemann, "El pensamiento económico de Prebisch."
38 Furtado gave Prebisch this title (*El Gran Heresiarca*) at the height of his fame in the early 1950s. *A Fantasia Organizada,* 99. Hodara called him a *profeta armado* and a *cuadillo intellectual*; Hodara, *Prebisch y la CEPAL,* 12.
39 Prebisch, *The Economic Development of Latin America and Its Principal Problems,* 59 and ff.
40 Ibid., 2. See Toye and Toye, "How the UN Moved from Full Employment to Economic Development," in their *Political Economy for a Divided World.*

CHAPTER TWELVE

1 Singer to David Pollock, 22 October 1990. Singer recalled the atmosphere: "Prebisch, as a Latin American and safely away in Santiago, was much less vulnerable during the McCarthy period than I was, sitting in New York, and the Prebisch-Singer thesis was considered subversive."
2 H.E. Caustin to David Owen, 8 October 1949, which clarifies the background to giving Prebisch credit (and responsibility) for his report, "which is contrary to the adopted policy." See also Magariños, *Diálogos,* 131, for Prebisch's account of the incident.
3 Caustin to Gustavo Martinez-Cabañas, 18 July 1949.
4 Raúl Prebisch to Adelita Prebisch, 26 June, 5 July 1950; Adelita Prebisch to Raúl Prebisch, 30 June 1950.
5 Acting OAS Secretary-General William Manger to Trygve Lie, 5 May 1950, for the formal communication of the OAS position.
6 Swenson to Caustin, 27 July 1948.
7 Hodara, *Prebisch y la CEPAL,* especially 176–83. Furtado, *A Fantasia Organizada,* for a more personal assessment of the early CEPAL years.
8 Singer, "Comments on 'Raúl Prebisch: The Continuing Quest,'" 44.
9 Prebisch, "Growth, Disequilibrium and Disparities."

10 US State Department office memorandum, "Development of US-Latin American Policy in Terms of US World Objectives, 1950–55"; Edward G. Miller to L. Halle, 24 March 1950.

11 See US State Department, "Supplement D: US Latin American Development Policy," 9 November 1950.

12 Halle to Miller, 27 March 1950.

13 Manger to Lie, 5 May 1950.

14 US State Department, memorandum of conversation, "Future of ECLA," 16 and 26 May 1950.

15 US State Department, "Confidential Report on the Third Session of the Economic Commission for Latin America," 7 September 1950. Regarding Prebisch's position on the European refugee issue, see Prebisch to David Owen, 19 June 1950.

16 Chris Ravndal, US State Department, confidential report, 7 September 1950.

17 Ibid.

18 *New York Times*, 4, 6, and 7 June 1950. Pierre Mendès-France, "Annual Report of the Economic Commission for Latin America," ECOSOC, 7 August 1950, 221–3. US State Department, "Comment by Under Secretary on Montevideo CEPAL Meeting," 12 July 1950.

19 Ravndal, US State Department, confidential report, 7 September, 1950.

20 United Nations, Economic and Social Council, Eleventh Session, 7 August 1950.

21 Prebisch's account of his accession to the position of executive secretary is related in Magariños, *Diálogos*, 132–3. US State Department, "Activities of Secretariat of United Nations Economic Commission for Latin America," Santiago, 27 June 1950.

22 Prebisch to Rist, 20 January 1950.

23 US State Department memorandum, 27 July 1950.

24 Furtado, interview with the author; Ganz, telephone interview with the author.

25 US State Department, "Activities of Secretariat of United Nations Economic Commission for Latin America," Santiago, 27 July 1950.

26 United Nations, Economic and Social Council, Eleventh Session, Geneva, 7 August 1950.

27 David Owen to Trygve Lie, 31 March 1951, "Report on the Fourth Meeting of Consultation of Ministers of Foreign Affairs of American States," Washington 26–30 March 1951. Compare US State Department, "Accomplishments of the Fourth Meeting of Consultation of Ministers of Foreign Affairs of American States," 12 April 1950.

28 "Energetica Intervención de Mexico (Lic. Carillo Flores) en Favor de la CEPAL," *El Popular*, Mexico City, 7 June 1951.

29 M. Bohan to US State Department, 14 June 1951.

30 "Report of the United States Delegation to the Fourth Session of the Economic Commission for Latin America," 17 July 1951. Compare with "Instructions to the US Delegation at the Fourth Meeting of ECLA, Mexico City, 28 May-14 June 1951."

CHAPTER THIRTEEN

1 *Avance,* 5 July 1951. The Prebisch Papers include the entire press commentary on his visit to Cuba.
2 *Informacion,* 5 July 1951.
3 *El Mundo,* 5 July 1951.
4 US State Department office memorandum, 24 October 1951.
5 Furtado, *A fantasia organizada,* 127–35.
6 Bohan, *Oral History Interview,* 52.
7 Interview of Dr Raúl Prebisch, executive director of ECLA, with President Vargas, Rio de Janeiro, 27 August 1951.
8 Interview of Dr Raúl Prebisch with Brazilian President Getulio Vargas, 27 August 1951.
9 Bohan, *Oral History Interview,* 52.
10 ECLA, *The Visit of Dr Raúl Prebisch, Executive Secretary of ECLA, to Brazil, 1951.* See also Furtado, *A fantasia organizada,* 162–71.
11 *O Estado de São Paulo,* 1 September 1951; *Diario de São Paulo e Rio,* 19 April 1953.
12 Alemann, "El pensamiento económico de Prebisch," for a personal account of Prebisch's critique of Viner at ECLA's 1953 session in Rio.
13 See Gudin, "A Mistica do Planjamento," *Diario de Noticias,* 29 May. Subsequent issues on 2, 6, 9, and 11 June carried the full text of this polemic. Prebisch's response began with the title, "A Mistica do Equilibrio Espontaneo na Economia."
14 Mallorquín, "Celso Furtado: um retrato intelectual."
15 *Folho da Manha,* São Paulo, 31 August 1951. Toye and Toye, "Raúl Prebisch and the Limits of Industrialization," 21–30.
16 *O Estado do São Paulo,* 1 September 1951.
17 Harrison, *A Strategy for Unification and US Disengagement,* 9.
18 Joint press conference held by UN Executive Secretaries, New York, 4 June 1952.
19 Ferguson, "ECLA, Latin American Development, and the United States," 45.
20 He spoke very positively regarding ECLA's fifth session, in Rio in April 1953: "We have been impressed not only with the caliber of ECLA's economic analysis but above all by the actual economic progress being made by Latin America. The development process is really under way. Its momentum must be maintained." *Omnipress,* New York, 28 April 1953.
21 US State Department memorandum, 13 March 1953.
22 Ferguson, "ECLA, Latin American Development, and the United States," 46.
23 *New York Times,* 22 November 1952.
24 Bohan, *Oral History Interview,* 84.

25 United States: Senate Sub-committee on Internal Security, Washington, 10 April 1954.

26 Alfonso Santa Cruz to Wladek Malinowski, 27 February 1953; Bohan, *Oral History Interview*, 49.

27 50 percent of the region's imports and 48 percent of its exports were with the US. "Latin America is our largest customer, supplier and field of foreign investment," a US State Department official explained, but also "an indispensable and irreplaceable ally. Latin America lies within our inner fortress; no error of omission or commission is permitted there." US State Department memorandum, *Informal Review of UN Paper on Integrated Economic Development*, Washington, 22 September 1954.

28 Garcia Márquez lamented the fate of Alberto Lleras: "A great writer led astray by politics." Cromos, 3 May 1993.

29 Technically the 8th Extraordinary Meeting of IA-ECOSOC.

30 John Foster Dulles to Milton Eisenhower, 14 September 1954. "I fully share your view of the importance of this conference and of developing hemispheric relations." Washington did, however, agree to reopen Export-Import Bank operations in Latin America.

31 *International Cooperation for a Latin American Development Policy*, E/CN.12/359, United Nations, 1954.

32 Lewis Swenson to Philippe de Seynes, 30 November 1955, retrospectively describing Prebisch's exceptional intervention at Quintandinha.

33 Discussed with characteristic energy in Toye and Toye, *The UN and Global Political Economy*.

34 Henry Holland, State Department office memorandum, 11 December 1954. Washington was convinced that Prebisch had supported a personal appeal by John Foster Dulles in mid-1954, just after the Guatemala fiasco, to defeat a Soviet invitation for Latin governmental officials to visit Moscow, merely as a ruse to divert attention from the bombshell he was preparing for Quintandinha. US Embassy Santiago to State Department, 31 July and 4 August 1954.

35 David McKey to Andrew Overby, 18 November 1954.

36 "If we are to demonstrate the worth of the free enterprise system to the Latin Americans, we must prove that our system will raise the standard of living which is far below that of his 'opposite number' in the US." Peter Grace to John Foster Dulles, 3 September 1954.

37 Prebisch to de Seynes, 23 January 1955.

38 Malinowski to Swenson, 3 April 1954.

39 Prebisch to de Seynes, 16 September 1955.

CHAPTER FOURTEEN

1 Crawley, *A House Divided: Argentina 1880–1980*, 166–74.

2 A. Echegoyen to Prebisch, 26 September 1955.

3 For example, *La Nacion,* 2 October 1955.
4 *La Nacion,* 4 October 1955.
5 *La Nacion,* 8 October 1955.
6 *La Nacion,* 7 October 1955; *El Mercurio,* 9 October 1955.
7 *El Mercurio,* 9 October 1955.
8 *La Nacion,* 8 October 1955.
9 Wladek Malinowski to Prebisch, 3 October 1955.
10 *El Mercurio,* 12 October 1955.
11 *La Nacion,* "Informe sobre el Estado Economico," 27 October 1955.
12 Norman Crump, "Argentine Hopes," *Times* (London), 6 November 1955.
13 US Embassy Buenos Aires to secretary of state, 31 October 1955. Sikkink, *Ideas and Institutions,* 78–80 in particular.
14 *Times* (London), 31 October 1955.
15 US Embassy Buenos Aires to secretary of state, 27 October 1957.
16 *Politica y Politicos,* 25 October 1955.
17 *Clarin,* 26 October 1955.
18 *La Prensa,* 18 October 1955.
19 Crawley, *A House Divided,* 168–9, for the initial response of the CGT, the base of Peronista power, to the Revolución Libertadora.
20 *La Mañana,* Montevideo, 12 November 1955.
21 Lewis, *Crisis of Argentine Capitalism,* 130.
22 *Clarin,* 16 November 1955.
23 *La Nacion,* 15 November 1955.
24 Prebisch, press conference, Buenos Aires, 15 November 1955.
25 *Manchete,* 21 July 1956.
26 L. Swenson to Philippe de Seynes, 27 November 1955.
27 Sikkink, *Ideas and Institutions,* 183.
28 Lewis, *Crisis of Argentine Capitalism,* 335.
29 *La Nacion,* 12 January 1956.
30 *Clarin,* 18 January 1956; *El Mercurio,* 4 February 1956.
31 *La Razon,* 24 January 2007.
32 Raúl Scalabrini Ortiz, 10 November 1955; *Federalista,* 23 December 1955. Scalabrini published a column in *QUE sucedio en 7 dias,* a weekly supporting Arturo Frondizi, dedicated to attacking the *Plan Prebisch.* See, for example, "La Carta de Scalabrini Ortiz," 15 January 1957.
33 *Siempre,* 18 January 1956. The most important attack, apart from Scalabrini Ortiz, came from Arturo Jauretche, *El Plan Prebisch: retorno al coloniaje* (Buenos Aires: Pena Lillo, 1984). Other critics included Abraham Guillen, Oscar Alende, Carlos Correa, and José V. Liceaga.
34 *Clarin,* 19 January 1956.
35 *La Razon,* 24 January 1956.

36 *La Nacion*, 29 January 1956.

37 Arturo Frondizi's book, *Petroleo y Politica* (Buenos Aires, 1954) featured an uncompromising defense of the state oil monopoly.

38 *La Nacion*, 27 February 1956.

39 Holland to Henry Cabot Lodge Jr, 27 January 1956.

40 Dulles to Cabot Lodge Jr, 3 February 1956.

41 Holland to Dulles, 2 February 1956.

42 Cabot Lodge Jr to Dulles, 24 January 1956. "Prebisch now in Argentina; appears to be in full charge of this operation from both ends and he seems person best able answer question on US personnel on this mission. Essential to discuss entire matter fully and frankly with him."

43 Lewis, *Crisis of Argentine Capitalism*, 289, 300–1.

44 *Manchete*, 21 July 1956.

45 *La Prensa*, 30 May 1956.

46 *Manchete*, 21 July 1956. Publication of *The Economic Development of Argentina* was delayed until the 23 February 1958 elections in the hope of interesting the new government, but the winner (Frondizi) had his own ideas about development in which Prebisch and ECLA had little part. Part I (a summary of the report) finally appeared on 9 July 1959. Apart from the National Institute of Agrarian Technology, the most lasting impact of Prebisch's work in Argentina in 1955–56 was the migration to Santiago of a cadre of young Argentine economists who would play a leading role in ECLA for the next generation. Internationally his most durable result was the eventual formation of the Paris Club.

47 *La Nacion*, 15 April 1956.

48 Prebisch's interview with Theophilo de Andrade, Reforma Cambial Argentina, *O Cruzeiro*, 28 January 1956, provided a preview of his critique of import substitution under Perón.

49 Decree 4161 tried to erase a decade of Argentine history by formally banning the use of Peronista symbols, including the mention of Juan or Eva Perón.

50 Bustelo, Bodegas Esmeralda, to Prebisch, 13 April 1956.

CHAPTER FIFTEEN

1 Noyola's work differentiated between "inflationary pressures" and "mechanisms of propagation" to distinguish between underlying weaknesses such as agrarian structure, a weak state or class system, and the visible inflationary process of declining currency values culminating in calling in the IMF. Aloof from the messiness of decision-making, his interest lay in the former so-called "root causes." See Danby, "Noyola's Institutional Approach to Inflation."

2 While Prebisch admitted to inherent "structural" problems facing Latin America (such as a built-in trade deficit given declining terms of trade), the central banker

in him feared the visible effects of inflation far more than his younger colleagues, and he concentrated more on the "permissive" behaviour of governments.

3 Furtado, *A fantasia organizada.*

4 Ibid., 177–85.

5 Raúl Prebisch, opening address to the first meeting of ECLA's Trade Committee, Santiago, 19 November 1956.

6 *El Mercurio,* 20 November 1956.

7 UN Secretary-General Dag Hammarskjöld to Louis Swenson, 9 December 1955.

8 ECLA, Resolution 101 [1] Sixth Session (Bogota, 1955). *El Mercurio,* 20 November 1956.

9 *Notas de la CEPAL, Summary: Latin American Working Group of Experts on the Iron and Steel Industry and Transformation of Iron and Steel* (Santiago, 15 December 1956).

10 *El Mercado Comun Latinamerican, Exposicion del Doctor Raúl Prebisch en la segunda reunion del comite especial para estudiar la formulacion de neuvas medidas para la cooperacion economica* (Buenos Aires, 28 April 1959).

11 Ibid.

12 Prebisch, *El Mercado Comun Latinoamericano.*

13 Swenson to Prebisch, 12 October 1956.

14 Prebisch to de Seynes, 24 December 1956.

15 They had become such close family friends that Monnet was the only foreigner invited to Dulles's funeral in 1959 and the person to whom Janet Dulles entrusted his private papers.

16 Edgar Jones, deputy director of the Fund's Exchange and Restrictions Department, to IMF Managing Director Per Jacobbson, Washington, 25 November 1956.

17 *Sumario: Primera Reunion del Comite de Comercio de la CEPAL, Notas de la CEPAL* (Santiago, 10 December 1956).

18 Prebisch to de Seynes, 29 May 1957.

19 Furtado, *A fantasia organizada,* 188–92. Furtado had a particular interest in Mexico since his first visit in 1951 and observed the profound US connection so different in impact from the Brazilian experience.

20 Furtado, *A fantasia organizada,* 189.

21 In any case he was heading another, more limited but equally controversial, study of the Venezuelan economy under the Jimenez dictatorship, which Prebisch also refused to release. "I felt blocked," he noted, "like an athlete having to change his sport to continue advancing." Furtado, *A fantasia organizada,* 201.

22 Raymond Mikesell, a delegate at the Bretton Woods Conference, was professor of Economics at the University of Oregon. Dudley Seers was acting chief, Economic Survey Division of ECLA, while Nicholas Kaldor worked with Furtado in the Development Division.

23 Central America was tiny, poor, and virtually without industry: ECLA's integration work here offered no guide for the more developed countries in the region like Argentina or Chile.

24 Prebisch to de Seynes, 10 February 1958. The two working groups would next meet in Rio (Central Banks, 24 November to 4 December 1958) and Mexico (Common Market, 16–25 February 1959) to finalize a package for back-to-back sessions of the Trade Committee and ECLA's eighth session, in Panama in 1959.

25 Williams to Irving S. Friedman, 24 January 1957.

26 A fact well remembered in Latin America as well.

27 F. Keesing to Irving S. Friedman, 15 January 1957.

28 The exchange reforms currently taking place made the payments problem one of "great urgency." All the research in this field was very political; Prebisch, for example, vetoed the publication of an ECLA paper on the EEC without first passing it by GATT and ECE. De Seynes and Hans Singer both thought it important not to risk angering the IMF.

29 Prebisch didn't want the loan of an IMF expert "until we have a clear idea of the possibilities and nature of a payments scheme for LA." De Seynes to Milic Kybal, 20 September 1957.

30 European integration provided one lesson – the importance of a payments system to facilitate trade in periods of balance-of-payments difficulties. In fact from 1950 to 1953 ECLA had studied the European Payments Union carefully to see how Latin America could enter the system, or cooperate with it to expand trade across the Atlantic. In Santiago at the first Trade Committee meeting, a resolution had been passed supporting the establishment of a regional payments system as a cornerstone of the future Common Market; the question was whether such a scheme on the European model was possible in the special circumstances of Latin America.

31 Prebisch to de Seynes, 17 September 1957.

32 Prebisch, *Address to ECLA's Committee of the Whole.* Despite this generally sour mood, however, he did not foresee that Nixon's visit would ignite hostile anti-US demonstrations. Rabe, *Eisenhower and Latin America*, 100–16.

33 On 17 May 1954 the US Supreme Court declared in *Brown vs Board of Education* that racial segregation violated the Equal Protection Clause of the US Constitution. But on 4 September 1957 Governor O. Faubus called out the National Guard to prevent the children from entering the school in Little Rock, Arkansas.

34 Kybal to Prebisch, 16 April 1958.

35 Richard M. Nixon, *Six Crises.* See the chapter titled "Caracas" for his personal account.

36 Scheman, ed., *The Alliance for Progress*, 63–6.

37 US State Department office memorandum, 15 June 1958.

38 The five points included: enhanced access to development capital; a financial and technical program for Latin American agriculture and food industries; raw materials and primary commodities stabilization and pricing; technological and productivity research for Latin American industrial development; and technical assistance for combating illiteracy and training in development. David Pollock to Guy Trancart, 18 February 1960.

39 Douglas Dillon made the announcement on that day so that it would precede a press conference featuring a similar US initiative for the Middle East. Rabe, *Eisenhower and Latin America*, 112. Christian Herter represented the US State Department given John Foster Dulles's illness, which led to his resignation on 25 February 1958.

40 Milton Eisenhower, *Report to the President on United States – Latin American Relations.*

41 Stephen G. Rabe, *Eisenhower and Latin America: The Foreign Policy of Anti-Communism*, 111–12.

42 Robert J. Dorr, US State Department, 30 December 1958.

43 Roy Rubottom, *Memorandum of Conversation*, US State Department, Washington, 18 November 1958.

44 US State Department Office memorandum, 18 November 1958.

45 Kybal to Prebisch, 15 October 1958.

46 At the September foreign ministers meeting, the US delegation had stood up for ECLA, repeating that it was and remained the lead international organization in the project as per Resolution 40 of the Buenos Aires Economic Conference.

47 Prebisch to Kybal, 6 October 1958.

48 Scheman, ed., *Alliance for Progress*, 40.

49 Levinson and Onis, *The Alliance That Lost Its Way*, 151.

50 In contrast, Filipe Herrera, the thrity-seven-year-old former Chilean finance minister and Central Bank manager who was elected as the first IDB president, acknowledged his debt to Prebisch and welcomed him as one of his closest associates, visiting ECLA during his first trip back to Chile after the Bank began operations. David Pollock to Louis Swenson, 19 May 1960.

51 US State Department Office memorandum, 18 November 1958.

52 US State Department memorandum, 18 November 1959.

53 Wyndham-White had suggested that a committee of experts meet in Washington to examine a joint US-Brazilian proposal for a standing forum comprising the six Latin members of GATT, the US, Canada, and several European countries that would examine regional economic integration in Latin America and report its findings to the GATT. Prebisch was neither informed nor invited.

54 Urquidi, "The Montevideo Treaty," 51–64. Only six Latin countries were in the GATT, and it was unlikely that Wyndham-White would repeat the endorsement he gave to the Treaty of Rome when it came to the proposed Latin American Common Market. Latin America remained on the periphery of the global system, with economic modernization just getting under way; the gaps between Latin America and Europe in infrastructure, education, human resources, state structures, and social and political cohesion were enormous. Latin American integration, Prebisch argued, therefore required a development model different from Europe, where growth could build from foundations already laid; Latin America had yet to build them, meaning that ECLA's project combined the opening of regional markets with

a strategy of industrialization to create competitive regional firms. To Wyndham-White this seemed like import-substitution at a regional level designed to keep out goods currently imported from Europe or the US, and therefore fell afoul of article XXIV of the GATT charter, which made the endorsement of regional free-trade agreements conditional on increasing overall international trade rather than diverting trade and investment. When asked if the Latin regional market would be "discomforting to free-traders," Urquidi replied: "Indeed it will! The facts of industrial development, and not only in the Latin part of the Hemisphere, are that it has to be carried out behind a protective tariff and similar measures."

55 In May 1957 Per Jacobsson visited Santiago on his first trip to Latin America and lodged with Raúl and Adelita in El Maqui. He thanked them for their hospitality but pointed out that his views "on the need for stability have not changed." Jacobsson to Prebisch, 20 September 1957.

56 "La influencia del Mercado comun en el desarrollo economico de America Latina" (ECLA, eighth session, Panama City, 1959; sent to Dr Milton Eisenhower, Johns Hopkins University on 1 June 1959); "The Latin American Common Market and the Multilateral Payments System"; and "ECLA's Annual Report to ECOSOC" (Geneva, 1959). See also Milic Kybal to R. Mikesell, 3 June 1959 and 1 June 1959.

57 Louis Swenson to OAS Secretary-General José A. Mora, 6 October 1956.

58 Del Canto to Jacobsson, 22 May 1959. While the Common Market project implied regional preferences and gradual and progressive reciprocity to achieve competitive regional industrialization, ECLA rejected the charge of "closed" regionalism: it aimed to intensify inter-American trade without prejudice to the expansion of trade with other areas, "bearing in mind the fundamental necessity to increase world trade in general." Regional import substitution would therefore replace – not limit – third-party exports to Latin America since rapidly developing economies would constantly require higher value-added imports to mature into developed economies.

59 In fact Del Canto became confused while sparring with Prebisch and had to be rescued (according to the World Bank representatives) by the US delegation. When challenged to explain how the IMF model of strict convertibility promoted regional trade without other measures such as reciprocal credit arrangements, he was unable to respond. With strict convertibility alone, Prebisch argued, Latin economies would be more than ever "water-tight compartments," competing for FDI (foreign direct investment) behind high tariff walls while depending on customs receipts to balance their budgets.

60 There were, of course, other divisions within the region; del Canto was correct that there was little political appetite for regional integration in Latin America.

61 Since the Perónist Party was banned and the Socialist Party was too small to be a factor, the choice was between Ricardo Balbin and Frondizi, the two Radical leaders heading separate factions of the party to fight the elections under different

banners. Frondizi negotiated a pact with Perón in January 1958 and won easily, revealing the strength of the Perónist revival.

62 Frondizi's economic program was based, he said, on "integration," but his concept implied social cohesion rather than trade liberalization.

63 ECLA, *Progress Report on ECLA Work Program* (Santiago, 6 October 1958). It was not clear at first whether Frondizi would continue his vendetta against the *Plan Prebisch* once elected, particularly after a successful four-power meeting of Argentina, Brazil, Chile, and Uruguay at the senior officials level in Santiago, which recommended a deepening of Southern Cone integration and the presentation of a common position to the GATT.

64 Hosted by Merle Cochran, the luncheon included Director of the Exchange Restrictions Department Irving Friedman, Director of Research Jacques J. Polak, and Jorge del Canto.

65 First-period decisions would require a two-thirds majority, provided there was no negative vote (i.e., each country retained a veto power). There was no IMF role; MFN (Most-Favoured-Nation) treatment was compulsory; and there was equal coverage of new and existing products.

66 Hammarskjöld to Prebisch, 18 February 1960.

67 After the signing of the Montevideo Treaty, US State Department officials repeated their support of its underlying principles but maintained sufficient reservations about its practicality to recommend the EEC rather than LAFTA to US private-sector investors. For his part Per Jacobsson scoffed at LAFTA in "*pocas palabras*" at the Annual IMF-World Bank Meeting in October 1960. There were no congratulations; and not one Latin American delegate spoke on its behalf. Pollock to Swenson, *Review of Raúl Prebisch's July 7–8 Visit to Washington*, 11 July 1960; H. Turkel, State Department *Office Memorandum*, 8 July 1960.

68 De Seynes in fact tried to persuade Prebisch, but Malinowski agreed that the job was not worth the effort.

69 For example: *El Colegio* in Mexico; the Getulio Vargas Institute in Brazil; and the Institute of Economic Research in Los Andes, Colombia. Chile and other countries were not far behind.

70 Robert Hausner to Prebisch, United Nations office memorandum, 29 September 1958. The calculated annual pension was $3,820 yearly after retirement on July 1 1963.

71 Malinowski to Prebisch, 17 May 1960.

72 The weakness of development planning was one obvious lesson from Perón's Argentina – and it was even more apparent in poorer countries. From Dag Hammarskjöld down, agencies were being asked find ways of accelerating growth in developing countries. Hammarskjöld pressed the need to move from theory to practice in international cooperation and to improve national planning to mobilize foreign and domestic capital since market forces would not lower their vulnerability.

He raised the spectre of two economic regions in the world growing apart unless the global community could agree on new measures to assist the Third World; ECLA, apparently, had an opportunity because advisory groups represented a logical continuation of its work in Santiago since the early years, capitalizing on its investment in training and development research. But the initiative was not easy to sell to Washington (where it was seen as another Prebisch attempt to extend ECLA's original mandate) or New York (where UN officials like de Seynes and Mosak insisted on keeping a tight leash on the Regional Commissions). UN Secretary-General Dag Hammarskjöld, *Remarks to the July 1956 ECOSOC Meeting* (Geneva, July 1956).

73 UN General Assembly, "Measures for the Economic Development of Under-Developed Countries" (New York, 1951).

74 Maizels, "Refining the World Commodity Economy," 108. Bello, "The Iron Cage," 27. Eugene R. Black in the World Bank finally accepted the IDA as a necessary bone to placate developing countries; while he disagreed with the concept the Bank at least would control it.

75 By December 1961 the Resolution had made its way through the UN system and been approved.

CHAPTER SIXTEEN

1 It was assumed (correctly) that Nixon was actively plotting the overthrow of Castro.

2 In autumn 1960 Richard Goodwin was busily exploring a campaign slogan that could evoke Roosevelt's "Good Neighbor Policy." In September he seized on the word "Alliance" and, with Karl Meyer at the *Washington Post* and Ernesto Betancourt at the OAS, broadened it to "Alliance for Progress." Kennedy liked it. By October it became a plank in the campaign, promising an initiative comparable to the Marshall Plan for Europe. Scheman, ed., *Alliance for Progress*, 195–6.

3 *Diario las Americas* (Miami), 22 September 1960. Milic Kybal to Jorge Ahumada, 2 September 1959.

4 Kybal to Reynold Carlson, Vanderbilt University, 17 April 1959.

5 ECLA office memorandum, 20 April 1959.

6 For a contemporary leftist account of the chronology see *New University Thought*, 4–8.

7 Included in Joaquin Martiz, *Recuento de Poemas, 1950–93*, 179.

8 US Mission to the UN to secretary of state, 8 July 1960. The meeting was convened following the earthquake in Chile with a solid front of Latin delegates confronting the US and European members. "From outset of session, perfectly clear that four non-Latin American members were tolerated in Commission solely on basis of being necessary evil."

9 Resuming work with E.M. Bernstein's economic consulting firm. David Pollock to Lewis Swenson, 30 August 1960.

10 Regino Boti Leon, interview with the author, 12 January 1995.
11 Che Guevara, quoted in ibid.
12 US Embassy Santiago to secretary of state, 20 April 1960.
13 Noyola to Pollock, 9 August 1960.
14 "Regino Boti Viaja a Estados Unidos," *Diario las Americas*, 22 September 1960.
15 *Allentown Chronicle*, 8 March 1960. A nine-nation technical committee was appointed by foreign ministers for the Committee of 21.
16 They wanted primary price stabilization; increased diversification; higher productivity in agriculture and industry; more technical assistance; and greater access to development capital.
17 Dillon, "The Prelude," 63–6. Considering his appointment of George Humphrey as treasury secretary in early 1953, Eisenhower's change of attitude toward Latin America was spectacular. It was also an unacknowledged compliment that both Kubitschek's Operation Pan America and the new principles adopted by the Committee of 21 were a flagrant poaching of ideas from ECLA in Santiago.
18 Fidel Castro Ruz, "The Problem of Cuba and Its Revolutionary Policy," United Nations General Assembly, 26 September 1960.
19 Walt W. Rostow's influential books, *A Proposal: Key to an Effective Foreign Policy* (with Max Milliken) and *Stages of Economic Growth: a Non-Communist Manifesto* brought him into the Kennedy team.
20 President John F. Kennedy, "Address at a White House Reception for Members of Congress and for the Diplomatic Corps of the Latin American Republics," Washington, 13 March 1961; the Prebisch Papers include the original draft of Prebisch's joint letter sent to President Kennedy.
21 But a key element of Prebisch's draft – his linkage of regional integration with the promotion of industrial exports – was dropped. His recommended text – "Without such arrangements, there can be no efficient, progressive industrialization, nor can industrial exports achieve appreciable proportions either within the Latin American area or as regards the rest of the world. Latin America must enter the industrial-export market" – was watered down into a bland endorsement of support for "all economic integration which is a genuine step toward larger markets and greater competitive opportunity." This was a defeat for Prebisch's efforts since 1956 to distinguish a rational import-substitution policy from its misapplication and errors of Argentina under Perón.
22 Schlesinger, "Myth and Reality," 68.
23 Prebisch, "Joint Responsibilities for Latin American Progress." It offered a tough message to donors and recipients. Development assistance from outside, he argued, was essential but secondary to the responsibilities of Latin countries themselves if they were to prosper. But the latter needed predictability in financing. "For planning to succeed, each country must know with certainty that for the duration of the plan it can count on those international resources which are indispensable for putting it into practice." In the same issue Jacob Viner agreed with Prebisch: long-term plans

had been the key to the success of the Marshall Plan, he concluded ("the outstanding success in the past history of foreign aid"), and long-term authorizations by the US Congress were also necessary for the success of the Alliance for Progress.

24 Lincoln Gordon, interview with the author.

25 White House memorandum, SECRET, *Conversation with Comandante Ernesto Guevara of Cuba*, 22 August 1961. Guevara thanked Goodwin for the "great political victory" of the Bay of Pigs invasion but called for a "*modus vivendi*" with the US Government.

26 Filipe Pazos had just walked out of a dinner with Moscoso and Prebisch when he arrived.

27 Lerdau, "The Alliance for Progress," 165–84.

28 Quoted in ibid., 167.

29 Prebisch, "*Vamos a tener mas recursos?*"

30 Ferguson, "ECLA and the Alliance for Progress." Frondizi had also intervened to prevent Prebisch being named executive director of the new OAS-ECLA-IDB Tripartite Committee, apparently to prevent its possible effectiveness in interfering with Argentina's direct access to the US and funding agencies.

31 US Embassy, Santiago to State Department, 2 September 1961. It repeated the rumour at Punta del Este that the US delegation had approached Prebisch to head the Panel.

32 Manuel J. Rios to Bodil Royem, 24 June 1962.

33 Sikkink, *Ideas and Institutions*, 101–10; Lewis, *Crisis of Argentine Capitalism*, 336–7, for an example of how Frondizi did not nurture Argentine domestic capitalists – in this case SIAM in the automobile sector, although his 1958 National Commission on Foreign Investment and Stabilization Plan had accommodated the US and the IMF according to script.

34 Prebisch's buoyant mood was confirmed in Ottawa (which had recently joined ECLA), where he briefed Canadian officials on new Alliance developments. "He was notably pro-United States in all his comments" and enthusiastic about the Alliance for Progress, Canada's Foreign Affairs noted, "and did not appear to be interested in any special self-advancement or in any special position for ECLA." US Embassy, Ottawa to US secretary of state, 1 December 1961.

35 Remarks by the Hon. Douglas Dillon, secretary of the US Treasury, at the Special Meeting of the InterAmerican ECOSOC, Washington, DC, 30 November 1961.

36 OAS press release, "Brazil Moves to Organize Its Alliance for Progress Short-Term Projects," 29 January 1962.

37 Bolivia and Colombia were the next countries to be reviewed by the panel.

38 Gilbert Burck, "Latin America: Bureaucracy and the Market," *Fortune* (February 1962).

39 Schlesinger, "Myth and Reality," 70.

40 Grunwald, "Invisible Hands in Inflation and Growth," 318. When *Business Week* declared its loyalty to the Alliance for Progress, the early reformist impulse was truly under siege.

41 Prebisch to los Senores Expertos del Comité de los Nueve, 12 June 1962.

42 A month earlier, in December 1961. Despite rumours of opposition lower down in the Special Fund staff, Hoffman went so far as to have a statement read at ECLA's ninth meeting, in Santiago on 5 May 1961 – immediately before the Punta del Este Conference – which literally guaranteed funding. In return, the government delegates at that meeting endorsed the project in principle with virtually no debate or discussion, leaving Raúl free to advance the institute project.

43 Benjamin Hopenhayn to Raúl Prebisch, 17 July 1963.

44 Richard E. Demuth to J. Burke Knapp, 1 May 1961.

45 Demuth to Burke Knapp, 10 July 1962.

46 Prebisch, *Address to ECLA's Eighth Plenary Meeting*, 14 February 1962.

47 To speed things up with Paul Hoffman, Prebisch had convinced five governments – Brazil, Bolivia, Chile, Venezuela, and Colombia – to submit a formal request to the Special Fund project. After it was approved in January 1962, Prebisch proposed a board of directors nominated from these five countries, the three sponsoring organizations (Special Fund, IDB, and ECLA) along with himself as director-general. Such a composition broke the rules in Latin America for a "regional" organization, ignoring Mexico and Argentina, which insisted on individual representation. He was compelled to back down in favour of an eleven-member council, with eight Latin representatives using the traditional selection from Argentina, Brazil, Mexico, and Chile, Venezuela/Colombia, as well as (collectively) Central America, Andean region, and the Southern Cone (Bolivia, Uruguay, or Paraguay). However Prebisch was successful in an agreement that the directors would act in their individual capacity rather than as government delegates.

48 Murray Ross to William Diamond, World Bank office memorandum, 15 June 1962.

49 David H. Pollock, interview with the author, 12 July 1992.

50 Record of meeting with US State Department Officials, Washington, DC, 15 February 1963, Pollock Papers, box 3.

51 Prebisch, *Address to the Tenth Session of the Economic Commission for Latin America*, Mar del Plata, 6 May 1963.

52 Lincoln Gordon, interview with the author. The US offensive against President Goulart, who opposed US sanctions against Cuba, began before October 1962. President Kennedy abruptly cancelled a visit to Brazil scheduled for 20 November, instead sending his brother for a humiliating public dressing-down of Goulart in his own capital.

CHAPTER SEVENTEEN

1 With US leadership, the newly founded ECOSOC invited eighteen countries to form a preparatory committee (the Interim Committee for International Trade Organization), for drafting an ITO. Rejected by Moscow, the committee met anyway in London and moved forward toward Havana.

2 *New York Times*, "About That Free Trade," 15 May 2006, for a retrospective a half-century later.

3 Although certain imperfections at the margin (such as excessive bureaucracy) were admitted.

4 Such as the UN Commission on International Commodity Trade. It was largely ineffective, only one of a host of new trade-related agencies that proliferated because the issue was of global importance, and filled the ITO vacuum with rampant bureaucratization.

5 Leaving the 1958 Coffee Agreement as the one US-developing country achievement in commodity trade.

6 Replacing the OEEC, which had been established in 1949 to guide European reconstruction. The developed market economies already had their own group serviced by the OECD in Paris; since 1945 they had learned the importance of working together on the key files whatever their individual policy differences, and they had deepened their international collaboration since 1960, when the OEEC was reshaped into the OECD.

7 One only had to look behind the flurry of resolutions in the UN General Assembly. GA Resolution 1421 (XIV), a general statement on trade and development for underdeveloped countries approved on 5 December 1959, followed by GA Resolution 1519 on 15 December 1960, *Strengthening and Development of the World Market and Improvement of the Trade Conditions of the Economically Less Developed Countries.* Neither implied action.

8 Formulated by UN officials led by Hans Singer, the UN Development Strategy set out a minimum annual growth target of 5 percent between 1960 and 1969. Three months after Kennedy's address, on 19 December 1961, GA Resolution 1707 (*International Trade as the Primary Instrument for Economic Development)* was approved, calling on the secretary-general to consult with member governments regarding the convening of a UN conference on international trade and development issues.

9 Toye and Toye, "From New Era to Neo-Liberal Era," 154–5.

10 Pollock, Love and Kerner, "Prebisch at UNCTAD," 46–7.

11 Final Report of the First Annual Meeting of the Inter-American Economic and Social Council at the Ministerial Level, OAS, Mexico, 27 October 1962.

12 UN General Assembly Resolution 1785, 8 December 1962.

13 Prebisch to de Seynes, 23 January 1963.

14 Prebisch still headed ECLA (to August 1963), and the new ILPES was just getting under way. He therefore decided to spend an initial three weeks in New York to claim the role of secretary-general, and then return for two months to prepare ECLA for the handover to José Antonio Mayobre. He decided to keep ILPES since his UNCTAD contract expired in mid-1964, appointing Cristóbal Lara as his deputy, bringing Benjamin Hopenhayn back from Washington to serve as secretary, and reassuring his team that he would be back as their leader.

15 In fact, de Seynes had opposed sending Prebisch to the Cairo Conference. Wladek Malinowski to Halina Malinowski (Malinowski personal correspondence), 8 July 1962.

16 As well as DESA's new World Model Projection Centre.

17 J. Mosak to Oscar Schachter, 9 January 1963.

18 David H. Pollock, resumé of meeting, 6 February 1963, 5 (Pollock Papers, Box 3). Subsequent Pollock references in this chapter are in the same location.

19 Mosak confided that Washington's support for holding UNCTAD had less to do with developing countries than with its disappointment in recent trade talks with Europe: UNCTAD would be a warning to the EEC to get serious, or the US would go elsewhere.

20 David Pollock, notes of meeting, 7 and 8 February 1963.

21 Although Dell's role in working on UNCTAD had been discussed since December, Mosak kept avoiding the issue.

22 UN Chief of Personnel Dharman, who was close to Mosak and de Seynes, cautioned Prebisch that it would be a "serious disruptive idea to certain governments."

23 Pollock to Prebisch, 23–25 April 1963.

24 But only through the personal intervention of U Thant, who persuaded the European UN Office to relocate meetings scheduled for WHO and the ILO.

25 Including Jan Tinbergen, T. Balogh, Ray Vernon, Nicholas Kaldor, Paul Rosenstein-Rodan, Ed Mason, Gerald Helleiner, Arthur Lewis, among other distinguished economists.

26 Chatham House, for example, followed up in October with a conference at Bellagio funded by the Carnegie Foundation, in which economists selected for "maximum impact upon governments" would propose recommendations for the Trade Conference. Pollock, *Notes,* 22 April 1963.

27 Originally seventy-five and subsequently including a far higher number of UN states as the years passed and membership increased.

28 For a detailed assessment of the pre-UNCTAD I negotiations, see: Dosman and Pollock, "Hasta la UNCTAD y de regreso: divulgando el evangelio, 1964–68," *Estudios Sociologicos del Colegio de México* 14 (September-December 1998), 48; Diego Cordovez, "The Making of UNCTAD: Institutional Background and Legislative History," *Journal of World Trade Law* I, no. 3 (May-June 1967), 243–328; and Thomas G. Weiss, *Multilateral Development Diplomacy in UNCTAD*.

29 New Zealand met with the G-77 until the end of the Conference before deciding that it belonged in Group B.

30 Pollock to Prebisch, 25 June 1964.

31 The trip began in Canberra, followed by two-to-four day visits in Tokyo, Bangkok, New Delhi, Karachi, Cairo, Belgrade, Warsaw, Moscow, Bonn, Paris, Brussels, and London.

32 De Gaulle had just rejected Britain's bid to join the EEC, the US and Europe were deadlocked on trade issues, and so forth, leaving some prospect of diverging Group

B approaches in Geneva. However the OECD secretariat in Paris played a skilful caucusing role, with the technical and analytical capacity to interpret complicated issues of international trade and finance for its members.

33 Statement by Dr Raúl Prebisch, informal meeting of the General Assembly Second Committee, 18 November 1963.

34 Ibid.

35 Ibid.

36 Record of meeting with US State Department Officials, Washington, DC, 1 November 1963, Pollock Papers, box 3.

37 Address by George W. Woods, luncheon in honour of Raúl Prebisch, 2 November 1963.

38 Ibid.

39 Dell worried that the report was too "Latin America-oriented" in criticizing "inward-looking development" and pressing for the promotion of exports of manufactured goods since most developing countries remained commodity producers (fully 90 percent of Third World trade) with large subsistence sectors. Dell and Krishnamurti also felt that Prebisch should tone down his sharp criticism of the GATT; a lower tone might "make our case for its improvement much stronger."

40 Ray Sternfeld, interview with the author. Mann had turned down Kennedy's offer to be assistant secretary of state for Latin America because he thought the Alliance for Progress to be softheaded. His appointment accelerated the Alliance fatigue evident before Kennedy's assassination: two weeks before Dallas, on 6 October, Assistant Secretary of State Edwin Martin decided to continue aid to the new military governments of Honduras and Dominican Republic despite their overturning democratically elected governments.

41 UNCTAD needed Washington's support so badly that Prebisch had rented an office in the OAS building to coordinate meetings with officials, legislators, and the private sector in the build-up to Geneva. Although falling to 39.4 percent in 1982, the US produced more than half of the developed world's GDP in 1960; it hosted the IMF, World Bank, and the IDB, and its immense influence gave it a de facto veto at the UN.

42 Pollock, notes of meeting on 1 November 1963, Department of State, Washington, DC. The argument was that developing countries were key to East-West relations – the swing-factor in US-USSR rivalry – and vulnerable to communist subversion. Rostow was convinced that he had constructed a new blueprint for US foreign policy, which the G-77 failed to grasp.

43 Statement at the 24th plenary meeting, 8 April 1964. Proceedings, vol. II, 436.

44 "I saw logic in the concept of the advanced countries opening their markets to Third World; the only problem was that they would never do it, and I did not want to be party to a fraud." George Ball, *The Past Has Another Pattern*, 193–5.

45 Arthur Karasz to Richard E. Demuth, 26 May 1964.

46 Heath, *The Course of My Life*, 602.
47 Helleiner, "The Southern Side of "Embedded Liberalism," 263–6.
48 Asia was even more complex but agreed to incorporate Yugoslavia, Israel, and the non-African Middle East countries. R. Krishnamurti laboured to maintain a united front among these governments during UNCTAD I, notwithstanding historical issues such as Kashmir and the difficulty of handling Japan, Australia, and New Zealand, who were members of ECAFE but also outside the G-77 as part of Group B.
49 Group C was a building block of UNCTAD itself – both in geography and ideology – and therefore vital to Prebisch's political credibility and overall strategy in the G-77. UNCTAD gave ECLA a new mission to coordinate a united Latin American position on trade and development for Geneva – taking the leadership in forming CECLA (Special Coordinating Committee for Latin America) in November 1963 as a model of regional consultation and caucusing for the other regional commissions – ECAFE in Bangkok or the ECA in Africa – which faced a similar challenge. Brazil was vital in carrying the UNCTAD initiative forward before Geneva. In November 1963 President Goulart told a meeting of the OAS that Latin unity at UNCTAD was vital; led by Minister of Planning Celso Furtado, Brazil facilitated the work of CECLA in early 1964 to prepare for Geneva. In January 1964, CECLA organized a Meeting of Experts, where Prebisch gave the lead paper, and a month later, at ECLA's Committee of the Whole, a position paper for UNCTAD I was accepted in principle with Mayobre announcing that integration had become "the meta, el eje y el centro," of ECLA's future activities (*El Clarin*, 16 February 1964). CECLA was again convened in Alta Gracia, Argentina, for a final Group C strategy session. The result was a Group C so prominent during UNCTAD I that many African and Asian delegations worried that their interests might be submerged by Latin America.
50 Krishnamurti to U Nyun, 29 May 1964. Jawaharlal Nehru's fatal heart attack and death on 27 May also stimulated Third World cohesion.
51 Cordovez, "UNCTAD and Development Diplomacy."
52 R. Krishnamurti, "Note on the Confidential Negotiations Convened by Dr Prebisch from 3–15 June, 1964 on the UNCTAD Recommendations on Institutional Machinery," June 1964.
53 Narisiham to de Seynes, 11 May 1964.
54 See Diego Cordovez, "UNCTAD and Development Diplomacy," *Journal of World Trade Law* I, no. 3 (May-June 1967).

CHAPTER EIGHTEEN

1 Celso Furtado, *Os Ares do Mundo*, 49.
2 This section relies heavily on the author's interviews with Celso Furtado and Fernando Henrique Cardoso.
3 Raúl Prebisch, unpublished recorded interview, Santiago, 19 December, 1973.

4 Celso Furtado, *Os Ares do Mundo*, 30–1.

5 De Seynes to Prebisch and C.V. Narasimhan, 30 October 1964.

6 DESA could not be allowed to dictate UNCTAD's policy or research, which had its own requirements: "what is needed is to combine variety and freedom of research with uniformity of methodology and consistency of basic data, results and interpretation." Prebisch to de Seynes and Narasimhan, 1 November 1964.

7 This was the notorious UN ACABQ (Advisory Committee on Administrative and Budgetary Questions). Essentially de Seynes proposed consolidating and merging services with DESA. The issue was critical for Prebisch in securing personnel, and the G-77 meeting was held on 14 January. The G-77 "will strongly support the submission of the Secretary General and would not be able to concur in the proposals of the Advisory Committee," Prebisch wrote to U Thant after the meeting. B.R. Turner, UN controller, wrote to C.V. Narasimhan regarding these "basic differences of opinion on matters of policy between Dr Prebisch and Mr de Seynes," and requesting advice from the secretary general on solving the crisis "in view of its importance within the organizational framework of the United Nations" (6 and 18 November; and Report of Secretary General to Advisory Committee, 8 December 1964). Staff needs were projected at seventy-one in 1965 and ninety-four in 1966, including twenty-one for work in commodities.

8 In the end he was worn down into accepting one of the pair. Twelve professional and eight general-service posts were to go from Mosak's bureau to UNCTAD. Dell was released to Prebisch on 10 November; while his area of specialization was finance related to development, he was also one of Prebisch's key overall advisors.

9 The new UNCTAD machinery was far too complex. The top organ remained the conference, initially to meet in 1966 but delayed until 1968, after which a four-year interval between conferences became the rule. Next in the hierarchy was the Trade and Development Board (TDB), encompassing no fewer than fifty-five members from the four regional groups, with its own president, and mandated to hold two sessions a year in New York and Geneva respectively. Reporting to the TDB were the three main UNCTAD committees: commodities, manufactures, and invisibles and financing. The complexity of these subject areas necessitated, in turn, subsidiary working groups and intergovernmental subcommittees. Although the secretariat expanded to 175 professionals by 1968, including a special division of conference affairs, there was too much perpetual motion for consistently high-quality work.

10 From the beginning African states complained that they were being excluded from senior positions in Prebisch's new secretariat. Some of them, like Tanzania and Ghana, openly attacked Prebisch for favouritism toward Latin Americans and for giving Africans jobs as, in their words, "elegant messenger boys." By February 1966 only six Africans had been hired in UNCTAD, Tanzania charged, and half at the lowest professional levels. Prebisch rejected the "serious accusations" as "fundamentally unjust." Out of a regional quota of thirteen, eight had been hired with five others to be

appointed soon, while only ten positions for Latins had been approved for UNCTAD. He had tried, immediately after Geneva, to locate qualified African candidates, but they were rare, high-priced, and with many other options. He thought he had two, including a D-2 appointment, lined up in 1965. But in July of that year U Thant asked him to back off since the economists were from Nigeria and Ghana, countries already over represented in the UN secretariat. Prebisch then tried to hire Michael Imru, Ethiopia's ambassador to Moscow, for the position of director, Trade Policies Division, earmarked for an African, but U Thant wrote unsuccessfully to Addis Ababa for his release. "In another case," Prebisch noted, "negotiations with an African were almost completed, when the person in question said that he would only accept a post as Under-Secretary. But unfortunately I hold this post."

11 Pollock, Love and Lerner, "Prebisch at UNCTAD," 44–6. Malinowski agreed to stand down but told Prebisch that he would consider the appointment of any other person as deputy secretary-general, even Sidney Dell, a personal betrayal. The debacle was a serious loss for Prebisch: in New York he had Dell, but his Geneva office was overburdened from the outset.

12 P. Spinelli to Secretary-General U Thant, European Office of the UN, Palais des Nations, Geneva, 10 May 1965.

13 A special TDB (Trade and Development Board) meeting later that month in New York approved the move.

14 World Bank, Karasz to File, 29 December 1965.

15 G.D. Arsenis to David Pollock, 6 October 1972. Note Walters, "International Organizations and Political Communication."

16 Bela Belassa, World Bank memorandum, 15 July 1965.

17 David Pollock, *Conversations with Raúl Prebisch*, Washington, 21–23 May 1985.

18 The Conference preceding the Fourth Trade and Development Board Meeting in Geneva; an agreement-in-principle would be approved at UNCTAD II in New Delhi.

19 Toye and Toye, "From New Era to Neo-Liberalism," 161–2.

20 Prebisch had raised the issue with the World Bank in July 1963 before the Geneva meeting, requesting a study of its potential role in "providing assistance to developing countries experiencing a secular decline in export receipts" (Prebisch to Richard H. Demuth, 17 July 1963).

21 Woods to Thant, 6 December 1965.

22 World Bank office memorandum, 29 December 1965.

23 World Bank office memorandum, 13–20 April 1966.

24 Even though, they argued, "a number of important questions of detail, administration and finance need further enquiry before an international agreement would be possible" (World Bank Report on the Meeting of the UNCTAD Committee on Invisibles and Financing, Geneva, 13–20 April 1966, 3). Both developed and developing countries also agreed that the new scheme should be coordinated with the IMF's short-term compensatory financing facility.

25 Moved to sweeping hopes for the UN Development Decade, Friedman "expressed his satisfaction at hearing a number of delegates from donor and recipient countries stress the need to increase the flow of development finance and to extend this assistance on more concessional terms" (World Bank Report on the Meeting of the UNCTAD Committee on Invisibles and Financing, Geneva, 13–20 April 1966, 6). Another meeting of the UNCTAD Committee on Invisibles and Financing Related to Trade was called for 21 November-2 December 1966, again in Geneva.

26 Prematurely established with three professional public relations officers, the ITC was not granted trust funds from donor governments for developing country projects until 1 May 1966 and was dismissed as insincere and ineffective.

27 Luis Augosto Castro Neves, interview with the author, 13 June 1991.

28 Raúl Prebisch to U Thant, 27 March 1967.

29 U Thant to Paul G. Hoffman, 16 May 1967. Washington was pleased, and even de Seynes and Mosak approved since they were convinced that Malinowski was behind the scheme of cornering export promotion for UNCTAD. The old rivals Prebisch and Wyndham-White had other interests in common, like their mutual dislike for the upstart UNIDO (United Nations Industrial Development Organization) based in Vienna. Both saw it as a UN throwback, committed to the worst features of inward-looking development. They agreed, therefore, to present a common front against the new UNIDO, because it was "ideologically opposed to regionalism" and might exercise excessive influence toward protectionist policies leading to "premature industrialization" (US Mission Geneva to State Department, 15 August 1967).

30 Bela Belassa to N. Sarma, 3 February 1967. This was an important symptom because the concept of supplementary financing originated from bank staff rather than its board representatives (Irving S. Friedman to George C. Woods, 5 December 1967).

31 Woods to Prebisch, 23 June 1967.

32 Speaking in Spanish without notes, he contrasted their "two distinct views on development policy and international cooperation. On the one hand there was the concept that to enable a country to implement its economic development effectively, its plan for investment and stabilization of domestic resources must not be subject to disturbing influences. On the other there was the concept that in such situations the country must adjust its economy and investment plans with a consequent decrease in its development rate." A corrected version toned down the dichotomy, merely stating that and that "if a country is to apply an economic development plan with some measure of efficiency, it is vital that its plan of investment and mobilization of internal resources should not be at the mercy of unforeseen external contingencies which have the effect of reducing its resources." (For the actual address, see Arthur Karasz to Michael L. Hoffman, 19 September 1967. The milder print version is Prebisch's Introductory Statement to the UNCTAD Trade and Development Board, Fifth Session, Geneva, 16 August 1967.)

33 Raúl Prebisch, address to the Trade and Development Board Fifth Session, UNCTAD Provisional Summary Record, Geneva, 16 August 1967.

34 Prebisch to Woods, 14 December 1967.

35 Sidney Dell to Raúl Prebisch, 18 March 1972.

36 UNCTAD, Fourth Meeting of the Trade and Development Board, Geneva, September 1966.

37 De Seynes to Woods, 26 May 1967.

38 Federico Consolo to Richard H. Demuth, 5 September 1966.

39 "Does he have an eye on U Thant's job?" the World Bank delegate mused (Consolo to Demuth, 5 September 1966). Prebisch had been considered for UN secretary-general in 1966.

40 V. Dubey to Files, IBRD office memorandum, 7 October 1966. Statement by Raúl Prebisch at the 93th Planning Meeting of the Trade and Development Board.

41 Consolo to Demuth, 7 August 1967.

42 After the 1964 election of Eduardo Frei as president of Chile, a popular Christian Democrat committed to development and support for UNCTAD, Prebisch drafted a letter for Frei to send to Filipe Herrera (IDB), José Antonio Mayobre (ECLA), and Carlos Sanz (CIAP) proposing a new program of action to relaunch the integration process in Latin America. But this promising mood in the Americas was soon reversed with the 1965 US invasion of the Dominican Republic, splitting Latin America between US allies (like the Brazilian generals) and anti-interventionist Mexico, Argentina, and Chile. This regional chill compounded the global impact of Johnson Administration's fixation with Southeast Asia after the August 1964 Tonkin Gulf Resolution and the ensuing military involvement in Vietnam.

43 Declaration of the Presidents of America Meeting of American Chiefs of State, Punta del Este, 12–14 April 1967.

44 Irving. S. Friedman to George D. Woods, 5 December 1967.

45 Prebisch, introductory statement to UNCTAD's second conference, New Delhi, 1968. S. Johnson to Friedman, 13 September 1967, had reported Prebisch's use of this term in his address to the UNCTAD Trade and Development Fifth Session on 17 August 1967. International ODA had declined from 0.83 percent GDP in 1961 to 0.69 percent in 1965, well off the 1 percent target of the UN Development Decade – and fully half was offset by debt and service repayments. Economic growth was barely 4 percent (as opposed to the UN minimum goal of 5 percent), and net import capacity from export earnings fell from $3.100 million in 1961 to $400 million 1965.

46 Although Prebisch's report to the second UNCTAD conference did contain certain new concepts: a distinction between less-developed and "more developed peripheral economies," for example, which he repeated it as an "obstacle," along with the "savings gap" (the chronic disparity between domestic savings and mounting investment requirements) and the more general external vulnerability of peripheral economies.

47 Prebisch, address to ECOSOC, 14 July 1966; Prebisch's Trade and Development Board text was delivered on 29 August 1967.

48 Arthur Karasz in the World Bank called Prebisch's recommendation "excellent." Karasz to Richard Demuth, 22 February 1968.

49 In March 1966 the original Panel of Nine was reduced from nine to five members and integrated into the CIAP machinery as a technical advisory group, prompting the resignation of the eight remaining members (See OAS, Declaración del CEAP sobre Resolución 27 – M/66, Washington 3 June, 1966; and P.N. Rosentein-Rodan to José A. Mora, 26 April 1966).

50 Arthur Karasz, report on UNCTAD II, World Bank, 18 April 1968.

51 *Wall Street Journal*, 21 January 1968.

52 "One thing that is new is supplementary financing," Prebisch claimed disingenuously in his opening address, "this, together with the financing of buffer stocks under commodity agreements, would be a fitting sequel to the great achievements of Bretton Woods."

53 Karasz to Demuth, 15 February 1968.

54 N.A. Sarna to Demuth, 12 March 1968.

55 Karasz to Demuth, 20 March 1968.

56 Pollock, Love, and Kerner, "Prebisch at UNCTAD," in Dosman, ed., *Raúl Prebisch: Power, Principle and the Ethics of Development*, 55.

57 Karasz to Demuth, 8 March 1968. India was equally ready to play at UNCTAD's expense, as were other developing countries, including Argentina after President Arturo Illia was overthrown in 1966.

58 Arthur Karasz to Richard E. Demuth, 8 March 1968.

59 The conference also accepted the UN goal of official development assistance equivalent to 1 percent GDP from developed to developing countries, but without specifying when the policy would come into effect.

60 Arthur Karasz to Richard E. Demuth, 20 March 1968. He reported that the Brazilian delegate "continues to talk about failure and would like to have the conference suspended."

61 Minutes, World Bank senior staff meeting, 29 March 1968.

62 *Washington Post*, 29 January 1969.

63 Prebisch, ACC report on UNCTAD II, Geneva, 24 April 1968; ECOSOC report on UNCTAD II, 10 July 1968.

64 Toye and Toye, "From New Era to Neo-Liberalism," 162–3.

65 Love, "Latin America, UNCTAD and the Postwar Trading System," especially 18–19.

66 By 1968 the group system of decision-making in UNCTAD was observed with religious conviction and impervious to change despite its rigidities. As Secretary of the Board Paul Berthoud noted to Prebisch in a confidential internal review, *The System of Groups in UNCTAD – Its Merits and Drawbacks. Suggestions for Improvement*, 10 June

1968: "The system of Groups which developed during the 1964 Conference has now become an integral part of the working machinery of UNCTAD."

67 Federico Consolo, World Bank Memorandum, 17 July 1968.

68 Consolo, World Bank Memorandum, 24 April 1968.

69 Three days of riots during the US Democratic Convention in Chicago, 26–29 August added to the chilling disillusionment.

70 To avoid what Prebisch called "a second Development Decade of even deeper frustration than the first" (Prebisch, Introductory Statement to the UNCTAD Trade and Development Board, Fifth Session, Geneva, 16 August 1967).

71 Prebisch to Woods, 13 December 1967.

72 Richard Demuth, World Bank memorandum, 12 April 1968.

73 Prebisch, report to the UN secretary-general, 1 May 1968.

74 Pearson's report, *Partners in Development* (1970), contained a list of sixty-eight recommendations – in effect a clinical inventory of useful measures deemed appropriate for all regions and countries to achieve a growth rate of 6 percent.

75 Karasz to Demuth, 20 March 1968. K.B. Lall of India was rumoured to be his likely successor.

76 In the amount of US$240,000 (Joaquin Gonzales to Prebisch, 20 June 1968).

77 Pedro Irañeta to Mario Mendivil, 13 November 1968.

78 These jobs, together with undertaking the major IDB commission, prompted doubts in some quarters that he quit UNCTAD for health reasons. U Thant's acceptance of his resignation on 26 November 1968 stated "mainly for reasons of health."

79 Prebisch to Michael Hoffman, associate director, Development Services Department, Word Bank, 13 December 1968. "We in the Bank will miss you greatly."

CHAPTER NINETEEN

1 US Embassy, Santiago to secretary of state, 2 and 4 December 1968.

2 *Economia*, Santiago, November/December 1968.

3 Prebisch, address to UNCTAD Trade and Development Board, 15 March 1969.

4 Prebisch declined a $100,000 salary offered by the Arthur D. Little management consulting firm to remain in the UN circuit.

5 CECLA, *Informe del Relator*, Reunion Extraordinario de CECLA a Nivel de Expertos, Viña del Mar, 7–14 May 1969, Anexo V Intervencion Inaugural del Ministro de Relaciones Exteriores de Chile senor Gabriel Valdes. Valdes's forum was much better organized and attended than ECLA's Lima session.

6 Valdes boasted that CECLA had been of "the highest importance" because it had clout, such as its success in persuading President Johnson to support the GSP in UNCTAD, and proposed strengthening their new forum with a permanent executive group. It took another meeting on 7–14 May to finalize the Viña del Mar

Consensus. Prebisch's letter to Nixon was grounded in mutual US-Latin American interests, while presenting the minimum needs for successful Latin development policies.

7 Armando Uribe, *The Black Book of American Intervention in Chile*, 31–2.

8 Echavarria to Prebisch, 23 February 1965.

9 ILPES, minutes of the emergency meeting of the board of directors, "Current Problems Facing the Institute and the Reorientation of Its Future Activities," 12–13 September 1969.

10 José Nun, interview with the author.

11 Cardoso and Faleto, *Dependency and Development in Latin America.* Fernando Henrique Cardoso returned to São Paulo in 1969 to co-found CEBRAP (Brazilian Centre of Analysis and Planning).

12 Mayobre, office memorandum, 18 October 1965.

13 Prebisch to Cristóbal Lara, 22 June 1968.

14 US Embassy, Santiago to secretary of state, 23 December 1968.

15 ILPES ninth annual meeting, in Santiago, 6–10 January 1970. Felipe Herrera agreed to join the board as a special mark of IDB confidence in the future of ILPES. De Seynes had the same idea. Other traditional missions would be recast. Training, for example, would move from basic courses to specialized seminars for business executives, trade unionists, or community leaders – particularly relevant for the smaller countries that clamoured for them; there were fifteen such applications for 1970 alone.

16 The *New York Times* (20 May 1969) advised Rockefeller to cancel visits to "the hard-pressed democracies of Chile and Uruguay" on a mission that "turns out to have been badly conceived and badly timed." Nor, the editorial argued, had the risky trip been necessary. "Before Mr. Rockefeller left," it argued, "two eminent economists – Carlos Sanz de Santamaria, Chairman of CIAP, and Raúl Prebisch – had underlined the needs of the region."

17 For example, Roberto Campos, Roundtable on Latin American Development, Boston University, 5 October 1972.

18 Prebisch, *Change and Development*, 7.

19 T. Graydon Upton to Mr Cecilio Morales, 10 November 1970, noting that the problem of capital flight from Latin America was ignored entirely. Examples from Asia were also not sufficiently used, although Prebisch was uniquely qualified to strengthen his report with comparative studies.

20 Prebisch, *Change and Development: Latin America's Great Task.* According to Paul Rosenstein-Rodan, the Prebish report was "like a seismographic apparatus sensitively registering social tremors." Pollock, "The Pearson and Prebisch Reports," 77. However, Prebisch did not share the widespread catastrophic view of North-South relations being promoted by prominent individuals such as philosopher C.P. Snow. "Disaster is quite avoidable provided we recognize the complexity,

the seriousness, and the urgency of the problem." Richard Holloran, "A Non Catastrophic View," *Washington Post*, 23 March 1969.

21 The Tupamaros had adopted the name of Tupac Amuru, the Indian nationalist who had resisted the Spanish invaders and was subsequently captured and quartered in 1781.

22 Unless changes were made quickly, Prebisch argued, "the course of events might lead to the socialist method of development even if that had not been the original intention of those who set themselves to strengthen the dynamic impetus of the economic system ... events themselves might impel the State to take over the very sources of income of the upper strata by a process of socialization – of the major enterprises at least – even if no ideological considerations were involved. Ideologies would come later to justify *faits accomplis* and strengthen their significance" (Raúl Prebisch, "Teme Prebisch una Explosión Social en IberoAmerica," *El Universal*, Mexico City, 27 April 1972).

23 *Change and Development: Latin America's Great Task*, 18–19. Already in 1961 ECLA had warned about the distortion occurring in Latin American economies with over-protected industries incapable of exporting, unlike the import-substitution model as applied in South Korea for example (Sunkel and Zuleta, "Neostructuralismo versus neoliberalismo," 44).

24 The figure of 8 percent had been established by an econometric model developed by the research team headed by ECLA's Manuel Balboa. ("I never understood computers," Prebisch remarked, "until I worked with Balboa.") Raúl warned that this would be an enormous challenge. Pollock and Ritter, "Pearson and Prebisch Reports," 6.

25 Hans Singer, transcript of oral statement presented at the Prebisch Symposium, Geneva, 2 July 1986, 4–5.

26 CERES, *FAO Review* 3, no 5 (September/October 1970), 8–7.

27 *Washington Post*, 18 September 1970.

28 Lewis Diuguid, "Latin Development Aid Boosted," *Washington Post*, 26 April 1970.

29 ECLA experts were already looking at informal markets; see Love, "The Rise and Decline of Economic Structuralism," 108–10.

30 *Washington Post*, 3 January 1971.

31 Adelita Prebisch, interview with the author.

32 Ibid.

33 William Lowenthal to Raúl Prebisch, 27 February 1970.

34 Prebisch to Andrew Cordier, 12 February 1970.

35 Prebisch to Paul Rosenstein-Rodan, 12 July 1972.

36 Latin governments remained as unwilling as ever to support the institute; at the meeting Brazil was deleted from the names of the eleven governments supporting the institute. At the most, they would provide $300,000 – but only for "contracted services."

37 *How the Institute Can Best Serve the UNDP and the IDB*, Santiago, 1971.

38 Haberler to Prebisch, 4 February 1972.

39 Cuban Vice-President Carlos Rafael Rodriguez and Charles Meyer, Nixon's new assistant secretary for Latin America, were the centre of attraction.

40 Prebisch to de Seynes, 17 January 1972. In recommending Iglesias for ECLA executive secretary, Prebisch noted that Furtado was also brilliant but that Washington would never accept him.

41 Prebisch to Alberto Morales, 23 February 1973.

42 Prebisch to Enrique Iglesias, 23 April 1973.

43 Herrera to Prebisch, 8 January 1973.

44 30 July 1973.

45 The appointment was heavily criticized throughout Latin America as patronage; in fact Raúl postponed the announcement until after ECLA's Quito session in March. His duties included attending major international meetings and drafting think pieces for the secretary general and Walter Sedwitz, executive director for economic and social affairs.

46 Prebisch to Laurencio Lopez, 18 July 1973.

47 United Nations Panel of Eminent Persons to Study the Impact of Multinational Corporations on the Development Process and on International Relations. David Pollock to Enrique Iglesias, 11 September 1973.

48 Valdez, *Pinochet's Economists.*

49 Prebisch to Hortensia Allende, 21 September 1973.

50 Prebisch, interview with *El Tiempo*, 11 July 1971.

51 *Jornal do Brasil*, 4 August 1973. Eugenio Gudin attended this BNDE conference on socio-economic development.

52 *El Tiempo*, "Raúl Prebisch: El populismo as negacion de una transformacion real," 11 July 1971.

53 But in the end Washington threw Latin America a bone, agreeing to create yet another OAS body, the Special Commission on Consultations and Negotiations, with the acronym CECON – quickly changed on the ground to "SECO" (dry).

54 New York *Times*, 23 October 1971.

55 Birns, ed., *The End of Chilean Democracy.*

56 Bodil Royem to Prebisch, 15 ovember 1972.

57 Adelita Prebisch, interview with the author.

58 Stephen S. Rosenfeld, "The Poor Nations Get Short Shrift," *Washington Post*, 7 April 1972. The US had unilaterally broken the postwar Bretton Woods monetary system on 15 August the previous year, and the Nixon Administration seemed unwilling to move on North-South issues. Quoting the *Journal of Commerce*, Rosenfeld continued, "just about every major proposal put forth in the interests of protecting the LDCS (less developed countries) from further deterioration in their terms of trade is drawing a negative response from Washington." UNCTAD was treated by Washington,

"not as a policy-making forum but as a sounding box for have-nots, malingerers and assorted other anti-Americans," and Santiago was probably its least preferred location on the globe aside from Hanoi.

59 Salvador Allende, "The Chilean Way," first message of President Allende to the joint session of Congress, 21 May 1971.

60 Although for certain opponents this undisputed political legitimacy made his UP more subversive than the Cuban Revolution. In contrast in Argentina, where Perónist and leftist guerrilla groups roamed the country despite repression, there were 417 shooting incidents in 1972, which left 356 killed and 286 wounded. Twenty million pesos were seized in 277 bank robberies. See E. J. Hobsbawm, "Chile: Year one," *New York Review of Books*, 23 September 1971, for an interesting assessment before the roof fell in on Allende's UP.

61 Prebisch's marginal comment scribbled on Endocio Ravines's article, "Culpa de quienes tienen es que otros no tengan," *La Prensa*, Buenos Aires, March 1973.

62 *El Mercurio*, 7 April 1973.

63 CIES, statement by Professor Paul N. Rosenstein-Rodan," Washington, 31 January, 1974.

64 Luis de Cervantes, "Pueden Surgir Otros Che Guevara si Continúa la Desigauldad," *Excelsior* (Mexico City), 20 January 1974.

65 United Nations, General Assembly Resolution 3202 (S-VI), May 1974. Barbara Ward, "First, Second, Third and Fourth Worlds," The *Economist*, 18 May 1974.

66 Juliet Halley to Raúl Prebisch, minutes of the meeting of the Inter-Agency Committee, 23 May 1974. US Department of State, secretary of state to US UN Mission, memorandum of conversation, 8 January 1975. Raúl Prebisch to US Mission, USUN, 1 August 1974.

67 Prebisch to Julio Silva, 6 October 1975.

68 For the US position see US Department of State, Raúl Prebisch to William B. Buffum, memorandum of conversation, 8 January, 1975. Also Department of State, Henry Kissinger, note to file, 14 August, 1974, instructing staff to observe a strict principle of noncommitment "in any case."

69 Waldheim to Prebisch, 18 August 1975.

CHAPTER TWENTY

1 The Summit Conference of Non-Aligned Nations held in Algiers in September 1973 was the catalyst for calling the sixth special session of the UN General Assembly and the subsequent NIEO initiative.

2 UN GA Resolution 3362, adopted by consensus, endorsed the concept of price indexation; a 0.7 percent aid target (0.7 percent of GDP of the developed countries); the linkage of development aid with the IMF's special drawing rights; and the management and pricing of core commodities.

3 However, the confidence of the West after the initial shock of the OPEC crisis was insufficiently restored for Kissinger to challenge the NIEO directly, as indicated by a conciliatory address to the special session of the UN General Assembly in September 1976. He also took the rare step of visiting ECLA headquarters in Santiago. But after UNCTAD's fourth meeting in June 1976 the outlook was uncertain – even more after the Paris Conference on the NIEO failed over oil security (*Financial Times*, 1 June 1976). The *Financial Times* reported that "Third World countries and the West are still on speaking terms." But that was all (*New York Times*, 19 September 1975). During the weak follow-on presidency of Gerald Ford, Henry Kissinger adopted an approach of "talking them to death" – of announcing vague proposals in support of North-South relations unlikely to be supported by the US Congress, waiting for differences among developing countries to emerge and curtail the promise of change.

4 *New York Times*, 19 September 1975.

5 Prebisch to Santa Cruz, 29 June 1977.

6 Robert McNamara established the Brandt Independent Commission on International Development in 1977 to help restore a momentum that had flagged since the 1960s.

7 Prebisch reassured Iglesias and the editorial board: "I will not forget the *Revista*," he wrote. "I wish to assure you that after all the bustle is over, I shall return to Santiago to take up the reins of the *Revista* – which I do not want to abandon for anything" (Raúl Prebisch to Enrique Iglesias, 24 May 1974). With this Raúl convinced the hold-outs among his authors ("the recalcitrants," he called them) to wait for his return.

8 Philippe de Seynes to Prebisch, 11 September 1976.

9 Lefeber and North, *Democracy and Development in Latin America*, 39. York University marked the opening of its Latin American and Caribbean Research Centre by conferring an honorary doctorate on Dr Prebisch.

10 Prebisch, *The New International Order and Cultural Values*, 5–26.

11 *The Guardian*, 26 March 1979.

12 Prebisch to José M. Lacalle, director of the Centre for Research and Promotion of Exports, Barcelona. He had attended the first Ibero American Conference on Planning and Development in 1973, where he met his retired friend Giner de los Rios. "What a pity that I do not know Spain better when I feel the attraction so strongly," Raúl exclaimed, his discovery of Spain a personal high point of his trip to Europe.

13 The Select Senate Committee to Study Governmental Operations with Respect to Intelligence Activities, chaired by Senator Frank Church, issued fourteen reports in 1975–76.

14 Santa Cruz to Prebisch, 21 April 1976.

15 Prebisch to Diego Cordovez, 23 December 1976.

16 *Financial Times,* 11 May 1977. Washington, in fact, was busy trying to reduce the US share of the OAS budget by cutting its bloated staff of 1,200 officials – with higher salaries than at the US State Department.

17 *Los Angeles Times,* 5 May 1977.

18 US Embassy in Guatemala to secretary of state, 6 May 1977.

19 Raúl Prebisch, address to ECLA's seventeenth session, Guatemala, 6 May 1977.

20 Ibid. The State Department Telegram quotes Prebisch's text at length.

21 C. Fred Bergsten, testimony to the Western Hemisphere Subcommittee of the Senate Foreign Relations Committee, October 5, 1978; *Financial Times,* 14 May 1979.

22 *Latin American Economic Report,* 27 July 1979.

23 Quoted in Scheman, ed., *Alliance for Progress,* 241.

24 *New York Times,* 2 February 1977.

25 Prebisch, "Pudiera Hacer Crisis Antes del 2000."

26 Ibid.

27 *El Sol de México,* 12 September 1976.

28 Prebisch, "Pudiera Hacer Crisis Antes del 2000."

29 For example, Sidney Weintraub to Prebisch, 9 February 1977; or L. Harrison to Robert E. Culbertson, "A Critique of the Prebisch Article 'Critique of Capitalism a la Periphery,'" US State Department memorandum, 27 January 1977.

30 *La Razon,* 13 June 1978. *Washington Post,* 9 September 1979.

31 Jack Anderson, "Argentina: Reality Contradicts Image," *Washington Post,* 6 September 1979. See also Karen deYoung and Charles A. Krause, "Our Mixed Signals on Human Rights in Argentina," *Washington Post,* 29 October 1978.

32 "Argentina: Reality Contradicts Image," *Washington Post,* 6 September 1979. See also *Financial Times,* 14 May 1979.

33 *Washington Post,* 29 October 1978. At the UNCTAD IV conference in Nairobi in May 1976, there had been apparent progress in beginning the implementation of commodity agreements – only the US and West Germany voted against the resolutions.

34 The Independent Commission on International Development Issues, chaired by Willi Brandt, issued its *North South Report* in 1980 and its second *Common Crisis Report* in 1983.

35 *Washington Post,* 20 May 1979; *Christian Science Monitor,* 21 November 1979.

36 *New York Times,* 18 May and 12 June 1981.

37 Prebisch replied, "There is not the slightest danger in relation to my insertion into the Northern establishment, nor in the establishment of the South, and as to the Nobel Prize, I will sign a piece of paper stating that I will not receive such distinction that does not correspond to an underdeveloped economist" (Raúl Prebisch to Abraham Mezarik, 18 June 1981).

38 *New York Times,* 31 March 1977. After Milton Friedman was awarded the prize in 1976, Gunnar Myrdal suggested that it be abolished.

39 Sir Arthur Lewis's *The Theory of Economic Growth* had, ironically, pre-empted Prebisch's scholarly recognition as the founder of structuralism. See chapter 13 above.

40 *El Litoral*, Santa Fe, 6 January 1982, "La Caida de la Economia Latinoamericano." Kuczinski, "The View from Latin America in the Mid-1980s," 229–34.

41 William J. Barber, "Chile con Chicago: A Review Essay," *Journal of Economic Literature* (33), December 1995, 1946.

42 *Presencia*, La Paz, 29 April 1979.

43 *El Mercurio* took up the crusade of "inoperancia del análisis de la CEPAL" (23 May 1981) until Prebisch felt compelled to set the record straight with a letter to the editor that pointed out that import substitution was a pragmatic response to the Great Depression and that he had already publicly warned about Latin governments' "excessive orientation toward the domestic market" and "their lack of stimuli for industrial exports." ISI had been merely a policy tool; he had never supported it as an ideology. "Unfortunately," he concluded, "this pragmatic policy ended by being transformed into dogma, just as export-oriented development is becoming dogma. It is necessary to export primary products and manufactured goods but at the same time to increase production for the home market" (5 June 1981).

44 *El Mercurio*, 23 May 1981 and 15 February 1982.

45 See for example Heraldo Muñoz to Raúl Prebisch, 5 August 1977; or Sidney Dell to Raúl Prebisch, 27 February 1979.

46 See Mallorquín, "Raúl Prebisch before the Ice Age," 101, including his reference to Armando Di Filippo, *Desarrollo y desigualidad social en América Latina.*

47 *New York Times*, 12 June 1981.

48 Prebisch to Weintraub, 27 April 1981.

49 Prebisch corresponded increasingly with Argentine scholars such as Guido Di Tella and Arturo O'Connell on Argentine history in the 1930s.

50 *La Nacion*, 27 February 1972.

51 Lewis, *Crisis of Argentine Capitalism*, 435–57. Filipe Herrera, who had resided in Rio since his retirement as coordinator general of an IDB-financed centre called ECIEL (Programme of Joint Studies on Economic Integration in Latin America), had returned to Santiago as president of the Banco Español.

52 Having lived in Washington for so many years Prebisch realized from the start that Galtieri's dreams of US support were ridiculous. But while opposing Galtieri's overt aggression he both strongly supported Argentina's historic claim to the Malvinas and opposed the economic sanctions imposed by European and North American governments after the outbreak of war. Between mid-May and September 1982 he worked on a volunteer basis with SELA (the Latin American Economic System), based in Caracas, to limit the damage of sanctions. But there was really nothing to be done: Argentina had violated international law, and Latin governments refused to go beyond rhetorical support; Chile actually assisted Britain.

53 *Wall Street Journal*, 17 October 1983.

54 Prebisch to Peter Dorner, 1 March 1984.
55 Prebisch, "Lineamientos de un programa."
56 Raúl Prebisch, "Lineamientos de un programa."
57 Bernardo Grinspun, interview with the author, 19 March 1992.
58 *Ambito Financiero*, 21 May 1984.
59 Lewis, *Crisis of Argentine Capitalism*, 480–1.
60 Julio Garcia del Solar, interview with the author, 18 March 1992.
61 "What do you want to know," Prebisch asked, "what age would you like me to say? I told you that I am about to celebrate my 83rd birthday, but I am working in the Church of the Merced, where they baptized me and took ten years from me, which they were able to do because they have burnt the archives and facts can be manipulated" (Raúl Prebisch, "Conferencia de prensa del Dr Prebisch en Casa de Gobierno," 10 April 1984, 26).
62 *Clarin*, 20 May 1984.
63 Republic of Argentina, *Senate Record*, Buenos Aires, 11 May 1984.
64 SELA co-organized the meeting with ECLA to discuss ideas ranging from creating an OELA (an OAS without the US) to improve informal contacts among central bankers. Enrique Iglesias, who had returned from ECLA and been appointed Uruguay's foreign minister a year earlier, was named secretary pro tem of the Cartegena Group on 5 October 1985.
65 Brokered by former US Treasury Secretary James Baker, whereby middle-income debtor countries could access World Bank and commercial bank lending in exchange for growth-oriented structural reforms.
66 Garcia del Solar, interview with the author. See also US Department of State, Embassy Buenos Aires to US secreetary of state, 3 November 1984.
67 Prebisch to David Pollock, 10 September 1984.
68 Department of Commerce, US Embassy to US secretary of state, "Raúl Prebisch Resigns as Presidential Advisor," 14 May 1985.

CHAPTER TWENTY-ONE

1 Eliana Diaz de Prebisch, interview with the author, 5 July 1989.
2 The Contadora Group, comprising Mexico, Venezuela, Colombia, and Panama, was formed in September 1983 to contain conflicts in Nicaragua, El Salvador, and Guatemala.
3 The Rio Group was formally created in 1986 on the invitation of Brazil.
4 The Treaty of Asunción was signed in 1991 by Argentina, Brazil, Paraguay, and Uruguay.
5 Hobsbawm, *Age of Extremes: The Short Twentieth Century*.
6 Raúl Prebisch, "Renovar el pensamiento económico latinoamericano," 537–9.

Bibliography

Prebisch's professional life was divided between the Argentine public service, where he worked until 1943, and senior United Nations appointments dating from 1949 until his death in 1986. Many records were lost in the political turbulence affecting Argentina, and important ECLA registry files in Santiago covering the years 1948–70 were also destroyed without copies. The resulting challenge of assembling documentation required detailed attention to archival sources, private collections, and interviews as well as books, articles, and other printed materials.

DOCUMENT COLLECTIONS

International Organizations

UNITED NATIONS SECRETARIAT ARCHIVES, NEW YORK AND SANTIAGO.

The documents assembled by these archives (in the following categories) are fully referenced individually in the notes, with enquiries to be directed to the UN.

UN General Assembly records

DESA (Department of Economic and Social Affairs) records

ECLA (Economic Commission for Latin America and the Caribbean):

Group 1 Registry and Personnel files
Group 2 Creation of ECLA
Group 3 ECLA Sessions 1949–86
Group 4 ECLA and DESA
Group 5 ECLA–OAS Relations
Group 6 Evolution of ECLA–US Relations
Group 7 ECLA and Regional Integration

Group 8 ECLA and the Alliance for Progress
Group 9 ECLA and UNCTAD
Group 10 Prebisch: Departure from ECLA

UNCTAD (UNITED NATIONS CONFERENCE ON TRADE AND DEVELOPMENT) ARCHIVES, GENEVA.

Each document provided by the UNCTAD Secretariat (in the following categories) is fully referenced in the notes.

Group 1 UNCTAD I Preparatory Conferences
Group 2 UNCTAD-GATT Relations
Group 3 Inter-Agency Memoranda: 1964–68

ILPES (LATIN AMERICAN INSTITUTE FOR ECONOMIC AND SOCIAL PLANNING), SANTIAGO.

The ILPES documentation begins in 1960, and each document used is fully referenced in the notes. The files fall into the following categories:

Group 1 Birth of ILPES
Group 2 ILPES in the UNCTAD Years
Group 3 The Joint ECLA-ILPES Office
Group 4 Inter-Office Correspondence, 1969–72

ORGANIZATION OF AMERICAN STATES:

Alliance for Progress Documents Consulted:

OEA. SER.H/X.3 Doc 227 Interamerican Economic and Social Council. Address of Raul Prebisch to the Second Session of the First Annual Meeting of Ministers. Mexico: 23 October 1962.

OEA. SER H/X.3 Doc 239 Interamerican Economic and Social Council. Review of the First Plenary Session of the First Annual Meeting of Ministers. Mexico: 23 October 1962.

OEA/SER.G/II C-d – 451 Interamerican Economic and Social Council: Minutes of the Regular Session. Washington: 9 October 1962.

OEA/SER.G/V C-d – 1001 The Secretary General's Note accompanying a Proposal to fill the Committee of Nine Vacancy, with Ing. Jorge Grieve's Biographical Background. Washington: 20 June 1962.

OEA/SER.L/VIII.1 Doc 1 Inauguration Ceremony of the OAS-IDB-ECLA Ad Hoc Trilateral Committee. Washington: 7 December 1940.

OEA/SER.H/X.2 Doc. 41 Inter-American Economic and Social Council. Statement of the General Secretariat of the Organization of American States with reference to coordination and secretariat functions. Washington: 7 December 1961.

OEA/SER.H/X.2 Doc. 40 Interamerican Economic and Social Council, Proposal to Establish the Group of Experts. Washington: November-December 1961.

OEA/SER.H/X.2 Doc. 60 Interamerican Economic and Social Council, Official Documents of the Extraordinary Meeting of Experts. Washington: 29 November 1961.

OEA/SER.H/XII.2 Inter-American Economic and Social Council. Official Documents Emanating from the Special Meeting at the Expert Level. Washington: 29 November to 9 December 1961.

OEA/SER.H/X.2 Doc 67 Dr. Raul Prebisch, Closing Address to the Group of Experts of the Interamerican Social and Economic Council. Washington: 9 December 1961.

OEA/SER.H/X.1 ES-RE-Doc. 8 Statements of the Secretary General of the Organization of American States, of the Executive Secretary of the United Nations Economic Commission for Latin America, and of the President of the Inter-American Development Bank regarding the Agenda of the Special Meeting. 12 July 1961. 7 p.

OEA/SER.H/X.1 ES-RE-Doc. 9 Prelininary List of Official Participants at Punta del Este. Washington: 14 August 1961.

OEA/SER.H/X.1 ES-RE-Doc.27 Address by Jorge Sol Castellanos, Executive Secretary of the Interamerican Economic and Social Council. Washington: 16 August 1961.

International Financial Institutions

IMF (INTERNATIONAL MONETARY FUND) ARCHIVES, WASHINGTON: Upon request, the IMF provided copies of inter-office letters and Prebisch correspondence concerning IMF-ECLA relations (1948–63). Each document used is referenced fully in the notes. For access to these files, please contact the IMF or author.

Group 1 IMF–ECLA Liaison 1948–56. Reports of Fund Missions to ECLA Sessions and Office Memoranda on topics including post-war EPU-Latin America payments and Dr Prebisch's *Economic Report* on Argentina (1955).

Group 2 Prebisch, the IMF and the Latin American Common Market. Inter-office correspondence and office memoranda including the Latin American Common Market, 1956–60 covering the period from ECLA's first Trade Committee meeting to the creation of the Latin America Free Trade Association.

WORLD BANK (INTERNATIONAL BANK FOR RECONSTRUCTION AND DEVELOPMENT), WASHINGTON, DC.

As with the IMF, the World Bank provided its collection of documents concerning its relationship with ECLA and UNCTAD. Each document specifically identified is referenced fully in the notes. For access to these files, please contact the World Bank Library.

Group 1 World Bank-ECLA Liaison, 1948–63. Topics include initial contacts and working relationships after 1958; joint activities; and training programs before and after President Kennedy's Alliance for Progress.

Group 2 World Bank-UNCTAD Liaison, 1963–68, including World Bank collaboration in UNCTAD, particularly the issue of supplementary financing and IDA replenishment, the transition from George Woods to Robert McNamara, and the calling of the Pearson Commission.

IBD INTER-AMERICAN DEVELOPMENT BANK, ARCHIVES

Documents released in consultation with IDB archivists (by category, with full individual referencing in the notes, and enquiries to be directed to the Bank.

Group 1 The Creation of the IDB, 1958–60: internal documents and correspondence.

Group 2 Growth and Development: Latin America's Great Task, 1968–70. Correspondence and papers clarifying the initial contacts with Prebisch in 1968, through the completion and evaluation of the report.

National Archives

UNITED STATES NATIONAL ARCHIVES, WASHINGTON, DC.

Department of State (Record Group 59). Central Files: Diplomatic Records. Decimal Files to 1963.

310.4 (Communications with US Mission to the United Nations)

340.1 (UN ECOSOC Economic and Social Council)

340.210 (ECLA Economic Commission for Latin America and the Caribbean)

361 (OAS Organization of American States)

365 (IA ECOSOC Inter-American Economic and Social Council)

394 (ITO International Trade Organizaton)

394.41 (GATT General Agreement on Tariffs and Trade)

398.13 (IMF International Monetary Fund)

398.14 (IBRD Internation Bank for Reconstruction and Development or WorldBank)

611.20 (Political Relations between Latin America and the United States)

835 (Internal Affairs of Argentina)

835.51 (Financial Affairs of Argentina)

835.516 (Banking in Argentina)

Security and Modern Military Branch Records of the Joint Chiefs of Staff

Department of Justice, Central Intelligence Agency and FBI (Under US Freedom of Information Act)

Economic Series (particularly the International Trade Administration (ITA) for US-Argentine Trade Policy and Negotiations 1939–43)

US Treasury (Freedom of Information Appeal FOIA denied)
Agency for International Development
Department of Commerce (Office of Multilateral Affairs).
Columbia University, Butler Library (Rare Book and Manuscript Collection)

ARGENTINA:
National Archives of Argentina (Buenos Aires)
Central Bank of Argentina (BCA): the Raul Prebisch Library
Argentine National Congress: Senate Debates (selected years to 1985)
La Nacion (Buenos Aires): Archives
Torcuato di Tella University: Oral History Project

Private Collections

PREBISCH PAPERS
Besa García, José F., ed. *Dr Raúl Prebisch, 1901–86: Archivo de Trabajo.* Santiago, Chile: ECLAC, 2003. Also available at the Inter-American Development Bank, Washington, DC, and the University of Illinois Library, Chicago. This archive contains Adela Moll de Prebisch's personal records on microfilm, edited by Besa, and is identified in the notes to this volume as Prebisch Papers. It includes:
Reel 1. 1920–44, folders 1–33: Personal and family correspondence from 1920 onwards; documentary collections covering Prebisch official visits to Rio de Janeiro and Washington in 1940–1; key unpublished and previously unknown Prebisch manuscripts; a complete file of Prebisch's extensive newspaper work written for *La Nacion* during the 1930s; documents on the evolution of the Argentine Central Bank during the Great Depression and World War II.
Reel 2. 1944–47, folders 34–55: Prebisch's correspondence with Robert Triffin, Victor Urquidi, Eugenio Gudin, and other economists and associates in the years after 1944. Press clippings from the 1930s to 1950s. Prebisch's letters with key diplomats and officials in Argentina, Washington, London and Latin America before joining ECLA in 1949; extensive manuscripts and notes; and Prebisch's work with the US Federal Reserve throughout Latin America from 1944 to 1947.
Reel 3. 1947–55, folders 56–84: the early CEPAL years; and Prebisch's return to Argentina in 1955.
Reel 4. 1956–65, folders 85–118: CEPAL and the first years of UNCTAD.
Reels 5–7. 1965–86, folders 119–85: ILPES and the *CEPAL* Review; Prebisch's return to Argentina.

THE PREBISCH FOUNDATION in Buenos Aires also houses valuable archival materials with particular reference to Prebisch's return to Argentina as advisor to President Raúl Alfonsín. Eliana Prebisch's succcessful initiative also produced

Prebisch's *Collected Works.* Published in four volumes under the editorial direction of Gregorio Weinberg and Manuel Fernandez Lopez and guided by the Foundation's publications committee headed by Enrique Garcia Vasquez, the *Obras 1919–1948* (Buenos Aires: Prebisch Foundation, 1991) established the Foundation as an irreplaceable destination for Prebisch scholars.

KRISHNAMURTI PAPERS

Rangaswami Krishnamurti, *Some UNCTAD Events and Reminiscences* (Geneva: 30 April 1991). The Krishnamurti Papers deal primarily with the Prebisch era of UNCTAD – the early years from 1964 to his resignation in 1968–69. Their meticulous preparation, together with Dr Krishnamurti's official position in Geneva within the UNCTAD team, make this private collection a valuable source for Prebisch scholars. The documents are organized in two boxes, and notes in the book from the Krishnamurti Papers include box references. For access please contact the author.

Box 1. Krishnamurti's narrative, in thirty-two chapters, of his UNCTAD experience, addressing key events and participants, and the evolution of UNCTAD from a concept to permanent UN organization. Special Topics include:

The UNCTAD Secretariat: Origins and Key Personalities

North-South Relations and the Group of 77

The UNCTAD-GATT Relationship

Commodity Negotiations and the GSP

Sydney Dell: his Role in UNCTAD

Box 2. Annexes: Internal memoranda and letters, 1964–68, with eleven entries between 1970 and 1984. Listings include:

Note on Confidential Negotiations on the establishment of UNCTAD, convened by Dr Prebisch, 3–14 June 1964.

UNCTAD Inter-Office Memoranda 1966–68.

Correspondence with the ECAFE (Economic Commission for Africa and the Far East) Executive Secretary.

Correspondence concerning the Council of Europe, 1966–67.

Raul Prebisch Correspondence, 1966–67.

Letters and other papers on UNCTAD-GATT relations, 1965–68.

POLLOCK PAPERS

David H. Pollock, ECLAC's Washington Office, *1956–91* (Ottawa, 2001). The Pollock Papers comprise over 2,500 internal documents and correspondence from the Washington Office of ECLAC between 1955 and 1980, personal letters and press clipping collections in English and Spanish, and memoranda from special advisory assignments for Prebisch before and after UNCTAD. This important source material has been organized into the following boxes, and all notes drawing on the Pollock Papers include box references. For access to these papers please consult the author.

Box 1 ECLAC Washington-Santiago Correspondence,1955–60.

Box 2 The Alliance for Progress Years, 1960–63.

Box 3 Prebisch and UNCTAD (1964).

Box 4 Prebisch in Washington, 1968–72.

Box 5 The UN Special Emergency Operation, 1974–75.

Box 6 ECLAC Inter-Office Correspondence, 1972–80.

Box 7 Press Clippings: Spanish and English.

Box 8 Other Correspondence: Hans Singer; Sidney Dell; Wladek Malinowski, Robert Muller; R. Krishnamurti; Hernan and Alfonso Santa Cruz; Anibal Pinto, Maurice Strong, Sidney Weintraub, Osvaldo Sunkel, etc.

INTERVIEWS

MAJOR PUBLISHED INTERVIEWS WITH PREBISCH:

Magariños de Mello, Mateo J. "Diálogos con Raúl Prebisch." Stockholm, 8 November 1971. Published with same title, Mexico: Fondo de Cultura Económica, 1991.

Gonzalez del Solar, Julio. "Conversaciones con Raúl Prebisch." Buenos Aires, 9 July 1983. Published as "Un texto de Raúl Prebisch," ed. Carlos Mallorquín. *Revista Aportes* (Benemérita Universidad Autónoma de Puebla), year V, no. 14 (May-August 2000).

Pollock, David, "Conversations with Raúl Prebisch," Washington, 21–23 May 1985. Published by David Pollock, Daniel Kerner and Joseph Love in three segments: "Aquellos Viejos Tiempos: la formación teorica y practica de Raúl Prebisch en la Argentina: Una entrevista con David Pollock." *Desarrollo Economico* 41, no. 164; "Entrevista inédita a Prebisch: logros y deficiencias de la CEPAL." *CEPAL Review* 75 (2001): 9–24; "Prebisch at UNCTAD." *Raúl Prebisch: Power, Principle and the Ethics of Development,* ed. Edgar J. Dosman. Washington and Buenos Aires: IDB/INTAL (2006): 37–63.

PERSONAL INTERVIEWS (All interviews were conducted by Edgar J. Dosman and/or David Pollock; an asterisk indicates that an individual has been interviewed several times, beginning with the date listed):

Abakoumoff, Alexis. UNCTAD. Geneva, 6 June 1989.

Abramovic, Dragoslav. World Bank. Washington, 16 November 1991.

Adebanjo, M.T. UNCTAD. Geneva, 6 June 1989.

Agosin, Manuel R. UNCTAD. Geneva, 7 June 1989.

Alfonsin, Raúl. President of Argentina. Washington, 27 January 1992.

Arendt, Carmen Vera. ECLAC. Santiago, 13 July 1989.

Assael, Hector. ECLAC. Santiago, 8 March 1992.

Balboa, Manuel. ECLAC. Santiago, 8 March 1989.
*Bardeci, Oscar. ILPES. Buenos Aires, 7 July 1989.
Bernstein, Edward M. IMF. Washington, 28 November 1990.
Bertholet, Yves. UNCTAD. Geneva, 5 June 1989.
*Besa Garcia, José. ECLAC. Santiago, 8 July 1989.
*Brown, Robert. ECLAC. Santiago, 8 March 1992.
Bunge, Mario. Prebisch Godson and McGill University. Montreal, 24 January 1992.
Cardoso, Fernando Henrique. President of Brazil. Belo Horizonte, Brazil, 21 May 2007.
Casillas, Luis A., Inter-American Development Bank. Washington, 8 March 1991.
Cassorla, Armando. Organization of American States. Washington, 13 February 1992.
Castro Neves, Luis Augosto. Brazil Diplomat. Ottawa, 13 June 1991.
Cavallo, Domingo. Argentine Official. Buenos Aires, 10 May 1991.
*Cibotti, Ricardo. ILPES. Buenos Aires, 10 May 1990.
*Cohen, Issac. ECLAC. Washington, 22 January 1990; 3 March 1991.
Cordovez, Diego. UN and UNCTAD. Quito, 8 May 1997.
Cox, Robert. ILO and York University. Toronto, 18 March 1989.
Dagum, Camilo. Economist, Ottawa University, 28 October 1987.
De Seynes, Philippe. UN undersecretary. New York, 20 May 1991.
*Devlin, Robert. ECLAC and Inter-American Development Bank. Santiago, 3 March 1991.
*Diaz de Prebisch, Eliana. Buenos Aires, beginning 5 July 1989.
Di Tella, Guido. Torcuato di Tella University. Ottawa, 17 May 1991.
*Domike, Arthur. United Nations and Esquel Group Foundation. Washington, 8 March 1991.
Dorfman, Adolfo. ECLAC. Buenos Aires, 13 March 1992.
Emmerij, Louis I. United Nations and Inter-American Development Bank. Washington, 30 March 1995.
Fajnzylber, Fernando. ECLAC. Santiago, 13 July 1989.
Ferrer, Aldo. ECLAC and Argentine official. Buenos Aires, 14 March 1992.
Fones, Marjery. ECLAC. 15 July 1989.
*Furtado, Celso. ECLAC. Rio de Janeiro, 10 July 1989.
Ganz, Alexander. ECLAC. Boston, 12 May 1998.
Garcia Vasquez, Enrique. Argentine Official. Buenos Aires, 13 March 1992.
Garcia del Solar, Julio. Argentine official. Buenos Aires, 18 March 1992.
Garritsen de Vries, Margaret. IMF. Washington, 8 March 1991.
*Gonzalez, Norberto. ECLAC. Buenos Aires, 5 March 1989.
Gonzalez-Cofino, Roberto. OAS, Washington, 12 February 1992.
Gonzalez del Solar, Julio. IMF and Argentine Central Bank. Buenos Aires, 1 May 1982.

Gordon, Lincoln. US State Department. Washington, 6 March 1991.
Grinspun, Bernardo. Argentine minister of finance. Buenos Aires, 19 March 1992.
Gulhati, Ravi. UNCTAD. Geneva, 5 June 1989.
*Gurrieri, Adolfo. ECLAC. Santiago, 14 July 1989.
Heuis, Pieter. ECLAC. Santiago, 18 July 1989.
*Hopenhayn, Benjamin. ILPES. Buenos Aires, 3–11 May 1990.
*Iglesias, Enrique. ECLAC executive secretary. Washington, 8 March 1990.
Izcue, Joaquin. Inter-American Development Bank. Bethesda, MD, 16 December, 1987.
Jull. Luci. ECLAC. Santiago, 15 July 1989.
Kamenetsky, Mario and Sofia. World Bank. Washington, 25 February 1987.
*Krishnamurti, Rangaswami. UNCTAD. Toronto, 16 July 1996.
Levinson, Jerome. Author and journalist. Washington, 5 March 1991.
Lleras Restrepo, Carlos. President of Colombia. Bogota, 19 November 1991.
*Lopez, Fernando. Prebisch Foundation. Buenos Aires, 6 July 1989.
Lowenthal, William. ILPES. Washington, 10 February 1992.
Machinea, José Luis. Argentine official. Washington, 15 April 1993.
*Malaccorto, Ernesto. Prebisch "Brains Trust". Buenos Aires, 11 May 1990.
Meller, Patricio. Economist. Santiago, 9 March 1992.
*Moll de Prebisch, Adela. Santiago, beginning 11 July 1989.
Nypan, Erling. UNCTAD. Geneva, 7 June 1989.
*Nun, José. ILPES, professor (Toronto and Buenos Aires) and Argentine secretary of culture. 16 March 1989.
*O'Connell, Arturo. Economist, consultant, and Argentine official. Mexico City, 25 January 1987.
Pezoa, Lillian. ECLAC. Santiago, 15 March, 1990.
*Pinto, Anibal. ECLAC. Santiago, 12 July 1989.
Polak, Jacques J. IMF. Washington, 5 March 1991.
Pollner, Marco. ECLAC. Washington, 15 November 1991.
Portales, Carlos. Chilean diplomat. Santiago, 9 March 1992.
Pulit, Francisco. Argentine diplomat. Ottawa, 25 November 1987.
Puppo, José Maria. ECLAC. Buenos Aires, 4 July 1989
Robichek, Walter. IMF. Washington, 22 April 1990.
Rodriquez, Octavio. ECLAC. Montevideo, 10 December 1999.
Rogers, William D. US State Department. Washington, 7 March 1991.
*Rosenthal, Gert. ECLAC. Santiago, 15 March 1990.
Royem, Bodil. ECLAC. Santiago, 15 March 1990.
Santa Cruz, Alfonso. ECLAC. Santiago, 18 March 1990.
Scott, Norman. UNCTAD. Geneva, 4 June 1989.
*Singer, Hans. UN and Institute for Development Studies, Sussex. Washington, 15 November 1991.

Sourrouille, Juan. Argentine finance minister. Buenos Aires, 13 March 1992.
Sternfeld, Ray. US State Department. Washington, 8 March 1991.
Sunkel, Osvaldo. ECLAC. Ottawa, 2 April 1991.
Tomassini, Luciano. ECLAC. Washington, 22 October 1991.
Thomson, Brian, Washington, 11 February 1992.
Tulchin, Joseph. Woodrow Wilson Centre. Washington, 4 March 1991.
Uribe, Manuel, Bank of Mexico and diplomat. Toronto, 21 April 2004.
*Urquidi, Victor. Economist and Bank of Mexico official, IMF, and economist. Mexico City, 28 January 1995.
Vaky, Viron P. US State Department and Inter-American Dialogue. Washington, 17 March 2003.
Valenzuela, Carlos. Chilean diplomat. 6 July 1989.
*Viteri de la Huerta, Jorge. UNCTAD and ECLAC. Santiago, 17 May 1990.
Weinberg, Gregorio. Prebisch Foundation. Buenos Aires, 10 May 1990.
Weintraub, Sidney. US State Department. Toronto, 4 November 2006.
Zamit Cutajar, Michael. UNCTAD. Geneva, 7 June 1989.

PREBISCH: PRIMARY PUBLICATIONS

Collections and Bibliographies:

Most of Prebisch's important works have been published in the following collections, and the location will be indicated in parentheses in the next section.

ECLAC. *Raúl Prebisch: Un Aporte al estudio de su pensamiento.* Santiago: ECLAC, 1987.
ECLA. *Raúl Prebisch: Discursos, declaraciones y documentos, 1952–63.* Santiago: ECLA, 1963.
Gurrieri, Adolfo, ed. *La obra de Prebisch en la CEPAL.* Mexico City: Fondo de Cultura Económica, 1982.
Mallorquín, Carlos. *Raúl Prebisch: The Complete Bibliography.* Mexico City, 2007.
Prebisch Foundation, *Raúl Prebisch: Obras 1919–1948,* ed. Manuel Fernández López. 4 vols. Buenos Aires: Prebisch Foundation, 1991.

Core Writings:

Prebisch, Raúl. "Cuestión social." *Revista de Ciencias Económicas,* no. 79–82 (January-April 1920). (Prebisch Foundation, *Obras,* vol. 1.)
– "Comentarios sobre el libro de Irving Fischer, Stabilizing the Dollar, New York, 1920." *Revista de Economía Argentina* 3, vol. 5, no. 27–28 (September-October 1920). (Prebisch Foundation, *Obras,* vol. 1)
– "La Conferencia financiera internacional de 1920." *Revista de Economía Argentina* 4, vol. 7, no. 37 (July 1921). (Prebisch Foundation, *Obras,* vol. 1)

- "Comentarios sobre el trabajo de Juan B. Justo, 'Estudios sobre la moneda', tercera edición, Buenos Aires." *Revista de Ciencias Económicas*, series 2, year 9, no. 1 (August 1921). (Prebisch Foundation, *Obras*, vol. 1)
- "Anotaciones sobre nuestro medio circulante. A propósito del último libro del Dr Norberto Piñero, caps. I-IX." *Revista de Ciencias Económicas*, series 2, year 9, no. 3–4, 6–7, 9–10 (October 1921–May 1922). (Prebisch Foundation, *Obras*, vol. 1)
- *Información estadística sobre el comercio de carnes. Primera parte: el mercado británico.* Buenos Aires: Sociedad Rural Argentina, Oficina de Estadística, 1922. (Prebisch Foundation, *Obras*, vol. 1)
- "Anotaciones sobre la crisis ganadera." *Revista de Ciencias Económicas*, series 2, year 10, no. 17 (December 1922). (Prebisch Foundation, *Obras*, vol. 1)
- "La sociología de Vilifredo Pareto." Speech given at the Faculty of Economic Sciences in honour of the memory of Vilfredo Pareto, 2 October 1923. *Revista de Ciencias Económicas*, Series 2, year 11, no. 27 (October 1923). (Prebisch Foundation, *Obras*, vol. 1)
- "El problema de la tierra." Address given at the Henry George Club, Melbourne, April 1924. (Prebisch Foundation, *Obras*, vol. 1)
- "Primer informe del Dr Raúl Prebisch sobre sus estudios financieros y estadísticos en Australia, 14 de agosto de 1924." *Revista de Economía Argentina*, year 7, vol. 13, no. 75–76 (September-October 1924). (Prebisch Foundation, *Obras*, vol. 1)
- "Anotaciones a la estadística nacional." *Revista de Economía Argentina*, year 8, vol. 15, no. 86 (August 1925). (Prebisch Foundation, *Obras*, vol. 1)
- "Anotaciones demográficas: A propósito de la teoría de los movimientos de la población, Parte I y II." *Revista de Economía Argentina*, year 9–10, vol. 18–19, no. 105 and 106 (March-April 1927). (Prebisch Foundation, *Obras*, vol. 1)
- "De cómo discurre el profesor Olariaga." *Revista de Ciencias Económicas*, Series 2, year 15, no. 75 (October 1927). (Prebisch Foundation, *Obras*, vol. 1)
- "Régimen de pool en el comercio de carnes: informe técnico." *Revista de Ciencias económicas*, Series 2, year 15, no. 77 (December 1927). (Prebisch Foundation, *Obras*, vol. 1)

Anuario de la Sociedad Rural Argentina: Estadísticas económicas y agrarias. 1928. Anuario de la Sociedad Rural Argentina, no. 1. Buenos Aires: Establecimiento Gráfico Luis L. Gotelli, 1928.

- "La posición de 1928 y las variaciones económicas de la última década." *Revista Económica* 2, no. 1 (January 1929). (Prebisch Foundation, *Obras*, vol. 1)
- "El Estado económico." *Revista Económica* 3, no. 1–3 (January-June 1930). (Prebisch Foundation, *Obras*, vol. 1)
- "Proyecto de Creación de un Banco Central." (1931) In *La creación del Banco Central y la experiencia Argentina.* Buenos Aires: Banco Central de la República de Argentina, 1972. (Prebisch Foundation, *Obras*, vol. 2)

– "La Acción de emergencia en el problema monetario." *Revista Económica* 5, no. 2 (February-March 1932). (Prebisch Foundation, *Obras*, vol. 2)
– "La Conferencia Económica y la crisis mundial." *Revista Económica* 6, no. 1 (January 1933). (Prebisch Foundation, *Obras*, vol. 2)
– "El convenio con Gran Bretaña." *La Nación* (Buenos Aires), 2 May 1933. (Prebisch Foundation, *Obras*, vol. 2)
– "El momento presente de nuestra economía." *Revista Económica* 7, no. 1–4 (January-April 1934). (Prebisch Foundation, *Obras*, vol. 2)
– "La inflación escolástica y la moneda Argentina." *Revista de Economía Argentina.* Buenos Aires, 1934. (Prebisch Foundation, *Obras*, vol. 2)
– *Reglamento Provisional del Banco Central de la República Argentina.* Buenos Aires: Banco Central de la República Argentina/Gotelli, 1935. (Prebisch Foundation, *Obras*, vol. 2)
– *Memoria Anual.* Primer a Octavo Ejercicios 1935–1942. Buenos Aires: Banco Central de la República de Argentina/Gotelli, 1942.
– "Ciclo de conversaciones en el Banco de México, S.A., ofrecidas por Raúl Prebisch entre el 24 de enero y el 7 de marzo de 1944." Buenos Aires: Banco Central de la República de Argentina, 1972. (Prebisch Foundation, *Obras*, vols. 3 and 4)
– "Panorama general de los problemas de regulación monetaria y crediticia en el continente americano: América Latina" and "Responsabilidad de los países de la periferia: palabras pronunciadas en la Mesa Redonda sobre Problemas Actuales y Futuros y Reformas Monetarias y Bancarias Recientes." *Memoria de la Primera Reunión de Técnicos sobre Problemas de Banca Central del Continente Americano.* Mexico City: Banco de México, 15–30 August 1946. (Prebisch Foundation, *Obras*, vol. 4)
– *Proyecto de Ley Organica del Banco Central de la Republica Dominicana.* Santa Domingo, 1946.
– *Introducción a Keynes.* Mexico City and Buenos Aires: Fondo de Cultura Económica, 1947.
– *Apuntes de Económica Politica,* Buenos Aires: Faculty of Economic Sciences, 1948.
– *The Economic Development of Latin America and its Principal Problems.* New York: United Nations, 1950. (Gurrieri, *CEPAL*)
– "Decálogo económico de Montevideo." *Revista de economía Argentina,* year 33, vol. 48, no. 386–387 (August-September 1950).
– "Growth, Disequilibrium and Disparities: Interpretation of the Process of Economic Development." New York: United Nations, 1951.
– *Theoretical and Practical Problems of Economic Growth.* Mexico City: ECLA, May 1951. E/CN.12/221. (Gurrieri, *CEPAL*)
– "La CEPAL y el desarrollo económico." *Revista de Economía* (Mexico City) (June 1951).

– "Notas sobre el desarrollo económico, la inflación y la política monetaria y fiscal." *Memoria de la Tercera Reunión de Técnicos de los Bancos Centrales del Continente Americano*, 377–93. Havana: Banco Nacional de Cuba, 1952.
– "El programa de integración. Informe preliminar del Director principal a cargo de la Secretaría ejecutiva de la CEPAL, sobre Integración y reciprocidad económica en el Istmo Centroamericano el 1° de agosto de 1952." *Revista de la Integración Centroamericana*, no. 6 (1952).
– *Introduction to the Technique of Programming,* and *Preliminary Study of the Technique of Programming Economic Development.* New York: United Nations, 1955. E/CN.12/292 and E/CN.12/363. (Gurrieri, *CEPAL*)
– "A mística do equilibrio espontáneo da economia." (Santiago, 9 September 1953). (ECLA, *Discursos*)
– *International Cooperation in a Latin American Development Policy.* New York: United Nations, 1954. (Gurrieri, *CEPAL*)
– "The Stimulus of Demand, Investment and Acceleration of the Rate of Growth." *ECLA: Economic Survey of Latin America 1954.* New York: United Nations, 1955.
– The Relationship between population growth, capital formation and employment opportunities in under-developed countries." *Proceedings of the World Population Conference, Rome, 1954,* vol. 5, 695–711. New York: United Nations, 1955.
– "The Prebisch Report." *Review of the River Plate* (Buenos Aires) 118, nos. 3235 and 3236 (October and November 1955). (ECLA, *Discursos*)
– "Comentario del informe económico-financiero del Dr Raúl Prebisch." *Boletín de la Bolsa de Comercio de Buenos Aires* 51, no. 2642 (26 December 1955).
– "Economic Recovery Program and Final Report: Sound Money or Uncontrolled Inflation." *Review of the River Plate,* 20 June 1956.
– "Theory and Practice in Economic Development: the Case of Argentina." *Panorama Económico* (Santiago) 10, no. 147 (June 1956). (ECLA, *Discursos*)
– "Principales tendencias del desarrollo económico en Latinoamérica." *Panorama Económico* 10, no. 148 (June 1956).
– "Soviet challenge to American leadership: America's role in helping developing countries." *Problems of United States Economic Development,* vol. 1. New York: Committee for Economic Development, 1958. (ECLA, *Discursos*)
– "Commercial Policy in the Underdeveloped Countries (from the point of view of Latin America)" *American Economic Review* 3 (1959). (Gurrieri, *CEPAL*)
– "La crisis estructural de la economía argentina y la orientación de sus soluciones." *CEPAL: Desarrollo económico de la Argentina.* Mexico City: United Nations, 1959. E/CN.12/429/Rev. 1. (ECLA, *Discursos*)
– "The Latin American Common Market and the Multilateral Payments System." *ECLA: The Latin American Common Market.* New York: United Nations, 1959. (ECLA, *Discursos*; Gurrieri, *CEPAL*, vol. 1)

– *El Mercado Comun Latinoamericano.* Montevideo: Academia Nacional de Economia del Uruguay, 1960.
– "The Structural Crisis in Argentina and its Prospects of Solution." *Economic Growth, Rationale, Problems, Cases,* ed. Eastin Nelson. Austin: University of Texas Press, 1960: 104–24. (ECLA, *Discursos*)
– "Panoramas y perspectivas de la industria siderúrgica en América Latina.", *Comercio Exterior* (Mexico City) 10, no. 1 (January 1960).
– "Economic Development or Monetary Stability: The False Dilemma." *Economic Bulletin for Latin America* (Santiago) 6 (March 1961).
– "Latin America: the Challenge and the Task Ahead." Office of Public Information, *The United Nations and Latin America.* New York: United Nations, 1961.
– "El principio de la reciprocidad." *Revista de Ciencias Económicas* (São Paulo) (June 1960).
– "Vamos a tener más recursos exteriores en América Latina, pero ¿estamos preparados para aprovecharlos al máximo?" *United Nations Review,* New York (October 1960).
– "CEPAL y sus tres principales problemas." *Mercado Común América Latina* (Montevideo) 2, no. 11 (February 1961).
– *La Marcha hacia el Mercado Común Latinoamericano.* Santiago: ILPES, 1961.
– "Economic Development, Planning and International Cooperation." Santiago: ECLA, 1961. (Gurrieri, *CEPAL*)
– *Memorándum presentado al presidente John F. Kennedy en marzo de 1961.* Washington, 8 March 1961.
– "Los obstáculos estructurales y la necesaria revisión de la política de desarrollo y de cooperación internacional." *Comercio Exterior* (Mexico City) 11, no. 5 (May 1961).
– "The Alliance for Progress: Joint Responsibilities for Latin American Progress." *Foreign Affairs* (July 1961).
– "Una política de estabilidad monetaria compatible con el desarrollo económico." *Economía y Finanzas* (Santiago), Year 25, no. 300 (October 1961).
– "Reflexiones sobre la integración latinoamericana." *Comercio Exterior* (Mexico City) 11, no. 11 (November 1961).
– *Towards a Dynamic Development Policy for Latin America.* New York: United Nations, 1963. E/CN.12/680. (Gurrieri, *CEPAL*, vol. 2)
– "Planning of Economic Growth in Latin America." *Review of the River Plate,* Buenos Aires, 11 June 1963.
– *Towards a New Trade Policy for Development.* Report by the Secretary-General of the United Nations Conference on Trade and Development. New York: UNCTAD, 1964. (Gurrieri, *CEPAL*, vol. 2)
– *Hacia la integración acelerada de América Latina: Proposiciones a los Presidentes latinoamericanos.* Document prepared at the personal request of José Antonio

Mayobre, Felipe Herrera, and Carlos Sanz de Santamaría. Mexico City: Fondo de Cultura Económica, 1965.

– *Economic Problems of Developing Countries: the Structural Reforms Needed to Solve Them. Commerce Annual.* Geneva: UNCTAD, 1966.

– "The Impact of Technological Progress on developing countries." Gustav Pollak Lecture, the John Fitzgerald Kennedy School of Government, Harvard University, 17 October 1966.

– *Toward a Global Strategy of Development.* Report of the Secretary-General of the United Nations Conference on Trade and Development at the second session of the Conference. New York: United Nations, 1968. TD/3/Rev. 1. (Gurrieri, CEPAL, vol. 2)

– *Reflections on International Cooperation for Latin American Development.* Document prepared the personal request of Messrs Galo Plaza, Felipe Herrera, Carlos Sanz de Santamaría and Patricio Rojas. Washington, 1969.

– "The System and the Social Structure of Latin America." *Latin American Nationalist Movements,* eds Irving Louis Horowitz et al. New York: Random House, 1969.

– *Change and Development: Latin America's Great Task.* Report Submitted to the Inter-American Development Bank. New York: Praeger, 1971. (Gurrieri, *CEPAL*)

– *Latin America: a Problem in Development.* Hackett Memorial Lecture, Institute of Latin American Studies, University of Texas, Austin, 5 April 1971.

– "Desarrollo económico, planeamiento y cooperación internacional." *Serie Conmemorativa del XXV Aniversario de la CEPAL.* Santiago: ECLAC, 1973. (Gurrieri, *CEPAL*)

– "A Critique of Peripheral Capitalism." *CEPAL Review* 1 (1976). (Gurrieri, *CEPAL*)

– "Desarrollo y política comercial internacional." *Pensamiento Político* (Mexico City) 22, no. 88 (August 1976).

– *UNCTAD and the New International Economic Order.* Address by Raúl Prebisch on receiving the Dag Hammarskjöld Honorary Medal. Berlin, 1978.

– *The New International Order and Cultural Values.* Madrid: Institute of International Cooperation, 1978.

– "Socio-economic Structure and Crisis of Peripheral Capitalism." *CEPAL Review* 6 (1978).

– "The Neo-classical Theories of Economic Liberalism." *CEPAL Review* 7 (1979).

– "Towards a Theory of Change." *CEPAL Review* 10 (1980).

– "Biosphere and Development." *CEPAL Review* 12 (1980).

– *Capitalismo periférico: crisis y transformación.* Mexico City: Fondo de Cultura Económica, 1981.

– "The Latin America Periphery in the Global System of Capitalism." *CEPAL Review* 13 (1981).

– "Dialogue on Friedman and Hayek from the Standpoint of the Periphery." *CEPAL Review* 15 (1981).

– "Capitalism: The Second Crisis." Report of the Third World Prize Presentation Ceremony, 2 April 1981. *Third World Quarterly* 3, no. 3 (July 1981).
– "Monetarism, Open-Economy Policies and the Ideological Crisis." *CEPAL Review* 17 (1982).
– "A Historical Turning Point for the Latin American Periphery." *CEPAL Review* 18 (1982).
– *Crisis in Peripheral Capitalism: Increasing Inequality in Latin America.* Distinguished Lecture Series, Madison, University of Wisconsin, 1983.
– "The Crisis of Capitalism and International Trade." *CEPAL Review* 20 (1983).
– "Hacia la recuperación económica y la equidad social." *Estudios Internacionales* (Santiago), year 16, no. 64 (October-December 1983).
– "Lineamientos de un programa inmediato de reactivación de la economía, majora del empleo y los salaries reales y ataque al obstáculo de la inflación." Santiago: CEPAL, 1984.
– "The Global Crisis of Capitalism and Its Theoretical Background." *CEPAL Review* 22 (1984).
– "Five Stages in My Thinking on Development." *Pioneers in Development,* eds G.M. Meier and Dudley Seers. New York: Oxford University Press, 1984.
– "The Latin American Periphery in the Global Crisis of Capitalism." *CEPAL Review* 26 (1985).
– Crisis del desarrollo argentino: de la frustración al crecimiento vigoroso, El Ateneo, Buenos Aires, 1986.
– "Renovar el pensamiento económico latinoamericano, un imperativo.", *Comercio Exterior* (Mexico City) 36, no. 6 (June 1986).

BOOKS, ARTICLES, AND OTHER SOURCES (SELECTED):

Abós, Alvaro, ed. *El libro de Buenos Aires: cronicas de cinco siglos.* Buenos Aires: Montadori, 2000.
Abreu, Marcelo De Paiva. "Foreign Debt Policies in South America, 1929–1945." *Brazilian Journal of Political Economy* 20, no. 3 (79) (July-September 2000).
Adelman, Jeremy, ed. *Essays in Argentine Labour History, 1870–1930.* Basingstoke: Macmillan, 1992.
Alemann, Roberto T. "El pensamiento económico de Prebisch." *Selección Contable.* Buenos Aires, April 1956.
Alexander, Robert J. *Juan Domingo Perón: A History.* Boulder, CO: Westview Press, 1979.
Alhedeff, Peter. "The Economic Formulas of the 1930s: A Reassessment." Oxford: St Anthony's College, July 1981.
Baer, Werner. "The Economics of Prebisch and ECLA." *Economic Development and Cultural Change* X, January 1962.

Bailey, Samuel L. *Immigrants in the Land of Promise: Italians in Buenos Aires and New York.* Ithaca, NY: Cornell University Press, 1989.

Baldinelli, Elvio. *Comercio exterior Argentino en el ultimo medio siglo.* Buenos Aires: ISEN (Instituto del Servicio Exterior de la Nacion), 1996.

Ball, George. *The Past Has Another Pattern.* New York: Norton, 1982.

Barber, William J. "Chile con Chicago: A Review Essay." *Journal of Economic Literature* (33), December 1995, 1946.

Barone, Enrico. "Studi di economia financiaria." *Giornale degli Economista* II [*Journal of Economics*] (1912).

Bejarano, Manuel. "Inmigración y estructuras tradicionales en Buenos Aires (1854–1930)." *Los fragmentos del poder,* eds Torcuato S. Di Tella and Tulio Halperin Donghi. Buenos Aires: Editorial Jorge Alvarez, 1969.

Belassa, Bela. "Regional Integration and Trade Liberalization in Latin America." *Journal of Common Market Studies* (September 1971).

Bello, Walden. "The Iron Cage: The WTO, the Bretton Woods Institutions and the South." Paper presented at the International Forum on Globalization. Seattle, November 1999.

Bhagwati, Jagdish. *The New International Economic Order: The North-South Debate.* Cambridge, MA: MIT Press, 1977.

Birns, L., ed. *The End of Chilean Democracy: An IDOC Dossier on the Coup and its Aftermath.* New York: Seabury Press, 1974.

Bohan, Merwin L. *Oral History Interview.* The Harry S. Truman Library, Independence, Missouri, February 1977.

Brennan, James P. *Peronism and Argentina.* Wilmington, SC: SR Books, 1998.

Bunge, Alejandro. *Una nueva Argentina.* Buenos Aires: Guillermo Kraft, 1940.

Bunge, Augusto. *El Culto de la vida.* Buenos Aires: Perrotti, 1915.

Calvert, Susan, and Peter Calvert. *Argentina: Political Culture and Instability.* Pittsburgh: University of Pittsburgh Press, 1989.

Canton, Dario. *Elecciones y partidos en la Argentina: historia, interpretación y balance.* Buenos Aires: Siglo Veintiuno Argentina Ediciones, 1973.

Cardoso, Fernando Henrique. "The Consumption of Dependency Theory in the USA." *International Organization* 32(1) (1978).

– and Enzo Faletto. *Dependency and Development in Latin America.* Berkeley: University of California Press, 1979.

Chenery, Hollis. "The Structuralist Approach to Development Policy." *American Economic Review* (May 1975).

Collier, Ruth Berins, and David Collier. *Shaping the Political Arena: Critical Junctures, the Labor Movement, and Regime Dynamics in Latin America.* Princeton: Princeton University Press, 1991.

Cordovez, Diego. "The Making of UNCTAD: Institutional Background and legislative history." *Journal of Trade Law* 1 (May-June 1967).

– "UNCTAD and Development Diplomacy." *Journal of Trade Law* (1971).

Corea, Gamani. "UNCTAD and the New Internacional Economic Order." *International Affaire* 53 (1977).

Cornejo, Benjamín. "The Social Doctrine in Prebisch's Thought." *Internacional Economics and Development: Essays in Honor of Raúl Prebisch*, ed. Luis Di Marco. New York: Academia Press, 1972.

Cortés Conde, Roberto. "Raúl Prebich: Los años de gobierno." CEPAL *Review* 75 (2001).

– and Ezequiel Gallo. *La formación de la Argentina moderna.* Buenos Aires: Paidós, 1967.

Cox, Robert W., and Harold K. Jacobson, eds. *The Anatomy of Influence: Decision-Making in International Organizations.* New Haven, CT: Yale University Press, 1973.

– "Ideologies and the New Internacional Economic Order." *International Organization* 33 (Spring 1979).

Crawley, Eduardo. *A House Divided: Argentina 1880–1980.* London: Hurst and Co., 1984.

Currie, Laughlin. *Accelerating Development: The Necessity and the Means.* New York: McGraw Hill, 1966.

Cutujar, Michael, ed. *UNCTAD and the North-South Dialogue: Essays in Honor of V.R. Malinowski.* New York: Pergamon Press, 1985.

Danby, Colin. "Noyola's Institutional Approach to Inflation." *Journal of the History of Economic Thought* 27, no. 2 (June, 2005).

Dell, Sydney. *Trade Blocs and Common Markets.* New York: Knopf, 1963.

Della Paolera, Gerardo, and Alan Taylor, eds. *The New Economic History of Argentina.* Cambridge: Cambridge University Press, 2003.

Devoto, Fernando J., and Torcuato Di Tella. *Political Culture, Social Movements and Democratic Transitions in South America in the XXth Century.* Milan: Fondazione Giangiacomo Feltrinelli, 1996.

Diaz Alejandro, Carlos. *Essays on the Economic History of the Argentina Republic.* New Haven, CT: Yale University Press, 1970.

Di Filippo, Armando. *Desarrollo y desigualdad social en América Latin.* Mexico: Fondo de Cultura Economica, 1981.

Di Tella, Guido. "Policy Changes in Argentina, 1920–1960." Oxford: St Anthony's College, July 1981.

– and D.C.M. Platt, eds. *The Political Economy of Argentina, 1880–1946.* Basingstoke: Macmillan and St Anthony's College, 1986.

Di Tella, Torcuato, and T. Halperin, eds. *Los Fragmentos del poder.* Buenos Aires: Editorial Jorge Alvarez, 1969.

– and Manuel Zymelman. *Las etapas del desarrollo económico argentino.* Buenos Aires: EUDEBA, 1967.

Dolores, Maria. *Uriburu y Justo; el auge Conservador.* Buenos Aires: Centro Editor de America Latina, 1983.

Dorfman, Adolfo. *Historia de la industria argentina.* Buenos Aires: Solar, 1970.

Dosman, Edgar J. "Markets and the State in the Evolution of the 'Prebisch Manifesto.'" *CEPAL Review* 75 (2001).

– ed. *Raúl Prebisch: Power, Principle and the Ethics of Development.* Washington and Buenos Aires: IDB/INTAL, 2006.

Dreier, John, ed. *Alianza para el Progreso.* Mexico City: Novaro, 1962. (See also *The Alliance for Progress: Problems and Perspectives,* Johns Hopkins, Baltimore, 1962.)

ECLAC. *Raúl Prebisch: Un aporte al studio de su pensamiento.* Santiago: ECLAC, March 1987.

Eichengreen, Barry. *Golden Fetters: The Gold Standard and the Great Depression, 1919–39.* New York: Oxford University Press, 1992.

Eisenhower, Milton. *Report to the President on United States–Latin American Relations.* Washington, December 1958.

Emmerij, Louis, Richard Jolly, and Thomas G. Weiss. "Generating Knowledge in the United Nations." *Reclaiming Development Agendas: Knowledge, Power and International Policy Making,* ed. Peter Utting. Basingstoke: Palgrave, 2006.

Escudé, Carlos Andres. "The Argentine Eclipse: The International Factor in Argentina's Post-World War II Decline." PhD dissertation, Yale University, December 1981.

Falcoff, M. and R.H. Dolcart, eds. *Prologue to Perón: Argentina in Depression and War, 1930–45.* Berkeley: University of California Press, 1975.

Felix, David. "Monetarists, Structuralists and Import Substituting Industrialization." *Inflation and Growth in Latin America,* eds Baer and Kerstenetzky. New York: Richard D. Irwin, 1964.

Ferguson, Yale H. "ECLA and the Alliance for Progress." Washington: State Department, 1962.

– "ECLA, Latin American Development, and the United States: A Broad View." Unpublished manuscript, Columbia University, Fall 1962.

Fishlow, Albert. *Rich and Poor Nations in the World Economy.* New York: McGraw Hill, 1978.

Fordor, Jorge, and Arturo O'Connell. "La Argentina y la economia Atlántica en la primera mitad del siglo XX." *Desarrollo económico* (Buenos Aires) 13, no. 49 (April-June 1973).

Frankenhoff, Charles. "The Prebisch Thesis: A Theory of Industrialism for Latin America." *Journal of Inter-American Studies* 4 (April 1962).

Fredeberg, A.S. *The UNCTAD of 1964.* Rotterdam: University Press, 1969.

Furtado, Celso. *Economic Development in Latin America.*
Cambridge: Cambridge University Press, 1970.

– *A fantasia organizada.* Rio de Janeiro: Editora Paz e Terra, 1985.

– *Os Ares do Mundo.* Rio de Janeiro: Paz e Terra, 1991.

Fajnzylber, Fernando. "Comentario sobre el articulo de Raúl Prebisch. Hacia una teoría de la transformacion. *Revista de la CEPAL* 11 (1980).

Garcia-Heras, Raúl. "World War II and the Frustrated Nationalization of the Argentine British-Owned Railways, 1939–1943." *Journal of Latin American Studies* 17 (May 1985).

Gibson, Edward L. *Class and Conservative Parties: Argentina in Comparative Perspectiva.* Baltimore: Johns Hopkins University Press, 1996.

González, Norberto. "Las ideas motrices de tres procesos de industrialización." CEPAL *Review* 75 (2001).

González, Fraga. "La Vision del Hombre y del Mundo en John M. Keynes y en Raul Prebisch." Documentos de Trabajo, Pontificia Universidad Católica Argentina, Buenos Aires, March 2006.

González, N. and David Pollock. "Del ortodoxo al conservador ilustrado: Raúl Prebisch en la Argentina, 1923–1943." *Desarrollo Económico* (Buenos Aires) 30, no. 120 (1991).

Gordon, Lincoln. "Inter-American Tensions and the Alliance for Progress." *Latin America: Evolution or Explosion,* ed. Mildred Adams. New York: Dodd Mead, 1963.

Gosovic, Branoslav. *UNCTAD: Conflict and Compromise.* Leiden: A.W. Sijthoff, 1972.

Gravil, Roger. "State Intervention in Argentina's Export Trade between the Wars." *Journal of Latin American Studies* 2, no. 2 (1970).

Grunwald, Joseph. "Invisible Hands in Inflation and Growth." Brookings Institution Reprint 89. Washington: Brookings, 1965.

– *Latin America and the World Economy: A Changing International Order.* Sage Publications, 1978.

Gurrieri, Adolfo. "Technical Progress and its Fruits: The Idea of Development in the Works of Raúl Prebisch." *Journal of Economic Issues* 17, no. 2 (June 1983).

– "Las ideas del joven Prebisch." CEPAL *Review* 75 (2001).

– *La Obra de* Prebisch *en* CEPAL. Mexico City: Fondo de Cultura Económica, 1982.

Haberler, Gottfried. "Terms of Trade and Economic Development." *El Desarrollo Economico y America Latina,* ed. Howard Ellis. Mexico City: Fondo de Cultura Economica, 1969.

Hanson, Simon G. "Case Study in Futility: The United Nations ECLA." *Inter-American Affairs* (Autumn 1948).

– "Preliminary Report to the United Nations Economic and Social Council on an Economic Commission for Latin America." *Inter-American Economic Affairs* 1, no. 3 (December 1947).

Harberger, Arnold. "Latin American Economists in the USA: A Comment." *Economic Development and Cultural Change* 15 (October 1966).

Harrison, Selig S. *A Strategy for Unification and US Disengagement.* Princeton: Princeton University Press, 2002.

Heath, Edward. *The Course of My Life. My Autobiography.* London: Hodder and Stoughton, 1998.

Helleiner, Eric. "The Southern Side of 'Embedded Liberalism.'" *Money Doctors: The Experience of International Financial Advising 1950–2000*, ed. Marc Flandreau. London and New York: Routledge, 2003.

Helleiner, Gerald K., Shahen Abrahamian, Edgar Bacha et al, eds. *Poverty, Prosperity and the World Economy: Essays in Memory of Sydney Dell.* New York: St Martin's Press, 1995.

– ed. *A World Divided: The LDCs in the International Economy*. Cambridge: Cambridge University Press, 1976.

Herrera, Felipe. *Nacionalismo latinoamericano.* Santiago: Editorial Universitaria, 1967.

Hirschman, Albert O. *Latin American Issues, Essays and Comments.* New York: Twentieth Century Fund, 1961.

Hobsbawm, Eric. *Age of Extremes: The Short Twentieth Century 1914–1991*. London: Michael Joseph, 1994.

Hodara, J. *Prebisch y la CEPAL*. Mexico City: El Colegio de México, 1987.

Hopenhayn, Benjamín. "Prebisch: pensador clásico y heterodoxo." *Revista de la CEPAL* 34 (1988).

Iglesias, Enrique V., ed. *The Legacy of Raúl Prebisch.* Washington: Inter-American Development Bank, 1994.

Jaguaribe, Helio. *Political Development: A General Theory and a Latin American Case Study*. New York: Harper and Row, 1973.

Jauretche, Arturo. *El Plan Prebisch: retorno al coloniaje.* Buenos Aires: Pena Lillo, 1984.

Kay, Cristóbal. *Latin American Theories of Development and Underdevelopment.* London: Routledge, 1989.

Keeling, David J. *Global Dreams, Local Crises.* Chichester, New York: Wiley, 1996.

Keynes, John Maynard. *The Means to Prosperity*. London: Macmillan, 1933.

– Essays on Persuasión. New York: Harcourt Brace, 1932.

Kindleberger, C. "Planning for Foreign Investment." *American Economic Review* 33 (1943).

Korzeniewicz, Robert. "Labor Unrest in Argentina." *Latin American Research Review* 24, no. 3 (1989).

Krishnamurti, R. "Some UNCTAD Events and Reminiscences." Geneva, 30 April 1991.

– "UNCTAD as a Negotiating Institution." *Journal of World Trade* 15 (January-February 1981).

Lalanne, Pedro Fernández. *Los Uriburu.* Buenos Aires: Emecé Editores, 1989.

Lefeber, Louis, and Liisa L. North. *Democracy and Development in Latin America.* Toronto: CERLAC-LARU, 1980.

Leontieff, Wassily. *The Future of the World Economy: A United Nations Study*. Oxford: Oxford University Press, 1977.

Leuchars, Chris. *To the Bitter End: Paraguay and the War of the Triple Alliance.* Westport, CT: Greenwood Press, 2002.

Levinson, Jerome, and Juan Onis. *The Alliance that Lost its Way.* Twentieth Century Fund, 1970.

Lewis, Sir Arthur. "Economic Development with Unlimited Supplies of Labour." *Manchester School of Economic and Social Studies,* May 1954.

– *The Evolution of the International Economic Order.* Princeton: Princeton University Press, 1977.

– *The Theory of Economic Growth.* Homewood, IL: Irwin, 1955.

Lewis, Paul H. *The Crisis of Argentine Capitalism.* Chapel Hill: University of North Carolina Press, 1990.

Llach, Juan José. "El Plan Pinedo de 1940, su significado historico y los origenes de la economia politica del Peronismo." *Desarrollo Económico* (Buenos Aires) 23, no. 92 (January-March 1984).

Lopez, Manuel Fernandez. "Hugo Broggi – A precursor in mathematical economics." *The European Journal of the History of Economic Thought* 10:2 (Summer 2003).

Lora, Jorge, and Carlos Mallorquín, eds. *Prebisch y Furtado. El Estructuralismo Latinoamericano.* Mexico City: Benemérita Universidad Autónoma de Puebla, Instituto de Ciencias Sociales y Humanidades, 1999.

Louro de Ortiz, Amalia A. *El grupo Pinedo-Prebisch y el neo-conservadorismo renovador.* Buenos Aires: Grupo Editor Latinoamericano, 1992.

Love, Joseph L. *Crafting the Third World: Theorizing Underdevelopment in Rumania and Brazil.* Stanford: Stanford University Press, 1996.

– "Economic ideas and ideologies in Latin America since 1930." *Ideas and Ideologies in Twentieth Century Latin America,* ed. Leslie Bethell. Cambridge: Cambridge University Press, 1996.

– "Latin America, UNCTAD and the Postwar Trading System." Paper presented to "The Regulation of Development," 23–24 April 2004.

– "Manoilescu, Prebisch, and Unequal Exchange." *Rumanian Studies* 5 (1986).

– "A New Look at the International Intellectual Environment of the Thirties and Forties." *The Legacy of Raúl Prebisch,* ed. Enrique V. Iglesias. Washington: Inter-American Development Bank, 1994.

– "Raúl Prebisch and the Origins of the Doctrine of Unequal Exchange." *Latin American Research Review* 15, no. 3 (November 1980).

– "The Rise and Decline of Economic Structuralism in Latin America: New Dimensions." *Latin American Research Review* 40, no. 3 (October 2005).

Lowenthal, Abraham. "Liberal, Radical and Bureaucratic Perspectivas on US-Latin American Policy: The Alliance for Progress in Retrospect." *Latin America and the US: Changing Policy Realities,* eds Julio Cotler and Richard Fagen. Stanford: Stanford University Press, 1974.

Luna, Félix. *Fuerzas hegemónicas y partidos politicos.* Buenos Aires: Editorial Sudamericana, 1989.

Maestri, Mario. "Guerra contra o Paraguai: Da Instauração a Restauração Historiografica." *Revista Espaco Academico,* Year 2, no. 2 (January 2003).

Maizels, Alfred. "Refining the World Commodity Economy." *UNCTAD and the North-South Dialogue,* ed. Michael Cutujar. New York: Pergamon Press, 1985.

Mallorquín, Carlos. "Un breve recuento de la deconstrucción del estructuralismo latinoamericano." *Estudios latinoamericanos,* year 1, no. 2 (1994).

– *Prebisch y Furtado. El Estructuralismo Latinoamericano.* Mexico City: Benemérita Universidad Autonomía de Puebla, Instituto de Ciencias Sociales y Humanidades, 1999.

– "Celso Furtado: um retrato intelectual." *Xama-Contraponto,* São Paulo, 2005.

– "Raúl Prebisch before the Ice Age." *Raúl Prebisch: Power, Principle and the Ethics of Development*, ed. Edgar J. Dosman. Washington and Buenos Aires: IDB/INTAL, 2006.

– "Los cuatro volúmenes de las *Obras de Raúl Prebisch.*" *Revista: Estudios Latinoamericanos, Nueva Epoca (UNAM)* year 2, no. 4 July-December 1995).

– "Textos y entrevista inedita de Raúl Prebisch." *Revista Paraguaya de Sociologíca* (December 1994).

– "The Unfamiliar Raúl Prebisch." *Ideas, Policies and Economic Development in the Americas,* eds Esteban Perez-Caldentey and Matias Vernengo. London: Routledge, 2007.

Manoilescu, Mihail. *The Theory of Protection and International Trade.* London: P.S. King & Son, 1931.

Manzetti, Luigi. *Institutions, Parties and Coalitions in Argentine Politics.* Pittsburgh: Pittsburgh University Press, 1993.

Mattera, Albert Alexander. "Twentieth Century Developments in Argentine Commercial Banking." MBA thesis, Graduate School of Business Administration, New York University, May 1948.

Meier, Gerald M. "Import Substitution and Industrial Protection." *Leading Issues in Development Economics,* ed. Gerald M. Meier. Oxford: Oxford University Press, 1964.

– and Dudley Seers, eds. *Pioneers in Development.* Oxford: Oxford University Press, 1984.

Meltzer, Allan H. *A History of the Federal Reserve, 1913–51.* Chicago: University of Chicago Press, 2004.

Metzger, Stanley. "UNCTAD: An Assessment." *American Journal of International Law* (July 1976).

Mowat, Charles Loch. *Britain between the Wars: 1918–1940.* London: Methuen, 1956.

Mikesell, Raymond. "Barriers to the Expansion of the United Nations Economic Functions." *Annals of the American Academy of Political and Social Sciences,* no. 302 (November 1954).

Mitchell, Christopher. "The Role of Technocrats in Latin American Integration." *Inter-American Economic Affairs* 21 (Summer 1967).

Muñoz, Heraldo. *Crisis y desarrollo alternativo en Latinoamérica.* Santiago: Editorial Aconcagua/CERC/lCL, 1985.

Murmis, Miguel, and Juan Carlos Portantiero. *Estudios sobre los origins del Peronismo.* Buenos Aires: Siglo XXI, 1971.

Myint, Hla. *The Economics of the Developing Countries.* London: Hutchison, 1964.

Myrdal, Gunnar. *Economic Theory and Underdeveloped Regions.* New York: Harper and Row, 1956.

Newton, Ronald C. *The Nazi Menace in Argentina, 1931–1947.* Stanford: Stanford University Press, 1992.

Nixon, Richard M. *Six Crises.* New York: Doubleday and Co. 1962.

Nurkse, Ragnar. "Trade Theory and Development Policy." *Economic Development for Latin America,* ed. Howard S. Ellis. London: St Martin's Press, 1961.

Ocampo, José Antonio. "Raúl Prebisch y la agenda del desarrollo en los albores del siglo XXI." *CEPAL Review* 75 (2001).

O'Connell, Arturo. "El regreso de la vulnerabilidad y las ideas tempranas de Prebisch sobre el 'ciclo argentino'." *CEPAL Review* 75 (2001).

O'Donnell, Guillermo. "Reflections on the Patterns of Change in the Bureaucratic-Authoritarian State." *Latin American Research Review* 13, no. 1 (1978).

Pasos, Lenorado. *Historia del Origen de los Partidos en la Argentina, 1810–1918.* Buenos Aires: Ediciones Centro de Estudios, 1972.

Peralta Ramos, M., and Carlos Waisman. *From Military Rule to Liberal Democracy in Argentina.* Boulder, CO: Westview Press, 1987.

Pinto, Anibal. "La Evaluacion del Pensamiento de la CEPAL." *Politica Economica y Desarrollo de America Latina.* Bonn: Verlag Neue Gessellschaft, GMBH, 1972.

– and Osvaldo Sunkel. "Latin American Economists in the USA." *Economic Development and Cultural Change* 15 (October 1966).

– and Jan Knakal. "The Center-Periphery System 20 Years Later." *International Economics and Development,* ed. Luis Di Marco. New York: Academic Press, 1972.

Polak, Jacques J. "Convertibility: An Indispensable Element in the Transition Process in Eastern Europe." Paper prepared for a conference organized by the Institute for International Economics and the Austrian National Bank, Vienna, 20–22 January 1991.

– "The IMF Monetary Model at Forty." Working Paper of the International Monetary Fund. IMF, 1997.

Pollock, David H. "Aquelles viejos tiempos: la formacion teorica y practica de Raúl Prebisch en Argentina: Una entravista con David Pollock." *Desarrollo Economico* 41.

– "Some Changes in United Status Attitudes toward CEPAL over the Past 30 Years." *CEPAL Review* 5 (1978).

– "Ideologies of Latin American Modernization." *Latin American Prospects for the 1970s*, eds David H. Pollock and Arch R. Ritter. New York: Praeger, 1973.

– "The Pearson and Prebisch Reports." *Latin American Prospects for the 1970s*, eds David H. Pollock and Arch R. Ritter. New York: Praeger, 1973.

Porcile, Gabriel. "The Challenge of Cooperation: Argentina and Brazil 1939–55." *Journal of Latin American Studies* 27 (1995).

Rabe, Stephan G. *Eisenhower and Latin America: The Foreign Policy of Anticommunism.* Chapel Hill: University of North Carolina Press, 1988.

Rapaport, Mario. *Gran Bretaña, Estados Unidos y las clases dirigentes argentinas: 1940–1945.* Buenos Aires: Editorial de Belgrano, 1980.

Rock, David. *Politics in Argentina, 1890–1930: The Rise and Fall of Radicalism.* Cambridge: Cambridge University Press, 1975.

– ed. *Latin America in the 1940s: War and Postwar Transitions.* Berkeley: University of California Press, 1994. http://ark.cdlib.org/ark:13030/ft567nb3f6

Rodríguez, Octavio. "Aprendizaje, acumulación, pleno empleo : las tres claves de desarrollo." *Desarrollo económico* 38, no. 151 (October-December 1998).

– "Prebisch: Actualidad de sus ideas básicas." CEPAL *Review* 75 (2001).

– *La Teoria del Subdesarrollo de la* CEPAL. Mexico City: Siglo Veintiuno Editores, Cuarta Edición, 1984.

Rogge, Benjamin A. "Economic Development in Latin America: The Prebisch Thesis." *Inter-American Economic Affairs* (Spring 1968).

Ruggiero, Kristin. *Modernity in the Flesh: Medicine, Law and Society in Turn-of-the Century Argentina.* Stanford: Stanford University Press, 2004.

Samuelson, P. "International Trade and Equalization of Factor Prices." *Economic Journal* 58 (1948).

Sangunetti, Horacio. *Los Sociolistas independientes.* 2 vols. Argentina: Centro Editor de America Latina, 1987

Sanjuan, Alfonso. "Camino al MERCOSUR: Antecedente poco conocido." *Cuadernos de Marcha* 141 (July 1998).

Santa Cruz, Hernán. *Cooperar o Perecer: El Dilema de la Comunidad Mundial.* Buenos Aires: Grupo Editor Latinoamericano, 1984.

– "Una página de la historia de las Naciones Unidas en sus primeros años: Recuerdos sobre el nacimiento de la CEPAL." Santiago: ECLAC, 1963.

Scheina, Robert. *Latin America's Wars: The Age of the Caudillo, 1791–1899.* Dulles, VA: Brassey's, 2003.

Scheman, L. Ronald, ed. *The Alliance for Progress: A Retrospective.* New York: Praeger, 1988.

Schlesinger, Jr, Arthur. "Myth and Reality." *The Alliance for Progress: A Retrospective,* ed. L. Ronald Scheman. New York: Praeger, 1988.

Scobie, James R. *Argentina: A City and a Nation.* New York: Oxford University Press, 1971.

– *Buenos Aires: From Plaza to Suburb, 1870–1910*. New York: Oxford University Press, 1974.

Seers, Dudley. "Why Visiting Economists Fail." *The Journal of Political Economy* 70 (August 1962).

– "What Are We Trying to Measure?" *Journal of Development Studies* (August 1972).

Shaw, John D. *Sir Hans Singer. The Life and Work of a Development Economist*. Basingstoke: Palgrave Macmillan, 2002.

Sikkink, Kathryn. *Ideas and Institutions: Developmentalism in Brazil and Argentina*. Ithaca, NY: Cornell University Press, 1991.

– "The Influence of Raúl Prebisch on Economic Policy Making in Argentina, 1950–1962." *Latin American Research Review* 23, no. 2 (1988).

Singer, Hans. "Comments on 'Raúl Prebisch: The Continuing Quest.'" *The Legacy of Raúl Prebisch*, ed. Enrique V. Iglesias. Washington: Inter-American Development Bank, 1994.

– "The Distribution of Gains between Investing and Borrowing Countries." *American Economic Review* (May 1950).

– "The Terms of Trade Controversy and the Evolution of Soft Financing: Early Years in the UN." *Pioneers in Development*, eds G.M. Meier and Dudley Seers. New York: Oxford University Press, 1984.

Smith, Peter H. *Argentina and the Failure of Democracy: Conflict among the Political Elites, 1904–1955*. Madison, WI: University of Wisconsin Press, 1974.

Smith, William C. *Authoritarianism and the Crisis of the Argentine Political Economy*. Stanford: Stanford University Press, 1991.

Solís, L. "Raúl Prebisch at ECLA: Years of Creative Intellectual Effort." Occasional Paper, no. 10. San Francisco: International Centre for Economic Growth, 1989.

Spraos, J. "The Statistical Debate on the Net Barter Terms of Trade between Primary Commodities and Manufactures." *Economic Journal* 90, no. 357 (1980).

Sprout, R. "The Ideas of Prebisch." *CEPAL Review* 46 (1992).

Tanzi, V., and K. Chu. *Fiscal Policy for Stable and Equitable Growth in Latin America*. IMF working paper, no. 1 93. Washington, DC: International Monetary Fund, 1989.

Teichman, Judith. "Interest Conflict and Entrepreneurial Support for Perón." *Latin American Research Review* 16, no. 1 (1981).

Streeten, Paul. "Development Ideas in Historical Perspective." *Regional Development Digest* 1 (1980).

Sunkel, Osvaldo. "National Development Policy and External Dependence in Latin America." *Journal of Development Studies* (October 1969).

– "Big Business and Dependencies: A Latin American View." *Foreign Affairs* (1972).

Thorp, Rosemary. *Progress, Poverty and Exclusion: An Economic History of Latin America in the 20th Century*. Washington: Johns Hopkins University Press and IDB, 1998.

Tinbergen, Jan. *Reshaping the International Order: A Report to the Club of Rome.* New York: Dutton, 1976.

Toye, John, and Richard Toye. "From New Era to Neo-Liberal era: US Strategy on Trade, Finance and Development in the United Nations, 1964–82." *Forum for Development Studies* 1 (5 June 154–55).

– "The Origins and Interpretation of the Prebisch-Singer Thesis." *Journal of Political Economy* 35 (2003).

– *Political Economy for a Divided World: Trade, Finance and Development.* Bloomington: Indiana University Press, 2004.

– "Raúl Prebisch and the Limits of Industrialization." *Raúl Prebisch: Power, Principle and the Ethics of Development*, ed. Edgar J. Dosman. Washington and Buenos Aires: IDB/INTAL, 2006.

– *The UN and Global Political Economy: Trade, Finance and Development.* Bloomington: Indiana University Press, 2004.

Triffin, Robert. "Central Banking and Monetary Management in Latin America." Washington: US Federal Reserve, 4 March 1944.

– *The World Money Maze: Nacional Currencies in International Payments.* New Haven and London: Yale University Press, 1966.

United Nations. *Relative Prices of Exports and Imports of Under-Developed Countries.* Lake Success, New York: Department of Economic and Social Affairs, 1949.

Urquidi, Victor L. *The Challenge of Development in Latin America.* Praeger, 1962.

– "The Montevideo Treaty: A Comment on Mr Sumberg's Views." *Inter-American Economic Affairs* 14, no. 1 (September 1960).

United States. Department of State: *Foreign Relations of the United Status, 1939–45.* 2 vols. Millwood, New York: Kraus International Publications, 1980.

Uribe, Armando. *The Black Book of American Intervention in Chile.* Boston: Beacon Press, 1975.

Valdez, Juan Gabriel. *Pinochet's Economists: The Chicago School in Chile.* Cambridge: Cambridge University Press, 1995.

Villanueva, Javier. "El origen de la industrialización argentina." *Desarrollo Económico* 12 (October-December 1972).

Viner, Jacob. *International Trade and Economic Development.* Glencoe, IL: Free Press, 1952.

– *International Trade and Economic Development. Lectures Delivered at the National University of Brazil.* Oxford: Clarendon Press, 1953.

– "Some Reflections on the Concept of Disguised Unemployment." *Leading Issues in Development Economics*, ed. Gerald Meier. Oxford: Oxford University Press, 1964.

Walter, Richard J. *Politics and Growth in Buenos Aires, 1910–1942.* Cambridge: Cambridge University Press, 1993.

– *The Socialist Party of Argentina, 1890–1930.* Austin: University of Texas at Austin, 1977.

Walters, Robert S. "International Organizations and Political Communication: The

Use of UNCTAD by Less Developed Countries." *International Organization* 24, no. 4 (1971).

Weiss, Thomas G. *International Bureaucracy: An Analysis of the Operation of Functional and Global International Secretariats.* Lexington Books, 1975.

– *Multilateral Development Diplomacy in UNCTAD.* London: Macmillan, 1986.

Whigham, Thomas L. and Barbara Potthast. "The Paraguayan Rosette Stone: New Insights into the Demographics of the Paraguayan War, 1864–70." *Latin American Research Review* 34:1 (1999).

Williams, John H. *Argentine International Trade under a Nonconvertible Exchange Regime.* Cambridge, MA: Harvard University Press, 1920.

Wionczek, Miguel. "The Latin American Free Trade Association." *International Conciliation* (January 1965).

Index

Abdel-Ghani, A.H., 389

"Absolute Imperative: New Economic Thinking in Latin America," 500

Acheson, Dean, 257–8, 265

Act of Bogotá, 356, 359

Ahumada, Jorge, 279–80, 333, 355

Alende, Oscar, 310

Alemann, Max, 36, 62–3, 70, 76, 101, 173

Alfonsín, Raúl, 491–2

Alfonsín Government (Argentina), 491–7

Algiers Charter, 427

Ali, Amjad, 407–8

Allende, Hortensia, 464–5

Allende, Salvador, 447, 457–8, 464–8; and Prebisch, 468

Alliance for Progress, 350, 357–60, 366, 369, 396, 533n2; waning US support for, 369–71, 539n40. *See also* Kennedy administration; OAS Panel of Experts; Punta del Este Conference

Altgelt, Oswaldo, 175

Alvear, Marcelo T., 41, 65, 74, 161–2

Anaya, Elbio, 165

Aramburu, Pedro Eugenio, 306–7, 455–6

Aramburu Government (Argentina), 306–7, 310–13, 317, 319. *See also Plan for Economic Restoration; Sound Money or Uncontrolled Inflation*

Aranha, Osvaldo, 125–7, 133, 140, 147

Argentina: and Brazil, 146–50, 222, 499; economic relations with Britain, 25–6, 45, 72, 82, 118–20, 129, 159–60 (*See also* Roca-Runciman Treaty); economic relations with Brazil, 125–7; economic relations with the US, 56, 119–25, 128–30, 133–6, 141, 149, 155, 157; economy 1896–1914, 11–12, 26; economy during the Great Depression, 70, 96–7; economy during World War II, 117–21, 136, 159–61; economy just before World War II, 109, 114; economy under Aramburu, 312–13; economy under Frondizi, 367; economy under Perón, 213–17; Exchange Control Commission, 72; Falklands/Malvinas War, 489–90; history, 15–16; and the IMF, 229–30, 317, 494–5; Independent Socialist Party, 67; Industrial Credit Fund, 170; the meat-packing industry 44–7, 58–9, 102–7; military coup of

1930, 68; military coup of 1943, 163–5; and Nazi Germany, 111–12, 135, 137–8, 152; the "Nazi menace," 149–55; neutrality during World War II, 145–9; politics in the 1970s, 489; return of democracy in 1983, 490; the Uriburu Government, 71; and the US, 147–8, 155, 169, 174–5, 196, 203, 206; World War II diplomacy, 139–40. *See also* Alfonsin Government, Marcelo T. Alvear, Aramburu Government, Argentine Central Bank, Argentine Export Promotion Corporation (CAPI), Argentine Industrial Union (UIA), Argentine Rural Society (SRA), Argentine Socialist Party, Argentine-US Trade Agreement (1941), Buenos Aires, Ramon S. Castillo, the Concordancia, Fabricaciónes Militares, Farrell Government, Arturo Frondizi, General Confederation of Workers (CGT), Group of United Officers (GOU), Institute for Production and Trade (IAPI), Lonardi Government, National Bank of Argentina (BNA), National Statistical Office, Roberto Ortiz, Radical Party, Ramirez Government.

Argentine Central Bank, 95, 105, 109, 124, 131–2, 199, 205–6; and the Farrell Government, 205–6; and the military coup of 1943, 163–165; opposition to, 137, 152, 165–6; and Perón, 210, 217; and pro-Nazi groups in Argentina, 137–8; and the Ramirez Government, 168, 170–4; structure, 97–9; and the US Federal Reserve, 131–2, 186; and World War II, 117–21, 144–5, 152–4, 157, 159. *See also* Argentine Export Promotion Corporation, Consignee Control, Pinedo Plan, Resolution V of the Rio Declaration

Argentine Export Promotion Corporation (CAPI), 129–30, 135, 149, 159, 186, 513n16

Argentine Industrial Union (UIA), 26, 44, 111. *See also* Luis Colombo

Argentine Rural Society (SRA), 43–5, 47, 57–9, 203

Argentine Socialist Party, 23–4, 33–5, 67, 74, 93

Argentine-US Trade Agreement (1941), 140–1

Armour, Norman, 122, 137, 151–2, 156, 175

Balbin, Ricardo, 306

Balboa, Manuel, 212

Baldwin, Gerald, 248

Ball, George, 394; at UNCTAD I, 400

Bank of Mexico, 185–6, 190–2, 211, 214–15, 220

Bardeci, Oscar, 449

Barone, Enrico, 28, 40

Barrientos, René, 440

Batista, Fulgencia, 285, 351

Bay of Pigs invasion, 353, 360

Bell, Daniel W., 128

Berger, René, 72, 96, 108, 113–14

Berle, Adolph, 132, 175, 357, 515n18

Bernstein, E.M., 230, 234

Berthaud, Paul, 389

Blanco, Eugenio, 307

Bohan, Merwin, 153, 158–9, 175; and ECLA, 270–1, 278; and "economic warfare" against Argentina, 157

Bolivia, 127

Bosch, Ernesto, 44, 47, 60, 69, 75, 99–100, 107, 152, 172–3, 186–7, 205

Boti, Regino, 255, 351–2

Botto, Carlos, 65
Boyle, Sir Edward, 437
Braden, Sproule, 203, 206
Brazil: and Argentina, 146–50, 222, 499; Castelo Branco military government and US MNCs, 413; and ECLA, 262, 271, 280–4, 325–6, 411–14; economic relations with Argentina, 125–7; and GATT, 422; opposition of Castelo Branco's military government to ILPES funding, 411–13; and UNCTAD, 412, 540n49; and the US, 281, 287, 536n52. *See also* João Goulart, Juschelino Kubitchek
Brazil-Argentine Economic Conference (1940), 126–7
Brazil-US Joint Commission, 281, 287
Brebbia, Carlos, 83, 85, 108, 113–16, 121, 141; Argentine loan negotiations in Holland, 115
Bretton Woods Conference, 190, 196
Britain. *See* Great Britain
Broide, Julio, 36, 64
Buenos Aires, 7–8, 24, 96; history, 15–16
Bulhões, Otavio, 126, 222, 234
Bunge, Alejandro, 26, 30, 54, 80, 163
Bunge, Augusto, 24, 32, 51, 94, 165–6; and Adelita, 76–7; and the Argentine coup of 1930, 67–8, 73; break with Prebisch, 94–5; gatherings at his home, 34–5, 63, 67; influence on Prebisch 34–5, 40
Bunge, Cesar, 303
Bunge, Mario, 35, 63, 94, 166
Buron, Robert, 246
Bushnell, John, 482
Bustillo, José Maria, 169, 196, 206

Cairo Conference on the Problems of Economic Development (1962), 379, 381–2
Campos, Roberto, 282, 332; and ILPES, 412–14; and the Pearson Commission, 437
Caputo, Dante, 496
Carcano, Miguel Angel, 83
Cardoso, Fernando Henrique, 547n11; and ILPES, 412–13, 448; MNCs and Latin American development, 413
Carter, Jimmy, 273; and Prebisch, 478
Carter administration, 473–4, 478–9, 482–3, 552n16
Cassel, Gustav, 80
Castillo, Eugenio, 229, 239, 242, 255, 275
Castillo, Ramon S., 122–4, 133, 135, 139, 144, 146, 148, 150–1, 155, 163
Castro, Fidel, 351, 353, 355–6
Caustin, Harold, 237, 253
CECLA. *See* ECLA: Special Coordinating Committee of Latin America
Central Intelligence Agency (CIA): involvement in overthrow of Arbenz, 290
centre and periphery. *See* Prebisch: centre and periphery
Centre for Economic Projections (CELADE), 346
CEPAL. *See* ECLA
Chamberlain, Neville, 86
Change and Development: Latin America's Great Task, *450–6*; terms of reference, 450–2
Chicago School: and Chile under Pinochet, 464–5
Chile, 147–8; in the Allende period, 457–8; military coup of September 1973, 464–5; and the OAS Panel of Experts, 368–9; sponsorship of UN resolution for creation of ECLA, 236
CIAP. *See* Inter-American Committee for the Alliance for Progress

Ciboti, Ricardo, 303
classical economic theory. *See* Prebisch and classical economic theory
Cochran, Merle, 336
Cohen, Benjamin, 194, 228–9
Cold War, 215, 234–5, 257–9, 267–9, 278, 284–90, 338–40, 352–3, 376–7. *See also* détente
Colombo, Luis, 91–2, 102, 136, 169, 186, 196, 203, 207
Concordancia (Argentina), 74. *See also* Aramburu Government, Ramon S. Castillo, Agustin P. Justo, Lonardi Government, Roberto Ortiz
Conference of Inter-American Foreign Ministers (1942), 145–9; Prebisch's role, 145, 148; US reaction to the outcome, 149. *See also* Resolution V of the Rio Declaration (1942)
Consensus of Viña del Mar, 446
Consignee Control, 154, 156–9, 169
Contadora Group, 554n2
Cordovez, Diego, 390
Cornejo, Julio, 9, 21
Cosío Villegas, Daniel, 191, 193, 195, 214, 238, 517n5
Croire, Francisco, 142, 151, 239–40, 242
Cuba: Revolution of 1959, 351–3; relations with the USSR, 352–3. *See also* Bay of Pigs invasion; Cuban Missile Crisis; Eisenhower administration; Kennedy administration
Cuban Missile Crisis, 376; and US-Latin American relations, 375–7. *See also* Kennedy administration

de Estrada, Tomas, 65
de la Torre, Lisandro, 24, 33, 59, 67, 71, 74, 102–7, 510n32; attack on Prebisch, 106
de Seynes, Philippe, 246, 270, 295, 330, 336, 348, 372; and Prebisch, 417; and preparations for UNCTAD, 386, 388–9; and Raúl Jr, 410; support for UNCTAD; and UNCTAD II; and UNCTAD's relationship with DESA
de Silveira, Azeredo, 422, 433–4
de Tomaso, Antonio, 24, 34, 67, 74, 88
del Canto, Jorge, 215, 343–4
Dell, Sidney, 388–9, 392, 415
Department of Economic and Social Affairs (UN) (DESA): turf war with UNCTAD, 386, 405–6, 414–15, 541n7
détente, 391–2
Diaz Alejandro, Carlos, 459
Diaz de Prebisch, Eliana, 366, 410–11, 439, 443
Dillon, Douglas, 337, 339–41, 356, 371, 396; and the OECD, 381; and the Pearson Commission, 437
Dorfman, Adolfo, 288, 309, 315–16
Dreier, John C., 258
Duhau, Luis, 55–61, 73, 88, 90, 93, 95–6, 103–7
Dulles, John Foster, 286, 315–16, 329, 338–9, 525n34, 528n15

Echavarria, José Medina, 481
Eckenstein, Christopher, 389
Eckhard, June, 232
ECLA First Session (Santiago 1948), 237–8
ECLA Second Session (Havana 1949), 246–9; *Economic Survey of Latin America*, 238–40, 246–7; importance of, 240–1. *See also The Economic Development of Latin America and its Principal Problems*
ECLA Third Session (Montevideo 1950), 260–2; *Economic Decalogue*, 263–4; *Economic Survey*, 256–7, 262–3

ECLA Fourth Session (Mexico City 1951), 269–72. *See also* "Theoretical and Practical Problems of Economic Growth"
ECLA Sixth Session (Bogotá 1955), 295–6, 324; Trade Committee, 325
ECLA Seventh Session (La Paz 1957), 323, 329–30
ECLA Eighth Session (Panama City 1959), 335, 343, 352
the ECLA Thesis, 269, 273–4
ECLA Trade Conference (1956). *See* ECLA and regional integration
Economic Commission for Africa (ECA), 404–5
Economic Commission for Africa and the Far East (ECAFE), 265, 289, 404–5
Economic Commission for Europe (ECE), 265, 289
Economic Commission for Latin America (ECLA): the *CEPAL Review*, 475; and Chilean politics, 447, 457–8, 464; and the Cuban Revolution, 351, 354–5; and DESA, 239, 289–90; and ECOSOC (UN), 251–89; and the FBI, 287; and IA-ECOSOC, 254–60; and the IDB (*See* Tripartite Commission); and the IMF, 329; lack of support in Latin America, 324; mandate, 238; and Mexico, 331–2; and new ideas, 331–3; and the OAS (*See* Tripartite Commission); origin, 236–7; position of strength in the UN, 288–9; and the Punta del Este Charter, 362; and regional integration, 325–6, 328–30 (*See also* Latin American common market); and Santiago, 250; Special Coordinating Committee of Latin America (CECLA), 446, 540n49, 546n5, 546n6; staffing, 266–7, 278–9, 288; training program for economists, 279–80; and UNCTAD I, 404–5, 540n49; Washington and Mexico City offices, 254. *See also* Quintandinha Conference; Truman administration and ECLA
The Economic Development of Latin America and Its Principal Problems, 243–5, 248–9, 251; reactions of economists, 248
Economic Journal (Revista Económica), 63–4, 66, 75
Economic Recovery Plan (1933) (Argentina), 90–3, 96
ECOSOC (UN Economic and Social Committee): and the origin of UNCTAD, 382; and the structure of UNCTAD, 405–6
Eisenhower, Dwight D. *See* Eisenhower administration
Eisenhower, Milton, 286, 339
Eisenhower administration, 285–6, 337–40, 351, 355, 534n17; Committee of 21, 355–6; and Cuba, 352–3; and Prebisch, 339–41. *See also* Act of Bogotá, Latin American common market project
Espil, Felipe, 129
Export-Import Bank (US), 287, 309, 525n30

Fabricaciónes Militares (FM) (Argentina), 169–80
Faculty of Economic Sciences, UBA, 25–6
Faleto, Enzo, 448
A Fantasia Organizada, 242. *See also* Celso Furtado
Farrell, Edelmiro Julian. *See* Farrell Government
Farrell Government (Argentina), 196, 203, 205–7, 210

Father Mendivel, 166
Fernandez, Anibal, 85
Ferrer, Aldo, 212, 303, 490–1
Fischer, Irving, 39
Fondo de Cultura Económica (Mexico), 214, 235
Ford administration, 478
Ford Foundation, 459–60
Frank, Isaiah, 340–1, 396
Frankel, Enrique, 212, 297
Fraser, Malcolm, 48, 54
Frei, Eduardo, 292, 447, 466
Friedman, Irving, 421, 434, 543n25, 552n38
Frondizi, Arturo, 338, 344, 361, 364–5, 367, 369, 532n62, 535n30, 535n33; and ILPES, 374; and the Plan Prebisch, 313, 532n63
Furtado, Celso, 255, 279–80, 528n19, 528n21; disagreements with Prebisch, 315, 322, 330–2; and ILPES, 374, 412–13; and ISI, 331; resignation from ECLA, 330

G-77 (Group of 77), 391, 393, 483; criticism of Prebisch, 408–9, 425; and GATT, 423; and UNCTAD I, 404–9, 418. *See also* "Towards a New Trade Policy for Development"
Gagneux, Edmundo G., 64, 96, 101, 108, 205
Gandhi, Indira, 427
Ganz, Alex, 266–7, 309, 315–16, 332
Garcia, Alizon, 307
Garcia, Teodoro, 21
Garcia Vasquez, Enrique, 492–3
Gardner, Richard: at UNCTAD I, 406–8
GATT (General Agreement on Trade and Tariffs): attempts to undermine UNCTAD, 421–3; creation of, 379–80; and developing countries, 380–1; influence of UNCTAD I on, 421; Kennedy Round, 421, 423; and Latin American common market project, 343. *See also* Eric Wyndham-White
General Confederation of Workers (CGT) (Argentina), 306–7
Generalized System of Preferences (GSP), 426–7, 435–6
Georges-Picot, Guillaume, 289, 324
Gerest, Abraham, 64, 70, 101
Getulio Vargas Foundation, 222
Global Strategy for Development, 428–30, 438, 544n46
Gomez, Rodrigo, 188–91, 254, 334
Gonzalez, Enrique, 168
Gonzalez, Norberto, 212, 303
Gonzalez del Solar, Julio, 142, 149, 195, 210, 212, 491
Good neighbor policy, 119–20, 127–32, 285
Goodwin, Richard, 358, 361, 371
Gordon, Lincoln, 357, 359, 396
Goulart, João, 376, 536n52
Great Britain, 89; and Argentina, 25–6, 45, 72, 82, 118–20, 129, 159–60. *See also* Imperial Economic Conference, Roca-Runciman Treaty
The Great Depression, 79–80
Grinspun, Bernardo, 492–7
Group of United Officers (GOU) (Argentina), 139
Grumbach, Eduardo, 128
Guani, Alberto, 127
Guatemala, military coup of 1954, 290–1
Gudin, Eugenio, 126, 221–4, 234, 283; and public vs private sector roles, 283
Guevara, Ernesto "Che," 354, 361, 440, 535n25; at UNCTAD I, 401
Guido, José Maria, 369
Gurrieri, Adolfo, 475

Guth, Wilfried, 437
Gutt, Camille, 230–2

Haberler, Gottfried,190, 219, 223, 248
Halle, Louis B. Jr, 258
Hammarskjold, Dag, 345, 347
Hanson, Simon G., 237
The Havana *Manifesto. See The Economic Development of Latin America and its Principal Problems*
Heath, Edward: at UNCTAD I, 402, 408
Helms, Richard, 466
Herrera, Felipe, 349, 358, 372, 440, 445, 452, 530n50, 547n15, 553n51
Hitler, Adolf, 113
Hoffman, Paul G., 372; and ILPES, 347–9, 536n42; support for UNCTAD, 423–4
Holland, Henry, 286, 309
Hoover, J. Edgar, 151–2, 155, 517n14
Hopenhayn, Benjamin, 367, 372, 447
Hueyo, Alberto, 74–5, 88, 90
Hueyo, Ernesto, 85
Hull, Cordell, 86, 128, 130, 133–4, 147, 169; anti-Argentine crusade, 149; and Prebisch, 156–7
Humphrey, George, 286–7, 294, 337

Iglesias, Enrique, 450, 469, 479; and the *CEPAL Review*, 475; secretary-general of ECLA, 462
Illia, Arturo, 401, 489
ILPES. *See* Latin American Institute for Social and Economic Planning
IMF (International Monetary Fund), 190, 424–5; and ECLA, 329; and Latin American common market project, 343
Imperial Economic Conference, 83
import substitution. *See* Prebisch and import substitution
Institute for Production and Trade (IAPI) (Argentina), 217, 513n16
Inter-American Committee for the Alliance for Progress (CIAP), 430, 463
Inter-American Conference (Bogotá 1948), 237
Inter-American Development Bank (IDB), 294–5, 377; and ECLA, *see* Tripartite Commission; IDB Commission on Latin American Development, 440, 442–3 (*see also Change and Development: Latin America's Great Task)*; formation, 339, 341
Inter-American Economic Conference (1957), 337
Inter-American Economic and Social Council (IA-ECOSOC), 236–7. *See also* OAS
International Coffee Agreement, 339
International Commodity Agreement (ICA) for cocoa, 418–20
International Co-operation for a Latin American Development Policy, 291–4
International Organizations Employees Loyalty Board (US), 332
International sugar agreement, 436
International Trade Organization, 379; Latin America and, 381
International Wheat Conference, 87
Irazusta, Rudolfo, 314–15
Ivanisevich, Oscar, 224

Jacobsson, Per, 336, 343, 531n55, 532n67
Jayawardena, Lal, 389
Jevons, Stanley, 39
Jeze, Gaston, 31, 50
Johnson administration, 396; and the GSP, 426–7; and the ICA for cocoa; invasion of Dominican Republic, 451; and Latin America, 396; and the

Presidents of America Summit (1967), 426–7; and UNCTAD I, 400–9; and UNCTAD II, 427
Journal of Economic Sciences, 28, 31, 36, 47
Journal of Economic Theory, 224–5
Judd, Percival, 389, 415, 419
Justo, Agustin P., 67, 71, 74, 91, 95, 99, 105, 107, 111–12, 161
Justo, Dr Juan B., 23–4, 35

Kafka, Alexandre, 282
Kaldor, Nicholas, 333
Keenleyside, Hugh, 264–5
Kemmerer, Edwin W., 39, 97
Kennan, George, 258
Kennedy, David M., 453, 455
Kennedy, John F., 350, 357–61, 365, 367; assassination, 396–7; and the Panel of Experts, 395. *See also* Kennedy administration
Kennedy administration, 368–9, 375; and the Bay of Pigs invasion, 360; and Brazil, 536n52; and Latin America, 371, 376; and UNCTAD, 392, 396. *See also* Alliance for Progress, Cuban Missile Crisis
Keynes, John M., 36, 85, 92, 195, 213–14, 218–19
Kindleberger, Charles, 219, 243, 248
Kissinger, Henry, 445–6; and Chile under Allende, 458; and the NIEO, 474
Klein, Walter, 101
Knibbs, Sir George, 50
Korean War, 285; and US-Latin American relations, 268, 278, 284
Korry, Edmund M., 460
Krieger Vasena, Adelberto, 310
Krishnamurti, R., 389–90, 392, 417, 539n39; at UNCTAD I, 406–7
Krushchev, Nikita, 352–3, 360
Kubitchek, Juschelino, 339–40, 355–6
Kybal, Milic, 255

LAFTA (Latin American Free Trade Association), 344–45
Lanusse, Gen. Alejandro, 489
Lara, Cristóbal, 385, 447
Latin America: in the 1970s, 480–1; in 1986, 499–500; anti-Americanism, 450–1; debt crisis, 486; importance to the US, 525n27; social and political instability 1968–70, 451–2
Latin American common market project, 333–6; concept of, 126–8, 140, 150; GATT position on, 343; and Frondizi, 344; IMF position on, 335–6, 343; obstacles to, 334; US position on, 329, 335, 340–3, 532n67. *See also* LAFTA, Latin American regional integration
Latin American identity, 241, 266, 296, 378
Latin American Institute for Social and Economic Planning (ILPES), 372–4, 348–9, 372, 445–50, 456–62, 547n15; and Chilean politics, 447, 457–8; funding problems, 460–61; Latin American reservations about, 373, 548n36; morale problems, 446–7, 458–9; and the Tripartite Committee, 373; and UNDP, 459–61
Latin American regional integration, 334, 343, 339; comparisons with Europe, 324–8. *See also* ECLA and Latin American regional integration
Le Breton, Tomas, 52–3, 56, 85
Leguizamon, Guillermo, 83–4
Leith-Ross, Sir Frederick, 80–1, 106
Lewis, Sir Arthur, 322, 437, 553n39
Lie, Trygve, 229, 246, 253, 265; and the Havana *Manifesto*, 251

Linares y Sansetena, Segundo, 8, 14
Lleras Restrepo, Carlos. 194, 292, 334, 440
Lobos, Eleodoro, 26–7, 43–4, 47–8, 53, 235
Lonardi Government (Argentina), 296, 298–304; National Advisory Board, 306; overthrow by Aramburu, 306
Lowenthal, William, 449, 458
Lurie, Samuel, 389

Maizels, Alfred, 389, 419
Malaccorto, Ernesto, 36, 62–4, 69–71, 76, 138, 164, 168, 173, 297, 307
Malbran, Manuel, 83, 85
Malinowski, 237, 253, 265, 290, 301, 347–9, 416–17, 542n11; attempt to get Prebisch to head UNCTAD, 382, 384; encouraging Prebisch to attend the Cairo Conference, 379, 381; and the origin of UNCTAD, 382; at UNCTAD I
Mann, Thomas, 337, 340–3, 356, 371; and UNCTAD, 396, 539n40; and US multinationals, 342–3
Manoilescu, Mihail, 80
El Maqui, 277–8, 321, 411, 488
Margolin, Robert E., 437
Marshall, Alfred, 25
Martin, Edwin, 371, 396
Martinez-Cabañas, Gustavo, 234, 238–9, 245, 251–2, 257
Martinez Zuveria, Gustavo, 171
Max, Herman, 194
Mayobre, José Antonio, 215, 332–3, 355, 461
McCarthyism, 287–8. *See also* International Organizations Employees Loyalty Board
McNamara, Robert: and the Pearson Commission, 437–8
Medina, José, 412, 447, 461
Meier, Gerald, 248
Mendès-France, Pierre, 263–4, 267–8
MERCOSUR, 499
Mexico: in the 1970s, 481–2; compared with Argentina, 189, 191–2; debt crisis, 486; police violence against students (1968), 440; and World War II, 189; and the US, 189–90
Mill, John Stuart, 25
Miranda, Miguel, 217
Mikesell, Raymond, 333
Molina, Sergio, 460
Moll, Carlos, 77, 121, 167, 202
Moll de Prebisch, Adela (Adelita), 176–7, 212, 253, 299; in Allende's Chile, 465, 468; courtship and marriage to Raúl, 76–9; and her family, 76–7, 79, 121, 131, 152, 167, 516n14; FBI allegations against her, 151; loyalty to Raúl, 411; and Raúl after his remarriage, 443–4; and Raúl's parents, 77, 91, 165
Monnet, Jean, 81, 289, 528n15
Montagu, Norman, 81
Mora, José Antonio, 358
Moreau, Alicia, 23, 312
Morgenthau, Henry, 128, 131–2
Mosak, Jacob, 289; and the future of UNCTAD, 405–6; and preparations for UNCTAD, 386–9; and UNCTAD's relationship with DESA, 414–15
Moscoso, Teodoro, 366
Muñoz, Heraldo, 487
Muschietti, A., 102
Myrdal, Gunnar, 240; *see also* ECE

Narasimhan, C.V., 406
National Bank of Argentina (BNA), 61, 63–4. *See also* Prebisch at the Office of Economic Research

National Statistical Office (Argentina), 30, 50, 53–5, 57
National University of La Plata (UNLP), 30–1
New International Economic Order (NIEO), 473, 483
Niemeyer, Sir Otto, 90, 97–8, 104, 122
Nierenstein, Mauricio, 27–8, 53, 58
Nixon, Richard, 337–9, 350–1, 442, 533n1
Nixon administration, 453, 455, 478; and Chile, 457, 466; and Latin America, 445–6, 549–50n58. *See also* Henry Kissinger
Non-Aligned Movement, 382, 482–3, 550n1. *See also* G-77
Notes on Demography, 54–5
"Notes on our Money Supply," 36–9
Notes Regarding the Beef Crisis, 47
Noyola, Juan, 322, 351, 354–5; and inflation, 527n1
Nun, José, 448

OAS (Organization of American States), 356–7, 451; and ECLA (*see* Tripartite Commission); formation, 237; and the Guatemala coup, 290–1. *See also* IA-ECOSOC; Inter-American Economic Conference (1957); OAS Panel of Experts; Quintandinha Conference (1954); Truman administration and the OAS
OAS Panel of Experts, 365–72, 430, 545n49
Ocampo, Victoria, 23
OECD (Organization for Economic Cooperation and Development), 381
Okito, Saburo, 437
Olariaga, Luis, 60–1
Ongania, Juan Carlos, 489
Operation Pan-America, 339, 355–6
Oria, Salvador, 27, 50, 100
Orradre, Pedro, 142, 492
Ortega y Gasset, José, 305
Ortiz, Roberto, 111, 118, 122–3, 128, 162
Osorio de Almeida, Miguel, 271
Owen, David, 228–9, 237, 253, 265; and the *Havana Manifesto*, 251

Palacios, Alfredo, 24, 33, 172
Pan-American Conference (Chapultepec, 1945), 236
Pan-American Union, 236
Panel of Nine. *See* OAS Panel of Experts
Paraguay, 127, 197–201, 518n16
Pareto, Vilfredo, 40–1, 51
Paris Club, 527n46
Parsons, M.L., 231–2
Partners in Development, See Pearson Commission
Patron-Costas, Robustiano, 1, 75, 162–4
Pazos, Filipe, 215, 275–6, 351, 354
Pearson, Lester B., 437–8
Pearson Commission, 437–8
Pedretti, Carlos, 198, 200, 202
Perez, Enrique S., 69–71
Perez-Guerrero, Manuel, 215, 441
Perez-Jimenez Government (Venezuela), 315
Peripheral Capitalism, Crisis and Change, 487
Perón, Juan Domingo, 67–8, 139, 164–5, 170–1, 196, 203; fall from power, 296, 298; prelude to taking power, 207–10. *See also* Perón Government
Perón Government (Argentina), 213, 216–17, 225; and Argentine Central Bank, 210
Peru, 440
Peterson, Rudolf, 459
Pierson, Lee, 123

Pinedo, Federico, 24, 67, 88, 90–1, 94–5, 99–100, 104–7, 122, 124, 128, 132–3, 158, 162, 175. *See also* Pinedo Plan
Pinedo Plan, 124–6, 128–9; failure of, 133; opposition to, 132–3
Pinero, Norberto, 36
Pinochet, Augusto, 486
Pinto, Anibal, 447
Plan for Economic Restoration, 303, 309–12
Plan Prebisch, 303–5; ECLA staff response, 315, 322; opposition to, 312
Plaza, Galo, 334, 445
Pollock, David, 385, 390, 392, 417, 419, 502
Prebisch, Adelita. *See* Moll de Prebisch, Adela.
Prebisch, Alberto, 19, 21, 39, 51, 62, 107–8, 457
Prebisch, Albin: business ventures, 11; death, 93; expectations of his children, 13; and his in-laws, 10–11; marriage to Rosa, 10; second family, 14, 29; and the Tucumán German Club, 13–14
Prebisch, Ernesto, 108
Prebisch, Julio, 19, 21
Prebisch, Raúl: acceptance of leadership of UNCTAD, 383–4; address on regional integration at ECLA Trade Conference (1959), 343–4; adolescence, 19; advisor to Tomas Le Breton, 52; and Raúl Alfonsin, 491–2, 498; and the Alfonsín Government, 492–7; and Salvador Allende, 465–7; and the Alliance for Progress, 358–9, 375, 378 (*See also* OAS Panel of Experts; Punta del Este Conference); and the Alvear Government (Argentina), 47–8, 50; anti-communism, 33, 350–5; "anti-patria" criticism in Argentina, 150, 152, 173, 305, 495–6; appointed Executive Secretary of ECLA, 264–5; and the Aramburu Government (Argentina), 307, 312–13 (*See also Plan for Economic Restoration; Sound Money or Controlled Inflation*); and the Argentine central bank concept, 73, 90, 95; and the Argentine economic crisis during the Revolución Libertadora, 318–19; and the Argentine media, 92, 300, 305–6, 308–9, 311–12, 495, 526n33; and the Argentine Rural Society, 44–7, 55–9; and the Argentine Socialist Party, 32, 33–5, 94; at the BNA (*See* Prebisch at the Office of Economic Research, BNA); "bohemian streak," 29, 249, 274, 323, 411; and the Bretton Woods Conference, 196–7; and Alejandro Bunge, 30–1; and Augusto Bunge, 34–5, 63, 69, 73–4, 78, 94–5; and the business cycle, 37–8, 65–6, 179–80, 226–7, 244; and the Cairo Conference (1962), 381; and Roberto Campos regarding ILPES, 413–14; and the Cartagena Consensus, 496–7; and the Carter administration, 473, 479–80; centre and periphery, 38, 214–15, 244, 276; and the *CEPAL Review*, 475, 551n7; charisma, 4, 247, 451, 262, 274, 399; childhood home, 12–14; and the Chilean coup, 464–5; and CIAP, 463; and classical economic theory, 60–1, 87, 179–83, 244, 248–9, 282–3; comparisons between Argentina and the British dominions, 40, 48–50, 57; conceptual struggles, 194–5, 241–2; and conditionality in foreign aid, 429–31, 479; and the *Consensus of Viña del Mar*, 446–7; consultancy to the OAS, 465, 549n40; consultancy

in Paraguay, 197–201; consultancy in Venezuela, 214–15; and "converging measures," 398–400; courtship and marriage to Adelita Moll, 77–9; and the creation of the Inter-American Development Bank, 341–2; and the Cuban revolution, 351, 353–5; death, 502; and debt-led growth, 481; decision to study economics, 19–20; and DESA, 386–8, 414–15; and dependency theory, 476–7; dismissal as general manager of the Argentine Central Bank, 168, 172–4; divorce from Adelita, 443; and the Dominican Republic, 215–16, 221; and John Foster Dulles, 290; early views of Argentine political parties, 33; and ECLA during the Lonardi/Aramburu period, 301, 309–10; ECLA farewell speech, 375; and ECOSOC, 267–8; and "elephantiasis of the state," 481; and the ethics of development, 477, 486–7, 500; and the Falklands/Malvinas War, 553n52; and his father, 14, 29, 58, 90, 93; and the FBI, 151, 515n18; financial difficulties, 176, 184–5, 444, 463, 469; first consultancy for ECLA (1949), 228–9, 234, 240 (*See also The Economic Development of Latin America and Its Principal Problems);* first visit to the Andean region, 194; flight from Buenos Aires after dismissal from the Central Bank, 175–6; and Eduardo Frei, 466; funeral, 4; and Celso Furtado, 322, 331–2, 549n40; and GATT under Wyndham-White, 422–3; general manager of the Argentine Central Bank, 100–2, 108–9, 112–21, 152; German relatives, 79; and the gold standard, 35, 39, 61, 65, 72; and his grandfather, 14–17; and the Great Depression, 64–6, 70–2, 96–7, 112; and the Group system in UNCTAD, 436–7; and Che Guevara, 401; and Harvard University, 197, 203–4; health issues, 107, 184, 220, 223–4, 384, 442, 269–70; honours, 473, 485; and Alberto Hueyo, 75; and the IDB Commission on Latin American Development, 440, 442–3, 450 (*See also Change and Development: Latin America's Great Task);* and ILPES, 347–9, 372–4, 378, 411–14, 442–50, 456–63, 536n47; and the IMF, 229–34, , 335–7, 343–4, 494–6; and import substitution industrialization, 92, 327–8, 453, 530–1n54, 534n21, 548n23, 553n39 (*See also* Prebisch and "inward-directed growth"); and the importance of statistics, 46, 54; and the independence of UNCTAD in the UN, 407–8, 541n6; and indigenous cultures, 201; and inflation, 322, 493–4, 527–8n2; and "inward-directed growth" (desarrollo hacia adentro), 160, 180; and Agustin P. Justo, 162; and the Kennedy administration, 357, 359, 534n21; and land reform, 33, 49; and the Latin American common market project, 333–4, 336–7, 342–4, 530–1n54; and Latin American regional integration, 326–8, 330, 544n42; at the League of Nations Preparatory Commission for the World Economic Conference, 1933, 77–8, 80–2; leave of absence from ECLA (1955), 301–2; and the Lonardi Government (Argentina), 298–306 (*See also* the *Plan Prebisch*); loss of faith, 28; and Martinez-Cabañas, 252, 265; and Marxism, 28; maternal ancestry, 8–9; and McCarthyism, 287–8; marriage to Eliana Diaz, 443; and Mexico, 188–9;

and the military coup of 1930 (Argentina), 67–8; military service, 52–3; and MNCS, 340, 412–13, 464, 469–70; and Jacob Mosak, 387–8; and his mother, 14, 165; and multilateralism, 181–2, 293–4, 361–3, 406–9; and the National Statistical Office (Argentina), 53–5, 57–8, 510n29; and the need for structural reforms in Latin America, 363, 375, 454–5, 488; as negotiator, 406, 409, 433, 436; and the NIEO, 429, 435; and the Nixon administration, 445–6; and the Nobel Prize in Economics, 485–6, 552n37; and the OAS Panel of Experts, 365–9, 372; at the Office of Economic Research, BNA, 61, 63–6, 69, 75; opening address at UNCTAD I, 398–9; opening address at UNCTAD II, 428–31; and the Perez-Jimenez dictatorship (Venezuela), 215; and Perón, 170–1, 206, 208, 217–18, 275; and the Perón Government (Argentina), 233, 298; and populism, 453, 465–6; and the position of UN secretary-general, 544n39; and the Pearson Commission, 438–9; and "progressive capitalism," 339; and the Quintandinha Conference, 291–4; and the presidency of the Argentine Central Bank, 205–6; primary education, 18; professor at UBA, 53, 58, 60, 75, 108, 177, 184, 194–5, 212–13, 216, 220, 224–6, 299; pro-US position during World War II, 145–6; and the Punta del Este Conference, 362–4; and Raúl Jr, 410–11, 439, 443; and the Reagan administration, 483–5, 488; relationship with Eliana Diaz, 366, 410–11, 439; research on the Argentine beef trade, 44–7, 59; resignation from UNCTAD, 441, 546n78; and the Roca-Runciman Treaty, 103; and the role of the public and private sectors, 179, 181–2, 283; and W.W. Rostow, 396–7; rumours of resignation from UNCTAD, 439–40; secondary school education, 18–19; secretary-general of UNCTAD, 384–411, 414–41; seminars at the Bank of Mexico, 185, 192–5, 517n21; seminar at UNAM, 232; and service to his country, 16, 18, 39–40, 42, 102, 211–12; and social crisis in Latin America, 481; social life, 60, 62–3, 108, 142, 500–1; special advisor to Lonardi, 301–2; "special relationship" with the US during World War II, 121–3, 145, 151, 158–9, 166–7; and Standard Oil, 304, 315–16, 340; and structuralism, 183, 243–5, 247–9, 273; student jobs, 29–30; support for private enterprise, 181, 282–3, 293–4, 318–19, 339–40; target of Nazi sympathizers, 138; and tax reform in Argentina, 50, 73; and technocratic elites, 40–2, 64, 76, 89, 95, 174, 273; and terms of trade (*See* Prebisch-Singer Theory); thumbnail biography, 5; and the "trade gap," 395, 418; and Triffin's offer of advisory work in Latin America, 204, 206–8; and UNCTAD's purpose, 417; UNCTAD secretary-general, 384–409, 410–11, 414–41; under-secretary of finance in the Uriburu military government (Argentina), 69–74; university education, 25–31, 36, 39; unpopularity in Argentina, 208–9, 313–15, 489 (*See also* Prebisch and the Argentine media); and the US Federal Reserve, 57; and US journalists, 285, 370; and Gabriel Valdes, 446–7, 460, 462; view of the

US, 484; visit to Australia and New Zealand (1923–4), 48–50; visit to Brazil (1951), 280–4; visit to Cuba (1951), 275–7; visit to Czechoslovakia, 436; visit to Europe (1924), 51; visit to the US and Canada (1926), 56–7; visit to Washington (1940–1), 127–34; and George Woods, 394, 400, 437; work habits, 22, 62–3, 108; world tour preceding UNCTAD I, 392–3, 538n31
Prebisch Manifesto. See The Economic Development of Latin America and Its Principal Problems
Prebisch Memorandum (1940), 128–9
Prebisch, Raúl Jr, 410–11, 439, 443
Prebisch, Rosa. *See* Uriburu de Prebisch, Rosa Linares
Prebisch-Singer Theory, 243–4, 521n29
Presidents of America Summit (1967), 426–7
Princeton Institute for Advanced Study, 219
Prio Socarras, Carlos, 275–6
Proclaimed List of Axis Companies. *See* US Board of Economic Warfare
Punta del Este Charter. *See* Punta del Este Conference
Punta del Este Conference (1961), 361–4, 535n31

Quintana, Carlos, 461–2
Quintandinha Conference (1954), 291–5. *See also International Cooperation for a Latin American Development Policy*

Radical Civic Union (Argentina) *See* Radical Party (Argentina)
Radical Party (Argentina), 22–3, 40–1, 64–7, 71, 132–3, 161–2
Ramirez, Gen. Pedro Pablo, 172
Ramirez Government (Argentina), 168–70, 191, 195–6
Ravndal, Chris, 108, 128, 136, 142, 154, 197, 234, 260–2
Rawson, Gen. Arturo, 163
Reagan administration, 484–6
Regional integration: *see* Latin American regional integration
Repetto, Nicolas, 24, 74
Resolution V of the Rio Declaration (1942), 148, 150–1, 153–4
Revista Económica. See Economic Journal
Revolución Libertadora (Argentina). *See* Aramburu Government, Lonardi Government
Ricardo, David, 25
Rio Conference (1940), *See* Brazil-Argentine Economic Conference
Rio Conference (1942), *See* Conference of Inter-American Foreign Ministers
Rio Group, 554n3
Roca, Julio A., 74, 82–3, 124–5, 127, 132–3, 162
Roca-Runciman Treaty, 3–4, 92, 102, 112, 119. *See also* Argentina: economic relations with Britain
Rockefeller, John D., 370–1
Rockefeller, Nelson, 128, 135, 258, 446
Rockefeller Commission, 446, 450–1
Rogers, William, 466
Roosevelt, Franklin D., 86, 127–9, 156, 189–90. *See also* Roosevelt administration
Roosevelt administration: and Argentina, 130–1, 133–4, 145–59, 169, 196, 203, 209; and Mexico, 189–90. *See also* Good Neighbor Policy
Roque-Gondra, Luis, 27, 53
Rosenstein-Rodan, Paul, 357, 368, 469, 547n20

Rostow, W.W., 371; and Latin American development 480; meeting with Prebisch about UNCTAD, 396–7; at UNCTAD II, 427–8, 431
Royem, Bodil, 367, 390, 411, 444
Rubottom, Roy R., 340
Ruiz-Guiñazú, E., 139, 145–8
Runciman, Walter, 72, 83–4

Saadi, Vicente, 496
Saavedra Lamas, Carlos, 60–1, 109–10, 160, 162, 165, 511n24
Saenz Peña, Luis Roque, 22
Samuelson, Paul, 243
Sanchez, Luis Alberto, 241
Santa Cruz, Alfonso, 474
Santa Cruz, Hernan, 236, 260
Sanz de Santamaria, Carlos, 169–71, 430, 445, 463
Savio, Gen. Mario A., 169
Scalabrini Ortiz, Raúl, 311
Schumpeter, Joseph, 190
Seers, Dudley, 333, 551n11
Shapiro, Louis, 242
Shevchenko, S., 389
Siewers, Enrique, 27, 36, 77
Silva, Julio, 36, 177
Silva, Patricio, 459, 461
Singer, Hans, 242–3, 256, 521n29
Smith, Reginald, 415
Social Progress Trust Fund, 356
Socialist Party of Argentina. *See* Argentine Socialist Party
Sociedad Rural (Argentina). *See* Argentine Rural Society
Sound Money or Uncontrolled Inflation, 303, 309–10
Sourrouille, Juan, 492, 497
Soviet Union: and Cuba, 352–3; and Czechoslovakia, 436; and the space race, 338, 352, 360, 370; and UNCTAD, 416; at UNCTAD I, 401–2; at UNCTAD II, 427; and the US (détente), 391–2. *See also* Cold War
Statistical Yearbook (1927), 57–9
Storni, Segundo V., 164, 169
Structuralism. *See* Prebisch and structuralism
Sunkel, Osvaldo, 447–8, 487
Supplementary Financing Mechanism, 418, 420–1, 424
Swenson, Louis, 255, 279, 328–9

Taborda, Damonte, 137–8
Taussig, F.W., 39
Terms of trade. *See* Prebisch-Singer Theory
Thant, U, 416; and the position of UNCTAD in the UN, 407, 415; and Prebisch, 384, 439–40; and Raúl Jr; support for UNCTAD, 423–4
Theoretical and Practical Problems of Economic Growth, 279
theory of comparative advantage, 25–6
von Thermann, Freiherr, 137–8
Thomas, Josiah B., 135
Tinbergen, Jan, 419, 485
Treaty of Asunción, 554n4
Treaty of Montevideo. *See* LAFTA
Triffin, Robert, 193, 195, 197–8, 202–5, 208, 211
Trimestre Economica, 219
Tripartite Committee, 357, 364–6, 448; and ILPES, 373; marginalization, 377
Truman administration, 234; and Argentina under Perón, 233; and ECLA, 236–7, 254, 259–64, 269–71, 284–6, 530n46; and Latin America, 215, 235, 240–1, 257–8, 278; and the OAS, 258–62, 270. *See also* Quintandinha Conference (1954)

Tucumán: history, 15–16, social conditions, 17–18

UN Advisory Committee on Administrative and Budgetary Questions (ACABQ), 541n7
UN Development Decade, 365, 382, 428, 437
UN Development Program (UNDP), 459
UN Emergency Operation (1974–5), 470–2
UN Mission to Argentina (1956), 315, 317–18, 527n46
UN Panel of Eminent Persons on MNCS, 464, 469–70
UN Special Fund: formation of ILPES, 347–9
UNCTAD (United Nations Committee on Trade and Development): and DESA,386, 405–6; and GATT, 423–4; Group of Experts, 387–8, 390; location of permanent headquarters, 416; origin, 381–2; Preparatory Committee meetings, 384–5, 387–8, 390–1, 397–8; selection of Prebisch as secretary-general, 383–4; staffing, 383–4 415–17, 541n7, 541n8, 541–2n10; structure, 541n9; successes, 435. *See also* ICA for cocoa; Supplementary Financing Mechanism; "Towards a New Trade Policy for Development"; UNCTAD I; UNCTAD II
UNCTAD I, 398–409; committees, 401–3, 406; divisions over future of UNCTAD, 405–8; G-77 response to Prebisch's compromise, 408–9; group system, 391, 540n48; growth of G-77 solidarity, 404–5; polarization between rich and poor countries, 403–5; Prebisch's compromise on structure, 406–8; US position, 400
UNCTAD II, 427–34; coolness of Group B countries, 426; evaluation of the conference, 434–5; last ditch negotiations, 433–4; preparations, 425. *See also* Algiers Charter, Generalized System of Preferences, *Global Strategy for Development*
Union of Argentine Industrialists. *See* Argentine Industrial Union
United States: anti-communism, 234, 259; and Brazil, 281, 287; and Cuba under Castro, 351–3, 357–62; and ECLA (*See* Truman administration and ECLA); economic relations with Argentina, 56, 119–25, 128–30, 133–6, 140–1, 149, 155, 157; and the Latin American common market project, 329, 335, 340–3, 532n67; and Latin American free trade, 127, 136; and Mexico, 189–90; strategic importance of Latin America for, 525n27; and UNCTAD (*See* Johnson administration and UNCTAD; Kennedy administration and UNCTAD). *See also* Alliance for Progress; Bay of Pigs invasion; Carter administration; Cold War; Consignee Control; Cuban Missile Crisis; Eisenhower administration; Export-Import Bank; International Organizations Employees Loyalty Board; Kennedy administration; Korean War; McCarthyism; Nixon administration; Rockefeller Commission; Roosevelt administration; Truman administration; US Board of Economic Warfare; US Federal Reserve Bank
Upton, T. Graydon, 341
Uriburu, Enrique, 44, 47, 56, 71, 73, 90, 142
Uriburu, Francisco, 17

Uriburu, José Evaristo, 17, 99
Uriburu, José Felix, 17, 66–8, 71, 73, 75
Uriburu de Garcia, Luisa, 21, 28
Uriburu de Prebisch, Rosa Linares, 8; influence on Raúl, 14; marriage to Albin, 10
Urquidi, Victor, 191, 193, 195, 214, 218–21, 238, 332, 343, 485
Uruguay, 127
US Board of Economic Warfare, 153–4, 159. *See also* Consignee Control
US Federal Reserve, 197–8; links with Argentine Central Bank, 131–2, 142
USSR. *See* Soviet Union

Vaky, Viron P., 478, 482
Valdes, Gabriel, 446; and ILPES, 447, 459–62
Vance, Cyrus, 474
Vargas, Getulio, 109–10, 125–6, 151, 156, 222, 280–1, 284, 293
Venezuela, 211
Verrier, Roberto, 102–3, 128, 303
Villaseñor, Eduardo, 188, 191, 211
Viner, Jacob, 190, 219, 248, 282–3, 534–5n23
Vining, Rutledge, 219
Viola, Gen. Roberto, 484
Viteri de la Huerta, Jorge, 390
Volcker, Paul, 497

Waldheim, Kurt, 464, 470
Wallich, Henry, 190, 235
Waugh, Samuel, 309
Welch, Leo, 108, 130, 135, 175, 211
Welles, Sumner, 127–8, 130, 135, 145, 148
White, Henry Dexter, 128
Williams, John, 2, 36, 122, 131
Woods, George D., 437; and UNCTAD, 394, 397, 420, 424–5; at UNCTAD I, 400
World Bank: and ECLA, 372–3; and ILPES, 372–3; and Supplementary Financing Mechanism, 418, 420, 424; and UNCTAD, 394, 397, 400, 424–5. *See also* Pearson Commission
World Economic Conference, 1933, 85–7
World War II, 121–2, 134–5; prelude to, 113–15
Wyndham-White, Eric, 379–80, 421–3; and Latin American integration, 343, 530n50, 530–1n54; at UNCTAD I, 400

Yearbook of the Rural Society: Economic and Agrarian Statistics
Young, Andrew, 474, 479
Yrigoyen, Hipolito, 22–3, 33, 64–8, 82